BIRDS OF PREY IN A
CHANGING ENVIRONMENT

THE NATURAL HERITAGE OF SCOTLAND

Each year since it was founded in 1992, Scottish Natural Heritage has organised or jointly organised a conference which has focused on a particular aspect of Scotland's natural heritage. The papers read at the conferences, after a process of refereeing and editing, have been brought together as a book. The eleven titles already published in this series are listed below (No. 6 was not based on a conference).

1. *The Islands of Scotland: a Living Marine Heritage*
    Edited by J.M. Baxter and M.B. Usher (1994), 286pp.

2. *Heaths and Moorlands: a Cultural Landscape*
    Edited by D.B.A. Thompson, A.J. Hester and M.B. Usher (1995), 400pp.

3. *Soils, Sustainability and the Natural Heritage*
    Edited by A.G. Taylor, J.E. Gordon and M.B. Usher (1996), 316pp.

4. *Freshwater Quality: Defining the Indefinable?*
    Edited by P.J. Boon and D.L. Howell (1997), 552pp.

5. *Biodiversity in Scotland: Status, Trends and Initiatives*
    Edited by L.V. Fleming, A.C. Newton, J.A. Vickery and M.B. Usher (1997), 309pp.

6. *Land Cover Change: Scotland from the 1940s to the 1980s*
    By E.C. Mackey, M.C. Shewry and G.J. Tudor (1998), 263pp.

7. *Scotland's Living Coastline*
    Edited by J.M. Baxter, K. Duncan, S.M. Atkins and G. Lees (1999), 209pp.

8. *Landscape Character: Perspectives on Management and Change*
    Edited by M.B. Usher (1999), 213pp.

9. *Earth Science and the Natural Heritage: Interactions and Integrated Management*
    Edited by J.E. Gordon and K.F. Leys (2000), 344pp.

10. *Enjoyment and Understanding the Natural Heritage*
    Edited by Michael B. Usher (2001), 224pp.

11. *The State of Scotland's Environment and Natural Heritage*
    Edited by Michael B. Usher, Edward C. Mackey and James C. Curran (2002), 354pp.

This is the twelfth book in the series.

BIRDS OF PREY IN A CHANGING ENVIRONMENT

Edited by D.B.A. Thompson, S.M. Redpath, A.H. Fielding,
M. Marquiss & C.A. Galbraith

SCOTTISH
NATURAL
HERITAGE

EDINBURGH: THE STATIONERY OFFICE

First published in 2003 by The Stationery Office Limited
71 Lothian Road, Edinburgh, EH3 9AZ

Applications for reproduction should be made to
Scottish Natural Heritage, 12 Hope Terrace,
Edinburgh EH9 2AS

British Library Cataloguing in Publication Data
A catalogue record for this book is available from the British Library

ISBN 0 11 4973083

Cover photography: Golden eagle *Aquila chrysaetos* (Laurie Campbell) set against the backdrop of Strath Dionard in north west Sutherland, Scotland (Des Thompson).

PREFACE

Birds of prey are among the most exciting, yet threatened, of all species on our planet. For many people they symbolise the majesty and sense of freedom to be found in wild places, and more recently they have come to be recognised as important indicators of the environment due to their place at the top of many food chains. Indeed, as predators, they are at the heart of some of the most contentious conservation conflicts of the day (e.g. Anon., 2000; Marren, 2002), and their interactions with game, and with wildlife generally, are hotly debated in the media and scientific press.

In December 2000, Scottish Natural Heritage (SNH), the British Ornithologists' Union (BOU) and the Joint Nature Conservation Committee (JNCC) held a conference on birds of prey in a changing environment. More than 200 people participated, providing one of the most lively events any of us have attended. This book provides an account of the conference, with the oral and poster papers updated, refereed and edited. The 41 chapters provide a substantial contribution to our current knowledge of birds of prey, and make an important broader contribution to our understanding of ecological and conservation issues in Britain.

The traditional term for a bird of prey, 'raptor', captures the essence of its predatory way of life. The word is derived from the Latin verb *rapere*, 'to take by force', in its past participle form *raptus*; hence also 'raptorial', meaning 'adapted for seizing prey'. The word 'raptor' has all the connotations of striking swiftly and plundering ruthlessly; but it also has much more romantic connotations, of 'rapture', of being 'rapt' or 'enraptured' – of the mental exaltation and intense delight of being transported into another sphere of experience.

There are two broad groups of raptor. The Accipitriformes (hawks, buzzards, eagles, kites, vultures, harriers and ospreys) and Falconiformes (falcons) are grouped together as diurnal species, because most of them hunt during daylight; the Strigiformes (owls) comprise the second group, the great majority of whose members hunt at night.

There is a rich pedigree of research on birds of prey in Britain. More than 25 years have elapsed since publication of the last significant overview of raptors in Britain (Brown, 1976) and an important book on raptor persecution (Bijleveld, 1974). Since then, several major reviews have appeared, notably by Newton (1979) on population ecology and by Mikkola (1983) on owls. In addition, several key monographs have been published on species such as the hen harrier (Watson, 1977), peregrine falcon (Ratcliffe, 1980, 1993), sparrowhawk (Newton, 1986), kestrel (Village, 1990), barn owl (Taylor, 1994) and, most recently, the golden eagle (Watson, 1997). Each of these has a strong Scottish emphasis, and is characterised by the investment of a huge amount of time in the field, when many days may be spent finding a nest or species. Raptors, after all, are among the most difficult and time consuming of animals to work on, and knowledge of nesting sites and feeding areas has to be accumulated over decades.

The chapters in this book derive from oral or poster presentations; many are reviews, some are national or local studies, and a few are summaries or collations of work published elsewhere. We have arranged the chapters under six themes.

Theme 1 contains reviews of the numbers and status of birds of prey in Britain and Ireland, and includes much information from elsewhere in Europe. We have taken the opportunity here of updating some of the population information given in the UK Raptor Working Group report (Anon, 2000).

Thirteen national/local studies of populations comprise Theme 2. Many of these studies have been ongoing for 10 years or more, and many are still continuing. Studies of behaviour and predation occupy Theme 3, which includes much previously unpublished material on ranging habits and social interactions.

Theme 4 considers the implications of land use change, while conservation and management issues (Theme 5) collectively embrace 11 studies. Finally, Theme 6 deals with conflicts between humans and birds of prey, and the search for solutions to these. Although the book focuses on raptors in Britain, it is important to consider this work in the context of a broader perspective. To this end we also include some of the excellent work undertaken in Spain, France and Iceland.

We hope that this book will engage bird watchers, researchers, decision-makers, land managers and the general public, because all of these in one way or another have a keen interest in birds of prey. Following the Earth Summit at Johannesburg, in August/September 2002, we have all come to realise the inextricable links between human health and well-being and environmental sustainability. That the focus of the Earth Summit was more on people than on biodiversity, compared with the United Nations Conference on Environment and Development in Rio de Janeiro in 1992, speaks volumes for the way in which politicians view the environment in the round. Solutions to environmental problems lie in improving health, education, energy production and transport, and reconciling social, economic and cultural differences, alongside action to conserve biodiversity and specific efforts such as the creation of National Parks and Nature Reserves. Work on the conservation of raptors transcends much of this. As the final part of the book shows, the solutions to some of the conservation issues will be found by linking novel science, changing attitudes to nature, and encouraging a shift in socio-economic policies for rural areas.

Most recently, in June 2002, the newly established Scottish Raptor Monitoring Scheme, involving Scottish Natural Heritage (in the chair), the Joint Nature Conservation Committee, the Scottish Raptor Study Groups, the British Trust for Ornithology, the Rare Breeding Birds Panel, the Royal Society for the Protection of Birds and the Scottish Ornithologists' Club, has set an important standard for monitoring birds of prey. This scheme marks an important development in monitoring raptors, for it formalises co-operative working between many organisations and individuals. The challenge will be to ensure that good quality information on raptor populations is deployed to improve conservation and management measures.

Beyond all this, however, we share the conviction that raptors remain important beacons for the changing state of our environment. These birds will continue to interest and inspire millions of people around the world.

Acknowledgements

We have to thank many people involved in the conference and in the preparation of this book. Ian Bainbridge, Steve Petty and David Stroud joined us on a steering group to direct the conference, and Jeremy Greenwood, Stuart Housden, Ian Newton, Derek Ratcliffe,

Patrick Stirling-Aird and Jeff Watson provided additional support and advice. The conference was held at the Scottish Police College, Tulliallan Castle, where the facilities were excellent; we thank Ron Bow and his colleagues for all their hard work and hospitality. We were particularly pleased that the Convener of Fife Council, John MacDougall, and the Chairman of SNH, John Markland, could join us on one evening for a splendid civic reception and dinner.

For the smooth planning and running of the conference we thank many of our colleagues in SNH, but especially Paul Robertson and Janette Munneke, who looked after us all with remarkable patience and efficiency. Joyce Garland, Lorne Gill, Helen Forster, Sally Johnson, Maureen Scott, Phil Shaw and Marion Whitelaw helped us in many ways. Magnus Magnusson has provided some deft touches, not least in clarifying the origins of the word 'raptor'. The BOU office provided logistical support, and we are grateful to Gwen Bonham, Steve Dudley and colleagues for their enthusiastic and willing involvement in the conference. In editing the book, we have had significant support from many referees (some of whom were not able to attend the conference); we thank them all for improving the quality of this book. Jo Newman helped enormously in the preparation of the book, for which the publisher and we are especially grateful. We appreciate also the extra technical support provided by Paul Robertson. Jane McNair of TSO Scotland has most ably and enthusiastically handled the publication process.

We thank the participants in the conference, for they collectively made it vibrant, enjoyable and special. We have to highlight Roy Dennis' evening illustrated talk on predators as part of natural systems; it was memorable for its vision, breadth and empathy with nature. It is a special pleasure to thank the two raptor 'masters', Ian Newton and Derek Ratcliffe, for their superb and distinctive keynote presentations. It was fitting that they were presented with delightful sketches of a sparrowhawk and a peregrine, penned by Keith Brockie. We extend particular thanks to the Scottish Raptor Study Groups, which comprise experienced fieldworkers who, largely on a voluntary basis, carry out monitoring of raptors throughout Scotland. The majority of their 200-plus membership attended the conference and contributed to the convivial atmosphere. Finally, we thank Derek Ratcliffe for providing a Foreword for the book.

Des Thompson and Colin A. Galbraith, Scottish Natural Heritage.
Steve Redpath and Mick Marquiss, Centre for Ecology and Hydrology,
Natural Environment Research Council.
Alan Fielding, Manchester Metropolitan University.

October 2003

References

Anon. (2000). *Report of the UK Raptor Working Group.* Department of the Environment, Transport and the Regions, and the Joint Nature Conservation Committee, Peterborough.

Bijleveld, M. (1974). *Birds of Prey in Europe.* Macmillan Press, London.

Brown, L. (1976). *British Birds of Prey.* Collins, London.

Marren, P. (2002). *Nature Conservation.* Harper Collins, London.

Mikkola, H. (1983). *Owls of Europe.* Poyser, Calton.

Newton, I. (1979). *Population Ecology of Raptors.* Poyser, Berkhamsted.

Newton, I. (1986). *The Sparrowhawk.* Poyser, Calton.

Ratcliffe, D. (1993). *The Peregrine Falcon.* Academic Press, London.

Scottish Raptor Monitoring Scheme Agreement (2002). Agreement involving Scottish Natural Heritage, Joint Nature Conservation Committee, Scottish Raptor Study Groups, British Trust for Ornithology (Scotland), Rare Breeding Birds Panel, Royal Society for the Protection of Birds (Scotland) and Scottish Ornithologists' Club. Scottish Natural Heritage, Battleby.

Taylor, I. (1994). *Barn Owls.* Cambridge University Press, Cambridge.

Village, A. (1990). *The Kestrel.* Poyser, Calton.

Watson, D. (1977). *The Hen Harrier.* Poyser, Berkhamsted.

Watson, J. (1997). *The Golden Eagle.* Academic Press, London.

Editorial note

All website addresses cited in chapters have been checked. However, as a matter of principle such addresses are given for information only, and are not viewed as a formal source of published information. Most chapters have cross-references to other chapters in this book; these are given as author(s), Chapter number(s), and are not cited in the References.

CONTENTS

List of Plates

(between pages 268 and 269)

LIST OF CONTRIBUTORS

David S. Allen, Countryside Council for Wales, Ladywell House, Park Street, Newtown, Powys, SY15 1RD.

Arjun Amar, Game Conservancy Trust, Hill of Brathens, Banchory, Aberdeenshire, AB31 4BW. Present address: Division of Fish of Wildlife – Rota, PO Box 1064, Rota, MP, Commonwealth of the Northern Mariana Islands, 06051.

Dave I.K. Anderson, Woodland Ecology Branch, Forest Research, Northern Research Station, Roslin, Midlothian, EH25 9SY.

Beatriz Arroyo, Centre for Ecology and Hydrology, Hill of Brathens, Banchory, Aberdeenshire, AB31 4BW.

Ian P. Bainbridge, Royal Society for the Protection of Birds, Dunedin House, 25 Ravelston Terrace, Edinburgh, EH4 3TP. Present address: Ecological Adviser's Unit, Scottish Executive Environment Group, SEERAD, 1-J77 Victoria Quay, Edinburgh, EH6 6QQ.

Vincent Bretagnolle, Centre d'Études Biologiques de Chizé, CNRS, 79630 Villiers en Bois, France.

R.A. Broad, Royal Society for the Protection of Birds Scotland, 10 Park Quadrant, Glasgow, G3 6B3.

David N. Carss, Centre for Ecology and Hydrology, Banchory, Aberdeenshire, AB31 4BY.

Ian Carter, English Nature, Northminster House, Peterborough, PE1 1UA.

Roger Clarke, The Hawk and Owl Trust, c/o Zoological Society of London, Regent's Park, London, NW1 4RY.

B.L. Cosnette, 50 Collieston Circle, Aberdeen, AB22 8UT.

K. Crane, Downbye Cottage, Glenbrittle, Isle of Skye, IV47 8TA.

Humphrey Q.P. Crick, British Trust for Ornithology, The Nunnery, Thetford, Norfolk, IP24 2PU.

C.H. Crooke, 6 George Street, Avoch, Ross-Shire, IV9 3PU.

Tony Cross, 'Samaria', Nantmel, Llandrindod Wells, Powys, LD1 6HG.

Peter Davies, Cumbria Raptor Study Group, c/o Snowhill Cottage, Caldbeck, Wigton, Cumbria, CA7 8HL.

Roy Dennis, Highland Foundation for Wildlife, Inchdryne, Nethybridge, Inverness-shire, PH25 3EF.

Andrew Dixon, The Malting House, Allendale, Hexham, Northumberland, NE47 9EE.

Nicholas Dixon, The Hawk and Owl Trust, c/o Zoological Society of London, Regent's Park, London, NW1 4RY.

Andrew Douse, Scottish Natural Heritage, 2 Anderson Place, Edinburgh, EH6 5NP.

Kevin Duffy, Royal Society for the Protection of Birds Scotland, 10 Park Quadrant, Glasgow, G3 6B3.

Brian Etheridge, Royal Society for the Protection of Birds, North Scotland Regional Office, Etive House, Beechwood Park, Inverness, IV2 3BW. Present address: Scottish Natural Heritage, 27 Ardconnel Terrace, Inverness, IV2 3AE.

R.J. Evans, Royal Society for the Protection of Birds, Dunedin House, 25 Ravelston Terrace, Edinburgh, EH4 3TP.

Chris J. Feare, WildWings Bird Management, 2 North View Cottages, Grayswood Common, Haslemere, Surrey, GU27 2DN.

Alan H. Fielding, Behavioural and Environmental Biology Group, Biological Sciences, Manchester Metropolitan University, John Dalton Building, Chester Street, Manchester, M1 5GD.

Colin A. Galbraith, Scottish Natural Heritage, 2 Anderson Place, Edinburgh, EH6 5NP.

Jesús T. García, Departamento de Zoología y Antropología, Facultad de Biología, Universidad Complutense, 28040 Madrid, Spain.

David W. Gibbons, Conservation Science Department, Royal Society for the Protection of Birds, The Lodge, Sandy, Bedfordshire, SG19 2DL.

R.E. Green, Royal Society for the Protection of Birds, The Lodge, Sandy, Bedfordshire, SG19 2DL. Present address: Department of Zoology, University of Cambridge, Downing Street, Cambridge, CB2 3EJ.

Jeremy J.D. Greenwood, British Trust for Ornithology, The Nunnery, Thetford, Norfolk, IP24 2PU.

Phil Grice, English Nature, Northminster House, Peterborough, PE1 1UA.

Jon Hardey, 23 Nellfred Terrace, Inverurie, Aberdeenshire, AB51 4TJ.

Paul F. Haworth, Bendoran Cottage, Bunessan, Isle of Mull, Argyll, PA67 6DU.

Mark Holling, The Old Orchard, Grange Road, North Berwick, East Lothian, EH39 4QT.

John Holmes, English Nature, Trevint House, Strangways Villas, Truro, Cornwall, TR1 2PA.

Julian Hughes, Royal Society for the Protection of Birds, The Lodge, Sandy, Bedfordshire, SG19 2DL.

David C. Jardine, 49 Bellfield Road, North Kessock, Inverness, IV1 3XX.

Xavier Lambin, Zoology Department, University of Aberdeen, Tillydrone Avenue, Aberdeen, AB24 2TZ.

Andrew Lawrence, South Wales Peregrine Monitoring Group, c/o 96 Yr Ysfa, Maesteg, Bridgend, CF34 9BE.

Gavin Legge, Forestry Commission, Kirkton of Durris, Banchory, Kincardineshire, AB3 3BP.

J.A. Love, Scottish Natural Heritage, 135 Stilligarry, South Uist, HS8 5RS.

Ed Mackey, Scottish Natural Heritage, 2 Anderson Place, Edinburgh, EH6 5NP.

Mike Madders, Natural Research, Carnduncan, Gruinart, Isle of Islay, PA44 7PS.

Mick Marquiss, Centre for Ecology and Hydrology, Hill of Brathens, Banchory, Aberdeenshire, AB31 4BY.

Amy Marsden, Institute of Genetics, University of Nottingham, Queens Medical Centre, Nottingham, NG7 2UH. Present address: National College for School Leadership, Triumph Road, Nottingham, NG8 1DH.

Wendy A. Mattingley, Scottish Raptor Study Groups, Cluny House, Aberfeldy, Perthshire, PH15 2JT.

Eric Meek, Royal Society for the Protection of Birds, 12/14 North End Road, Stromness, Orkney, KW16 3AG.

D.H. Morgan, Behavioural and Environmental Biology Research Group, Biological Sciences, Manchester Metropolitan University, Manchester, M1 5GD.

K. Morton, Royal Society for the Protection of Birds, Dunedin House, 25 Ravelston Terrace, Edinburgh, EH4 3TP.

Greg Mudge, Scottish Natural Heritage, The Governor's House, The Parade, Fort William, PH33 6BA.

E.J. Macdonald, Ardslignish, Glenborrodale, Ardnamurchan, Argyll, PH36 4JG.

Mike J. McGrady, Natural Research Ltd., Am Rosenhügel 59, A-3500 Krems, Austria.

David R.A. McLeod, GIS Solutions, 14 Crailinghall Cottages, near Crailing, Jedburgh, TD8 6LU.

Fiona A. McPhie, Highland Foundation for Wildlife, Inchdryne, Nethybridge, Inverness-shire, PH25 3EF.

K. Nellist, Downbye Cottage, Glenbrittle, Isle of Skye, IV47 8TA.

Peter Newbery, Royal Society for the Protection of Birds, The Lodge, Sandy, Bedfordshire, SG19 2DL.

Ian Newton, Centre for Ecology and Hydrology, Monks Wood, Abbots Ripton, Huntingdon, Cambridgeshire, PE28 2LS.

Ólafur K. Nielsen, Icelandic Institute of Natural History, PO Box 5320, IS-125, Reykjavik, Iceland.

Duncan Orr-Ewing, Royal Society for the Protection of Birds, Dunedin House, 25 Ravelston Terrace, Edinburgh, EH4 3TP.

Lorcan O'Toole, Irish Raptor Study Groups, Carrowtrasna, Churchill, County Donegal, Ireland.

David T. Parkin, Institute of Genetics, University of Nottingham, Queen's Medical Centre, Nottingham, NG7 2UH.

Steve J. Petty, Woodland Ecology Branch, Forest Research, Northern Research Station, Roslin, Midlothian, EH25 9SY. Present address: Craigielea, Kames, Tighnabruaich, Argyll, PA21 2AE.

D.A. Ratcliffe, 34 Thornton Close, Girton, Cambridge, CB3 0NG.

G.W. Rebecca, Royal Society for the Protection of Birds, 10 Albyn Terrace, Aberdeen, AB10 1YP.

Steve M. Redpath, Centre for Ecology and Hydrology, Hill of Brathens, Banchory, Aberdeenshire, AB31 4BW.

Colin Richards, South Wales Peregrine Monitoring Group, c/o 96 Yr Ysfa, Maesteg, Bridgend, CF34 9BE.

Gordon S. Riddle, Swinston, Culzean Country Park, Maybole, KA19 8JX.

Helen T. Riley, Scottish Natural Heritage, 2 Anderson Place, Edinburgh, EH6 5NP.

Paul Robertson, Scottish Natural Heritage, 2 Anderson Place, Edinburgh, EH6 5NP.

Geoff Shaw, Forest Enterprise, Creebridge, Newton Stewart, DG8 6AJ.

Phil Shaw, Scottish Natural Heritage, Battleby, Redgorton, Perth, PH1 3EW.

Colin R. Shawyer, The Hawk and Owl Trust, c/o Zoological Society of London, Regent's Park, London, NW1 4RY.

Mike Shewry, Scottish Natural Heritage, Battleby, Redgorton, Perth, PH1 3EW.

Innes M.W. Sim, Conservation Science Department, Royal Society for the Protection of Birds, Dunedin House, 25 Ravelston Terrace, Edinburgh, EH4 3TP.

D. Simpson, c/o The Estate Office, Harewood Yard, Leeds, West Yorkshire, LS19 7LF.

Nigel Snell, Southern England Kite Group, 2 Hambleden Mill, Hambleden, Henley-on-Thames, Oxon, RG9 3AF.

Malcolm Stott, Royal Society for the Protection of Birds, Geltsdale Nature Reserve, 9 Coalfell Terrace, Hallbankgate, Brampton, Cumbria, CA8 2PY.

David A. Stroud, Joint Nature Conservation Committee, Monkstone House, City Road, Peterborough, PE1 1JY.

Ron W. Summers, Royal Society for the Protection of Birds, North Scotland Regional Office, Etive House, Beechwood Park, Inverness, IV2 3BW.

Iain R. Taylor, Applied Ornithology Group, Johnstone Centre, Thurgoona Campus, Charles Sturt University, PO Box 789, Albury, New South Wales, 2640, Australia.

Andy Tharme, Royal Society for the Protection of Birds, Dunedin House, 25 Ravelston Terrace, Edinburgh, EH4 3TP. Present address: Economic Development & Environmental Planning, Scottish Borders Council, Newton St. Boswells, Melrose, TD6 0SA.

Simon Thirgood, Game Conservancy Trust, ICAPB, University of Edinburgh, Kings Buildings, West Mains Road, Edinburgh, EH9 3JT. Present address: Frankfurt Zoological Society, FZS Regional Office in the Serengeti, PO Box 14935, Arusha, Tanzania.

Chris J. Thomas, Department of Biological Sciences, University of Durham, Science Laboratories, South Road, Durham, DH1 3LE.

Mike Thomas, South Wales Peregrine Monitoring Group, c/o 96 Yr Ysfa, Maesteg, Bridgend, CF34 9BE.

D.B.A. Thompson, Scottish Natural Heritage, 2 Anderson Place, Edinburgh, EH6 5NP.

Michael P. Toms, British Trust for Ornithology, The Nunnery, Thetford, Norfolk, IP24 2PU.

Rafael Villafuerte, Instituto de Investigación en Recursos Cinegéticos (CSIC-UCLM-JCCLM), Ronda de Toledo s/n, 13005 Ciudad Real, Spain.

Javier Viñuela, Instituto de Investigación en Recursos Cinegéticos (CSIC-UCLM-JCCLM), Ronda de Toledo s/n, 13005 Ciudad Real, Spain.

David Walker, Cumbria Raptor Study Group, c/o Snowhill Cottage, Caldbeck, Wigton, Cumbria, CA7 8HL.

Jeff Watson, Scottish Natural Heritage, 9 Culduthel Road, Inverness, IV2 4AG.

D. Phil Whitfield, Scottish Natural Heritage, 2 Anderson Place, Edinburgh, EH6 5NP.

FOREWORD

Birds of prey have been closely connected with human affairs for a very long time. They were held in special esteem during the thousands of years in which people cultivated their assistance in the taking of game through the ancient sport of falconry, and became elevated to cherished status symbols. Their fall from grace began when the firearm gave a more efficient means of killing wild quarry, and as they appeared increasingly in competition with humans for this bounty of nature. Despite their rise to popularity again in modern ornithology, as among the most spectacular form of life which evolution has thrown up, this malign legacy of enmity from game preservers remains alive in parts of the country to this day.

Birds have been pre-eminent in the enormous growth in popular interest in wildlife during the last 50 years, and the birds of prey have become a special focus of attention. During this time some of them were, by quirk of chance, the particular victims of the organochlorine pesticide episode, and achieved a symbolic importance in the dawning of the era of environmental awareness. The recovery of the affected species after the banning of these chemicals has been a major success story in wildlife conservation. The remedial action did not happen easily; it came about as the result of a painstakingly assembled body of evidence for the harmful effects of these chemicals, which finally over-rode the agro-chemical opposition, and the doubters who sat in judgement. It was the field data obtained by a large number of voluntary helpers which gave the British Trust for Ornithology's Peregrine Enquiry of 1961-62 the lead in pointing the way to the crucial scientific studies of cause and effect. The efforts became truly international, giving rise to global sharing of knowledge of these birds.

This happy cooperation between amateur and professional has continued to grow, as studies of the birds of prey have expanded to include all the British breeding species. The network of Raptor Study Groups, which now covers much of Britain and is especially strong in Scotland, plays a major role in following the fortunes of these birds and increasing understanding of the influences which rule their lives. The monitoring of populations has become routine and comprehensive, as the collaborative effort in the Preface shows, and an impressive database informs both research and conservation. The work of the Royal Society for the Protection of Birds in practical protection and public education has been an important factor in raising the level of acceptance – and, indeed, affection – for the birds of prey and promoting their increase and recovery over the last few decades. Many of the purists who once opposed meddling with nature have been won over to the re-introductions which have restored the sea eagle and goshawk as residents and seen the red kite re-occupy an increasing part of its long-lost range.

The birds of prey as a whole are a success story. The osprey and honey buzzard have made their own way back; the hobby is expanding northwards, perhaps in response to warmer summers; and the common buzzard has shown a remarkable spread in many lowland areas which must mean that some formerly hostile parties have finally accepted that it should be left alone. While knowledge of land use effects has explained the decline of some species through loss of food supply and nesting habitat, remedial measures are possible in some cases. The supplementary feeding of large raptors has been tried with some success in places, and the provision of nest boxes for kestrels, barn owls and tawny owls has boosted the numbers of these species locally. Studies to increase the ecological insight on which management depends are an important part of the research programme. Yet there is still a small number of raptors whose presence arouses a reflex hostility from certain interests. When we come to the hen harrier on the grouse moors it would seem that we live in an era which goes back a century or more. Despite all the fine words from some landowners' spokespeople, this bird continues to be destroyed relentlessly in some areas in a bare-faced violation of the law. Golden eagles and peregrines are also not tolerated on some grouse moors, and goshawks are put down in certain pheasant preserves. Peregrines are detested by many pigeon-racing folk, and even the humble sparrowhawk – always the keepers' foe – is now accused of both pigeon-killing and depleting garden song-bird populations.

Addressing these problems rationally becomes more difficult against a background of prejudice against the birds of prey which exaggerates and distorts the facts – or simply shows unwillingness to consider any other point of view. No amount of carefully marshalled evidence that natural control mechanisms prevent the predators from outgrowing their food supply will cut any ice with those determined to maximise their shootable stocks of game. It is a matter of simple reflection that, if some of the wilder allegations about raptor predation were true, many songbirds would have ceased to exist long ago, and the predators themselves would then have died out through lack of food. But this will not persuade those with unshakeable bees in their bonnets.

This book is a timely presentation of scientific evidence, argument and discussion on most of the matters I have touched upon, and a good many more besides. It is a remarkable distillation of knowledge across a very wide field, and gains from the community of interest focused by so many devotees of birds of prey gathered together under one roof. It builds on much valuable work undertaken by the country conservation agencies, NGOs and of course the raptor workers themselves. It is gratifying to know that so much work is under way to develop our understanding of the ecology of these birds. Yet it should be clear that science is only the essential first step, and for birds of prey to become a complete success story in Britain, there is still a long way to go in conservation politics and action. Raptor enthusiasts will have to speak up, and assert their simple conviction that birds of prey are as important as gamebirds or homing pigeons.

D.A. Ratcliffe
Former Chief Scientist,
Nature Conservancy Council

July 2003

THEME ONE

NUMBERS AND STATUS

THEME ONE

NUMBERS AND STATUS

More than any other group of birds, raptors have experienced considerable fluctuations in number throughout Europe. Historically in Britain and Ireland, there are four broad phases which define changes in number and status of raptors: Medieval times, when some species were strictly protected; the Victorian era of the mid- to late 19th century, when most birds of prey were heavily persecuted to preserve game, notably red grouse *Lagopus lagopus scoticus* and pheasants *Phasianus colchicus* (resulting in some raptor species becoming extinct); the pesticides period of the 1950s-1970s, when many species suffered significantly as a result of the accumulation of persistent organochlorine pesticides in food chains; and the 'conservation and recovery' phase of the 1980s to the present time, when legislation and public awareness gave rise to more stringent protection, species re-introduction programmes and recovery in range of some species (e.g. Brown, 1976; Newton, 1979; Anon., 2000). Today, there is comprehensive survey and monitoring of some raptor species, and there are periodic national surveys or population assessments of all species (e.g. Scottish Raptor Monitoring Scheme Agreement, 2002; Gregory *et al.*, 2003). Some studies of owls (Strigiformes) and the diurnal raptors have even provided textbook examples of how factors such as habitat, prey density and competition influence variation in numbers of animals over space and time (e.g. Begon *et al.,* 1996).

In the opening chapter, Newton reviews the evidence for the role of natural factors in the limitation of birds of prey numbers. He presents four lines of evidence to support the view that for some raptor species breeding densities do not fluctuate at random, but are limited principally by food supplies and/or nest sites. Much of the public interest in birds of prey focuses on the rarer species. Greenwood *et al.* (Chapter 2) provide the most detailed assessment to date of population sizes and trends of 20 species of birds of prey in Britain and Ireland. They note that in the European context, the British populations of the following species are particularly important: peregrine *Falco peregrinus*, kestrel *Falco tinnunculus*, sparrowhawk *Accipiter nisus*, golden eagle *Aquila chrysaetos*, merlin *Falco columbarius* and hen harrier *Circus cyaneus*. Whilst populations of most of the diurnal birds of prey species have increased in Britain and Ireland over the last 50 years, the owls appear to have either declined or remained fairly stable. Indeed, across Europe the majority of owl species appear to be experiencing population declines. Greenwood *et al.* outline requirements for improvements in monitoring of raptor populations, and note the importance of the Scottish Raptor Monitoring Scheme Agreement (2002).

Thirty-nine species of diurnal raptor and 13 species of owl breed regularly in Europe. A comparison of the population sizes of these birds with other birds breeding in Europe points to the relatively small populations of raptors. This is important in terms of conservation legislation, for it is the rarer and more vulnerable species which have received most protection under legislation. Stroud (Chapter 3) provides a thorough overview of the status and legislative protection of birds of prey and their habitats in Europe. He explores the historical context of existing legislation, and provides a revealing commentary on the environmental and social factors which have given rise to changes in legislation. Two international treaties provide for the conservation of raptors in Europe: the EC Directive on the Conservation of Wild Birds (79/409/EEC, known as the 'Birds Directive'), and the 1979 Convention on the Conservation of European Wildlife and Natural Habitats (known as the 'Berne Convention'). A review of issues currently affecting the conservation status of Europe's birds of prey leads Stroud to conclude that most species remain adversely affected through human impacts, with around 90% of the most vulnerable diurnal raptor species being adversely affected by habitat change or fragmentation.

Taken together, these three chapters provide an important assessment of the numbers and status of birds of prey. Collectively, they reveal the considerable amount of information we now have on populations of birds of prey nationally, and indeed internationally. It is striking that many research studies encounter difficulties in determining the importance of prey supplies, habitat or some other factor in influencing raptor numbers because human persecution can be prevalent, yet difficult to quantify. In 1979, Newton stated that: 'The last 10-15 years have seen an enormous expansion in research and conservation efforts devoted to raptors in many parts of the world. This has come mainly from a realisation of the drastic declines in the numbers of such birds since the last century, and of the poor and endangered status that many now have.' Since that observation was made, legislation has been introduced across Europe to provide a wider framework for conserving and indeed managing raptor populations. However, as we shall see from the studies in much of the rest of this book, the evidence points to the need for changes in environmental policies, and more effort to enforce the legislative protection of birds of prey.

References

Anonymous (2000). *Report of the UK Raptor Working Group*. Department of the Environment, Transport and Regions, and Joint Nature Conservation Committee, Peterborough.

Begon, M., Harper, J.L. & Townsend, C.R. (1996). *Ecology: Individuals, Populations and Communities*. Blackwell, Oxford.

Brown, L. (1976). *Birds of Prey*. Collins, London.

Gregory, R.D., Eaton, M.A., Noble, D.G., Robinson, J.A., Parsons, M., Baker, H., Austin, G. & Hilton, G.M. (2003). *The State of the UK's Birds 2002*. The RSPB, BTO, WWT and JNCC, Sandy.

Newton, I. (1979). *Population Ecology of Raptors*. Poyser, Berkhamsted.

Scottish Raptor Monitoring Scheme Agreement (2002). Agreement involving Scottish Natural Heritage, Joint Nature Conservation Committee, Scottish Raptor Study Groups, British Trust for Ornithology (Scotland), Rare Breeding Birds Panel, Royal Society for the Protection of Birds (Scotland) and Scottish Ornithologists' Club. Scottish Natural Heritage, Battleby.

1. THE ROLE OF NATURAL FACTORS IN THE LIMITATION OF BIRD OF PREY NUMBERS: A BRIEF REVIEW OF THE EVIDENCE

Ian Newton

Summary

1. Bird of prey populations are normally limited, rather than fluctuating at random. In the absence of human intervention, the limitation in many species comes through competition for breeding space, and is helped by the presence of surplus adults, which breed only when an existing nesting territory becomes vacant.

2. In habitats where nest sites are freely available, breeding density is often limited by food supply. This may be inferred from the following findings: (a) species that exploit fairly stable (often varied) food sources show fairly stable densities, which differ between regions where food abundance differs; (b) species that exploit annually fluctuating (often restricted) food supplies show fluctuating densities; and (c) species that are exposed to a long-term or step-wise change in food supply show a long term or step-wise change in density. In other areas, however, breeding density may be restricted by shortage of nest sites to a lower level than would normally occur with the available food-supply. This may be inferred from: (a) the absence of breeding pairs in areas that lack nest sites but are otherwise apparently suitable; (b) the provision of artificial nest sites is sometimes followed by a big increase in breeding density; and (c) the loss of nest sites is sometimes accompanied by a decline in breeding density. Hence, in the habitat available in any one region, breeding density is naturally limited by food supply or nest sites, whichever is most restricting.

3. As a consequence of persecution (past or present) or other human actions, many modern populations are below the level that would be permitted by the habitat. Some species may also be limited in numbers and distribution by other birds of prey, which eat them or compete for food or nest-sites.

4. Aspects in need of further study include: (a) effects of widescale food manipulation experiments on population density and individual behaviour; (b) behavioural mechanisms that lead birds to adjust their spacing (and density) to prevailing food-supply; (d) effects of interactions (competitive or predatory) between different predator species on raptor and owl breeding densities; and (d) movements of nomadic species between successive nesting areas, best done by the satellite-tracking of radio-tagged individuals.

1.1 Introduction

Although raptor populations over much of the world have been reduced by human activities - by habitat destruction, deliberate persecution, and by pesticides and other toxic chemicals - enough studies of intact populations have now been made to suggest how densities are naturally limited. In this chapter I shall be concerned primarily with the natural limitation of breeding density in birds of prey and only peripherally with human impacts. The chapter is intended as a scene setter, and the approach is comparative; it is partly an update of earlier reviews (Newton, 1979, 1991a,b), focussing on more recent research, but also draws on studies of owls (Strigiformes) as well as those of diurnal raptors (Falconiformes).

1.2 Evidence that densities are regulated

For some raptor species, the idea that breeding density is regulated, rather than fluctuating at random, is based on four main findings: (1) the stability of the breeding populations of many species, in both size and distribution, over periods of many years; (2) the existence of surplus adults, physiologically capable of breeding, but attempting to do so only when a territory is made available through the death or removal of a previous occupant; (3) the re-establishment of populations, after their removal by man, to the same level as previously; and (4) in areas where nest sites are not restricted, in many species a regular spacing of breeding pairs. In the sections below, these points are examined in turn.

1.2.1 Stability of breeding population

Some raptor species show some of the most stable breeding densities known among birds, as can be documented from long-term studies (Newton, 1979, 1991b). An example is the golden eagle *Aquila chrysaetos* in which the density of territorial pairs in some sizeable areas may vary by no more than 15% of the mean level over periods up to several decades (Newton, 1979; Watson, 1996; Steenhof *et al.*, 1997). Compared to findings on others birds (Lack, 1954, 1966), and to what is theoretically possible, this represents a remarkable degree of stability. Similar evidence for such relative stability over fewer years is available for at least a dozen other raptor species in various parts of the world (Newton, 1979).

Evidence for long-term stability also comes from studies of the total raptor fauna of particular areas. Near Berlin, Wendland (1952-53) found constancy in the numbers of individual species, and hence of the raptor population as a whole, over an 11 year period. Craighead & Craighead (1956) obtained similar results in three study years covering a seven-year period in Michigan.

Stability of breeding densities, as shown in the above studies, would be expected only in stable environments. It would not be expected in habitats that were changing rapidly through vegetation succession or human action, or in which prey densities were changing. Nor would it be expected in those populations recovering from past persecution or pesticide impacts.

In practice, the degree of variability in any bird population tends to increase with the span of years over which counts are made (Newton, 1998). This is partly because the chance of including an unusual year increases with the length of study, and also because the year-to-year fluctuations may be superimposed on a long-term upward or downward trend. In fact, wherever bird species have been studied over periods of several decades, their abundance and distribution patterns are often found to have changed greatly. Peregrines in Britain provide a well-documented example, for even in regions where they have not previously been heavily persecuted, they are much more numerous now than 70 years ago (Ratcliffe, Chapter 4).

1.2.2 Surplus birds

In some populations, non-breeding, non-territorial adults can be seen near nest sites, occasionally fighting with breeders, and even killing and replacing them (Gargett, 1975; Monneret, 1988; Bowman *et al.*, 1995, Haller, 1996). However, the main evidence for the existence of surplus birds, which breed only when a place becomes available, is that lost mates are often replaced in the same season by other individuals, which then breed themselves. Replacement sometimes occurs within a few days, and is evidently widespread among raptors. Specific instances, reported incidentally in the literature, involve at least 26 species, from small falcons to large vultures, and include both solitary and colonial species (Newton, 1979). At some nest sites, more than one replacement was recorded (where shooting was continued), and at other sites individuals of both sexes were replaced. Most instances referred to females, perhaps because they were more easily shot than males, or because they were more numerous among surplus birds. Replacements included some birds in adult plumage and others in immature plumage.

Documented instances were mainly from the early literature and, as evidence for the existence of surplus birds, were often equivocal. In recent years, properly controlled removal experiments, of the kind done on other birds, have been conducted on at least three species of raptors, namely the common kestrel *Falco tinnunculus*, the American kestrel *Falco sparverius* and the Eurasian sparrowhawk *Accipiter nisus* (Table 1.1; Village, 1983; Bowman & Bird, 1986; Newton & Marquiss, 1991). In all of these species, replacement of removed individuals occurred, sometimes within days, indicating the presence of surplus birds of both sexes, mostly in the younger age groups, capable of breeding when a vacancy appeared. In each case, birds from neighbouring territories were marked, so it could be shown that the replacement individuals had not simply moved from other territories nearby.

Table 1.1. Results of experimental removal of breeders from nesting territories in early spring (pre-laying). Details from Newton & Marquis (1991), Village (1983) and Bowman & Bird (1986).

	Sparrowhawk		Kestrel		American kestrel	
	Male	*Female*	*Male*	*Female*	*Male*	*Female*
Number removed	7	7	10	11	16	4
Number replaced	3	3	3	7	8	1
Number produced eggs	1	3	2	7	4	
Number produced young	0	1	0	6	?	

Few attempts have been made to estimate the numbers of floaters in raptor populations. However, Newton & Rothery (2001) calculated that at least 22% of female sparrowhawks present at the start of the breeding season were floaters. From radio-tracking data, Kenward *et al.* (1999, 2000) calculated the proportion of non-breeders in a common buzzard population in spring at 75% or more, and in a goshawk population at 29% of males and 60% of females (which had higher survival than males), but these latter estimates included territorial non-breeders, as well as floaters. All three populations were judged to be close to the level that the habitat could support, and in depleted or expanding populations the expected proportions of floaters would be lower.

1.2.3 Re-establishment of populations

In Britain, instances are known of local breeding populations being removed or depleted by human action, and then recolonizing or recovering to about the same level as previously, with pairs in the same nesting places. This occurred with peregrine falcons *Falco peregrinus* shot during 1939-45 on the south coast of England, and depleted by pesticide poisoning during the 1960s in many other regions (Ratcliffe, 1993). In each case, not only did the newcomers use the same cliffs as their predecessors, but also the same nest ledges. One of the most remarkable examples involved the merlin *Falco columbarius* (Rowan, 1921-22), in which four or five pairs of this small falcon settled each year on an area of the North York Moors in eastern England. For more than 20 consecutive years, all of the pairs were shot and no young were raised. Yet each year four or five new pairs settled in the same places as their predecessors. Such events imply constancy in the carrying capacity of the environment over the years, with the same limitations on breeding numbers. Again this would be expected only in landscapes that remained reasonably stable over the years, and not in those altered by human action. In some parts of Britain, peregrines now breed at greater density than previously, but this has been attributed to increase in their food supply in the form of racing pigeons (Crick & Ratcliffe, 1995).

1.2.4 Regular spacing

In continuously suitable nesting habitats, a regular spacing of breeding pairs has been documented in many kinds of raptors and owls, and is evidently widespread in solitary nesting species (for common buzzard, see Tubbs, 1974; for golden eagle *Aquila chrysaetos*, see Watson, 1996; for peregrine falcon, see Ratcliffe, 1993; for sparrowhawk, see Newton *et al.*, 1977, 1986; for tawny owl *Strix aluco*, see Southern, 1970). Such spacing, reflecting the territorial behaviour of individual pairs, is consistent with the idea of density limitation, especially when the same pattern holds over many years. It would not, of course, be expected where nest sites were sparse and irregular in distribution, constraining the distribution of breeding pairs.

These four arguments, taken together, provide circumstantial evidence that: (a) breeding density is limited, (b) the limitation results from competition for breeding space (or 'territories'); and (c) stability of breeding density is helped by the existence of surplus birds, encouraged to breed only when a territory is vacated and a gap is made available. We should not assume that surplus birds are available at all times in all populations; or that all non-breeders are capable of breeding that year if a place were made available to them. In species in which individuals do not breed until they are several years old, many birds in the non-territorial sector are likely to be immature, and perhaps unable to defend a territory, let alone breed.

In many studies of fairly stable populations, in each year some previous territories remained vacant. The usual occupancy of British peregrine territories pre-1939 was 85% (Ratcliffe, 1972), and in some common buzzard territories it was 77-83% (Tubbs, 1974). Territories vary in quality - that is in the opportunities they offer for survival and successful breeding - and possibly some poor territories are suitable for occupation only in certain years, or only by certain birds (Newton, 1988). In the removal experiments on sparrowhawks reported above, birds taken from known good territories were quickly replaced, while those taken from known poor territories nearby were not. Also, when given the opportunity to breed, replacement birds bred much less well than other first-time settlers. This was especially true of males. Findings from raptors thus underline the importance of both site features and bird features in influencing whether settlement, defence and breeding occur.

1.2.5 *Regulation of breeding density around a constant level*

Research on sparrowhawks in south Scotland revealed how breeding density was regulated around a constant level over a 20 year period. In this 200 km² area, nest numbers fluctuated from year to year but remained throughout within 15% of the mean level, with no long-term upward or downward trend. Each year almost all of the breeding females were trapped for ringing and identification, so each year the new breeders could be separated from the established ones remaining from previous years. In general, the numbers of new breeders added each year matched the numbers of older ones lost from the previous year (Figure 1.1). In this way, long-term stability of the population was maintained by density-dependent recruitment (Newton, 1991a). Such a regulatory system can operate only while there are enough floaters to fill the gaps, otherwise breeding numbers would decline.

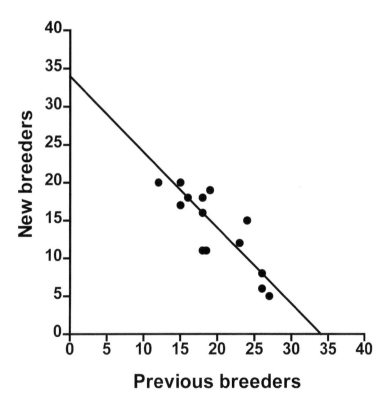

Figure 1.1. Density-dependent recruitment to a breeding population of the Eurasian sparrowhawk, south Scotland, 1975-89. The breeding population remained fairly stable during this period, and the numbers of new breeders recruited each year (y) were inversely related to the numbers of established breeders remaining from the previous year (x). Regression relationship: y = 31.7-0.90x, r=0.69, N=14, P<0.003. Population stability was itself a consequence of a fairly stable territorial system, in which the landscape was apparently occupied to a similar level each year. From Newton (1991).

1.3 Density limitation in relation to food supplies

In the limitation of breeding numbers within suitable habitat, two resources seem of major importance to birds of prey, namely food supplies and nest sites (Newton, 1979). Consider first the relationship between breeding densities and food supplies in areas where nest sites are freely available.

1.3.1 Regional variations in breeding density

In some species, regional variations in breeding density are associated with regional variations in prey supplies. Sparrowhawk nesting densities in the woods of 12 different regions of Britain varied in relation to the local densities of prey birds. The hawks nested closer together, at higher densities, in areas where their prey were most numerous. The woods in all of these areas were of roughly similar structure, and the differences in prey densities were associated with variation in elevation and soil type (Newton *et al.*, 1977, 1986). Similar relationships between regional breeding densities and prey densities have been documented for common kestrel (Village, 1990), common buzzard (Newton, 1979; Graham *et al.*, 1995), golden eagle (Watson *et al.*, 1992) and peregrine in Britain (Ratcliffe, 1969), and in these and other species elsewhere.

In solitary nesting raptors the link between density and food supply is apparently brought about by spacing behaviour, as birds adjust their spacing (territory sizes) to correspond with the food situation. In permanent residents, such as golden eagles in Scotland, density is most closely related to food supply (carrion) in winter when food is scarcest (Watson *et al.*, 1992), but in summer migrants, such as kestrels in Scotland, it is adjusted to food supply in spring, at the time of settling (Village, 1990).

Unusually high densities of raptors are invariably associated with an unusual abundance of food. Examples of natural situations are the abundance of peregrines around large seabird colonies (Beebe, 1960), of ospreys *Pandion haliaetus* around fisheries (Henny, 1988), and of black eagles *Aquila verreauxii* around hyrax concentrations (Gargett, 1975), but even greater densities of raptors occur in some African and Asian cities, where human activity provides the food. The city of Delhi, in India, covers 150 km^2 and in 1967 held an estimated 2,900 raptor pairs, a density of more than 19 pairs per km^2 (Galushin, 1974). These were mainly scavenging species, such as black kite *Milvus migrans* (15 pairs per km^2) and white-backed vulture *Gyps africanus* (four pairs per km^2), but also included some other species. This high density was associated primarily with a huge amount of food within the city (mainly garbage and animal carcasses), but also with an abundance of nesting sites, and an unusual tolerance by the human population.

The implications from such natural variation are that raptors respond to the food situation, and that solitary species space themselves more widely, in larger territories, where food is sparse. An earlier argument, on whether food or behaviour limits density, becomes redundant if the birds adjust the spacing to the resources available (Marquiss & Newton, 1982; Village, 1983). So one line of evidence that breeding density is limited in relation to food supply comes from the long-term stability of populations, but at different densities in different regions.

1.3.2 Annual variations in breeding density

For other species, the idea that breeding density is adjusted in relation to food supply comes not from long-term stability in density, but from annual fluctuations in density which parallel fluctuations in food. Most species in the regions concerned have restricted diets based on cyclic prey. Two main cycles are recognised: (a) an approximate four-year cycle of rodents on northern tundras, boreal forests and temperate grasslands; and (b) an approximate ten-year cycle of snowshoe hares *Lepus americanus* in the boreal forests of North America. Some gamebirds are also cyclic, but whereas in northern Europe they follow the four-year rodent cycle, in North America they follow the ten-year hare cycle (Lack, 1954; Keith, 1963). The main raptor and owl species that depend on such prey show great year-to-year fluctuation in breeding density in parallel with fluctuation in their food supply (Table 1.2). Moreover, some species, such as the northern goshawk, fluctuate in density where they feed on cyclic prey, but remain fairly stable in density where their food-supply is more stable (often through being more varied). Such regional variation within species provides further circumstantial evidence for a link between breeding density and food supply.

Table 1.2. Annual variation in breeding numbers of raptors and owls that exploit greatly fluctuating food sources.

Species that eat rodents (approximately 4 year cycles)

Rough-legged hawk *Buteo lagopus*
- 0-9 pairs during 9 years, North Norway (Hagen, 1969)*
- 26-90 pairs during 34 years, Colville River, Alaska (Mindell *et al.*, 1987)
- 10-82 pairs during 5 years, Seward Peninsula, Alaska (Swartz *et al.*, 1974)
- 0-27 pairs during 6 years, NW Territories (Court *et al.*, 1988)

Hen harrier *Circus cyaneus*
- 10-24 females in 33 km^2 during 22 years, Orkney, Scotland (Balfour, in Hamerström, 1969)
- 13-25 females in 160 km^2 during 5 years, Wisconsin (Hamerström, 1969)*†
- 0-9 pairs in 6 years between 1938 and 1946 (Hagen, 1969)*
- 8-22 pairs during 8 years, Scotland (Redpath *et al.*, 2002)*

Common kestrel *Falco tinnunculus*
- 35-109 clutches during 4 years; Netherlands (Cavé, 1968)*
- Approximately 20-fold fluctuation in index of number of broods ringed in Britain over 42 years, with peaks every 4-5 years (Snow, 1968)*
- 1-14 pairs during 5 years, North Norway (Hagen, 1969)*
- 1-16 nests during 12 years, Swabian Alps (Rockenbauch, 1968)*
- 28-38 pairs during 4 years, south Scotland, 9-28 pairs and 12-22 pairs in two areas during 6 years, southern England (Village, 1990)*
- 2-46 pairs during 11 years, western Finland (Korpimäki & Norrdahl, 1991)*
- 2-29 pairs during 23 years, northern England (Petty *et al.*, 2000)*

Black-shouldered kite *Elanus axillaris*
- Increase from 1 to 8 nests in one year, associated with rodent plague, South Africa (Malherbe, 1963)*
- 19-35 individuals, during 3 years, Transvaal, South Africa (Mendelsohn, 1983)*

Long-eared owl *Asio otus*

- 1-19 pairs during 11 years, western Finland (Korpimäki & Norrdahl, 1991)*
- 9-18 pairs during 4 years, south Scotland (Village, 1981)*

Short-eared owl *Asio flammeus*

- 0-28 pairs during 2 years, northern Alaska (Pitelka *et al.*, 1955)*
- 0-49 pairs during 11 years, western Finland (Korpimäki & Norrdahl, 1991)*
- 0-27 pairs (index) during 23 years, northern England (Petty *et al.*, 2000)*

Snowy owl *Nyctea scandiaca*

- 3 and 7 pairs during 2 years, northern Alaska (Pitelka *et al.*, 1955)*

Tengmalm's owl *Aegolius funereus*

- 3-63 pairs during 7 years, western Finland (Korpimäki, 1985)*

Barn owl *Tyto alba*

- 14-94 pairs during 13 years, south Scotland (Taylor, 1994)*

Species that eat gallinaceous birds and rabbits (4-year or 10-year cycles)

Ferruginous hawk *Buteo regalis*

- 5-16 pairs during 8 years in one area, 1-8 pairs during 3 years in another area, Utah (Woffinden & Murphy, 1977)*

Northern goshawk *Accipiter gentilis*

- 0-4 nests during 13 years; 2-9 nests during 7 years, in two areas of Sweden (Höglund, 1964)
- 1-9 nests during 4 years, Alaska (McGowan, 1975)
- 0-11 pairs during 7 years, Yukon (Doyle & Smith, 1994)*
- 11-28 pairs during 13 years, Finland (Wikman & Lindén, 1981)*

Gyr falcon *Falco rusticolus*

- 13-49 pairs during 5 years, Seward Peninsula, Alaska (Swartz *et al.*, 1974)*
- 19-31 occupied cliffs and 12-29 successful nests during 4 years, Alaska (Platt, 1977)*
- 8-19 pairs during 27 years, Colville River, Alaska (Mindell *et al.*, 1987)
- 19-31 pairs during 4 years, Brooks Range, Alaska (Platt, 1977)
- 39-63 occupied territories during 17 years, north-east Iceland (Nielsen, 1999)*

Great horned owl *Bubo virginianus*

- 20-40 territory holders, 20-86 total birds during 6 years, Yukon (Rohner, 1995)*

* Prey population also assessed and related to raptor numbers.
† Excluding one year when population dropped from DDT poisoning.

Populations of microtine rodents do not reach a peak simultaneously over their whole range, but the cycles may be synchronised over tens, hundreds or many thousands of square kilometres, out of phase with those in more distant areas. However, peak populations may occur simultaneously over many more areas in some years than in others, giving a measure of synchrony, for example, to lemming cycles over large parts of northern Canada, with few regional exceptions (Chitty, 1950). In addition, the periodicity of vole cycles tends to increase northwards, from about three years between peaks in temperate and southern boreal regions, increasing to four or five years in northern boreal regions. The amplitude of the cycles also increases northwards from barely discernible cycles in some temperate regions to marked fluctuations further north, where peak densities typically exceed troughs by more than a hundred-fold (Hanski *et al.*, 1991). Even further north, on the tundra, the periodicity of lemming cycles is in some places even longer (five to seven years between peaks on Wrangel Island (Menyushina, 1997)), and the amplitude is even greater, with peaks sometimes exceeding troughs by more than a thousand-fold (Shelford, 1945). In most places, the increase phase of the cycle usually takes two to three years, and the crash phase one to two years. Importantly, the crash phase often overlaps with spring and summer, a time when rodent predators are breeding.

The longer hare cycles have been less extensively studied, but peaks in numbers can exceed troughs by more than a hundred-fold (Adamcik *et al.*, 1978). Unlike the situation in rodents, the cycle is more or less synchronised over much of boreal North America, with populations across the continent peaking in the same years (Keith & Rusch, 1988).

Raptors and owls show two main types of response to cyclic fluctuations in their food-supply (Figure 1.2). One type is shown by resident species, which tend to stay on the same territories year-round and from year to year. While preferring rodents (or lagomorphs), they eat other prey, so they can remain in the same area through low rodent years. However, their survival may be poorer, and their productivity much poorer, in low than in high prey years. In low prey years, the majority of territorial pairs may make no attempt to breed, and those that do, lay relatively small clutches and raise small broods. The common buzzard, tawny owl, Ural owl *Strix uralensis*, barn owl *Tyto alba* and great horned owl *Bubo virginianus* are in this category, responding functionally to prey numbers, and numerically chiefly in terms of the numbers of young raised (Mebs, 1964; Southern, 1970; Saurola, 1989; Petty, 1992; Taylor, 1994; Rohner, 1996). This type of response, shown by resident populations, produces a lag between prey and predator numbers, so that high predator densities follow good food-supplies and low densities follow poor supplies (Figure 1.2). Prey and predator densities fluctuate in parallel, but with the predator behind the prey (up to two years behind in the snowshoe hare-great horned owl system (Rohner, 1995)). The lag period depends partly on the age at which first-breeding in the predator occurs. In the tawny owl, young produced in a peak vole year often breed in the following year, just before vole numbers crash (Petty, 1992), but in the great horned owl most individuals reach two or more years before they attempt to breed (Rohner, 1995)). The same holds for gyr falcons *Falco rusticolus* in Iceland, where the main prey species (rock ptarmigan *Lagopus mutus*) fluctuates with roughly ten-year periodicity and where the total numbers of falcons showed a two year lag, and the numbers of territorial falcons a three year lag, behind the peak ptarmigan year (Nielsen, 1999, Chapter 24).

The second type of response is shown by 'prey-specialist' nomadic species, which concentrate to breed in different areas in different years, depending on where their food is plentiful at the time. Typically, individuals might have one to two years in the same area in each three to five year vole cycle, before moving on when prey decline. They thus respond

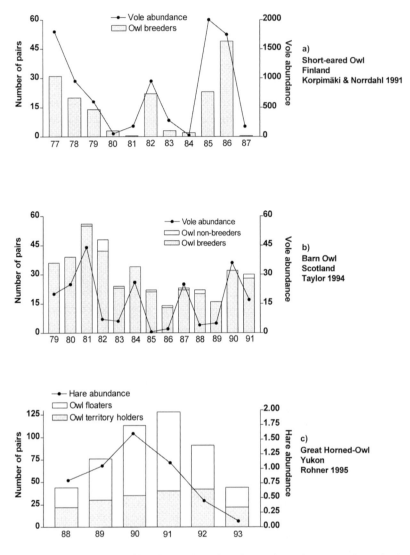

Figure 1.2. Fluctuations in the numbers of breeding and non-breeding owls in relation to indices of vole densities. (a) Short-eared owl, immediate response; (b) barn owl, lag in response in decline years; (c) great horned owl, long lag in response, with the peak in total owl numbers one year behind the peak in prey numbers, and in breeding owl numbers two years behind. From Korpimäki & Norrdahl (1991), Taylor (1994), and Rohner (1995).

to their food supplies more or less immediately, so that their local densities can match food supplies at the time, with minimal lag. Familiar examples from among owls include the short-eared owl *Asio flammeus*, long-eared owl *Asio otus*, northern hawk owl *Surnia ulula*, and to some extent, snowy owl *Nyctea scandiaca* and great grey owl *Strix nebulosa*, and from among raptors the rough-legged buzzard *Buteo lagopus* and in some areas the common kestrel, hen harrier *Circus cyaneus*, Montagu's harrier *Circus pygargus* and black-winged kite *Elanus caeruleus* (Table 1.2).

The local densities of most such species can vary from nil in low rodent years to several tens of pairs per 100 km² in intermediate (increasing) or high rodent years. In an area of western Finland, for example, over an 11 year period, numbers of short-eared owls varied between 0 and 49 pairs, numbers of long-eared owls between 0 and 19 pairs, and numbers of kestrels between 2 and 46 pairs, in accordance with spring densities of *Microtus* voles (Korpimäki & Norrdahl, 1991). When voles are plentiful, such species tend to raise large broods, so if they are successful in finding prey-rich areas year after year, individuals could in theory breed well every year, buffered from effects of local fluctuations in their prey. In practice, however, they may not always find suitable prey-rich areas. In all of the owl species mentioned, individuals have sometimes been seen in areas with low prey populations, typically as single wide-ranging non-breeders, rather than as territorial pairs (e.g. Pitelka *et al.*, 1955; Menyushina, 1997). In addition, if previously high rodent numbers crash during the course of a breeding season, nest desertion and chick mortality can be high. Under these conditions, 22 out of 24 nests of short-eared owls in south Scotland failed, and most of the adults left the area in early summer, when they would normally be raising young (Lockie, 1955).

Relationships between nomadic owl and microtine densities have been studied mainly in particular areas, monitored over a number of years. Such studies have revealed temporal correlations between predator and prey numbers. However, spatial correlations were found by Wiklund *et al.* (1998), who counted predators and prey in 15 different localities on the Eurasian tundra in a single year. These areas extended from the Kola peninsula in the west, through 140° of longitude, to Wrangel Island in the east. Comparing areas, densities of snowy owl (and two skua *Stercorarius* species) were correlated with densities of lemming, which were at different stages of their cycle in different areas.

The two responses (delayed and simultaneous) are not completely distinct, and different species of owl and raptor may be better described as showing a graded response, from the most sedentary at one end to the most mobile at the other. Moreover, the same species may show regional variation in behaviour depending on food supply, and the extent to which alternative prey are available when favoured prey are scarce. The more varied the diet, the less the chance of all prey types being scarce at the same time. Korpimäki (1986) examined the population fluctuations, movements and diet of Tengmalm's owls *Aegolius funereus* from studies at 30 different European localities extending from about 50°N to 70°N. The amplitude and cyclicity of owl population fluctuations increased northwards, while diet breadth and degree of site fidelity decreased northwards. This fitted the fact that microtine fluctuations became more pronounced and more synchronised northwards, while the number of alternative prey decreased. Furthermore, snow conditions were more important in the north, because this small owl cannot easily get at voles under deep snow. According to Korpimäki (1986), then, Tengmalm's owl could be described as a resident generalist predator of small mammals and birds in central Europe, as partially nomadic (with males resident and females moving around) in south and west Finland, and as a highly nomadic microtine specialist in northern Fennoscandia, in areas with the most pronounced vole cycles.

Among lagomorph feeders, the great horned owl and goshawk seem to show much greater fluctuation in breeding density in the north of their North American range, where they depend primarily on snowshoe hares, than further south where they have a wider range of prey, but I know of no detailed studies in the southern parts. There would be little value in great horned owls or goshawks in northern areas breeding nomadically, because, as mentioned above, snowshoe hares seem to fluctuate in synchrony over their whole range.

Birds leaving one area because of a shortage of hares would be unlikely to find many more hares anywhere else. This is in marked contrast to the situation in microtine-feeding species.

1.3.3 Long-term or step-wise changes in food supplies

Some raptor species, which are normally fairly stable in numbers, have shown a marked change in breeding density following a marked change in food supply. Often such population changes result from human impacts on habitats, but not always. An example is provided by the buzzard in Britain, in which breeding densities fell after the viral disease myxomatosis reduced the number of rabbits that formed the main prey. In one area, numbers dropped from 21 pairs to 14 pairs between one year and the next, as rabbit numbers were reduced (Dare, 1961).

Lest anyone think from the foregoing that marked temporal changes in breeding density occur only in species that eat microtines or lagomorphs, consider the peregrine. In parts of Britain nesting densities have increased greatly in recent decades (to well above any previously recorded levels), in association with the increased availability of homing pigeons, a favourite prey (Ratcliffe, 1993; Crick & Ratcliffe, 1995).

1.3.4 Modifying influence of weather

In much of northern Eurasia and North America, winter snow provides a protective blanket over small rodents that live and breed in the vegetation beneath. The level of protection that snow provides depends on its depth, the hardness of the surface crust and the duration of lie, all of which tend to increase with latitude. Different species of rodent-eating raptors and owls vary in their ability to detect and secure rodents under snow, and in general the larger (heavier) species are better able to penetrate snow than smaller ones. The great grey owl is renowned for its ability to smash through hard deep snow (45 cm or more) to catch rodents which it apparently detects by ear (Nero, 1980), while small species, such as Tengmalm's owl, are disadvantaged by even very shallow snow (Sonerud, 1984). The behaviour of the rodents themselves also affects their accessibility to their avian predators, particularly the frequency with which they emerge and run along the surface.

Prolonged snow cover can sometimes stop rodent-eaters from responding in the usual way to a rodent peak in early spring, affecting breeding density, proportion of pairs nesting and clutch sizes (for snowy owl, see Menyushina, 1997), and in some winters it can lead to large-scale starvation even when voles are plentiful (for barn owl, see Shawyer, 1987; Taylor 1994; and for tawny owl, see Jedrzejewski & Jedrzejewski, 1998; Saurola, 1997).

In some areas, year-to-year changes in resident breeding populations of common kestrel have been linked with winter weather, which influences food availability (Village, 1990; Kostrzewa & Kostrzewa, 1991). Marked declines in kestrel numbers, associated with heavy mortality, occur in years of prolonged snow cover, when rodents remain hidden for long periods. Larger species, which can withstand longer periods on reduced rations, seem much less affected by hard winters.

1.4 Density limitation in relation to nest sites

In some districts, bird of prey breeding densities are held by shortage of nest sites below the level that the available food supply would be expected to support. The evidence is of two kinds: (a) breeding raptors are scarce or absent in areas in which nesting places are scarce or absent, but which otherwise appear suitable (non-breeders may live in such areas); and (b) the provision of artificial nest sites is sometimes followed by an increase in breeding density, while removal of nest sites can lead to a decrease in breeding density. Kestrel numbers increased from a few pairs to more than 100 pairs when nesting boxes were provided in a Dutch polder area with few natural sites (Cavé, 1968). Similar results were obtained with other populations of kestrel, and also with American kestrels, ospreys and prairie falcons *Falco mexicanus* (Reese, 1970; Rhodes, 1972; Hamerström *et al.*, 1973; R. Fife, pers. comm.). Among owls, increases in breeding density following nest site provision have been noted in little owls *Athene noctua*, barn owls, Ural owls and others (Mikkola, 1983; Exo, 1992; Petty *et al.*, 1994). The results from a controlled experiment on common kestrel are given in Table 1.3.

Table 1.3. Results of experimental provision of nest sites for European kestrels in areas previously devoid of breeding kestrels. All birds used the boxes provided and included both first year and adult breeders. From Village (1983).

	No. of nest sites provided	No. of pairs nesting in same year
Experimental areas	17	8
Control areas	0	0

Sometimes the provision of nesting sites has facilitated an extension of breeding range, as exemplified by the Mississippi kite *Ictinia mississippiensis* and other species which nest in tree plantations on North American grasslands (Parker, 1974). Likewise, nesting on buildings has allowed peregrines and other cliff nesters to breed in areas otherwise closed to them through lack of nest sites. On the other hand, the destruction of nesting sites has sometimes led to reductions in breeding density, as in certain eagles when large free-standing trees were felled (Bijleveld, 1974), in peregrines when cliffs providing nest sites were destroyed by mining (Porter & White, 1973) and in barn owls when old buildings were demolished or renovated (Taylor & Walton, Chapter 32). In addition, when nest sites are scarce, species may compete for them, and the presence of one dominant species may restrict the numbers and distribution of another (Newton, 1979).

1.5 Winter densities

Some raptors stay on their breeding sites all year, but others spread over a wider area after breeding, or migrate to a completely different area. Outside of the breeding season, nest sites are less important, so in theory the birds have greater freedom to move around, and can exploit temporary food sources in a way not possible while breeding. Some Palaearctic raptors, which winter in Africa, may spend most of their time between breeding seasons on the move, following rain belts, and exploiting temporary abundances of termites, locusts, and other prey (Newton, 1979). At this season, therefore, food can take over as the all-important limiting factor.

The few studies that have been made of species that remain in an area all winter again imply that food supply has a major influence on density. For example, Craighead & Craighead (1956) compared the raptor population in an area of Michigan over two years, in one of which there was a high vole population and in the other a low one. In the good vole year, 96 raptors of seven species were present in the area, but in the poor year only 27 individuals of five species were counted. Other studies involve individual species over longer periods (e.g. Village, 1990). Evidently, within the habitats that are occupied, food supply can be an important limiting factor at all seasons.

1.6 Discussion

1.6.1 Food and nest sites

To judge from available evidence, the carrying capacity of any habitat for raptors and owls is set by two main resources, food and nest sites, and whichever is most restricted is likely to limit breeding density. On this basis, much of the natural variation in breeding densities can probably be explained. However, much of the relevant research has been done on resident populations, and it is possible that some migrant populations may be limited on winter quarters, and so be unable to occupy their breeding habitat to the full. The European honey buzzard *Pernis apivorus* provides a possible example. This situation is analogous to that of some small resident species which, at mid-to-high latitudes are in some years reduced by winter severity below the level that nesting habitat would support.

Most of the evidence presented above on the role of food and nest sites is based on correlations, but experiments have confirmed the existence of surplus birds in some populations, and the provision of nest sites has confirmed their importance as potential limiting factors. So far, to my knowledge, no proper experiments have been made that involve manipulation of the food supply of whole populations (as opposed to individuals). This is an obvious gap in the study of raptor populations, the results of which could have applications in management; for however good a habitat in other respects, raptors cannot occupy it without the prey to support them.

Another aspect in need of further study concerns the precise mechanism which leads individuals to take larger territories (giving lower densities) where food is scarce. Do territory owners have to forage more widely in such conditions, simply extending their defence accordingly and 'forcing out' their weaker neighbours; or are owners obliged to take smaller territories in areas of high food density because the many birds attracted to such areas push up the defence costs of large territories to unsustainable levels (Temeles, 1987; Newton, 1998, pp. 46-48)? These are only two of several possible mechanisms, and food provision experiments, together with observations on marked birds, might help to decide between them.

In the so-called 'nomadic' rodent-eating species, which concentrate to breed in widely separated areas in different years, little is known of how individuals find prey-rich areas, or of how far they move between breeding seasons. Although some revealing ring recoveries are available (see Newton, 2002, for owls), such questions would be better addressed by use of satellite tracking of radio-tagged individuals.

1.6.2 Other limiting factors

Food and nest sites are, of course, not the only factors limiting the current numbers and distributions of raptors in Britain and elsewhere. Many populations are held by persecution (past or present), or by pesticides and other toxic chemicals, below the level that the contemporary landscape would support. In addition, most raptor populations in Britain are currently in the process of change, either in recovery from past persecution or pesticide impacts, or in decline from renewed persecution or habitat degradation and decline in food-supplies. Nonetheless, study of the natural limiting factors, as discussed above, provides a useful framework within which to organise our thinking and to plan our management efforts.

A largely unexplored aspect is the extent to which the numbers and distributions of some raptor and owl species may be limited by the presence of other species. Such limitation could occur either through competition for a shared food supply, by direct predation of small species by large ones, or by small species avoiding large ones, and thereby having less habitat or fewer nest sites available to them. Such matters are likely to require more attention in Britain as goshawks extend their range, with potential effects on smaller raptors and owls, and if eagle owls establish themselves (nesting recorded in at least three widely separated areas in recent years). Both these species include many smaller raptors in their diets, and could influence their population levels.

Instances are on record of golden eagles displacing peregrines from cliff nest-sites, and peregrines displacing kestrels (Newton, 1979). In addition, some owl species have been suspected of limiting the distribution of others (for Eurasian eagle owl possibly affecting Ural owl, see Saurola (1992); for Ural owl possibly affecting Tengmalm's owl, see Hakkarainen & Korpimäki (1996); for tawny owl possibly affecting Tengmalm's and Eurasian pygmy owls, see Koenig (1998); and for Ural owl and tawny owl possibly affecting one another, see Lundberg (1980)). It is clear, therefore, that while food supply is the primary limiting factor for many raptors and owls, nest site shortages, adverse weather or other secondary factors can sometimes reduce breeding densities and performance substantially below what the food supply would otherwise permit.

Acknowledgements

I am grateful to two anonymous referees for helpful comments.

References

Adamcik, R.S., Todd, A.W. & Keith, L.B. (1978). Demographic and dietary responses of great horned owls during a snowshoe hare cycle. *Canadian Field Naturalist*, **92**, 156-166.

Beebe, F.C. (1960). The marine peregrine of the Pacific northwest coast. *Condor*, **62**, 145-189.

Bijleveld, M. (1974). *Birds of Prey in Europe*. MacMillan Press, London.

Bowman, R. & Bird, D.M. (1986). Ecological correlates of mate replacement in the American kestrel. *Condor*, **88**, 440-445.

Bowman, T.D., Schempf, P.F. & Bernatowicz, J.A. (1995). Bald eagle survival and population dynamics in Alaska after the Exxon Valdez oil spill. *Journal of Wildlife Management*, **59**, 317-324.

Cavé, A.J. (1968). The breeding of the kestrel, *Falco tinnunculus* L., in the reclaimed area Oostelijk Flevoland. *Netherlands Journal of Zoology*, **18**, 313-407.

Chitty, H. (1950). Canadian arctic wildlife enquiry, 1943-49, with a summary of results since 1933. *Journal of Animal Ecology*, **19**, 180-193.

Court, G.S., Bradley, D.M., Gates, C.C. & Boag, D.A. (1988). The population biology of peregrine falcons in the Keewater District of the Northwest Territories, Canada. In *Peregrine Falcon Populations. Their Management and Recovery*, ed. by T.J. Cade, J.H. Enderson & C.M. White. The Peregrine Fund, Boise. pp. 729-739.

Craighead, J.J. & Craighead, F.C. (1956). *Hawks, Owls and Wildlife*. Stackpole Co., Pennsylvania.

Crick, H.Q.P. & Ratcliffe, D.A. (1995). The peregrine *Falco peregrinus* breeding population of the United Kingdom in 1991. *Bird Study*, **42**, 1-19.

Dare, P. (1961). Ecological observations on a breeding population of the common buzzard *Buteo buteo*. Ph.D. thesis, Exeter University.

Doyle, F.I. & Smith, J.M.N. (1994). Population responses of northern goshawks to the 10-year cycle in numbers of snowshoe hares. *Studies in Avian Biology*, **16**, 122-129.

Exo, K.M. (1992). Population ecology of little owls *Athene noctua* Central Europe: a review. In *The Ecology and Conservation of European Owls*, ed. by C.A. Galbraith, I.R. Taylor & S. Percival. Joint Nature Conservation Committee, Peterborough. pp. 64-75.

Galushin, V.M. (1974). Synchronous fluctuations in populations of some raptors and their prey. *Ibis*, **116**,127-134.

Gargett, V. (1975). The spacing of black eagles in the Matopos, Rhodesia. *Ostrich*, **46**, 1-44.

Graham, I.M., Redpath, S.M. & Thirgood, S.J. (1995). The diet and breeding density of common buzzards *Buteo buteo* in relation to indices of prey abundance. *Bird Study*, **42**, 165-173.

Hagen, Y. (1969). Norwegian studies on the reproduction of birds of prey and owls in relation to micro-rodent population fluctuations. *Fauna*, **22**, 73-126.

Hakkarainen, H. & Korpimäki, E. (1996). Competitive and predatory interactions among raptors: an observational and experimental study. *Ecology*, **77**, 1134-1142.

Haller, H. (1996). Der Steinadler in Graubünden. *Ornithologische Beobachter*, **9**, 1-167.

Hamerström, F. (1969). A harrier population study. In *Peregrine Falcon Populations. Their Biology and Decline*, ed. by J.J. Hickey. University of Wisconsin Press, Madison. pp. 367-383.

Hamerström, F., Hamerström, F.N. & Hart, J. (1973). Nest boxes: an effective management tool for Kestrels. *Journal of Wildlife Management*, **37**, 400-403.

Hanski, I., Hansson, L. & Henttonen, H. (1991). Specialist predators, generalist predators, and the microtine rodent cycle. *Journal of Animal Ecology*, **60**, 353-367.

Henny, C.J. (1988). Large osprey colony discovered in Oregon in 1899. *Murrelet*, **69**, 33-36.

Höglund, N. (1964). Der Habicht *Accipiter gentilis* Linné in Fennoscandia. *Viltrevy*, **2**, 195-270.

Jedrzejewski, B. & Jedrzejewski, W. (1998). *Predation in Vertebrate Communities. The Bialowieza Primeval Forest as a Case Study*. Springer-Verlag, Berlin.

Keith, L.B. (1963). *Wildlife's Ten-Year Cycle*. University Wisconsin Press, Madison.

Keith, L.B. & Rusch, D.H. (1988). Predation's role in the cyclic fluctuations of ruffed grouse. *Proceedings of the International Ornithological Conference*, **19**, 699-732.

Kenward, R.E., Marcström, V. & Karlbom, M. (1999). Demographic estimates from radio-tagging: models of age-specific survival and breeding in the goshawk. *Journal of Animal Ecology*, **68**, 1020-1033.

Kenward, R.E., Walls, S.S., Hodder, K.H., Pahkala, M., Freeman, S.N. & Simpson, V.R. (2000). The prevalence of non-breeders in raptor populations: evidence from rings, radio-tags and transect surveys. *Oikos*, **91**, 271-279.

Koenig, C. (1998). Ecology and population of pygmy owls *Glaucidium passerinum* in the Black Forest (SW Germany). In *Holarctic Birds of Prey*, ed. by R.D. Chancellor, B.-U. Meyburg & J.J. Ferroro. World Working Group on Birds of Prey and Owls, Berlin. pp. 447-450.

Korpimäki, E. (1985). Rapid tracking of microtine populations by their avian predators: possible evidence for stabilising predation. *Oikos*, **45**, 281-284.

Korpimäki, E. (1986). Gradients in population fluctuations of Tengmalm's owl *Aegolius funereus* in Europe. *Oecologia*, **69**, 195-201.

Korpimäki, E. & Norrdahl, K. (1991). Numerical and functional responses of kestrels, short-eared owls and long-eared owls to vole densities. *Ecology*, **72**, 814-825.

Kostrzewa, R. & Kostrzewa, A. (1991). Winter weather, spring and summer density and subsequent breeding success of Eurasian kestrels, common buzzards, and northern goshawks. *Auk*, **108**, 342-347.

Lack, D. (1954). *The Natural Regulation of Animal Numbers.* University Press, Oxford.

Lack, D. (1966). *Population Studies of Birds.* University Press, Oxford.

Lockie, J.D. (1955). The breeding habits and food of short-eared owls after a vole plague. *Bird Study*, **2**, 53-69.

Lundberg, A. (1980). Why are the Ural owl *Strix uralensis* and the tawny owl *S. aluco* parapatric in Scandinavia? *Ornis Scandinavica*, **11**, 116-120.

Malherbe, A.P. (1963). Notes on the birds of prey and some others at Boshoek north of Rustenburg during a rodent plague. *Ostrich*, **34**, 95-96.

Marquiss, M. & Newton, I. (1982). A radio-tracking study of the ranging behaviour and dispersion of European sparrowhawks *Accipiter nisus*. *Journal of Animal Ecology*, **51**, 111-133.

McGowan, J.D. (1975). *Distribution, Density and Productivity of Goshawks in Interior Alaska.* Department of Fish & Game Report, Alaska.

Mebs, T. (1964). Biologie und Populationsdynamik des Mausebussards (*Buteo buteo*). *Journal für Ornithologie*, **105**, 247-306.

Mendelsohn, J.M. (1983). Social behaviour and dispersion of the black-shouldered kite. *Ostrich*, **54**, 1-18.

Menyushina, I.E. (1997). Snowy owl (*Nyctea scandiaca*) reproduction in relation to lemming population cycles on Wrangel Island. In *Biology and Conservation of Owls of the Northern Hemisphere*, ed. by J.R. Duncan, D.H. Johnson & T.H. Nicholls. Second International Symposium, February 5-9, 1997, United States Department of Agriculture, Winnipeg, Manitoba, Canada. pp. 572-582.

Mikkola, H. (1983). *Owls of Europe.* Poyser, Calton.

Mindell, D.P., Albuquerque, J.L.B. & White, C.M. (1987). Breeding population fluctuations in some raptors. *Oecologia*, **72**, 382-388.

Monneret, R.-J. (1988). Changes in the peregrine falcon populations of France. In *Peregrine Falcon Populations. Their Management and Recovery*, ed. by T.J. Cade, J.H. Enderson, C.G. Thelander & C.M. White. The Peregrine Fund Inc., Boise. pp. 201-213.

Nero, R.W. (1980). *The Great Grey Owl: Phantom of the Northern Forest.* Smithsonian Institution Press, Washington, D.C.

Newton, I. (1979). *Population Ecology of Raptors.* Poyser, Berkhamsted.

Newton, I. (1988). Individual performance in sparrowhawks: the ecology of two sexes. *Proceedings of the International Ornithological Congress*, **19**, 125-154.

Newton, I. (1991a). The role of recruitment in population regulation. *Proceedings of the International Ornithological Congress*, **20**, 1689-1699.

Newton, I. (1991b). Habitat variation and population regulation in sparrowhawks. *Ibis*, **133**, supplement 1, 76-88.

Newton, I. (1998). *Population Limitation in Birds.* Academic Press, London.

Newton, I. (2002). Population limitation in Holarctic owls. In *Ecology and Conservation of Owls*, ed. by I. Newton, R.K. Kavanagh, J. Olsen & I.R. Taylor. CSIRO, Canberra. pp. 3-29.

Newton, I. & Marquiss, M. (1991). Removal experiments and the limitation of breeding density in sparrowhawks. *Journal of Animal Ecology*, **60**, 535-544.

Newton, I., Marquiss, M., Weir, D.N. & Moss, D. (1977). Spacing of sparrowhawk nesting territories. *Journal of Animal Ecology*, **46**, 425-441.

Newton, I. & Rothery, P. (2001). Estimation and limitation of numbers of floaters in a Eurasian sparrowhawk population. *Ibis*, **143**, 442-449.

Newton, I., Wyllie, I. & Mearns, R.M. (1986). Spacing of sparrowhawks in relation to food supply. *Journal of Animal Ecology*, **55**, 361-370.

Nielsen, O.K. (1999). Gyrfalcon predation on ptarmigan: numerical and functional responses. *Journal of Animal Ecology*, **68**, 1034-1050.

Parker, J.W. (1974). Populations of the Mississippi kite in the Great Plains. *Raptor Research Foundation, Raptor Research Report*, **3**, 159-172.

Petty, S.J. (1992). Ecology of the tawny owl *Strix aluco* in the spruce forests of Northumberland and Argyll. Ph.D thesis, Open University, Milton Keynes.

Petty, S.J., Lambin, X., Sherratt, T.N., Thomas, C.J., Mackinnon, J.L., Coles, C.F., Davison, M. & Little, B. (2000). Spatial synchrony in field vole *Microtus agrestis* abundance in a coniferous forest in northern England: the role of vole-eating raptors. *Journal of Applied Ecology*, **37**, 136-147.

Petty, S.J., Shaw, G. & Anderson, D.I.K. (1994). Value of nest boxes for population studies and conservation of owls in coniferous forests in Britain. *Journal of Raptor Research*, **28**, 134-142.

Pitelka, F.A., Tomich, P.Q. & Treichel, G.W. (1955). Breeding behaviour of jaegers and owls near Barrow, Alaska. *Condor*, **57**, 3-18.

Platt, J.B. (1977). The breeding behaviour of wild and captive gyr falcons in relation to their environment and human disturbance. Ph.D. thesis, Cornell University.

Porter, R.D. & White, C.M. (1973). The peregrine falcon in Utah, emphasising ecology and competition with the Prairie Falcon. *Brigham Young University Science Bulletin*, **18**, 1-74.

Ratcliffe, D.A. (1969). Population trends of the peregrine falcon in Great Britain. In *Peregrine Falcon Populations*, ed. by J.H. Hickey. University of Wisconsin Madison, Milwaukee & London Press. pp. 239-269.

Ratcliffe, D.A. (1972). The peregrine populations of Great Britain in 1971. *Bird Study*, **19**, 117-156.

Ratcliffe, D.A. (1993). *The Peregrine Falcon. Second edition.* T. & A.D. Poyser, London.

Redpath, S.M., Thirgood, S.J. & Clarke, R.G. (2002). Field vole *Microtus agrestis* abundance and hen harrier *Circus cyaneus* diet and breeding success in Scotland. *Ibis*, **144** (on line), E33-E38.

Reese, J.G. (1970). Reproduction in a Chesapeake Bay osprey population. *Auk*, **87**, 747-759.

Rhodes, L.I. (1972). Success of osprey nest structures at Martin National Wildlife Refuge. *Journal of Wildlife Management*, **36**, 1296-99.

Rockenbauch, D. (1968). Zur Brutbiologie des Turmfalken (*Falco tinnunculus* L.). *Anzeiger der Ornithologischen Gesellschaft in Bayern*, **8**, 267-76.

Rohner, C. (1995). Great horned owls and snowshoe hares - what causes the time-lag in the numerical response of predators to cyclic prey. *Oikos*, **74**, 61-68.

Rohner, C. (1996). The numerical response of great horned owls to the snowshoe hare cycle: consequences of non-territorial 'floaters' on demography. *Journal of Animal Ecology*, **65**, 359-370.

Rowan, W. (1921-22). Observations on the breeding habits of the merlin. *British Birds*, **15**, 122-129, 194-202, 222-231, 246-253.

Saurola, P. (1989). Ural owl. In *Lifetime Reproduction in Birds*, ed. by I. Newton. Academic Press, London. pp. 327-345.

Saurola, P. (1992). Population studies of the Ural owl *Strix uralensis* in Finland. In *The Ecology and Conservation of European Owls*, ed. by C.A. Galbraith, I.R. Taylor & S. Percival. Joint Nature Conservation Committee, Peterborough. pp, 28-31.

Saurola, P. (1997). Monitoring Finnish owls 1982-1996: methods and results. In *Biology and Conservation of Owls of the Northern Hemisphere*, ed. by J.R. Duncan, D.H. Johnson & T.H. Nicholls. Second International Symposium, February 5-9, 1997. United States Department of Agriculture, Winnipeg, Manitoba, Canada. pp. 363-380.

Shawyer, C.R. (1987). *The Barn Owl in the British Isles. Its Past, Present and Future.* The Hawk Trust, London.

Shelford, V.E. (1945). The relation of snowy owl migration to the abundance of the collared lemming. *Auk*, **62**, 592-596.

Snow, D.W. (1968). Movements and mortality of British kestrels *Falco tinnunculus*. *Bird Study*, **15**, 65-83.

Sonerud, G. (1984). Effect of snow cover on seasonal changes in diet, habitat and regional distribution of raptors that prey on small mammals in boreal zones of Fennoscandia. *Holarctic Ecology*, **9**, 33-47.

Southern, H.N. (1970). The natural control of a population of tawny owls (*Stix aluco*). *Journal of Zoology*, **162**, 197-285.

Steenhof, K., Kochert, M.N. & MacDonald, T.L. (1997). Interactive effects of prey and weather on golden eagle reproduction. *Journal of Animal Ecology*, **66**, 350-362.

Swartz, L.G., Walker, W., Roseneau, D.G. & Springer, A.M. (1974). Populations of gyrfalcons on the Seward Peninsula, Alaska, 1968-1972. *Raptor Research Foundation, Raptor Research Report*, **3**, 71-75.

Taylor, I. (1994). *Barn Owls*. University Press, Cambridge.

Temeles, E.J. (1987). The relative importance of prey availability and intruder pressure in feeding territory size regulation by harriers *Circus cyaneus*. *Oecologia*, **74**, 286-297.

Tubbs, C.R. (1974). *The Buzzard*. David & Charles, London.

Village, A. (1981). The diet and breeding of long-eared owls in relation to vole numbers. *Bird Study*, **28**, 215-224.

Village, A. (1983). The role of nest-site availability and territorial behaviour in limiting the breeding density of kestrels. *Journal of Animal Ecology*, **52**, 635-645.

Village, A. (1990). *The Kestrel*. T. & A.D. Poyser, Calton.

Watson, J. (1996). *The Golden Eagle*. Academic Press, London.

Watson, J., Rae, S.R. & Stillman, R. (1992). Nesting density and breeding success of golden eagles in relation to food supply in Scotland. *Journal of Animal Ecology*, **61**, 543-550.

Wendland, V. (1952-53). Populationsstudien an Raubvögeln 1 & 2. *Journal für Ornithologie*, **93**, 144-153; **94**, 103-13.

Wiklund, C.G., Kjellén, N. & Isakson, E. (1998). Mechanisms determining the spatial distribution of microtine predators on the Arctic tundra. *Journal of Animal Ecology*, **67**, 91-98.

Wikman, M. & Lindén, H. (1981). The influence of food-supply on goshawk population size. In *Understanding the Goshawk*, ed. by R.E. Kenward & I.M. Lindsay. International Association for Falconry and Conservation of Birds of Prey, Oxford. pp. 105-113.

Woffinden, N.D. & Murphy, J.R. (1977). Population dynamics of the ferruginous hawk during a prey decline. *Great Basin Naturalist*, **37**, 411-425.

2. NUMBERS AND INTERNATIONAL IMPORTANCE OF RAPTORS AND OWLS IN BRITAIN AND IRELAND

Jeremy J.D. Greenwood, Humphrey Q.P. Crick & Ian P. Bainbridge

Summary

1.   Although there have been various recent tabulations of populations of predatory birds in Britain and Ireland, they have been so condensed that the uncertainties, details and caveats associated with the data have sometimes not been apparent. Available information on the population sizes and trends of raptors and owls (Strigiformes) in Britain and Ireland is summarized here, using more precise terms than the usual 'breeding pairs' given, which is ambiguous.

2.   The methods on which these estimates are based range from occasional surveys of distribution (combined with educated guesses about mean densities) to full annual censuses. The relationship between the counts of breeding birds and the total number of birds present at the start of the breeding season is considered.

3.   The British and Irish populations, and their trends, are set in a European context. The populations of peregrine *Falco peregrinus*, kestrel *F. tinnunculus*, sparrowhawk *Accipiter nisus*, golden eagle *Aquila chrysaetos* and hobby *Falco subbuteo* moorland species are particularly important internationally.

4.   Owl populations tend to be declining all over Europe.

5.   Most raptor populations have increased in Britain and Ireland (though some have not, especially in more recent years).

6.   Fewer raptor species have increased in Europe as a whole.

7   It is important to establish nationally integrated raptor monitoring, to support the considerable amount of fieldwork which is carried out and to use the data that it provides more effectively to provide better information about national population sizes and trends.

2.1 Introduction

Birds of prey form an important, high-profile component of the biodiversity of Britain and Ireland. Although many of the species have relatively small population sizes, their potential impact on certain prey species has been the subject of considerable controversy. Such controversy has been particularly evident with respect to game-keeping and pigeon-fancying. However, although there have been various recent tabulations of populations of predatory birds in Britain and Ireland, they have been so condensed that the uncertainties, details and caveats associated with the data have sometimes not been apparent. Such information is important in providing a properly informed debate and, without it, can lead to ambiguity and disagreement about basic facts. Most recently, Gregory *et al.* (2002) have provided a comprehensive overview of the population status of birds in the United Kingdom, giving an analysis of conservation concern over the period 2002-2007.

In this chapter, we not only attempt to summarize the most recent estimates of numbers and trends in recent decades but also to describe how they were obtained. We clarify the units of counting used for each species (noting the ambiguity of 'breeding pairs') and consider what the estimates might mean in terms of the total population of full-grown birds in the country at the beginning of the breeding season. In addition, with the full publication of the European Bird Database (BirdLife International/European Bird Census Council, 2000), it is now possible to set British and Irish populations in a wider geographical context, in terms of both their sizes and their trends.

Consideration of the results and the methods used to obtain them allows us to explore the adequacy of current monitoring and to suggest improvements.

2.3 Methods

The estimates presented here are of breeding populations. We have avoided the use of the term 'breeding pair', since this means different things to different people, in favour of more precise terms.

So as to allow for a range of biogeographic and administrative interests, estimates are given for each species in respect of the following geographical units: Great Britain (GB), Ireland (I), United Kingdom (UK), England (E), Scotland (S), Wales (W), Isle of Man (M), Northern Ireland (NI), and Republic of Ireland (RI). Where figures are not shown, they can either be worked out from the figures given (e.g. I = NI+RI) or they should be taken as zero. Ranges shown in parentheses are 95% confidence limits.

In some cases, indirect estimates for the political divisions of GB or of Ireland have been based on estimates for the whole island; the overall estimate has been divided according to the numbers of hectads (10 x 10 km squares) in which the species was recorded in the 1988-91 breeding bird atlas (Gibbons *et al.*, 1993), each hectad being weighted according to the proportion of its tetrads in which the species was recorded. These are referred to as 'atlas-based estimates'.

The methods used to estimate populations and their trends in the UK fall into eight categories, with relevant species given as follows (scientific names are given in Section 2.4):–

1. Annual complete counts or systematic sample censuses. Red kite, white-tailed eagle, osprey.
2. Annual data-gathering by the Rare Breeding Birds Panel (RBBP) (Spencer *et al.*, 1992; Ogilvie, 1997; Ogilvie *et al.*, 2001). Since this relies largely on the unprompted submission of data by observers, the data are, to varying degrees, unsystematic and patchy; they are not controlled for variations in recorder effort. Honey buzzard, marsh harrier, Montagu's harrier.
3. Populations estimated by special non-annual surveys, but with trends derived from:

   - RBBP data and from coverage by Raptor Study Groups (RSGs). Hen harrier, golden eagle.
   - Trends from local RSG studies and other special study sites (but data not necessarily readily available). Merlin, peregrine.
   - The British Trust for Ornithology (BTO) Common Birds Census (CBC) and BTO/Joint Nature Conservation Committee/Royal Society for the Protection of

Birds Breeding Bird Survey (BBS) (Marchant *et al.,* 1990; Baillie *et al.,* 2001; Raven *et al.,* 2002). Buzzard, barn owl, little owl, tawny owl.

4. Population estimated by careful extrapolation from intensive localized studies. Trends from CBC and BBS. Sparrowhawk, kestrel.
5. Population estimated by educated guesswork.

   - Trends from CBC and BBS. Hobby.
   - Trends from changes in range recorded in the two atlases of breeding birds (Sharrock, 1976; Gibbons *et al.,* 1993: hereafter, the 1968-72 and 1988-91 atlases). Goshawk, short-eared owl, long-eared owl.

In most cases, surveys depend on fairly direct observations of breeding activities. For two, they depend on surveying behaviour that is thought, with more (tawny owl) or less (buzzard) justification, to be related to the holding of breeding territory (see species accounts below). A similar range of methods is used in the Republic of Ireland. We have used the Irish Raptor Study Group's Annual Round-up for 2000, with further details supplied by Lorcan O'Toole, referred to hereafter as IRSG data. Coverage in Ireland is generally less complete than in GB.

For most raptors, and some owls, there is a population of immature and non-breeding birds present, but rarely counted, during the breeding season. We have presented what information is available to relate the size of the total population of breeders and non-breeders at the start of the breeding season to the estimates of breeding numbers. Because direct information is generally sparse, we have used indirect methods to provide rough estimates of the extent of the non-breeding population.

To place the British and Irish populations in their European context we have used the European Bird Database (EBD) of BirdLife International and the European Bird Census Council. Data-gathering for the EBD was conducted in 1992-93 but some of the data are from earlier periods and others have been updated. They have been partially published by Tucker & Heath (1994) and Hagemeijer & Blair (1997) and fully documented by BirdLife International/European Bird Census Council (2000). The three publications differed somewhat both in the extent of updating of the database and in their definition of Europe. We used the most recent update, provided directly to us in November 2000. We used the definition of Europe in BirdLife/EBCC (2000) (their Figure 1), except that we excluded Greenland, Turkey and Cyprus. (Note that the book excluded Armenia, Azerbaijan and Georgia and, because of recent difficulties in gathering data, Bosnia & Herzegovina, Kosovo, Macedonia, Montenegro, and Serbia).

Full details of the questionnaires used to gather the data are given by Tucker & Heath (1994) (their Appendix 5). Respondents were asked to record the number of breeding pairs (not defined) in their country, in terms of both a minimum and a maximum estimate (or an exact count, if available). They were told that even 'very rough estimates' were useful and figures were provided by every country for all of the species considered here. We summed the means of the minima and maxima to get estimates of the European populations. Because European Russia holds such a high proportion of the total population of some species, we also made estimates excluding Russia. We have quoted estimates to no more than three significant figures because some of the national figures are very approximate.

Respondents were also asked to estimate the population trends of each species during 1970-90 in their countries, on the scale -2 = decrease greater than 50%, -1 = decrease of 20-50%, 0 = change of less than 20%, +1 = increase of 20-50%, and +2 = increase greater than 50%. We also scored special cases on this scale: fluctuating, without clear trend = 0, gone extinct in that country during 1970-90 = -2, and new breeder during 1970-90 = +2. We calculated a mean trend over all countries, weighted by population size, to get a measure of the overall European population change. In view of the approximate nature of the trend information, we have used a precision of only one decimal place for those means.

2.4 Population estimates and trends

2.4.1 Honey buzzard (Pernis apivorus)
Pairs with nests (2000): GB = 29; country breakdowns not available because of confidentiality (Batten, 2001).

This species is under-recorded and under-reported. The observations submitted to RBBP represent a combination of casual records and of systematic watches for displaying and nesting birds at known localities. In 2000, there was exhortation for more recording and more submission of data; all known current workers on the species were contacted, as were RSGs and other likely sources of information. Guidance on how to find honey buzzards was provided in articles in journals and in an advice page sent out to interested people. However, data were not obtained from all areas and a further 32 pairs or single birds were reported but without nests being confirmed, so the above total is certainly too low. Roberts *et al.* (1999) made an informal estimate of 50-60 territorial pairs.

Non-breeding birds are observed but it is not clear how many there are. The limited available information suggests that there are probably fewer non-breeders than breeders as, although breeding at one year old may occur, it is not normal (Kostrzewa, 1998), and probably the majority of yearlings and some adult birds over-summer in Africa (Bijlsma, 1993).

RBBP records suggest a large increase (Figure 2.1) but it is clear that the species is not only currently under-reported but that it was even more under-reported in the past. However, Steve Roberts (pers. comm.), who is working on the species, believes that there has been a real increase.

2.4.2 Red kite (Milvus milvus)
Pairs producing eggs (2000): E = 131 (118-146), S = 39, W = 259 (200-318); territorial pairs 153, 44, 337 respectively (Wotton *et al.*, 2002).

Production of eggs was confirmed by either the presence of a bird sitting on a nest, or a nest seen to contain eggs or young. The figures are reliable: the distribution of this species is well-known and most of the population is monitored each year. In 2000, all occupied areas outside of the two strongholds in Wales and the Chilterns (central England) were surveyed; in the Chilterns, a full survey was made of the core area and of sample squares around the edge; in Wales stratified samples were made of both the core and the range edge.

Although a few English birds have bred when one year old, the usual age at first breeding is two years (S. Wotton, pers. comm.), so there are some non-breeders in the population,

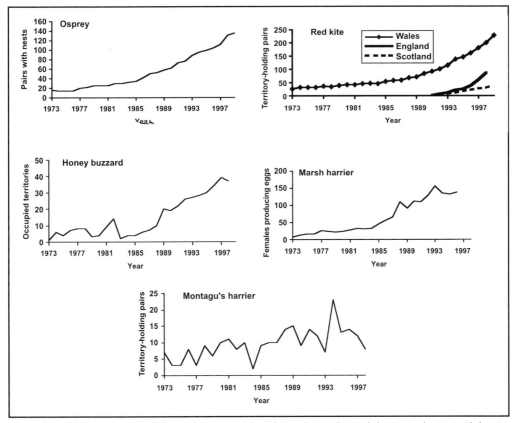

Figure 2.1. UK breeding populations of osprey, red kite, honey buzzard, marsh harrier and Montagu's harrier reported to the Rare Breeding Birds Panel 1973-1999. (Dr Ian Carter supplied data for red kites in England in 1996). For some species, the units are not the same as those used for current population estimates (see text) because comparable data are not available. Note that 'occupied territories' includes territories occupied by singletons, whereas 'territory-holding pairs' excludes singletons. (Data supplied by M.A. Ogilvie).

even though the species is still expanding into vacant habitat. If we assume that all birds breed when two years old, then demographic data for the Chilterns suggest that there are about 1.1 non-breeding first-years for every breeding pair (I. Carter, pers. comm.). However, less than half of the birds in the established (though growing) Welsh population breed at two years old, some not until their seventh summer, and some birds breed intermittently (Davis *et al.*, 2001), indicating a higher proportion of non-breeders. The British populations are clearly too much influenced by re-introductions and too different from each other in demography to provide an overall estimate of the number of non-breeders at present.

RBBP records for this species provide a good indication of the trend in its British population though the species has increased so much that complete annual counts have been impossible for some time in Wales and have now become so in the Chilterns (Figure 2.1)

2.4.2 White-tailed eagle (Haliaeetus albicilla)
Pairs with nests (2000): S = 22 (23 pairs occupied territory; 18 pairs laid eggs) (Bainbridge *et al.,* Chapter 30).

This re-introduced population is closely monitored every year. All known territories are visited and a large area of potential range checked in early spring; it is possible that there are a very few pairs undetected in remote locations.

The total population is thought to be 80-90 birds (Bainbridge *et al.*, Chapter 30).

The population increased from two nesting pairs in 1983 to 22 in 2000 (Bainbridge *et al.*, Chapter 30).

2.4.4 Marsh harrier (Circus aeruginosus)

Females producing eggs (1995): GB = 156 (Underhill-Day, 1998). Females with nests (1999): E = 145 (RBBP). Additional possible breeding females (1999): E = 14, S = 4, W = 1 (RBBP).

In Ireland, breeding has not been confirmed since 1917 (Hutchinson, 1989) but juveniles have recently been seen very early in the summer, prompting speculation that they may have come from Irish nets (L. O'Toole, pers. comm.).

The 1995 census was based on an exhortation for more complete recording by observers. Underhill-Day (1998) thought that it probably underestimated the true population because of missed early failures (it only accepted records where breeding was proved) and because it was not based on any formal sampling strategy. Nonetheless, RBBP figures for the years around 1995 were 20-25 lower, showing the even greater extent of under-recording by RBBP for this species. The core areas are well-monitored, however, so the RBBP data do provide reliable trends.

This species does not breed until 2 or 3 years old, implying a sizeable non-breeding population (Cramp & Simmons, 1979; J. Underhill-Day in Wernham *et al.*, 2000). However, although some birds return to the breeding grounds in their first year (J. Underhill-Day in Wernham *et al.*, 2000), others appear to wander, so it is difficult to know how many of them summer in Britain. The number of non-breeders recorded appears to have been relatively small during the early stages of the expansion of the British population but during 1977-86 the total number of birds reported was c. 30% greater than the number breeding (Day, 1988): since females made up 53% of the breeding population during 1983-95 (Underhill-Day, 1998), this implies that the total population of full-grown birds present (including breeding males) is c. 2.4 times greater than the number of breeding females.

The history of this species in Britain has been documented by Day (1988) and by Underhill-Day (1984, 1998). Following extinction at the end of the 19th century, it recolonized in 1911 but increased only slowly until 1945; it then increased at almost 10% per annum until 1958 before declining at over 10% per annum until 1971. From then until 1995 it increased at c. 20% per annum but numbers have since appeared to level off (Figure 2.1).

2.4.5 Hen harrier (Circus cyaneus)

Territorial pairs (counting secondary females of polygynous males as pairs) (1998): E = 19, S = 436 (365-506), W = 28, NI = 38, M = 49 (Sim *et al.*, 2001). Pairs (1999/2000): RI = 86-99 (D. Norriss, pers. comm.).

The UK survey combined areas covered completely by RSGs with randomly selected 10 km squares from the rest of the likely range; the intended coverage was almost complete. The estimate from the Republic of Ireland is based on recent surveys of most parts of the range: 86 pairs were holding territory and a further 13 pairs or singletons were recorded in suitable habitat.

It is almost impossible to estimate the number of non-breeders because this species is so widely persecuted (Etheridge *et al.*, 1997): not only does the demography vary according to the level of persecution but it is impossible to measure productivity because nests may be destroyed after observations have been made. The number of apparently single birds recorded in the 1998 survey, which is the minimum estimate of the number of non-breeders, averaged 0.28 per territorial pair (Sim *et al.*, 2001).

Between 1988/89 and 1998 the size of the total population in Great Britain did not change, though there were marked regional changes. That in Northern Ireland increased substantially (Sim *et al.*, 2001), but the species may be declining in the Republic (IRSG data). Annual data are too patchy, at least in collated form, to provide reliable information.

2.4.6 Montagu's harrier (Circus pygargus)

Territorial females (1999): E = 9 (RBBP).

The RBBP figure is based on records routinely submitted to county recorders; the extent of under-recording and under-reporting is unknown.

The species has only ever bred sporadically in Ireland, most recently in 1971 (Hutchinson, 1989).

Although most females do not breed until they are two to three years old and males not until they are three, there is evidence that many of the non-breeders over-summer in Africa (Cramp & Simmons, 1979), so it is not clear how many non-breeders one would expect in Britain. In 1998, there were 13 males and eight territorial females reported to RBBP but in 1999 only eight males were reported; in an intensive study area in Sweden there were 5-11 non-breeding immature birds annually in a population of 40 breeding pairs (Clarke, 1996; Rodebrand, 1996). The proportion of breeding females in the total population of fully grown birds present in England was c. 45% during both 1945-54 (rising population) and 1975-84 (low numbers) (Underhill-Day, 1990).

An investigation of post-breeding numbers (Underhill-Day, 1990) found that no more than 17 recorded breeding attempts were made in any year up to 1944, after which there was an increase to 30 breeding attempts in 1953. The population then fell until 1974, when no breeding was reported, and has since fluctuated between one and 12 nests p.a. It is not clear how much of the small increase in reports to the RBBP (Figure 2.) is a result of better reporting.

2.4.7 Goshawk (Accipiter gentilis)

Occupied home ranges (1995): E = 120, S = 80, W = 200 (Petty, 1996). Pairs with nests (1994-2000): NI = 5-10 (D. Scott, pers. comm.). Occupied home ranges (2000/01): RI = 3 (IRSG data).

The 1995 estimate was based on collation of data from various correspondents, who covered most of the species' British range at the time, and from an unpublished PhD thesis that provided the estimate for Wales (Petty, 1996 and pers. comm.). A very small proportion of the territories may have been occupied by singletons (S.J. Petty, pers. comm.). Comparison of these figures with RBBP data shows that the latter suffer from serious under-recording and under-reporting, associated with the species being both cryptic and persecuted.

The Northern Ireland figure is based on extensive fieldwork by Don Scott (Scott, 2001a). Pairs or singles were recorded from three scattered counties in RI but there has been little systematic work to find other sites or confirm nesting (L. O'Toole, pers. comm.).

In a population on Gotland, Sweden, 56% of all males and 33% of all females attempt to nest (Kenward *et al.*, 1999), so there is a total of 4.8 birds for each pair that lay eggs. The non-breeding population in Britain is likely to be slightly higher at saturation because of higher male survival, possibly occasioned by greater availability of prey and milder winters than in Gotland (R. Kenward, pers. comm.) but it is still expanding into suitable habitat, so the proportion of non-breeders is probably low at present.

It is clear that this species has increased substantially in numbers in Britain since its re-establishment (largely or wholly through its informal re-introduction), which began in 1950 (Petty, 1996). Because of widespread under-reporting, the details of the increase are, however, unknown and there are substantial local variations, dependent on the level of persecution (Marquiss *et al.*, Chapter 9). The species is colonizing Ireland, having probably nested first there in 1994 (Scott, 2001a).

2.4.8 Sparrowhawk (Accipiter nisus)

Pairs with new nests (1988-91): GB = 32,000, I = 11,000 (1988-91 atlas). (Atlas-based: E = 22,000, S = 7,000, W = 3,200, M = 55, NI = 2,400, RI = 8,600).

The GB estimates were based on extrapolation from intensive study areas, which provided information on the relationship between sparrowhawk nest spacing, altitude and forest area (Newton, 1986), using Forestry Commission data on the extent of forests of appropriate age at different altitudes. Although re-colonization of the south-east of England (following recovery from pesticides) was not complete at the time of the atlas fieldwork, it was considered that the population would have fully recovered by the time that the atlas was published, so that the extrapolated figure would probably have been reached (I. Newton, pers. comm.). The Ireland figure was calculated from estimates of the area of woodland, assuming the same nest spacing as in Britain (I. Newton, pers. comm.). Pairs with new nests provide a good index because the nest remains recognizable as such for the rest of the season, and often in subsequent years, giving tangible evidence of a breeding attempt long after the builders have given up (I. Newton., pers. comm.).

Newton (1986) concluded that 25,000 breeding pairs implied a further 30,000 non-breeding birds. More recent demographic evidence is that there are 0.28 non-nesting females for each nesting female; because the birds are monogamous, there are probably similar numbers of males, so the total population is c. 1.28 times greater than the number nesting (Newton & Rothery, 2001).

CBC data indicate, following reductions in organochlorine pesticide use, that sparrowhawk numbers have increased substantially since the 1960s, particularly in the mid-1980s to mid-1990s, but have stabilized or even declined since then (Figure 2.2, Table 2.1). However, CBC coverage was biased to the south-east of Britain, which is where numbers have increased more recently and more steeply. Furthermore, data from carcasses received at Monks Wood Research Station indicate that the increase at the national level was less steep, that the peak was a few years earlier, and that there has been a subsequent decline (Newton *et al.*, 1999). BBS results (regionally corrected) are consistent with stability (Table 2.1). Trends in Ireland are not known.

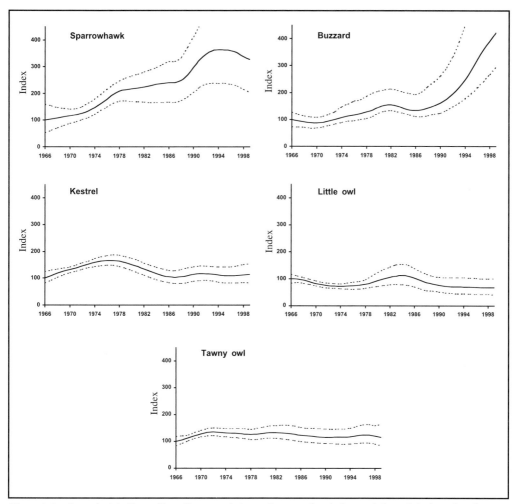

Figure 2.2. Smoothed indices of breeding populations of sparrowhawk, buzzard, kestrel, little owl and tawny owl, the raptors and owls monitored in the United Kingdom by the Common Birds Census, 1966-1999 (Marchant *et al.*, 1990; Baillie *et al.*, 2001). The index is set arbitrarily at 100 in 1966. Pecked lines indicate 95% confidence limits.

Table 2.1. Common Birds Census trends for sparrowhawk, buzzard, kestrel, little owl and tawny owl in the UK over standard 30, 10 and 5 year periods (with 90% confidence limits). The figures are percentage changes relative to the index in the first year of each period (Baillie *et al.*, 2001). Those in bold are significantly different from zero.

	CBC						*BBS*	
	1968-98		*1988-98*		*1993-98*		*1994-99*	
Sparrowhawk	**+212**	(+64-+487)	**+35**	(+10-+62)	-6	(-21-+12)	+1	(-15-+18)
Buzzard	**+332**	(+204-+954)	**+175**	(+107-+363)	**+78**	(+52-+131)	**+29**	(+16-+44)
Kestrel	-5	(-31-+36)	+7	(-9--25)	-2	(-13-+11)	**-30**	(-38--21)
Little owl	-29	(-56-+12)	-22	(-44-+6)	-4	(-26-+20)	-8	(-31-+23)
Tawny owl	+6	(-2-+48)	+1	(-19-+26)	3	(-11-+23)	+11	(-6-+77)

2.4.9 *Buzzard (Buteo buteo)*

Apparently territorial pairs (1983): UK = 12,000-17,000, "perhaps in the lower half of that range" (Taylor *et al.*, 1988) (Atlas-based: E = 4,200-5,900, S = 4,600-6,500, W = 3,300-4,700); RI = 120-150 (2000 IRSG data); NI = 150-300 (2000: IRSG data and J. Wells, pers. comm.).

Soaring birds were counted in a stratified random sample of tetrads in the UK and the number of breeding pairs taken to be half the number of soaring birds recorded (24,500-33,800), though with the caveat that this might underestimate numbers because some females may have been incubating during the later stages of the survey. Coverage was only 74%, with evidence of bias towards occupied squares, so the true figure was probably in the lower end of the range given (Taylor *et al.*, 1988). Irish figures are based on the collation of records, mostly of soaring birds.

The key question is how the number of soaring birds relates to the number of territory-holding birds. Evidence from one intensive study area (Sim *et al.*, 2000) is that the number of soaring birds (provided the survey is done at the right time of year and under the right conditions) is a fairly close estimate of the number of birds in pairs holding territory (not the number of pairs, *contra* their Table 1; I. Sim, pers. comm.). Some experienced buzzard observers believe that non-territorial birds rarely soar but others believe that they often do (extensive correspondence with Peter Dare, Robert Kenward, Robin Prytherch and Innes Sim; see also Dare, 1998). Overall, it is clear both that some of the birds seen soaring are not birds that have established territories and that not all pairs that hold territory in an area will be observed soaring in the time available to the surveyors. Thus, even in regions where the numbers of birds soaring is close to twice the number of pairs with territories, this agreement could be little more than coincidence. Furthermore, it is clear from the comments of experienced observers, and as already noted by Tubbs (1974), that there may be considerable regional variation in the soaring behaviour of buzzards, perhaps related to the proportion of non-breeders locally, and to habitat, so that the coincidence between soaring numbers and territories may not hold nationally.

Hence, while counts of numbers of soaring birds (at the right time of year and under the right conditions) may be the best practical way of indexing the national population, such counts are unlikely to provide more than a rough estimate of the number of territorial pairs.

It is very difficult to know how many non-breeders (i.e. birds that do not even hold territory) there are, in relation to the number of territory-holding pairs. The mean age at first breeding in Wales is c. 3 years (Davis & Davis, 1992). In one area only a minority of the total full-grown population (in the region of 15-30%) lays eggs (Kenward *et al.*, 2000). Given that various studies indicate that a substantial proportion (30% or more) of the birds holding territory do not lay eggs in some populations, perhaps the number of territorial pairs needs to be multiplied by 2.3-4.6 to get an estimate of the total full-grown population. But the proportion of territorial birds that does not lay eggs may vary from year to year, depending on food supply (Mebs, 1964). Furthermore, it seems to be much lower in some places than in others (e.g. Sim *et al.*, 2000), perhaps because populations there are growing more rapidly. This implies that the multiplier should be lower in such places. Overall, the total population is probably more than twice the number of territorial pairs, perhaps three or four times the number.

The general, though not consistently sustained, eastward expansion of this species in Britain after the First World War accelerated during the 1990s (1968-72 and 1988-91 atlases; Clements,

2000), though, because of its south-eastward bias in coverage, the CBC must exaggerate the scale of increase (Figure 2.2, Table 2.1). The BBS (which is corrected for regional variation in coverage) also records recent increases, but not as steep (Table 2.1). Buzzard numbers are also increasing rapidly in Ireland (Norriss, 1991; IRSG data; J. Wells, pers. comm.).

2.4.10 Golden eagle (Aquila chrysaetos)

Home ranges occupied by pairs (1992): E = 1, S = 421 (Green, 1996).

This species' British distribution is well known. All but 13 home ranges and all potential nesting areas within the species' British range were systematically surveyed. Of the 13 home ranges not visited, ten had apparently held no birds in the 1982/83 survey. A home range was considered to be occupied by a pair if two adult birds were seen together or if there was evidence of eggs having been laid.

An attempt to re-introduce this species to Ireland began in 2001.

Of 491 occupied home ranges that were recorded, 69 held single birds (Green, 1996). It is likely, however, that singletons will have been under-recorded.

Perhaps following some increase (Watson, 1997), the size of the British population did not change between 1982 and 1992, though there was some regional variation in trend. Subsequent monitoring has been too patchy, at least in collated form, to provide reliable national information.

2.4.11 Osprey (Pandion haliaetus)

Pairs with nests (1999): S = 136 (RSPB, unpublished data). At least four pairs nested in England in 2001 (A. Brown, pers. comm.).

There is an annual census of all known sites in GB (which are consistently re-used), plus searching of likely areas and checking of sightings by the public, so only a few sites may be missed each year.

Apparent pairs have been over-summering in Ireland recently (L. O'Toole., pers. comm.).

The demography of this population has not been sufficiently worked out to attempt estimates of how many non-territory-holders there are in Britain. Ospreys do not attempt to breed until they are at least three years old (Cramp & Simmons, 1979) and the population has been growing at c. 9% per annum, so there must be a significant number of immature birds associated with the population. However, most first-year birds and many second-year ones do not over-summer in the breeding areas (Cramp & Simmons, 1979).

Ospreys were at very low numbers or extinct in Scotland during 1917-53 but have increased rapidly following their recolonization in 1954 (Dennis, 1995). They became extinct in England before 1850 (A. Brown, pers. comm.) but recently recolonized naturally, as well as breeding at Rutland Water in 2001, following re-introduction. There is full annual monitoring (Figure 2.1).

2.4.12 Kestrel (Falco tinnunculus)

Pairs producing eggs (1988-91): GB = 50,000, I = 10,000 (1988-91 atlas). (Atlas-based: E = 35,000, S = 11,000, W = 3,500, M = 140, NI = 1,600, RI = 8,400).

The GB figure was based on densities observed in intensive study areas and the proportion of the country occupied by the species. The Irish figure was based on extrapolation from the GB data. However, this extrapolation did not take into account the apparently lower densities of kestrel in Ireland, within occupied areas (1988-91 atlas), which is consistent with the virtual absence of voles from Ireland; it should perhaps be revised downwards (A. Village, pers. comm.).

In upland areas, numbers breeding vary according to the abundance of prey (Village, 1990). Over a period of seven years, Village (1990) estimated that at least 30% of a tagged population in lowland English farmland was non-breeding (i.e. did not belong to a pair that produced eggs). In the same area, direct counts showed mean densities to be 47 and 32 birds/100 km², a proportion of 32% non-breeders.

Since the survival-rate of females after their first year is 66% (Village, 1990), 34% of birds in a stable population are first-years. Carcasses gathered nationwide over a period of 20 years indicated that 41% of first-year females do not breed (Wyllie & Newton, 1999), which would be compatible with Village's overall figure of 31% if 26% of older females did not breed in any one year. Were non-breeding in any one year to be independent of previous breeding, this figure is exactly compatible with the figure of 3% of females older than one year having never bred, derived from carcass analysis (Wyllie & Newton, 1999), assuming a stage age-distribution and the 66% post-first-year survival rate. This agreement suggests that it is safe to conclude that for every pair of breeding kestrels in Britain there is an additional non-breeding bird.

Kestrels had recovered from the deleterious effects of organochlorine pesticides by the mid-1970s but subsequently declined and are now no more common than in the early 1960s (Figure 2.2, Table 2.1). Furthermore, although the CBC indicates that abundance has been stable for the last 15 years, the BBS suggests that a further decline has occurred since 1994 (Table 2.1). Irish trends are not known.

2.4.13   Merlin (Falco columbarius)

Pairs with nests: E = 400, S = 800, W = 80 (1993-4: Rebecca & Bainbridge, 1998); NI = 25-40 (1992-5: UK Raptor Working Group, 2000); RI = at least 200 (2000: D. Norriss, pers. comm.). Isle of Man: very small numbers breed irregularly (UK Raptor Working Group, 2000).

The GB total of c. 1,300 was thought to be accurate within +/-200 (Rebecca & Bainbridge, 1998). In areas where long-term intensive studies guaranteed 100% coverage, independent checks during the 1993-94 census showed that they provided unbiased estimates of population size. In the rest of the country, a random selection from a regular grid of squares was surveyed using standardized techniques, and population size was extrapolated from these data. The NI estimate was based on unpublished data from RSGs and RSPB fieldworkers. The estimate for RI, thought to be vague, is based on extrapolation from local surveys; it accords roughly with the 1998-91 atlas view that Ireland held one-fifth as many merlin as GB.

Rebecca & Bainbridge (1998) found that there were an extra 10% of sites that were occupied by one or two birds without breeding being confirmed. This equates to c. 200 extra birds (including both sexes). It is likely that there are further non-breeders that do not even occupy sites but there is no direct evidence as to their number and little indirect evidence. Thus, in an intensive study of urban merlin in Canada, males generally did not breed until their second year but females usually bred in their first (Lieske *et al.*, 1997), implying that, if breeding pairs fledge 2.2 young per attempt (Bibby & Nattrass, 1986; Crick, 1993) and if first-year survival is equal to that of the kestrel at 35% (Village, 1990), the population of non-breeding males is about 500 first-year birds plus an unknown number of adults. The proportion of first-year birds among breeders in a Northumberland study (Newton *et al.,* 1986), at 8% in males and 18% in females, was lower than reported in kestrels (above) but this would be compatible with either a greater or a smaller proportion of non-breeders overall, dependent on the pattern of age-specific mortality, which is unknown.

Between the British surveys of 1983-84 and 1993-94, merlin numbers increased in most areas and were stable elsewhere (Rebecca & Bainbridge, 1998). The species may be declining in Ireland (IRSG data).

2.4.14 Hobby (Falco subbuteo)

Pairs producing well-grown young (2000): 2,200 (Rob Clements, 2001 and pers comm.). Occupied territories (including singletons) (1999): E = 518, W = 19 (RBBP) (probably a great underestimate, see below). Apparently occupied territories (1990-99): S = 0-6 (RBBP). (1990 was the first year since 1887 that hobbies appeared to hold territory in Scotland, and 1994 had the only confirmed egg-laying yet).

Clements' estimate was based on an assessment of the species' distribution (drawn from the 1988-91 atlas, and from information from workers into whose areas hobbies have subsequently expanded), and in typical densities in occupied areas (based on published and unpublished surveys); densities used for particular regions were adjusted to take into account the extent of suitable habitat. This figure is substantially higher than previous estimates, partly because the species is increasing and partly because earlier estimates were too low. The hobby is cryptic in its habits and Rob Clements (pers. comm.) believes that densities may often be further underestimated because surveyors do not search what they mistakenly believe to be unsuitable habitat. He believes that even his estimate should be treated as a minimum.

The RBBP figures are clearly too low (Prince & Clarke (1993) estimated from sample surveys that the RBBP missed 50% of the hobbies in Cambridgeshire, for example). They do, however, indicate the relative proportions nesting in the countries of the UK (unless the species' particular scarcity in Wales and Scotland, combined with its recency of spread in those countries, has led to particularly marked under-reporting there).

Hobbies' nests are easiest to find when they hold well-grown young, which is why Clements' estimate is couched in those terms. He estimates that the number of pairs laying eggs may be over 2,500, based on limited information on breeding failures.

The evidence on the number of non-breeding hobbies is too indirect and scant to allow quantitative assessment. However, although females may breed at one year old, males do not though all return to Europe rather than over-summering in Africa (Cramp & Simmons, 1979; Brown *et al.,* 1982). There must therefore be significant numbers of non-breeding birds.

Since the proportion of CBC plots on which hobbies occur is small, the change in that proportion over time is a fair indicator of the scale of increase in the hobby population (Figure 2.3). Data from RBBP and county bird reports also reflect this rapid increase (Parr, 1994; see also Fuller *et al.,* 1985).

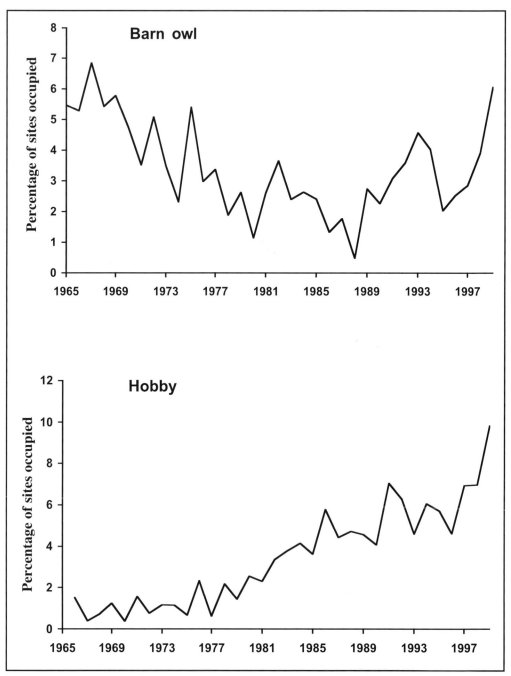

Figure 2.3. Percentage of Common Birds Census plots occupied annually by barn owl and by hobby, 1966-1999. (Data supplied by BTO).

2.4.15 *Peregrine (Falco peregrinus)*

Territorial pairs (1991): E = 278, S = 611, W = 254, M = 20, NI = 93 (Crick & Ratcliffe, 1995). Occupied territories (1991): RI = 350-355, including those occupied by single birds (Norriss, 1995). (Singletons occupied a further 4% of territories in the UK).

The UK survey achieved almost full coverage except in north and west Scotland. It attempted to visit all known sites and also to check potentially suitable areas, emphasis being given to checking potential sites early in the season in order to assess site occupancy before any pairs departed their sites. Extrapolations of occupancy in unsurveyed areas were based on occupancy rates in the surrounding region. In the Republic of Ireland, a sample survey of 50% of the peregrine's breeding range was conducted, with extrapolations to areas of similar ecology. Again, early visits were used to assess occupancy.

Some territorial peregrines do not breed and other full-grown birds do not even hold territories. There are enough non-breeders in British peregrine populations for any paired birds that die to be replaced quickly and "theoretical calculations from the known mortality and productivity rates suggest that the number of non-breeders could be as large as the breeding population" (Ratcliffe, 1993).

The pesticide-associated declines of the 1950s were largely reversed by 1981 and by 1991 most populations were higher than ever before recorded (Table 2.2), though not in north and west Scotland (Crick & Ratcliffe, 1995; also Ratcliffe, Chapter 4). Annual data are too patchy, at least in collated form, to provide more detailed monitoring.

Table 2.2. Numbers of occupied peregrine territories in the UK, Isle of Man and Ireland. Data from Ratcliffe (1993) and Crick & Ratcliffe (1995).

	1930-39	*1961*	*1962*	*1971*	*1981*	*1991*
England	158	55	34	47	131[1]	288
Scotland	513	446	388	366	489	639
Wales	135	46	30	30	125	263
Isle of Man	14	7	4	2	6[1]	20
NI	54	-	40[2]	40[2]	53	99
RI	180-200	-	-	127[2]	225	350

Notes:
1. The data for the Isle of Man are from 1979, when three to six occupied territories were estimated; we have assumed six for 1981 and subtracted this figure from the England figure given in Ratcliffe (1993), which included the Isle of Man.
2. These figures are based on occupancy rates of a subsample of the 1930-39 sites.

Derek Ratcliffe (pers. comm.) receives reports from a number of observers, and Denis Corley (pers. comm.) has collated information from published sources; these indicate continued growth in some areas (e.g. southern England), stabilization in others, and probably decline in a few places, with continued low numbers in north and west Scotland.

2.4.16 Barn owl (Tyto alba)

Pairs producing eggs (1995-97): E = 3,400, S = 300, W = 300 (Toms *et al.*, 2000a,b); M = less than 10 breeding records per year, but under-reported (Craine & Moore, 1997; Cullen, 2000); I = 600-900 (1982-85, Shawyer, 1987). (Atlas-based: NI = 140-210, RI = 460-690).

The British figures represent the first replicable baseline population estimate, based on a stratified randomized sample survey with validation of the results by independent observers. The total of 4,000 has approximate 95% confidence limits of +/-1,200. The Irish figures are based on densities obtained in four sample areas, extrapolated to those 10 km squares where barn owls were recorded (Shawyer, 1987). Coverage was relatively poor and it is not clear how representative were the four sample areas.

In many areas, this species relies on prey whose numbers fluctuate markedly. When prey are abundant, most barn owls breed; when they are scarce, not only does the total population decline because of increased mortality but many of the survivors do not breed (Taylor, 1994). The 1995-97 census revealed marked differences in numbers breeding from year to year, attributed by observers largely to variations in prey numbers. These variations were not synchronous across the country. If we assume that the number breeding in the year that produced the largest estimates in a region represented 100% of the total population, with non-breeding accounting for the lower figures in the other two years, then it is possible to calculate how the three-year mean relates to the total population. A weighted average across all regions indicates that, in order to estimate the total number of individuals (breeding and non-breeding) in the population, the mean number of breeding pairs over the three years should be multiplied by 2.6. This multiplier will be biased downwards if the whole population was not breeding in the year with the largest number of breeders recorded and upwards if (through sampling error) the estimate for that year exceeded the total population size.

Since the proportion of CBC plots on which barn owls occur is small, the change in that proportion over time is a fair indicator of the decline in the barn owl population from the mid-1960s and its apparent recovery since the late 1980s (Figure 2.3), changes attributed by Newton *et al.* (1991) to the pattern of organochlorine pesticide use. It is thought still to be decreasing in Ireland (IRSG data).

2.4.17 *Little owl (Athene noctua)*
Occupied nest sites (1995-97): E = 6,347 (5,800-7,000), W = 366 (330-420). Toms *et al.* (2000a) provided estimates for each of the three years, from which we have calculated these means and approximate confidence limits. Probably less than 10 pairs occupy sites in Scotland annually (Thom, 1986, and Scottish Bird Reports).

Likely nest sites were examined in a stratified random sample of tetrads, aimed at surveying barn owls. Observers were not asked to provide evidence of breeding and it is possible that some cavities used only for roosting or for preparing food (Hibbert-Ware, 1938) were included in the count, which may therefore overestimate breeding numbers. Coverage was incomplete but did not vary with stratum and there was no evidence of serious bias.

We do not know what proportion the birds that occupy nest sites make up of the total population. Some little owls breed when only a year old but some territory-holders do not lay eggs (Glue & Scott, 1980).

CBC data show some variation in numbers over time but no significant long-term trends (Figure 2.2, Table 2.1). Unfortunately, crepuscular species are poorly monitored by general schemes such as CBC and BBS, so the population indices have wide confidence limits.

2.4.18 *Tawny owl (Strix aluco)*
Territorial pairs (1988-91): GB = 20,000 (1988-91 atlas). (Atlas-based: E = 14,000, S = 3,900, W = 2,000).

A national survey in 1989, comprising 2,521 10-minute point-counts in 122 hectads, yielded habitat-specific densities of autumn territories (Percival, 1990). The hectads counted were not an obviously biased sample. From the habitat-specific figures, an average GB density of ten territories per hectad was calculated to give the Atlas estimate. Productivity in 1989 may have been low, which would have reduced autumn territorial activity (Percival, 1990). Reasonable margins of error on the estimate (not formal confidence limits) are 15,000-40,000 (S. Percival, pers. comm.).

Most tawny owls that fail to secure a territory in their first autumn or winter starve to death (Southern, 1970; Hirons, *et al.*, 1979), so the number of territories in autumn is a measure of the population at the start of the breeding season. But note that on average (with very marked annual variations), one-third of territory-holders do not lay eggs (Southern, 1970), so the number of territories is much greater than the number of pairs producing eggs.

There has been some variation in numbers indexed by CBC and BBS but no significant long-term trends (Figure 2.2, Table 2.1).

2.4.19 Short-eared owl (Asio otus)

'Pairs' (1988-91): GB = 1,000-3,500 (1988-91 atlas). (Atlas-based: E = 210-740, S = 780-2,700, W = 10-40). Small numbers nest on the Isle of Man, though there are usually less than five localities from which birds are reported during any one breeding season (Craine & Moore, 1997; Cullen, 2000). Pairs producing eggs (1997-2000): NI = 1, 0, 3, 2 (annual figures) (Scott, 1999, 2001b; Don Scott, pers. comm.). Has bred occasionally in RI (Hutchinson, 1989) but there have been no recent records (D. Norriss, pers. comm.).

These are probably the most unreliable estimates for any species except the next. Data on this species are so scant that the distinction between territory-holding, nest-building and egg-laying pairs cannot usually be made. The British estimate is based on the number of hectads with evidence of occupancy and breeding, multiplied by general knowledge of typical densities in occupied squares. The Welsh figure is consistent with more direct information (Lovegrove *et al.*, 1994).

Short-eared owls breed at one year old and are usually monogamous (Cramp, 1985), so all birds in a population could be breeders. However, this species is highly nomadic and the numbers present and breeding vary widely according to local abundance of prey (Mikkola, 1983; Village, 1987; Ratcliffe, 1990; Korpimäki, 1994; D.E. Glue in Wernham, *et al.*, 2002) so birds breeding in Britain one year may have bred elsewhere in the previous year. The range given for the population reflects this variation at least as much as uncertainty over the true figure.

There was a 15% decline in number of hectads with breeding evidence between the 1968-72 and 1988-91 atlases, though this could be a result of annual variations in the proportion breeding. There is no other evidence on population changes of this species, except for the recent sporadic colonization of Ireland.

2.4.20 Long-eared owl (Asio flammeus)

'Pairs' (1988-91): GB = 1,100-3,600, I = 1,100-3,600 (1988-91 atlas). (Atlas-based: E = 550-1,800, S = 530-1,750, W = 10-40, M = 4-14, NI = 530-1,730, RI = 570-1,870). Territorial pairs (1997): Britain & Ireland = 2,000-4,000 (Scott, 1997).

The numbers of this species are probably less well known than those of any other British owl or raptor. The 1968-72 atlas estimate for Britain & Ireland was based on the number of hectads in which there was evidence of breeding, multiplied by general knowledge of typical densities in occupied squares. The second atlas estimate, shown above, was derived from this by assuming that densities had remained constant within occupied squares. The separate GB and Ireland figures in the Atlas were obtained from comparing the numbers observed in timed counts, which averaged approximately the same over the two islands. The Atlas-based estimate from Wales is probably too great, because four confirmed breeding pairs were found during atlas-fieldwork (Lovegrove *et al.,* 1994); that for the Isle of Man fits with the numbers routinely reported (Craine & Moore, 1997; Cullen, 2000). Scott's 1997 estimate was based on up-to-date information from a number of people conducting local studies (Derick Scott*,* pers. comm.).

The species is usually monogamous (Scott, 1997). At least some breed at one year old (Glue, 1977). Indeed, numbers breeding in one study varied according to breeding success in the previous year (Williams, 1998), suggesting that first-year birds are roughly as likely to breed as older birds. Hence all birds in a population could be breeders. Derick Scott (pers. comm.) states that he tries to find any non-breeders in his study area but finds very few. However, Glue (1977) stated that long-eared owls were regularly found occupying woods in the breeding season without nesting; the proportion of population that bred was only 83% on average over four years at Eskdalemuir and varied according to vole abundance (Village, 1981); and the numbers breeding in a Finnish study area varied similarly (Korpimäki, 1994). The range given for the total population reflects this uncertainty at well as uncertainty over the number of birds nesting.

There was a 24% decline in the number of hectads with breeding evidence between the 1968-72 and 1988-91 atlases. Although this could be a result of annual variations in proportions breeding, there is anecdotal evidence of a real decline. There is no other evidence on population changes of this species. It may be declining in Ireland, from anecdotal evidence (IRSG data).

2.5 The European context: numbers

British and Irish populations are placed in their European context in Table 2.3.

Key conclusions are the importance of these islands for peregrine, whose total European population is so small, and for kestrel, sparrowhawk, and golden eagle. In addition to the more generalist hobby, moorland species (hen harrier, merlin and short-eared owl) are also commoner here than in much of Europe, except Russia, emphasizing the importance of moorland habitat in Britain and Ireland.

2.6 The European context: population trends

Little owl and tawny owl numbers have been roughly stable in the United Kingdom over the last 30 years, kestrel and barn owl have fluctuated, short-eared owl may have declined, long-eared owl has probably done so and the evidence for an increase in golden eagles is tenuous (Watson, 1997). Of the remaining 13 or 14 species, red kite, white-tailed eagle, marsh harrier, buzzard, osprey, hobby, goshawk, honey buzzard and merlin have continued to increase in the UK in the last ten years, though the last two (or three) only slowly. (These increases represent recovery from the effects of persecution and pesticides). The recent

Table 2.3. Population estimates of raptors and owls that breed in Britain and Ireland. European figures are "breeding pairs"; Britain and Irish figures are in units described in the text for individual species Where original estimates were given as ranges, the mid-range value is shown. ** indicates populations comprising at least 5% of the European total, * those comprising at least 5% of the total for Europe excluding Russia (with the exception of the golden eagle which comprises 4.8%).

	Europe	*Europe (excl. Russia)*	*GB*	*Ireland*	*UK*	*RI*
Honey buzzard	125,000	40,000	29	0	29	0
Red kite	21,500	21,500	429	0	429	0
White-tailed eagle	4,350	3,350	22	0	22	0
Marsh harrier	70,000	37,500	156	0	156	0
Hen harrier	26,500	9,000	483*	136	521*	99
Montagu's harrier	38,000	13,000	9	0	9	0
Goshawk	155,000	70,000	400	9	407	2
Sparrowhawk	330,000	170,000	32,000**	11,000*	34,400**	8,600*
Buzzard	845,000	345,000	14,000	335	14,200	135
Golden eagle	9,300	8,800	422*	0	422*	0
Osprey	9,000	6,000	136	0	136	0
Kestrel	370,000	300,000	50,000**	10,000	51,600**	8,400
Merlin	46,000	16,000	1,280*	230	1,310*	200
Hobby	92,500	37,500	2,200*	0	2,200*	0
Peregrine	9,300	8,300	1,143**	445*	1,236**	352
Barn owl	155,000	155,000	4,000	750	4,175	575
Little owl	360,000	305,000	6,713	0	6,713	0
Tawny owl	595,000	540,000	20,000	0	20,000	0
Short-eared owl	73,500	18,500	2,250*	2	2,250*	0
Long-eared owl	485,000	210,000	2,350	2,350	3,480	1,220

changes in hen harrier and peregrine populations have been geographically variable. Numbers of Montagu's harrier have fluctuated, those of golden eagle have been stable, and those of sparrowhawk may have started to go down in the last decade.

Hen harriers, merlins and barn owls appear to be declining in Ireland, but other species appear to be faring much as in Britain.

Table 2.4 shows European population trends. They are not affected substantially by the exclusion of Russian populations, except for Montagu's harrier and short-eared owl (of which the very large Russian populations are increasing and decreasing respectively, in contrast to some other populations).

Whereas more species have increased than decreased in Britain, decreases are as numerous as increases in Europe as a whole. There is little correlation between British and European trends - except that owls are generally faring badly.

The importance of British and Irish hen harrier and kestrel populations is emphasized by their declines in other parts of Europe. This is true to a lesser degree for golden eagle and merlin.

Table 2.4. European population trends of raptors and owls. Species are arranged according to their trends in the UK. The European index ranges from −2.0 (decline of at least 50% in all countries) to +2.0 (increase of at least 50% in all countries). Russian data are excluded: species where this has a marked effect are marked * and discussed in the text.

UK trend			European trend
30-year	**10-year**		
Increase	Increase	Honey buzzard	0.0
		Red kite	0.2
		White-tailed eagle	1.3
		Marsh harrier	0.8
		Osprey	0.4
		Goshawk	1.3
		Buzzard	0.7
		Merlin	-0.1
		Hobby	-0.1
Increase	Stable or variable	Hen harrier	-0.6
		Montagu's harrier	0.4*
		Golden eagle	-0.1
		Sparrowhawk	1.0
		Peregrine	0.2
Stable, variable or unknown	Stable or variable	Kestrel	-0.6
		Barn owl	-0.4
		Little owl	-0.4
		Tawny owl	0.0
Declining?	Unknown	Long-eared owl	-1.5
		Short-eared owl	0.0*

2.7 Monitoring

Current monitoring of raptors in the UK may be summarized as follows.

1. Species which are fully or almost fully censused annually: red kite, white-tailed eagle, osprey. Note that red kites and ospreys are becoming so widespread that they will increasingly move into the next category.
2. Species which are extensively studied by RSGs, with additional data from various sources, collated by RBBP: hen harrier, goshawk, golden eagle, merlin, peregrine. All but goshawk are also censused once every five years (hen harrier) or ten years (golden eagle, merlin, peregrine) so as to provide better long-term monitoring.
3. Species for which the RBBP provides annual reporting, often supported by intensive local monitoring by RSGs and other specialists: honey buzzard, Montagu's harrier, hobby, marsh harrier (the latter also surveyed decadally).

4. Species that are adequately covered by the BBS (i.e. that occur on at least 50 survey squares): sparrowhawk, buzzard, kestrel. (Hobby may also turn out to be adequately covered by BBS because, although it occurs on only about 30 squares at present, this is fair coverage within its core range).

Tawny owl and little owl are covered by BBS (each occurring on about 100 sites) but, given their nocturnal habits, it is not clear how adequate this coverage is. The barn owl is now the subject of a special monitoring scheme (Crick *et al.*, 2001). Long- and short-eared owls are scarcely monitored at all, though there are a few local studies of the former.

In Ireland, coverage tends to be less complete than in the UK, although it has improved considerably and the Countryside Bird Survey (the equivalent of the BBS) should provide data on the commoner species.

There are problems with this monitoring. RBBP coverage for a number of species is clearly incomplete and unsystematic. If it were possible to make it more formal - even only to the extent of more systematic data collection from existing studies - the value of the information would be greatly improved. The RSGs obtain much detailed data of high quality but their coverage is often based on localized study areas and varies between years, so the information arising from them is more difficult to draw together than it would be if the data-gathering and analysis were more standardized at the national level. It is unfortunate that so much good fieldwork is not supported by a system that allows it to be used to deliver the best scientific and conservation-related results.

We believe that what is needed for better monitoring of raptor populations is not so much more fieldwork but an optimization of the considerable effort already being made.

1. More of the data being used to contribute to national monitoring, especially data from nest-recording and ringing.
2. More standardized methods for fieldwork and data-gathering.
3. More integration of data from different study areas.
4. More effective sampling strategies, to ensure adequate coverage of each species' range.
5. More cost-effective collation of the results.
6. More comprehensive, standardized and accessible reporting.
7. More financial support for fieldwork, to ensure that the programme is comprehensive and coherent.

These needs could be met if there was a properly integrated national system that had the aim of supporting the work of the RSGs and other fieldworkers, of delivering better information, and of curating the data. This ought to be a collaboration between all of those currently involved in monitoring raptors and owls: RSGs and other volunteer fieldworkers, voluntary conservation bodies, research organizations and government agencies. A system imposed from above would not work. The new Scottish Raptor Monitoring Scheme Agreement (2002) is an important step towards devising a national monitoring scheme for raptors.

2.8 Conclusions

From the above survey, we conclude that there is a need to address the adequacy of the methods used to estimate numbers and trends of many raptors and owls, particularly those that rest on unsystematic collation of data. It is important that those who report on population sizes should specify clearly what count units they have used. 'Breeding pairs' is too vague. Our knowledge of the total population of full-grown birds is generally very poor, because non-breeding birds are difficult to count. To get better estimates of population sizes of some species may be so demanding of effort as not to be worthwhile. We need coherent monitoring of raptors and owls at the national level, to make cost-effective use of the fieldwork effort. Britain and Ireland have internationally significant numbers of golden eagle, sparrowhawk, kestrel, peregrine and hobby. Our moorlands are important, partly because they contain internationally significant numbers of hen harrier, merlin and short-eared owl.

Acknowledgements

We thank all those who have provided us with information, advice and criticism: Andy Brown, Ian Carter, Rob Clements, Denis Corley, Peter Dare, Peter Davis, David Glue, Rhys Green, Tony Hardy, Robert Kenward, Mick Marquiss, Ian Newton, David Norriss, Lorcan O'Toole, Steve Percival, Robin Prytherch, Derek Ratcliffe, Derick Scott, Don Scott, Innes Sim, Patrick Stirling Aird, John Underhill-Day, Andy Village, Jeff Watson, Jim Wells and Simon Wotton. We have benefited from the comments of two anonymous referees.

For access to databases, we thank the European Bird Census Council and Bird Life International (*per* Melanie Heath) and the British Trust for Ornithology (*per* David Noble).

Lastly, we thank the many ornithologists, mainly amateurs, who conducted the fieldwork on which this work rests.

References

Baillie, S.R., Crick, H.Q.P., Balmer, D.E., Bashford, R.I., Beaven, L.P., Freeman, S.N., Marchant, J.H., Noble, D.G., Raven, M.J., Siriwardena, G.M., Thewlis, R. & Wernham, C.V. (2001). *Breeding Birds in the Wider Countryside: their conservation status 2000. BTO Research Report No. 252.* BTO, Thetford.

Batten, L.A. (2001). European Honey-buzzard Survey 2000 and 2001: preliminary results and requests for further surveys. *British Birds,* **94**, 143-144.

Bibby, C.J. & Nattrass, M. (1986). Breeding status of the Merlin in Britain. *British Birds,* **79**, 170-185.

Bijlsma, R.G. (1993). *Ecologische Atlas van de Nederlandse Roofvogels.* Schuyt & Co, Haarlem.

Birdlife International/European Bird Census Council (2000). *European Bird Populations: Estimates and Trends. BirdLife Conservation Series No. 10.* BirdLife International, Cambridge.

Brown, L.H., Urban, E.K. & Newman, K. (1982). *The Birds of Africa. Vol. 1.* Academic Press, London.

Clarke, R. (1996). *Montagu's Harrier.* Arlequin Press, Chelmsford.

Clements, R. (2000). Range expansion of the Common Buzzard in Britain. *British Birds,* **93**, 242-248.

Clements, R. (2001). The Hobby in Britain: a new population estimate. *British Birds,* **94**, 402-408.

Craine, G.D. & Moore, A.S. (1997). The Manx Bird Report for 1994. *Peregrine,* **7**, 296-356.

Cramp, S. & Simmons, K.E.L. (Eds). (1979). *The Birds of the Western Paleartic. Vol. II.* Oxford University Press, Oxford.

Cramp, S. (Ed.) (1985). *The Birds of the Western Palearctic. Vol. IV.* Oxford University Press, Oxford.

Crick, H.Q.P. (1993). Trends in breeding success of Merlins (*Falco columbarius*) in Britain from 1937-1989. In *Biology and Conservation of Small Falcons,* ed. by M.K. Nicholls & R. Clarke. Hawk and Owl Trust, London.

Crick, H.Q.P. & Ratcliffe, D.A. (1995). The Peregrine *Falco peregrinus* breeding population of the United Kingdom in 1991. *Bird Study,* **42**, 1-19.

Crick, H.Q.P., Shawyer, C.R., Siriwardena, G.M., Balmer, D.E. & Toms, M.P. (2001). *The BTO Barn Owl Monitoring Programme: 1st Report: Pilot Year 2000. BTO Research Report No. 258.* British Trust for Ornithology, Thetford.

Cullen, P. (2000). The Manx Bird Report for 1996. *Peregrine,* **8**, 2-42.

Dare, P.J. (1998). A Buzzard population on Dartmoor, 1955-1993. *Devon Birds,* **51**, 4-15.

Davis, P., Cross, T. & Davis, J. (2001). Movement, settlement, breeding, and survival of Red Kites *Milvus milvus* marked in Wales. *Welsh Birds,* **3**, 18-43.

Davis, P.E. & Davis, J.E. (1992). Dispersal and age of first breeding of buzzards in Central Wales. *British Birds,* **85**, 578-587.

Day, J. (1988). Marsh Harriers in Britain. *RSPB Conservation Review,* **2**, 17-19.

Dennis, R. (1995). Ospreys *Pandion haliaetus* in Scotland - a study of recolonization. *Vogelwelt,* **116**, 193-196.

Etheridge, B., Summers, R.W. & Green, R.E. (1997). The effects of illegal killing and destruction of nests by humans on the population dynamics of the Hen Harrier *Circus cyaneus* in Scotland. *Journal of Applied Ecology,* **34**, 1081-1105.

Fuller, R.J., Baker, J.K., Morgan, R.A., Scroggs, R. & Wright, M. (1985). Breeding populations of the Hobby *Falco subbuteo* on farmland in the southern Midlands & England. *Ibis,* **127**, 510-516.

Gibbons, D.W., Reid, J.B. & Chapman, R.A. (1993). *The New Atlas of Breeding Birds in Britain and Ireland: 1988-1991.* T. & A. D. Poyser, London.

Glue, D. (1977). Breeding biology of Long-eared Owls. *British Birds,* **70**, 318-331.

Glue, D. & Scott, D. (1980). Breeding biology of the Little Owl. *British Birds,* **73**, 167-180.

Green, R.E. (1996). The status of the Golden Eagle in Britain in 1992. *Bird Study,* **43**, 20-27.

Gregory, R.D., Wilkinson, N.I., Noble, D.G., Robinson, J.A., Brown, A.F., Hughes, J., Procter, D., Gibbons, D.W. & Galbraith, C.A. (2002). The population status of birds in the United Kingdom, Channel Islands and Isle of Man: an analysis of conservation concern 2002-2007. *British Birds,* **95**, 410-448.

Hagemeijer, E.J.M. & Blair, M.J. (Eds). (1997). *The EBCC Atlas of European Breeding Birds: Their Distribution and Abundance.* T. & A.D. Poyser, London.

Hibbert-Ware, A. (1937). Report of the Little Owl food inquiry 1936-37. *British Birds,* **31**, 162-187.

Hirons, G., Hardy, A. & Stanley, P. (1979). Starvation in young Tawny Owls. *Bird Study,* **26**, 59-63.

Hutchinson, C.D. (1989). *Birds in Ireland.* T. & A.D. Poyser, Calton.

Kenward, R.E., Marcstrom, V. & Karlblom, M. (1999). Demographic estimates from radio-tagging: models of age-specific survival and breeding in the goshawk. *Journal of Animal Ecology,* **68**, 1020-1033.

Kenward, R.E., Walls, S.S., Hodder, K.H., Pahkala, M., Freeman, S.N. & Simpson, V.R. (2000). The prevalence of non-breeders in raptor populations: evidence from rings, radio-tags and transect surveys. *Oikos,* **91**, 271-279.

Korpimäki, E. (1994). Rapid or delayed tracking of multi-annual vole cycles by avian predators? *Journal of Animal Ecology,* **63**, 619-628.

Kostrzewa, A. (1998). *Pernis apivorus* Honey Buzzard. *BWP Update,* **2**, 107-120.

Lieske, D.J., Oliphant, L.W., James, P.C., Warkentin, I.G. & Espie, R.H.M. (1997). Age of first breeding in Merlins *(Falco columbarius). Auk,* **114**, 288-290.

Lovegrove, R., Williams, G. & Williams, I. (1994). *Birds in Wales.* T. & A.D. Poyser, London.

Marchant, J.H., Hudson, R., Carter, S.P. & Whittington, P. (1990). *Population Trends in British Breeding Birds.* British Trust for Ornithology, Tring.

Mebs, Th. (1964). Zur Biologie und Populationsdynamik des Mäusebussards *(Buteo buteo). Journal für Ornithologie,* **105**, 247-306.

Mikkola, H. (1983). *Owls of Europe.* T. & A.D. Poyser, Calton.

Newton, I. (1986). *The Sparrowhawk.* T. & A.D. Poyser, London.

Newton, I, Meek, E. & Little, B. (1986). Population and breeding of Northumbrian Merlins. *British Birds,* **79**, 155-170.

Newton, I, Wyllie, I. & Asher, A. (1991). Mortality causes in British Barn Owls *Tyto alba*, with a discussion of aldrin-dieldrin poisoning. *Ibis,* **133**, 162-169.

Newton, I, Wyllie, I. & Dale, L. (1999). Trends in the numbers and mortality patterns of Sparrowhawks (*Accipiter nisus*) and kestrels (*Falco tinnunculus*) in Britain, as revealed by carcass analyses. *Journal of Zoology,* **248**, 139-147.

Newton, I. & Rothery, P. (2001). Estimation and limitation of numbers of floaters in a Sparrowhawk population. *Ibis,* **143**, 442-449.

Norriss, D.W. (1991). The status of the Buzzard as a breeding species in the Republic of Ireland, 1977-1991. *Irish Birds,* **4**, 291-298.

Norriss, D.W. (1995). The 1991 survey and weather impacts on the Peregrine *Falco peregrinus* breeding population in the Republic of Ireland. *Bird Study,* **42**, 20-30.

Ogilvie, M. (1997). Rare Breeding Birds Panel. *British Birds,* **90**, 351-352.

Ogilvie, M. & Rare Breeding Birds Panel (2001). Rare breeding birds in the United Kingdom in 1999. *British Birds,* **94**, 344-381.

Parr, S.J. (1994). Population changes of breeding Hobbies *Falco subbuteo* in Britain. *Bird Study,* **41**, 131-135.

Percival, S.M. (1990). Population trends in British Barn Owls, *Tyto alba,* and Tawny Owls, *Strix aluco,* in relation to environmental change. *BTO Research Report No. 57.* British Trust for Ornithology, Tring.

Petty, S.J. (1996). History of the northern goshawk *Accipiter gentilis* in Britain. In *The Introduction and Naturalisation of Birds,* ed. by J.S. Holmes & J.R. Simons. HMSO, London.

Prince, P. & Clarke, R. (1993). The Hobby's breeding range in Britain. *British Wildlife, 4,* 341-346.

Ratcliffe, D. (1990). *Bird Life of Mountain and Moorland.* Cambridge University Press, Cambridge.

Ratcliffe, D. (1993). *The Peregrine. Second edition.* T. & A.D. Poyser, London.

Raven, M.J., Noble, D.G. & Baillie, S.R. (2002). *The Breeding Bird Survey 2001: Report No. 7.* British Trust for Ornithology, Joint Nature Conservation Committee and Royal Society for the Protection of Birds, Thetford.

Rebecca, G.W. & Bainbridge, I.P. (1998). The breeding status of the Merlin *Falco columbarius* in Britain in 1993-94. *Bird Study,* **45**, 172-187.

Roberts, S.J., Lewis, J.M.S. & Williams, I.T. (1999). Breeding European Honey-buzzards in Britain. *British Birds,* **92**, 326-345.

Rodebrand, S. (1996). Ängshöken *Circus pygargus* på Öland. *Calidris,* **1996**, 99-116.

Scott, D. (1997). *The Long-eared Owl.* The Hawk and Owl Trust, London.

Scott, D. (1999). Breeding Short-eared Owls migrate across the sea to Northern Ireland. *Peregrine,* **Autumn 1999**, 5.

Scott, D. (2001a). Goshawk – breeding in Northern Ireland. *Northern Ireland Bird Report 1999,* 114-119.

Scott, D. (2001b). Influx of Short-eared Owls and Hen Harriers into Northern Ireland during 1999. *Northern Ireland Bird Report 1999,* 120-127.

Scottish Raptor Monitoring Scheme (2002). Agreement involving Scottish National Heritage, Joint Nature Conservation Committee, Scottish Raptor Study Groups, British Trust for Ornithology (Scotland), Rare Breeding Birds Panel, Royal Society for the Protection of Birds (Scotland), and Scottish Ornithologists' Club. Scottish Natural Heritage, Perth

Sharrock, J.T.R. (1976)). *The Atlas of Breeding Birds in Britain and Ireland.* T. & A.D. Poyser, Calton.

Shawyer, C.R. (1987). *The Barn Owl in the British Isles.* The Hawk Trust, London.

Sim, I.M.W., Campbell, L., Pain, D.J. & Wilson, J.D. (2000). Correlates of the population increase of Common Buzzards *Buteo buteo* in the West Midlands between 1983 and 1996. *Bird Study,* **47**, 154-164.

Sim, I.M.W., Gibbons, D.W., Bainbridge, I.P. & Mattingley, W.A. (2001). Status of the Hen Harrier *Circus cyaneus* in the UK and the Isle of Man in 1998. *Bird Study,* **48**, 341-353.

Southern, H.N. (1970). The natural control of a population of tawny owls *(Strix aluco). Journal of Zoology,* **162**, 197-285.

Spencer, R. & The Rare Breeding Birds Panel (1992). The Rare Breeding Birds Panel. *British Birds,* **85**, 117-122.

Taylor, K., Hudson, R. & Horne, G. (1988). Buzzard breeding distribution and abundance in Britain and Northern Ireland in 1983. *Bird Study,* **35**, 109-118.

Taylor, I.R. (1994). *Barn Owls: Predator-prey Relationships and Conservation.* Cambridge University Press. Cambridge.

Thom, V. (1986). *Birds in Scotland.* T. & A.D. Poyser, Calton.

Toms, M.P., Crick, H.Q.P. & Shawyer, C.R. (2000a). The status of breeding Barn Owls *Tyto alba* in the United Kingdom 1995-97. *Bird Study,* **48**, 23-37.

Toms, M.P., Crick, H.Q.P. & Shawyer, C.R. (2000b). *Project Barn Owl - Final Report. BTO Research Report No. 197/HOT Research Report No. 98/1.* British Trust for Ornithology, Thetford. The Hawk and Owl Trust, London.

Tubbs, C. (1974). *The Buzzard.* David & Charles, Newton Abbot.

Tucker, G.M. & Heath, M.F. (1994). *Birds in Europe: their Conservation Status.* BirdLife International, Cambridge.

UK Raptor Working Group (2000). *Report of the UK Raptor Working Group.* Department of the Environment, Transport and the Regions, Bristol and Joint Nature Conservation Committee, Peterborough.

Underhill-Day, J.C. (1984). Population and breeding biology of Marsh Harriers in Britain since 1900. *Journal of Applied Ecology,* **21**, 773-787.

Underhill-Day, J.C. (1990). The status and breeding biology of Marsh Harriers *Circus aeruginosus* and Montagu's Harrier *Circus pygargus* in Britain since 1900. PhD Thesis, Council for National Academic Awards, London.

Underhill-Day, J. (1998). Breeding Marsh Harriers in the United Kingdom, 1983-95. *British Birds,* **91**, 210-218.

Village, A. (1981). The diet and breeding of Long-eared Owls in relation to vole numbers. *Bird Study,* **28**, 215-224.

Village, A. (1987). Numbers, territory-size and turnover of Short-eared Owls *Asio flammeus* in relation to vole abundance. *Ornis Scandinavica,* **18**, 198-204.

Village, A. (1990). *The Kestrel.* T. & A.D. Poyser, London.

Watson, J. (1997). *The Golden Eagle.* T. & A.D. Poyser, London.

Wernham, C.V., Toms, M.P., Marchant, J.H., Clark, J.A., Siriwardena, G.M. & Baillie, S.R. (2002). *The Migration Atlas: Movements of the Birds of Britain and Ireland.* T. & A.D. Poyser, London.

Williams, R. (1998). Ecology and population dynamics of the Long-eared Owl. *The Raptor,* **25**, 34-37.

Wotton, S.R., Carter, I., Cross, A.V., Etheridge, B., Snell, N., Duffy, K. & Gregory, R.D. (2002). Red Kites *Milvus milvus* in the UK in 2000. *Bird Study,* **49**, 278-286.

Wyllie, I. & Newton, I. (1999). Use of carcasses to estimate the proportions of female Sparrowhawks and Kestrels which bred in their first year of life. *Ibis,* **141**, 489-506.

3. THE STATUS AND LEGISLATIVE PROTECTION OF BIRDS OF PREY AND THEIR HABITATS IN EUROPE

David A. Stroud

Summary

1. Compared with other breeding birds, the population sizes of European raptors are small. Indeed, raptor populations comprise a significant proportion of the rarest European birds. These small populations are a consequence not only of naturally low natural densities of these top predators, but also result from widespread persecution, and adverse consequences of land-use changes.

2. Current conservation provision for raptors in Europe derives from two international treaties both entering into force in 1979. The main provisions of the EC Directive on the Conservation of Wild Birds (79/409/EEC) relevant to the conservation of European raptors are outlined. These relate to habitat protection, general species protection, sale of live and dead birds, and means of derogating from some obligations. Within the European Union, the Directive implements the ornithological aspects of the Convention on the Conservation of European Wildlife and Natural Habitats (the Berne Convention), developed by the Council of Europe (CoE). This Convention applies widely to CoE signatories. The habitat conservation provisions of the EEC Directive on the conservation of Habitats and Species will also have general benefits for birds of prey.

3. The main relevant provisions of the Convention on International Trade in Endangered Species of Wild Fauna and Flora (CITES) and the Bonn Convention on migratory species are also summarised. There is scope for a better focus of activities under the Bonn Convention that would benefit the conservation of migratory raptors at an international scale.

4. A brief review of issues currently affecting the conservation status of European birds of prey indicates that, despite a sound legislation basis for their protection, many — indeed most — remain adversely affected through interactions with man. Of the 29 most vulnerable European diurnal raptor species, 27 are adversely affected by changes, losses or fragmentation of their habitats. Major issues include the intensification of agricultural habitats, as well as the abandonment of traditional pastoral agriculture. Persecution (shooting, trapping, direct and indirect poisoning, nest destruction) affects most diurnal raptor species, with egg-robbing, disturbance at nest sites, and illegal hunting on migratory routes being significant adverse factors for many species. Contamination with pesticide residues is a significant issue for at least 13 species. The theft of eggs and young for falconry purposes is a major conservation problem for the larger falcons. The high mortality rate following collision with pylons and powerlines and/or electrocution is a significant factor for nearly a third of species, especially in eastern Europe.

5. Despite high levels of legal protection across most of Europe, there remain major challenges in practice to ensure the implementation and enforcement of conservation legislation, so as to reverse the currently unfavourable conservation status and trends of many species.

3.1 Introduction

In Europe, birds of prey have had a long history of interaction with people. In earliest times, the largest raptors were persecuted owing to predation of stock. In contrast, during mediaeval periods, the larger falcons were highly prized for falconry, leading to the provision of strict protective measures in many countries (as described by Ratcliffe, 1993). The advent of game rearing in the 19th century led to widespread persecution and, in Britain, the partial or complete extinction of several species (Anon., 2000). Birds of prey were some of the first bird species to be afforded strict protection under national and international law. They have become totemic species, highly valued by some sectors of society. In part at least this has been because of their importance as wider indicators, not only of chemical pollution in the environment (Newton, 1998; Ratcliffe, Chapter 4), but also because their conservation status tells us something about the wider health of landscapes (Amar *et al.*, Chapter 29; Thompson *et al.*, Chapter 25).

This chapter reviews the current population levels and conservation status of birds of prey in Europe and the principal factors that influence this. It then outlines the main international legislative instruments for birds of prey conservation in Europe, and looks at their domestic implementation, using the United Kingdom as an example. It finally reviews the effect that this legislative provision has had on current European status. Where appropriate a distinction is made between owls (Strigiformes) and other birds of prey (Acciptriformes, Falconiformes; sometimes referred to as non-owl or diurnal birds of prey). All Latin names for birds of prey species are included in Appendix 3.1.

3.2 Current population status of raptors in Europe

3.2.1 Population status

There are 39 species of diurnal birds of prey and 13 species of owl that breed regularly in Europe. Based on population data from the *European Breeding Bird Atlas* (Hagemeijer & Blair, 1997; Appendix 1) the most abundant diurnal raptor species is the buzzard (371,000-472,000 pairs found across 36 countries), with steppe eagle *Aquila nipalensis* being the rarest (two pairs in Russia). Amongst owls, tawny owl *Strix aluco* is most abundant (416,000-562,000 pairs in 33 countries), with snowy owl *Nyctea scandiaca* being the rarest (33 pairs in four countries).

A comparison between the population sizes (in orders of magnitude) of birds of prey, owls and other European breeding birds (Figure 3.1) shows that the former have relatively small populations. This is clearly a consequence of their ecological position as top predators which will naturally result in occurrence at low densities relative to other bird species, notably their prey. It is also, however, a consequence of centuries of direct persecution and the indirect effects of other anthropogenic impacts — such as negative consequences of land use change or in some cases pesticide use. Many of those raptors with smallest populations are also those which have the greatest number of threats.

Owls are generally more abundant than diurnal raptors. Most species of owl (10 of 13) have populations of more than 10,000 pairs in Europe, whilst for diurnal species only three of 39 species are so abundant (Figure 3.1).

These data also show that a high proportion of the rarest of all European birds are birds of prey. Of all European birds with populations of fewer than 1,000 pairs, 46% are diurnal birds of prey. Indeed, nearly a quarter (24%) of all species with populations of fewer than

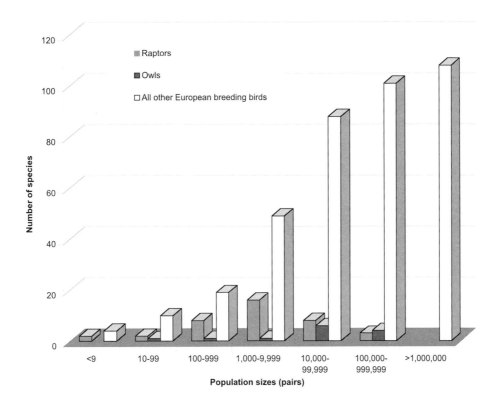

Figure 3.1. Population sizes of all regularly breeding European raptors, compared to all other European breeding birds. Data from European Breeding Bird Atlas (Hagemeijer & Blair, 1997).

10,000 pairs in Europe are diurnal birds of prey. It is not surprising, therefore, that public awareness of raptors links their special and rare appeals.

3.2.2 Conservation status

BirdLife International's SPEC (Species of European Conservation Concern: Tucker & Heath, 1994) assessments of conservation status provide a biologically based international context for the prioritisation of conservation actions. The categorisation is based on the interaction of two factors – the degree to which the species' global distribution is concentrated in Europe, and whether or not the species has favourable conservation status in Europe (itself indicated by European Threat Status — Tucker & Heath, 1994).

Table 3.2 summarises relevant categorisations for all birds of prey. It shows that nearly 80% (30 of 38) of non-owl birds of prey are in unfavourable conservation status (SPEC categories 1-3), whilst almost half the owls (six of 13 species) are similarly categorised.

Four raptors categorised as globally threatened occur in Europe — greater spotted eagle *Aquila clanga*, imperial eagle *Aquila heliaca*, Spanish imperial eagle *Aquila adalberti* and lesser kestrel *Falco naumanni*. Two non-owl birds of prey (Levant sparrowhawk *Accipiter brevipes* and Eleonora's falcon *Falco eleonorae*) and one owl (Scops owl *Otus scops*) are categorised as SPEC 2, that is both with unfavourable conservation status *and* being globally concentrated in Europe. The remaining 29 species which have unfavourable conservation status in Europe are not globally confined to, or concentrated on, the continent (Appendix 3.1).

Table 3.1. Contracting Parties to international treaties that influence conservation status of birds of prey in Europe (as at January 2001). ✓ indicates Contracting Party to treaty; ✱ indicates that the country is not a party to CITES but monitors and controls trade in CITES-listed species.

	CITES	Bonn Convention	Birds Directive (only EU Member States)	Berne Convention
Albania				✓
Andorra				✓
Armenia				
Austria	✓	✓	✓	✓
Azerbaijan	✓			✓
Belarus	✓			
Belgium	✓	✓	✓	✓
Bosnia-Herzegovina				
Bulgaria	✓	✓		✓
Burkina Faso	✓	✓		✓
Croatia	✓	✓		✓
Cyprus	✓			✓
Czech Republic	✓	✓		✓
Denmark	✓	✓	✓	✓
Estonia	✓			✓
European Union	✓	✓		✓
Finland	✓	✓	✓	✓
France	✓	✓	✓	✓
FYR Macedonia	✓	✓		✓
Georgia	✓	✓		
Germany	✓	✓	✓	✓
Greece	✓	✓	✓	✓
Hungary	✓	✓		✓
Iceland	✓			✓
Ireland	✓	✓	✓	✓
Italy	✓	✓	✓	✓
Latvia	✓	✓		✓
Liechtenstein	✓	✓		✓
Lithuania	✱			✓
Luxembourg	✓	✓	✓	✓
Malta	✓			✓
Moldova				✓
Monaco	✓	✓		✓
The Netherlands	✓	✓	✓	✓
Norway	✓	✓		✓
Poland	✓	✓		✓
Portugal	✓	✓	✓	✓
Romania	✓	✓		✓
Russian Federation	✓			
Senegal	✓	✓		✓
Serbia				
Slovakia	✓	✓		✓
Slovenia	✓	✓		✓
Spain	✓	✓	✓	✓
Sweden	✓	✓	✓	✓
Switzerland	✓	✓		✓
Tunisia	✓	✓		✓
Turkey	✓			✓
Ukraine	✓			✓
United Kingdom	✓	✓	✓	✓

Table 3.2. SPEC categorisation of European birds of prey (data from Tucker & Heath, 1994).

	Diurnal birds of prey	Owls
SPEC 1 — Species of global conservation concern	4	
SPEC 2 — Species with unfavourable conservation status and concentrated in Europe	2	1
SPEC 3 — Species with unfavourable conservation status but not concentrated in Europe	23	5
SPEC 4 — Species with favourable conservation status and concentrated in Europe	3	1
Not SPEC listed	4	6
Total species	36	13

3.3 International conservation treaties

In legislative terms, European birds of prey are arguably one of the most legislated for groups of species anywhere in the world. They benefit from the highest levels of legislative protection under both national and international laws. Typically, this legislation addresses both protection of birds and their nests, as well as requirements to maintain habitats.

Two main international treaties address the conservation of birds of prey in Europe: the 1979 EEC Council Directive 79/409/EEC on the Conservation of Wild Birds (known as the 'Birds Directive') and the 1979 Convention on the Conservation of European Wildlife and Natural Habitats (known as the 'Berne Convention').

3.3.1 Birds Directive

In 1979, the European Community adopted the Birds Directive to provide for the protection, management and control of all species of naturally occurring wild birds in the European territory of Member States. It is the main means by which the European Union has implemented the Berne Convention (below). Accordingly, many of its provisions are similar, if not identical. It provides a key framework for biodiversity conservation in the European Union.

Elements of this 1979 Directive have since been modified with the accession of additional Member States. This has mainly involved revision to the lists of species given in the Directive Annexes. The revisions of 1985 and 1992 (following the expansion of the European Union in those years) were significant, adding a significant number of birds of prey and owl to Annex I (Table 3.3). The Birds Directive seeks to conserve bird populations through several mechanisms (Temple-Lang, 1982). Fundamental aims are set out in Article 2 which requires Member States to *"maintain the population of the species referred to in Article 1 [i.e. all wild birds] at a level which corresponds in particular to ecological, scientific and cultural requirements, while taking account of economic and recreational requirements, or to adapt the population of these species to that level.".*

Article 3 requires Member States to preserve, maintain or re-establish a sufficient diversity and area of habitats to meet the obligations in Article 2.

Table 3.3. Progressive additions of birds of prey to Annex I of the Birds Directive.

Year of addition to Annex I	Species	Legal text
1979	Honey buzzard, black-shouldered kite, black kite, red kite, white-tailed eagle, lammergeier, Egyptian vulture, griffon vulture, black vulture, short-toed eagle, marsh harrier, hen harrier, Montagu's harrier, sparrowhawk (*A. n. granti* only), Spanish imperial eagle, golden eagle, booted eagle, Bonelli's eagle, osprey, Eleonora's falcon, lanner falcon, peregrine, eagle owl, snowy owl and short-eared owl	Council Directive 79/409/EEC on the conservation of wild birds (OJ No L 103, 25 April 1979, p. 1)
1985	Pallid harrier, Levant sparrowhawk, Corsican/Sardinian goshawk, long-legged buzzard, lesser spotted eagle, spotted eagle, imperial eagle, lesser kestrel, merlin, pygmy owl and Tengmalm's owl	Commission Directive (85/411/EEC) of 25 July 1985 amending Council Directive 79/409/EEC on the conservation of wild birds (OJ No L 233, 30 August 1998, pp. 33-41)
1995	Gyrfalcon, hawk owl, great grey owl and Ural owl	Act of accession of Austria, Finland and Sweden - Council Decision 95/1/EC (OJ No L 1, 1 January 1995, p.1-)

Article 4 requires Member States to classify, in particular, the most suitable territories as special protection areas for the rare or vulnerable species listed in Annex I (Article 4.1), for regularly occurring migratory species (Article 4.2), and for the protection of wetlands, especially wetlands of international importance (the Directive also lists some sub-species (e.g. the Corsican-Sardinian race of goshawk *Accipiter gentilis arrigonii* and the Macaronesian race of sparrowhawk *Accipiter nisus granti*) on Annex I). These sites have become known as Special Protection Areas (SPAs). Within SPAs, Member States are obliged to take necessary steps to avoid deterioration of natural habitats and any disturbance of the species, where this disturbance would be significant having regard to the objectives of the Directive. The Directive envisages that the establishment of SPAs, when taken collectively across the EU, will result in a European network of protected sites.

A large proportion of European non-owl birds of prey (33 of 39) and owl (eight of 13) species are currently listed on Annex I (Appendix 3.1). Annex I lists species which "*shall be the subject of special conservation measures concerning their habitat in order to ensure their survival and reproduction in their area of distribution*".

Of the remaining birds of prey, most are regular migrants and thus require (where site-based protection is an appropriate conservation measure – Stroud *et al.*, 2001) the classification of SPAs under Article 4.2. These species include goshawk *Accipiter gentilis* (northern populations only), sparrowhawk *Accipiter nisus* (northern populations only), buzzard *Buteo buteo* (northern and eastern populations), rough-legged buzzard *Buteo lagopus*, kestrel *Falco tinnunculus* (migratory in north and east of Europe, partial migrant or dispersive elsewhere, red-footed falcon *Falco vespertinus*, hobby *F. columbarius* and saker *F. cherrug*.

The only non-Annex I listed species which are sedentary (and so may not require SPAs under European legislation) are some populations of goshawk (*A. g. buteoides* and *A. g. gentilis*), sedentary populations of sparrowhawk (*A. n. nisus*), island (including the UK) and central mainland Europe races of buzzard, and island (including the UK) races of kestrel (*F. t. alexandri, neglectus, canariensis* and *dacotiae*).

Thus, for virtually all European birds of prey, Member States are required to classify SPAs under Article 4 (where site-based protection is an appropriate conservation measure), either because they are listed on Annex I or because they are migratory. This conservation of important sites is a mandatory action required of Member States by the Directive. Article 4 indicates that a Member State has a degree of discretion as to which are "*the most suitable territories*" that it will classify. However, European Court of Justice case-law (e.g. ECJ Case C-3/96 — Commission of the European Communities v. The Kingdom of The Netherlands supported by The Federal Republic of Germany (Judgement of the Court). OJ, 25 July 1998, C234/8) indicates that this discretion is strictly limited.

The Directive also establishes a general system of bird species protection under Article 5 (including their eggs and nests), prohibits trade in live or dead birds (Article 6), provides for certain species to be hunted provided it is compatible with the aims of the Directive (Article 7), and bans large-scale or non-selective means of capture or killing (Article 8) in particular those listed in Annex IV(a). It also establishes a system of derogation from some parts of the Directive including for the killing and taking of certain species (Article 9).

The derogation procedures ('exceptions') from the provisions of species protection measures allowed under Article 9 are strictly limited, as follows.

"Member States may derogate from the provisions of Article 5, 6, 7 and 8, where there is no other satisfactory solution, for the following reasons:

- *in the interests of public health and safety,*
- *in the interests of air safety,*
- *to prevent serious damage to crops, livestock, forests, fisheries and water,*
- *for the protection of flora and fauna,*
- *for the purposes of research and teaching, of re-population, of re-introduction and for the breeding necessary for these purposes,*
- *to permit, under strictly supervised conditions and on a selective basis, the capture, keeping or other judicious use of, certain birds in small numbers."*

The Birds Directive also encourages research in support of bird species conservation (Article 10).

3.3.2 Habitats Directive

The 'Habitats Directive' (Council Directive 93/43/EEC on the conservation of natural habitats and of wild fauna and flora) is of significance also. European raptors will benefit indirectly from the habitat protection measures (including the classification of a European network of Special Areas of Conservation). Article 6 of the Directive also has direct implications for the management and conservation of SPAs identified under Article 4 of the Birds Directive.

3.3.3 Berne Convention

The Berne Convention provides a broad framework for the conservation of fauna and flora within signatory countries (Table 3.1, Figure 3.2) of the Council of Europe. The main provisions with respect to vertebrate species protection and pest management are summarised in Table 3.4.

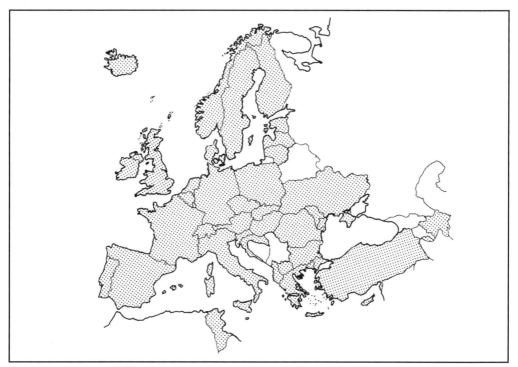

Figure 3.2. The extent of Europe covered by the provisions of either the European Union's Birds Directive and/or the Berne Convention, and thus the area over which these treaties require strict protection for birds of prey (including control of deleterious changes in land use).

The European Union is a Contracting Party to the Convention. This provides for necessary intra-Community co-ordination in order to fulfil the objectives of the Convention which has a wider geographical scope. One consequence has been the important linkage between the Conventions and its European Union implementation by means of Directives. As they relate to birds of prey, the species protection regime (including derogation measures) of the Berne Convention (Table 3.4) is virtually identical to that of the Birds Directive.

3.3.4 Convention on Trade in Endangered Species (CITES)

CITES entered into force in 1975 and regulates the international trade in specimens of species of wild fauna and flora, i.e. export, re-export and import of live and dead animals and plants and parts and derivatives of these. It is based on a system of permits and certificates which can only be issued if certain conditions are met.

Table 3.4. Main species protection provisions of the 1979 Berne Convention.

Basic provisions apply to all species through Article 2: *"The Contracting Parties shall take requisite measures to maintain the population of wild flora and fauna, at or adapt it to, a level which corresponds in particular to ecological, scientific and cultural requirements, while taking account of economic and recreational requirements and the needs of sub-species, varieties or forms at risk locally.".*

Article 6: Comprehensive protection of species listed in Appendix II (strictly protected fauna).

Article 7: Protection for species listed under Appendix III (protected fauna) *"any exploitation of wild fauna specified in Appendix III shall be regulated in order to keep the populations out of danger, taking into account the requirements of Article 2.".* Note that in regulating taking, Contracting Parties must have regard for sub-species and varieties that are at risk locally, without necessarily being threatened at European level.

Regulation of means of taking through Article 8, in particular banning the use of large-scale and non-selective means of capture and killing: *"In respect of the capture or killing of wild fauna species specified in Appendix III and in cases where, in accordance with Article 9, exceptions are applied to species specified in Appendix II, Contracting Parties shall prohibit the use of all indiscriminate means of capture and killing and the use of all means capable of causing local disappearance to, or serious disturbance to, populations of a species, and in particular, the means specified in Appendix IV."*

Prohibited means of capture and killing are listed under Appendix IV.

Article 9 provides for derogation procedures ('exceptions') from the provisions of species protection measures:

1.   Each Contracting Party may make exceptions from the provisions of Articles 4, 5, 6, 7 and from the prohibition of the use of the means mentioned in Article 8 provided that there is no other satisfactory solution and that the exception will not be detrimental to the survival of the population concerned:
- *for the protection of flora and fauna;*
- *to prevent serious damage to crops, livestock, forests, fisheries, water and other forms of property;*
- *in the interests of public health and safety, air safety or other overriding public interests;*
- *for the purposes of research and education, of repopulation, or reintroduction and for the necessary breeding;*
- *to permit, under strictly supervised conditions, on a selective basis and to a limited extent, the taking, keeping or other judicious exploitation of certain wild animals and plants in small numbers.*

2.   The Contracting Parties shall report every two years to the Standing Committee on the exceptions made under the preceding paragraph. These reports must specify:
- *the populations which are or have been subject to the exceptions and, when practical, the number of specimens involved;*
- *the means authorised for the killing or capture;*
- *the conditions of risk and the circumstances of time and place under which such exceptions were granted;*
- *the authority empowered to declare that these conditions have been fulfilled, and to take decisions in respect of the means that may be used, their limits and the persons instructed to carry them out;*
- *the controls involved.*

Species are subject to different degrees of regulation and are listed in three appendices. Appendix I lists species threatened with extinction and for which trade must be subject to strict regulation and authorised only in exceptional circumstances. Appendix II lists species not necessarily threatened with extinction now, but which may become so unless trade is strictly regulated.   It also contained so-called 'look-alike' species that are controlled because of their similarity in appearance to other regulated species. Appendix III contains species that are subject to regulation with the jurisdiction of a Party and for which co-operation of other Parties is needed to prevent or restrict their exploitation.

All European birds of prey are listed in Appendix II of CITES with the exceptions of white-tailed eagle *Haliaeetus albicilla*, imperial eagle *Aquila heliaca*, Spanish imperial eagle *A. adalberti*, peregrine *Falco peregrinus* and gyrfalcon *F. rusticolus* which are all listed on Appendix I.

The European Union is not yet a Party to CITES, although has been fully implementing the Convention since 1984 through its own Regulations (which in various regards are actually stricter than those of CITES). The most recent of these is Council Regulation (EC) No. 338/97 on the Protection of Species of Wild Fauna and Flora by regulating Trade therein. This Regulation goes beyond CITES and allows for the inclusion of non-CITES listed species in its Annexes.

Most European countries are signatories to CITES (Table 3.1).

3.3.5 Convention on the Conservation of Migratory Species (Bonn Convention)

The Bonn Convention entered into force in 1983 and provides a framework through which its Contracting Parties may act and co-operate to conserve migratory species and their habitats by:

- adopting strict protection measures for migratory species that have been categorised as endangered;
- concluding Agreements for the conservation and management of migratory species that have an unfavourable conservation status or would benefit significantly from international co-operation; and
- undertaking joint research activities.

There are two appendices to the Convention that list migratory species that would benefit from conservation measures. Appendix I lists species that are in danger of extinction throughout all or a significant proportion of their range. Range States are required to prohibit the taking of these animals, with few exceptions, so as to give them full protection. Appendix II lists migratory species whose conservation status (which need not necessarily be endangered) requires, or would benefit from, the implementation of international co-operative Agreements.

A number of Agreements have been agreed and are in force, including the Agreement on the Conservation of African-Eurasian Migratory Waterbirds (AEWA), the European Bats Agreement (EUROBATS), and the Agreement on the Conservation of Small Cetaceans in the Baltic and North Seas (ASCOBANS). Most recently, an Agreement on the Conservation of Albatrosses and Petrels has been concluded.

A large number of European countries are signatories to the Bonn Convention (Table 3.1), including the European Union.

All European diurnal birds of prey are listed in Appendix II of the Bonn Convention, and the white-tailed eagle is additionally listed in Appendix I. Owls, however, are not currently listed under the Convention – a consequence of the sedentary nature of most owl species.

3.4 Legislation and domestic implementation in the UK: an example

3.4.1 Historic context

In mediaeval times some species were subject to strict protection in England as a consequence of their role in high status sports such as falconry (Yapp, 1982; Ratcliffe, 1993). Indeed, as reviewed by Marchant & Watkins (1897), there were a number of strict Tudor laws relating to the protection of birds of prey. For example, the Act of 11 Henry VII, cap. 17, stated that eggs of any falcon, goshawk, laner, or swan should not be taken out of the nest on pain of imprisonment of a year and a fine at the King's will. According to Marchant & Watkins (1897):

> *"The Act 31 Henry VIII, c. 12, made it a felony punishable with death for a person wrongfully to take or cause to be taken any egg or eggs of any "falcon, goshawk, or laner, or the birds (i.e. the young) of any falcon, goshawk, or laner or laneret" out of or from any nest or nests of any "falcon, goshawk, or laner" within any of the King's honours, castles, manors, lands, tenements, woods or other grounds".*

The rise of Victorian game shooting, however, led to changed attitudes and increased persecution in the 19th century. The resulting major population declines which led to national extinctions for some species in turn resulted in enhanced legal protection from 1880 onwards (Table 3.5), and at least some consequential slow recovery of populations. Initial protection came through local provision (at county and county borough level) for the protection of birds of prey under the 1880 Wild Birds Protection Act (Marchant & Watkins, 1897). The Schedule of the Act listed species for which a national close season was established and the eggs of which were protected. County administrative authorities could apply to the Secretary of State for the establishment of Orders extending protection for named species to specific counties. No birds of prey were nationally listed in the Schedule of the Act, an omission noted at the time. Again, according to Marchant & Watkins (1897):

> *"Many rare birds, which are in danger of being exterminated, have been left out, e.g. the kite, the osprey, the buzzard, and the hen harrier, and there might well have been added birds such as the kestrel, the golden eagle, the rose-coloured pastor, the heron and the crossbill."*

Although the 1880 Act did not give national protection, in the decade following, local protection in some counties was extended to many birds of prey through subsequent Statutory Instruments. The extent of protection for eggs and the close season for killing hen harrier *Circus cyaneus*, peregrine, osprey *Pandion haliaetus* and buzzard are shown in Figures 3.3-3.6, respectively. Several points can be noted.

- Generally, those areas where protection was given in the 1880s were those where the species concerned had already become extinct (c.f. Parslow, 1973; Holloway, 1996), or indeed, may never have occurred (as in the protection of osprey eggs in southern England).
- Protection of adults extended only to the provision of a close season, extending generally from February or March, until August. Outside of this period, birds could be legally killed in most counties.

Table 3.5. Sequence of national and international legislative developments during the last two centuries, and the changing status of birds of prey in the UK.

Decade	Year	Status of birds of prey in UK (Anon., 2000)	Monitoring of status	Developments in UK conservation policy and legislation	European/international (from legislative developments)
1800s		Onset of management of moorlands for red grouse involving rotational burning and intensive predator control.			
1810s					
1820s					
1830s		Development of driven grouse shooting.			
1840s		Widespread adoption of intensive management of heather moorland for red grouse following introduction of rapid fire cartridge in 1848.			
1850s		Montagu's harrier virtually extinct (to 1920s).			
1860s		Increased red grouse shooting as development of railways leads to easier access to uplands: major impacts apparent on most upland raptor species. Elimination by persecution of buzzards from most of Britain other than a few western districts.			
1870s					
1880s	1880			Wild Birds Protection Act – allows for protection of birds and eggs at county and county borough level. First move towards providing at least partial legal protection, but incomplete geographic and species coverage.	

Decade	Year	Status of birds of prey in UK (Anon., 2000)	Monitoring of status	Developments in UK conservation policy and legislation	European/international (from legislative developments)
1890s		UK extinction of goshawk through persecution.			
1900s	1900	UK extinction of marsh harrier through persecution and drainage of reedbed habitat.			
		Hen harrier restricted to Orkneys and Western Isles owing to persecution in mainland Britain.			
		Honey buzzard probably extinct in Britain.			
1910s	1910-14	Golden eagle population minimum in Scotland.			
	1914-18	Reduction of levels of persecution during WWI.			
	1916	UK extinction of white-tailed eagle and osprey through persecution and egg-collecting.			
1920s	1927	Regular breeding of marsh harriers commences in East Anglia.			
1930s	1931-35	Red kite population minimum in Wales.			
1940s	1939-45	Reduction of levels of persecution during WWII.			
	late 1940s	Introduction of DDT into major agricultural use.			
1950s		Major declines in birds of prey owing to accumulation of DDT and other persistent organochlorine pesticides in food chains. By 1960 sparrowhawk virtually extinct in eastern Britain.			
		Unofficial re-establishment of goshawks.			

Decade	Year	Status of birds of prey in UK (Anon, 2000)	Monitoring of status	Developments in UK conservation policy and legislation	European/international (from legislative developments)
	1954	Re-colonisation by ospreys.		Protection of Birds Act: UK-wide protection for all birds of prey (other than sparrowhawk).	
1960s		Declines due to bio-accumulation of pesticides continue for many species.			
	1961		First national peregrine survey.		
	1962		Second national peregrine survey.		
	1963	Peregrine population minimum.	1968–1972: first BTO *Breeding bird atlas of Britain and Ireland* enables assessment of distribution.	Sparrowhawk protected by Statutory Order following declining population.	
1970s		Recovery of many birds of prey following controls of use of persistent organic chemicals.			
	1971		Third national peregrine survey.		
	1972		Establishment of Rare Breeding Birds Panel to collate information on locations of Britain's rarest breeding birds.		
	1975	White-tailed eagle re-establishment commences.			CITES enters into force.
	1979				EEC Birds Directive & Berne Convention enter into force – the first Europe-wide comprehensive legislative provision for bird conservation.
1980s		Declining extent of moorland management for red grouse through much of the British uplands.	Development of Raptor Study Groups in Scotland (and later elsewhere) to provide local co-ordination of raptor monitoring.		

Decade	Year	Status of birds of prey in UK (Anon., 2000)	Monitoring of status	Developments in UK conservation policy and legislation	European/international (from legislative developments)
	1981		Fourth national peregrine survey.	Wildlife & Countryside Act implements Birds Directive in GB.	
	1982		First national golden eagle survey.		
	1983		National buzzard survey.		Bonn Convention on migratory species enters into force.
	1984				European Communities CITES Regulation.
	1985	First white-tailed eagle chick reared since 1916.		Wildlife (Northern Ireland) Order implements aspects of Birds Directive in NI.	
	1989	red kite re-establishment in England and Scotland commences.			
1990s		Decline of kestrels possibly linked to agricultural intensification. Strong re-establishment of red kite populations in England and Scotland through 1990s.	1988-1991: second BTO *Breeding bird atlas of Britain and Ireland* enables reassessment of distribution against late 1960s data.		
	1991		Fifth national peregrine survey.	Government launches inter-departmental Campaign Against Illegal Poisoning of Wildlife in response to NCC/RSPB report *Death by Design*.	
	1992	First red kites to rear young in England for over 100 years.	Second national golden eagle survey.	EEC Habitats Directive enters into force.	
	1993		1993 & 1994: national merlin survey.		

Decade	Year	Status of birds of prey in UK (Anon., 2000)	Monitoring of status	Developments in UK conservation policy and legislation	European/international (from legislative developments)
	1994		BTO/JNCC/RSPB Breeding Bird Survey established to monitor trends in commoner breeding birds.	The Conservation (Natural Habitats, &c.) Regulations implements Habitats Directive in GB.	
	1995			Government establishes DETR/JNCC Raptor Working Group to advise on policies and conflict resolution.	
				The Conservation (Natural Habitats, etc.) Regulations (Northern Ireland) implements Habitats Directive in NI.	
	1996				Publication of first international species action plans by EU/Council of Europe for globally threatened raptors in Europe.
	1997			*Action for Scotland's Moorlands: a statement of intent* signed by 14 organisations pledging to oppose illegal killing of birds of prey and seek solutions to conflict situations.	Revision of European Communities CITES Regulation.
	1998		National hen harrier survey. Statutory Conservation Agency /RSPB Annual Breeding Bird Scheme (SCARABBS) finalised to provide timetable and funding for future surveys of scarce/rare raptors in UK.	Substitute feeding of hen harriers on moorland demonstrated as a practical means of resolving some conflicts with red grouse managers. The Partnership Against Wildlife Crime publish desirable enhancements to legislation. Biodiversity Action Plan for British Uplands published.	

Decade	Year	Status of birds of prey in UK (Anon., 2000)	Monitoring of status	Developments in UK conservation policy and legislation	European/international (from legislative developments)
2000s	2000		National honey buzzard survey co-ordinated by RBBP.	DETR/JNCC Raptor Working Group publishes conclusions and recommendations.	Action Plans for five priority species published by European Commission.
				Countryside and Rights of Way Act introduced (England and Wales only).	
	2001			UK SPA review (Stroud *et al.*, 2001) published by JNCC.	
	2002		Launch of Scottish Raptor Monitoring Scheme by SNH, JNCC, Scottish Raptor Study Groups, BTO, RBBP, RSPB & SOC.	Major recovery programme for hen harriers in northern England launched by English Nature.	Action Plans for four more priority species published by European Commission.
				Scotland's Moorland Forum formed in March 2002 with 22 member organisations working to sustain and enhance moorland.	
			National peregrine survey.		

Figure 3.3. a) Counties that gave protection to hen harriers by means of a summer close season through Orders under the 1880 Protection of Birds Act. b) Counties that gave protection to hen harrier eggs and nests through Orders under the 1880 Protection of Birds Act.

Figure 3.4. a) Counties that gave protection to ospreys by means of a summer close season through Orders under the 1880 Protection of Birds Act. b) Counties that gave protection to osprey eggs and nests through Orders under the 1880 Protection of Birds Act.

Figure 3.5. a) Counties that gave protection to peregrines by means of a summer close season through Orders under the 1880 Protection of Birds Act. b) Counties that gave protection to peregrine eggs and nests through Orders under the 1880 Protection of Birds Act.

Figure 3.6. a) Counties that gave protection to buzzards by means of a summer close season through Orders under the 1880 Protection of Birds Act. b) Counties that gave protection to buzzard eggs and nests through Orders under the 1880 Protection of Birds Act.

• Where counties had chosen to protect birds of prey, protection was generally more extensive for eggs and nests than it was for birds (which typically could still legally be killed outside a closed (breeding) season).

Thus, whilst it started to establish principles and maybe to change opinions, the 1880 Act in itself probably did little to reverse ongoing declines then apparent in many of the British populations of large raptors.

UK-wide protection for all birds of prey (except sparrowhawk, which was given protection by Statutory Order in 1963 following its widespread decline because of the effects of organochlorine pesticides) occurred only following the 1954 Protection of Birds Act (Table 3.5). This Act also established the principle of special penalties for the killing of rarer species.

In 1979, both the Berne Convention and the Birds Directive came into force. As noted above, these established a variety of legal principles regarding the protection of threatened birds, including requirements for site conservation and the regulation of taking and killing. To bring UK domestic legislation into line with these obligations, in 1981 the Wildlife and Countryside Act was passed (for Great Britain), and in 1985 the equivalent provisions came into force in Northern Ireland through the Wildlife (Northern Ireland) Order. In the 1990s, there have been several Statutory Instruments to better reflect the provisions of the Birds Directive in domestic legislation.

There have been problems implementing aspects of the Wildlife and Countryside Act (British Trust for Ornithology *et al.*, 1995, 1997). The introduction of the Countryside and Rights of Way Act 2000 (in England and Wales) significantly enhanced a number of aspects related to legislative enforcement, in particular, it introduced the possibility of custodial sentences for certain offences under the Wildlife and Countryside Act. Similar measures have been proposed for Scotland.

There has been a recent review of the UK network of SPAs (Stroud *et al.*, 2001). The review has derived targeted suites of SPAs for each Annex I and migratory bird in the UK for which site-based conservation measures are appropriate. Provisions for birds of prey are summarised in Table 3.6, whilst Figure 3.7 shows the location of the 47 SPAs that have been individually selected for one or more birds of prey.

In the UK, as probably in other European countries, the fulfilment of international obligations in domestic law can be through a range of different pieces of pre-existing legislation. It is relatively rare that international legislation is sufficiently novel to warrant comprehensive primary legislation to enact its provisions domestically — although this can sometimes occur. The scope of domestic legislation can be both broader in application and more restrictive in detail than corresponding international obligations since a general tenet of all such treaties is that they set minimum standards: Member States are free to establish stricter regulations at national level should this be desired.

Most recently, the process of ongoing political devolution with the UK opens the potential for differing species legislation in different countries. The degree of legislative divergence within the UK, however, will be constrained by the over-arching requirements of international legislation, especially the Birds Directive.

Table 3.6. Population coverage of UK migratory and Annex 1 birds of prey within SPA suites (from Stroud *et al.*, 2001). This table lists all regularly occurring migratory birds of prey in the UK (and species listed in Annex I of the Directive where these are regularly occurring within the UK). Medium shading indicates that, although the species is present in the UK during the season, no SPAs have been selected (i.e. present but no SPAs). Black indicates that, for some migrants, the species does not regularly occur in the UK during the season concerned (i.e. not present thus no SPAs). Light shading indicates Annex 1 status. For full explanation of data sources, see Stroud *et al.* (2001).

Name	*Breeding season*					*Non-breeding season*				
	Number of breeding sites in species' UK SPA suite	Total numbers in species' UK SPA suite (pairs)	% British (GB) breeding population	% all-Ireland breeding population in Northern Ireland	% international population	Number of non-breeding sites in species' UK SPA suite	Total numbers in species' UK SPA suite (individuals)	% British (GB) non-breeding population	% all-Ireland non-breeding population in Northern Ireland	% international population
Honey Buzzard	1	2	13%		<0.1%					
Red Kite	1	15	9.3%		<0.1%					
White-tailed Eagle										
Marsh Harrier	10	116	74%		0.4%					
Hen Harrier	14	229	47.4%		2.8%	20	244	32.5%		1.0%
Montagu's Harrier										
Goshawk										
Sparrowhawk										
Buzzard										
Rough-legged Buzzard										
Golden Eagle	8	60	15%		1.2%			Largely resident on breeding areas		
Osprey	9	39	39%		0.8%					
Kestrel										
Red-footed Falcon										
Merlin	14	426	32.8%		4.2%	1	15	1.2%		<0.1%
Hobby										
Peregrine	9	93	7.7%	1.6%	1.7%					
Snowy Owl										
Long-eared Owl										
Short-eared Owl	6	131	13.1%		1.0%					

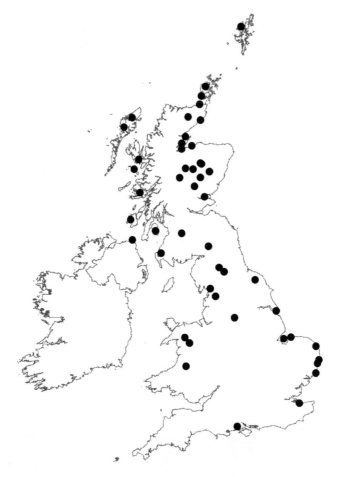

Figure 3.7. The network of the 47 Special Protection Areas identified for breeding raptors in the UK (from Stroud *et al.,* 2001).

3.5   Conservation status of raptors in Europe: the effect of legislative provision

3.5.1 *Threats*

The conservation status of most European birds of prey remains poor. For species listed as SPEC 1, SPEC 2 or SPEC 3, main negative factors for each species were identified from the species accounts of BirdLife International's European review of bird conservation (Tucker & Heath, 1994), and international action plans (Heredia *et al.,* 1996; European Commission, 2000, 2001). These are summarised in Tables 3.7 and 3.8 for diurnal birds of prey and owls, respectively. The assessment made here is far from consistent or systematic. Many of the identified negative factors are not mutually exclusive, and indeed some specifics (for example declines in prey items) are usually consequences of wider issues (such as land use change). The approach does, however, serve to identify the main important conservation issues for European birds of prey.

Threats can be categorised into four groups: a) land use and habitat issues, the effects of b) direct and c) indirect interactions with people, and d) natural (i.e. non-anthropogenic related) issues (also Thompson *et al.,* Chapter 25).

Land use changes affect populations through a variety of direct and indirect means (see Donázar *et al.,* 1997), including loss of favoured habitats and nest sites, and decline in availability of prey. Habitat loss, change and fragmentation affects nearly all species (27 of 29 diurnal birds of prey, although not Egyptian vulture *Neophron percnopterus* and peregrine). Major issues include the intensification of forest and agricultural habitats on the one hand, as well as the abandonment of traditional pastoral agriculture on the other.

Direct interactions with man include the widespread effects of persecution (including shooting, trapping, direct and indirect poisoning and nest destruction), egg-robbing, illegal trade in live birds, the effects of pesticide contamination, disturbance at nest sites, and illegal hunting on migration.

The main indirect interaction with man is collisions with powerlines and pylons (especially an issue in Eastern Europe), and for owls in particular, collisions with vehicles along roads.

Adverse natural factors are limited to the effects of inter-specific competition identified as a factor for three species.

It might be supposed that different threats might be faced within different countries in the European Union, not least because of the wide-scale negative impacts of the Common Agricultural Policy on land use patterns. However, the number and type of threats facing birds of prey with distributions that occur largely within the European Union are not significantly different to those whose distributions lie substantially outside the European Union (pallid harrier *Circus macrourus*, Levant sparrowhawk *Accipiter brevipes*, long-legged buzzard *Buteo rufinus*, greater spotted eagle, steppe eagle, imperial eagle, red-footed falcon and saker falcon).

3.5.2 International action plans

In response to the continuing decline in numbers and range of many globally threatened bird species in Europe, the Council of Europe and the European Commission have jointly initiated international action plans for several species. Plans have been published jointly for black vulture *Aegypius monachus,* imperial eagle, Spanish imperial eagle and lesser kestrel *Falco naumanni* (Heredia *et al.,* 1996). More recently (2000), the Birds Directive's Ornis Committee (the main international forum for taking forwards the implementation of the Directive) has agreed international plans for the Corsican-Sardinian race of goshawk *Accipiter gentilis arrigoni,* the Macaronesian race of sparrowhawk *Accipiter nisus granti,* Eleonora's falcon *Falco eleonorae,* lanner *Falco biarmicus* and gyrfalcon.

Whether these plans are an effective means of delivering improved status for the species concerned has still to be assessed.

3.6 Discussion

The governments of Europe have agreed to uniform and strong provisions for the conservation of birds of prey through the Berne Convention and for EU Member States through the Birds Directive. The provisions are among the strongest for any group of species anywhere in the world, and apply over a huge extent of Europe, from North Africa to high Arctic Svalbard, and from the Iberian Peninsula to the shores of the Caspian Sea (Figure 3.2). They include the prohibition of negative influences such as all forms of deliberate capture and keeping, deliberate killing, the collection of eggs, and disturbance at the nest and during the breeding season.

Table 3.7. Factors identified by Tucker & Heath (1994) as negatively influencing European diurnal bird of prey species that have unfavourable conservation status in Europe (i.e. SPEC 1-3).

	Number of species (out of 29)	Black-winged kite	Black kite	White-tailed eagle	Lammer-geier	Egyptian vulture	Griffon vulture	Cinereous vulture	Short-toed eagle	Hen harrier	Pallid harrier	Levant sparrow-hawk	Long-legged buzzard	Lesser spotted eagle	Greater spotted eagle	Steppe eagle
SPEC status		3	3	3	3	3	3	3	3	3	3	2	3	3	1	3
Habitat related																
Habitat loss, change & fragmentation	27	1	1	1	1		1	1	1	1	1	1	1	1	1	1
Agricultural intensification (abandonment of low intensity agricultural land)	18	1	1		1		1	1	1	1		1	1	1		1
Agricultural abandonment	7	1			1		1		1							
Modern/inappropriate forestry practises (incl. open ground afforestation)	16	1	1	1			1	1	1	1				1	1	
Forest fires	3							1	1							
Wetland loss and degradation	7		1	1						1				1	1	
Reduced carrion availability (from better stock husbandry & waste disposal)	4				1		1	1								
Loss of nest sites	0															
Decline in natural prey items	11											1		1		

	Number of species (out of 29)	Black-winged kite	Black kite	White-tailed eagle	Lammergeier	Egyptian vulture	Griffon vulture	Cinereous vulture	Short-toed eagle	Hen harrier	Pallid harrier	Levant sparrow-hawk	Long-legged buzzard	Lesser spotted eagle	Greater spotted eagle	Steppe eagle
Direct interactions with man																
Persecution (shooting, trapping, direct and indirect poisoning, nest destruction)	25	1	1	1	1	1	1	1		1			1		1	1
Egg-robbing	11			1	1										1	
Illegal trade in live birds (falconry)	6															
Pesticide contamination	15		1	1	1				1		1					
Disturbance (especially at nest sites)	18		1	1	1			1	1				1	1	1	1
Illegal hunting on migration	10					1			1					1		
Introduced predators	1															
Indirect interactions with man																
Powerline and pylon collisions/electrocution	12		1						1				1			1
Climate change	1															
Collisions with vehicles	0															
Natural																
Inter-specific competition	3														1	
No. of factors/spp.		5	8	7	8	2	6	7	10	5	2	3	5	7	7	5

Table 3.7 (contd.). Factors identified by Tucker & Heath (1994) as negatively influencing European diurnal bird of prey species that have unfavourable conservation status in Europe (i.e. SPEC 1-3).

	Imperial Eagle	Spanish imperial eagle	Golden eagle	Booted eagle	Bonelli's eagle	Osprey	Lesser kestrel	Kestrel	Red-footed falcon	Eleonora's falcon	Lanner	Saker	Gyrfalcon	Peregrine
SPEC status	1	1	3	3	3	3	1	3	3	2	3	3	3	3
Habitat related														
Habitat loss, change & fragmentation	1	1	1	1	1	1	1	1	1	1	1	1	1	
Agricultural intensification (abandonment of low intensity agricultural land)	1	1	1	1		1	1		1		1			
Agricultural abandonment					1		1					1		
Modern/inappropriate forestry practises (incl. open ground afforestation)	1	1	1	1		1				1	1	1		
Forest fires				1										
Wetland loss and degradation			1						1					
Reduced carrion availability (from better stock husbandry & waste disposal)														
Loss of nest sites														

	Imperial Eagle	Spanish imperial eagle	Golden eagle	Booted eagle	Bonelli's eagle	Osprey	Lesser kestrel	Kestrel	Red-footed falcon	Eleonora's falcon	Lanner	Saker	Gyrfalcon	Peregrine
Decline in natural prey items	1	1			1	1	1	1	1			1	1	
Direct interactions with man														
Persecution (shooting, trapping, direct and indirect poisoning, nest destruction)	1	1	1	1	1	1	1	1	1	1	1	1	1	1
Egg-robbing	1	1	1	1		1				1	1	1	1	1
Illegal trade in live birds (falconry)	1		1	1						1	1	1	1	1
Pesticide contamination		1	1	1	1	1	1		1	1	1	1		1
Disturbance (especially at nest sites)	1	1			1	1	1		1	1	1	1	1	
Illegal hunting on migration	1							1	1	1	1	1	1	
Introduced predators										1				
Indirect interactions with man														
Powerline and pylon collisions/electrocution	1	1		1	1	1					1	1	1	
Climate change								1						
Collisions with vehicles														
Natural														
Inter-specific competition							1				1			
No. of factors/spp.	9	9	5	7	8	9	8	7	6	10	10	9	7	4

Table 3.7. Factors identified by Tucker & Heath (1994) as negatively influencing European diurnal bird of prey species that have unfavourable conservation status in Europe (i.e. SPEC 1-3).

	Number of species (out of 6)	Barn owl	Scops owl	Eagle owl	Snowy owl	Little owl	Short-eared owl
SPEC status		3	2	3	3	3	3
Habitat related							
Habitat loss, change & fragmentation	4	1	1			1	1
Agricultural intensification (abandonment of low intensity agricultural land)	3	1				1	1
Agricultural abandonment	0						
Modern/inappropriate forestry practises (incl. open ground afforestation)	1						1
Forest fires	0						
Wetland loss and degradation	1						1
Reduced carrion availability (from better stock husbandry & waste disposal)	0						
Loss of nest sites	3	1	1			1	
Decline in natural prey items	2	1					1
Direct interactions with man							
Persecution (shooting, trapping, direct and indirect poisoning, nest destruction)	3		1	1			1
Egg-robbing	1			1			
Illegal trade in live birds (falconry)	0						
Pesticide contamination	4	1	1			1	1
Disturbance (especially at nest sites)	2			1	1		
Illegal hunting on migration	1		1				
Introduced predators	0						
Indirect interactions with man							
Powerline and pylon collisions/electrocution	2			1	1		
Climate change	0						
Collisions with vehicles	3	1		1		1	
Natural							
Inter-specific competition	0						
No. of factors/spp.		6	5	5	2	5	7

Both the Birds Directive and the Berne Convention also require strong measures to be taken with regards to the establishment of protected areas and the conservation of appropriate habitats outside of protected sites. The Berne Convention, in particular, requires *"Contracting Parties ..... to ensure the conservation of the habitats of the wild flora and fauna species especially those specified in Appendices I and II"* [i.e. all birds of prey].

Why, despite these strong legal measures which have been agreed and should have been implemented by virtually all European governments, is such a high proportion of all of Europe's birds of prey and owls in unfavourable conservation status? Indeed, the factors identified as negatively affecting most European birds of prey (persecution, including shooting, trapping, direct and indirect poisoning, nest destruction; disturbance at nest sites; egg-robbing; illegal trade in live birds for falconry; habitat change, loss and fragmentation) are exactly those that the Convention and Directive explicitly aims to control. Clearly, there seems to be a widespread failure in the effectiveness of direct conservation action in support of these treaties given the current poor European status of most raptors. This failure is particularly notable in the light of the important aspirations set out in the Preambles of both treaties. As with other international environmental treaties, the effectiveness of implementation by signatories is a fundamental and important issue (Victor *et al.,* 1998).

There are, in addition, needs at international level. Article 4(3) requires the co-ordination of nationally classified SPAs so as to *"form a coherent whole which meets the protection requirements of these* [= Annex I and migratory] *species in the geographical sea and land area where this Directive applies"*. This activity has never occurred, although it is necessary to assess the effectiveness of SPA provision at European scale. Indeed, there have been few assessments of species-related requirements for protected area networks at either national or European scales. Whilst BirdLife International have comprehensively identified Important Bird Areas in Europe (Heath & Evans, 2000) they do not address the adequacy of this proposed network for individual bird species. The only such national network assessments have been undertaken by Denmark (Rasmussen, 1999) and by the UK (Stroud *et al.,* 2001). An international assessment of protected area requirements for birds of prey remains a pressing need, as only this will provide a means of assessing the adequacy of national provision.

The Eurogroup Against Bird Crime (2000), an international network of non-governmental organisations, summarises different national systems of legislation for wild birds for 26 European countries. This highlights the wide interpretation of international treaty provisions. Undoubtedly major issues that influence the effectiveness of the two treaties are first, inadequate enforcement measures in many countries, and second, and more fundamentally, inadequate environmental education and public awareness programmes. As with any legislation, for environmental legislation to be effective, it has to have the consent of the broad body of the public. In those cases where individuals deliberately persist in breaking the law, then effective enforcement is needed, with appropriate deterrent penalties.

Major steps in broad environmental awareness have been made in most European countries, yet much more needs to be achieved. This is perhaps highlighted by the example of the UK where, although it has been illegal to kill deliberately or disturb at the nests of some raptors for over 120 years (Marchant & Watkins, 1897; Figures 3.3-3.6 above), the practice persists (RSPB & NCC, 1991a,b; RSPB, 1999a,b; Raptor Roundup, in press). This has been described by Government Ministers as "a national disgrace" (Anon., 2000).

Elimination of illegal persecution is especially difficult in situations where there is real or, more usually, perceived conflicts with vested interests such as stock-keeping (Marquiss *et al.*, Chapter 36), or game-rearing (Allen & Feare, Chapter 33; Redpath & Thirgood, 1997, Chapter 39; Galbraith *et al.*, Chapter 41). Lessons from the UK indicate that, in such circumstances, the mere passage of legislation protecting species which are considered by some to be causing conflicts is unlikely to be effective in itself in stopping the illegal persecution. Such legislation needs to be actively supported by programmes which address and, where possible, remove or ameliorate the causes of conflict. A milestone in the UK was the publication of the Department of the Environment, Transport and the Regions/Joint Nature Conservation Committee Raptor Working Group's report (Anon., 2000). This clearly outlined the nature of conflicts with some birds of prey and presented management options that would solve these problems. An essential element of such activity is the working in partnership with those interest groups affected by activities of protected species. In Scotland, at least two such partnerships have been formed since the late 1990s (Galbraith *et al.*, Chapter 41). In contrast to the UK, this seems scarcely to have started in much of Europe.

Such activity can enhance the effectiveness of legislation that seeks to protect species from the direct or indirect effects of persecution. An issue that is more intractable is the negative effects of land use changes on birds of prey — especially those agricultural policies that result in changes from extensive and low-intensity farming systems to more intensive and monocultural forms of agriculture (e.g. Beaufoy *et al.*, 1994; Donázar *et al.*, 1997). Indeed, such influences are not unique to raptors, but are a general cause of declines in a large number of Europe's birds (Tucker & Heath, 1994; Hagemeijer & Blair, 1997; Pain & Pienkowski, 1997). Indeed, European agricultural policy has degraded not just the wider countryside, but also sites of international importance (Heath & Evans, 2000).

The UK has recently adopted a 'Skylark Index' to provide a national 'headline' indicator for sustainable agricultural practices and quality of life in the UK. This index is a combined index of the trends of 20 widespread farmland bird species (Department of the Environment, Transport and the Regions, 1999). The index is currently in steep decline, indicating the severe population reductions now being experienced by many formerly common farmland birds (Gregory *et al.*, 2000, 2002). Given the ecological sensitivity of birds of prey, and especially given that their population trends can provide information on land use practices at landscape scales (Donázar *et al.*, 1997; Newton, Chapter 1), there would be merit in adopting a European 'Eagle Index'.

An 'Eagle Index' could, in similar fashion to the UK's Skylark Index, integrate information on the trends of several birds of prey across many countries. Indeed, it would surely be welcomed as an objective means of allowing the Birds Directive and Berne Convention to monitor their effectiveness in implementing their stated objectives.

3.6.1 An African-Eurasian Raptor Agreement?

The main mode through which the Bonn Convention operates 'on the ground' is the formalisation and subsequent implement of international Agreements. Extant Agreements for European white storks *Ciconia ciconia*, European bats and small cetacea have been highly effective, and the African-Eurasian Waterbird Agreement shows great promise (Boere & Lenten, 1998). This Agreement entered into force in late 1999 and already has been instrumental in the development of a major funding proposal under the Global Environment Facility (potentially raising $12,000,000 over four years on projects related to the conservation of migratory waterbirds and the conservation of their wetland habitats in Africa and eastern Europe). A major element is the transfer of information on conservation 'best practice' between countries – for example in monitoring, habitat and species protection, and conflict resolution. There would be great benefits for such an international focus to birds of prey conservation – both practically and politically.

Given the large number of European raptors which migrate to Africa in the non-breeding season, conservation actions seeking to restore status would be greatly supported by the formulation of an African-Eurasian Raptor Agreement. The development of such an international treaty should be an active international priority.

Acknowledgements

I am grateful to Des Thompson, Colin Galbraith and two anonymous referees for helpful comments on the draft text.

References

Anonymous (2000). *Report of the UK Raptor Working Group.* Department of the Environment, Transport and the Regions/Joint Nature Conservation Committee, Peterborough.

Beaufoy, G., Baldock, D. & Clark, J. (1994). *The Nature of Farming. Low Intensity Farming Systems in Nine European Countries.* Institute for European Environmental Policy, London.

Boere, G.C. & Lenten, B. (1998). The African-Eurasian Waterbird Agreement: a technical agreement under the Bonn Convention. In *Migration and International Conservation of Waders. Research and Conservation on North Asian, African and European Flyways*, ed. by H. Hötker, E. Lebedeva, P.S. Tomkovich, J. Gromadzka, N.C. Davidson, J. Evans, D.A. Stroud & R.B. West. *International Wader Studies*, **10**, 45-50.

British Trust for Ornithology, Hawk and Owl Trust, National Trust, Royal Society for the Protection of Birds, Scottish Raptor Study Groups, Wales Raptor Study Group & The Wildlife Trusts (1995). *Birds of Prey in the UK: a Review and Implications for Future Policies.* Report to DETR/JNCC Raptor Working Group.

British Trust for Ornithology, Hawk and Owl Trust, National Trust, National Trust for Scotland, Royal Society for the Protection of Birds, Scottish Raptor Study Groups, Wales Raptor Study Group, The Wildlife Trusts, Scottish Ornithologists' Club, Wildfowl & Wetlands Trust, & World Wide Fund for Nature (WWF–UK) (1997). *Birds of Prey in the UK: Back from the Brink.* British Trust for Ornithology, Thetford.

Department of the Environment, Transport and the Regions (1999). *A Better Quality of Life – a Strategy for Sustainable Development for the United Kingdom.* Department for the Environment, Transport and the Regions, London.

Donázar, J.A., Naveso, M.A., Tella, J.L. & Campión, D. (1997). Extensive grazing and raptors in Spain. In *Farming and Birds in Europe: the Common Agricultural Policy and its Implications for Bird Conservation*, ed. by D.J. Pain & M.W. Pienkowski. Academic Press, London. pp. 117-149.

Eurogroup Against Bird Crime (2000). *Wild Bird Legislation in Europe.* RSPB and NOF, Sandy.

European Commission (2000). Action plans for Annex I bird species considered as 'priority for funding under life'. http://europa.eu.int/comm/environment/nature/directive/birdspriority.htm.

European Commission (2001). Action plans for Annex I bird species considered as 'priority for funding under life'. European Union action plans for eight priority bird species: bittern (*Botaurus stellaris*), ferruginous duck (*Aythya nyroca*), Steller's eider (*Polysticta stelleri*), lammergeier (*Gypaetus barbatus*), greater spotted eagle (*Aquila clanga*), lesser spotted eagle (*Aquila pomarina*), Bonelli's eagle (*Hieraaetus fasciatus*), little bustard (*Tetrax tetrax*). European Commission, Brussels. Also available at http://europa.eu.int/comm/environment/nature/directive/birdshome_en.htm.

Gregory, R.D., Noble, D.G., Campbell, L.H. & Gibbons, D.W. (2000). *The State of the UK's Birds 1999.* RSPB and BTO, Sandy.

Gregory, R.D., Wilkinson, N.I., Noble, D.G., Robinson, J.A., Brown, A.F., Hughes, J., Procter, D., Gibbons, D.W. & Galbraith, C.A. (2002). The population status of birds in the United Kingdom, Channel Islands and Isle of Man: an analysis of conservation concern 2002-2007. *British Birds,* **95**, 410-448.

Hagemeijer, E.J.M. & Blair, M.J. (Eds) (1997). *The EBCC Atlas of European Breeding Birds: their Distribution and Abundance.* T. & A.D. Poyser, London.

Heath, M. & Evans, M.I. (Eds). (2000). Important Bird Areas in Europe: Priority Sites for Conservation. 2 volumes. *BirdLife Conservation Series No. 8.* BirdLife International, Cambridge.

Heredia, B., Rose, L. & Painter, M. (1996). *Globally Threatened Birds in Europe. Action Plans.* Council of Europe Publishing, Strasbourg.

Holloway, S. (1996). *The Historical Atlas of Breeding Birds in Britain and Ireland, 1875-1900.* T. & A.D. Poyser, London.

Marchant, J.R. & Watkins, W. (1897). *Wild Birds Protection Acts, 1880–1896. Second edition.* R.H. Porter, London.

Newton, I. (1998). *Population Limitation in Birds.* Academic Press, London.

Pain, D.J. & Pienkowski, M.W. (Eds). (1997). *Farming and Birds in Europe: the Common Agricultural Policy and its Implications for Bird Conservation.* Academic Press, London.

Parslow, J.F.L. (1973). *Breeding Birds of Britain and Ireland.* T. & A.D. Poyser, Berkhamsted.

Raptor Roundup (in press). Roundup of raptor monitoring in Scotland, 2000-2002. *Scottish Birds.*

Rasmussen, J.F. (1999). *Birds of Danish SPAs: Trends in Occurrence.* Miljø- og Energiministeriet, Skov- og Naturstyrelsen, Denmark.

Ratcliffe, D.A. (1993). *The Peregrine Falcon. Second edition.* T. & A.D. Poyser, London.

Redpath, S.M. & Thirgood, S.J. (1997). *Birds of Prey and Red Grouse.* The Stationery Office, London.

RSPB (1999a). *Persecution: a Review of Bird of Prey Persecution in Scotland in 1998.* Royal Society for the Protection of Birds, Edinburgh.

RSPB (1999b). *Birdcrime '98. Offences Against Wild Bird Legislation 1998.* Royal Society for the Protection of Birds, Sandy.

RSPB & NCC (1991a). *Death by Design. The Persecution of Birds of Prey and Owls in the UK 1979–1989.* Royal Society for the Protection of Birds, Sandy and Nature Conservancy Council, Peterborough.

RSPB & NCC (1991b). *Persecution. Birds of Prey and Owls Killed in the UK 1979–1989.* Royal Society for the Protection of Birds, Sandy and Nature Conservancy Council, Peterborough.

Stroud, D.A., Chambers, D., Cook, S., Buxton, N., Fraser, B., Clement, P., Lewis, P., McLean, I., Baker, H. & Whitehead, S. (Eds). (2001). *The UK SPA network: its scope and content.* Joint Nature Conservation Committee, Peterborough.

Temple-Lang, J. (1982). The European Community Directive on bird conservation. *Biological Conservation,* **22**, 11-25.

Tucker, G.M. & Heath, M. (1994). *Birds in Europe: their Conservation Status.* BirdLife International, Cambridge.

Victor, D.G., Rausiala, K. & Skolnikoff, E.B. (Eds). (1998). *The Implementation and Effectiveness of International Environmental Commitments. Theory and Practice.* International Institute for Applied Systems Analysis. MIT Press, Cambridge, Massachusetts.

Yapp, W.B. (1982). Birds in captivity in the Middle Ages. *Archives of Natural History,* **10**, 479-500.

Appendix 3.1. Population, conservation and legal status of European birds of prey. Data and information, *inter alia*, from Hagemeijer & Blair (1997), Heredia *et al.* (1996), and Tucker & Heath (1994).

Species		Population status					Conservation status			Legal status			
		European population size (prs)	European Russian population size (prs)	Turkish population size (prs)	No. of populated countries in Europe	SPEC status	European threat status	Other status (Birds to Watch 2)	European conservation Action Plan	CITES	Bonn Convention	Birds Directive Annex I	Berne Convention
ACCIPITRIFORMES													
Honey buzzard	*Pernis apivorus*	44,424	83,666	158	33	4	S			Appendix II	Appendix II	Annex I	Appendix II
Black-winged kite	*Elanus caeruleus*	1,318			3	3	V			Appendix II	Appendix II	Annex I	Appendix II
Black kite	*Milvus migrans*	27,348	59,161	316	29	3	V			Appendix II	Appendix II	Annex I	Appendix II
Red kite	*Milvus milvus*	21,777	7		24	4	S			Appendix II	Appendix II	Annex I	Appendix II
White-tailed eagle	*Haliaeetus albicilla*	2,419	995	17	20	3	R	Near threatened		Appendix I	Appendix I; Appendix II	Annex I	Appendix II
Lammergeier	*Gypaetus barbatus*	86	28	224	4	3	E		2001	Appendix II	Appendix II	Annex I	Appendix II
Egyptian vulture	*Neophron percnopterus*	1,853	49	2,236	10	3	E			Appendix II	Appendix II	Annex I	Appendix II
Griffon vulture	*Gyps fulvus*	9,064	296	316	10	3	R			Appendix II	Appendix II	Annex I	Appendix II
Black vulture	*Aegypius monachus*	967	39	224	3	3	V	Near threatened	1996	Appendix II	Appendix II	Annex I	Appendix II
Short-toed eagle	*Circaetus gallicus*	4,760	1,732	2,236	20	3	R			Appendix II	Appendix II	Annex I	Appendix II
Marsh harrier	*Circus aeruginosus*	29,197	31,623	1,581	29	3	S			Appendix II	Appendix II	Annex I	Appendix II
Hen harrier	*Circus cyaneus*	9,391	17,321		22	3	V			Appendix II	Appendix II	Annex I	Appendix II
Pallid harrier	*Circus macrourus*	23	1,414		4	3	E	Near threatened		Appendix II	Appendix II	Annex I	Appendix II
Montagu's harrier	*Circus pygargus*	8,069	24,495	447	26	4	S			Appendix II	Appendix II	Annex I	Appendix II
Goshawk	*Accipiter gentilis*	75,221	83,666	316	33		S	Appendix II	2000 - Corsican-Sardinian goshawk	Appendix II	Appendix II	Annex I - *A. g. arrigonii* only	
Sparrowhawk	*Accipiter nisus*	156,078	158,745	5,477	37		S	Appendix II	2000 - Macaronesian Sparrowhawk	Appendix II	Appendix II	Annex I - *A. n. granti* only	
Levant sparrowhawk	*Accipiter brevipes*	2,176	2,121	71	7	2	R			Appendix II	Appendix II	Annex I	Appendix II
Buzzard	*Buteo buteo*	413,101	489,898	2,236	36		S			Appendix II	Appendix II		Appendix II
Long-legged buzzard	*Buteo rufinus*	291	1,095	3,162	4	3	(E)			Appendix II	Appendix II	Annex I	Appendix II
Rough-legged buzzard	*Buteo lagopus*	16,142	97,980		3		S			Appendix II	Appendix II		Appendix II
Lesser spotted eagle	*Aquila pomarina*	7,571	100	122	16	3	R		2001	Appendix II	Appendix II	Annex I	Appendix II
Greater spotted eagle	*Aquila clanga*	7	79	800	7	1	E	Vulnerable	2001	Appendix II	Appendix II	Annex I	Appendix II
Steppe eagle	*Aquila nipalensis*	2	19,365	3	1	3	V			Appendix II	Appendix II	Annex I	Appendix II
Imperial eagle	*Aquila heliaca*	182	212	22	8	1	E	Vulnerable	1996	Appendix I	Appendix II	Annex I	Appendix II
Spanish imperial eagle	*Aquila adalberti*	155			1	1	E	Vulnerable	1996	Appendix I	Appendix II	Annex I	Appendix II

Species		Population status				Conservation status				Legal status			
		European population size (prs)	European Russian population size (prs)	Turkish population size (prs)	No. of populated countries in Europe	SPEC status	European threat status	Other status (Birds to Watch 2)	European conservation Action Plan	CITES	Bonn Convention	Birds Directive Annex I	Berne Convention
FALCONIFORMES													
Golden eagle	*Aquila chrysaetos*	5,412	283	316	26	3	R			Appendix II	Appendix II	Annex I	Appendix II
Booted eagle	*Hieraaetus pennatus*	3,604	283	224	13	3	R			Appendix II	Appendix II	Annex I	Appendix II
Bonelli's eagle	*Hieraaetus fasciatus*	856		32	7	3	E		2001	Appendix II	Appendix II	Annex I	Appendix II
Osprey	*Pandion haliaetus*	4,981	2,958	3	17	3	R			Appendix II	Appendix II	Annex I	Appendix II
Lesser kestrel	*Falco naumanni*	7,484	102	5,292	13	1	(V)	Vulnerable	1996	Appendix II	Appendix II	Annex I	Appendix II
Kestrel	*Falco tinnunculus*	282,127	67,082	11,180	39	3	D			Appendix II	Appendix II		Appendix II
Red-footed falcon	*Falco vespertinus*	3,304	24,495		11	3	V			Appendix II	Appendix II		Appendix II
Merlin	*Falco columbarius*	12,586	29,580		12		S			Appendix II	Appendix II	Annex I	Appendix II
Hobby	*Falco subbuteo*	20,942	52,915	2,236	33		S			Appendix II	Appendix II		Appendix II
Eleonora's falcon	*Falco eleonorae*	3,910		42	4	2	R		2000	Appendix II	Appendix II	Annex I	Appendix II
Lanner	*Falco biarmicus*	207		32	3	3	(E)		2000	Appendix II	Appendix II	Annex I	Appendix II
Saker	*Falco cherrug*	316	110	32	9	3	E			Appendix II	Appendix II		Appendix II
Gyrfalcon	*Falco rusticolus*	905	100		4	3	V		2000	Appendix I	Appendix II	Annex I	Appendix II
Peregrine	*Falco peregrinus*	5,824	566	447	27	3	R			Appendix I	Appendix II	Annex I	Appendix II
STRIGIFORMES													
Barn owl	*Tyto alba*	141,218	15,811	158	36	3	D			Appendix II			Appendix II
Scops owl	*Otus scops*	83,238	15,811	12,247	19	2	(D)			Appendix II			Appendix II
Eagle owl	*Bubo bubo*	11,308	6,325	1,581	32	3	V			Appendix II		Annex I	Appendix II
Snowy owl	*Nyctea scandiaca*	33	32		4	3	V			Appendix II		Annex I	Appendix II
Hawk owl	*Surnia ulula*	8,208	31,623		3		(S)			Appendix II		Annex I	Appendix II
Pygmy owl	*Glaucidium passerinum*	31,671	31,623		19		(S)			Appendix II		Annex I	Appendix II
Little owl	*Athene noctua*	246,921	31,623	15,811	29	3	D			Appendix II			Appendix II
Tawny owl	*Strix aluco*	469,968	31,623	10,000	33	4	S			Appendix II			Appendix II
Ural owl	*Strix uralensis*	12,147	316,228		16		(S)			Appendix II		Annex I	Appendix II
Great grey owl	*Strix nebulosa*	866			1		S			Appendix II		Annex I	Appendix II
Long-eared owl	*Asio otus*	205,741	158,114	316	37		S			Appendix II			Appendix II
Short-eared owl	*Asio flammeus*	17,249	31,623	7	26	3	(V)			Appendix II		Annex I	Appendix II
Tengmalm's owl	*Aegolius funereus*	48,159	31,623	16	28		(S)			Appendix II		Annex I	Appendix II

Key and sources:

Population sizes – Hagemeijer & Blair (1997)

Action plans - Heredia *et al.* (1996)

European Threat status
E = Endangered
V = Vulnerable
R = Rare
D = Declining
S = Secure
( ) = Status provisional

SPEC (*Species of European Conservation Concern*) (after Tucker & Heath, 1994)
SPEC 1 = Species of global conservation concern
SPEC 2 = Species with unfavourable conservation status and concentrated in Europe
SPEC 3 = Species with unfavourable conservation status but not concentrated in Europe
SPEC 4 = Species with favourable conservation status and concentrated in Europe

THEME TWO

POPULATION STUDIES

THEME TWO

POPULATION STUDIES

Detailed studies of national and local populations of raptors have made significant contributions to the advancement of ornithology, and indeed to ecology, in Britain and further afield. Some of the more recent studies have provided important insights into the vulnerability of raptor populations to human and natural influences (e.g. Real & Mañosa, 1997; Watson, 1997; Whitfield *et al.,* in press) which have even challenged some of the paradigms of animal population ecology (e.g. Ebenhardt, 2002). The 13 studies described here testify to the richness and diversity of raptor monitoring and research in Britain.

It is appropriate to open a theme on 'population studies' with Ratcliffe's account of what he terms 'The Peregrine Saga' (Chapter 4). The peregrine falcon *Falco peregrinus* remains one of the beacon species for indicating the state of our environment. Ratcliffe (1993) described the painstaking survey, monitoring and research work which led, first, to an understanding of the impacts on peregrines of persistent organochlorine insecticide used in agriculture, and second, eventually, to the ban on the use of DDT throughout the whole of the USA in 1972, and in the European Union in 1986. Here, Ratcliffe reflects on the effects of game shooting, egg collecting, pigeon racing and agro-chemical pollution on the mixed fortunes of peregrines. Ultimately, the peregrine has proved itself to be a resilient species, capable now of surviving at times in almost any part of Britain. Hardey *et al.* (Chapter 5) have compared the breeding success of inland peregrines in three regions of Scotland over a 10-year period. Their study points to variation in weather giving rise to differences between years in clutch size and brood size, and to variation in breeding success between localities being due to differences in levels of human persecution.

Three studies of owls (Strigiformes) reveal the complex influences of food supply, habitat and weather conditions in influencing distribution, numbers and breeding performance. Petty & Thomas (Chapter 6) describe a long-term study of the tawny owl *Strix aluco* in Kielder Forest, Northern England. They describe both short-term and long-term changes in foraging habitat, and the impacts of these on the population dynamics of the owls. Overall, the tawny owl population produced 4.5 times more fledged chicks during increasing field vole *Microtus agrestis* years than during low vole years, largely as a result of fewer pairs breeding, and brood sizes being smaller when vole numbers were low. This is a fine example of painstaking research on the population ecology of a species which many people rarely see in the field. Shaw & Riddle (Chapter 7) compare the responses of the barn owl *Tyto alba* and the kestrel *Falco tinnunculus* to cyclical variation in their preferred prey, the field vole *Microtus agrestis,* in south west Scotland. Interestingly, barn owls showed the stronger numerical response to their prey, and only the barn owl showed extreme fluctuations in productivity which matched the vole cycles. The relationship between time of laying and vole numbers each year was striking, with the mean first-egg date differing by up to 50 days in barn owls between consecutive years depending upon the stage of the vole cycle. Looking broadly at the barn owl population in the UK as a whole, Toms *et al.* (Chapter 8) report on the results of Project Barn Owl undertaken during 1995-1997. Given the cyclical variation in barn owl numbers from year-to-year, it is important to have population estimates over a three-year period; Toms *et al.* point out that their study provides a baseline against which future population changes can be measured.

There are two population ecological studies. Marquiss *et al.* (Chapter 9) contrast the population dynamics of northern goshawks *Accipiter gentilis* in the Scottish/English Borders and North-East Scotland. In both areas monitoring began in 1972, around when there was the first evidence of breeding in both areas (the species having become extinct in Scotland by the 1880s due to persecution). Whilst the population in the Borders rose exponentially in the 1980s, to reach 87 pairs in 1996, the north-east Scotland population did not start increasing until 1990, and by 1997 only 17 pairs were found. Marquiss *et al.* suggest that persecution around pheasant *Phasianus colchicus* release pens in north-east Scotland suppressed a recovery of the goshawk population there. In a study of the golden eagle *Aquila chrysaetos* in three study areas (Skye, Mull and Lochaber) in western Scotland, Watson *et al.* (Chapter 10) analyse patterns in breeding performance over a 20-year period. Their detailed analysis found relationships between eagle productivity and weather, which were different in each of the three areas, although there was a general tendency for productivity to be higher in years when some part of the preceding winter was mild, and when there was less rainfall in spring. There are important comparisons here with other studies of weather effects on eagles (e.g. Gargett, 1990; Steenhof *et al.*, 1997) which have broader implications for other population studies of raptors.

The protection and associated recovery of the osprey *Pandion haliaetus* in Britain is one of the best known conservation success stories. Dennis & McPhie (Chapter 11) chart the growth of the Scottish osprey population from 1954 through to 2000. This analysis has shown that human persecution, in the form of egg collecting, reached a peak in the late 1980s when around a quarter of active nests were robbed. It will be interesting to see how the recently established osprey population in England develops.

Two studies of common buzzard *Buteo buteo* populations in Scotland show how much interesting information can be derived from individual efforts. Holling (Chapter 12) charts the increase in the breeding population in Lothian and Borders, from just a scatter of pairs in the 1970s through to an estimate of perhaps as many as 1,000 pairs today. The rapid recovery of the buzzard population in Britain, especially eastwards, has been noted by several studies (e.g. Anon., 2000; Sim *et al.*, 2000). This may be due to an increase in the abundance in rabbits *Oryctolagus cuniculus*, the main prey, a reduction in persecution of buzzards in the lowlands, and an increase in breeding productivity since the late 1980s (Sim *et al.*, 2000). Jardine (Chapter 13) has studied buzzards on the Island of Colonsay, in the Inner Hebrides, for over 10 years. The population there grew from 3-4 pairs in the 1930s to around 20 pairs at the present time. Whilst Jardine found a significant relationship between the annual proportion of rabbits in prey remains and a measure of the rabbit population, he found no significant influence of rabbits on the breeding parameters of buzzards, though more detailed work is planned to investigate this and the possible effects of weather.

The merlin *Falco columbarius* is arguably one of the most challenging diurnal raptors to study because it is so easily overlooked on its breeding grounds. The first two studies here report long-term monitoring. Rebecca & Cosnette (Chapter 14) studied merlins in Aberdeenshire over a 20 year period. Their study has demonstrated long-term changes in distribution linked with afforestation, and short-term changes influenced by land management practices, notably intensive muirburn of some heather *Calluna vulgaris* dominated moorland. Fielding & Haworth (Chapter 15) made a 13-year study of a merlin population in the south Pennines. They found a steady increase in their study population from 5 pairs in 1983 to 17 pairs in 1990, correlated with more favourable weather conditions during the period immediately following egg laying through to when nestlings were present in the nest.

The final chapter here shows how micro-satellite DNA profiling can be applied to a population of merlins to investigate aspects of mate and nest fidelity. Marsden *et al.* (Chapter 16) worked on Rebecca and Cosnette's study population, and analysed DNA extracted from feathers collected in the area over a 19-year period. Marsden *et al.* were able to show that the turnover of individuals occupying nest sites was high, with over 70% of females occupying nests for just one year. This approach has significant implications for quantifying turnover of individuals and populations of birds, which are otherwise difficult to identify uniquely. In particular, genetic profiling may help in identifying particular localities or individuals which contribute to population declines or increases. The national survey of golden eagles in Britain in 2003 has involved collection of feathers to support genetic profiling, and other such surveys may employ this technique.

Taken together, these studies straddle a huge range of approaches to understanding the population ecology of birds. Human persecution emerges as a significant factor responsible for low populations at the beginning of some studies, or in terms of influencing year-to-year changes in breeding production in some areas.

References

Anonymous (2000). *Report of the UK Raptor Working Group.* Department of the Environment, Transport and the Regions, and the Joint Nature Conservation Committee, Peterborough.

Ebenhardt, L.L. (2002). A paradigm for population analysis of long-lived vertebrates. *Ecology*, **83**, 2841-2854.

Gargett, V. (1990). *The Black Eagle.* Acorn Books, Johannesburg.

Ratcliffe, D.A. (1993). *The Peregrine Falcon. Second edition.* Poyser, London.

Real, J. & Mañosa, S. (1997). Demography and conservation of western European Bonelli's eagle populations. *Biological Conservation*, **79**, 59-66.

Sim, I.M.W., Campbell, L., Pain, D.J. & Wilson, J.D. (2000). Correlates of the population increase of common buzzards (*Buteo buteo*) in the West Midlands between 1983 and 1996. *Bird study*, **47**, 154-164.

Steenhof, K., Kochert, M.N. & Macdonald, T.L. (1997). Interactive effects of prey and weather on golden eagle reproduction. *Journal of Applied Ecology*, **66**, 350-362.

Watson, J. (1997). *The Golden Eagle.* Poyser, London.

Whitfield, D.P., Fielding, A.M., McLeod, D.R.A. & Haworth, P.F. (in press). Modelling the effects of persecution on the population dynamics of golden eagles *Aquila chrysaetos* in Scotland. *Biological Conservation*.

4. THE PEREGRINE SAGA

D.A. Ratcliffe

Summary

1. This chapter provides an outline of the peregrine falcon's *Falco peregrinus* relationships with people, which had their origins several thousand years ago.

2. Game shooting, egg collecting, racing of homing pigeons, and agro-chemical pollution have all affected the fortunes of peregrines.

3. The post-war impact of pesticides on peregrines is recorded by a combination of national surveys and detailed field and laboratory research. The results of this work awakened the world to the potential consequence of environmental pollutants for wildlife and people.

4. The peregrine remains an important symbol of the state of our countryside, and more recently our towns and cities.

4.1 The esteem of falconers

The earliest associations were through falconry, known from the time of the ancient Egyptians and Chinese in 2000 BC, and widely practised across Asia in the pre-Christian era (Michell, 1900). There is no telling at just what point earlier peoples saw that the hunting skill of the birds of prey could be turned to their own advantage in obtaining food, but perhaps falconry soon became regarded as a sport as well as a practical activity. Speed, agility and strength combined with trainability made the peregrine a favourite to fly at quarry, and during the feudal times after the Norman Conquest it became treated as the sovereign or nobleman's bird, protected by harsh penalties. The earliest records of peregrine nesting places date from the Middle Ages, when they supplied eyasses for falconry, and some eyries figure in the annual tribute of estates to the Crown. This Golden Age of falconry, during which the Emperor Frederick II of the Holy Roman Empire wrote his remarkable treatise on the subject, continued until the early 1600s, but a century later it was only a minority interest, and has survived in Britain as the sport of a relatively small number of devotees. In parts of the Middle East it continues as an elite recreational interest.

4.2 The hatred of game preservers

The development of the firearm sounded the death-knell for falconry as a popular activity in Britain, for it provided a more efficient means of taking game. The birds of prey came, moreover, increasingly to be seen as competitors with humans in this business of hunting, and the new weapons were turned against the former accomplices. Game shooting became the fashionable pursuit by the late 1700s and the great age of game preservation was ushered in, with special custodians to wage war on any creature which could harm the prized targets for the shotgun. And so the peregrine became an outcast, detested now almost above all raptors for its predatory prowess, and hunted down relentlessly wherever bird-game was preserved. In particular, an onslaught was made on the peregrine in its breeding haunts, for this was an easy bird to shoot or trap at the usually traditional eyries, though it was less vulnerable to the poison so deadly to the carrion-feeders.

The 'vermin-lists' of the large estates have catalogued many examples of the scale of destruction meted out to this and other predators during the Victorian and Edwardian hey-day of game-bird preservation. Peregrines were ruthlessly destroyed on most estates, and many were the breeding haunts where one or both birds were killed in each successive year over a long period (Ratcliffe, 1993). This persecution banished the bird from all its more accessible lowland haunts, especially inland, so that the more precipitous coasts and lofty crags of the remoter mountains became its refuge. Its distribution became more skewed towards the north and west of Britain than formerly, though the species had probably always been restricted by the availability of good cliffs, which were mainly in these regions. But many keepered cliffs continued to act as magnets to new birds seeking territories, and their repeated removal each year helped to drain the population and restrict its capacity for increase or recovery of its original range. Yet, despite this drag on recruitment, the peregrine breeding population appeared to show a remarkable long-term stability at this reduced level (Ratcliffe, 1962).

4.3 The rapacity of collectors

Whether or not the late 19th century enthusiasm for displays of stuffed birds gave an added inducement to killing peregrines, they figured frequently in the collections on show. The bird was also a desirable addition to the many skin collections that were amassed during this time. It did, however, have its admirers and became a favourite subject for the bird painters of those days, such as Thorburn and Lodge.

The peregrine also had the misfortune to lay particularly handsome and variable eggs, and when egg collecting rose to popularity, from about 1860 onwards, it suffered especially from the attentions of 'oologists'. For almost 100 years, in certain districts, such as south and south-west England, parts of Wales, and northern England, a majority of eyries was raided annually and often for repeat clutches as well. Few young were reared in these popular egging districts, so that recruitment was further depressed. Whether the local output of young was sufficient to maintain the relatively constant breeding populations found in the species' main refuges, or whether this depended on recruitment from more successful areas in Scotland and Ireland, egging doubtless reinforced keeper persecution in limiting the peregrine's capacity for recovering its former range. The occasional puzzling desertion of perfectly good nesting places may have been because there were not enough new birds to fill all of the gaps in breeding territories that normal mortality inevitably created.

4.4 The hostility of pigeon fanciers

When the racing of homing pigeons rose to popularity, also in the late 19th century, the peregrine incurred the enmity of those concerned, for the homer exercised a fatal fascination as favourite prey. This became more serious a matter during the 1914-1918 War, when military use of message-carrying pigeons led to measures to reduce peregrine number in certain areas, though no record of details has survived. Grumbles and desultory persecution by fanciers continued during the 1920s and 1930s. Then came World War II and a much more systematic campaign of destruction in certain districts, to protect the carrier pigeons belonging to airmen on sea operations. At least 600 birds were reckoned to have been shot and many eggs and young taken during this time (Ferguson-Lees, 1951). Some of the victims ended up in the national skin collection at Tring, Hertfordshire, and so were not wholly wasted.

Peregrines of the south and south-west England coast were almost wiped out, and those of some parts of Wales, Scotland and Northern Ireland much reduced, showing that even previous refuges were vulnerable to increased persecution. Yet, in compensation, gamekeeping almost ceased during both war periods, and at many breeding places where the birds previously never had a chance, there was successful breeding during these times. Overall, the UK breeding population was probably reduced to 87% of its pre-war level by 1945 (Ratcliffe, 1993).

4.5 The irresponsibility of the agro-chemical industry

After the war, there was fairly rapid recovery to pre-war levels, but no more, in some depleted districts, though others failed to reach this level, as on the south-east England coast. By 1956, symptoms of decline appeared, first in the far south of England (Treleaven, 1961) but extending to Wales by 1957-58. Providentially, the pigeon-fanciers' outcry against peregrine predation on homing pigeons in 1960 led to the BTO Enquiry of 1961-1962, which revealed that the species was in the middle of a headlong crash in numbers, almost countrywide. Continuing survey in 1963 suggested that numbers nationally were down to 44% of pre-1940 levels (Ratcliffe, 1993). In some parts of southern England and Wales, the peregrine had almost disappeared, while even in Scotland it was much reduced in many areas, and only the east-central Highland population was little affected. Dire predictions were made about the species' prospects for survival in Britain and Ireland. As well as disappearance of the adults, other associated symptoms of decline were thin eggshells, leading to frequent breakage or disappearance of eggs; failure to lay; death of embryos or chicks; and small broods of fledged young (Ratcliffe, 1993).

Parallel declines had also been detected in populations of other birds of prey – sparrowhawk, kestrel and barn owl (Prestt, 1965). The cause was soon identified as the persistent organochlorine insecticides of agriculture, used especially as cereal seed dressings, though it took a good many years of painstaking research before the sceptics in the agro-chemical camp were finally overwhelmed by the evidence for cause and effect. The Government's Advisory Committee on Pesticides reluctantly brought in voluntary restrictions on the use of the organochlorines, first in 1962, which appeared to halt the crash by 1964. Further restrictions were made in 1964, 1969 and 1976, but it was not until the European Union introduced mandatory bans, beginning with dieldrin in 1981 (then DDT in 1986, and aldrin and endrin in 1991) that these chemicals were finally phased out in the UK (except for lindane). The problems for wildlife caused by the organochlorines had proved to be almost world-wide and many other countries had more quickly taken effective action against them, notably in the United States where first Administrator of the Enviromental Protection Agency, William Ruckelshaus, having considered all of the evidence, courageously banned the use of DDT throughout the whole country in 1972 (Peregrine Fund, 1999).

4.6 The lessons of history

There were a number of lessons to be learned from this episode in the peregrine's history, which can be regarded as the forerunner of the new wave of environmental concern that has become so prominent a feature of life today. Perhaps the first point was that the thoughtless release of poisons against particular targets may have quite unforeseen and disastrous effects on other organisms. Many of the substances introduced as agricultural and horticultural pesticides had such a wide spectrum of toxic effects that the term 'biocides' was coined for them. In the case of eggshell thinning, the effects were not detected until 20 years after the first release of the causal agent, DDT, which had until then been defended against allegations of damage to wildlife in the UK. The introduction of the Pesticides Safety Precautions Scheme in Britain has had some beneficial effect in screening against the release of many other chemicals potentially damaging to wildlife, but cannot be a complete filter, since effects can be tested on only a few experimental species (Moore, 1987).

The next lesson was the need for monitoring of wildlife – or, at least, certain key species – so that changes in numbers and/or distribution could be readily detected. It so happened that for the peregrine, a good deal of relevant information already existed and could be put together retrospectively, but for most species this happy circumstance did not obtain. The population surveys and mapping schemes of the British Trust for Ornithology and other bodies were given impetus by this realisation. The need for parallel monitoring of numerous environmental factors besides toxic chemical residues has been widely accepted by both government and industry, and practised by the relevant bodies. Besides this, the value of stored biological material in museums and elsewhere became clear. Many egg collectors felt exonerated when their illegal activities became instrumental in identifying the eggshell thinning phenomenon, and – like it or not – the onset of this important issue gave a difficult philosophical problem with which to wrestle. But the answer here, surely, is that the need for such material should be foreseen, planned scientifically, and collection made legally under licence.

At the technical level, the importance of chemical residue persistence, fat solubility and bioaccumulation in animal tissues, and secondary poisoning, became clear in the studies of impact of pesticides on predators. The chance variations in sensitivity of different species to any one chemical also emerged as an influential but unpredictable factor. It became important to understand the varying toxicity and precise effects of the different substances within the cocktail of residues typically found in avian tissues, especially those at the top of the food chain. In Britain, the contribution of the more acutely toxic cyclodienes (dieldrin, aldrin, endrin, heptachlor) was judged more important in causing the peregrine crash, by greatly increasing adult mortality, than DDT with its lower acute toxicity but significant sub-lethal effects on breeding performance. In North America, the reverse view was taken – that DDT and widespread breeding failure were the main factors in peregrine decline, with the dieldrin group playing a much smaller role because they were far less widely used.

In the debate between scientists, the validity of circumstantial, correlative and convergent evidence was argued by the conservation side against the agro-chemical apologists' insistence on the need for experimental data obtained under controlled conditions. These considerations also helped to define the crucial experimentation on some aspects (e.g. eggshell-thinning and DDT) that was later undertaken, but the practical difficulties of using birds such as peregrines in controlled experiments were never overcome. Conservationists had a lesson in the politics of wildlife conservation and learned to sharpen and focus their arguments accordingly. It was necessary to separate the science of understanding causation from the value judgements about the importance of impacts on wildlife and environment, versus the undeniable benefits of the synthetic pesticides to humankind, especially in the

Third World. One revelation was that not even the greatest wilderness on Earth, Antarctica, was free from pesticide contamination, because volatile residues entered the atmosphere, circulated and spilled out again all over the globe (Sladen *et al.,* 1966).

Some commentators saw the peregrine-pesticide case as the classic example of the 'canary down the mine', with its portents not only for other wildlife but also for human beings. Certainly, this case sounded the alert for possible adverse effects on other organisms, and raised awareness of the potential dangers of environmental pollutants in general. It probably made medical researchers look harder at the hazards of pesticides to human health, and establish more rigorous tolerance limits to residues in foodstuffs. Whether it gave a longer-term validity to the notion of birds of prey as environmental indicators is more open to question. In the first place, it was the catastrophic effects of primary poisoning of granivorous birds by organochlorines that led to the thought that secondary poisoning could be affecting the birds of prey which fed upon these victims. The decline of the peregrine had little significance for other birds or mammals except predators likely to be suffering parallel effects through bioaccumulation. And as time went by, environmental factors of all kinds became increasingly watched for change and for possibly adverse impacts on animals and plants exposed to them; so that the situation was reversed, with change in the physical/chemical environment detected first, and then biological effects sought later. The ecological barometer value of wild species has thus become ever less relevant, though our concern for affected wildlife remains undiminished.

4.7 The conservation success

The final proof of the hypothesis that organochlorine pesticides caused decline in birds of prey populations was in the steady recovery of the affected species as contamination levels fell. The peregrine in Britain and Ireland was back to its pre-1940 numbers by 1985, and has shown at least substantial recovery in most parts of the world where it had seriously declined. In the United States it was formally removed from the Endangered Species List in 1999. In the UK the peregrine has gone on to a super-recovery. The 1991 survey (Crick & Ratcliffe, 1995) showed that the breeding population nationally was at 145% of its pre-1940 level, though the geographical pattern was not quite the same as before. In some districts, numbers were still higher, and in Lakeland stood at 272% of the pre-1940 level (Horne & Fielding, 2002), whereas in the northern Highlands and the Scottish Islands they were lower than during the height of the crash, as instanced by the virtual disappearance of the species from Shetland (Ellis & Okill, 1990). Not only territory occupation but also eggshell thickness, brood size and success rate of pairs laying eggs showed recovery to, or close to, the pre-war norms. Continued monitoring of organochlorine residues also showed decline to low levels which were unlikely to have appreciable pathological effects on raptors (Newton *et al.,* 1993).

One would expect the peregrine population to recover to its normal level if the influences responsible for decline were removed, but increase to perhaps the highest level ever known requires some further explanation – as does failure to reach pre-1940 levels in some areas. The complex pattern of increase suggests that more than one factor was involved. In parts of Wales, northern England and southern Scotland there has obviously been an increase in breeding density, with many previous territories now shared between two or even three pairs instead of held by single pairs. Since it had previously appeared that breeding density was geared to food supply, this suggests that food supply in these areas had increased substantially. There is indeed evidence for an increased number of racing pigeons and for a greater availability of homers as prey during the breeding season over the last 20 years or so (Ratcliffe, 1993), which may be a sufficient explanation of the increase in peregrine breeding density.

There has also been a great expansion of breeding distribution. First, there was a reoccupation of many nesting places on the grouse moors, which were previously only irregularly or occasionally tenanted, because the birds were not allowed to survive there for long (see Hardey *et al.*, Chapter 5). This pointed to a relaxation of hostility on the part of game preservers. Whereas peregrine distribution had previously always appeared to be limited by the availability of good cliffs for nesting, there has been a remarkable increase in the use of tiny rocks, broken banks or even flat ground for nest-sites, when the more suitable breeding places with inaccessible sites became fully occupied. Peregrines have increased greatly in the lowlands inland, using crags close to human presence, quarries (used as well as old) and man-made structures of various kinds (buildings, pylons, etc.). Tree-nests have been reported in three widely separated areas.

This new elasticity in choice of nest-site is an interesting ecological development, since it gives the peregrine the potential for an enormously expanded breeding distribution. It suggests that the species could nest almost anywhere in Britain or Ireland, provided the food supply is adequate. It also implies that the species has relaxed its needs for security and distance from humans through a reduction in persecution. The super-recovery thus reflects the success of the educational campaign by conservationists – led by the RSPB – aimed at winning greater public tolerance and, indeed, enthusiasm, for this and other birds of prey. Protection of nesting pairs, and the decline of egg collecting and illegal taking of young, have also greatly boosted breeding success in many areas, leading to a large annual output of young. The sheer pressure from numbers of new birds, seeking a place of their own in which to breed, has evidently been another important factor in occupation of once-marginal habitats and the expansion of peregrine range.

In North America, where the peregrine had disappeared from the eastern part of the continent, the bird has been given a large helping hand in recovery, through programmes of captive breeding and release to the wild (6,769 birds by 1999). Here, cities and buildings have deliberately been used to re-establish birds in relatively pesticide-free environments, and with great success. In the eastern US there are now well over 200 nesting pairs of peregrines, and recovery is proceeding under its own steam, in one of the most successful hands-on rescue interventions that wildlife conservation has yet recorded. It has also shown a steady increase in most western states and in Alaska and the Canadian Arctic where numbers had become depressed. In 1998 there were at least 1,650 known pairs of the anatum race in North America (Peregrine Fund, 1999). Peregrines have recovered over most parts of Europe where they declined (i.e. virtually everywhere except Spain), but have been slowest to do so in Fennoscandia, where the whole population is migratory and exposed outside of the breeding season to residual pesticide problems in the farmlands of Europe south of the Baltic (Tucker & Heath, 1994).

4.8 The future

The peregrine story has gone full circle, with complaints from both pigeon fanciers and grouse preservers about predation now back at almost their previous levels (Galbraith *et al.*,

Chapter 41). The conservationists are not going to give up their victory, so hard-won over so many years, and the original problem is thus back again. The pigeon and grouse people have increasingly been taking the law into their own hands by killing peregrines and destroying nests again, and this cannot be countenanced. The pigeon fanciers have also evidently tackled the problem by the more responsible means of adjusting race routes and times to reduce their birds' exposure to predation in districts where the risks are high, as a report by the Hawk and Owl Trust recommended (Anon., 2000; Shawyer *et al.,* Chapter 21). Slight decline in breeding population has been reported during the last two years in certain high density peregrine areas, and could be explained by decrease in food supply (e.g. Dixon *et al.,* Chapter 20); while a more marked reduction in grouse moor areas reflects renewed persecution there. Failure to recover in northern Scotland looks like continuing toxic chemical effects, perhaps through marine pollutants obtained from seabird prey, or from movement to winter quarters where pesticide contamination risks are still high (Anon., 2000).

The peregrine has thus shown itself to be a robust and resilient species, capable of living in almost any part of Britain. It has bounced back while many birds of lowland and especially farmland habitats have appeared to be much more sensitive to changes in land use and with bleaker long-term prospects. How ironic if the peregrine proved to be one of the toughest survivors, better able than most species to cope with the environmental vicissitudes of the 21st century.

In closing, I pay tribute to all those many people who have given so devotedly of their time and energy, and freely of their information, in peregrine recording during recent decades. They are far too numerous to name here, but have, I hope, all been acknowledged elsewhere, at some time or another. Some have made an outstanding contribution to our knowledge of the bird over many years. Without this combined effort there would have been little to tell of the peregrine saga over the crucial period of the past 40 years or so. In acting as their mouthpiece I have always been aware how much this is their story, and can only hope that I have told it accurately and fairly.

To this small army of helpers I also offer a further thought. Monitoring of the UK peregrine population must continue, and the facts on predation should inform debate on the problems it causes. There has to be an objective basis on which the value judgements can be made, but those who love peregrines will have to realise that their interest is as valid as the interests of those who dislike them, and to speak up accordingly. They should become as single-minded and vehement as the opposition in defending their interest. Retirement from the official machine brings me the luxury of no longer having to see other viewpoints. I have my own viewpoint to promote, and it is that I like the birds of prey greatly, I wish the persecution of them to cease, and I believe that man's treatment of them over the last 300 years is one of the most shameful episodes in the whole of our natural history. They deserve something better in the third millennium, and we should take measures to achieve this.

We look forward to seeing the results of the fifth national population census undertaken in 2002 (deferred from the previous year due to the outbreak of Foot and Mouth Disease which imposed restrictions on countryside activities). Yet, whatever the outcome, we may be sure that the peregrine's future will continue to be closely enmeshed with the doings of human beings.

References

Anonymous (2000). Report of the UK Raptor Working Group. Department of the Environment, Transport and the Regions, Bristol and Joint Nature Conservation Committee, Peterborough.

Crick, H.Q.P. & Ratcliffe, D.A. (1995). The peregrine *Falco peregrinus* breeding population of the United Kingdom in 1991. *Bird Study,* **42**, 1-19.

Ellis, P.M. & Okill, J.D. (1993). Breeding numbers and breeding success of the peregrine *Falco peregrinus* in Shetland, 1961-1991. *Scottish Birds,* **17**, 40-49.

Ferguson-Lees, I.J. (1951). The peregrine population of Great Britain, Parts I and II. *Bird Notes,* **24**, 200-05; 309-14.

Horne, G. & Fielding, A.F. (2002). Recovery of the peregrine falcon *Falco peregrinus* in Cumbria, UK, 1966-99. *Bird Study.* **49**, 229-236.

Michell, E.B. (1990). *The Art and Practice of Hawking.* Methuen, London.

Moore, N.W. (1987). *The Bird of Time. The Science and Politics of Nature Conservation.* Cambridge University Press, Cambridge.

Newton, I., Wyllie, I. & Asher, A. (1993). Long-term trends in organochlorine and mercury residues in some predatory birds in Britain. *Environmental Pollution,* **79**, 143-151.

Peregrine Fund (1999). Restoration. *Newsletter No. 30,* **Summer/Fall 1999**, 3.

Prestt, I. (1965). An enquiry into the recent breeding status of some of the smaller birds of prey and crows in Britain. *Bird Study,* **12**, 196-221.

Ratcliffe, D.A. (1962). Breeding density in the peregrine *Falco peregrinus* and raven *Corvus corax. Ibis,* 104, 13-39.

Ratcliffe, D.A. (1993). *The Peregrine Falcon. Second edition.* Poyser, London.

Sladen, W.J.L., Menzie, C.M. & Reichel, W.L. (1966). DDT residues in Adelie Penguins and a Crabeater Seal from Antarctica. *Nature,* **210**, 670-73.

Treleaven, R.B. (1961). Notes on the peregrine in Cornwall. *British Birds,* **54**, 136-142.

Tucker, G.M. & Heath, M.F. (1994). *Birds in Europe: their Conservation Status.* Birdlife International, Cambridge, UK.

5. VARIATION IN BREEDING SUCCESS OF INLAND PEREGRINE FALCON (*FALCO PEREGRINUS*) IN THREE REGIONS OF SCOTLAND 1991-2000

Jon Hardey, Chris J. Rollie
& Patrick K. Stirling-Aird

Summary

1.   Breeding success of inland peregrines *Falco peregrinus* was compared in three regions of Scotland between 1991 and 2000. The primary land use within 3 km of each breeding site was identified.

2.   Clutch size and brood size did not differ significantly between the three regions, but did differ between years, evidently due to variation in the weather.

3.   Breeding success per territorial pair differed significantly between peregrines breeding on grouse moors (land managed primarily for shooting red grouse *Lagopus lagopus scoticus*) and on areas with other primary land uses. Mean brood size per successful nest did not differ significantly between peregrines breeding on these two areas.

4.   It is suggested that the lower breeding success of peregrines breeding on grouse moors was linked to higher levels of persecution.

5.   In South-west Scotland, peregrines which nested on sheepwalk close to towns with large numbers of homing pigeon *Columba livia* lofts, were significantly less successful than peregrines nesting on sheepwalk elsewhere in the region.

6.   Primary land use, other than grouse moors, significantly affected peregrine productivity and site occupation, presumably due to differences in the abundance and availability of prey as altitude is not known for many sites.

5.1 Introduction

This chapter examines breeding success in peregrine falcon *Falco peregrinus* populations in South-west, Central and North-east Scotland (Table 5.1) between 1991 and 2000. In each

Table 5.1. Study areas - description of area covered and associated Raptor Group.

Region	Description	Raptor Study Group
North-east	Moray east of the River Spey	
	Aberdeenshire, Aberdeen	North East of Scotland
Central	Perthshire west of the A9	Tayside
	Clackmannanshire	Central Scotland
	Stirlingshire, Dunbartonshire	
	Kinrossshire west of the M90	
South-west	Dumfries and Galloway	Dumfries and Galloway
	Ayrshire south of the A70	South Strathclyde

of these three regions, the peregrine breeding population increased markedly between 1981 and 1991 (Hardey, 1991; Ratcliffe, 1993; Crick & Ratcliffe, 1995; Rollie, 2000). Land use affects the peregrine's breeding success indirectly through changes in prey abundance (Ratcliffe, 1993) and directly through land management (Scottish Raptor Study Groups, 1998; Anon., 2000; Ratcliffe, Chapter 4). In this chapter, we discuss the effect of land management practices on the breeding success of peregrines in the three regions.

5.2 Study area

The three regions are defined in Table 5.1. These differ in the composition of primary land use within 3 km of peregrine breeding sites (Figure 5.1). Primary land use categories are described in Table 5.2. The South-west has the lowest proportion of grouse moors (areas

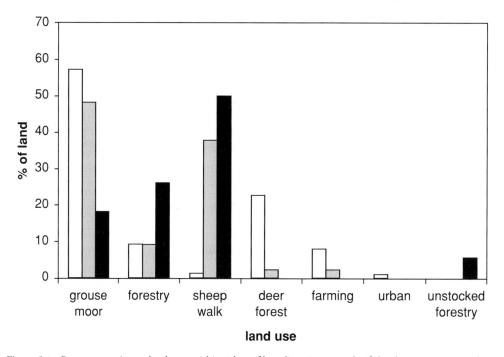

Figure 5.1. Percentage primary land uses within 3 km of breeding sites in each of the three regions: North-east – white; Central = grey; South-west - black.

Table 5.2. Categories of primary land uses within 3 km of peregrine eyries.

Land use	Description
Forestry	Planted with trees (size not recorded), usually conifers, with open ground for agricultural stock grazing.
Unstocked forestry	Planted with trees (size not recorded), usually conifers, with no agricultural stock grazing.
Sheepwalk	Open hill used for sheep grazing.
Deer forest	Sporting estate managed for shooting red deer *Cervus elaphus*.
Urban	Within built up area.
Grouse Moor	Active management for grouse shooting with muirburn and well maintained grouse butts.
Farming	Land below 300 m with mixed arable and stock farming.

managed primarily for grouse shooting, 18.2%). The proportions of grouse moors are greater in Central (48.3%) and North-east (57.3%) regions. Sheepwalk (open hill grazing for sheep) is the main land use around sites in the South-west (50.0%). This is a common land use in Central region (37.9%) but is virtually absent from the North-east (1.3%). In the latter, sheepwalk is replaced by deer forest. Deer forests are sporting estates managed primarily for deer stalking (22.7%), and are not found in the South-west. Land dominated by commercial forestry is another common land use in the South-west (26.1%), but is less frequent further north (Central 9.2%, North-east 9.3%).

5.3 Method

The Scottish breeding population of peregrines is monitored by members of a network of Raptor Study Groups (RSG). These consist of experienced field workers, both amateur and professional, who visit known eyries and locate new ones from which to collect data on breeding success and population size (e.g. Scottish Raptor Study Groups, 1998; Scottish Raptor Monitoring Scheme, 2002).

This chapter presents data collected in three regions by five RSGs (Table 5.1) between 1991 and 2000 at inland breeding sites. In each region, raptor workers visited breeding sites in late March or early April so as to establish occupancy. Occupancy was confirmed if adults were seen or if signs were found that peregrines were active at the site (kills, feathers, active roost). Later visits were made in order to record breeding success. Clutch size was only recorded when the eyrie could be clearly viewed without causing excessive disturbance. The minimum brood size at fledging was also established. Productivity was measured as the number of young fledged per occupied territory (see Ratcliffe, 1993).

Not all sites were visited annually (Appendix 5.1) and later visits could not always be made. The percentage of sites checked varied annually and between the different areas. South-west (92%–100%) and North-east (85%–100%) achieved higher coverage than Central (48%–100%). These differences were caused by changes in the number of field workers available to a particular RSG. For each breeding site, the primary land use within 3 km of the eyrie was identified and recorded by the local RSG. Grouse moors were assessed against all other land uses. Percentage occupancy and productivity were compared. Variation within the other land uses was also analysed. These included areas where grouse were shot but were not managed for grouse shooting. The categories for identifying primary land uses are described in Table 5.2.

In the South-west region, the main land use around inland peregrine sites was sheepwalk. The productivity of peregrines breeding on sheepwalk within 6.4 km (4 miles) of urban areas, where there are large numbers of racing pigeon fanciers, was compared to peregrines breeding on sheepwalk elsewhere in the region. Analysis of variance was used to make comparisons between sites. Standard deviations, sd, are given where appropriate.

5.4 Results

Any known inland breeding site which was not used for breeding by peregrines at any time between 1991 and 2000 was excluded from the analysis. Coastal sites were not included in the analysis.

5.4.1 Clutch size

Recorded clutch sizes ranged from one to five (Table 5.3a) and varied significantly between years (F = 2.15, P <0.05). The differences in clutch size between areas was not significant (F = 0.69, ns) although clutches of four eggs were more frequently recorded in Central and North-east than in South-west regions. There was no difference in clutch size in pairs breeding on ground largely managed for grouse and those breeding on land managed for other purposes (F = 2.24, ns).

5.4.2 Brood size

Brood size (Table 5.3b) in successful nests, which fledged at least one young, again varied significantly between years (F = 2.06, P <0.05). There was no significant difference between regions, or between grouse moors and other primary land use practices. Brood size per territorial pair (Table 5.3b) varied significantly between years (F = 33.5, P <0.001), between regions (F = 15.48, P <0.001), and between other land uses (F = 38.60, P <0.001).

Mean productivity (fledged young per occupied site) for all occupied sites (Table 5.4) was lower in each of the three areas for peregrines breeding on grouse moors than other land uses. Brood sizes for successful nests did not show this difference.

Table 5.3. Clutch and brood sizes in South-west, Central and North-east Scotland, 1991–2000.

a)

Clutch size	North-east		Central		South-west	
	n	%	*n*	%	*n*	%
1	9	5.8	0	0.0	14	4.3
2	17	11.0	7	15.5	44	13.6
3	55	35.5	17	37.7	153	47.4
4	73	47.1	21	46.7	110	34.0
5	1	0.6	0	0.0	2	0.6
Mean	3.11		3.22		3.06	
SD	0.07		0.13		0.05	

b)

Brood size	North-east		Central		South-west	
	n	%	*n*	%	*n*	%
0	227	52	143	33	298	48
1	52	12	74	17	91	15
2	92	21	120	29	126	21
3	91	12	79	18	83	13
4	10	2	15	3	23	17
5	0	0	0	0	1	0
Mean	0.99		1.37		0.99	
SD	0.06		0.06		0.05	

Table 5.4. Mean brood size per territorial pair and per successful pair in North-east, Central and South-west Scotland, 1991-2000 (gr – land managed for grouse shooting, ngr – other land uses).

	North-east			Central			South-west		
	gr	ngr	all	gr	ngr	all	gr	ngr	all
Number of territorial pairs	233	201	434	200	231	431	123	499	622
Mean brood size/territorial pair	0.64	1.36	0.96	0.90	1.51	1.22	0.81	1.02	0.94
Number of successful pairs	81	126	207	115	173	288	51	273	324
Mean brood size/successful site	2.12	2.29	2.22	1.85	2.25	2.09	2.07	1.75	1.84

5.4.3 Site occupation

The percentage of occupied peregrine breeding sites on grouse moors has declined steadily over the last ten years (Table 5.5). This decline was greatest in the North-east and the South-west regions. The percentage occupation of breeding sites by pairs or single birds varied significantly between years, regions and between grouse moor and areas of other land uses (Table 5.6).

Table 5.5. Annual variation in percentage occupancy by peregrines breeding in grouse moor (gr) and other land uses (ngr) sites in North-east, Central and South-west Scotland, 1991–2000.

Year	North-east		Central		South-west	
	gr	ngr	gr	ngr	gr	ngr
1991	80	88	86	95	100	93
1992	86	72	87	96	100	91
1993	70	67	86	96	100	92
1994	83	82	84	85	88	87
1995	70	78	67	86	88	92
1996	67	83	79	80	88	89
1997	71	68	70	88	75	84
1998	71	84	81	81	75	77
1999	56	78	68	89	75	80
2000	51	59	73	84	69	84

Table 5.6. Analysis of variance of percentage occupation of breeding sites.

Factor	F	P	Degrees of freedom
Year	5.06	<0.001	9
Region	11.08	0.002	2
gr/ng	17.20	<0.001	1

There have been similar declines in percentage occupation by peregrines occupying sites where there were other land uses (Table 5.5) although these declines were more gradual. They were similar in the South-west and Central areas. The decline in the North-east was more marked.

5.4.4 Variation in the percentage failed sites

Table 5.8 shows that peregrines breeding in areas managed for grouse shooting (gr) had a significantly higher failure rate than those breeding in areas with other primary land uses (ngr) (F = 42.97, P <0.001). There were also significant differences between regions (F = 15.88, P <0.001) and between years (F = 2.10, P <0.05).

5.4.5 Productivity of peregrines breeding near homing pigeon areas in South-west Scotland

In South-west Scotland, peregrines breeding on sheepwalk within 6.4 km of urban areas with a large number of pigeon lofts were significantly less successful than those peregrines breeding on sheepwalk over 6.4 km from these areas (0.42 young territorial pair^{-1}, sd = 0.21, cf 1.35 young territorial pair^{-1}, sd = 0.75; F = 17.12, P = <0.001).

5.4.6 Effect of land use on productivity and occupancy of breeding sites

The mean brood sizes per territorial pair and the percentage occupation differed significantly with land uses round peregrine eyries (Table 5.7; F = 9.8, P <0.01 and F = 9.99, P <0.01, respectively). Occupancy and productivity were highest on farmland. Productivity was lowest on unstocked forestry and grouse moors whilst occupancy was lowest on deer forests, forestry, unstocked forestry and grouse moors. Urban areas, which had the highest percentage occupancy and mean brood size per territorial pair (2.31, sd = 0.54), were omitted from the analysis as the sample size was low.

Table 5.7. Effect of land use around the breeding site on mean brood size/territorial pair - all regions 1991–2000. Table 5.2 gives details on land uses. Number, n, is the number of breeding sites checked.

Land use	Brood size			Percentage occupancy		
	n	*Mean brood size/territorial pair*	*sd*	*n*	*Percentage occupancy*	*sd*
Deer forest	149	1.48	1.49	195	81.9	2.50
Farmland	57	1.63	1.26	59	100.0	4.26
Forestry	269	1.09	1.33	332	77.8	4.26
Grouse moor	689	0.93	1.34	885	76.5	1.13
Sheepwalk	545	1.35	1.42	600	85.9	1.47
Unstocked forestry	39	0.84	1.27	47	78.4	4.88

5.5 Discussion

5.5.1 Clutch size and brood size

Variation in clutch size (Figure 5.2) and brood size (Figure 5.3) between years was possibly associated with variation in the weather during the breeding season. Heavy rainfall or snow in late March and April have been observed to cause clutch desertion or non-laying in all three regions; heavy rainfall in May can affect hatching success (unpublished observations).

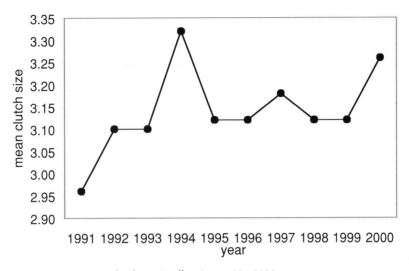

Figure 5.2. Variation in mean clutch size in all regions, 1991-2000.

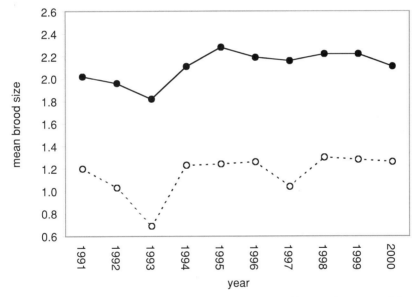

Figure 5.3. Annual variation in brood size per territorial pair (dotted line) and per successful pair (solid line) for all regions, 1991-2000.

The effect of poor weather has been observed in other peregrine populations (Ratcliffe, 1993). In America, Hagar (1969) and White (1975) noted that severe weather reduced breeding success. Norriss (1995) suggested that the breeding range in Ireland was limited by weather and that exceptionally heavy rainfall in April reduced productivity. Horne & Fielding (2002) found a similar relationship in Cumbria where the mean number of young fledging per occupied range was negatively correlated to rainfall in both April and May. Mearns & Newton (1988) also showed that the proportion of clutches producing young in South-west Scotland varied according to the May rainfall. High rainfall reduced the number of young fledged. The relationship between weather and variation in clutch and brood size in the three regions will be analysed in a separate paper.

5.5.2 Areas managed for grouse shooting - site occupation and percentage breeding failure (1991-2000)

The significant variation in brood size per territorial pair between regions and between areas managed primarily for grouse shooting (grouse moors) and for other land uses reflects the lower productivity of peregrines breeding in grouse moor-dominated areas. Mean brood size was similar in successful nests in both grouse shooting areas and other land use areas (Table 5.4). We suggest that the significantly higher failure rate of peregrines in grouse shooting areas is due to persecution. The higher levels of persecution on grouse moors are well documented (Hardey, 1998; Scottish Raptor Study Groups, 1998; Royal Society for the Protection of Birds, 2000).

Over the ten year period, the number of known peregrine breeding sites within each region has increased (Appendix 5.1). The peregrines have responded differentially in each of the primary land use categories, presumably linked to differences in land management. We believe that changes did not result from a shift by falcons from one area within each region to another, but rather that increases and decreases within each land use category reflect a genuine change in peregrine numbers within that category.

Site occupancy of peregrines breeding on grouse moors has decreased. This trend is common to all three regions (Table 5.5). The decline was linked to illegal persecution (Scottish Raptor Study Groups, 1988; Anon., 2000; Royal Society for the Protection of Birds, 2000). Peregrines breeding in areas not managed for grouse shooting also showed a decrease in site occupancy (Table 5.5) and this was most marked in the North-east. Ratcliffe (1993) and Hunt (1988) both suggest that there is normally a surplus of non-breeding birds which can quickly replace adult losses. Etheridge *et al.* (1997) showed that the hen harrier *Circus cyaneus* population in Scotland was limited by persecution, with grouse moors acting as a sink for birds. The effect on peregrine populations in the three Scottish study regions appears to be similar. Indeed, persecution may have limited peregrine breeding density, as suggested by Ratcliffe (1993). High levels of persecution may also be removing the non-breeding surplus leading to population decline in areas dominated by other land uses.

Predation by peregrines on red grouse *Lagopus lagopus* has been linked to population limitation of the latter (Hudson, 1992; Thirgood *et al.*, 2000; Redpath & Thirgood, 2000). This is of concern to land managers attempting to produce sufficient surplus grouse to allow 'driven' shooting. Driven shooting provides an important source of revenue for grouse moor estates (McGilvray, 1995, Fraser of Allendar Institute, 2001). It is suggested that the recent increase in persecution is a direct result of this conflict and that the higher percentage failure of breeding peregrines in areas managed for grouse shooting (Table 5.8) is also linked to persecution. Scottish Raptor Study Groups have obtained over 20 records where clear or probable evidence of persecution was obtained for grouse moor peregrines (unpublished data).

5.5.3 Homing pigeon areas and peregrine breeding success

Persecution of peregrines as a result of their predation on homing pigeons is well documented (Ratcliffe, 1993, Chapter 4; Shawyer *et al.*, 2000). Peregrines in South-west Scotland that bred on sheepwalk within 6.4 km (4 miles) of towns where there are large

Table 5.8. Annual variation in percentage of failed sites in North-east, Central and South-west Scotland, 1991–2000.

Year	North-east		Central		South-west	
	gr	*ngr*	*gr*	*ngr*	*gr*	*ngr*
1991	60	28	33	27	54	44
1992	63	44	43	26	69	44
1993	64	47	53	38	75	75
1994	57	41	55	19	50	38
1995	88	28	57	24	73	37
1996	74	26	33	15	44	51
1997	83	50	44	29	65	49
1998	77	36	40	17	33	39
1999	33	30	61	41	42	45
2000	67	32	32	25	60	40

numbers of homing pigeon lofts were significantly less successful than those breeding on sheepwalk not close to large numbers of homing pigeon lofts. This difference could be due to persecution in the former areas. Shawyer *et al.* (2000) gave instances of such persecution but stressed that the majority of pigeon fanciers are law abiding and do not interfere with peregrines. Our comparison was restricted to sheepwalk in South-west Scotland as there is no recognised problem with 'the fancy' in the other regions.

5.5.4 *Effect of land use round the nest site on productivity and percentage occupation*

The effect of grouse shooting management on percentage occupation by peregrines and on productivity of their breeding sites has been discussed. The percentage occupation and productivity on grouse moors, which are an excellent habitat for peregrines with good prey populations (Tharme *et al.*, 2001), were reduced by persecution.

Other forms of land use around nest sites influence percentage occupation of nest sites and productivity. Effects of these land uses may be linked to the abundance and availability of prey populations. Afforestation appears to be adversely affecting peregrines as both percentage occupancy and productivity are low on forestry (stocked and unstocked) compared to sheepwalk, possibly through prey availability. Mearns (1981) suggests that afforestation may influence peregrine breeding success by reducing available prey populations. This effect may be reduced, to some extent, by peregrines travelling longer distances to hunt. Weather can also influence percentage occupation and productivity. Peregrines which breed in deer forests have a low percentage occupancy, attributable to the fact that many sites, especially at high altitude, are unoccupied in years of high snowfall (personal observations). However, the productivity of occupied deer forest sites is high (Table 5.7), possibly due to lower persecution.

Acknowledgements

We thank all of the raptor workers of the Dumfries and Galloway, South Strathclyde, Central, Tayside and North-East of Scotland Raptor Study Groups for their time and dedication in visiting peregrine sites and collecting the data; Dr Mick Marquiss for his help and advice with the analysis of our data; Dr Innes Sim, Dr Ian Bainbridge and two anonymous referees for their comments on the analysis; and local landowners and their staff for their assistance.

References

Anonymous (2000). *Report of the UK Raptor Working Group*. DETR/JNCC, Peterborough.

Crick, H.Q.P. & Ratcliffe, D.A. (1995). The Peregrine breeding population of the United Kingdom in 1991. *Bird Study*, **42**, 1-19.

Etheridge, B., Summers, R.W. & Green, R.E. (1997). The effects of illegal killing and destruction of nests by humans on the population dynamics of the hen harrier in Scotland. *Journal of Applied Ecology*, **34**, 1081–1105.

Fraser of Allendar Institute (2001). *An Economic Study of Scottish Grouse Moors: an Update*. Game Conservancy Ltd, Fordingbridge.

Hagar, J.A. (1969). History of the Massachusetts Peregrine Falcon population. In *Peregrine Falcon Populations: Their Biology and Decline*, ed. by J.J. Hickey. The University of Wisconsin Press, Madison. pp. 123-131.

Hardey, J.J.C. (1991). Increase in the numbers of breeding peregrines in North East Scotland 1981–1991. *North East of Scotland Bird Report 1991*. The North-East of Scotland Bird Club, Aberdeen.

Hardey, J.J.C. (1998). Peregrine Falcon NE Scotland. Breeding Success. Unpublished report by North East of Scotland Raptor Study Group.

Hudson, P.J. (1992). *Grouse in Space and Time*. Game Conservancy Ltd., Fordingbridge.

Horne, G. & Fielding, A.F. (2002). Recovery of the peregrine falcon *Falco peregrinus* in Cumbria, UK, 1966-99. *Bird Study*. **49**, 229-236.

Hunt, W.G. (1988). The Natural Regulation of Peregrine Falcon populations. In *Peregrine Falcon Populations – Their Management and Recovery*, ed. by T.J. Cade, J.H. Enderson, C.G. Thelander & C.M. White. The Peregrine Fund Inc., Boise, Idaho. pp. 667–676.

McGilvray, J. (1995). *An Economic Study of Grouse Moors*. University of Strathclyde, Glasgow.

Mearns, R. (1981). The diet of the Peregrine in south Scotland in the breeding season. *Bird Study*, **30**, 81–90.

Mearns, R. & Newton, I. (1988). Factors affecting breeding success of peregrines in South Scotland. *Journal of Animal Ecology*, **57**, 903–916.

Norris, D.W. (1995). The 1991 survey and weather impacts on the Peregrine Falcon breeding population in the Republic of Ireland. *Bird Study*, **42**, 20–30.

Ratcliffe, D.A. (1993). *The Peregrine Falcon. Second edition*. Poyser, Berkhamsted.

Redpath, S.M. & Thirgood, S.J. (2000). Numerical and functional responses in generalist predators: hen harriers and peregrines on Scottish grouse moors. *Journal of Animal Ecology*, **68**, 879–892.

Rollie, C.J. (2000). Inland breeding peregrines in south-west Scotland – some notes. Unpublished report.

Royal Society for the Protection of Birds (2000). *Persecution – a Review of Bird of Prey Persecution in Scotland in 1999*. RSPB, Sandy.

Scottish Raptor Monitoring Scheme (2002). *Scottish Raptor Monitoring Scheme Agreement*. Scottish Natural Heritage, Perth.

Scottish Raptor Study Groups (1998). *The Illegal Persecution of Raptors in Scotland*. Scottish Office Central Research Unit, Edinburgh.

Shawyer, C., Clarke, R. & Dixon, N. (2000). A study into raptor predation of domestic pigeons. Unpublished report. DETR, London.

Tharme, A.P., Green, R.E., Baines, D., Bainbridge, I.P. & O'Brien, M.O. (2001). The effect of management for red grouse shooting on the population density of breeding birds on heather-dominated moorland. *Journal of Applied Ecology,* **38**, 439-457.

Thirgood, S.J., Redpath, S.M., Rothery, P. & Aebischer, N.J. (2000). Raptor predation and population limitation in red grouse. *Journal of Animal Ecology,* **69**, 504–516.

White, C.M. (1975). Studies on Peregrine Falcons in the Aleutian Islands. *Raptor Research Report,* **3**, 33–50.

Appendix 5.1. Peregrine breeding sites checked in North-east, Central and South-west Scotland, 1991-2001. Data include all known sites used between 1991-2000.

Year	1991	1992	1993	1994	1995	1996	1997	1998	1999	2000
Region										
North-east										
Sites known	66	72	75	79	79	81	83	83	83	83
Sites checked	66	67	68	72	67	78	76	80	82	82
% of known sites checked	100	93	91	91	85	96	92	96	99	99
Sites occupied	59	53	45	58	46	55	49	56	48	44
% of checked sites occupied	80	73	58	72	61	58	58	63	53	48
Central										
Sites known	94	96	97	99	100	100	100	101	102	102
Sites checked	94	64	50	72	66	71	68	68	61	70
% of known sites checked	100	67	52	78	66	71	68	67	59	69
Sites occupied	77	54	48	59	48	57	54	54	47	51
% of checked sites occupied	92	84	96	82	73	80	79	79	77	73
South-west										
Sites known	71	74	78	83	83	83	87	87	88	88
Sites checked	68	68	74	78	77	80	82	82	88	84
% of known sites checked	96	92	95	94	93	96	94	94	100	95
Sites occupied	65	61	67	68	70	70	69	63	70	65
% of checked sites occupied	96	90	91	87	91	88	84	77	80	77

6. Distribution, Numbers and Breeding Performance of Tawny owls (*Strix aluco*) in Relation to Clear-Cutting in a Conifer Forest in Northern England

Steve J. Petty & Chris J. Thomas

Summary

1. The study was undertaken in Kielder Forest, northern England. This is an extensive spruce forest established since the late 1920s on grass and heather moorland. Clear-cutting started in the late 1960s and soon became the main method of harvesting timber. Today, older parts of the forest comprise a mosaic of tree stands of different ages created by the temporal and spatial separation of clear-cuts.

2. Tawny owl *Strix aluco* population dynamics were studied in this rapidly changing forest environment for 18 years (1981-1998). The owls bred in nest boxes and fed largely on field voles *Microtus agrestis* with cyclic populations, which peaked every 3-4 years. Clear-cuts provided the main habitat for voles for around 12 years after replanting.

3. Owl territories were distributed along the lower parts of valley systems where the better quality soils and the best vegetation for voles were located. Numbers of territorial tawny owls increased from 1981 to 1991 and then declined until 1998. The area of vole habitat on clear-cuts below 300 m altitude explained 44% of this variation in owl numbers. Thus, the extent and quality of foraging habitat for tawny owls showed both short-term changes associated with vole cycles and long-term changes linked to changes in the overall area of young plantations.

4. Vole abundance each spring was placed into one of three abundance classes; low, increasing or declining. Overall, the owl population produced 4.5 times more fledged chicks in increasing vole years than in low vole years, a result of fewer pairs breeding and successful brood sizes being smaller when vole numbers were low.

5. We compare our results with similar studies in boreal forests, and discuss ways of enhancing conifer forests in Britain for tawny owls and their prey.

6.1 Introduction

Extensive forests of fast growing, non-native coniferous species have been established in the British uplands during the last 80 years on sites that had been largely treeless since the clearance of native forests (Petty & Avery, 1990). Many forests were planted over a short time scale (Ford *et al.*, 1979). Wildlife studies initially concentrated on how successional changes influenced the development of communities within these novel habitats (Moss, 1978, 1979; Hill, 1979, 1986; Moss *et al.*, 1979; Petty & Avery, 1990) and the response of individual species of moorland and woodland habitats to such changes (Marquiss *et al.*, 1978, 1985; Newton *et al.*, 1981, 1982; Thompson *et al.*, 1988; Newton, 1991).

Early indications that wind would be a major disturbance factor came in 1953 and 1968 when around 1.8 and 1.6 million m³ of timber, respectively, was windblown in two major gales (Holtam, 1971). Clear-cutting developed as a response to these catastrophic events to ensure that timber was harvested prior to crops reaching a crucial height, after which their susceptibility to windthrow increased and their profitability declined. In an attempt to break up large tracts of even-aged forest at the end of the first rotation, the patch size of clear-cuts was often considerably smaller than when initially planted (McIntosh, 1995). In some of our oldest forests, clear-cutting is producing a dynamic mosaic of different-aged stands of trees.

The ecological significance of creating such spatio-temporal patterns in novel habitats is little understood, but is generally considered to improve biological diversity (Petty *et al.*, 1995a; Peterken, 1999). To some extent, clear-cutting mimics natural gap forming processes in native forest, due to factors such as fire, wind and pathogens (Peterken, 1996). However, the size, structure and distribution of gaps formed naturally differ substantially from those created by clear-cutting (Quine *et al.*, 1999; Ulanova, 2000). Nevertheless, one would expect some species to be adapted to exploit such ephemeral gaps, whether created by nature or man.

More recently, research has focussed on how wildlife has adapted to the diversification of stand ages brought about by clear-cutting and how such practices might be improved to enhance biological diversity (Lurz *et al.*, 1995; Patterson *et al.*, 1995; Wallace & Good, 1995; Humphrey *et al.*, 1999, 2000; Ferris *et al.*, 2000). Not surprisingly, the study of raptors and carnivores has been a profitable area, as these species either collectively or individually reflect how forest management influences a wide range of food resources upon which predators depend (Petty, 1992; Petty *et al.*, 1995b, 2000; Shaw, 1995; O'Mahony *et al.*, 1999; Coles *et al.*, 2000).

In this analysis we use data from a long-term study to investigate the impact of clear-cutting on numbers, distribution and breeding performance of tawny owls (*Strix aluco*) in a large spruce forest in northern England. Tawny owls are birds primarily of broadleaved woodland, but have adapted well to a range of man-altered habitats (Southern, 1970; Cramp, 1985; Percival, 1993; Redpath, 1995; Petty & Saurola, 1997). These include open habitats, such as urban areas, farmland and moorland, which remain suitable for foraging, roosting and breeding so long as they retain some woodland fragments. Tawny owls have also colonised many upland conifer forests once they have reached a suitable age (Petty, 1992).

Food supply is one of the most important factors influencing the demography and distribution of raptors (Newton, 1979, 1998). Tawny owls are no exception and have a life history shaped by rodent populations that vary in abundance from year-to-year (Southern, 1970; Petty, 1992). Their main prey in temperate broadleaved forests and woodlands of central Europe are mice *Apodemus sylvaticus* and *A. flavicollis*, and bank voles *Clethrionomys glareolus* (Southern & Lowe, 1982; Wendland, 1984; Cramp, 1985; Jedrzejewski *et al.*, 1994, 1996). These woodland rodents exhibit multiannual fluctuations in numbers linked to the seed production patterns of the main tree species (*Quercus* spp. and *Fagus sylvatica*) (Jensen, 1982, 1985; Hansson, 1985; Gurnell, 1993).

In areas with fewer broadleaved trees or where mast production is less pronounced, rodents of open grassy habitats, such as *Microtus* voles, often feature more in tawny owl diet (Delmée *et al.*, 1979; Mikkola, 1983). This is the case in our study area, where field voles

Microtus agrestis are their most important food (Petty, 1999). Here, vole populations exhibit cyclic dynamics with peak numbers occurring every 3-4 years (Petty, 1992, 1999; Lambin *et al.*, 2000). Tawny owls are highly philopatric and overcome years with few voles by ceasing to breed and by utilising alternative prey, such a common frogs *Rana temporaria* and birds (Petty, 1992, 1999).

6.2 Study area

Kielder Forest, in northern England, is one of the largest man-made conifer forests in Europe, with a total area of 620 km², of which 500 km² is planted with trees (McIntosh, 1995). It comprises largely Sitka spruce *Picea sitchensis* and Norway spruce *Picea abies* managed on a 40-60 year rotational clear-cutting system, which over the last 25 years has created a mosaic of different-aged stands of trees. Clear-cuts ranged in size from 5 ha to more than 100 ha, with the smallest in valley bottoms. The study area was situated in the centre of Kielder Forest and was defined by a north-south, east-west rectangle encompassing all tawny owl nest sites used during 1979-1998 (Figure 6.1a). This area included moorland and other open areas that were unsuitable breeding habitat for tawny owls. The forested part of the study area within this rectangle was 176 km² (centre of the study area, 55°13′N, 2°33′W).

(a)   (b)

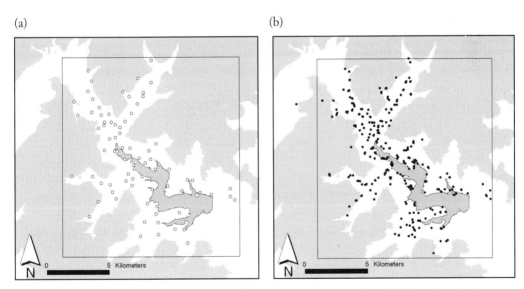

Figure 6.1. The box outlines the study area in Kielder Forest, Northumberland, with Kielder Water in the centre and the 300 m contour (shaded above and not shaded below 300 m); (a) the distribution of 77 tawny owl nesting territory centres (open circles); (b) the distribution of all nest sites (closed circles) used at least once during the study period (1981-1998).

6.3 Methods

6.3.1 The tawny owl population

Forty tawny owl territories were identified during 1975-1979 by listening for calling birds and finding pellet/roost locations, nest sites, fledged broods and moulted feathers. Subsequently, nest boxes of a design suitable for tawny owls were erected near to the centre of these 40 territories, with an additional box placed between territories (Petty, 1992).

Other boxes were sited in parts of the forest that lacked owls, at a similar spacing to boxes in the forest with owls. Most nest boxes were erected during winters 1979/80 and 1980/81, and subsequently boxes were removed prior to clear-cutting and re-erected in the nearest suitable patch of trees. Thus, there was ample opportunity for new pairs to settle in the study area, as at any one time there were at least twice as many boxes available as pairs of owls. The entire population had switched to using nest boxes by 1983, and subsequently no natural sites were used for breeding, although natural sites that had been used in the past were checked annually, together with potential natural sites that had never been used, at least to our knowledge. Most females were caught each time they bred and were identified individually from ring numbers, and from 1988 most breeding males were also caught (Petty, 1992). Over time, it was possible to determine from these recaptures which nest site belonged to which territory.

Territory occupancy and breeding success were recorded each year during 1981-1998. Up to one month before the first egg was laid, each pair visited most potential nest sites (mainly nest boxes) in their territory and left traces of down or small body feathers around the entrance hole. Closer to laying, a deep scrape was formed in the debris at the bottom of the chosen site, often with down and small body feathers around the edge. In years when pairs failed to lay, they still went through this process. A territory was classified as occupied when a fresh scrape with down or feathers was found in at least one nest site in that territory during the last two weeks of March and the first two weeks of April. Territories were classified as unoccupied when no signs of owls were found at nest sites. To validate this method of recording occupancy, tape-recorded 'hoot' calls of male owls were broadcast at 101 locations that were evenly distributed throughout the forested part of the study area in 1991 and 1992 during late February–early March (Redpath, 1994). This method identified just over 90% of the occupied territories as determined from nest site signs, but failed to locate any additional territories, suggesting that the 'nest site signs method' was more effective (Petty, unpublished data). Kloubec (2000) also showed that the use of broadcast calls was not 100% successful in locating territorial tawny owls, with the success rate apparently influenced by a number of environmental variables.

Additional inspections were undertaken to determine clutch size and the number of chicks successfully leaving each nest site. Some female owls deserted during laying or incubation and often relaid at another nest site, or exceptionally in the same nest (Petty, 1992). In these instances, only one breeding attempt per territory/year was used in the analysis (Petty & Fawkes, 1997). Clutch size was calculated from pairs that laid at least one egg. Successful brood size was calculated from pairs that fledged (chick leaving the nest site) at least one chick. Overall brood size was calculated from all occupied territories; with pairs that failed to lay or those that failed in a breeding attempt being assigned a brood size of zero. The latter statistics reflected the overall performance of the territorial population.

The number of territories monitored annually increased from 45 in 1981 to 77 in 1998, not all of which were occupied annually (see above). Most of this increase (21 territories) was the result of more territories being established in the original study area of 1981, with pairs using existing nest boxes. However, 11 territories were added during 1982-1997 due to the study area being progressively enlarged. The past history of these territories was unknown and so they were excluded in the analysis of population trend (850 occupied and 180 unoccupied territory/years), but included in the analysis of breeding performance (939 occupied territory/years).

For analyses using the spatial distribution of territories (Figure 6.1a), the mean territory centre was calculated weighted by frequency of nest site use. For example, the territory centre for three nests located at NY205602, NY209610 and NY204605 was calculated from the mean northing (205+209+204)/3 = 206, and the mean easting (602+610+605)/3 = 606, to give the range centre at NY206606. If the same nest was used on two occasions, its grid reference was entered twice into the calculation.

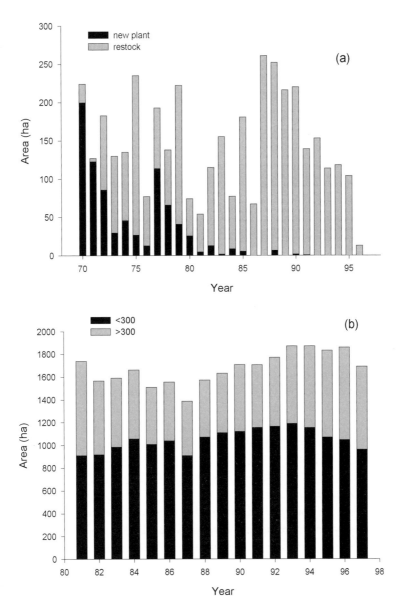

Figure 6.2. (a) Area of first (new planting) and second generation (restocking) planting undertaken annually in the tawny owl study area during 1970-1996. (b) The total amount of vole habitat (1-11 year old, first and second rotation plantations) split by elevation in the same area during 1981-1997.

6.3.2 Field vole habitat

We constructed annual habitat coverages within a Geographical Information System (GIS, Arc/Info version 7.1.2). Polygon boundaries of uniformly planted areas were derived from the Forestry Commission's (FC) 1:10,000 scale digital stock maps for 1996. These did not include internal rides <10 m wide. Attribute data for polygons were obtained from a FC digital database, including tree species, planting year and rotation. First rotation described the planting of previously treeless moorland hereafter called afforestation whilst second generation described the planting of clear-cuts hereafter called restocking. Clear-cuts were usually restocked within 18 months of being felled. Young plantations suitable for field voles were defined as crops between 1-11 years after planting (Figure 6.2b), after which the growing trees gradually shaded out the ground vegetation. We retrospectively mapped the extent of these habitat types for each year from 1975-1996 using query tools within the GIS. Other less suitable field vole habitats, such as grass pasture and moorland, were also identifiable in the GIS. These formed permanent open habitats interspersed throughout the study area. Most were grazed by domestic stock and as a result field vole densities were generally low (Charles, 1981).

In the analysis, afforested sites were treated the same as restocked sites. The amount of afforestation in the study area declined during the 1970s, with virtually none after 1980 (Figure 6.2a). In contrast, the amount of clear-cutting and restocking increased until the late 1980s and subsequently declined. Thus, young restocked and afforested sites provided ephemeral islands of vole habitat embedded within a matrix of older crops that were largely unsuitable for voles (Thomson, 1996).

6.3.3 Field vole abundance

Vole abundance was assessed during March-May, when tawny owls were breeding, using a subjective score based on vole signs (faeces, grass clipping and runways) in young plantations (Petty, 1992). This enabled each spring to be placed in one of following three vole abundance classes that encompassed a complete vole cycle: low (the trough in the cycle, after which numbers usually started to increase by the summer, but after owls had bred); increasing (numbers increasing throughout the year and peaking in the autumn/winter); or declining (numbers high overwinter followed by a rapid decline during spring/summer). This subjective score was significantly related to spring vole density (r_s = 0.84, N = 7, P <0.05) determined from trapping during 1985-1991 (Petty, 1992).

6.4 Results

6.4.1 Distribution of tawny owl territories

Centres of territories were not evenly distributed throughout the study area, but dispersed along the main valley systems feeding into Kielder Water (Fig 6.1a). The nearest neighbour distance (NND) between territory centres (mean = 730 m, N = 77, SE = 35.2 m) was related to altitude, but while this relationship was significant (r = 0.42, N = 77, P <0.01), altitude only explained 18% of the variability in NND (Figure 6.3).

The location of territory centres in the lower part of each valley suggested that owls avoided nesting on higher ground. In fact, most nest sites were below the 300 m contour (Figures 6.1b and 6.3). This distribution pattern might have been an artefact of where nest boxes had been sited. To investigate if this was the case or not, the mean altitude of territory

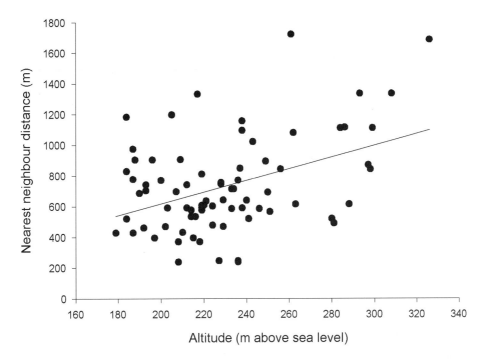

Figure 6.3. The relationship between the spacing (nearest neighbour disturbunce, m) and altitude of 77 tawny owl territory centres (Y = -145.51 + 3.82X, r^2 = 0.18, P <0.001) in Kielder Forest, Northumberland.

centres was compared between territories that had been located before nest boxes were erected (prior to 1979/80 winter) with territories established after nest boxes were available. There was no significant difference in altitude between these two groups (Table 6.1), indicating that nest box placement had little influence on the altitudinal distribution of territories.

Table 6.1. The mean altitude (m) of tawny owl territory centres in Kielder Forest, Northumberland. A comparison between territories occupied before (existing) and after the erection of nest boxes (new).

	Existing	*New*	*P (t-test)*
Mean	224.4	237.4	0.44
N	40	26	-
SD	34.45	35.93	-
Range	184-326	187-308	-

6.4.2 Trend in the number of owl territories

The best measure of population trend in the territorial population was provided by the temporal variation in the number of occupied territories. Numbers increased from 44 in 1981, peaked at 58 in 1991 and then declined to 46 in 1998 (top of the light bar, Figure 6.4). In contrast, the number of territories monitored annually in the original study area (see section 6.3.1) increased gradually from 45 to 66 (top of the bar, Figure 6.4)

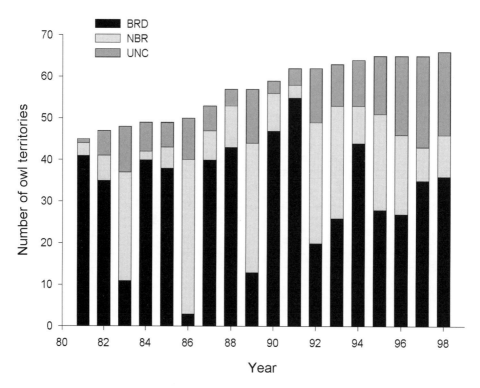

Figure 6.4. The number of tawny owl territories split into three categories by year; BRD - breeding attempt where at least one egg was laid, NBR - occupied but with no breeding attempt (bird/s present) and UNC - unoccupied.

In the absence of soil maps, we arbitrarily split the study area by altitude to determine whether the distribution pattern of breeding owls was linked to suitable field vole habitat. Areas below 300 m altitude included most of the better quality soils, on which grew the best vegetation for field voles (Wallace & Good, 1995). Above this altitude, peaty soils were widespread, but these produced much poorer vegetation for voles. There was a highly significant relationship between the number of occupied owl territories and the extent of young plantations below 300 m altitude (Figure 6.5a), but not above 300 m (Figure 6.5b). This relationship indicated that just less than half (44%) of the annual variation in the number of territorial pairs could be accounted for by the availability of ephemeral vole habitat in the lower valleys. This linked well with the distribution of territory centres and nest sites (Figures 6.1a and 6.1b).

6.4.3 Breeding performance

Occupied territories were split into three categories; (i) those with no breeding; (ii) those where a breeding attempt failed; and (iii) those that successfully reared at least one chick (Figure 6.4). Overall, there was a significant difference among these three occupancy categories related to vole year class (Table 6.2). In particular, a lower proportion of territorial pairs (35%) laid eggs in low vole years than in increasing (86%) or declining (81%) vole years. Breeding success followed the same trend, with only 28% of territories successful in

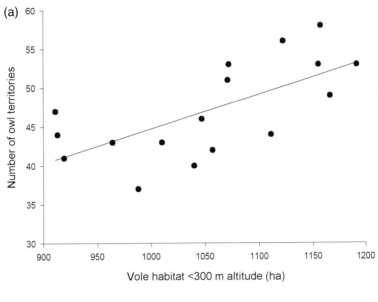

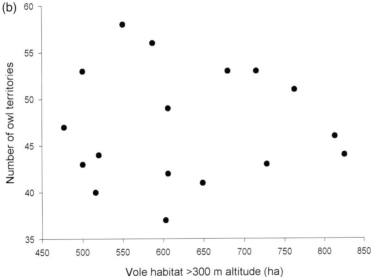

Figure 6.5. The number of occupied tawny owl territories in relation to the area of field vole habitat present on afforested and restocked sites (see text). There was a significant relationship between the number of owl territories and the extent of vole habitat below 300 m altitude (a) (Y = 0.46 + 0.04X, r^2 = 0.44, P <0.004, but not above 300 m altitude (b) (r^2 = 0.00, P=0.997). Each point represents one year.

low vole years compared to 76% and 69% respectively in increasing and declining vole years. Interestingly, a lower proportion of pairs failed in a breeding attempt (7%) during low vole years than during increasing (10%) or declining vole years (13%) (Table 6.2).

A more detailed scrutiny of breeding success showed similar trends (Table 6.3). In low vole years, incubation started later and clutch, successful brood and overall brood sizes were significantly smaller than in the other two vole year classes. In contrast, incubation started

Table 6.2. Breeding status of occupied tawny owl territories (N = 963 territory years) by vole year class in Kielder Forest during 1981-1998. Overall, there was a significant difference in breeding status in relation to vole year class (χ^2_4 = 234.31, P <0.001).

Breeding status[1]	Vole year class[2] (%)						Total	
	Low		Increase		Decrease			
No breeding	197	(64.8)	44	(13.6)	62	(18.5)	303	(31.4)
Failed breeding	21	(6.9)	33	(10.2)	42	(12.5)	96	(10.0)
Successful	86	(28.3)	247	(76.2)	231	(69.0)	564	(58.6)
Total	304	(100.0)	324	(100.0)	335	(100.0)	963	(100.0)

1   No breeding = evidence of bird/s present and nest scrape formed, but no eggs laid; failed breeding = breeding attempt failed during egg laying, incubation or the nestling period; successful; at least one chick leaving the nest.
2   Low vole years = 1983, 1986, 1989, 1992, 1993, 1996; increasing vole years = 1981, 1984, 1987, 1990, 1994, 1997; decreasing vole years = 1982, 1985, 1988, 1991, 1995, 1998.

Table 6.3. Mean (SE) breeding parameters of occupied tawny owl territories by vole year class in Kielder Forest during 1981-1998. The text describes how clutch and brood sizes were calculated (section 6.3.1).

Breeding parameter[1]	Vole year class[2]			N	P (three-way)[3]	P (two-way)[4]
	Low	Increase	Decrease			
SIC	39.1	26.2	24.1	647	***	NS
	(1.05)	(0.74)	(0.66)			
CLT	2.17	3.11	3.04	656	***	NS
	(0.05)	(0.05)	(0.05)			
SBR	1.72	2.85	2.34	561	***	***
	(0.06)	(0.06)	(0.06)			
OBR	0.49	2.22	1.66	939	***	***
	(0.05)	(0.08)	(0.07)			

1   SIC = start of incubation (1st March = 1); CLT = clutch size; SBR = successful brood size; OBR = overall brood size.
2   See Table 6.2.
3   Kruskal-Wallis (low, increase and decrease vole year classes); ***P <0.001, NS, not significant.
4   Mann-Whitney (increase and decrease vole year classes); ***P <0.001, NS, not significant.

around the same time and clutch sizes were similar in the increasing and decreasing phases of the vole cycle. The main difference in these latter two vole year classes was that successful brood and overall brood sizes were significantly larger in increasing than decreasing vole years. Taken as a whole, the territorial owl population produced 4.5 times more chicks in the increasing vole years than in low vole years, a result of both fewer pairs breeding and successful brood sizes being smaller in low vole years.

6.5 Discussion

6.5.1 The distribution of territorial tawny owls

Most nest sites were below 300 m altitude and situated along valley systems feeding into Kielder Water; the lowest point in the study area at 185 m altitude (Figure 6.1a). Within this altitude band, territory centres were 240-1,724 m apart. The spacing of territories was influenced by altitude, but as this relationship explained only 18% of the variation (Figure 6.3) other factors were evidently involved, such as the size and spatial arrangement of clear-cuts (Petty, 1989; Coles *et al.*, 2000). Fine-grained habitat mosaics, created by small clear-cuts, provide more edge habitat per unit area than do large clear-cuts, and tawny owls concentrate their hunting along such edges. Additional analyses on temporal trends in habitat composition around individual territories are planned to explore this aspect further.

Owls appeared to avoid nesting in higher parts of the forest. One reason might be that better soils were more frequent below 300 m, and these produced the grass-dominated vegetation preferred by field voles (Hansson, 1971; Hansson & Larsson, 1978; Gipps & Alibhai, 1991). Wallace & Good (1995) showed that soil type distribution in Kielder varied with altitude. Mineral soils covered only 10% of the area above 300 m, but 65% of the area below 250 m. Thus, suitable vegetation for voles was more likely to colonise clear-cuts on low ground where mineral soils were widespread.

A similar distribution on lower and wetter ground has been noted in tawny owl studies in Switzerland (Eiberle, 1970), Finland (Lahti & Mikkola, 1974; Lundberg, 1980), Scotland (Petty, 1992) and elsewhere (Mikkola, 1983; Cramp, 1985). Eiberle (1970) also thought this preference for low ground was related to prey availability. In many upland areas, broadleaved woodlands are more abundant in valley bottoms. These habitats not only provide prey, such as mice and bank voles, but often contain suitable tree cavities for breeding. Presumably there are also energetic advantages for owls to nest in low-lying areas, apart from nest sites being more sheltered. Most prey are relatively small (less than 40 g) and during a breeding attempt many journeys are made between the nest and foraging areas. The tawny owl is not designed for soaring flight. So, it must be easier to glide downhill with prey and return unladen, than *vice versa*.

Another factor that might have influenced the distribution of owls in Kielder was the use of nest boxes. Tawny owls do not build their own nests and are dependent on finding a suitable site in which to breed; they prefer to nest in large, dry tree cavities (Cramp, 1985). When these are absent or scarce, they will use a variety of alternative sites. Prior to nest boxes being available in Kielder, tawny owls bred in tree cavities, crag ledges, buildings, disused stick nests of other species and ground sites (Petty, 1992; Petty *et al.*, 1994). Some of these nest sites were abundant, such as old stick nests of red squirrel *Sciurus vulgaris* and carrion crow *Corvus corone*. Thus, it was considered unlikely that nest site availability limited the distribution and numbers of tawny owls before nest boxes were available. At the start of our study, more nest boxes were provided than pairs of owls, so that any increase in the breeding population could be quickly located and monitored. The owls' response was to abandon poor quality natural sites and switch entirely to using nest boxes within three years (Petty *et al.*, 1994). With a surplus of boxes available, pairs had a choice about where to settle and breed. A comparison of altitude at territory centres before and after nest box provision indicated that nesting altitude had changed little with the use of nest boxes (Table 6.1). Moreover, there was another advantage of using nest boxes, apart from the ease of collecting demographic data. Nest site quality was standardised and could be discounted as a factor affecting breeding success (Newton, 1979, 1998).

6.5.2 Population trend of tawny owls

Tawny owls are highly philopatric and respond functionally rather that numerically to multiannual fluctuations in rodent abundance (Southern, 1970; Cramp, 1985; Petty, 1992). In other words, they overcome rodent scarcity by switching to alternative prey and ceasing to breed. This strategy contrasts to the numeric response of mobile vole specialists, such as short-eared owls *Asio flammeus* and long-eared owls *Asio otus* that track changes in vole abundance over large geographical areas, and as a result are largely absent from areas where voles are scarce (Village, 1981, 1987; Korpmäki & Norrdahl, 1985, 1991; Korpmäki, 1992). Therefore, with little temporal change in the overall area of vole habitat one would predict relative stability in tawny owl numbers, but less stability if temporal changes occurred. The latter appears to be the case in Kielder. Variation in the extent of ephemeral vole habitat below 300 m altitude had a fairly strong influence on owl numbers (Figure 6.5a). However, as this relationship explains only 44% of the variation in owl numbers, other factors were evidently involved that will be explored in future analyses.

6.5.3 Clear-cuts, vole abundance and breeding performance of tawny owls

Although clear-cuts were ephemeral they clearly provided an important habitat for small mammals in Kielder, of which field voles were by far the most abundant (Petty, 1992, 1999). The importance of clear-cuts as foraging habitat for owls was shown by the relationship between vole abundance on clear-cuts and breeding performance of owls (Tables 6.2 and 6.3). Field voles are also present on permanent grasslands interspersed throughout the study; however, such populations were likely to be less cyclic and less abundant due to the impact of heavy grazing by domestic animals. Charles (1981) recorded densities of 0-10 vole ha^{-1} on grazed hill ground in south Scotland. This was lower than mean vole densities (20-50 ha^{-1}) recorded on clear-cuts in the trough years between cycle peaks in Kielder, and very much lower than mean densities in peak years (150-200 voles ha^{-1}) (Lambin *et al.*, 2000; Petty *et al.*, 2000). Thicket and pole stage plantations provide little additional rodent prey for tawny owls (Charles, 1981; Thomson, 1996). Thus, the dynamics of vole populations on clear-cuts strongly influenced the demography of tawny owls (Petty, 1992).

6.5.4 The impact of clear-cutting on owls in boreal forests

Our results indicate that clear-cutting is important for tawny owls in man-made spruce forests in Britain. In the absence of clear-cutting, vole-dependent predators would have lower densities because they would be more reliant on rodent populations within older parts of the forest and on adjacent farmland, where densities are substantially lower (see previous). So, how do our results compare to similar studies in the boreal forest of Fennoscandia?

Clear-cutting has become widespread in Fennoscandia since the 1940s and has important ecological implications for the diversity of wildlife communities (Rolstad & Wegge, 1987; Esseen *et al.*, 1992, 1997; Wegge *et al.*, 1992; Edenius & Elmberg, 1996). Recent studies are beginning to show that fragmentation of boreal forests, by clear-cutting and agriculture, leads to an increase of many common species (including those avian and mammalian predators that eat small mammals) and a corresponding decline in scarce species, such as large predators (that also kill small predators) and species susceptible to predation from small predators (for example, woodland grouse) (Kurki *et al.*, 2000; Lindén *et al.*, 2000). The main rodent species to increase on clear-cuts are *Microtus* spp.; similar to the response of field voles in our study. However, unlike spruce forests in Britain, conifer forests in Fennoscandia are more open and contain much more pine, birch and ericaceous vegetation (Esseen *et al.*, 1992, 1997). The latter is especially important as it provides habitat for *Clethrionomys* voles, which often exhibit cyclic populations that are synchronised with *Microtus* cycles (Hörnfeldt, 1978; Angelstam *et al.*, 1985; Sonerud, 1997; Stenseth, 1999). Thus, vole-dependent predators already have a food-supply within older parts of the forest, but at a lower density than on clear-cuts, unlike spruce forests in Britain. The higher density of small mammals on clear-cuts than in later successional stages also appears to be widespread in North America (Kirkland, 1990).

Many small to medium sized owls that occur in boreal forests are to some extent dependent on small mammals for food (Mikkola, 1983; Cramp, 1985; Nero *et al.*, 1987; Johnsgard, 1988; Duncan *et al.*, 1997). As already discussed, clear-cutting often improves the food supply, by providing suitable habitat for a higher density of small mammals than found in old forest. Thus, it is not surprising that most studies conclude that clear-cutting is mainly beneficial to owls, but with reservations about detrimental impacts on nest site quality and increased predation risk (Hakkarainen *et al.*, 1996, 1997; Duncan, 1997; Sonerud, 1997; Whitfield & Gaffney, 1997). One of the most noticeable impacts of clear-cutting in pristine forests is the progressive reduction in the extent of old forest, and with it the loss of large tree cavities that are preferred by many species of owl for nesting. In younger forests, some species resort to less secure nest sites, such as stick nests and tree stumps, where they are more exposed to predation from larger owls and northern goshawk *Accipiter gentilis* (Mikkola, 1976, 1983).

6.5.5 Management implications for conifer forests in Britain

Our results indicate that small mammal populations are likely to be more abundant in British conifer forests where clear-cutting is the main method of harvesting timber than in forests where systems other than clear-cutting are used. Clear-cutting is thus advantageous to many vole-dependent predators, as young plantations often provide rich foraging areas. In addition, tawny owls benefit from fine-grained habitat mosaics created by relatively small clear-cuts, because they hunt from perches provided by older trees around the edge (Petty, 1989; Coles *et al.*, 2000).

One negative aspect of clear-cutting is that it perpetuates relatively young forest, and this restricts nesting opportunities for cavity-nesting birds. Without nest boxes, tawny owls use inferior nest sites where they are more exposed to predation. Red foxes *Vulpes vulpes* are likely predators of ground nests and other nest sites within their reach (some crag ledges), while these, stick nests and nests in open tree holes are more vulnerable to predation by northern goshawks and pine marten *Martes martes*, both of which are expanding their range in Britain (Valender, 1991; Marquiss, 1993; Petty, 1996). This also happens in European boreal forests, which have additional avian predators such as eagle owls *Bubo bubo* and Ural owls *Strix uralensis* (Hakkarainen & Korpmäki, 1996). Early in our study, tawny owls nesting in exposed natural sites were as successful as those using nest boxes, but this was when goshawks were scarce. This is unlikely be the case now that goshawk are far more abundant, but something we have been unable to demonstrate as all pairs have bred in nest boxes since 1983, where they are relatively secure from goshawks (Petty *et al.*, 1994). Even so, goshawks kill both adult and fledging tawny owls and may be implicated in the population decline, which started in 1992 (Petty *et al.*, in press). This aspect is being investigated in a separate analysis of recruitment and survival rates.

A linked network of old tree stands would be advantageous to tawny owls (and other wildlife) because it would provide both secure nesting sites and foraging areas in the future. Our study shows that tawny owls prefer to nest in the valley bottoms and this is ideally where old stands should be located, as these are some of the most productive and wind-resistant sites in most landscapes. This links well to the current policy of establishing broadleaved trees in riparian habitats (Forestry Commission, 1998) and proposals to establish forest habitat networks (Peterken *et al.*, 1992). In these areas it is important to include tree species that are likely to create large natural cavities, and which are suited to upland sites (Low, 1986; Rodwell & Paterson, 1994). Common alder *Alnus glutinosa*, sycamore *Acer pseudoplatanus* and ash *Fraxinus excelsior* are particularly useful in this respect. Patches of old conifers, managed on continuous cover systems (Hart, 1995; Mason *et al.*, 1999) and linked to these riparian woodlands, would provide additional cavities for nesting. Another advantage of establishing a network of old forest habitats, including both coniferous and broadleaved trees, is that woodland rodents would benefit too. In old woodland, wood mice and bank voles are often more important to tawny owls than field voles.

To summarise, tawny owls in upland conifer forests benefit most from appropriate management of low ground habitats. Key elements to include are a linked network of old tree stands managed on a continuous cover system and small clear-cuts temporally and spatially separated to create a fine-grained mosaic of different-aged tree stands.

Acknowledgements

We thank Forest Enterprise in Kielder Forest District for allowing us to carry out this study and encouraging our work over the years. Chris Quine, Linda Petty and two anonymous referees made some helpful suggestions on an earlier draft, and David Anderson helped with some of the fieldwork.

References

Angelstam, P., Lindström, E. & Widén, P. (1985). Synchronous short-term population fluctuations of some birds and mammals in Fennoscandia - occurrence and distribution. *Holarctic Ecology*, **8**, 285-298.

Charles, W.N. (1981). Abundance of the field vole (*Microtus agrestis*) in conifer plantations. In *Forest and Woodland Ecology*, ed. by F.T. Last. Institute of Terrestrial Ecology, Cambridge. pp. 135-137.

Coles, C.F., Petty, S.J. & Thomas, C.J. (2000). Relationships between foraging range, prey density and habitat structure in the tawny owl *Strix aluco*. In *Raptors at Risk (Proceedings of the 5th World Conference on Birds of Prey and Owls)*, ed. by R.D. Chancellor & B.-U. Meyburg. World Working Group on Birds of Prey and Owls, Berlin. pp. 803-812:

Cramp, S. (1985). *The Birds of the Western Palearctic. Volume IV.* Oxford University Press, Oxford.

Delmée, E., Dachy, P. & Simon, P. (1979). Etude comparative du régime alimentaire d'une population forestière de Chouettes hulottes (*Strix aluco*). *Gerfaut*, **69**, 45-77.

Duncan, J. (1997). Great gray owls (*Strix nebulosa nebulosa*) and forest management in North America: a review and recommendations. *Journal of Raptor Research*, **31**, 160-166.

Duncan, J.R., Johnson, D.H. & Nicholls, T.H. (1997). Biology and conservation of owls of the northern hemisphere. United States Department of Agriculture, Forest Service General Technical Report NC-190. North Central Research Station, St. Paul, Minnesota.

Edenius, L. & Elmberg, J. (1996). Landscape level effects of modern forestry on bird communities in north Swedish boreal forests. *Landscape Ecology*, **11**, 325-338.

Eiberle, K. (1970). Zur Wahl des Brutplatzes durch den Waldkauz im Lehrrevier der EHT. Schweiz. *Zeitschrift für Forstwesen*, **121**, 148-150.

Esseen, P.-A., Ehnström, B., Ericson, L. & Sjöberg, K. (1992). Boreal forests - the focal habitats of Fennoscandia. In *Ecological Principals of Nature Conservation: Applications in Temperate and Boreal Environments*, ed. by L. Hansson. Elsevier Applied Science, Conservation Ecology Series, London & New York. pp. 252-325.

Esseen, P.-A., Ehnström, B., Ericson, L. & Sjöberg, K. (1997). Boreal forests. *Ecological Bulletins*, **46**, 16-47.

Ferris, R., Peace, A.J., Humphrey, J.W. & Broome, A.C. (2000). Relationships between vegetation, site type and stand structure in coniferous plantations in Britain. *Forest Ecology and Management*, **136**, 35-51.

Ford, E.D., Malcolm, D.C. & Atterson, J. (1979). *The Ecology of Even-aged Plantations*. Institute of Terrestrial Ecology, Cambridge.

Forestry Commission (1998). *The UK Forestry Standard: the Government's Approach to Sustainable Forestry*. Forestry Commission, Edinburgh.

Gipps, J.H.W. & Alibhai, S.K. (1991). Field vole *Microtus agrestis*. In *The Handbook of British Mammals, Third Edition*, ed. by G.B. Corbet & S. Harris. Blackwell Scientific Publications, Oxford. pp. 203-208.

Gurnell, J. (1993). Tree seed production and food conditions for rodents in an oak wood in southern England. *Forestry*, **66**, 291-315.

Hakkarainen, H. & Korpimäki, E. (1996). Competitive and predatory interactions among raptors: an observational and experimental study. *Ecology*, **77**, 1134-1142.

Hakkarainen, H., Korpimäki, E., Koivunen, V. & Kurki, S. (1997). Boreal owl response to forest management: a review. *Journal of Raptor Research*, **31**, 125-128.

Hakkarainen, H., Vesa, K., Korpimäki, E. & Kurki, S. (1996). Clear-cut areas and breeding success of Tengmalm's owl *Aegolius funereus*. *Wildlife Biology*, **2**, 253-258.

Hansson, L. (1971). Habitat, food and population dynamics of the field vole *Microtus agrestis* (L) in south Sweden. *Viltrevy*, **8**, 267-378.

Hansson, L. (1985). The food of bank voles, wood mice and yellow-necked mice. In *The Ecology of Woodland Rodents; Bank Voles and Wood Mice. Symposia of the Zoological Society of London Number 55*, ed. by J.R. Flowerdew, J. Gurnell & J.H.W. Gipps. Clarendon Press, Oxford. pp. 141-168.

Hansson, L. & Larsson, T.-B. (1978). Vole diet on experimentally managed reforestation areas in northern Sweden. *Holarctic Ecology*, **1**, 16-26.

Hart, C. (1995). *Alternative Silvicultural Systems to Clear Cutting in Britain: a Review*. Forestry Commission Bulletin 115. HMSO, London.

Hill, M.O. (1979). The development of flora in even-aged plantations. In *The Ecology of Even-aged Plantations*, ed. by E.D. Ford, D.C. Malcolm & J. Atterson. Institute of Terrestrial Ecology, Cambridge. pp. 175-192.

Hill, M. (1986). Ground flora and succession in commercial forests. In *Trees and Wildlife in the Scottish Uplands*, ed. by D. Jenkins. Institute of Terrestrial Ecology, Huntingdon. pp. 71-78.

Holtam, B.W. (1971). *Windblow of Scottish forests in January 1968*. Forestry Commission Bulletin 45. HMSO, Edinburgh.

Hörnfeldt, B. (1978). Synchronous population fluctuations in voles, small game birds, owls, tularemia in northern Sweden. *Oecologia (Berlin)*, **32**, 141-152.

Humphrey, J.W., Hawes, C., Peace, A.J., Ferris-Kaan, R. & Jukes, M.R. (1999). Relationships between insect diversity and forest habitat characteristics in plantation forests. *Forest Ecology and Management*, **113**, 11-21.

Humphrey, J.W., Newton, A.C., Peace, A.J. & Holden, E. (2000). The importance of conifer plantations in northern Britain as a habitat for native fungi. *Biological Conservation*, **96**, 241-252.

Jedrzejewski, W., Jedrzejewska, B., Szymura, A. & Zub, K. (1996). Tawny owl (*Strix aluco*) predation in a pristine deciduous forest (Bialowieza National Park, Poland). *Journal of Animal Ecology*, **65**, 105-120.

Jedrzejewski, W., Jedrzejewska, B., Zub, K., Ruprecht, A.L. & Bystrowski, C. (1994). Resource use by tawny owls *Strix aluco* in relation to rodent fluctuations in Bialowieza National Park, Poland. *Journal of Avian Biology*, **25**, 308-318.

Jensen, T.S. (1982). Seed production and outbreaks of non-cyclic rodent populations in deciduous forests. *Oecologia (Berlin)*, **54**, 184-192.

Jensen, T.S. (1985). Seed-seed predator interactions of European beech, *Fagus silvatica* and forest rodents, *Clethrionomys glareolus* and *Apodemus flavicollis*. *Oikos*, **44**, 149-156.

Johnsgard, P.A. (1988). *North American Owls: Biology and Natural History*. Smithsonian Institution Press, Washington.

Kirkland, G.L., Jr. (1990). Patterns of initial small mammal community change after clearcutting of temperate North American forests. *Oikos*, **59**, 313-320.

Kloubec, B. (2000). Spring calling activity of the tawny owl (*Strix aluco*) in southern Bohemia. *Buteo*, **11**, 87-96 (with English summary).

Korpimäki, E. (1992). Population dynamics of Fennoscandian owls in relation to wintering conditions and between-year fluctuations of food. In *The Ecology and Conservation of European Owls*, ed. by C.A. Galbraith, I.R. Taylor & S. Percival. Joint Nature Conservation Committee, Peterborough. pp. 1-10.

Korpimäki, E. & Norrdahl, K. (1985). Rapid tracking of microtine populations by their avian predators: possible evidence for stabilising predation. *Oikos*, **45**, 281-284.

Korpimäki, E. & Norrdahl, K. (1991). Numerical and functional responses of kestrels, short-eared owls and long-eared owls to vole densities. *Ecology*, **72**, 814-826.

Kurki, K., Nikula, A., Helle, P. & Lindén, H. (2000). Effects of forest fragmentation and composition on breeding success in grouse. *Ecology*, **81**, 1985-1997.

Lahti, E. & Mikkola, H. (1974). Nest sites and nesting habitats of the Ural, tawny and great grey owls. *Savon Luonto*, **6**, 1-10.

Lambin, X., Petty, S.J. & MacKinnon, J.L. (2000). Cyclic dynamics in field vole populations and generalist predation. *Journal of Animal Ecology*, **69**, 106-118.

Lindén, H., Danilov, P.I., Gromtsev, A.N., Helle, P., Ivanter, E.V. & Kurhinen, J. (2000). Large-scale forest corridors to connect the taiga fauna to Fennoscandia. *Wildlife Biology*, **6**, 179-188.

Low, A.J. (1986). *Use of Broadleaved Species in Upland Forests*. Forestry Commission Leaflet 84. HMSO, London.

Lundberg, A. (1980). Why are the Ural owl *Strix uralensis* and the tawny owl *S. aluco* parapatric in Scandinavia? *Ornis Scandinavica*, **11**, 116-120.

Lurz, P.W.W., Garson, P.J. & Rushton, S.P. (1995). The ecology of squirrels in spruce dominated plantations: implications for forest management. *Forest Ecology and Management*, **79**, 79-90.

Marquiss, M. (1993). Goshawk *Accipiter gentilis*. In *The New Atlas of Breeding Birds in Britain and Ireland: 1988-1991*, ed. by D.W. Gibbons, J.B. Reid & R.A. Chapman. Poyser, London. pp. 108-109.

Marquiss, M., Newton, I. & Ratcliffe, D.A. (1978). The decline of the raven *Corvus corax* in relation to afforestation in southern Scotland and northern England. *Journal of Applied Ecology*, **15**, 129-144.

Marquiss, M., Ratcliffe, D.A. & Roxburgh, R. (1985). The numbers, breeding success and diet of golden eagles in southern Scotland in relation to changes in land use. *Biological Conservation*, **34**, 121-140.

Mason, W.L., Kerr, G. & Simpson, J.M.S. (1999). *What is Continuous Cover Forestry?* Forestry Commission Information Note 29. Forestry Commission, Edinburgh.

McIntosh, R. (1995). The history and multi-purpose management of Kielder Forest. *Forest Ecology and Management*, **79**, 1-11.

Mikkola, H. (1976). Owls killing and killed by other owls and raptors. *British Birds*, **69**, 144-154.

Mikkola, H. (1983). *Owls of Europe.* Poyser, London.

Moss, D. (1978). Song-bird populations in forestry plantations. *Quarterly Journal of Forestry*, **72**, 5-14.

Moss, D. (1979). Even-aged plantations as a habitat for birds. In *The Ecology of Even-aged Plantations*, ed. by E.D. Ford, D.C. Malcolm & J. Atterson. Institute of Terrestrial Ecology Cambridge. pp. 413-427.

Moss, D., Taylor, P.N. & Easterbee, N. (1979). The effects on song-bird populations of upland afforestation with spruce. *Forestry*, **52**, 129-147.

Nero, R.W., Clark, R.J., Knapton, R.J. & Hamre, R.H. (1987). *Biology and conservation of northern forest owls.* General Technical Report RM-142. United States Department of Agriculture, Forest Service, Rock Mountain Forest and Range Experimental Station, Fort Collins.

Newton, I. (1979). *Population Ecology of Raptors.* Poyser, Berkhamsted.

Newton, I. (1991). Habitat variation and population regulation in sparrowhawks. *Ibis*, **133 Suppl. 1**, 76-88.

Newton, I. (1998). *Population Limitation in Birds.* Academic Press, San Diego.

Newton, I., Davis, P.E. & Davis, J.E. (1982). Ravens and buzzards in relation to sheep farming and forestry in Wales. *Journal of Applied Ecology*, **19**, 681-706.

Newton, I., Davis, P.E. & Moss, D. (1981). Distribution and breeding of red kites in relation to land-use in Wales. *Journal of Applied Ecology*, **18**, 173-186.

O'Mahony, D., Lambin, X., MacKinnon, J.L. & Coles, C.F. (1999). Fox predation on cyclic field vole populations in Britain. *Ecography*, **22**, 575-581.

Patterson, I.J., Ollason, J.G. & Doyle, P. (1995). Bird populations in upland spruce plantations in northern Britain. *Forest Ecology and Management*, **79**, 107-131.

Percival, S. (1993). Tawny owl *Strix aluco*. In *The New Atlas of Breeding Birds in Britain and Ireland: 1988-1991*, ed. by D.W. Gibbons, J.B. Reid & R.A. Chapman. Poyser, London. pp. 250-251.

Peterken, G.F. (1996). *Natural Woodlands: Ecology and Conservation in Northern Temperate Regions.* Cambridge University Press, Cambridge.

Peterken, G.F. (1999). Applying natural forestry concepts in an intensively managed landscape. *Global Ecology and Biogeograhy*, **8**, 321-328.

Peterken, G.F., Ausherman, D., Buchenau, M. & Forman, R.T.T. (1992). Old-growth conservation within British upland conifer plantations. *Forestry*, **65**, 127-144.

Petty, S.J. (1989). Productivity and density of tawny owls (*Strix aluco*) in relation to the structure of a spruce forest in Britain. *Annales Zoologic Fennici*, **26**, 227-234.

Petty, S.J. (1992). Ecology of the tawny owl *Strix aluco* in the spruce forests of Northumberland and Argyll. Ph.D. thesis. The Open University, Milton Keynes.

Petty, S.J. (1996). History of the northern goshawk *Accipiter gentilis* in Britain. In *The Introduction and Naturalisation of Birds*, ed. by J.S. Holmes & J.R. Simons. The Stationery Office, London. pp. 95-102.

Petty, S.J. (1999). Diet of tawny owls (*Strix aluco*) in relation to field vole (*Microtus agrestis*) abundance in a conifer forest in northern England. *Journal of Zoology, London*, **248**, 451-465.

Petty, S.J., Anderson, D.I.K., Davison, M., Little, L., Sherratt, T.N., Thomas, C.J. & Lambin, X. (in press). The decline of common kestrels *Falco tinnunculus* in a forested area of northern England: the role of predation by northern goshawks *Accipiter gentilis? Ibis.*

Petty, S.J. & Avery, M.I. (1990). *Forest Bird communities: a Review of the Ecology and Management of Forest Bird Communities in Relation to Silvicultural Practices in the British Uplands.* Forestry Commission Occasional Paper 26. Forestry Commission, Edinburgh.

Petty, S.J. & Fawkes, B.L. (1997). Clutch size variation in tawny owls (*Strix aluco*) from adjacent valley systems: can this be used as a surrogate to investigate temporal and spatial variations in vole density? In *Biology and Conservation of Owls of the Northern Hemisphere*, ed. by J.R. Duncan, D.H. Johnson & T.H. Nicholls. General Technical Report NC-190. United States Department of Agriculture, Forest Service, North Central Research Station, St. Paul, Minnesota. pp. 315-324.

Petty, S.J., Garson, P.J. & McIntosh, R. (Eds) (1995a). Kielder: the ecology of a man-made spruce forest. *Forest Ecology and Management*, **79**, 1-160.

Petty, S.J., Lambin, X., Sherratt, T.N., Thomas, C.J., MacKinnon, J.L., Coles, C.F., Davison, M. & Little, B. (2000). Spatial synchrony in field vole *Microtus agrestis* abundance in Kielder Forest, northern England: the role of vole-eating raptors. *Journal of Applied Ecology*, **37**, 136-147.

Petty, S.J., Patterson, I.J., Anderson, D.I.K., Little, B. & Davison, M. (1995b). Numbers, breeding performance and diet of the sparrowhawk *Accipiter nisus* and merlin *Falco columbarius* in relation to cone crops and coniferous seed-eating finches. *Forest Ecology and Management*, **79**, 133-146.

Petty, S.J. & Saurola, P. (1997). Tawny owl *Strix aluco*. In *The EBCC Atlas of European Breeding Birds: their Distribution and Abundance*, ed. by E.J. Hagemeijer & M.J. Blair. Poyser, London. pp. 410-411.

Petty, S.J., Shaw, G. & Anderson, D.I.K. (1994). Value of nest boxes for population studies and conservation of owls in coniferous forests in Britain. *Journal of Raptor Research*, **28**, 134-142.

Quine, C.P., Humphrey, J.W. & Ferris, R. (1999). Should the wind disturbance patterns observed in natural forests be mimicked in planted forests in the British Uplands? *Forestry*, **72**, 337-358.

Redpath, S.M. (1994). Censusing tawny owls *Strix aluco* by the use of imitating calls. *Bird Study*, **41**, 192-198.

Redpath, S.M. (1995). Habitat fragmentation and the individual: tawny owls (*Strix aluco*) in woodland patches. *Journal of Animal Ecology*, **64**, 652-661.

Rodwell, J. & Patterson, G. (1994). *Creating New Native Woodlands.* Forestry Commission Bulletin 112. HMSO, London.

Rolstad, J. & Wegge, P. (1987). Distribution and size of capercaillie leks in relation to old forest fragmentation. *Oecologia*, **72**, 389-394.

Shaw, G. (1995). Habitat selection by short-eared owls *Asio flammeus* in young coniferous forests. *Bird Study*, **42**, 158-164.

Sonerud, G.A. (1997). Hawk owls in Fennoscandia: population fluctuations, effects of modern forestry, and recommendations on improving foraging habitats. *Journal of Raptor Research*, **31**, 167-174.

Southern, H.N. (1970). The natural control of a population of tawny owls (*Strix aluco*). *Journal of Zoology, London*, **162**, 197-285.

Southern, H.N. & Lowe, V.P.W. (1982). Predation by tawny owls (*Strix aluco*) on bank voles (*Clethrionomys glareolus*) and wood mice (*Apodemus sylvaticus*). *Journal of Zoology, London*, **198**, 83-103.

Stenseth, N.C. (1999). Population cycles in voles and lemmings: density dependence and phase dependence in a stochastic world. *Oikos*, **87**, 427-461.

Thompson, D.B.A., Stroud, D.A. & Pienkowski, M.W. (1988). Afforestation and upland birds: consequences for population ecology. In *Ecological Change in the Uplands*, ed. by M.B. Usher & D.B.A. Thompson. Blackwell Scientific Publications, Oxford. pp. 237-260.

Thomson, L. (1996). Abundance of small mammals in relation to tree stand age. MSc Ecology thesis. University of Durham, Durham.

Ulanova, N.G. (2000). The effects of windthrow on forests at different spatial scales: a review. *Forest Ecology and Management*, **135**, 155-167.

Valender, K.A. (1991). Pine marten *Martes martes*. In *The Handbook of British Mammals, Third Edition*. ed. by G.B. Corbet & S. Harris. Blackwell Scientific Publications, Oxford. pp. 368-376.

Village, A. (1981). The diet and breeding of long-eared owls in relation to vole numbers. *Bird Study*, **28**, 215-224.

Village, A. (1987). Numbers, territory size and turnover of short-eared owls *Asio flammeus* in relation to vole abundance. *Ornis Scandinavica*, **18**, 198-204.

Wallace, H.L. & Good, J.E.G. (1995). Effects of afforestation on upland plant communities and implications for vegetation management. *Forest Ecology and Management*, **79**, 29-46.

Wegge, P., Rolstad, J. & Gjerde, I. (1992). Effects of boreal forest fragmentation on capercaillie grouse: empirical evidence and management implications. In *Wildlife 2001: Populations*, ed. by D.R. McCullough. & R.H. Barrett. Elsevier Science Publishers Ltd, Oxford. pp. 738-749.

Wendland, V. (1984). The influence of prey fluctuations on the breeding success of the tawny owl *Strix aluco*. *Ibis*, **126**, 284-296.

Whitfield, M.B. & Gaffney, M. (1997). Great gray owl (*Strix nebulosa*) breeding habitat use within altered forest landscapes. In *Biology and Conservation of Owls of the Northern Hemisphere*, ed. by J.R. Duncan, D.H. Johnson & T.H. Nicholls. General Technical Report NC-190. United States Department of Agriculture, Forest Service, North Central Research Station, St. Paul, Minnesota. pp. 498-505.

7. COMPARATIVE RESPONSES OF BARN OWL (*TYTO ALBA*) AND KESTREL (*FALCO TINNUNCULUS*) TO VOLE CYCLES IN SOUTH-WEST SCOTLAND

G. Shaw & Gordon S. Riddle

Summary

1. This study compared breeding parameters of kestrel *Falco tinnunculus* and barn owl *Tyto alba* in response to annual variations in their preferred prey base.

2. There are interesting differences in the way the two species respond to their preferred prey, with barn owls showing a stronger numerical response.

3. Only the owls showed extreme fluctuations in productivity which matched vole *Microtus* cycles.

7.1 Introduction

In grassland areas of south-west Scotland, the field vole *Microtus agrestis* is the preferred prey of barn owls *Tyto alba* and kestrels *Falco tinnunculus*. These *Microtus* populations are cyclic, typically building to a peak level of abundance every third year, followed by a collapse in numbers and subsequent recovery to the next peak (see Petty & Thomas, Chapter 6). The predators therefore experience large variations in their preferred prey from year to year. This paper compares the breeding strategies adopted by kestrels and barn owls to survive on an unstable food resource.

7.2 Study area and methods

Barn owls were studied from 1985 to 2000 in the upland conifer forests of Galloway and south Ayrshire. Rough grasslands on forest margins and in young plantations provided extensive habitat for field voles. The large cavities required by nesting barn owls were scarce in managed forests. Existing nest sites (old buildings) were supplemented by nest boxes. Each year 14–55 (mean 33) territories were occupied. For further details see Shaw (1994).

A breeding population of kestrels was studied from 1972 on the border of Ayrshire and Dumfries & Galloway. The breeding habitat was a mixture of upland rough grassland, grazed mainly by sheep, and adjacent young conifer plantations. Kestrel pairs bred in old stick nests of carrion crows *Corvus corone* and in nest boxes in shelter belts and on forest edges, on cliff and quarry ledges and in buildings. An annual sample of around 40 nesting territories was monitored, and 21–41 (mean 31) territories were occupied in each year of the study. For further details see Riddle (1993).

A vole sign index (Petty, 1999) was used to assess the abundance of field voles on the barn owl study area, in March and April each year. The two study areas were contiguous and partly overlapping, and it was assumed that the same trends in vole numbers were common to both. We compared barn owl and kestrel breeding performance over five vole cycles (1986 to 2000), looking in particular at

(a)   the proportion of the population which attempted to breed in each year (measured as the percentage of occupied territories in which at least one egg was laid);

(b)   the timing of egg-laying (measured as the mean of the first-egg dates for the first clutches laid in all territories in which eggs were produced);

(c)   clutch size (mean size of all first clutches laid in each year); and

(d)   productivity (total young fledged each year, from all breeding attempts, divided by the number of territories occupied at the start of the season).

The degree of association between the breeding parameters for each species was measured using Spearman rank correlations (r_s).

7.3 Results

7.3.1 *Trends in the number of occupied territories*

Both species showed considerable variation in breeding numbers from year to year, and each followed an approximate three-year cycle (Figure 7.1). However, there was a contrasting pattern for each species. Barn owl numbers tended to reach a peak in the year following a good vole year, and declined the next season. Kestrel numbers peaked in the good vole year, and always declined steeply in the following year.

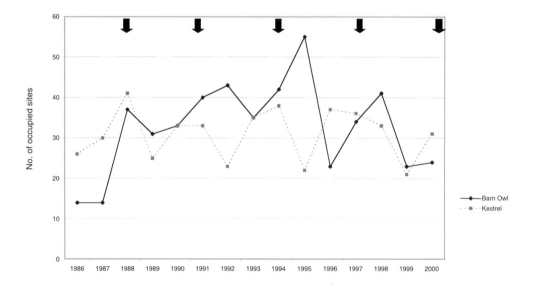

Figure 7.1. Barn owl and kestrel in south-west Scotland: annual number of occupied sites 1986-2000 (arrows = peak voles years)

7.3.2 *Breeding attempts*

In most years, eggs were laid in 90-100% of occupied kestrel territories (Figure 7.2). In contrast, while most barn owls produced eggs in years when vole numbers were high, in low vole years up to half the breeding attempts were abandoned before eggs were laid. Overall, the correspondence between the two predators was weak ($r_s = 0.31$; P >0.1; NS).

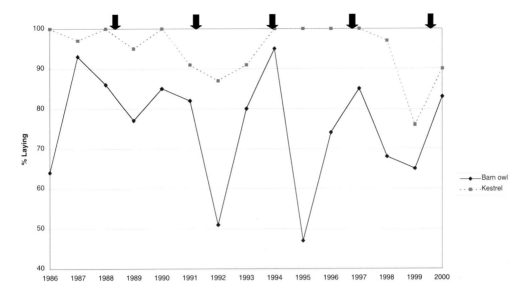

Figure 7.2. Barn owl and kestrel in south-west Scotland: annual percentage of occupied sites producing clutches 1986-2000 (arrows = peak vole years).

7.3.3 Timing of laying

There was a close relationship between the two species for the start of laying in each year (r_s = 0.62; P <0.05). The timing of laying was strongly associated with vole numbers (Figure 7.3), with clutches started earlier in peak vole years. A 3-year cycle was most pronounced in barn owls, where the mean first-egg date differed by up to 50 days between consecutive years. Kestrels showed a tighter laying pattern, but generally followed the same trend.

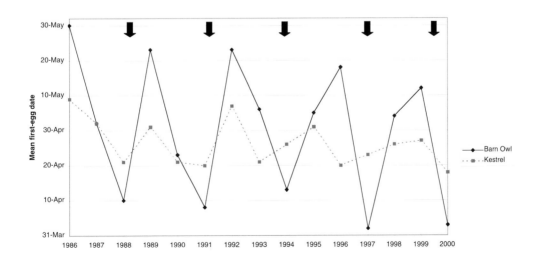

Figure 7.3. Barn owl and kestrel in south-west Scotland: mean annual first-egg dates 1986-2000 (arrows = peak vole years).

7.3.4 Clutch size

There was a similar close relationship for the number of eggs laid each year (r_s = 0.72; P <0.01). Clutch size decreased with later mean laying dates in both barn owl (r_s = -0.84; P <0.01) and kestrel (r_s = -0.59; P <0.05). Again, barn owls showed the most extreme variation between years, in particular showing a stronger response than kestrels in low vole years (Figure 7.4).

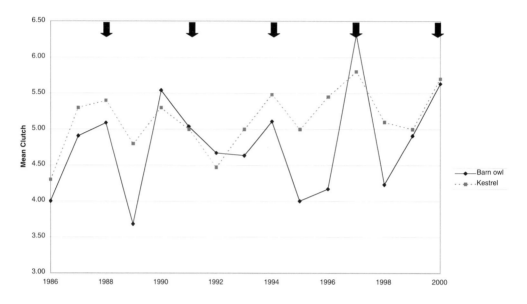

Figure 7.4. Annual variation in mean clutch size of barn owl and kestrel 1986-2000 (arrows = peak vole years).

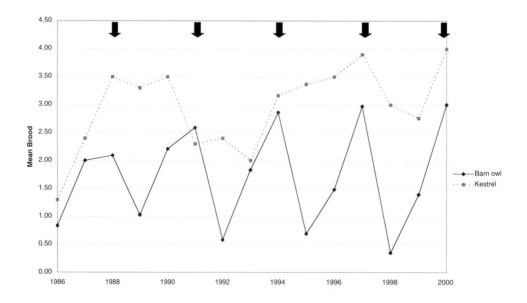

Figure 7.5. Annual variation in productivity (mean brood size per occupied territory) in barn owl and kestrel in south-west Scotland 1986-2000 (arrows = peak vole years).

7.3.5 *Productivity*

The mean number of young fledged by barn owls and kestrels each year was poorly correlated ($r_s = 0.45$; $P > 0.05$, NS). While both species fledged most young in peak vole years (Figure 7.5), kestrels consistently fledged more young than barn owls, with little evidence for the same cycles of production.

7.4 Discussion

Overall, barn owl breeding performance showed a stronger association with the annual trends in field vole numbers. Although both species bred earlier and produced more eggs in peak vole years, only the owls exhibited extreme fluctuations in productivity which matched vole cycles. Following a collapse in vole numbers, many barn owls did not breed at all; those that did laid small clutches late in the season, and productivity was very low. Most kestrels in the study area laid eggs every year, and reared young even in those years when the owls were least productive.

Barn owls were dependent on field voles in our study. Although vole abundance varied between years, both pellet analysis and fresh prey at nests showed that the diet typically comprised 70-80% *Microtus* by number. Common shrew *Sorex araneus* was the only other significant prey species (up to 20%, by number). Other small mammals present in the forest were rarely taken, possibly because they avoided the open areas hunted by owls. Kestrel diet was dominated by field voles when these were numerous, but other small mammals, birds, lizards and invertebrates featured prominently in other years. Kestrels appeared to behave as vole specialists when conditions were right, but became generalist predators, switching to alternative prey when voles were scarce.

Kestrel numbers always fell following a good vole year, while barn owl numbers increased. One possible explanation could have been an asynchrony in the vole cycle between the two study areas (Lambin *et al.*, 1998). However, the close associations for early laying and maximum clutch size over 15 years suggest that both study areas experienced vole peaks and troughs at the same time. An alternative explanation is that, following a year of high productivity, many kestrels responded to a vole crash by moving elsewhere, while most barn owls remained in the study area.

Ringing recoveries demonstrated that barn owls were resident in the study area; territories were occupied all year round. As a result, when vole numbers were high barn owls always started to breed earlier than kestrels. In such years, up to 20% of pairs reared a second brood, with young leaving the nest as late as November. As largely nocturnal hunters, barn owls could maximise their foraging time by extending their breeding season before and after the period of maximum day length. Although productivity in barn owls was depressed every third year, the birds were able to respond rapidly to increase chick production when vole numbers were high.

Kestrels were highly mobile, and from ringing recoveries it was found that the young birds dispersed to winter in southern England, Ireland and northern Europe. Returning birds had more flexibility to select areas where food resources were sufficient to support a breeding attempt. The kestrel breeding season was restricted to a single brood, and few clutches were started after mid-May. On rare occasions pairs which failed early in the clutch stage re-laid and fledged young. As diurnal predators, kestrels may be constrained to the period of greatest day length to meet the foraging demands of a brood. Nevertheless, in general productivity was higher for kestrels, but this may have been balanced by the extra risks involved in migration, and in the need to secure a territory each year.

Acknowledgements

We are grateful to two referees, Steve Petty and Mike Toms, for their constructive comments on an earlier draft.

References

Lambin, X., Elston, D., Petty, S.J. & MacKinnon, J. L. (1998). Spatial patterns and periodic travelling waves in cyclic Field Vole, *Microtus agrestis*, populations. *Proceedings of the Royal Society of London, Series B,* **265**, 1491-1496.

Petty, S.J. (1999). Diet of tawny owls (Strix aluco) in relation to field vole (Microtus agrestis) abundance in a conifer forest in northern England. *Journal of the Zoological Society of London*, **248**, 451-465.

Riddle, G.S. (1993). Research Progress Report: A 20 year study of Kestrels in Ayrshire. *Scottish Birds*, **17**, 9-13.

Shaw, G. (1994). Research Progress Report: A ten year study of Barn Owl conservation in conifer forests. *Scottish Birds,* **17**, 187-191.

8. The Status of Breeding Barn Owls (*Tyto alba*) in the United Kingdom 1995-97: Project Barn Owl

Michael P. Toms, Humphrey Q.P. Crick
& Colin R. Shawyer

Summary

1. This chapter reports on the results of Project Barn Owl Tyto alba, a three-year national survey of breeding barn owls *Tyto alba* within the United Kingdom, providing a baseline population estimate of c. 4,000 breeding pairs and based on standardized and repeatable methods.

2. It also demonstrates the occurrence of spatial and temporal patterns in the estimates, most likely linked to variations in habitat quality, climatic conditions during the breeding season and fluctuations in prey abundance.

3. Collectively, the results from the project, together with ongoing monitoring work, provide a means by which future changes in barn owl populations can be monitored and conservation objectives addressed.

8.1 Introduction

The barn owl *Tyto alba* population within the United Kingdom is widely acknowledged to have undergone a long-term decline in numbers during the past 100-150 years (Blaker, 1934; Shawyer, 1987; Gibbons *et al.*, 1993, Tucker & Heath, 1994). The decline is thought to be linked to the loss of hunting habitats and nest sites, mediated through the process of agricultural intensification (Shawyer, 1987; Taylor, 1994; Taylor & Walton, Chapter 32). The most recent survey, which estimated c. 4,500 breeding pairs (Shawyer, 1987), included a recommendation that periodic surveys should be carried out in order to monitor future population change. It was to address this objective, and to develop a repeatable and statistically precise survey methodology, that Project Barn Owl was established.

8.2 Methods

As a consequence of their distribution, ecology and behaviour, barn owls are difficult to survey accurately (Sharrock, 1976; Bibby *et al.*, 1992; Taylor, 1994). Therefore, in order to develop a suitable survey methodology, a range of survey designs was discussed by a working group involving a number of organisations; additionally, a year of pilot work involving field trials and computer simulation was carried out (see Crick *et al.*, 1994 for details). The methodology suggested by the pilot work involved the stratified-random allocation of 1,100 surveys tetrads (2 x 2 km squares), which were to be covered by volunteer fieldworkers. The stratification was based on the presence/absence of barn owls in the two periods covered by the BTO atlases of breeding birds (Gibbons *et al.*, 1993; see Toms *et al.*, 2001 for details).

Within each tetrad, fieldwork was carried out over three years (1995-1997) to allow for the effects of any short-term fluctuations in the number of breeding pairs that may have arisen from changes in prey populations (Taylor, 1994).

Fieldworkers were asked to visit their tetrads during two periods in the first and last years of the survey and during one summer period in the second year. During the first period (termed 'winter' fieldwork – November-January) fieldworkers were asked to locate and record all sites that could potentially be used by breeding barn owls. During the second fieldwork period (termed 'summer' fieldwork – mid-June to the end of August) fieldworkers were asked to revisit, under a Schedule 1 licence, all 'potential' sites and to determine their occupancy by barn owls or other species. Detailed validation work was undertaken to determine whether fieldworkers were correctly locating all breeding barn owls within their survey squares (see Toms *et al.*, 2000).

National population estimates were calculated individually for each of the three survey years using the number of confirmed breeding pairs found and knowledge of the sampling intensity. A bootstrapping procedure was used to calculate the confidence intervals (Efron & Tibshirani, 1986; Greenwood, 1991) and a Jackknife approach was adopted to examine the potential effects of regional variations in observer coverage (see Toms *et al.*, 2001).

8.3 Results

8.3.1 Coverage and survey efficiency

Over 80% of tetrads were covered at least once during the survey period and more than 55% were visited in at least two 'summer' field sessions (Table 8.1). Although levels of coverage varied regionally, reflecting the availability of fieldworkers, there was no bias associated with the presence of breeding barn owls: both time spent on fieldwork (Table 8.2) and continuation rates (from one year to the next) were similar for observers who found

Table 8.1. Barn owl population estimates derived from Project Barn Owl survey work, 1995-1997. Stratum 0 = no breeding barn owls found during either Atlas survey period; stratum 1 = breeding barn owls found in one or other Atlas survey period; and stratum 2 = breeding barn owls found in both Atlas survey periods

Year	Stratum	Number of confirmed breeding pairs	Number of squares surveyed	Total number of squares available	National estimate of breeding pairs	Lower Confidence Limit	Upper Confidence Limit
	0	0	58	18,119			
1995	1	8	243	23,617	2,830	1,951	3,761
	2	30	346	23,669			
	0	0	58	18,119			
1996	1	11	219	23,617	3,967	2,785	5,252
	2	39	332	23,669			
	0	0	52	18,119			
1997	1	13	208	23,617	3,951	2,769	5,214
	2	32	306	23,669			

Table 8.2. Time spent on 'summer' fieldwork in tetrads where confirmed breeding by barn owls took place and in tetrads where it did not (after Toms *et al.*, 2001). NS, not significant.

Year	Breeding barn owls found	Time spent (min)		Interquartile range	Mann-Whitney test results
		n	*Median*		
1995	Yes	30	375	180-570	
	No	308	352	198-565	*U*=0.021, *P*=0.88, NS
1996	Yes	36	325	158-592	
	No	271	360	210-570	*U*=0.51, *P*=0.47, NS
1997	Yes	37	360	210-615	
	No	237	330	180-525	*U*=0.96, *P*=0.33, NS

breeding owls and those who did not. The results of the validation work, which showed that no breeding barn owls were missed by fieldworkers, supported a high degree of confidence in fieldworker ability.

8.3.2 Estimates of breeding pairs

One hundred and thirty-three confirmed breeding attempts were recorded during the survey, with 79% of these coming from England, 12% from Scotland and 9% from Wales. National estimates for the individual survey years suggested a breeding population of c. 4,000 breeding pairs (Table 8.2). Although this figure is not directly comparable with the estimate derived from the 1982-1985 Hawk Trust survey (Shawyer, 1987), the latter estimate of 4,457 pairs falls within the bootstrapped confidence intervals of the current survey.

Regional differences in the estimates derived from Project Barn Owl suggested that East Anglia, south-west England, south-east England and southern Scotland supported the highest densities of barn owls per unit area, while there were also clear temporal differences between years in the number of breeding pairs reported (Table 8.3). These temporal differences were matched by corresponding patterns in a regional analysis of Nest Record

Table 8.3. Regional density estimates for barn owl breeding pairs derived from Project Barn Owl survey data, 1995-1997. Density is shown as the number of breeding pairs per 10 km square.

Region	Breeding density		
	1995	1996	1997
South-west England	3.06	3.37	4.50
Southern and Central England	1.42	3.15	2.30
East Anglia	4.05	5.60	4.55
Northern England	0.72	0.53	0.95
Wales	0.74	2.24	1.82
Southern Scotland	2.40	0.79	1.62
Northern Scotland	-	0.26	0.30
Northern Ireland	-	-	-

Scheme data: 1996 had high productivity in England but low productivity in Scotland, with almost the reverse in 1997 (Toms *et al.*, 2001). Productivity in 1995 was generally poor across both England and Scotland, something that may have contributed to the lower estimate derived for 1995, although reduced levels of coverage in several key areas also contributed to the difference between the estimate produced for 1995 and those for 1996 and 1997. This is something that was tested using a Jackknife approach, supporting the effect of reduced coverage on the 1995 estimate (Toms *et al.*, 2001).

8.4 Discussion

It would be inappropriate to make comparisons between the current survey results and those from either of the two previous studies in the United Kingdom because of the different methods employed and differences in the way in which the national estimates were calculated. Consequently, the results of Project Barn Owl provide a baseline against which future population changes can be assessed and conservation objectives judged (such as the RSPB Species Action Plan for barn owl target to increase the population size by 50% by 2010), rather than a comparison with previous estimates. However, evidence from a number of local studies suggests that in some areas barn owl populations are benefiting from targeted conservation efforts (Johnson, 1990), although other studies highlight a continued decline (Grant *et al.*, 1994a,b; Taylor *et al.*, 1999).

Importantly, the current work provides a backbone for future work on this species within Britain and sets a standard which can be adopted by other researchers across much of Europe and beyond. In addition, the study has demonstrated that volunteer fieldworkers can survey a difficult species, and that statistical precision can also be maintained using a repeatable methodology.

The regular and systematic survey of barn owl populations in the United Kingdom is an important component of future conservation work, but it must be supported by the collection of information on population parameters, nest site occupancy and habitat associations (also Taylor & Walton, Chapter 32). Such additional information is currently being gathered through an annual monitoring programme, whose basis was developed as part of Project Barn Owl (Toms, 1997).

Acknowledgements

We would like to thank the sponsors, Bayer AG, LIPHA SA, Sorex Ltd and Zeneca Agrochemicals, for their support for the project and, in particular, their representatives for their advice and help. We are also especially grateful to the hundreds of volunteers who carried out and co-ordinated the fieldwork and to the landowners who allowed us access to their land. Finally, we are equally grateful to the members of the Barn Owl Advisory Committee and to JNCC's Barn Owl Liaison Group who provided advise on the design of the survey. We also thank two anonymous referees for comments on the draft manuscript.

References

Bibby, C.J., Burgess, N.D. & Hill, D.A. (1992). *Bird Census Techniques.* Academic Press, London.

Blaker, G.B. (1934). *The Barn Owl in England and Wales.* RSPB, London.

Crick, H.Q.P., Dockerty, T., Shawyer, C.R. & Hall, B. (1994). *Project Barn Owl Pilot Year Report.* British Trust for Ornithology Research report No. 163. British Trust for Ornithology, Thetford.

Efron, B. & Tibshirani, R. (1986). Bootstrap methods for standard errors, confidence intervals and other measures of statistical accuracy. *Statistical Science*, **1**, 54-77.

Gibbons, D.W., Reid, J.B. & Chapman, R.A. (Eds). (1993). *The New Atlas of Breeding Birds in Britain and Ireland 1988-1991*. Poyser, London.

Grant, K., Lord, D. & Ramsden, D. (1994a). *The 1994 barn owl survey of Cornwall – a joint project by the Barn Owl Trust and the Cornwall Bird Watching and Preservation Society*. Barn Owl Trust research report. The Barn Owl Trust, Ashburton, Devon.

Grant, K., Pearce, G. & Ramsden, D. (1994b). The 1993 barn owl survey of Devon: a joint project by the Barn Owl Trust and the Devon Bird Watching and Preservation Society. *Devon Birds*, **47**, 31-39.

Greenwood, J.J.D. (1991). Estimating the total number and its confidence limits. *Bird Study*, **39**, 35-37.

Johnson, P.N. (1990). Barn owls in North Norfolk. Norfolk Bird and Mammal Report for 1990. Transactions of the Norfolk & Norwich Naturalists' Society, **29**, 91-95.

Sharrock, J.T.R. (1976). *The Atlas of Breeding Birds in Britain and Ireland*. Poyser, Calton.

Shawyer, C.R. (1987). *The Barn Owl in the British Isles: Its Past, Present and Future*. The Hawk Trust, London.

Taylor, I.R. (1994). *Barn Owls: Predator-Prey Relationships and Conservation*. Cambridge University Press, Cambridge.

Taylor, M., Seago, M., Allard, P. & Dorling, D. (1999). *The Birds of Norfolk*. Pica Press, Mountfield.

Toms, M.P. (1997). *Project Barn Owl: Evaluation of an Annual Monitoring Programme*. British Trust for Ornithology Research Report No. 177. British Trust for Ornithology, Thetford.

Toms, M.P., Crick, H.Q.P. & Shawyer, C.R. (2000). *Project Barn Owl: Final Report*. British Trust for Ornithology Research Report No. 197. British Trust for Ornithology, Thetford.

Toms, M.P., Crick, H.Q.P. & Shawyer, C.R. (2001) . The status of breeding Barn Owls *Tyto alba* in the United Kingdom 1995-97. *Bird Study*, **48**, 23-37.

Tucker, G.M. & Heath, M.F. (1994). *Birds in Europe: Their Conservation Status*. Bird Life Conservation Series No. 3. Bird Life, Cambridge.

9. Contrasting Population Trends of the Northern Goshawk (*Accipiter gentilis*) in the Scottish/English Borders and North-East Scotland

Mick Marquiss, Steve J. Petty,

Dave I.K. Anderson & Gavin Legge

Summary

1. Following re-colonisation in the early 1970s, goshawk *Accipiter gentilis* populations in the north-east of Scotland and the Scottish/English Borders were monitored.

2. The population in the north-east grew very slowly, at less than half the rate of that in the Borders. The occupancy of known nesting areas in the north-east was also much lower, suggesting inadequate recruitment.

3. Breeding production was high and similar in both populations so low recruitment in the north-east was due to higher losses of full-grown goshawks there.

4. It is reasoned that high losses in the north-east were unlikely to be due to environmental factors, and that persecution by game interests was responsible.

9.1 Introduction

Following deforestation and intensive persecution by game interests, the northern goshawk *Accipiter gentilis* became extinct in Scotland by the 1880s (Marquiss & Newton, 1982; Petty, 1996). Re-colonisation took place from the mid-1960s to early 1970s with the sporadic breeding by birds which had either escaped from captivity or been released (Marquiss, 1981). Two populations became established in Britain, with annual breeding from 1972 in the 'Borders' (southern Scotland and northern England) and from 1973 in north-east Scotland. Initial breeding was detected in both areas as they were systematically searched during studies of Eurasian sparrowhawks *Accipiter nisus* (Newton *et al.*, 1977). Goshawk population expansion was successful in the Borders and by 1990 the species was widespread and not uncommon (Gibbons *et al.*, 1993). In contrast, the bird remained rare in north-east Scotland. Here we detail breeding performance and trends in breeding numbers, and suggest that persecution by game managers is the most plausible explanation for the geographical difference in status.

9.2 Study areas and methods

In both areas, population monitoring began in 1972 and has continued to date. Study areas each covered approximately 500 km² of coniferous plantation forest, centred on Kielder in the Borders, and on Banchory in north-east Scotland. Maps of these areas and their patterns of land use and ecology are given in Petty *et al.* (1995) and Jenkins (1985), respectively. The main differences in woodlands were that forest blocks were smaller in the north-east where there were more tree species and a greater predominance of Scots pine *Pinus sylvestris* (Newton *et al.*, 1977, 1986; Marquiss & Rae, 2002). There was also less state-owned forest in the north-east (Forestry Authority, 1997) where much privately owned woodland and intervening terrain was used for game shooting (pheasants *Phasianus colchicus* in farmland and grouse and deer on moorland).

Woodland was systematically traversed to detect the kills, faeces, moulted feathers and nests of goshawks (Petty, 1989). As each nesting territory was newly discovered, histories were derived from the condition and content of extant nests. The layers of material from previous years' attempts were examined. If nest lining and moulted feathers were present, it was assumed that eggs had been laid and incubation started – this was confirmed where unhatched eggs were uncovered. Nest attempts were classified as successful (if the top layer contained copious nestling down, faeces and the bones of prey) and unsuccessful (if these were absent). These signs were easily discernible up to three years after a breeding attempt.

Most suitable nesting terrain was searched at least every three years, so few newly-found nesting places contained more than two or three previous attempts. The main problem was not in the interpretation of evidence from extant nests, but in the lack of evidence where nests had been lost due to windblow, forest thinning or felling. Over the years nesting attempts might thus have gone undetected where a nesting place was occupied intermittently. Where an area of forest was consistently occupied we could have missed the earliest attempts but not later ones because, after detection, the nest territory was checked annually to record occupancy and breeding performance. If, in any one year, a site of previous nesting lacked signs or nest refurbishment, it was classified as unoccupied and the surrounding woodland was searched thoroughly to detect alternative nesting places or to confirm their absence.

9.3 Results

9.3.1 Population trends

There was good evidence that both populations started with a few birds which had escaped or been deliberately released (Marquiss, 1981; Petty, 1996). The population in the Borders rose exponentially in the 1980s, following the first known production of young in 1977, to reach 87 pairs in 1996 (Figure 9.1). Birds in the north-east first raised a brood four years earlier (1973), but that population did not start increasing until 1990. The subsequent population growth rate in the north-east was half that of the Borders' population and in 1997, even with exhaustive searching, only 17 pairs could be found.

9.3.2 Occupancy of known nesting areas

Despite an abundance of nest sites in the north-east, there were large areas of woodland that lacked goshawks. Moreover, occupancy of known nesting areas was low. Only 29-81% of previously recorded nesting areas in the north-east were occupied in individual years, compared with 89-100% for the Borders' population. Even when restricting the comparison to similar stages in population growth (years with between 5 and 17 pairs), a median of 100% of nesting territories were occupied annually in the Borders, but only 70% in the north-east; a significant difference (Mann-Whitney test, adjusted for ties, $W_{5, 10} = 55$, P <0.005).

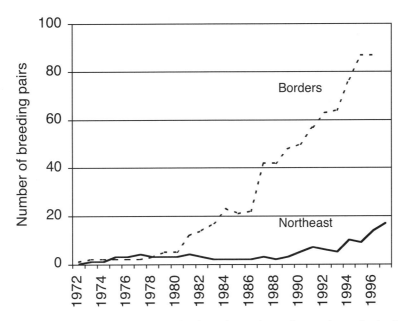

Figure 9.1. Population trends in northern goshawks in the Borders and in north-east Scotland, 1972-1997.

Table 9.1. Breeding performance of northern goshawks in the Borders and in north-east Scotland. NS, not significant.

	Borders *(n = 522)*	*North-east* *(n = 127)*	
% Failed to lay	6.9%	5.5%	χ^2 = 2.04, NS
Mean clutch size	3.79	3.69	t = 0.92, NS
% Reared young	86.2%	84.3%	χ^2 = 0.93, NS
Mean brood size	2.89	2.89	t = 0.01, NS
Young/pair	2.49	2.44	

9.3.3 Breeding performance

The breeding performance of goshawks was similar in both areas (Table 9.1) and high compared with figures from elsewhere. Other studies in Europe have found 2.3 young per pair per year in lowland Britain (Anon, 1990), 1.9 in Wales (Toyne, 1994), 3.0 in Switzerland (Buhler *et al.*, 1987), 1.6 in The Netherlands (Bijlsma, 1994) and 1.8 in Sweden (Widén, 1985). Both of our study areas have therefore produced potential recruits at a similar and relatively high rate.

9.3.4 Recruitment to the breeding population

Most goshawks mature and breed in their second year (Cramp & Simmons, 1977). Thus, at least in the colonisation phase, population growth should be linked to the number of young produced two years previously. We tested this idea using multiple regression of year-to-year breeding population change against the total production of young in each of the three previous years. We used data from both populations but only from comparable periods (during population increase up to 17 pairs). As predicted, the annual increase was significantly related to production two years previously (t = 3.21, P<0.005), the relationship explaining 26% of the overall variation. There was no significant association between annual increment and production one year (t = 1.38, NS) or three years (t = -0.93, NS) previously.

In the north-east, the breeding population increased on average by one pair for every 9.5 young fledged two years earlier. In contrast, in the Borders over the same phase of population growth, only 6.0 young had to fledge to produce each additional breeding pair. This suggested that the loss of full-grown birds was higher in the north-east.

9.4 Discussion

The goshawk population in the north-east grew very slowly compared with that in the Borders. We probably missed some breeding attempts in the north-east as previously used nests were destroyed by timber operations before we discovered the nesting site. However, this was insufficient explanation for the very low population 25 years after initial colonisation. Neither could it account for the high proportion of previously recorded nesting areas that were searched annually but remained unoccupied. The latter suggested a shortage of recruits to maintain the occupancy of existing nest areas, let alone fuel rapid population increase in the north-east.

Fledged young were produced at a similar rate per breeding attempt in the two populations, suggesting that the loss of full-grown birds was greater in the north-east. This could have been because more of them dispersed from the area or because fewer of them survived. Goshawks in Britain are not migratory and the median natal dispersal distance is only 21 km (Petty, 2002), so the pattern of breeding range increase is one of creeping expansion (Lensink, 1997). The size of the study areas was sufficient to encompass average natal dispersal. The high breeding performance of the two populations in the present study suggests that food supply was good, so it is unlikely that birds in the north-east dispersed farther or survived less well because of food shortage.

We suggest that the different population growth rates reflect different levels of post-fledging mortality due to persecution. Goshawk persecution is common in Britain. Forty-two percent of the known deaths of ringed birds were classified as 'deliberately taken by man' (Petty, 2002). In the Borders, extensive state-owned forests provide secure nesting places for goshawks, but far-dispersing juveniles are still killed at pheasant release pens (Petty & Anderson, 1996). In the north-east, more than half of the forest area is privately owned and is often used to harbour pheasant release pens. Other forests are close to moorland or farmland, and are used for shooting game.

Pheasant release pens attract goshawks (Kenward, 1977; Allen & Feare, Chapter 34) and in a UK-wide questionnaire survey for the British Association for Shooting and Conservation, goshawks were said to be a problem in the north-east of Scotland (Harradine *et al.*, 1997). This is consistent with our records of at least 23 birds reported killed (Table 9.2). This information came from our own observations and also from local bird recorders and the Royal Society for the Protection of Birds (RSPB, unpublished). In the 1970s and early 1980s we also received reports from gamekeepers who sometimes additionally produced goshawk remains or a ring to support their claims of a large 'novel' predator at pheasant pens.

Table 9.2. Reported incidents of the illegal persecution of northern goshawks in north-east Scotland, 1973-1997. These records are a likely underestimate of actual persecution (Petty, 2002).

Reported details on persecution	*First year birds*	*Older birds*	*Age unknown*	*Total*
Birds at pheasant pens	10	1	1	12
Birds at crow traps	4	1	1	6
Birds 'shot'	2	2	-	4
Birds 'killed'	1	-	-	1
Total	17	4	2	23

Goshawks may indeed be a problem for game rearing in the north-east, but persecution is illegal and the situation is clearly unsatisfactory for both game managers and hawks. Effective non-lethal methods of deterring predation by goshawks at pheasant release pens are required (Allen & Feare, Chapter 34; Galbraith *et al.*, Chapter 41). If such methods can be developed and implemented in the north-east, we predict that the breeding population should increase at a rate similar to or even higher than that of the Borders' population. We also predict that known nesting areas in the north-east would then be occupied almost continuously, as occurs within the Borders' forest.

Acknowledgements

We acknowledge the help of landowners, tenants and land managers, particularly Forest Enterprise, for access to study areas; Nick Picozzi, Robert Rae, Keith Duncan, Eddie Duthie, Mick Canham, Rodney Hislop and Neil Cook for help in the north-east; the Borders Goshawk Study Group for help in the Borders; local bird recorders and the RSPB for information on persecution incidents; Scottish Natural Heritage and English Nature for issuing licences to disturb goshawks for the purposes of monitoring; and David Jardine and Chris Quine for comments on an earlier draft of the manuscript.

References

Anonymous (1990). Breeding biology of goshawks in lowland Britain. *British Birds*, **83**, 527-540.

Bijlsma, R.G. (1994). *Ecologishe Atlas van de Nederlandse Roofvogels.* Haarlem (NL), Schuyt.

Buhler, U., Klaus, R. & Schlosser, W. (1987). Brutbestand und Jungenproduktion des Habichts *Accipiter gentilis* in der Nordostschweiz 1979-1984. *Der Ornithologische Beobachter*, **84**, 95-110.

Cramp, S. & Simmons, K.E.L. (Eds) (1980). *The Birds of the Western Palearctic, Volume II.* Oxford University Press, Oxford.

Forestry Authority (1997). *National Inventory of Woodland and Trees, Scotland – Grampian Region.* Forestry Commission. Edinburgh.

Gibbons, D.W., Reid, J.B. & Chapman, R.A. (Eds) (1993). *The New Atlas of Breeding Birds in Britain and Ireland: 1988-1991.* T. & A.D. Poyser, London.

Harradine, J., Reynolds, N. & Laws, T. (1997). *Raptors and Gamebirds – a Survey of Game Managers Affected by Raptors.* British Association for Shooting and Conservation. Marford Mill.

Jenkins, D. (Ed). (1985). *The Biology and Management of the River Dee.* Institute of Terrestrial Ecology

Symposium Number 14. Institute of Terrestrial Ecology. Huntingdon.

Kenward, R. (1977). Predation on released pheasants (*Phasianus colchicus*) by goshawks in Central Sweden. *Viltrevy*, **10**, 79-112.

Lensink, R. (1997). Range expansion of raptors in Britain and the Netherlands since the 1960s: testing an individual-based diffusion model. *Journal of Animal Ecology*, **66**, 811-826.

Marquiss, M. (1981). The Goshawk in Britain – its provenance and current status. In *Understanding the Goshawk*, ed. by R.E. Kenward & M.I. Lindsay. International Association for Falconry, Oxford. pp. 43-55.

Marquiss M. & Newton, I. (1982). The Goshawk in Britain. *British Birds*, **75**, 243-260.

Marquiss, M. & Rae, R. (2002). Ecological differentiation in relation to bill size amongst sympatric, genetically undifferentiated Crossbills *Loxia* spp. *Ibis*, **144**, 494-508.

Newton, I., Marquiss, M., Weir, D.N. & Moss, D. (1977). Spacing of sparrowhawk nesting territories. *Journal of Animal Ecology*, **46**, 425-441

Newton, I., Wyllie, I. & Mearns, R. (1986). Spacing of sparrowhawks in relation to food supply. *Journal of Animal Ecology*, **55**, 361-370.

Petty, S.J. (1989). *Goshawks: their Status, Requirements and Management*. Forestry Commission Bulletin No. 81. HMSO, London.

Petty, S.J. (1996). History of the northern goshawk *Accipiter gentilis* in Britain. In *The Introduction and Naturalisation of Birds*, ed. by J.S. Holmes & J.R. Simons. HMSO, London. pp. 95-102.

Petty, S.J. (2002). Northern goshawk (Goshawk) *Accipter gentilis*. In *The Migration Atlas: Movements of the Birds of Britain and Ireland*, ed. by C. Wernham, M.P. Toms, J.P. Marchant, J.A. Clark, G.M. Siriwardena & S.R. Baillie. T. & A.D. Poyser, London. pp. 232-234.

Petty, S.J. & Anderson, D.I.K. (1996). Population growth and breeding performance of goshawks in the English/Scottish Borders during 1987-1996. *Forestry Commission Research Division Report*. HMSO, Edinburgh.

Petty, S.J., Garson, P.J. & McIntosh, R. (Eds) (1995). Kielder – the ecology of a man-made spruce forest. *Forest Ecology and Management* (special issue), **79**, 1-2.

Toyne, E.P. (1994). *Studies of the Ecology of the Northern Goshawk Accipiter gentilis in Britain*. PhD Thesis, University of London, London.

Widén, P. (1985). Breeding and movements of goshawks in boreal forests in Sweden. *Holarctic Ecology*, **8**, 273-279.

10. GOLDEN EAGLE (*AQUILA CHRYSAETOS*) BREEDING PERFORMANCE IN RELATION TO CLIMATE IN WESTERN SCOTLAND DURING THE PERIOD 1981-2000

J. Watson, A.H. Fielding, D.P. Whitfield, R.A. Broad, P.F. Haworth, K. Nellist, K. Crane & E.J. Macdonald

Summary

1.   This chapter considers the effects of weather on golden eagle *Aquila chrysaetos* breeding performance in three study areas (Skye, Mull and Lochaber) in Western Scotland over a 20 year period.

2.   Three measures of breeding success were used in the analysis: fledging success (number of young fledged/territorial pair/year); the proportion of occupied ranges that fledged at least one young; and the proportion of successful pairs rearing twins.

3.   Over the course of the study, eagle breeding performance was consistently highest on Skye with an average 0.58 young fledged/pair/year and 19% of successful pairs rearing twins.   Equivalent figures for Mull were 0.46 and 11%, and for Lochaber, 0.31 and 5%.   No study area showed significant long-term trends in performance although all three showed marked between year variation.

4.   Relationships between productivity and weather were different in each of the three areas, although there was a general tendency for productivity to be positively correlated with temperature during some part of the preceding winter, and to be negatively correlated with rainfall in spring.

5.   The diet of golden eagles during the breeding season in each of the three study areas is different. In Skye the predominant prey animals are rabbits *Oryctolagus cuniculus* and fulmars *Fulmaris glacialis*; in Mull substantial prey comprise mountain hares *Lepus timidus*; and in Lochaber eagles display a catholic diet with no particular prey species predominant.

6.   Our paper describes the possible links between weather effects, food availability and productivity in different parts of the golden eagle's range in Western Scotland.

10.1 Introduction

A range of potentially interacting factors influences the productivity of Scottish golden eagles *Aquila chrysaetos*. If events such as intentional disturbance are excluded they can be summarized as prey availability and the ability of the birds to obtain sufficient food to satisfy parental and offspring requirements. Previous studies (e.g. Gargett, 1990; Watson, 1997; Steenhof *et al.*, 1997) indicated that weather can make a significant contribution overall to golden eagle reproductive success. Weather may help to determine the amount of available food, including carrion, and in certain conditions, such as heavy rainfall or high wind speeds, may make prey capture and transport difficult or energetically expensive. Extreme weather events, such as late frosts, which coincide with critical periods of eagle reproductive phenology, can have direct impacts, particularly on eggs or chicks. Understanding the contribution weather makes to between-years variability in golden eagle productivity is important, not least because it can help to clarify the impact of other important processes, such as land use change, which may be operating over the same timescale.

Although it now seems certain that the world is experiencing a period of relatively rapid climate change, it is less certain how these changes will be manifested at the local scale. Harrison (1997) presented evidence for changes in the Scottish climate (1964-1993) that were consistent with more westerlies during winter, a trend that could be linked to global warming effects. The dominant westerly airflows across the Atlantic Ocean are important determinants of the north-west of Scotland's oceanic climate. In addition, ameliorating influences of the North Atlantic Drift mean that winters are much milder than would be expected from Scotland's latitude. The oceanic nature of the west of Scotland's climate may have two potentially important influences on golden eagle productivity. First, because the annual temperature curve is relatively flat, a small change in average temperature could affect the length of the plant-growing season (Pepin, 1995). Therefore, even small changes in average temperatures may alter the quantity of live prey and carrion. For example, Bell & Webb (1991) showed that reproductive changes in the rabbit *Oryctolagus cuniculus* probably depend on the effects of climate on food quality and quantity. Second, north-western Scotland has a high temperature lapse rate. For example, during the daytime it may reach 1°C 100 m^{-1}, resulting in an increase of 17 frost-affected days per 100 m rise (Harrison & Harrison, 1988). Consequently, if there is a relationship between weather and golden eagle productivity we might expect it to be particularly strong in mountainous oceanic regions, such as Western Scotland.

In this chapter we describe a study of the effects of climate on golden eagle productivity in three regions: Skye, Mull and Lochaber. The main aim of this study was to provide answers to three questions:- 1) What, if any, productivity trends are apparent? 2) If trends are apparent are they synchronized across the three regions? 3) Can golden eagle productivity be linked to spatial or temporal climatic variability?

10.2 Methods

10.2.1 *Study areas*

Skye is the largest of the Inner Hebridean Islands (57°23′N 06°12′W, area 1,656.0 km²). For the purposes of this study the islands of Raasay (57°25′N 06°03′W, area 64.0 km²) and Scalpay (57°18′N 05°58′W, area 24.8 km²) are included as part of the Skye region. Skye is dominated by heather and bog with only around 10% of the land under conifer afforestation. Skye has a variety of rock types, with a large extent of Tertiary basalts, gabbros and granites in the north and centre. Jurassic sediments predominate along the north-east coast of Trotternish, whilst Sleat comprises mainly gneiss, schist and Torridonian sandstone. Mull (56°27′N 06°00′W) covers 875.0 km² (924.0 km² including all subsidiary islands such as Ulva and Gometra) and is the second largest of the Inner Hebridean islands. Much of Mull has a characteristic terraced landscape, derived from the predominant basaltic lava flows that form most of the island. There are also significant regions of schist, granite and sedimentary rock. Most of Mull is used for sheep and cattle grazing, although sheep densities are lower than many areas in the western Highlands and

Islands of Scotland (Fuller & Gough, 1999). There are also large numbers of red deer *Cervus elaphus* and feral goats *Capra hircus*. Numbers of red grouse *Lagopus lagopus scoticus* and ptarmigan *Lagopus mutus*, common prey of golden eagles in many parts of Scotland (Watson, 1997) are low, but there are high numbers of the introduced Irish mountain hare *Lepus timidus hibernicus* and rabbits are common in some coastal locations. Approximately 15% of the island is covered with commercial conifer plantations (including recently felled plantation). The Lochaber study area (56°50'N 05°30'W) included the southern half of that district, from Ardnamurchan in the west to Ardgour in the east, and south to Morvern and the Sound of Mull. The region is composed of a complex series of Moine schists to the north and east. Basic intrusive rocks predominate in Ardnamurchan, whilst Morvern comprises granite outcrops, schists and some Tertiary basalts. The majority of the land is dominated by acidic grassland, bog, patchy heather and montane vegetation. Approximately 10% of the land is commercial conifer forest and there are quite extensive areas of semi-natural oak woodland in both Morvern and Ardnamurchan. The major land use is deer forest in the higher hills with sheep on lower hills and near the coast. Numbers of red grouse and mountain hare are extremely low. There are small numbers of ptarmigan on the higher hills of Morvern and Ardgour and rabbits occur in some coastal areas, notably at the west end of Ardnamurchan.

10.2.2 Productivity data

Fieldwork methods were essentially those used on the two national surveys of golden eagles in Britain (Dennis *et al.*, 1984; Green, 1996) and involved visiting all, or a large subset, of known home ranges with a history of nesting or occupation by golden eagles together with potential nesting areas. Each home range was given a name and a unique code, and each nest site within a range was assigned a letter in order to maintain co-ordination between observers. Actual and potential nest sites were first visited in January to early March to establish presence or absence of eagles. All observations of eagles were recorded including, if possible, the age of individuals (adult or subadult based on the amount of white markings on the wings and tail). Any indications of nests having been built up with the addition of sticks or fresh lining material were also recorded with the appropriate nest site codes if possible. If no eagles were noted on the first visit, then subsequent visits were usually attempted to reduce the chances that any birds had been overlooked.

For occupied ranges later visits were made at appropriate times to follow the fate of possible breeding attempts. The number of eggs and/or chicks in a nest was recorded if it was possible to do so without disturbance to the breeding birds and if the nest site was readily accessible. Otherwise, observations of a bird apparently incubating or brooding on a nest were taken to be indicative of an active breeding attempt. Final visits were made to nest sites in July or early August to determine the number of chicks close to fledging. If no chicks were in the nest but fledglings were observed close by, these were assumed to have fledged from the focal nest site (Bahat, 1992). Chicks near to fledging were assumed to have fledged successfully (see also Kochert *et al.*, 1999; McIntyre & Adams, 1999). Reasonably comprehensive data are available for all regions between 1981 and 2000.

In order to assess the possible influence of weather it is necessary to have some measure of productivity. Because the number of surveyed ranges differed between years (Table 10.1), it is inappropriate to use a simple count of the observed number of fledged eagles. The basic

Table 10.1. Productivity data from three regions. 'Occupied' is the number of ranges containing a pair of eagles; 'Bred' is the number of ranges fledging at least one young; 'Fledged' is the number of young fledged; 'FR' is the fledging rates (fledged/occupied ranges); and 'Twins' is the number of ranges fledging two young.

Region	Year	Occupied	Bred	Fledged	FR	Twins
Skye	1982	28	15	16	0.57	1
	1983	19	9	9	0.47	0
	1984	27	15	17	0.63	2
	1985	30	15	17	0.57	2
	1986	30	10	13	0.43	3
	1987	30	15	16	0.53	1
	1988	30	15	21	0.70	6
	1989	29	19	25	0.86	6
	1990	29	15	20	0.69	5
	1991	28	13	15	0.54	2
	1992	30	12	13	0.43	1
	1993	29	12	15	0.52	3
	1994	29	14	14	0.48	0
	1995	31	19	21	0.68	2
	1996	32	14	19	0.59	5
	1997	32	13	14	0.44	1
	1998	32	16	24	0.75	8
	1999	32	15	17	0.53	2
	2000	31	14	17	0.55	3
Mull	1982	24	12	14	0.58	2
	1983	23	6	6	0.26	0
	1984	27	9	10	0.37	1
	1985	27	14	14	0.52	0
	1986	29	6	6	0.21	0
	1987	30	8	10	0.33	2
	1988	31	12	15	0.48	3
	1989	30	14	16	0.53	2
	1990	27	10	12	0.44	2
	1991	30	16	18	0.60	2
	1992	31	10	10	0.32	0
	1993	19	10	11	0.58	1
	1994	27	12	13	0.48	1
	1995	23	8	9	0.39	1
	1996	21	10	11	0.52	1
	1997	25	14	15	0.60	1
	1998	27	12	14	0.52	2
	1999	27	9	9	0.33	0
	2000	27	10	12	0.44	2
Lochaber	1982	20	7	8	0.40	1
	1983	20	4	4	0.20	0
	1984	20	5	5	0.25	0
	1985	20	6	6	0.30	0
	1986	18	3	3	0.17	0
	1987	18	6	6	0.33	0
	1988	15	5	6	0.40	1
	1989	16	7	7	0.44	0
	1990	15	6	6	0.40	0
	1991	18	7	7	0.39	0
	1992	20	4	4	0.20	0
	1993	16	6	6	0.38	0
	1994	19	4	4	0.21	0
	1995	20	5	6	0.30	1
	1996	18	3	3	0.17	0
	1997	21	7	7	0.33	0
	1998	20	6	8	0.40	2
	1999	20	5	5	0.25	0
	2000	20	6	6	0.30	0

productivity measure was the number of young fledged per territorial pair per year (fledging rate). However, two separate elements determine this figure: the number of ranges fledging twins and the number of ranges fledging young. Consequently, two other measures were also investigated: (i) proportion of successful ranges fledging twins; and (ii) proportion of occupied sites fledging at least one chick (proportion successful). Surveyed ranges were excluded if no adult birds were seen or eggs were known to have been stolen.

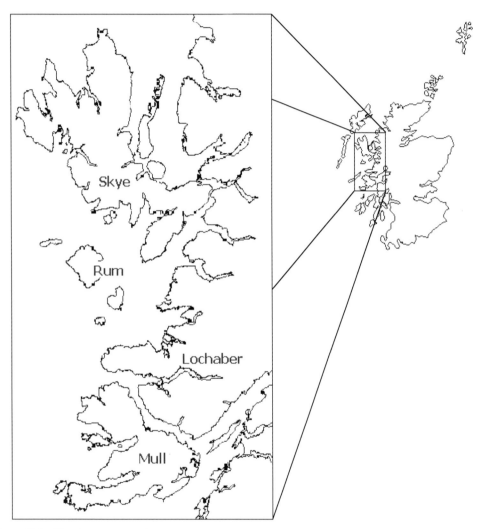

Figure 10.1. The three survey regions.

10.2.3 Weather data

All weather data were obtained from the British Atmospheric Data Centre (BADC) (http://www.badc.rl.ac.uk/). Comprehensive weather data were available on Mull from the Aros weather station (56.53°N, -5.98°W). There were no long-term weather records of sufficient continuity to allow separate treatment for Skye and Lochaber. The closest weather station to both was on the island of Rum (57.01°N, -6.28°W). Daily records (1981-1999) were extracted from BADC data files. However, because of missing data, weather analyses were restricted to 1981-1998 (6,575 days). Although five weather variables were available most were closely correlated. Consequently, only two variables considered most likely to affect eagles and their prey were retained: mean maximum daily temperature (0.1°C precision) and mean daily rainfall (0.1 mm precision). These data were summarized in two formats for use in subsequent analyses. The first are monthly averages calculated for each calendar year or month. As calendar month boundaries are rather arbitrary, and relationships may not be detected if they cross months, a more comprehensive approach is to calculate the equivalent of 365 overlapping 'months'. Thirty-day running means were obtained for each day in turn by starting on January 1st and finding weather means for the period January 1st to January 30th, this was repeated for January 2nd to January 31st, January 3rd to February 1st, etc. The end of the year was wrapped around into the next year, e.g. December 31st to January 29th. Data for February 29th were excluded. Three hundred and sixty-five 30-day means are generated, 12 of which almost coincide with the usual monthly boundaries; these are called 'running means'. The 30-day period was used to provide comparability with the monthly summaries. Shorter durations introduced statistical noise, while longer runs smoothed the weather patterns.

10.2.4 Statistical methods

The simplest approach involved the calculation of all possible correlations (0.05 significance level) between weather variables and productivity measures. These correlations were restricted to individual calendar months October to July (weather for the period between October and December was correlated with eagle productivity in the subsequent year). This is a useful exploratory technique but only linear relationships will be detected and many coefficients will lack power so Type II errors are quite likely, making it difficult to detect relationships unless they are quite strong and coincide with calendar boundaries. Productivity measures were also correlated with the running means (October to July) and plotted as correlograms, effectively a simplified cross-correlation (e.g. Legendre & Legendre, 1998, p. 661). Although spurious significant correlations are inevitable given the number of tests, it is clear that seasonal patterns in the correlograms combined with relationships between the magnitudes of the correlation coefficients and reproductive events (phenology) that will provide support for hypotheses which then require additional confirmatory investigations.

10.3 Results

The number of pairs monitored varied between area and between years, and was between 19 and 32 on Skye (mean 29.4 per year), 15 and 21 in Lochaber (mean 18.6 per year) and 19 and 31 on Mull (mean 26.6 per year). In most years over 90% of known ranges were surveyed. Skye had consistently the highest success (0.58 young/pair and 19% of successful pairs rearing twins). Mull was next with 0.46 and 11%, respectively. Lochaber was the poorest with 0.31 and 5%, respectively (Table 10.1). Fledging rates were significantly related to the percentage of successful ranges in all three regions (R^2 values: Skye 62.0%; Mull 93.8%; Lochaber 88.1%). On Skye, fledging rate (FR) had a significant linear relationship with the twin frequency (FR = 0.481 + 0.503 twin frequency, R^2 = 34.2%). Thus the magnitude of the Skye fledging rate was closely related to the proportion of ranges fledging twins. On Mull, the relationship between the fledging rate and twin frequency was non-linear (FR = 0.331 + 3.145 twin frequency − 11.43 twin frequency^2, R^2 = 42.6%). Thus, on Mull, the maximum proportion of successful ranges fledging twins occurred when fledging rates were around the average. There were insufficient twins in Lochaber for a valid analysis, but the trend appears to be linear. Twin production was particularly good in all regions between 1987 and 1991.

There were no significant long-term trends in performance in any of the three areas over the three years (regression lines of productivity versus year were all insignificant with P >0.25). There was no serial autocorrelation in the productivity measures (Durbin Watson statistic >1.5 in all cases). In all three regions overall fledging success showed marked fluctuations between years, but there was some between-region synchrony that becomes clearer if fledging rates are replaced by standardized (*z*) values (Figure 10.2a). In Figure 10.2a, a standardized fledging rate of 0 is equal to the regional mean, negative values are

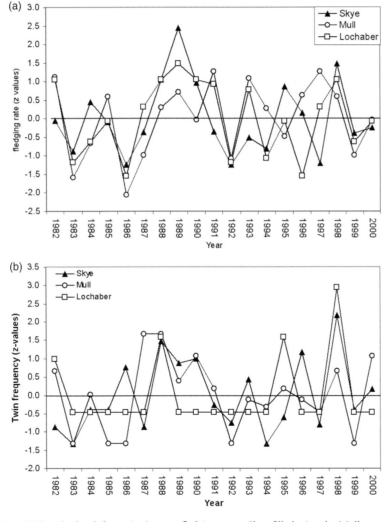

Figure 10.2. (a) Standardised (by region) mean fledging rates: Skye filled triangle; Mull open circle; Lochaber open square. (b) Mean standardized (by region) twin frequency: Skye filled triangle; Mull open circle; Lochaber open square.

below average for that region and *vice versa*. Between-region productivity synchrony was investigated by correlating regional productivity across years. Good years in Skye tended to be good in Lochaber and *vice versa* (P <0.01), and good years in Mull tended to be good in Lochaber and *vice versa* (P <0.01). There were, however, no significant between-years correlations on Skye and Mull, mainly due to a loss of synchrony between 1995-1997 inclusive. There is less obvious synchrony in twin frequency (Figure 10.2b). Although there were years which were consistently good or bad across the regions, none of the between-regions correlations were significant.

No significant correlations were found between the two weather variables, based on calendar month data, and breeding performance in the three areas. However, when productivity measures were correlated with the running means, several periods of significant correlations became apparent (Figures 10.3, 10.4 and 10.5). On Skye (Figure 10.3) there was a significant positive correlation between temperature and performance in the following year for the 30-day periods beginning 20th October through to 2nd November and again from 6th December to 26th December. There were no other significant correlations with temperature on Skye. For rainfall, there was a significant negative correlation from 27th October to 5th November, a significant positive correlation from 6th January until 28th January, and a significant negative correlation from 2nd April until 27th April. The only significant correlation with twin production was a negative correlation with temperature from mid-November to early December. In summary, warm autumn/early winter, wet midwinter and dry April are 'good' for eagle breeding success on Skye.

On Mull (Figure 10.4) there was no significant correlation (positive or negative) between temperature and fledging rate in autumn/winter, but there was a highly significant positive correlation between fledging rate and temperature in March (15th to 28th). There was significant negative correlation between fledging rate and rainfall in December (11th to 15th and 22nd to 24th). Unlike Skye and Lochaber there was no link between rainfall and fledging rate in spring, but there was a significant negative correlation with twin production and rainfall for the period 17th to 24th April, and 5th to 6th May. In summary, dry weather in December, warm weather in March are 'good' for fledging rate on Mull, and dry weather in April is 'good' for twin production.

In Lochaber (Figure 10.5) there was no 'autumn' link between weather and fledged young/pair (although there was a significant positive correlation between temperature from 23rd October to 1st November and twin production in the following year). There was a significant positive correlation with temperature and fledging rate in January/February (20th January to 5th February) and in March (7th to 10th and 20th to 28th). Like Skye, there was a positive link with rainfall in January (17th to 20th) and more prolonged negative links with rainfall in late March/April (twin frequency – 29th March to 3rd April and fledging rate – 8th to 18th April) with further significant negative correlations with rainfall in May (16th to 26th May). In summary, warm autumn/early winter is 'good' for twin production, but the strongest links between temperature and fledging rate are later than in Skye (January and March). A dry April is 'good' for fledging rate, as is dry weather in May.

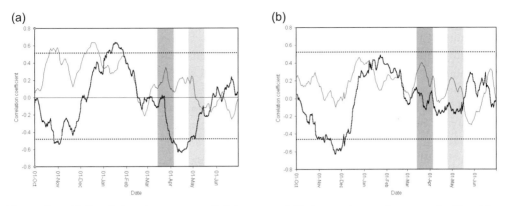

Figure 10.3. (a) Correlations between mean fledging rate and 30-day running weather means for Skye: Mean daily rainfall – thick line; Mean daily maximum temperature – thin line. The darker shaded section shows the approximate laying dates and the lighter shaded section marks the approximate hatching dates. Horizontal dotted lines are notional critical values for the correlation coefficient (0.05, 2-tailed). (b) Correlations between mean twin frequency and 30-day running weather means for Skye: Mean daily rainfall – thick line; Mean daily maximum temperature – thin line.

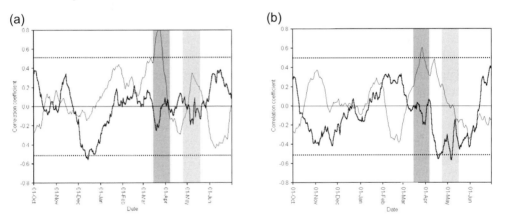

Figure 10.4. (a) Correlations between mean fledging rate and 30-day running weather means for Mull. (b) Correlations between mean twin frequency and 30-day running weather means for Mull.

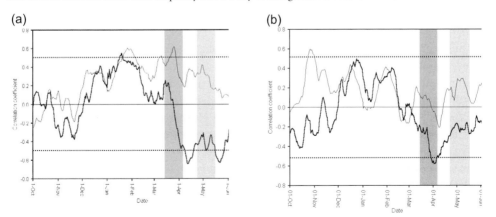

Figure 10.5. (a) Correlations between mean fledging rate and 30-day running weather means for Lochaber. (b) Correlations between mean twin frequency and 30-day running weather means for Lochaber.

10.4 Discussion

The results of this study may be indicative of a large proportion of the western Scottish golden eagle population since the surveyed pairs represent almost 20% of the total Scottish population. Overall, the Scottish population remained stable from 1982 to 1992 (Green, 1996), and there is no indication that the number of breeding pairs of golden eagles in Skye, Mull or Lochaber has changed throughout the period 1982-2000. Despite the considerable between-year fluctuations there was no evidence for any trends in overall golden eagle productivity in any of the regions. Unfortunately there are no comparable data, covering the same period for Scottish breeding pairs from other regions, that can be used to put these results into a national context.

Generic differences in performance between the three areas are linked to known differences in the amount of 'live prey' available to eagles in the three areas, but not to the total amount of available food. On Skye there is an estimated 27 kg live prey/20 km transect, 7 kg of live prey/20 km transect on Mull and 2 kg of live prey/20 km in Lochaber. If carrion is included the amounts increase to 124 kg (Skye), 75 kg (Mull) and 91 kg (Lochaber) (Watson *et al.,* 1992). Between-years differences in productivity appear to be a function of the proportion of ranges fledging young (all regions), although on Skye these differences are also strongly linked to changes in twin frequency. Steenhof *et al.* (1997) also noted that the overall breeding success of a golden eagle population was related to the proportion of pairs that bred.

Fledging rate synchrony, and the obvious good and bad years for twins, is suggestive of widespread rather than local influences on productivity. One obvious candidate for a wide scale effect is the weather. There are at least four periods in golden eagle reproductive phenology that could be influenced by the weather. First, there is the period before eggs are laid when females must accumulate sufficient resources to maintain body condition. The second period begins once eggs have been laid. Watson (1997) suggests that two-thirds of Scottish birds lay eggs between the 16th March and 4th April. The laying date appears to have some plasticity and may be influenced by the February weather (Watson, 1997). Unfortunately we did not have sufficient data on laying dates to confirm this finding. Once eggs have been laid they must be protected from weather extremes (the third period) and the male must usually obtain sufficient food for both parents (Collopy, 1984). Chicks seem to be particularly susceptible to weather events during their first 20 days (early to late May; the fourth period). For example, the female spends more time brooding young chicks when wind-chill is greater (Ellis, 1979). The potential effects of weather on the chicks should be expected to decline as the chicks grow, with fledging occurring from mid-July onwards.

Previous studies have suggested that the most detrimental effects of adverse weather occur during the incubation and early brood rearing periods (e.g. Clouet, 1981; Tjernberg, 1983; Watson, 1997; Steenhof *et al.,* 1997). These effects could operate directly on the parents or young birds. However, most studies suggest that weather operates through indirect effects on food availability and its accessibility. For example, there is evidence that declines in other eagles, such as the black eagle *Aquila verreauxii* in the Matobo Hills of Zimbabwe, can be linked to the weather. In this example it is thought that the decline was a consequence of the effects of drought on hyrax (Procaviidae) numbers (Gargett, 1990; Goodwin, 2000). Since the black eagle is a specialist predator we might expect it to be more susceptible to the weather than the more generalist golden eagle.

Discrepancies between calendar month and running mean correlations between weather variables and productivity measures could arise in two ways. Firstly, the large number of running mean correlations may generate spurious significant correlations. Secondly, discrepancies could arise because weather effects are not synchronized with calendar month boundaries. The clear seasonal patterns in the magnitude and direction of the correlation coefficients (Figures 10.3 to 10.5), combined with the coincidence between the significant running mean correlations and important dates in the reproductive phenology of golden eagles, tends to support the hypothesis that the correlations are real and cross calendar month boundaries. For example, on Mull significant positive relationships between temperature and fledging cover the 30-day periods beginning the 11th to 29th March, which coincide with Watson's (1997) incubation dates, suggesting that weather during this period has a direct effect on egg viability, possibly because the female is forced to abandon the eggs in order to feed herself (Collopy, 1984).

If the correlations between temperature, rainfall and golden eagle productivity are related to food supply they do not appear to be operating through effects on carrion (an important source of food for eagles in all three areas in winter). Warm winters and dry springs would be expected to produce less rather than more carrion. More likely, any effect on food supply is on the availability of live prey. The live prey component of diet is different for eagles in the three localities. The most important single prey items are rabbits in Skye, grouse in Lochaber, and mountain hares in Mull. There is some evidence that mild autumn/early winters allow rabbits to breed longer (Bell & Webb, 1991), and if this is happening on Skye, and these rabbits are subsequently more numerous in late winter/early spring, this may explain the link with breeding success in the year after a mild autumn/early winter. Mild late winter/early spring could again affect eagles directly if more grouse and hares survive into spring or simply through an effect on eagle condition.

The main rainfall effects are moderately consistent across the three areas. Wet spring weather is linked either to poorer overall fledging rate (Skye and Lochaber) or to a reduced proportion of twins (Mull). It is unclear if these relationships are a consequence of direct effect on the parents, or indirect effects operating via prey abundance and/or availability in the following spring. Steenhof *et al.* (1997) also noted that winter weather influenced productivity, possibly via changes in prey availability or vulnerability rather than through an effect on prey abundance. Thus, the effect is likely to be on food supply, either as a result of reduced abundance of key prey species or as a result of poor hunting success caused by poor weather at a critical period in the eagle's breeding cycle (notably the late incubation/early hatching period when male eagles must do all the hunting at a time before many of the key prey species have themselves bred and increased in numbers).

These analyses have highlighted some potentially important relationships between golden eagle productivity and weather in western Scotland. Although annual productivity appears to show no trend this masks some large between-year fluctuations and some important between-range differences. Overall the pattern of correlations tends to support the hypothesis that warm winters and dry springs are likely to favour good breeding performance by eagles in western Scotland.

An interesting outcome from this work is to consider the possible effects of climate change on eagle performance. For example, over the past 20 years the mean daily rainfall in the 30-day period from 30th March on Mull has increased steadily (Figure 10.6). This

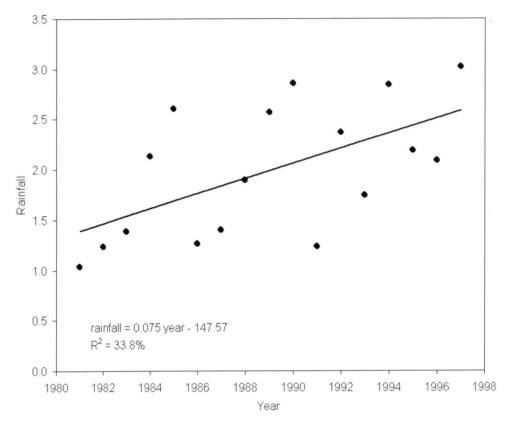

Figure 10.6. Relationship between mean daily April rainfall (mm) and year for the Aros weather station on Mull.

may or may not be linked with the recent tendency for fewer twins on Mull in the late 1990s. The weather data on Rum (and presumably therefore Skye) show a similar tendency for wetter springs in recent years, but also drier and somewhat warmer autumns. These two trends are pushing in opposite directions on Skye. Warmer autumn/early winter periods appear to be 'good' for eagles and wetter springs not so. The lack of any discernable trend in breeding performance over time is therefore, perhaps not surprising.

Acknowledgements

Special thanks are due to Mike Madders and Richard Evans who conducted much of the golden eagle monitoring on Mull. AHF was in receipt of a Leverhulme Research Fellowship during the writing of this paper. Weather data were provided by the United Kingdom Meteorological Office. Adam Watson and two anonymous referees made helpful improvements to the manuscript.

References

Bahat, O. (1992). Post-fledging movements of golden eagles Aquila chrysaetos in the Negev desert, Israel, as determined by radio-telemetry. In *Wildlife Telemetry*, ed. by I.G. Priede & S.M. Swift. Ellis Horwood, Chichester. pp. 612-621.

Bell, D.J. & Webb, N.J. (1991). Effects of climate on reproduction in the European wild rabbit (*Oryctolagus cuniculus*). *Journal of Zoology*, **224**, 639-648.

Clouet, M. (1981). L'Aigle royal (*Aquila chrysaetos*) dans Les Pyrénées françaises. Resultats de 5 ans d'observations. *L'Oiseau et R.F.O.*, **51**, 89-100.

Collopy, M.W. (1984). Parental care and feeding ecology of golden eagle nestlings. *Auk*, **101**, 753-760.

Dennis, R.H., Ellis, P.M., Broad, R.A. & Langslow, D.R. (1984). The status of the golden eagle in Britain. *British Birds*, **77**, 592-607.

Ellis, D.H. (1979). Development of behavior in the golden eagle. *Wildlife Monographs No. 70*. The Wildlife Society, Bethesda, Maryland.

Fuller, R.J. & Gough, S.J. (1999). Changes in sheep numbers in Britain: implications for bird populations. *Biological Conservation*, **91**, 73-89.

Gargett, V. (1990). *The Black Eagle*. Acorn Books, Johannesburg.

Goodwin, W. (2000). Black eagle studies in the Matobo Hills. *Scottish Bird News*, **58**, 8-9.

Green, R.E. (1996). The status of the golden eagle in Britain in 1992. *Bird Study*, **43**, 20-27.

Harrison, S.J. (1997). Changes in the Scottish climate. *Botanical Journal of Scotland*, **49**, 287-300.

Harrison, S.J. & Harrison, D.J. (1988). The effect of elevation on the climatically determined growing season in the Ochil Hills. *Scottish Geographical Magazine*, **104**, 108-115.

Kochert, M.N., Steenhof, K., Carpenter, L.B. & Marzluff, J.M. (1999). Effects of fire on golden eagle territory occupancy and reproductive success. *Journal of Wildlife Management*, **63**, 773-780.

Legendre, P. & Legendre, L. (1998). *Numerical Ecology. Second English edition*. Elsevier Science, Amsterdam.

McIntyre, C.L. & Adams, L.G. (1999). Reproductive characteristics of migratory golden eagles in Denali National Park, Alaska. *The Condor*, **101**, 115-123.

Pepin, N.C. (1995). The use of GCM scenario output to model effects of future climatic change on the thermal climate of marginal maritime uplands. *Geografiska Annaler Series A-Physical Geography*, **77A**, 167-185.

Steenhof, K., Kochert, M.N. & McDonald, T.L. (1997). Interactive effects of prey and weather on golden eagle reproduction. *Journal of Applied Ecology*, **66**, 350-362.

Tjernberg, M. (1983). Prey abundance and reproductive success of the golden eagle *Aquila chrysaetos* in Sweden. *Holarctic Ecology*, **6**, 17-23.

Watson, J. (1997). *The Golden Eagle*. T. & A.D. Poyser, London.

Watson, J., Rae, S.R. & Stillman, R. (1992). Nesting density and breeding success of golden eagles *Aquila chrysaetos* in relation to food supply in Scotland. *Journal of Animal Ecology*, **61**, 543-550.

11. GROWTH OF THE SCOTTISH OSPREY (*PANDION HALIAETUS*) POPULATION

Roy Dennis & Fiona A. McPhie

Summary

1.   In this chapter, we present preliminary results detailing the growth of the osprey *Pandion haliaetus* population in Scotland from 1954 until 2000.

2.   The number of nests has grown exponentially, and there are now 145 known pairs in Scotland.

3.   Productivity has remained constant from 1970 with considerable annual variation.

4.   Calculating the potential for population growth on the basis of the number of chicks produced each year indicates that the actual population growth is significantly less than that predicted from the annual productivity.

5.   The impact of nest robberies by egg collectors is discussed: the peak of nest robberies occurred in 1989, when a quarter of active nests were robbed.

6.   The Scottish osprey population is growing at a rate that is typical of a new, establishing population. However, the rate of increase is less than that predicted from its annual productivity. Future work will investigate this further, with particular emphasis on the role of individual variation in lifetime reproductive success in the growth and spread of the Scottish osprey population.

11.1 Introduction

The protection and associated recovery of the osprey *Pandion haliaetus* as a breeding species in Scotland has been a much publicised conservation success story in the latter half of the 20th century. Annual breeding success has been reported in the annual reports of the Rare Birds Breeding Panel (e.g. Ogilvie & The Rare Breeding Birds Panel, 1998, 1999), as well as in the journal *Scottish Birds* and unpublished annual osprey newsletters (available from R.H. Dennis). Since a pair nested at Loch Garten in 1954, the Scottish osprey population has grown to 145 known pairs in 2000. Detailed records of nest occupation and breeding success have been kept throughout this period. Some of this data has been analysed (Dennis, 1983, 1995), but so far little research has been done on the pattern of population spread in Scotland.

Here, we present preliminary results detailing the growth of the Scottish osprey population from 1954 until the present day. We examine the rate at which the population has grown, and how this compares to the rate of spread that would be predicted from its annual productivity. We discuss the apparent shortfall between annual productivity and population growth, and suggest possible explanations for this discrepancy. We conclude by outlining our plans for future research into the dynamics of the Scottish osprey population.

11.2 Data collection

Data on osprey nest numbers, occupancy and breeding success have been collected each year since 1954. All known nests are checked for occupancy from early March onwards; suitable areas are searched systematically for new nests. Information on new sites obtained from local sources is followed up and, similarly, opportunistic observations of birds flying in directions where there was not known to be a nest were investigated.

11.3 Results

11.3.1 Number of nests

The population of ospreys breeding in the Scotland has grown steadily from just one pair in 1954 to at least 145 in 2000 (Figure 11.1). Its growth follows an exponential curve, which implies that the population is still in its initial phase of growth and is not yet subject to limitation by environmental or density dependent factors. However, since the early 1990s, the actual increase in nests has begun to deviate from that predicted by an exponential growth rate, and lies below the trend-line, which suggests that limiting factors may have begun to operate. Plotting the number of nests on a log scale reinforces this, as the rate of increase in numbers appears to slow down with time.

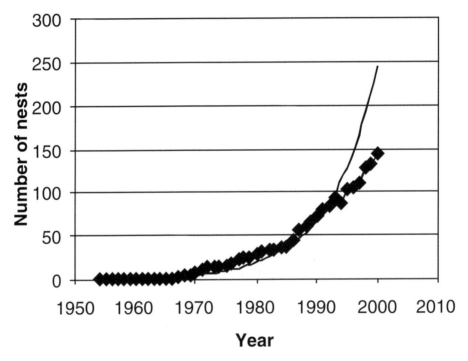

Figure 11.1. Number of osprey nests in Scotland 1970-2000. This shows an initial exponential increase ($R^2 = 0.9435$, $y = 2E-109e^{0.128x}$). The points show the actual rate of growth of the number of nests, and the solid line shows the fit of the exponential curve.

11.3.2 Productivity and population growth

Productivity (the number of young produced per nest) has remained constant throughout the last 30 years, although there has been strong year-to-year variation (Figure 11.2). All

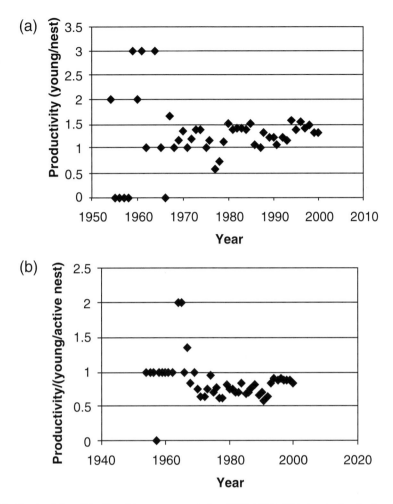

Figure 11.2. Productivity of the Scottish osprey population 1970-2000. This is calculated using a) all pairs that occupied a nest for a breeding season, and b) using only pairs that laid eggs. Both plots show that mean productivity has remained constant although there has been strong year-to-year variation.

statistics in this section are calculated using data from 1970 onwards, due to the small numbers of nests in the preceding years.

The growth rate of the population (change in number of nests calculated as a proportion of the number of nests in the previous year) fluctuates considerably about the mean, and seems to peak every three to four years (Figure 11.3a), suggesting that there is some degree of population cycling, and raising the possibility that these peaks may be predicted from the productivity of the population in previous years. However, calculating the autocorrelation function for population change (Figure 11.3b) shows that all of the coefficients lie within the confidence limits of the analysis and that, in fact, there is no significant pattern in the time series of data. However, patterns of breeding success specific to individuals within the population may affect the way in which the population changes. For instance, the autocorrelation for the population as a whole may mask trends at the individual level: this possibility will be explored in more detail elsewhere.

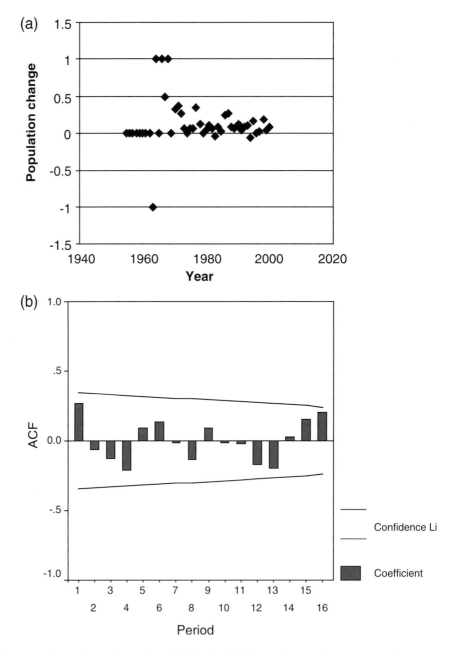

Figure 11.3. a) Annual change in population from 1954-2000. This is calculated as the proportional increase relative to the number of nests the previous year (simple linear regression 1970-2000: $R^2 = 0.121$, $F = 3.98$, $P < 0.06$). b) Autocorrelation function (ACF) for population change 1954-2000. All coefficients lie within the confidence limits of the analysis.

It might be expected that there would be a relationship between annual productivity and population growth. However, as young ospreys do not recruit into the breeding population until they are at least three years old, and because juvenile mortality before this is high

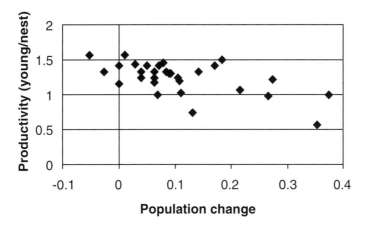

Figure 11.4. Productivity and population growth are negatively correlated (Pearson's product moment correlation: r = -0.61, P <0.01).

(approximately 60% (Poole, 1989)), population growth will be determined by several different factors. In fact, productivity and population growth are negatively correlated (Figure 11.4), suggesting that in years where the population has increased most, productivity decreases. This could be because new breeders are less productive, and because there is a higher proportion of non-breeding pairs in the population in these years. The data presented in Figure 11.2 support this idea, as there is greater year-to-year variation in productivity/nest than in productivity/active pair. Increased competition between breeding pairs for access to feeding sites may also affect productivity in years where the population has increased most.

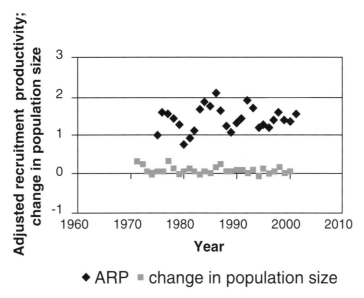

Figure 11.5. Change in population size of the Scottish osprey population in comparison to the potential for population growth (adjusted recruitment productivity, ARP), calculated on the basis of previous productivity. The observed change in population size is significantly lower than that predicted from the number of birds available for recruitment in any given year (t-test: $t_{0.05, 55}$ = 21.8, P <0.001).

11.4 Potential for population growth in comparison to observed growth rate

The potential for growth of a population may be predicted in philopatric species from the annual productivity of the population in previous years. This value is often referred to as the recruitment standard (Newton, 1979), and can be used to determine whether the current growth of a population matches its potential, calculated from the number of young it produces.

Spitzer (1980) used data from a population of osprey breeding in the north-eastern United States to produce a formula to calculate the Adjusted Recruitment Productivity (ARP) for the population in any given year. The ARP estimates the number of young birds that could potentially recruit into the breeding population in any given year on the basis of the number of young produced three, four and five years previously, and the proportions of young in the population that commence breeding at ages three, four and five.

Figure 11.5 shows that the ARP of the Scottish population shows a similar pattern to observed productivity (i.e. remains constant but with considerable annual fluctuations about the mean). However, there is no significant relationship between the ARP and the observed rate of population increase (Figure 11.5; $r = 0.23$, $n = 25$, $P > 0.05$). Additionally, the ARP is consistently larger than the observed population growth (Figure 11.5). There are several possible reasons for this trend. Firstly, it is possible that the Scottish osprey population does not meet all of the assumptions of Spitzer's (1980) ARP model. If the proportions of birds commencing breeding at ages three, four and five differ from Spitzer's, the calculated ARP may be an overestimate. Alternatively, there may be greater juvenile mortality than accounted for by the ARP calculations. Shooting on migration, as well as collisions with electricity power lines, are known causes of death, and initial results from recent satellite tracking studies suggest that losses of potential breeders on migration are higher than usual from the Scottish population due to the long sea crossings undertaken by some young birds (R.H. Dennis, unpublished data). Additionally, the Scottish population may not be as isolated as Spitzer's population which, at the time of his study, was in a phase of rapid recovery following a decline due to pesticides. Finally, it is possible that birds fledging from the Scottish population may nest elsewhere in Europe and thus the assumption of equal emigration and immigration is unlikely to be satisfied. We are unsure of losses due to emigration into the mainland European populations, but we do know that birds immigrating from Scandinavia continue to be part of the Scottish breeding population.

The population figures used in these analyses are based on known breeding pairs and nests, but there is an unknown number of other nests that have not been found or reported. Some nests are found several years after they were established, and in many cases details of previous years' breeding can be obtained through local knowledge. In such cases the database has been amended accordingly. In the early decades of the study, we were reasonably certain that we knew all of the nests, but as numbers have grown, we believe that we are missing some new nests. This may amount to 5% in the last decade (R.H. Dennis, pers. obs.). We have examined the data based on such assumptions and found that, even if this level of nests has been missed each year for the last ten years, the overall number of nests recorded over the last ten years would not be significantly different from our present figures (t-test: $t_{0.05,20} = -0.5$, $P > 0.50$) and therefore would not affect our conclusions about the growth of the population.

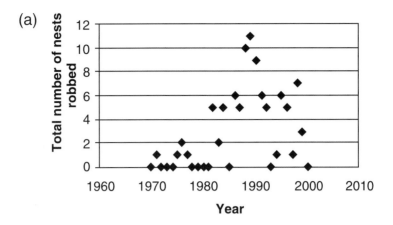

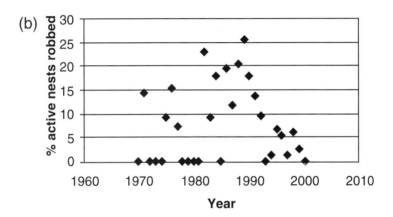

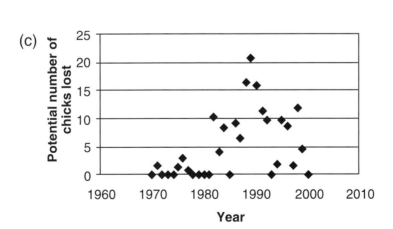

Figure 11.6. a) Number of osprey nests robbed each year, b) percentage of active nests robbed each year, and c) potential number of fledglings lost due to robberies per year (productivity per active nest x number of nests robbed).

11.5 Identifiable losses

In 19 out of the 30 years from 1970-2000, at least one active nest has been robbed by egg collectors. It is likely that these figures are underestimates as it can be impossible to distinguish between a failed breeding attempt and a nest that has been robbed. Detailed information collected by the RSPB Investigations Department has allowed us to check back and correct unexplained losses due to egg thefts, so we believe the figures are now accurate. The peak of nest robberies occurred in 1989, when 25.6% of active nests were robbed (Figure 11.6b). The number of chicks potentially lost to the population annually as a result of robberies can be calculated on the basis of the productivity of the population on any given year, by multiplying the productivity per active nest in that year by the number of active nests robbed (Figure 11.6c). Nests which were robbed were often potentially productive nests rather than first time breeders (R.H. Dennis, pers. obs.). However, comparison of the number of chicks fledged in each year with the potential number that might have fledged had there been no robberies shows that in fact there is no significant difference between theses two figures ($t_{0.05, 92} = 0.272$, P >0.70). Although this suggests that egg collecting has not had a significant impact on population growth over all, it is possible that in the mid-1980s to early 1990s (when pressure from nest robberies was greatest) productivity may have been reduced.

11.6 Discussion and future work

The above analyses suggest that the Scottish osprey population is growing at a rate that would be expected from a new, establishing population, although it appears that it may have started to be subject to density-dependent effects in recent years. Our estimates of the potential for recruitment of young birds to the population show that the actual rate of increase is markedly less than the rate that would be predicted from yearly productivity. There are several possible explanations for this discrepancy, and we will investigate these further.

It is known that, as the Scottish osprey population has increased, it has done so in distinct sub-populations which have built up around an original pioneering pair in each particular area, and that the rate of range expansion is slow (Dennis, 1995): because of this, it is likely that further insight into the relationship between the potential and observed increases in osprey breeding numbers can be gained by looking at each sub-population in isolation. We also intend to use data on age of first breeding in the Scottish osprey population to calculate recruitment productivity in line with the proportions of birds breeding for the first time at ages three, four and five in this population. Additionally, we will incorporate mortality data, the estimated percentage of unlocated breeding pairs and the continuing immigration of birds from Scandinavia into our analysis of population expansion. Finally, we will take into account the effects of repeatability of individual breeding success, and the consequent variation in lifetime reproductive success between pairs and possibly sub-populations on the way the Scottish osprey population has grown and spread.

Acknowledgements

Many people have contributed to the collection of data on the breeding success of ospreys in Scotland since 1954, including staff of the RSPB, SNH (and previously Nature

Conservancy), SWT and the Forestry Commission. In the last decade, the majority of the information has been collected by Roy Dennis and Colin Crooke in northern Scotland; Ian Francis and Stuart Rae in north-east Scotland; Keith Brockie in Perthshire and Angus; and Roger Broad in south-west Scotland. We express our sincere thanks to all of the field-workers. We would also like to thank Graeme Ruxton, Stuart Humphries and two anonymous referees for helpful comments on the manuscript.

References

Dennis, R.H. (1983). Population studies and conservation of Ospreys in Scotland. In *Biology and Management of Bald Eagles and Ospreys*, ed. by D.M. Bird. Harpell Press, Quebec. pp 207-214.

Dennis, R.H. (1995). Ospreys *Pandion haliaetus* in Scotland - a study of recolonization. *Vogelwelt*, **116,** 193-196.

Newton, I. (1979). *Population Ecology of Raptors*. Poyser, Berkhamsted.

Ogilvie, M.A. & The Rare Breeding Birds Panel (1998). Rare breeding birds in the United Kingdom in 1995. *British Birds*, **91**, 417-447.

Ogilvie, M.A. & The Rare Breeding Birds Panel (1999). Rare breeding birds in the United Kingdom in 1996. *British Birds*, **92**, 120-154.

Poole, A.F. (1989). *Ospreys: A Natural and Unnatural History*. Cambridge University Press, Cambridge.

Spitzer, P.R. (1980). Dynamics of a discrete coastal breeding population of Ospreys in the northeastern USA, 1969-1979. Unpublished PhD thesis, Cornell University, Cornell.

12. Buzzards (*Buteo buteo*) on the Increase in Lothian and Borders, Scotland

Mark Holling

Summary

1. During the 1990s, the population of buzzards *Buteo buteo* in both Lothian and the Borders increased dramatically.

2. In the 1970s there was just a scatter of pairs across the two regions, and in the mid-1980s there were still less than 20 pairs, mostly in Borders. The first detailed population estimate for the area in 1992 gave a minimum of 126 pairs.

3. Monitoring of the subsequent increase across both regions has led to an estimate of at least 835, but probably as many as 1,000 pairs.

4. This chapter documents this increase and discusses some of the reasons thought to have led to such a major change in status.

12.1 Introduction

Buzzards nesting in Britain have shown interesting changes in distribution, related in part to reductions in persecution, a marked decline of one of their major prey animals, the rabbit (*Oryctolagus cuniculus*) due to myxomatosis, and pesticide contamination of other prey animals (also Sim *et al.*, 2000; Sim, Chapter 28). Local studies have recorded changes in distribution and status. This chapter records changes in Lothian and Borders, in central and southern Scotland.

12.2 The Lothian and Borders study area

The study area is the whole of the former regions of Lothian and Borders (now the administrative areas of City of Edinburgh, West Lothian, Midlothian, East Lothian and Scottish Borders). This is the same area as that covered by *The Breeding Birds of South-east Scotland* (Murray *et al.*, 1998), which documented the breeding distribution of birds in the area during 1988-1994 (as part of 'the SE Scotland Breeding Bird Atlas'). Breeding distributions of birds were mapped for all 1,756 tetrads (2 x 2 km squares) in the area. That study provided a baseline on distribution and status against which subsequent changes can be mapped and described.

12.3 Methods

Published details of buzzard status in the Borders up to 1974 were reviewed (e.g. Evans, 1911; Blackwood, 1925; Baxter & Rintoul, 1953; Morrison, 1978). All known records for the region from 1975 to 1997 inclusive were then collated and added to a database. Most of these records came from the *Borders Bird Reports* published from 1979 to the present day (Murray, 1980 onwards), supplemented by the original detailed records held by Ray Murray, the Scottish Ornithologists' Club (SOC) Local Bird Recorder. Local birdwatchers were encouraged to report all buzzard sightings on a specially prepared form, or via the Local Bird Recorder. The period 1988-1994 was when the intensive fieldwork for the SE Scotland Breeding Bird Atlas was undertaken, resulting in all tetrads in the Borders being visited, and most buzzards being located. I visited some selected areas to confirm absence or to fill in gaps in coverage. This enabled the fullest possible picture to be compiled. The history of the buzzard in the Borders up to 1992 has been well documented (Holling & McGarry, 1994). Since 1998, intensive record keeping has been restricted to 44 10 km squares in the south and east of the region, owing to the ubiquity of the buzzard in the remainder of the Borders. Distributions have been mapped and analysed at tetrad level on an annual basis. The recording unit of the tetrad was chosen to build upon the work of the SE Scotland Breeding Bird Atlas, and because it was felt that an area of 4 km² minimised the risk of duplication of records. More intensive fieldwork by me in a study area north of Galashiels (unpublished) demonstrated that this coarse methodology balanced the effects of the data being largely based on casual records rather than thorough searching.

In parallel, George Smith has followed the fortunes of the buzzard population in Lothian. The history of Lothian buzzards has been well documented (Smith, 1994). Since 1993, all known buzzard territories were searched for nests and nest contents examined, enabling the collection of nest productivity data and accurate mapping of the spread of buzzards in Lothian. However, no attempt was made to collate other casual sightings, which may well refer to additional territorial pairs, thus under-estimating the overall status in Lothian.

For the purposes of this analysis, a territory within Lothian equates to a site where nesting was at least attempted. For Borders, a broader definition applies; any buzzard record from a tetrad during the months February to August inclusive is assumed to relate to a single territory, unless there is evidence that there is more than one territory in the tetrad (such evidence would be the presence of more than one nest or pairs displaying against each other). Records from the remainder of the year are also included if more than one bird is involved, or if there are repeated sightings in separate months.

12.4 Results

Table 12.1 shows the dramatic rise in the numbers of territorial buzzard pairs in both Lothian and Borders since the mid-1980s.

Breeding performance of the Lothian buzzard population has been closely monitored since 1993 (Table 12.2) and has shown an average productivity of 2.40 young per productive pair, and 1.69 young per territorial pair. On a smaller sample of nests (n = 90) in the Borders for which data were available over the period 1996-2000, a slightly lower average of 2.26 young per productive pair was calculated.

Table 12.1. Estimated numbers of buzzard territories in Lothian and Borders 1984–1999.

	1984	1992-3	1997	1999
Borders	16	100-298	500	750
Lothian	1-2	26	60	85-250

Table 12.2. Productivity of Lothian buzzards 1993–2000.

	1993	1994	1995	1996	1997	1998	1999	2000	Average
Territories monitored	26	33	50	52	62	82	86	23	
Young recorded	28	37	92	102	128	120	159	49	
Young/productive pair	2.15	1.76	2.76	2.68	2.86	2.14	2.40	2.45	2.40
Young/territorial pair	1.08	1.12	1.84	1.96	2.06	1.46	1.85	2.13	1.69

12.5 Discussion

12.5.1 Borders

In the middle of the 19th century, buzzards were still 'numerous' in the hilly parts of the Borders (Blackwood, 1925). However, 50 years later they were all gone, leading Evans (1911) to summarise the status as 'formerly common, still occasionally seen, appears to have gone by late 19th century; became scarce, then a rare straggler'. This period of loss, of course, coincided with the rearing of game for sport becoming fashionable and gamekeepers becoming numerous.

It was only in the late 1960s that buzzard display was again noted (in Peeblesshire). Morrison (1978) reported that an increasing number were being seen during the 1970s in the north-west of the region. The first confirmed breeding in the 20th century was not until 1981 (two nests), but even then one of these was shot out (Murray, 1982: Borders Bird Reports). The population seemed to expand slowly through the 1980s, but was poorly recorded. The distribution appeared to be limited to parts of Peeblesshire, having presumably re-colonised the Borders from Dumfriesshire. Fortunes seemed to pick up at the end of the 1980s and the fieldwork for the SE Scotland Breeding Bird Atlas (Murray *et al.*, 1998) began to discover new pairs in new sites, especially in 1990 and 1992. A review of the status to 1992 (Holling & McGarry, 1994) indicated a minimum of 100 territories in the Borders. A baseline picture was produced, using data for the five year period 1988-1992. With additional information available, the SE Scotland Atlas estimated 500 pairs of buzzards in the Borders by 1997 (Holling in Murray *et al.*, 1998).

Since that time this study has documented the continued spread of the population from the core areas in Peeblesshire and parts of Selkirkshire over to the Lammermuirs in the north east of the region, out to the Cheviots in the south and most recently into the low-lying areas of Berwickshire in the east. A five year snapshot following the previous review, covering 1993-1997, and subsequent changes reported for 1998 and 1999, further confirmed this spread and revealed that in fact the population was closer to 750 territories (unpublished). The increase is due both to the spread to southern hills and lower-lying ground to the east, but also because of consolidation in the core range. In 2000, 2001 and 2002 it became noticeable that territories were being established in previously vacant areas at the heads of the valleys.

In 1992, density in occupied areas was close to one pair per tetrad (0.25 pairs km^{-2}). In a detailed study area in the Gala Water area north of Galashiels (15 tetrads), density now exceeds 0.4 pairs km^{-2} and these densities are probably typical for much of the region now. In the West Midlands, a survey of soaring buzzards (Sim *et al.*, 2000) found a density of 0.41 pairs km^{-2}, including core and edge parts of the range.

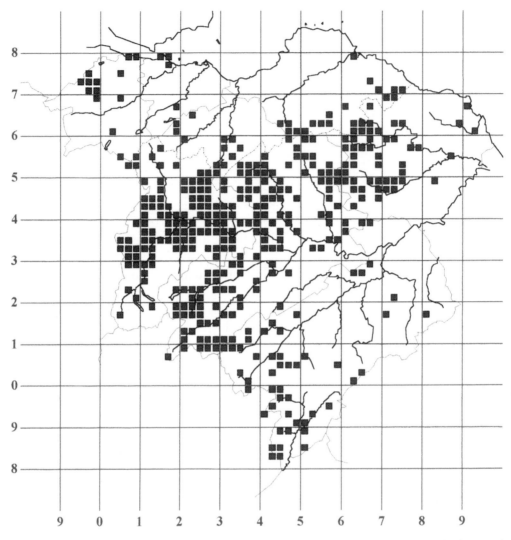

Figure 12.1. The distribution of breeding buzzards based on *The Breeding Birds of South-east Scotland: a Tetrad Atlas 1988-1994* (Murray *et al.*, 1998, pp. 92-93), covering the seven-year period 1988-1994.

12.5.2 Lothian

From a total extinction in Lothian around 1820, a very small pioneering breeding population of one or two pairs persisted from around 1968 until around 1987, despite severe persecution. During the period 1988 to 1999, the number of known breeding pairs in Lothian increased from two in 1988 to 85 in 1999. The birds in East Lothian and Midlothian are thought to have originated from the expanding Borders populations to the south, but the West Lothian population has its origins in the Stirling/Clackmannanshire area.

In 1993 it was estimated that a peak of 250 pairs of buzzard could be reached in Lothian (Smith, 1994), but this now seems to have been an understatement. The 1999 figures are certainly an underestimate of the true number of the breeding buzzards in the area, based

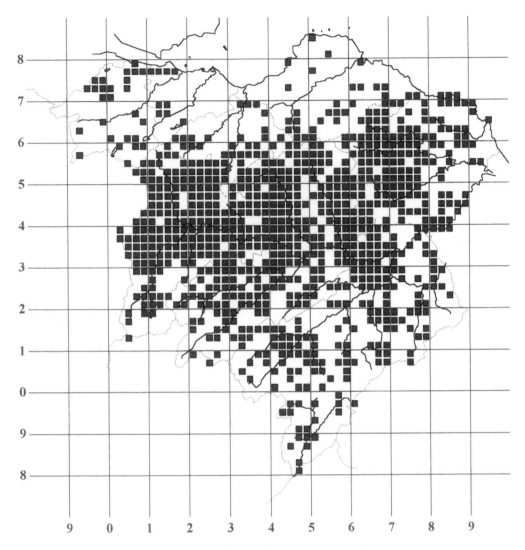

Figure 12.2. The distribution of buzzards in all seasons for the six-year period 1995-2000.

as they are on confirmed nest sites. Casual reports submitted to the Lothian Bird Recorder provide evidence that there are now many additional territories. It is thought that there may already be as many as 250 pairs now breeding in Lothian, with the bulk (150-200) in West Lothian (G.D. Smith, pers. obs.). By 1999 in East Lothian, birds were restricted to hill edge habitats and low-lying policy woodlands, but are now much more widespread.

12.5.3 Reasons for the increase

Although populations of buzzards in Borders appear to have been increasing slowly during the 1980s, it seems to have been only in the late 1980s that fortunes really changed. A significant further expansion occurred between 1992 and 1994 when many new areas were colonised and the Lothian population began to pick up. This period of increase coincided with the intensive fieldwork for the SE Scotland Breeding Bird Atlas (Murray *et al.,* 1998), which will have exaggerated the change. However, buzzards were certainly being located during 1992-1994 in areas which had been surveyed earlier and which at that time had not held buzzards. Personal observations since that study have shown that buzzards are now occurring in woodlands in low-lying, mainly arable areas of East Lothian and Berwickshire, and are becoming widespread in the Cheviots, where they were almost absent in 1988-1994.

Sim *et al.* (2000) studied the expanding buzzard population in the West Midlands. They found that the increase there could be ascribed to three factors: (1) an increase in the abundance of the main prey species, the rabbit *Oryctolagus cuniculus*, over the period 1985-89; (2) an increase in nest productivity since the late 1980s; and (3) a reduction in persecution of buzzards, thought also to be related to the introduction of the Larsen trap. It seems likely that the same factors would apply to Lothian and Borders.

For buzzards, a recruitment standard of 1.15 young per productive pair is required to maintain a stable population (Newton, 1979). The productivity analysis (Table 12.2) shows that in Lothian the number of young leaving the nest is 2.40 per productive pair. With reduced persecution, it would seem that sufficient young are reaching breeding age and are colonising new areas or occupying additional territories within the current breeding areas. Nest sites are not a limiting factor in much of the area as a range of tree species (and heights) have been used locally. It would appear likely that within a few years buzzards will be breeding in all parts of the region, except for treeless hills and built-up areas. Monitoring continues.

Acknowledgements

I would like to thank all members of the Lothian & Borders Raptor Study Group for their support and information about buzzards, and local members of the Scottish Ornithologists' Club for the many casual records reported via the Local Bird Recorders. George Smith kindly supplied summaries of his work on buzzards in Lothian. Special thanks must also go to Ray Murray for allowing access to the Borders bird record database and for his many useful observations, and to Pete Gordon for his encouragement in continuing with the study. Many Borders nest histories were supplied by Malcolm Henderson in the south of the Borders, and Alan Heavisides and his team of raptor workers in the Lammermuirs.

References

Baxter, E.V. & Rintoul, L.J. (1953). *The Birds of Scotland*. Oliver and Boyd, Edinburgh.

Blackwood, W.T. (1925). Vertebrate Fauna of Peeblesshire. In *A History of Peeblesshire Vol 1*, ed. by J.W. Buchan & Rev. H. Paton. Wylie, Jackson & Co., Glasgow.

Evans, A.H. (1911). *A Fauna of the Tweed Area*. David Douglas, Edinburgh.

Holling, M. & McGarry, O.C. (1994). A review of the changing status of the buzzard in the Borders. *Borders Bird Report*, **14**, 76-82.

Morrison, C.M. (Ed.) (1978). *Checklist of the Birds of Tweeddale*. Scottish Wildlife Trust, Peebles.

Murray, R.D. (Ed.) (1980-2000). *Borders Bird Report*, **1-18** covering 1979-1998.

Murray, R.D., Holling, M., Dott, H.E.M. & Vandome, P. (1998). *The Breeding Birds of South-east Scotland: a Tetrad Atlas 1988-1994*. Scottish Ornithologists' Club, Edinburgh.

Newton, I. (1979). *Population Ecology of Raptors*. T. & A.D. Poyser, Berkhamsted.

Sim, I.M.W., Campbell, L., Pain, D.J. & Wilson, J.D. (2000). Correlates of the population increase of Common Buzzards *Buteo buteo* in the West Midlands between 1983 and 1996. *Bird Study*, **47**, 154-164.

Smith, G.D. (1994). Buzzards in Lothian - a success story. *Lothian Bird Report*, **1993**, 108-110.

13. BUZZARDS (*BUTEO BUTEO*) ON COLONSAY 1990-2000: NUMBERS AND BREEDING PERFORMANCE

David C. Jardine

Summary

1. Results of a long-term study of a high density island population of buzzard *Buteo buteo* in the Scottish Inner Hebrides are presented.
2. Breeding productivity was slightly lower than that reported in two short-term studies in Argyll.
3. On Colonsay there was a link between the proportion of rabbits in prey remains found at buzzard nests and a simple measure of the rabbit population (based on faecal counts), indicating the possible usefulness of this low input measure of prey abundance.

13.1 Introduction and study area

Colonsay, and the adjoining island of Oronsay, lie in the southern Inner Hebrides, and their small size (4,500 ha) means that they are ideally suited to a raptor study which could be conducted with limited time availability. These islands comprise a wide range of habitats including machair, coastal heath and low intensity pasture.

In the 1930s, only three to four pairs of buzzard bred on Colonsay, and by the early 1960s the population had risen to five to six pairs. Since then, there have been changes on the islands that have led to a significant increase in the population to around 20 pairs in the 1980s (Jardine *et al.*, 1984).

13.2 Methods

In 1990-2000 an attempt was made to monitor every breeding pair of buzzard. Nests were located, wherever possible, and details of breeding performance and prey were recorded. Young were measured in order to establish hatching date (Austin *et al.*, 1997).

Estimates of summer prey were made from remains found at the nest. Rabbit *Oryctolagus cuniculus* prey mass was established using foot length (derived from Cowan, 1983), rats *Rattus norvegicus* by measurement and birds through Hickling (1983). A measure of the rabbit populations was made annually using 27-51 faecal count quadrats (30 cm x 30 cm) in areas of short turf in low-lying ground. Monthly weather records for Colonsay were used to explore the relationship between annual buzzard breeding and various climate parameters (spring rainfall, early summer sunshine).

13.3 Results

Buzzards nested at high densities (38 to 53 per 100 km^2), with between 17 to 24 pairs present each year. The number of successful pairs varied between six and 20, leading to significant variation in the number of young reared. Annual average brood size varied between 1.4 to 2.5 young per successful pair (mean of all successful nests = 1.79 (n = 101)). Annual median hatching dates varied between 22nd and 31st May (median date of all nests = 27th May (n = 97)) with extreme hatching dates of 13th May and 15th June.

Rabbit prey comprised the main food item found at nests (Table 13.1). There was a significant relationship between the annual proportion of rabbit in prey remains and the measure of the rabbit population (r = 0.597, P <0.05). No significant relationships were found between the annual breeding parameters of buzzards (hatch date, average brood) and the annual measures of rabbit population. Neither were any significant relationships found between the monthly weather records and annual breeding parameters.

Table 13.1. Summary of prey items found at buzzard nests, Colonsay 1990-2000.

Prey item		Number	Percentage	Estimated mass (g)	Percentage
Rabbit	*Oryctolagus cuniculus*	150	(47.9)	57,774	(81.2)
Rat	*Rattus norvegicus*	43	(13.8)		(6.6)
Total mammals		**193**	**(61.7)**	**62,474**	**(87.8)**
Birds					
Meadow pipit	*Anthus pratensis*	56		1,102	
Starling	*Sturnus vulgaris*	10		740	
Song thrush	*Turdus philomelos*	10		704	
Wheatear	*Oenanthe oenanthe*	8		184	
Blackbird	*Turdus merula*	7		602	
Snipe	*Gallinago gallinago*	6		690	
Wren	*Troglodytes troglodytes*	4		36	
Rock dove	*Columba livia*	3		810	
Robin	*Rubus erithracus*	2		34	
Pheasant	*Phasianus colchicus*	2		1,864	
Corncrake (chick)	*Crex crex*	1		15	
Oystercatcher	*Haematopus ostralegus*	1		467	
Lapwing	*Vanellus vanellus*	1		205	
Curlew	*Numenius arquata*	1		662	
Kittiwake	*Rissa tridactyla*	1		387	
Dunnock	*Prunella modularis*	1		19	
Mistle thrush	*Turdus viscivorus*	1		130	
Goldcrest	*Regulus regulus*	1		5	
Chaffinch	*Fringilla coelebs*	1		18	
Linnet	*Carduelis cannabina*	1		13	
Total birds		**118**	**(37.7)**	**8,635**	**(12.1)**
Common lizard	*Lacerta vivipara*	1	(0.3)	10	(0.1)
Northern Eggar moth	*Lasiocampa quercus callunae*	1	(0.3)	1	
Grand total		**313**	**(100.0)**	**71,120**	**(100.0)**

13.4 Discussion

Both of the previously published studies of buzzard in Argyll were conducted over short (two year) periods. The breeding performance of buzzard in this study is below that reported by Austin *et al.* (1997) and Maguire (1979) (1.79 fledged young per successful nest, c.f. 2.13 and 2.36 young respectively). However, the breeding performance reported by these authors lies within the range of annual variation in breeding performance found in this study. This study confirms that care is required in interpreting results for short-term studies that may not reflect the longer term position.

The median hatch date in this study was 27th May which, by allowing 36 days for incubation, gives an average laying date of 21st April; this is seven days later than that reported by Austin *et al.* (1997) but similar to that of Maguire (1979).

Graham *et al.* (1995) noted the correlation between lagomorph abundance (through counts of live rabbits and brown hares *Lepus europaeus*) and the composition on buzzard prey. This study has repeated this finding, but has substituted the use of live counts of prey with the use of faecal counts. This prey assessment method, which can be done at any time of day, may prove to be a useful technique in other studies where establishing prey abundance is not straightforward.

It is surprising that no correlations were found between breeding parameters and monthly weather records (c.f. Watson *et al.*, Chapter 10). It is believed that this was a consequence of using monthly records rather than more detailed records and further study is proposed in order to check this.

Acknowledgements

I am indebted to the owners of Colonsay and Oronsay, Mr A. Howard and Mrs Coburn, and the tenant farmers for access to study. Janet Jardine and friends have assisted with fieldwork, Des Thompson encouraged me to write up this study, and Kevin Byrne kindly provided weather records for Colonsay. I thank them all.

References

Austin, G.E. & Houston, D.C. (1997). The breeding performance of the buzzard *Buteo buteo* in Argyll, Scotland and a comparison with other areas in Britain. *Bird Study*, **44**, 146-155.

Cowan, D. (1983). Aspects of the behavioural ecology of the European wild rabbit *Oryctolagus cuniculus L.* in southern England. Unpublished Ph.D. thesis. University of London, London.

Graham, I.M., Redpath, S.M. & Thirgood, S.J. (1995). Diet and breeding density of common buzzards *Buteo buteo* in relation to indices of prey abundance. *Bird Study*, **42**, 165-173.

Hickling, R.E. (1983). *Enjoying Ornithology*. Poyser, Calton.

Jardine, D.C., Clarke, J. & Clarke, P.M. (1984). *The Birds of Colonsay and Oransay*. Stornoway Gazette, Stornoway.

Maguire, E.J. (1979). Notes on the breeding buzzards in Kintyre. *Western Naturalist*, **8**, 3-13.

14. Long-Term Monitoring of Breeding Merlin (*Falco columbarius*) in Aberdeenshire, North-East Scotland 1980-2000

G.W. Rebecca & B.L Cosnette

Summary

1.   Around 100 merlin *Falco columbarius* breeding territories were identified in Aberdeenshire during 1968 to 2000, with 130 1 km squares occupied at some stage.

2.   There were an estimated 45 to 55 breeding pairs in the 1990s, comprising a relatively stable population from year to year, which was about 4% of the British population.

3.   The number of breeding territories monitored annually increased, but did not result in a proportional increase in the number of pairs located. In two study areas (lower Deeside and upper Donside) the number of pairs fluctuated, but over different periods.

4.   A decrease in occupation and subsequent abandonment of breeding territories in lower Deeside was linked to the afforestation of former moor. Excessive burning of heather *Calluna vulgaris* temporarily affected the occupation of breeding territories in upper Donside.

5.   Between 1983 and 2000, an average of 20 pairs successfully fledged young each year.

14.1 Introduction

In Britain, breeding merlin *Falco columbarius* usually nest in remote areas and can be elusive and easily overlooked (Brown, 1976; Sharrock, 1976; Newton *et al.,* 1978; Cramp & Simmons, 1980). In the mid-1970s the merlin was considered to have been one of the least known of the diurnal raptors in Britain (Brown, 1976). There had also been reported declines over its British breeding range since at least 1900. Loss of suitable breeding habitat, persecution and disturbance were given as plausible reasons for the declines (Alexander & Lack, 1944; Parslow, 1967; Brown, 1976; Sharrock, 1976) with environmental pollutants also implicated in the later years (Newton, 1973; Newton *et al.,* 1978). The negative effects of pesticides also impacted on North American and Scandinavian merlin during the 1970s, with researchers reporting that contamination was a serious problem and recommending that international restrictions and local bans should be introduced for some persistent biocides (Risebrough *et al.,* 1970; Fox, 1971; Temple, 1972; Trimble, 1975; Fyfe *et al.,* 1976; Fox & Donald, 1980; Olsson, 1980). By the mid-1980s the merlin was reported as the most heavily contaminated raptor in Britain, and was still declining despite a wide reduction in pesticide use (Newton, 1984; Newton & Haas, 1988).

In Aberdeenshire and Kincardineshire, 27 merlin breeding territories were located during 1968 to 1979 with breeding confirmed at 19 areas and considered probable at eight areas (Figure 14.1). In view of the large area of apparently suitable merlin breeding habitat

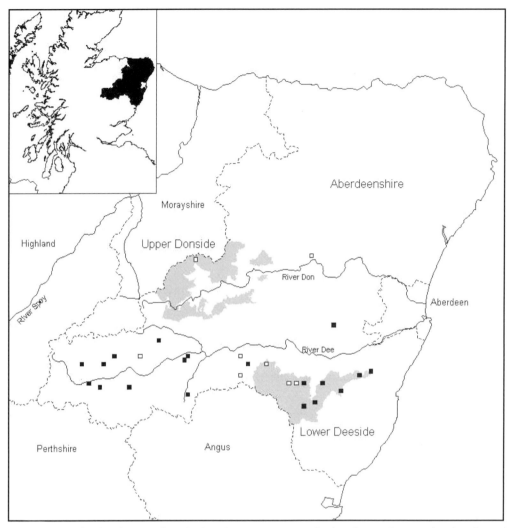

Figure 14.1. The distribution of merlin breeding territories in Aberdeenshire and Kincardineshire located between 1968 and 1979. Solid 1 km squares represent confirmed breeding and open 1 km squares represent probable breeding. Shaded blocks define detailed study areas, lower Deeside covered 1980 to 2000 and upper Donside covered 1986 to 2000.

in north-east Scotland (Brown, 1976; Newton *et al.*, 1978; Cramp & Simmons, 1980; Buckland *et al.*, 1990) it seemed likely that the 1979 figure was minimal. This study was initiated on Deeside in 1980, and in 1981 the North-East Scotland Raptor Study Group (NESRSG) was formed to monitor raptors in the former Grampian Region (excluding west Moray District, see Figure 1 in Rebecca *et al.*, 1992). This chapter details merlin monitoring until 2000 in the Local Authority area of Aberdeenshire (formerly Aberdeenshire and Kincardineshire) (Figure 14.1). The main aims of the study were to: 1) survey suitable breeding habitat in north-east Scotland, locate merlin and confirm breeding; 2) monitor a sample of known breeding territories annually; 3) identify and establish areas where full ecological studies would be practical; and 4) assess the status of the population and contribute to the conservation of the species.

During the study period, the merlin was given formal protection in Britain as a Schedule 1 species within the Wildlife and Countryside Act 1981 and as an Annex 1 species within the 1979 European Union Directive on the Conservation of Wild Birds (79/409/EEC). The merlin was also included in Britain's Red Data bird list between 1990 and 2000 (Batten *et al.,* 1990; Gibbons *et al.,* 1996).

14.2 Study areas

The first study area was established on lower Deeside in 1980 covering 215 km², and the second study area was established on upper Donside in 1986 covering 237 km² (Figure 14.1). Some results of the work have been published (e.g. Cosnette, 1984, 1991; Rebecca *et al.,* 1988, 1990, 1992; Rebecca, 1992, 1993, 1998; Cosnette & Rebecca, 1997).

14.3 Methods

The methods for survey and monitoring (Rebecca *et al.,* 1992; Cosnette & Rebecca, 1997) were generally consistent with other long-term merlin studies in Britain (Newton *et al.,* 1986; Meek, 1988; Ellis & Okill, 1990; Little & Davison, 1992; Wright, 1997). Suitable areas, including native Caledonian pine forests and some coniferous plantations bordering moorland, were searched between March and August for the presence of merlin. Local ornithologists and bird-watchers were encouraged to take an interest in merlin and to contribute to the study, and information received from them and others such as hill-walkers and gamekeepers was followed up.

By the late 1980s merlins were known to be frequently nesting in old carrion crow (*Corvus corone*) nests at the edges of coniferous plantations in Northumberland (A. Bankier, M. Davison and B. Little, pers. comms., 1986-1989; Little & Davison, 1992), Wales (Parr, 1991) and south-west Scotland (Orchel, 1992). There were also two records of merlin nesting in old crow nests in plantations in north-east Scotland, from Morayshire in 1987 (B. Etheridge, pers. comm.) and Kincardineshire in 1991 (Rebecca, 1992). G.W.R. visited Northumberland in 1992 and south-west Scotland in 1993 to see a sample of typical plantation nesting sites and to assess the habitat adjoining them (so as to consider further potential habitat in Aberdeenshire). Most sites visited were in thicket plantations adjoining grass dominated moor. Following these visits, coniferous plantation edges that bordered moorland were methodically surveyed in 1993 to 1996 for signs of merlin. Foresters, gamekeepers and ornithologists were also alerted to this change in nesting behaviour. In addition, most of the raised bogs in Aberdeenshire were checked in 1995 to 1997 for the presence of merlin as part of general ornithological and habitat surveys (I.S. Francis & G.W.R., unpublished data).

Confirmed breeding was recorded if any of the following was observed: courtship display, including the male bringing food to the female; copulation or nest site scraping (Feldsine & Oliphant, 1985); adults going to or leaving a nest; eggs or eggshells found; or young seen or heard. Probable breeding was recorded if fresh signs of occupation were found on at least two occasions separated by at least one week during May or June, or if it was obvious, from experience, that the signs found indicated that a breeding attempt had probably occurred. These signs included the presence of prey remains, pellets, droppings or moulted merlin feathers. Successful breeding was recorded when at least one young was fledged or if the young were capable of flight when last observed. Annual productivity was calculated by dividing the number of fledged young by the number of confirmed and probable breeding attempts.

For the two study areas, all of the known breeding territories were monitored annually with visits made until a conclusion concerning occupancy and success was reached. The remaining suitable habitat, including plantation edges, was resurveyed on a regular basis. All breeding attempts during 1980 to 2000 were plotted on 1:25,000 maps to the nearest 5 m and the average altitude calculated for each territory.

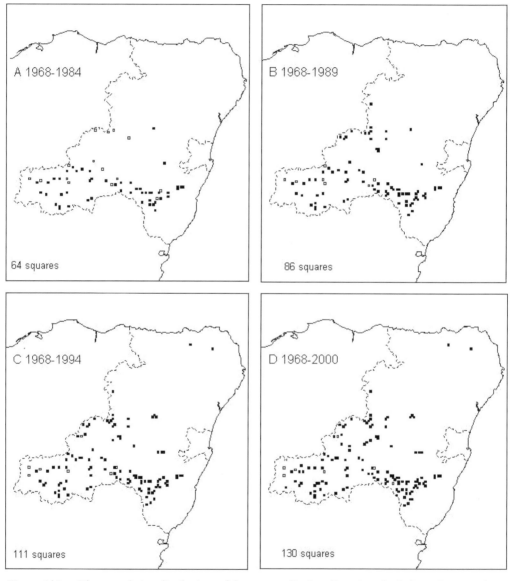

Figure 14.2. The cumulative distribution of known merlin breeding sites (including alternatives) in Aberdeenshire mapped as 1 km squares: solid squares represent confirmed breeding and open squares represent probable breeding.

14.4 Results

14.4.1 Distribution of breeding territories and population estimate

Progress of the survey work is evident from the cumulative distribution of breeding sites mapped as 1 km squares up to 1984, 1989, 1994 and 2000 (Figure 14.2). Most breeding territories had more than one nesting site within the 1 km square and some had obvious alternative sites in a different square, which occasionally was not an adjacent square. By 2000, 130 different 1 km squares had been used (Figure 14.2d). Using experience, and knowledge from the Deeside and Donside study areas, the likelihood of further alternative nesting sites was assessed annually. The basis of this assessment was whether squares in the same glen or catchment area were used in different years but only one pair was ever present. In total, 29 squares were judged as alternatives and, that being the case, approximately 100 merlin breeding territories were known in Aberdeenshire by 2000.

Most of the merlin breeding habitat, including plantation edges, in Aberdeenshire was well surveyed during 1993 to 1996, when the population was estimated at 45 to 55 breeding pairs (after allowing for areas not covered due to access restrictions; Cosnette & Rebecca, 1997). Resource limitations meant that it was not possible to monitor every breeding territory every year (Figure 14.3) and that situation is unlikely to change. The population in 2000 was estimated to be similar to the mid-1990s: 45 to 55 pairs.

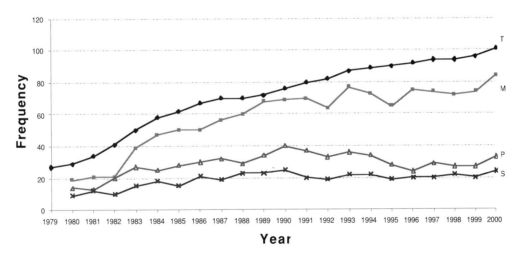

Figure 14.3. The cumulative total of merlin breeding territories in Aberdeenshire between 1979 and 2000. The number of territories monitored, pairs located and successful during 1980 to 2000. T = cumulative number of known merlin breeding territories; M = number of territories monitored; P = number of breeding pairs located; and S = number of pairs with at least one fledged young.

14.4.2 Territories monitored, number of pairs and success

As the study progressed, the number of known breeding territories and the number monitored increased; from 19 in 1980, 50 in 1986, 77 in 1993, to 84 in 2000 (Figure 14.3). The largest annual increase in monitoring was in 1983, the first year of the first national survey of breeding merlin in Britain (Bibby & Nattrass, 1986).

The mean number of territories monitored, pairs located and successful, and occupancy rate from 1983 to 1988, 1989 to 1994, and 1995 to 2000 are shown in Table 14.1. The mean number of territories monitored increased in each of these periods, from 50 to 70 to 74, whereas the mean occupancy rate, by breeding pairs, decreased from 58% to 51% to 38%. The annual percentage occupancy rate decreased significantly over the study period (Figure 14.4).

Table 14.1. Mean number of merlin territories monitored, breeding pairs located and successful, and occupancy rate of territories in Aberdeenshire in 1983-1988, 1989-1994 and 1995-2000.

Years	Mean number of territories monitored (range)		Mean number of breeding pairs located (range)		Mean number of successful pairs (range)		Mean percentage occupancy of territories by pairs (95% confidence limits)	
1983-1988	50	(39-60)	29	(25-32)	19	(15-23)	58	(44-72)
1989-1994	70	(64-77)	36	(33-40)	22	(19-25)	51	(38-62)
1995-2000	74	(65-84)	28	(24-33)	21	(19-24)	38	(27-49)

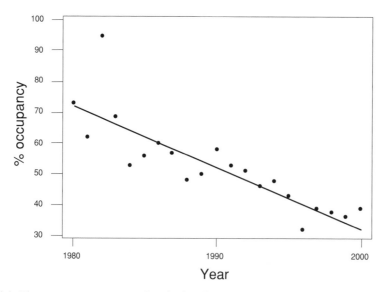

Figure 14.4. The percentage occupancy of merlin breeding territories in Aberdeenshire between 1980 and 2000 (regression $F_{1,19}$ = 46.03 P <0.001).

Between 1983 and 2000 the mean number of successful pairs was 20, with an annual range of 15 (in 1983 and 1985) to 25 (in 1990) (Figure 14.3). The mean number of successful pairs in the last three six-year periods of study were similar at 19, 22 and 21, respectively (Table 14.1).

14.4.3 Lower Deeside and upper Donside study areas

Details of the study areas are given in Tables 14.2 and 14.3. Full coverage of lower Deeside was complete by 1982 and upper Donside by 1989. Some aspects of breeding biology could therefore be compared after 1989. The main habitat difference was that lower Deeside had approximately 30% of coniferous plantations by 1990, covering the eastern third of the area, whereas upper Donside had no young plantations (Table 14.2). Lower Deeside breeding territories were on average 135 m lower than upper Donside (Table 14.3). On upper Donside, 20 breeding territories were located, with 24 1 km squares being used for nesting (Figure 14.5a); on lower Deeside 25 territories were located, with 41 1 km squares used for nesting (Figure 14.5b). On average, lower Deeside had a larger number of pairs and a higher equivalent density per 10 km^2 than upper Donside, whereas average productivity was very similar in the two areas (Table 14.3).

Table 14.2. Study dates, areas, habitats and land use changes in the Aberdeenshire merlin study areas.

Study areas	Study period	Year complete coverage achieved	Area (km^2)	Main habitats in 1990-2000 to nearest 5%			Land use change
				Managed grouse moor	Remnant moor	Coniferous plantation	
Lower Deeside	1980-2000	1982	215	55	15	30	Plantations at thicket stage by 2000 (14-25 years)
Upper Donside	1986-2000	1989	237	90	10	0	Relatively little; some excessive burning

Table 14.3. Number of territories, altitude and population trends in the Aberdeenshire merlin study areas. Number of pairs, density per 10 km^2 and productivity during 1990 to 2000.

Study areas	No. of 1 km squares used for breeding	No. of breeding territories	Mean altitude (m) of breeding territories ± standard error (range)	Population trend	Human persecution	Mean number of breeding pairs 1990-2000 (range)	Mean pairs per 10 km^2 in 1990-2000 (range)	Mean fledged young per pair per year 1990-2000 ± standard error (range)
Lower Deeside	41	25	310 ±12 (190-450)	Stable: 1982-1992 Decline: 1993-2000	Nil	10.6 (7-14)	5.0 (3.3-6.5)	2.08 ±0.17 (1.0-3.0)
Upper Donside	24	20	445 ±16 (330-570)	Stable: 1989-1994 Crash: 1995-1996 Recovery: by 2000	Believed to have occurred 6 times	7.8 (4-11)	3.3 (1.7-4.6)	1.98 ±0.15 (1.1-2.7)

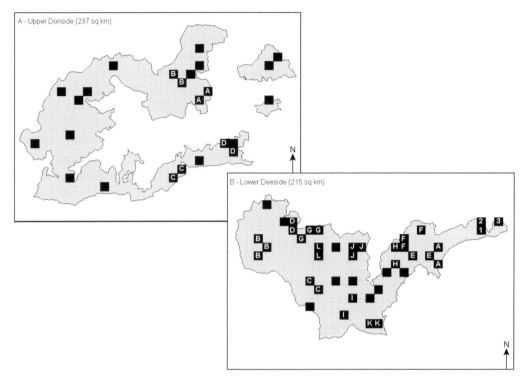

Figure 14.5. The distribution of 1 km squares where merlins were confirmed breeding in a) upper Donside during 1986 to 2000 and b) in lower Deeside during 1980 to 2000. Letters A-L are alternative nesting squares. Adjacent squares with no lettering had breeding pairs in the same year. Numbers 1 to 3 are detailed in Appendix 1.

The number of pairs fluctuated in both study areas but over different periods (Figure 14.6). The lower Deeside population was relatively stable during 1982 to 1992 at 11 to 14 pairs, but an overall decline was evident between 1993 and 2000, from 12 to seven pairs. The upper Donside population was relatively stable during 1989 to 1994, at seven to 11 pairs, but fell to four and five pairs, respectively, in 1995 and 1996; there was then a steady recovery to 11 pairs by 2000. As detailed comparisons could be made between study areas after 1989, the distribution of breeding pairs was mapped in 1990 and 2000 (Figures 14.7 and 14.8). By 2000, the coniferous plantations in lower Deeside were approximately 14 to 25 years old, (trees were assumed to be three to five years old when planted) and were largely at the thicket stage. In upper Donside, excessive burning of heather *Calluna vulgaris* rendered some nesting sites unusable because most merlin nests in north-east Scotland are on the ground in heather 30 to 70 cm deep (Rebecca *et al.*, 1992).

In lower Deeside maximum occupancy occurred in 1982 and 1990, when 14 pairs bred, and the distribution of breeding squares in 1990 is shown in Figure 14.7a. The lowest occupancy was in 2000 when only seven pairs bred, and the distribution of these squares is shown in Figure 14.7b. Examination of Figure 14.7 shows the eastern third of the study area to have held seven pairs in 1990 and three in 2000. The habitat surrounding the southern-most breeding territory did not change between the periods mapped. By 2000, the remaining six eastern territories were dominated by thicket plantations. One of the occupied territories in 2000 was in an area that had not been planted following discussions with Fasque Estates;

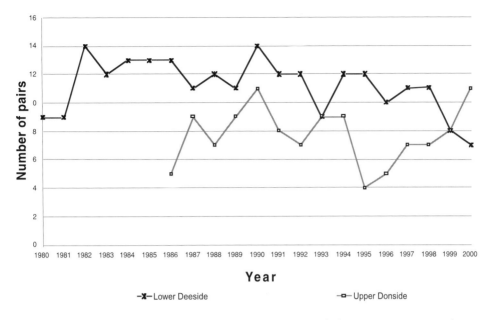

Figure 14.6. The number of breeding pairs of merlin in lower Deeside during 1980 to 2000 and in upper Donside during 1986 to 2000.

(G.W.R. negotiated with the head forester of Fasque Estates to leave the traditional nesting sites of three pairs unplanted and some additional areas of open ground were built into the forest design plan as potential merlin hunting ground). The other occupied territory in 2000 was in an area that was not planted and which was retained for sheep and cattle grazing. The breeding territory in the far north-east of the lower Deeside study area (Figure 14.7a) was last occupied by a pair in 1995 after which the area was considered unsuitable due to maturing plantations (Rebecca, 1998). The breeding territory in the far north-west of lower Deeside (Figure 14.7a) was occupied by a pair each year from 1979 to 1998. However, in the spring of 1999 Dunecht Estate felled hundreds of scattered self-sown Scots pine *Pinus sylvestris* trees over a period of about two months. This unexpected disturbance occurred over both sides of the glen where merlin had previously nested, and the territory was not occupied in 1999 or 2000.

In upper Donside during the late 1980s to early 1990s, most of the occupied breeding territories were found along the northern part of the study area, with eight out of 11 pairs there in 1990 (Figure 14.8a). During 1989 to 1992 occupancy in the north-east of the main moorland block was consistent with three, four, four and three pairs in successive years. In contrast, no breeding territories were located during the late 1980s to early 1990s in the south-west of the study area. There was a marked reduction in the number of occupied territories over the whole study area by the mid-1990s with only four pairs located in 1995, and five in 1996. The greatest reduction was in the north-east of the main moorland block, with no pairs in 1995 and only one in 1996. A recovery then began, and by 2000 the number of occupied territories had risen to 11 (Figure 14.8b). The distribution of occupied territories changed between 1990 and 2000 with two previously unknown breeding territories located in the south-west, one in 1999 and one in 2000 (Figure 14.8) - both on an estate where a reduction in moorland management had taken place during the late 1990s.

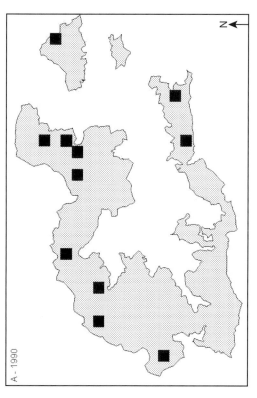

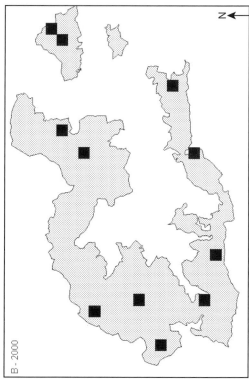

Figure 14.8. The distribution of merlin nesting sites as 1 km squares in upper Donside: a) in 1990 and b) in 2000.

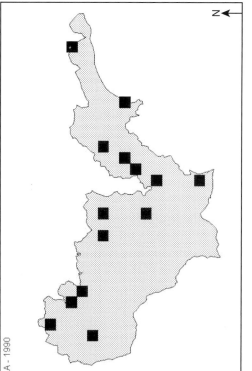

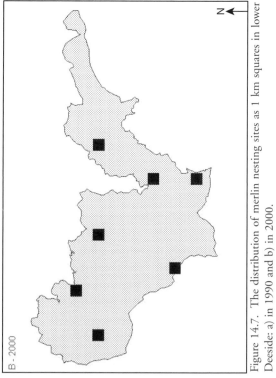

Figure 14.7. The distribution of merlin nesting sites as 1 km squares in lower Deeside: a) in 1990 and b) in 2000.

14.5 Discussion

14.5.1 Survey coverage and population estimate

During the 21 year study period, virtually all of the suitable merlin breeding habitat was searched many times. However, a few remote areas were only visited occasionally. There were also many areas which appeared suitable, but where merlin were not located. Feedback was requested from estates staff, in particular gamekeepers or countryside rangers, and hill-walkers and other naturalists. Nevertheless, with the resources available it was not possible to visit every known breeding territory every year so there are probably still a few unrecorded breeding territories.

In the 1993/1994 national survey of breeding merlin in Britain, the results from detailed survey methods, designed to locate all merlin, were compared with the previous knowledge of merlin in 10 km squares from well studied areas. The number of pairs located in 11 out of 14 study areas was within the range expected, indicating that in most well studied areas (including north-east Scotland) the numbers were accurately estimated (Rebecca & Bainbridge, 1998). The estimate for Aberdeenshire, of 45 to 55 breeding pairs in the 1990s, was calculated taking into account annual occupancy rates and fluctuations in the detailed study areas; it represents about 4% of the British merlin population in 1993 to 1994 (estimated at 1,300 ±200 breeding pairs (Rebecca & Bainbridge, 1998)). The Aberdeenshire population was believed to have been relatively stable during the study period and can therefore be considered important for merlin in a national context.

The progressive increase in the number of territories monitored did not result in a proportional increase in the number of pairs located. As a result, the average occupation of territories decreased throughout the study period. One interpretation could be that the population may have been in decline, but another explanation may be that merlin in Aberdeenshire have alternative nesting sites further apart than was observed or judged, for example in different catchment areas or glens, at perhaps six to ten kilometres apart. A detailed study with individually marked birds would be necessary to validate this possibility. In an effort to quantify nest site fidelity and movements, merlin broods were colour-ringed in Aberdeenshire, Morayshire and Angus in 1996 to 2000. In addition, in 1998 DNA analysis began on moulted adult feathers from Deeside from 1980 to 1999, and blood and feathers from broods from 1997 to 1999 (Marsden *et al.*, Chapter 16).

In lower Deeside, there was a population decrease associated with land use change and disturbance. However, such land use change was not widespread in Aberdeenshire during the study period and only a few territories were believed to be unsuitable for merlin by the late 1990s. The fluctuating status in upper Donside may have been more typical for the overall area. Similarly, the change in distribution of occupied breeding territories could indicate that merlin often switch breeding sites, possibly because of subtle or temporary habitat changes such as excessive burning of heather, predation pressure or changes in prey density. Alternatively, different merlins might, by chance, choose different areas in which to breed, in what is generally homogenous habitat. The study period could have encompassed the lifespan of five or six generations of merlin (if British merlins have similar longevity levels to those in Sweden; average female age 2.2 years, range 1 to 6 (Wiklund, 1995), and average male age 4.0 years, range 1 to 10 (Wiklund, 1996)). Merlins that were ringed as nestlings on Deeside moved to Morayshire, Perthshire, Angus and Donside to breed, and ringed young from all of these areas were found breeding on Deeside (G.W.R., unpublished data). The annual occupancy of breeding territories in Aberdeenshire and in these surrounding areas (Figure 14.1) may be related to the overall productivity within the region. Irrespective of the factors affecting the occupancy and distribution of breeding territories in Aberdeenshire, the mean numbers of successful pairs, for six year periods, varied little over the last 18 years of the study.

14.5.2 Effects of habitat change in lower Deeside

The three 1 km squares (numbers 1 to 3) in the far north-east of lower Deeside (Figure 14.5b) were discrete breeding territories. In 1980 and 1981, two of these territories were the first in the study area to be afforested with conifers. The third territory was planted up during 1986 and 1987. By 1990 only one territory was regularly occupied (Figure 14.7a) and the last breeding attempt was in 1995. In 1996 and 1997, an unmated female was present for about three weeks and two or three days, respectively. The details of occupancy, nest site and breeding success for these three territories during 1979 to 1997 was given in Rebecca (1998) and is reproduced here as Appendix 14.1. No merlins were seen or heard, nor were any signs of occupation found, in the three territories during 1998 to 2000. The general area was believed to be unsuitable for breeding merlin by the late 1990s due to the lack of open ground for hunting. There were eight discrete breeding territories in the eastern third of lower Deeside, which were affected by afforestation between 1980 and 1989. Six pairs were breeding in 1990 but this had declined to two by 2000, and these two were in areas that had not been planted.

14.5.3 Effects of habitat management on upper Donside

The upper Donside study area was under the influence of nine sporting estates, the largest of which were situated in the west. During the late 1980s only four of these estates were extensively managed for game. However, it was apparent by the early 1990s that heather management was undergoing radical change on some estates. Several moors, on which heather burning had been minimal in the 1980s, were extensively burned (not by the traditional strip method). Some steep heather banks where merlin had previously bred were entirely burnt out. Much of this burning was carried out well into April when the birds would have been established on their territories and would almost certainly have caused disturbance. Gamekeeper activity on some of the smaller estates also increased and although not previously suspected, human persecution of merlin nests became apparent at three territories. By 1995, the number of extensively managed estates had risen to eight. There was a partial recovery of merlins in the north-east of the main moorland block as the heather regenerated and by 2000 two territories were occupied. However, other breeding sites will remain largely unsuitable until there is improved heather cover.

14.6 Conservation initiatives

All of the data were made available to the Royal Society for the Protection of Birds (RSPB) and Scottish Natural Heritage (SNH) for conservation casework purposes. Details of the breeding territories were provided for the Grampian Regional Councils' Indicative Forestry Strategy in 1988, as the merlin was one of the key species identified by the compilers. In 1987 it was established that 12% to 14% of the then known merlin breeding territories in the NESRSG area were within or adjacent to Sites of Special Scientific Interest (SSSIs). Six further areas with a relatively high density of breeding merlin were recommended as potential SSSIs (Rebecca, 1988). In 1991, 13% of merlin breeding territories were within or adjacent to SSSIs (Rebecca, 1993). The locations of relevant breeding territories in Glen Tanar National Nature Reserve (mid-Deeside) were forwarded to SNH and those in Mar Lodge Estate (upper Deeside) were forwarded to the National Trust for Scotland (NTS). Staff from SNH and NTS were guided on the methods of locating and monitoring breeding merlin and assistance was given with the monitoring where necessary.

Acknowledgements

For encouragement and advice at the beginning of the study we thank: B. Little, M. Marquiss, E.R. Meek, N. Picozzi and P.H. Shaw. Merlins can be elusive on their breeding grounds and in certain remote areas are difficult to study, so a considerable amount of commitment, energy and time were needed to cover an area the size of Aberdeenshire. The following people assisted with the survey and monitoring over various periods for which we are very grateful: D.J. Bain, M.V. Bell, D. Calder, E. Cameron, the late J. Chapman, N. Cook, W. Craigie, A. Duncan, K. Duncan, J. Duncan, R. Duncan, E. Duthie, I.S. Francis, C. Geddes, P. Glennie, J.J.C. Hardey, M. Kimber, A. MacHardy, M. Marquiss, I. McLeod, P.J. Newman, J. Parkin, A.G. Payne, N. Picozzi, R. Rae, G. Ruthven, K.D. Shaw, P.H. Shaw, I.M.W. Sim, L.D. Steele, B.J. Stewart, J.L. Swallow, I. Thomson and A. Thorpe.

We also thank: the local bird recorders and everyone who passed on records; Fasque Estates, and in particular head forester F. Sheridan, for their co-operation in trying to maintain merlin breeding territories within their forest design plan; many other estates and their staff for their co-operation and in some cases active interest; E. Kelly for helping to produce the maps and S. Adair for typing the draft manuscript. The Scottish Ornithologists' Club, Hawk and Owl Trust, RSPB and SNH gave us grants to offset travel expenses, and these were much appreciated. Finally, we thank P. Haworth, D. Jardine and M. Marquiss for constructive comments on the draft and M. Marquiss for advice on statistics. We have found studying merlins to be challenging, exciting and at times frustrating, but never dull. We agree with Leslie Brown (1976) who suggested that whoever tackled a detailed study of the merlin would find it a rewarding and splendid little bird.

References

Alexander, W.B. & Lack, D. (1944). Change in status among British breeding birds. *British Birds*, **38**, 62-69.

Batten, L.A., Bibby, C.J., Clement, P., Elliot, G.D. & Porter, R.F. (1990). *Red Data Birds in Britain*. Poyser, London.

Bibby, C.J. & Nattrass, M. (1986). Breeding status of the Merlin in Britain. *British Birds*, **79**, 170-185.

Brown, L. (1976). *British Birds of Prey*. Collins, London.

Buckland, S.T., Bell, M.V. & Picozzi, N. (Eds) (1990). *The Birds of North-East Scotland*. North-East Scotland Bird Club, Aberdeen.

Cosnette, B.L. (1984). Successive use of same site by two female Merlins. *Scottish Birds*, **13**, 118.

Cosnette, B.L. (1991). Apparent bigamy in Merlins and co-operation of two females with large young. *North-East Scotland Bird Report*, **1990**, 74-75.

Cosnette, B.L. & Rebecca, G.W. (1997). Breeding Merlins in Aberdeenshire during 1993-1996. *North-East Scotland Bird Report*, **1996**, 71-80.

Cramp, S. & Simmons, K.E.L. (1980). Merlin. In *The Birds of the Western Paleartic Vol. 2*, ed. by S. Cramp & K.E.L. Simmons. Oxford University Press, Oxford. pp. 308-316.

Ellis, P.M. & Okill, J.D. (1990). Breeding ecology of the Merlin *Falco columbarius* in Shetland. *Bird Study*, **37**, 101-110.

Feldsine, J.W. & Oliphant, L.W. (1985). Breeding behaviour of the Merlin: the courtship period. *Raptor Research*, **19**, 60-67.

Fox, G.A. (1971). Recent changes in the reproductive success of the Pigeon Hawk. *Journal of Wildlife Management*, **35**, 122-128.

Fox, G.A. & Donald, T. (1980). Organochlorine pollutants, nest-defence behaviour and reproductive success in Merlins. *Condor*, **81**, 81-84.

Fyfe, R.W., Risebrough, R.W. & Walker, W. (1976). Pollutant effects on the reproduction of the Prairie Falcons and Merlins of the Canadian Prairies. *Canadian Field Naturalist*, **90**, 346-355.

Gibbons, D.W., Avery, M.I., Baillie, S.R., Gregory, R.D., Kirkby, J., Porter, R.F., Tucker, G.M. & Williams, G. (1996). Bird Species of Conservation Concern in the United Kingdom, Channel Islands and Isle of Man: Revising the Red Data List. *RSPB Conservation Review*, **10**, 7-10.

Little, B. & Davison, M. (1992). Merlins *Falco columbarius* using crow nests in Kielder Forest, Northumberland. *Bird Study*, **39**, 13-16.

Meek, E.R. (1988). The breeding ecology and decline of the Merlin *Falco columbarius* in Orkney. *Bird Study*, **35**, 209-218.

Newton, I. (1973). Egg breakage and breeding failure in British Merlins. *Bird Study*, **20**, 241-244.

Newton, I. (1984). Raptors in Britain - a review of the last 150 years. *BTO News*, **131**, 6-7.

Newton, I., Meek, E.R. & Little, B. (1978). Breeding ecology of the Merlin in Northumberland. *British Birds*, **71**, 376-398.

Newton, I., Meek, E.R. & Little, B. (1986). Population and breeding of Northumbrian Merlins. *British Birds*, **79**, 155-170.

Newton, I. & Haas, M.B. (1988). Pollutants in Merlin eggs and their effects on breeding. *British Birds*, **81**, 258-269.

Olsson, B.O. (1980). *Project Stenfalk Rapport 1975-1978*. Svenska Naturskyddsforemingen, Stockholm.

Orchel, J. (1992). *Forest Merlins in Scotland: Their Requirements and Management*. Hawk and Owl Trust, London.

Parr, S.J. (1991). Occupation of new conifer plantations by Merlins in Wales. *Bird Study*, **38**, 103-111.

Parslow, J.L.F. (1967). Changes in status among breeding birds in Britain and Ireland. *British Birds*, **60**, 2-49.

Rebecca, G.W. (1988). *Merlins in Grampian*. Unpublished report. Royal Society for the Protection of Birds, Edinburgh.

Rebecca, G.W. (1992). Merlins breeding at the edge of a mature conifer plantation. *North-East Scotland Bird Report*, **1991**, 61-62.

Rebecca, G.W. (1993). The importance of the breeding population of the Merlin *Falco columbarius* in North-East Scotland. In *Biology and Conservation of Small Falcons*, ed. by M.K. Nicholls & R. Clarke. Hawk and Owl Trust, London. pp. 39-41.

Rebecca, G.W. (1998). Repeated use of an artificial crow nest by Merlins. *The Raptor*, **25**, 22-24.

Rebecca, G.W. & Bainbridge, I.P. (1998). The breeding status of the Merlin *Falco columbarius* in Britain in 1993-1994. *Bird Study*, **45**, 172-187.

Rebecca, G.W., Cosnette, B.L. & Duncan, A. (1988). Two cases of a yearling and an adult male Merlin attending the same nest site. *Scottish Birds*, **15**, 45-46.

Rebecca, G.W., Cosnette, B.L., Duncan, A., Picozzi, N. & Catt, D.C. (1990). Hunting distance of breeding Merlins in Grampian indicated by ringed wader chicks taken as prey. *Scottish Birds*, **16**, 38-39.

Rebecca, G.W., Cosnette, B.L., Hardey, J.J.C. & Payne, A.G. (1992). Status, distribution and breeding biology of the Merlin in north-east Scotland, 1980-1989. *Scottish Birds*, **16**, 165-183.

Risebrough, R.W., Florant, G.L. & Berger, D.D. (1970). Organochlorine pollutants in Peregrines and Merlins migrating through Wisconsin. *Canadian Field Naturalist*, **84**, 247-253.

Sharrock, J.T.R. (1976). *The Atlas of Breeding Birds in Britain and Ireland*. BTO/IWC, Poyser, Berkhamsted.

Temple, S.A. (1972). Chlorinated hydrocarbon residues and reproductive success in eastern north American Merlins. *Condor*, **74**, 105-106.

Trimble, S.A. (1975). Habitat management series for unique or endangered species. Report No 15, Merlin *Falco columbarius*. US Department. of the Interior, Bureau of Land Management, Denver, Colorado.

Wiklund, C.G. (1995). Nest predation and life-span: components of variance in LRS among Merlin females. *Ecology*, **76**, 1994-1996.

Wiklund, C.G. (1996). Breeding lifespan and nest predation determine lifetime production of fledglings by male merlins *Falco columbarius*. *Proceedings of the Royal Society of London*, **263**, 723-728.

Wright, P.M. (1997). Distribution, site occupancy and breeding success of the Merlin on Barden moor and fell, North Yorkshire. *Bird Study*, **44**, 182-193.

Appendix 14.1. Occupation and breeding success at merlin nesting areas at the Slug Moors, 1979-1987 (see Figure 14.5b). G = nest on ground, T = nest in old crow nest in tree (1985-1990) or artificial basket nest in tree (1992-1995) (from Rebecca, 1998).

Year	NESTING AREA 1			NESTING AREA 2			NESTING AREA 3		
	Nest site	No. of young	Comments	Nest site	No of young	Comments	Nest site	No. of young	Comments
1979	G	3		-	-	Not occupied	?	?	Pair probably bred
1980	G	5	Moved 500 m, 1979 site planted	-	-	Not occupied, ploughed/planted	?	?	Female seen
1981	-	-	1980 area burnt, female seen	-	-	Not occupied, ploughed/planted	G	1	Nest near 1979 area
1982	G	4	30 m from 1980 nest, planting complete	G	0	Young predated	G	0	20 m from 1981 nest, egg breakage
1983	G	3	Moved back to 1979 site	G	0	Eggs failed to hatch	G	0	Near 1981 and 1982 sites, egg breakage
1984	G	0	Female killed on nest near to 1980 and 1982 sites, second female present but breeding not confirmed	-		Not occupied	G	0	Eggs predated by crow
1985	G	3	200 m from 1984 nest	-		Not occupied	GGG	0	3 attempts, all egg breakage
1985	G	0	Second pair, near 1979 site, eggs predated by crow, pair moved to area 2 for relay	T	0	Pair moved from area 1 and re-laid, egg breakage			
1986	G	0	Near 1984 site, eggs taken by crow	T	4		G	4	Moved 400m, 1979-1985 sites burnt out
1986	T	0	Re-lay, eggs disappeared						
1987	-	-	Pair present then moved to area 2	T	4	Crow nest repaired at chick stage	-	-	Not occupied, 1979-1985 sites now planted, 1986 area burnt
1988	-	-	Pair present then moved to area 2	G	5	No suitable crow nest	-	-	Not occupied
1989	-	-	Not occupied	G	4	No suitable crow nest	-	-	Not occupied

Year	NESTING AREA 1			NESTING AREA 2			NESTING AREA 3		
	Nest site	No. of young	Comments	Nest site	No of young	Comments	Nest site	No. of young	Comments
1990	T	0	Pair moved from area 2 and re-laid	G	0	Moved to area 1 for re-lay	-	-	Not occupied
1991	G	0	Egg breakage, pair moved to area 3	-	-	Not occupied	-	-	Pair from area 1 after failure, but no re-lay
1992	T	1	Artificial nest installed and used, plantation now thicket	-	-	Not occupied	-	-	Not occupied
1993	T	4	Artificial nest used	-	-	Not occupied	-	-	Not occupied
1994	T	2	Artificial nest used	-	-	Not occupied	-	-	Not occupied
1995	T	4	Artificial nest used	-	-	Not occupied	-	-	Not occupied
1996	-	-	Female present for about 3 weeks	-	-	Not occupied	-	-	Not occupied
1997	-	-	Female present for 2-3 days, plantation restructured	-	-	Not occupied, plantation restructured	-	-	Not occupied

15. RECOVERY OF THE SOUTH PENNINE MERLIN (*FALCO COLUMBARIUS*) POPULATION

Alan H. Fielding & Paul F. Haworth

Summary

1. The South Pennine merlin *Falco columbarius* population underwent a severe decline, dropping to only five pairs in 1983. Since then the population has recovered, peaking at 17 pairs in 1990.

2. The recovery was not associated with changes in foraging or nesting habitats.

3. The number of occupied sites, the proportion of successful sites and the total clutch size were all correlated with the number of degree-days (using a 6°C threshold) between early February and the mean laying date (5th May).

4. The number of young fledged in sites with eggs was negatively correlated with the maximum temperature in the period immediately following egg laying and the amount of rainfall when nestlings were present in the nest.

5. It is suggested that the recovery may be related to the warmer springs, which have resulted in extra prey.

15.1 Introduction

The South Pennine merlin population has been studied in detail since 1982 (Haworth & Fielding, 1988; Haworth & Thompson, 1990). This chapter examines year-to-year variations in numbers and breeding success, notably in relation to fluctuations in weather conditions.

The study area is a geologically uniform tract of upland (152 km², 2.08°W, 53.80°N) dominated by land between 250 and 430 m. Major land uses are water catchment, sheep farming and grouse moor (Haworth & Thompson, 1990). The region supports a significant proportion of the national merlin population (Stillman & Brown, 1994). In common with most of Britain, merlins in the South Pennines underwent a severe decline prior to the mid-1980s (Brown & Stillman, 1998); the recent recovery is largely due to re-occupancy of traditional sites (Nattrass, 1994, 1996). We investigate the hypothesis that merlin productivity is indirectly affected by spring weather, which may influence prey availability.

15.2 Methods

Breeding pairs were established through field surveys (during March-July, 1982-1995). Occupation was assumed if pairs showed site-attachment on at least two occasions. Sites were labelled 'used' if at least one egg was laid and, where appropriate, clutch size, brood size and fledging success was recorded (see also Rebecca & Cosnette, Chapter 14). Productivity measures (e.g. mean clutch size) were expressed in relation to successful breeding attempts and occupancy. Weather data (1982–1995) were extracted from Meteorological Office databases (Bradford, 1.33°W, 53.82°N, altitude 134 m). One potential problem with using monthly means to link weather and bird productivity is that significant relationships can only be detected if they coincide with calendar boundaries. In this study two different approaches were used: 'running means' and 'degree-days'. Running means overcome the boundary problem by correlating annual productivity with weather in 30-day 'moving-windows' (see Watson *et al.*, Chapter 10). Plant and insect growth are related to the number of degree-days, i.e. accumulated temperature above a developmental threshold. Degree-days quantify the amount by which daily temperatures exceed this threshold, and large excesses result in greater development. In a degree-day model only fluctuations above the threshold are important. In order to test the hypothesis that merlin productivity is indirectly affected by spring weather, we examined degree-days for 1st January-31st May, using a 6°C threshold, which corresponds to the plant growing season (MAFF, 1976).

15.3 Results

Table 15.1 lists site occupancy and productivity details. Most clutches were laid in early May (mean = 5th May, n = 31, 95% confidence limit: 3rd–7th May). Eggs were stolen from four nests, and two nests failed because of fox predation and one because of trampling. There was a significant linear trend towards greater occupancy (Figure 15.1. Occupancy = -28.1 + 0.431 year, R^2 = 38.3%, P <0.05) and better breeding success (used sites = -47.3 + 0.613 year, R^2 = 64.7%, P <0.001) in more recent years. No occupancy or productivity variables were significantly correlated with altitude. Mean nearest neighbour distances were negatively correlated with the number of occupied sites (r = -0.604, P <0.05) and the number of used sites (r = -0.797, P <0.005). There was no correlation between mean nearest neighbour distances and clutch size, brood size or the number of young fledged from used nests (P >0.9). The numbers of occupied sites, successful sites and total clutch size were positively correlated with the degree-days between early February and the mean laying date (Figure 15.2). The mean number of young fledged was negatively correlated with the maximum temperature for the period immediately after the mean laying date and with the amount of rainfall when nestlings were present (Figure 15.3).

15.4 Discussion

Concerns were raised for the merlin in Britain following the 1983-1984 national survey (Bibby & Nattrass, 1986), which indicated a significant decline from the 1950s. Explanations for this decline included habitat loss, disturbance and pesticide accumulation from wintering grounds (e.g. Bibby, 1986; Newton *et al.*, 1986). Unequivocal evidence is unavailable for any hypothesis and additional, but unidentified, factors have been implicated (Thom, 1986; Bibby & Nattrass, 1986). Except for pollutant levels (e.g. Nygård, 1999), there is little evidence for environmental improvements that would support a sustained recovery. However, in common with other studies (e.g. Little *et al.*, 1995), and the results of the second national survey (Rebecca & Bainbridge, 1998), it seems that earlier concerns for the South Pennine merlin population were unfounded given its recovery from the 1983 low point (Figure 15.1). These recoveries occurred despite the absence of targeted conservation strategies, and Parr (1994) considered the overall recovery of the merlin in Britain sufficient to remove the species from the British Red Data list.

The recovery of the South Pennine merlin is unrelated to changes in habitat or nesting preferences. Habitat re-surveys identified no major changes since the earlier study by Haworth

Table 15.1. Occupancy and productivity of 24 known merlin sites for the period 1982-1995, (nnd is the distance to the nearest site). Annual usage is indicated by 0 (not used), 1 (occupied, but no eggs laid), 2 (at least 1 egg laid).

Site	Altitude (m)	nnd (km)	Occupied	Used	Total Clutch	Total Brood	Total Fledged	Clutch/ Success	Brood/ Success	Fledge/ Success	82	83	84	85	86	87	88	89	90	91	92	93	94	95
1	370	0.7	3	2	9	9	9	4.50	4.50	4.50	0	0	0	0	0	0	0	0	1	2	0	0	2	0
2	330	0.8	6	6	21	12	11	3.50	2.00	1.83	2	2	2	2	2	2	2	0	0	0	0	0	0	0
3	390	1.4	4	3	13	11	11	4.33	3.67	3.67	0	0	0	0	0	2	2	0	2	2	2	2	0	0
4	350	1.7	2	1	4	0	0	4.00	0.00	0.00	0	0	0	0	0	0	0	0	1	0	0	0	2	0
5	310	0.8	7	5	19	9	9	3.80	1.80	1.80	0	0	0	0	0	0	2	2	2	2	2	2	1	2
6	350	0.6	7	4	16	12	12	4.00	3.00	3.00	0	0	0	0	0	0	0	0	1	2	2	1	2	1
7	350	0.6	1	1	4	0	0	4.00	0.00	0.00	0	0	0	0	0	0	0	0	0	0	2	2	0	0
8	370	1.4	4	3	9	4	4	3.00	1.33	1.33	0	0	2	2	0	0	0	1	0	0	0	0	0	2
9	410	0.9	5	4	17	15	15	4.25	3.75	3.75	0	0	0	0	0	0	0	0	1	2	2	2	2	2
10	410	1.2	7	5	22	15	15	4.40	3.00	3.00	1	0	2	0	0	0	0	0	1	2	0	2	2	2
11	340	0.3	2	2	8	8	8	4.00	4.00	4.00	0	0	0	0	0	0	0	2	2	0	0	0	0	2
12	310	1.7	4	1	2	2	2	2.00	2.00	2.00	1	0	0	1	0	0	2	0	0	1	0	1	0	0
13	330	0.7	8	7	32	24	19	4.57	3.43	2.71	0	0	0	0	2	2	2	2	2	2	2	2	0	2
14	420	1.2	6	4	16	10	10	4.00	2.50	2.50	0	0	0	0	1	1	2	2	2	0	0	0	0	0
15	360	1.2	9	4	18	9	9	4.50	2.25	2.25	1	0	1	0	1	1	1	1	2	0	0	2	2	2
16	320	0.3	1	1	4	3	3	4.00	3.00	3.00	0	0	0	0	0	0	0	0	2	0	0	0	0	0
17	350	1.3	1	1	3	2	2	3.00	2.00	2.00	0	0	0	0	0	0	0	0	0	0	0	0	0	2
18	400	1.5	13	9	40	37	37	4.44	4.11	4.11	0	2	2	1	2	2	2	2	2	1	2	2	2	2
19	350	0.6	13	13	56	49	41	4.31	3.77	3.15	2	2	2	2	2	2	2	2	2	2	2	2	2	0
20	380	1.6	2	0	0	0	0	-	-	-	1	0	0	0	0	0	0	0	0	0	0	0	0	0
21	370	1.0	4	3	14	8	8	4.67	2.67	2.67	0	0	0	0	0	0	0	1	2	2	0	0	0	0
22	410	1.8	12	8	35	20	19	4.37	2.50	2.37	1	2	1	2	1	1	2	2	2	0	0	0	2	2
23	380	1.2	12	6	25	18	18	4.17	3.00	3.00	2	0	1	1	1	1	2	0	1	0	2	1	2	2
24	390	1.5	12	9	37	35	29	4.11	3.89	3.22	0	2	2	2	1	1	1	0	1	2	2	2	2	2

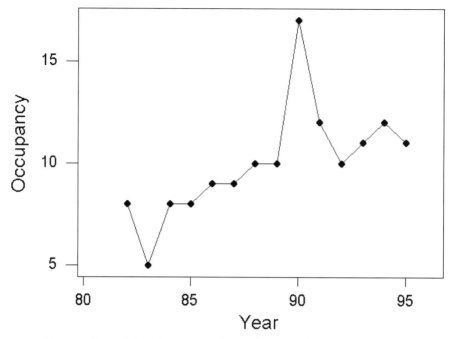

Figure 15.1. Number of occupied merlin ranges in the South Pennines, 1982–1995.

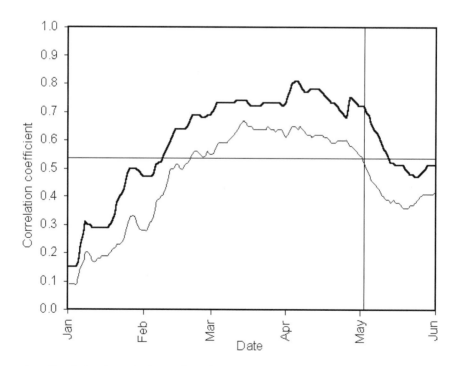

Figure 15.2. Correlations between the number of degree-days and occupied sites (heavy line) and total clutch size (thin line). The horizontal line is the notional P = 0.05 (2-tailed) critical value for *r*. The vertical line marks the mean laying date. Degree days were calculated using the mean air temperature and a 6°C threshold (See section 15.2 Methods).

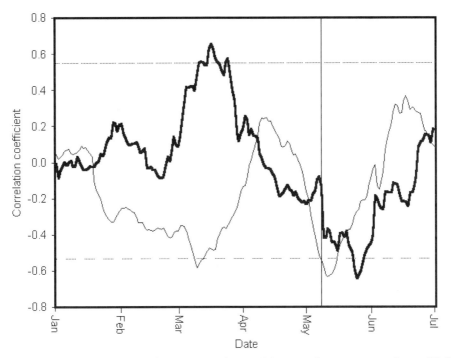

Figure 15.3. Correlations between the fledging rates of successful nests and running means for rainfall (heavy line) and maximum temperature (thin line). The dotted horizontal lines are the notional P = 0.05 (2-tailed) critical values for *r*. The vertical line marks the mean laying date. Running means are for the 30 days from the start date.

& Fielding (1988) and, unlike the Kielder and Welsh populations (Parr, 1994; Little *et al.,* 1995), there was no increase in the use of crow nests. However, the main part of this population's recovery (1985-1990) was characterised by a period of increasingly warmer springs.

Weather, particularly extreme events, can directly affect bird mortality and productivity (e.g. Franklin *et al.,* 2000). Indirect effects may result from the influence of weather on the amount and availability of food (e.g. Mearns & Newton, 1988; Kostrzewa & Kostrzewa, 1990). Anecdotal accounts of the weather's influence on merlins are common (e.g. Cosnette, 1984). Ratcliffe (1990) suggested that between-year variations in merlin numbers are partly explicable by passerine population fluctuations which may be related to winter and spring weather. Although Meek (1988) concluded that weather was not the prime factor in the decline of Orkney's merlin (1981-1986) he noted that cold late springs could prevent birds from reaching peak breeding condition. A link between weather and merlin population dynamics is important given the predictions of actual or impending climatic change. In this study, we postulate that indirect effects of early spring weather may be one of many factors influencing the occupancy and productivity of merlin territories. The mechanism could operate via the effect that weather, particularly temperature, has on plants and invertebrates that are food for the merlin's potential prey. However, it is unlikely that short-term studies could separate out weather effects from other important factors (Steenhof *et al.,* 1997). Therefore, data are required from long-term studies of populations such as that in the South Pennines that have not been subjected to changes in foraging or nesting habitat (c.f. Rebecca & Cosnette's study in Aberdeen, Chapter 14).

There is evidence from the degree-day correlations (Figure 15.2) that both occupancy and total clutch size are correlated with pre-laying weather conditions. Prior to laying, sufficient food is required to bring the female into suitable condition (or nesting attempts may be abandoned). Newton *et al.* (1978) noted that 37% of merlin sites, showing evidence of occupation in April, were vacant by May, possibly because the pair failed to reach breeding condition. The significant linear trend towards more occupancy (Figure 15.1) is obscured by the large peak in 1990. This anomaly supports the potential spring weather link since it coincides with a number of extreme climate events. The winters of 1988/89 and 1989/90 were the second and sixth warmest winters since 1659. February 1990 was the second warmest in the same series and was followed by the third warmest March (Jones & Hulme, 1993). Similarly, the worst year in the series, 1983, had one of the wettest springs on record (Farmer, 1983). Presumably heavy rainfall reduces a merlin's ability to catch prey, leaving females in poor breeding condition. Warm early spring weather allows earlier breeding of the merlin's potential prey species. For example, Glue (1995) noted that the mild winter of 1994/95 generated large, early populations of aerial insects and soil invertebrates. This was subsequently reflected in large, early broods of many birds including the meadow pipit (*Anthus pratensis*).

Once eggs have been laid there is evidence of more direct effects on reproductive success. The significant negative correlation between fledging rate and maximum temperature immediately after laying (Figure 15.3) is suggestive of thermal stress on the eggs. The later negative correlation between fledging rate and rainfall (in the period when nestlings are present) is consistent with other raptor studies (e.g. Mearns & Newton, 1988; Franklin *et al.*, 2000) and is probably related to constraints on parental foraging or direct chick or egg mortality through chilling.

Although this study demonstrates that the size and productivity of the South Pennine merlin population is significantly correlated with spring weather, the relationship is apparently not universal. For example, Parr (1994) suggested that the Welsh population was relatively stable between 1970 and 1991. Similarly, the North-East Scotland population appears to have been stable during the 1980s and early 1990s (Rebecca *et al.*, 1992; Rebecca, 1993; Rebecca & Cosnette, Chapter 14). Little *et al.* (1995) described how the Kielder Forest (North-East England) population rose from 10 to 29 pairs between 1982 and 1991, but this was thought to result from the exploitation of new nesting opportunities along forest edges. There has been no significant forest expansion in the South Pennines and only one breeding attempt in a crow's nest. The plant growing season (temperature >6°C) in the oceanic uplands of Britain is considered to be sensitive to changes in mean temperature (Pepin, 1995). The onset of spring weather accounts for most of the variation in the growing season's duration (Jones & Thomasson, 1985). Pepin (1995) demonstrated that differences in the mean annual temperature curves were likely to produce more significant climatic effects on plant growth in maritime and oceanic regions of Britain compared with the more continental eastern regions. This may explain the discrepancy between our results and those for other populations.

Irrespective of how success was measured, some territories were particularly successful (Table 15.1). Unpublished investigations, into the relationships between productivity and habitat (using data from Stillman & Brown (1994)), have not yet identified any significant correlations. Thus, the characteristics underlying the most successful territories remain unknown. As in the Newton *et al.* (1986) study, there was no evidence for the expected relationship between occupancy rate and nest success, perhaps suggesting that differences are due to the characteristics of territory-holding individuals rather than the territory.

It is unfortunate that the two national merlin surveys coincided with particularly bad and good years for spring weather. Confidence about the status of the merlin in Britain, resulting from a doubling of the population's estimated size, may be unjustified if the earlier decline and subsequent expansion are partially weather dependent. Effective conservation depends on an ability to manipulate conditions to ensure increasing or stable populations (Newton, 1994). A species such as the merlin, which appears susceptible to climatic trends, may therefore be difficult to manage effectively. More generally, the results demonstrate that if population trends are used as a conservation status criterion (e.g. Avery *et al.*, 1994), any interpretation should take account of recent climatic trends.

Acknowledgements
We thank John Watts for providing much valuable data on breeding merlin from 1990, Richard Stillman for providing habitat data for our study region, the United Kingdom Meteorological Office for providing weather data, and two anonymous referees for comments. Alan Fielding was in receipt of a Leverhulme Fellowship during the writing of this manuscript.

References
Avery, M., Gibbons, D.W., Porter, R., Tew, T., Tucker, G. & Williams, G. (1994). Revising the British Red Data List for birds: the biological basis of U.K. conservation priorities. *Ibis*, **137**, S232-S239.

Bibby, C.J. (1986). Merlins in Wales: site occupancy and breeding in relation to vegetation. *Journal of Applied Ecology*, **23**, 1-12.

Bibby, C.J. & Nattrass, M. (1986). Breeding status of the merlin in Britain. *British Birds*, **79**, 170-185.

Brown, A.F. & Stillman, R.A. (1998). The return of the merlin to the south Pennines. *Bird Study*, **45**, 293-301.

Cosnette, B.L. (1984). Successive use of the same site by two female merlins. *Scottish Birds*, **13**, 118.

Farmer, G. (1983). Exceptional climatic events for the year 1983. *Climate Monitor*, **12**, 134-141.

Franklin, A.B., Anderson, D.R., Gutiérrez, R.J. & Burnham, K.P. (2000). Climate, habitat quality, and fitness in northern spotted owl populations in northwestern California. *Ecological Monographs*, **70**, 539-590.

Glue, D.E. (1995). The combined influences of the mild 1994/95 winter and protracted hot dry summer on Britain's breeding birds in 1995. *Journal of Meteorology*, **20**, 339-342.

Haworth, P.F. & Fielding, A.H. (1988). Conservation and management implications of habitat selection in the merlin *Falco columbarius* L. in the South Pennines, UK. *Biological Conservation*, **46**, 247-260.

Haworth, P.F. & Thompson, D.B.A. (1990). Factors associated with the breeding distributions of upland birds in the South Pennines, England. *Journal of Applied Ecology*, **27**, 562-577.

Jones, P.D. & Hulme, M. (1993). Temperature and windiness. In *Impacts of the Mild Winters and Hot Summers in the United Kingdom in 1988-1990*, ed. by M.G.R. Cannell & C.E.R. Pitcairn. HMSO, London. pp. 3-8.

Jones, R.J.A. & Thomasson, A.J. (1985). *An Agroclimatic Databank for England and Wales*. Technical Monograph No. 16. Soil Survey, Harpenden.

Kostrzewa, A. & Kostrzewa, R. (1990). The relationship of spring and summer weather with density and breeding performance of the buzzard *Buteo buteo*, goshawk *Accipiter gentilis* and kestrel *Falco tinnunculus*. *Ibis*, **132**, 550-559.

Little, B., Davison, M. & Jardine, D. (1995). Merlins *Falco columbarius* in Kielder Forests - influences of habitat on breeding performance. *Forest Ecology and Management*, **79**, 147-152.

MAFF (1976). *The Agricultural Climate of England and Wales*. Ministry of Agriculture, Fisheries and Food Technical Bulletin 35. HMSO, London.

Mearns, R. & Newton, I. (1988). Factors affecting breeding success of peregrines in South Scotland. *Journal of Animal Ecology*, **57**, 903-916.

Meek, E.R. (1988). The breeding ecology and decline of the merlin *Falco columbarius* in Orkney. *Bird Study*, **35**, 209-218.

Nattrass, M. (1994). *Summary of the Analysis of English Nature Licences Issued in 1993 for Schedule 1 Birds*. English Nature, Peterborough.

Nattrass, M. (1996). *Summary of the Analysis of English Nature Licences Issued in 1994 for Schedule 1 Birds*. English Nature, Peterborough.

Newton, I. (1994). Experiments on the limitation of bird breeding densities: a review. *Ibis*, **136**, 397-411.

Newton, I., Meek, E.R. & Little, B. (1978). Breeding ecology of the merlin in Northumberland. *British Birds*, **71**, 376-398.

Newton, I., Meek, E.R. & Little, B. (1986). Population and breeding of Northumberland merlins. *British Birds*, **79**, 155-170.

Nygård, T. (1999). Long term trends in pollutant levels and shell thickness in eggs of merlin in Norway, in relation to its migration pattern and numbers. *Ecotoxicology*, **8**, 23-31.

Parr, S.J. (1994). Changes in the population size and nest sites of merlins *Falco columbarius* in Wales between 1970 and 1991. *Bird Study*, **41**, 42-47.

Pepin, N.C. (1995). The use of GCM scenario output to model effects of future climatic change on the thermal climate of marginal maritime uplands. *Geografiska Annaler, Series A - Physical Geography*, **77A**, 167-185.

Ratcliffe, D.A. (1990). *Bird Life of Mountain and Upland*. Cambridge University Press, Cambridge.

Rebecca, G.W. (1993). The importance of the breeding population of the Merlin (*Falco columbarius*) in North East Scotland. In *Biology and Conservation of Small Falcons*, ed. by M.K. Nicholls & R. Clarke. Zoological Society of London, London. pp. 39-41.

Rebecca, G.W. & Bainbridge, I.P. (1998). The breeding status of the merlin *Falco columbarius* in Britain in 1993-1994. *Bird Study*, **45**, 172-187.

Rebecca, G.W., Cosnette, B.L., Hardey, J.J.C. & Payne, A.G. (1992). Status, distribution and breeding biology of the merlin in north east Scotland, 1980-1989. *Scottish Birds*, **16**, 165-183.

Steenhof, K., Kochert, M.N. & McDonald, T.L. (1997). Interactive effects of prey and weather on golden eagle reproduction. *Journal of Applied Ecology*, **66**, 350-362.

Stillman, R.A. & Brown, A.F. (1994). Population sizes and habitat associations of upland breeding birds in the South Pennines, England. *Biological Conservation*, **69**, 307-314.

Thom, V.E. (1986). *Birds in Scotland*. Poyser, Calton.

16. A NON-INVASIVE TECHNIQUE FOR MONITORING RAPTOR POPULATIONS USING GENETIC PROFILING: A CASE STUDY USING MERLIN (*FALCO COLUMBARIUS*)

Amy Marsden, Graham W. Rebecca
& David T. Parkin

Summary

1. Microsatellite DNA profiling was applied to a population of merlins *Falco columbarius* in North-East Scotland in order to investigate aspects of mate and nest fidelity.

2. Cast feathers were used as a non-invasive source of DNA to identify individuals occupying nest sites over a period spanning 20 years. The data suggest that both males and females may hold nest sites over successive years.

3. Turnover of individuals occupying nest sites in this population was high, with 77% of females occupying nests for just one year.

4. Where females were found at the same nest site in consecutive years, it was likely to be with the same mate (71% of males were the same), whereas if the female changed the male was likely to change also (85% of males changed).

16.1 Introduction

The advent of molecular techniques such as DNA profiling has revolutionised the study of species often regarded as 'difficult' from a behavioural point of view (e.g. Amos *et al.*, 1993). Whilst much information is available regarding the population biology of raptors, their study has always been hampered due to difficulties in capturing (and therefore individually identifying) adult birds, and the near-impossibility of reading rings in the field. Here we show how the breeding behaviour of birds can be studied through microsatellite profiling of DNA extracted from moulted feathers. The identity of adults at a site may be inferred from the genetic profiles of the nestlings collected over a number of years, as a change in the pair composition may be indicated by the appearance of a new array of alleles (Wetton & Parkin, 1997). The focus of this chapter is to outline the use of feathers as a source of DNA in order to monitor a merlin population in the Deeside region of Aberdeenshire, North-East Scotland (Rebecca & Cosnette, Chapter 14). Microsatellite DNA profiling was carried out so as to identify individuals occupying nest sites over a period spanning 20 years. This is one of the first studies to have utilised molecular data from cast feathers in order to investigate aspects of mate and nest site fidelity in an avian species.

16.2 Methods

Blood and feather samples were taken from more than 150 young from all known nests (n = 56) in the Deeside area in the breeding seasons 1997-1999 and used to infer the identity of breeding adults. Cast feathers from potential parents were collected from the same nest sites, and approximately 500 of these, dating back to 1980, were analysed. DNA was extracted from blood using a standard phenol/chloroform approach (e.g. Nesje & Røed, 2000). DNA extraction from feathers followed a Chelex resin protocol. All individuals were typed at eight microsatellite loci: NVH fp49 (Nesje & Røed, 2000), NVH fp89, NVH fp92-1, NVH fp74-4, NVH fp31, NVH fp46-1 (Nesje *et al.*, 2000), Fµ1 and Fµ2 (J.H. Wetton, unpublished.). NVH fp49 is sex-linked and hence can also be used to sex individuals.

16.3 Results

Summary statistics are shown in Table 16.1. The probability of identity was 1.16×10^{-8}, hence there is less than a 1 in 100 million chance that two unrelated birds will have the same genetic profile. Occupancy of nest sites by individuals was analysed by creating a table denoting the females and males recorded at a nest each year from 1980-1999 (illustrated for five of the nest sites in Table 16.2). The maximum number of years for which an individual male or female was recorded at a particular nest was four. Maximum occupancy of nest sites by females is illustrated in Figure 16.1. At nest sites where the occupants were typed in consecutive years, the genetic profiles were compared so as to establish whether this involved the same individual(s). The percentage change in occupancy (turnover) was calculated for each adjacent pair of years for which a genetic profile was available. On average there was a 69% (range 28%-100%) turnover of individuals from one year to the next.

Table 16.1. Polymorphism, parentage exclusion and identity for the Deeside merlin population revealed by eight microsatellite loci.

Locus	No. of alleles	Heterozygosity[1] Observed	Expected	Parentage exclusion probability[2] First parent	Second parent	Probability of identity[3]
NVH fp49	5	0.59	0.53	0.13	0.24	0.32
NVH fp89	9	0.78	0.82	0.47	0.64	0.06
NVH fp92-1	5	0.80	0.77	0.37	0.55	0.09
NVH fp79-4	9	0.92*	0.84	0.50	0.67	0.05
NVH fp31	6	0.58	0.56	0.18	0.36	0.22
NVH fp46-1	6	0.74	0.66	0.25	0.43	0.16
Fµ1	5	0.78	0.70	0.26	0.42	0.16
Fµ2	16	0.92	0.89	0.62	0.77	0.02
Total for all 8 loci:				0.97	0.99	1.16×10^{-8}

1. Conformity to Hardy-Weinberg equilibrium was analysed using GENEPOP version 3.1 (Raymond & Rousset, 1995). * indicates significant heterozygote excess (p<0.05).
2. Calculated by the program CERVUS (Marshall *et al.*, 1998).
3. Calculated according to Hanotte *et al.* (1991).

Table 16.2. Turnover of merlin at five sites in the Deeside study area. Numbers denote females and letters denote males identified at each site. Identical number or letter at a site indicates that the female or male returned to the nest site. Blank spaces denote nest unoccupied or no feathers available for that year. Letters and numbers are unique to rows; i.e. there was no movement of birds between these sites.

Site	Year																			
	80	81	82	83	84	85	86	87	88	89	90	91	92	93	94	95	96	97	98	99
1	1	2		3		3	3		4	5		6			7	7		7	8	9
		A		B		B				C								D	E	F
2					1					2	3						4	5	5	5
					A													B	C	C
3	1	2		3	3	3	3		4	5					6	6	6	6		
	A	B				C											D	E		
4					1			2			2	3						4		5
					A		B				C	D	E					F		G
5						1			2	3	4				5		6	7	7	7
																			A	A

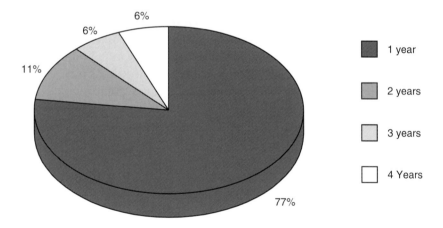

Figure 16.1. Maximum occupancy of nest sites by female merlins (n=84) in the Deeside population between 1980 and 1999. The mean length of nest occupancy by female merlins was 1.4 years during this study period.

Where females were site faithful over two consecutive years, 71% (10/14) of their male partners were also site faithful. Where the female occupying the nest changed, the male also changed on 85% (11/13) of occasions. Thirty-seven percent (10/27) of all pairings contained the same birds for two successive years. These results suggest that there is a significant association between the behaviour of both sexes (Fisher's exact test, p = 0.028). Information regarding movement is beyond the scope of this chapter and is presented elsewhere (Marsden, 2002).

16.4 Conclusions

Despite the widespread decline of the merlin in Britain during the middle part of the 20th century (Rebecca & Bainbridge, 1998), high levels of heterozygosity remain in the Deeside population. Turnover of individuals occupying nest sites in this population was high. Our results are similar to other work on merlin, both in Canada (James *et al.*, 1989; Warkentin *et al.*, 1991) and Britain (Wright, 1997). James *et al.* (1989) found turnover in a suburban population in Canada to be 80% for females and 59% for males. This result was confirmed by Warkentin *et al.* (1991), who found that occupancy of nests for three or four years was very rare, and that the average length of territory occupation was only 1.1 years for females. Similar results were obtained for merlin in the UK (Ellis & Okill, 1990; Wright, 1997). Our results, obtained through genetic identification, strongly support traditional ringing and recapture studies.

In conclusion, genetic profiling of cast feathers using microsatellites has been successfully applied to the study of mate and site fidelity in merlin. Until recently this type of study would have been impossible. In many countries, taking blood samples from wild birds is beset with legal complexities, but the collection of feathers is less proscriptive. It saves time and resources as the collection of feathers from a live bird is less invasive than taking a blood sample. Genetic profiling can then be based upon feathers collected from nestlings at the time of ringing or cast by adults at roosting or plucking sites, or (especially for females) from the nest itself. This is particularly valuable in the study of rare and endangered species. Many raptors have suffered declines as a result of pesticide contamination, in addition to persecution either by direct killing, egg collection or removal of the young for the captive hawk trade. DNA profiling has allowed enforcement agencies to tackle areas of wildlife crime, such as the unlawful taking of birds of prey from the wild (Shorrock, 1998). As part of this study, 'at risk' nests have been routinely visited by conservationists, and feathers collected from the chicks. In addition to providing genetic data relating to the structure of contemporary raptor populations, DNA profiles also provide a potential source of evidence should nest contents be robbed, and should serve as a deterrent to wildlife crime.

Acknowledgements

We are grateful to Dr Marit Nesje and Dr Jon Wetton for making the primers available to us. Amy Marsden was funded by a Natural Environment Research Council studentship whilst undertaking a Ph.D. at the University of Nottingham. Graham Rebecca is funded by the Royal Society for the Protection of Birds.

References

Amos, B, Schlötterer, C. & Tautz, D. (1993). Social structure of pilot whales revealed by analytical DNA profiling. *Science*, **260**, 670-672.

Ellis, P.M. & Okill, J.D. (1990). Breeding ecology of the merlin *Falco columbarius* in Shetland. *Bird Study*, **37**, 101-110.

Hanotte, O., Burke, T., Armour, J.A.L. & Jeffreys, A.J. (1991). Hypervariable minisatellite DNA sequences in the Indian peafowl *Pavo cristatus*. *Genomics*, **9**, 587-597.

James, P.C., Warkentin, I.G. & Oliphant, L.W. (1989). Turnover and dispersal in urban merlins *Falco columbarius*. *Ibis*, **131**, 426-447.

Marsden, A. (2002). *Population Studies of Falcons Using Microsatellite DNA Profiling*. Ph.D. Thesis, University of Nottingham, Nottingham.

Marshall, T.C., Slate, J., Kruuk, L.E.B. & Pemberton, J.M. (1998). Statistical confidence for likelihood-based paternity inference in natural populations. *Molecular Ecology*, **7**, 639-655.

Nesje, M. & Røed, K.H. (2000). Sex identification in falcons using microsatellite DNA markers. *Hereditas*, **132**, 261-263.

Nesje, M., Røed, K.H., Lijfeld, J.T., Lindberg, P. & Steen, O.F. (2000). Genetic relationships in the peregrine falcon (*Falco peregrinus*) analysed by microsatellite DNA markers. *Molecular Ecology*, **9**, 53-60.

Raymond, M. & Rouset, F. (1995). GENEPOP (Version 1.2): population genetics software for exact tests and ecumenicism. *Journal of Heredity*, **86**, 248-249.

Rebecca, G.W. & Bainbridge, I.P. (1998). The breeding status of the merlin *Falco Columbarius* in Britain in 1993-94. *Bird Study*, **45**, 172-187.

Shorrock, G. (1998). The success of DNA profiling in wildlife law enforcement. *International Journal of Biosciences and the Law*, **1**, 327-341.

Warkentin, I.G., James, P.C. & Oliphant, L.W. (1991). Influence of site switching in urban-breeding merlins (*Falco columbarius*). *The Auk*, **108**, 294-302.

Wetton, J.H. & Parkin, D.T. (1997). A suite of falcon single-locus minisatellite probes: a powerful alternative to DNA fingerprinting. *Molecular Ecology*, **6**, 119-128.

Wright, P.M. (1997). Distribution, site occupancy and breeding success of the merlin *Falco columbarius* on Barden Moor and Fell, North Yorkshire. *Bird Study*, **44**, 182-193.

THEME THREE

BEHAVIOURAL INTERACTIONS, PREDATION AND RANGING BEHAVIOUR

THEME THREE

BEHAVIOURAL INTERACTIONS, PREDATION AND RANGING BEHAVIOUR

Important, recent work on birds of prey is unravelling the effects of competition, predation and inter-specific interactions on the composition and distribution of some birds of prey assemblages. Newton (Chapter 1) refers to this, and detailed studies by Bechard *et al.* (1990), Solonen (1993), Hakkarainen & Korpimäki (1996) and Petty *et al.* (2003) have all investigated interactions between raptor species, pointing to some significant influences of direct and indirect interactions between species. These studies are particularly interesting because there had been a traditional view in some quarters that there was little competition between raptor species in the same habitat (e.g. Lack, 1946; Jaksić & Braker, 1983). We should see a growing body of research on interactions between predatory birds.

Several raptor workers have noted that golden eagles *Aquila chrysaetos*, in particular, appear to prevent peregrines *Falco peregrinus* nesting in some suitable areas (see Ratcliffe, 1993), and that hen harriers *Circus cyaneus* tend to occur at lower density, or indeed may be absent, on moors with golden eagles. Fielding *et al.* (Chapter 17) provide a detailed study of the impacts of golden eagles on the distribution of raven *Corvus corax*, buzzard *Buteo buteo* and peregrine on the Island of Mull. They find significant effects on the distribution of all three species, and indeed suggest that nest site selection by buzzard and raven may be constrained by golden eagle foraging activities. They raise the fascinating point that human persecution of golden eagles in some parts of Scotland may be giving rise to a somewhat artificial assemblage of birds of prey, and suggest that if golden eagles were free from current levels of persecution (Whitfield *et al.* in press), there could be a reduction in hen harrier *Circus cyaneus* and peregrine densities on and around some managed grouse moors.

Crane & Nellist (Chapter 18) have made a painstaking study of the winter ranging behaviour and social interactions in three neighbouring pairs of golden eagles on Skye. This research builds on their early work published in *Island Eagles* (Crane & Nellist, 1999), which is based on observations made since 1981 on birds which could be recognised individually. Their observations suggest that unsettled, single eagles give rise to many territorial interactions; the sheer number of observations made of displaying golden eagles is exceptional. Another study of interactions between raptors was made further south, on the Isle of Mull, by Morgan *et al.* (Chapter 19). This study looked in particular at the function of inter-specific mobbing behaviour, and found it to be prevalent between some raptor species.

Five studies deal with predation by raptors. Dixon *et al.* (Chapter 20) quantified peregrine predation on racing pigeons *Columba livia* in Wales. They found that both breeding density and the level of territory occupation by peregrines were influenced by the availability of racing pigeons. They propose that the decline in the number of pigeon fanciers in Wales, and the possible restructuring of the pigeon racing seasons, could give rise to a reduction in racing pigeon availability, which would have significant implications for peregrine conservation. Shawyer *et al.* (Chapter 21) review the causes of racing pigeon losses (including predation by raptors) across the UK. Their study is important, because it puts into context the losses of racing pigeons to raptors. The two chapters provide a timely contribution to the ongoing debate about the impacts of raptors on racing pigeons. It is somewhat ironic that Ratcliffe (Chapter 4) reminds us that concerns about racing pigeon losses to peregrines following the Second World War gave rise to the first national peregrine survey, which went on to reveal the inimical impacts of organochlorine pesticides on peregrines. Further research on the extent and causes of racing pigeon losses in Scotland is under way, funded by Scottish Natural Heritage and the Scottish Homing Union, and undertaken by the Central Science Laboratory.

In winter, many raptors move to the coast. Whitfield (Chapter 22) has made a fascinating study of sparrowhawk *Accipiter nisus* predation on the behaviour and population dynamics of wintering redshanks *Tringa totanus* in south east Scotland. He has found that competition between redshanks for feeding areas down from the high tide line (where predation risk is greatest) causes strong density-dependent predation effect on adults and juveniles. This study may have wider applicability to coastal wader populations, with far reaching consequences for the population dynamics of waders on their breeding grounds thousands of miles from the coast.

For many raptor species we still have only the most basic of information on their ranging behaviour. Madders (Chapter 23) has studied the foraging behaviour of hen harriers, and provides a model which predicts the relative use made of different parts of their range by foraging birds during the breeding season. These sorts of models are proving to be valuable in evaluating the potential impact of land use change on harriers and many other birds. However, such models make important assumptions, some of which still need to be refined.

The theme of predation in this book is rounded-off with an extraordinary study by Nielson (Chapter 25) of gyr falcons *Falco rusticolus* in north-east Iceland during 1981-2000. Rock ptarmigan *Lagopus mutus* adults are the most important prey for gyr falcons, and Nielson has quantified in great detail the functional response of gyr falcons to ptarmigan abundance. Comparisons with other studies of gyr falcons in Arctic regions reveal the importance of ptarmigans to these birds. However, the lengthy list of species recorded (counted, aged and weighed) in the diet of these raptors shows what effective predators they are. This is a penetrating study of the world's largest falcon, and is an excellent role model for research on predation elsewhere.

References

Bechard, M.J., Knight, R.L., Smith, D.G. & Fitzner, R.E. (1990). Nest sites and habitats of sympatric hawks *Buteo* (spp.) in Washington. *Journal of Field of Ornithology*, **61**, 159-170.

Crane, K. & Nellist, K. (1999). *Island Eagles*. Cartwheeling press, Skye.

Hakkarainen, H. & Korpimäki, E. (1996). Competition and predator re-interactions among raptors: an observational and experimental study. *Ecology*, **77**, 1134-1142.

Jaksić, F.M. & Braker, H.E. (1983). Food-niche relationships and guild structure of diurnal birds of prey: competition versus opportunism. *Canadian Journal of Zoology*, **61**, 2230-2241.

Lack, D. (1946). Competition for food by birds of prey. *Journal of Animal Ecology*, **15**, 123-129.

Petty, S.J., Andeson, D.I.K., Davison, M., Little, B., Sherrat, T.N., Thomas, C.J. & Lambin, X. (2003). The decline of common kestrels *Falco tinnunculus* in a forested area of northern England: the role of predation by northern goshawks *Accipiter gentilis*. *Ibis*, **145**, 472-483.

Ratcliffe, D.A. (1993). *The Peregrine Falcon. Second Edition.* Poyser, Calton.

Solonen, T. (1993). Spacing of birds of prey in southern Finland. *Ornis Fennica*, **70**, 129-143.

Whitfield, D.P., Fielding, A.H., McLeod, D.R.A. & Haworth, P.F. (in press). Modelling the effects of persecution on the population dynamics of golden eagles *Aquila chrysaetos* in Scotland. *Biological Conservation*.

17. THE IMPACT OF GOLDEN EAGLES (*AQUILA CHRYSAETOS*) ON A DIVERSE BIRD OF PREY ASSEMBLAGE

A.H. Fielding, P.F. Haworth, D.H. Morgan, D.B.A. Thompson & D.P. Whitfield

Summary

1. We propose that golden eagles *Aquila chrysaetos* impose a threat to other raptors to the extent that they influence the distribution and behaviour. Three predictions are tested: (a) smaller raptors nest further than expected from golden eagle range centres; (b) golden eagles are disproportionately represented in interspecific interactions with other raptors; and (c) smaller raptors avoid areas used by foraging golden eagles.

2. Information was available for the distributions of four birds of prey (golden eagle, raven *Corvus corax*, buzzard *Buteo buteo* and peregrine falcon *Falco peregrinus*) on the island of Mull (875 km²). Their spatial distributions suggest that buzzard, raven and peregrine falcon nest further than expected from golden eagle range centres.

3. Detailed information on habitat use and interspecific interactions was available for the Ross of Mull (174 km²) and was used to investigate the effects that golden eagles may have had on habitat use by buzzard, raven, hen harrier *Circus cyaneus*, kestrel *Faclo tinnunculus* and short-eared owl *Asio flammeus*.

4. Hierarchical models demonstrated that nest site selection by buzzard and raven may be constrained by golden eagle foraging activities. Habitat use maps and interspecific interaction frequencies support the hypothesis that smaller birds of prey react to the presence of golden eagle in a way which is consistent with a predation threat. Indeed, all five raptors were known to be predated by golden eagles on the Ross of Mull.

5. We discuss the implications of golden eagle persecution in other regions of Scotland for the structure of bird of prey assemblages. If golden eagles were released from current levels of persecution, there may be a reduction in hen harrier and peregrine falcon densities around managed grouse moors.

17.1 Introduction

When species coexist where resources are limiting it is normally presumed that they must have different requirements. Consequently, species with overlapping geographical ranges are assumed to diverge in habitat requirements, morphology or feeding behaviour, thus reducing the potential for competition (Newton, 1998: p. 351). Bechard *et al.* (1990) stated that coexistence in three sympatric hawks (Acciptridae) was related to differences in nesting habitats. However, it is unclear if coexistence occurred because there were fundamental *a priori* differences in nesting habitats or because coexistence produced consequential shifts in nesting habitats. Evidence of resource partitioning in raptor foraging habitat and diet is more equivocal than that for nest sites. Although some examples demonstrate little overlap in prey, other studies have found considerable overlap. Lack (1946) found limited evidence for food competition between congeneric raptors in the same habitat. Similarly, in a review of published data, Jaksić & Braker (1983) found that food niche breadths of raptors were little affected by the presence of potentially competing species, and that there was little support for predictions based on competition-structured assemblages. However, apparent coexistence amongst potential competitors is possible if habitat is spatially or indeed temporally heterogeneous. The obvious example is the shared use of the same habitat by diurnal falcons (Falconidae) and crepuscular owls (Strigiformes). Consequently, coexistence should only be judged at appropriate spatial and temporal scales.

Many raptor studies are essentially autecological and, although there are exceptions (e.g. Hakkarainen & Korpimäki, 1996), most discussions of interspecific effects are anecdotal. Nonetheless there is a consensus that some raptors are restricted by the presence of others. For example, Ratcliffe (1993) states that golden eagles restrict the distribution of peregrine falcons, possibly because of the predation risk to peregrine fledglings. Peregrines are said to respond to this latent threat by avoidance reactions in their choice of nest site.

Although interspecific competition for food is considered to be a major process controlling the dynamics of groups of coexisting raptors, other interactions, such as nest site competition, may also play a significant role in structuring multi-species assemblages (and determining species presence/absence, or precise patterns of habitat use and diet expressed). However, it has become increasingly apparent that smaller carnivores may be restricted by the need to avoid predation by larger species (intraguild predation). For example, Fedriani *et al.* (1999) showed that Iberian lynx (*Lynx pardinus*) killed red foxes (*Vulpes vulpes*), and that foxes reduced this risk by niche segregation. Since there is considerable published evidence that some raptors depredate smaller species, it is possible that similar processes may offer an additional/alternative mechanism operating to constrain particular species in raptor assemblages. Solonen's (1993) study of the spatial distribution of the nests of 14 raptor species suggested that the assemblage's spatial structure might have been affected by the avoidance of predation risk, with interspecific competition being less evident. Similarly, Hakkarainen & Korpimäki (1996) thought that both predation risk and interspecific competition could have major influences on habitat selection and the fitness of individual raptors. Therefore, although habitat or prey partitioning theories may explain raptor distribution patterns, the avoidance of intraguild predation is also implicated. Additionally, the presence of a predator may have indirect effects on the behaviour of other predators and prey. For example, Durant (2000) showed that the perceived presence of competitors, lions (*Panthero leo*) and spotted hyena (*Crocuta crocuta*), had a noticeable impact on the foraging rate of competitively inferior cheetahs (*Acinonyx jubatus*). Unfortunately it is difficult to disentangle the relative roles of competition and predation in an undisturbed community since behavioural and ecological responses minimise the incidence of both resource overlap and intraguild predation (Durant, 1998, 2000).

Undoubtedly the best way of demonstrating interspecific effects is by controlled experiments (e.g. Hakkarainen & Korpimäki, 1996). However, manipulative experiments, with sufficient statistical power, are impractical or unethical for large, protected raptors. A less satisfactory approach is interpreting the outcomes of 'natural experiments'. For example, Ratcliffe (1993) described how re-colonisation of the Galloway Hills by golden eagles resulted in the systematic abandonment of peregrine breeding sites as the number of eagle pairs increased. Later, the golden eagles declined and peregrines returned to the original, now deserted, crags. However, as Newton (1998: p. 351) warns, such observations only provide circumstantial evidence for competition. Indeed, the evidence is only circumstantial for an interaction that could be competition for food, competition for nest sites or intraguild predation. Support for interaction effects (including competition and predation) can also be obtained from inductive studies of the distributions and behaviour of different species. Although the absence of controlled experimental conditions precludes the identification of cause and effect, such studies can be used to develop theories whose predictions can be tested.

If predation risk, within a raptor assemblage, is related to size differences it might be expected that, in Britain, golden eagles would be the species most likely to restrict the distribution of other species (Poole & Bromley, 1988; Ratcliffe, 1993, 1997). In this study we test the hypothesis that the distribution and abundance of smaller raptors is influenced by golden eagles. The island of Mull is unusual, in a British context, because it supports a rich raptor assemblage (Table 17.1) in a relatively small area, little affected by persecution or disturbance. The possible effects of golden eagles on Mull's raptor assemblage are investigated across several spatial and temporal scales. We predict that, on the island scale, the distribution of raven, buzzard and peregrine falcon should be affected by golden eagles so that they nest further than expected from occupied golden eagle nest sites. At a smaller scale we examine the shared use of habitat patches and direct inter-specific interactions within the diurnal raptor assemblage. We predict that golden eagles should be involved in more interactions than expected, and that smaller species will avoid areas used by foraging golden eagles.

Table 17.1. The Ross of Mull (including Iona) raptor assemblage (1991-2000). Home ranges refer to distinct ranges occupied at least once between 1991-2000. * Seen, but non-breeding on the Ross of Mull in 1998.

Common name	Scientific name	Number of home ranges	
		Ross of Mull	*All of Mull*
Golden eagle	*Aquila chrysaetos*	6	31
Buzzard	*Buteo buteo*	34	132
Raven	*Corvus corax*	22	84
Kestrel	*Falco tinnunculus*	24	> = 80
Hen harrier	*Circus cyaneus*	12	> = 24
Merlin	*Falco columbarius*	1	> = 5
Short-eared owl	*Asio flammeus*	25	> = 70
Barn owl	*Tyto alba*	> = 5	?
Tawny owl	*Strix aluco*	> = 8	?
Long-eared owl	*Asio otus*	> = 1	?
Sparrowhawk	*Accipter nisus*	> = 3	?
Peregrine falcon	*Falco peregrinus*	0[*]	5
White-tailed eagle	*Haliaeetus albicilla*	0[*]	6

17.2 Methods

17.2.1 Study area

Mull (56°27'N 06°00'W) covers 875 km² (924 km² including all subsidiary islands) and is the third largest Scottish Hebridean island. Much of Mull is used for sheep and cattle grazing, although sheep densities are lower than in many areas in the western Highlands and Islands of Scotland (Fuller & Gough, 1999). There are large numbers of red deer (*Cervus elaphus*) and several hundred feral goats (*Capra hircus*). Red grouse (*Lagopus lagopus scoticus*) and ptarmigan (*Lagopus mutus*), common prey of golden eagles in many parts of Scotland (Watson, 1997), are scarce, but introduced Irish mountain hare (*Lepus timidus hibernicus*) and rabbit (*Oryctolagus cuniculus*) are locally common. The Ross of Mull (174 km²) is a low altitude (<400 m, average 100 m) peninsula which has been the location for an intensive study of raptor productivity and habitat use since 1994.

17.2.2 Species

The list of species and the number of occupied ranges are given in Table 17.1. Ravens are included because of their ecological position as a functional raptor (Smith & Murphy, 1982). Although 35 golden eagle ranges have been identified on Mull only 31 were active during the period of this study, giving an estimated average range area of 2,500 ha, a figure at the low end of the values given by McGrady (1997). Ravens were intensively surveyed across the island in 1990 and 1998 (Haworth, 1999), when occupied ranges increased from 61 to 84; most of these were coastal (46 and 67, respectively). Information on the island-wide distribution of buzzards was obtained during the 1998 raven survey, supplemented with additional surveys where required. The distribution of peregrine falcon nests was obtained during other surveys and from other raptor workers. All raptors on the Ross of Mull have been systematically surveyed each year since 1994.

17.2.3 Spatial distribution

Distances to the nearest extant golden eagle range centre (mean of nest locations from Fielding & Haworth (1995)) were calculated for buzzard, raven and peregrine falcon nests. However, land area increases non-linearly with distance and so distance data were converted to density estimates for each 1 km band, up to 6 km, away from golden eagle range centres using a GIS (Arcview 3.2, ESRI). Sea was excluded from the analyses.

Mean intra-specific nearest neighbour distances (between nest locations) were calculated for buzzard (1998 data), raven (1990 and 1998) and golden eagles (range centres). Although the mean nearest neighbour distance is a useful measure for analyzing range distributions, it only provides information about first-order spatial patterns. Because spatial patterns are scale-dependent, more information is available if spatial pattern is investigated at more than one scale. One method of investigating multi-scale patterns is to find the distances to the 2nd, 3rd, … kth nearest neighbours. Therefore, k-order effects were investigated by calculating the $L(r)$ function (Besag, 1977). If a pattern is random (a Poisson process) at a measurement scale (r) then $L(r) = 0$. If there is clustering, $L(r) > 0$, and if $L(r) < 0$ then regularity is implied. The significance of the $L(r)$ measures, i.e. significant departure from a random pattern, were obtained by generating 95% confidence intervals for $L(r)$ using the Ripley module from the ADE-4 package (Thioulouse *et al.*, 1997). Peregrine falcons were excluded from these analyses because of the small sample size. We give standard errors (SE) where appropriate.

17.2.4 Predictive modelling

If golden eagles restrict the distribution of other raptors, then apparently suitable, but unoccupied, nesting habitat should be available close to eagle nests or within regions extensively used by foraging eagles. This can be tested by comparing the predictions from models that differ only with respect to the inclusion of golden eagle distribution information as a predictor. If habitat in areas used by golden eagles consists of suitable nesting habitat for a second species, a habitat-only model should incorrectly predict locations for nest sites (i.e. false positives) which are subsequently corrected when the model is augmented with golden eagle distribution data.

We investigated the effect of golden eagle activity on the nest site distributions of buzzard and raven using two methods to ensure that predictions were not methodologically biased. The two methods were linear discriminant analysis and Quest (Quick, Unbiased, Efficient, Statistical Tree version 1.8.10: Loh & Shih, 1997), a classification tree. Linear discriminant analysis is one of the better methods for predicting species' distributions (Fielding, 1999a; Manel *et al.*, 1999a,b; Lim *et al.*, 2000). However, concerns have been raised about techniques that rely on covariances between predictor variables rather than the ecologically more defensible constraints modelled by recursive partitioning methods, such as decision trees (e.g. O'Connor, 2002). Regression and classification trees, or decision tree methods, are better able to deal with outliers (Bell, 1999) and the frequent multimodal nature of distribution data. Decision trees also produce rules which can easily be incorporated into an ecological context. We used Quest, which was the best of the decision tree methods tested by Lim *et al.* (2000).

Table 17.2. Predictor variables and sample sizes used in Quest and discriminant analyses. GEPref is the area (ha) of habitat preferentially used by golden eagles. All others are areas (ha) of vegetation named after the National Vegetation Classification (*sensu* Rodwell, 1991, 1992) class with the highest loading (>0.75 in all cases) on the principal component.

	Buzzard	**Raven**
Nests	30	20
Non-nests	101	27
Predictors	GEPref	GEPref
	Agrostis/Festuca/Pteridium	Fellfield and land area
	Rush pasture	Conifer plantation, wet heath and *Calluna*
	Young plantation	Bracken and *Calluna*
	Wet heath	
	Bracken/*Calluna*	
	Mire	
	Wet heath/bracken	
	Wet heath/mire complex	
	Wet heath/*Calluna*/bracken	
	Agrostis/Festuca	

Predictive models were restricted to the Ross of Mull because detailed foraging data were unavailable for the rest of the island. Potential nest location predictors were obtained for two groups: nests and non-nest areas. Predictor data were obtained from circular buffers centred on the locations of all nests used in 1998 and random non-nest locations. All buffer operations used the X-tools extension (DeLaune, 1999) for Arcview 3.2. Non-nest samples were obtained by allocating random coordinates and pruning these to produce a set of buffers that had minimal (<5%) overlap. Sample sizes are given in Table 17.2. A 0.5 km radius buffer was used for buzzards to reflect the nest spacing and observed habitat use by territorial pairs (unpublished data). Ravens did not exhibit similar territorial behaviour but nests were more widely spaced, so a 1 km radius buffer was used. Implementation details are given in Appendix 17.1.

17.2.5 Inter-specific interactions, habitat utilisation and range overlap

Observations of raptor location and behaviour, including inter-specific interactions, were obtained as part of a long-term study of the Ross of Mull raptor and scavenging bird assemblage (Morgan *et al.*, Chapter 19). Two experienced field workers (PFH and DHM) gathered data between August 1994 and December 1998 inclusive. Random sampling was impossible because of access and safety constraints. Sampling effort was greatest, and approximately constant (weather permitting), between July and October. Observations were collected using binoculars and spotting telescopes and plotted on 1:25,000 maps of the study area and used to identify 'preferred' areas (Appendix 17.2). Observational data were also used to identify pairs of species that co-occurred more or less than expected (Appendix 17.3). Individual raptors involved in interactions were classified as instigators or recipients. If a bird flew directly towards another, prior to an interaction, it was labelled the instigator. For example, a buzzard flying towards, and interacting with, a golden eagle that had entered its range would be the instigator.

The resource partitioning analysis (Appendix 17.3) only measures spatial overlap and hence mainly measures exploitation or 'diffuse' competition. A more refined measure of resource overlap, which is better able to detect interference competition, should incorporate time. Two individuals are more likely to interact if they co-occur within a minimum distance (d_m) of each other and within a certain time window (t_m). The main problem is selecting appropriate values for d_m and t_m. The chosen values (200 m and 15 minutes) took account of the precision of the spatial and temporal observational data combined with the need to produce sufficiently large samples. Since all of the raptors have excellent vision, and an ability to move quickly over quite large distances, it is likely that most individuals would have been aware of the presence of the other within this spatial and temporal window. A cross-tabulation of inter-specific overlap 'incidents' or co-occurrences was obtained by searching through the database of observations. Expected overlap frequencies were obtained by multiplying the product of the two species proportions in the overall observation database (Table 17.3) by the observed number of overlap incidents. Standardised differences (residuals) between observed and expected frequencies were obtained by calculating $(o - e)^2/e$. This enables across-species comparisons to be made after correcting for differences in abundance.

17.3 Results

17.3.1 Spatial distribution

Golden eagle ranges had a mean nearest neighbour distance of 4.6 km (SE ±0.3 km) and showed evidence of regular spacing at measurement scales between 1 km and 3 km (Figure 17.1a). There

Table 17.3. Number of observations and inter-specific interactions (1994-1999) for each raptor on the Ross of Mull. Species with fewer than 200 observations are not shown. [a] Inter-specific interactions excludes interactions with rare raptors (e.g. peregrine falcons) and non-raptors (e.g. crows). * marks those species in which the number of interactions differs from that expected (P <0.05; based on 95% confidence intervals for their proportion of all sightings).

Species	Sightings (percentage of all sightings)		[a]Inter-specific interactions (percentage of all interactions)	Percentage of a species sightings as inter-actions
Golden eagle*	1,955	(10.3)	29.7	17.5
Buzzard*	9,284	(49.1)	23.6	2.9
Hen harrier	897	(4.7)	5.1	6.6
Kestrel*	2,807	(14.9)	20.2	8.3
Raven	3,543	(18.7)	17.8	5.8
Short-eared owl	406	(2.1)	3.6	10.1

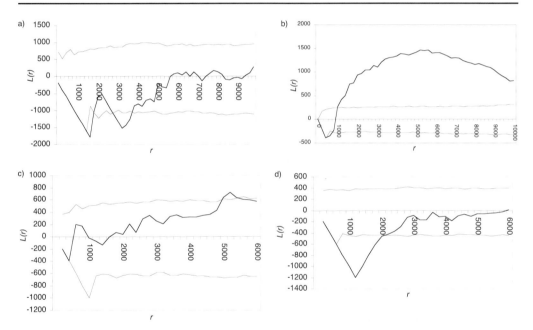

Figure 17.1. Multiscale pattern analyses for (a) active golden eagle ranges, (b) buzzard nests, (c) raven nests – 1990, and (d) raven nests – 1998. Thick lines are the *L(r)* values; thin lines are the upper and lower confidence intervals obtained from 2000 Monte Carlo simulations; and *r* is the scale of the pattern analysis (effectively the 'quadrat size').

was no evidence, over the measurement scales used, that golden eagle ranges were aggregated. Almost the entire island (96.5%) is within 6 km of a golden eagle range and 60% is within 3 km of the centre of an occupied golden eagle range. Distances between buzzard nests and the centre of the nearest occupied golden eagle range (Figure 17.2, mean = 3.4 km, SE ±0.12 km) showed a slight positive skew. Buzzard nests showed some evidence of regular spacing over small distances (0.5 km–0.8 km) but strong evidence of aggregation at all scales above 1 km (Figure 17.1b). For both raven surveys, the distribution of distances (Figure 17.3)

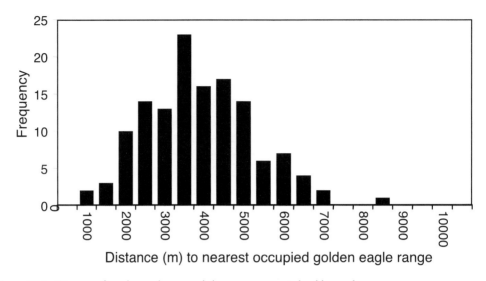

Figure 17.2. Distances from buzzard nests and the nearest occupied golden eagle range centre.

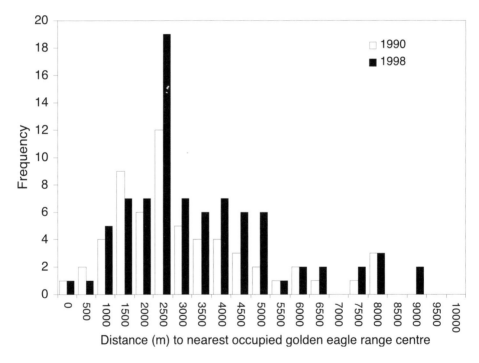

Figure 17.3. Distances between raven nests (1990 and 1998 surveys) and the nearest occupied golden eagle range centre.

showed a positive skew. The change in the mean distance to the nearest golden eagle range was insignificant (1990 mean = 3.1 km, SE ±0.25 km; 1998 mean = 3.3 km, SE ±0.25 km). Even though the raven population expanded there was some range turnover. There were no significant differences, in distances to golden eagle range centres, between new and continuously occupied raven ranges. However, abandoned coastal raven ranges were significantly closer (P <0.05) to golden eagle ranges than either the new or unchanged ranges. Distances from abandoned inland ranges to golden eagle range centres did not differ from either new or unchanged inland raven ranges (Table 17.4). Thus, although raven density increased, new nests were, on average, no closer to golden eagle ranges. The way in which this happened is apparent in Figures 17.1c and 17.1d. In 1990, raven ranges were randomly spaced over almost all measurement scales. However, in 1998, raven ranges exhibited regular spacing over the range 0.60 km–2.20 km. Therefore, the increased density was achieved by

Table 17.4. Distance (m) from occupied raven nests to nearest occupied golden eagle range centre. Gains and losses refer to changes between the 1990 and 1998 raven surveys (lcl, lower confident limit; ucl, upper confidence limit).

Location	Status	Mean	SE	n	95% lcl	95% ucl
Coastal	Gained	3,857	362	31	3,119	4,596
	Lost	1,808	351	9	1,014	2,601
	Unchanged	3,515	382	36	2,741	4,290
Inland	Gained	2,680	282	13	2,071	3,289
	Lost	2,633	300	7	1,924	3,342
	Unchanged	2,855	344	9	2,076	3,633

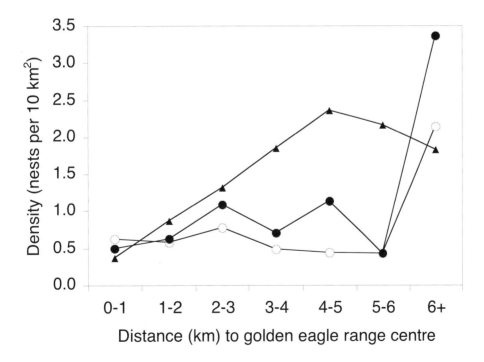

Figure 17.4. Density (number 10 km^{-2}) of buzzard (triangle) and raven (filled circle - 1998 survey, open circle – 1990 survey) nests in seven distance bands to active golden eagle range centres.

filling spaces between existing ranges, and thereby producing the apparent regularity that may be expected as a consequence of territorial behaviour (Figure 17.1d). Buzzard nest density increased linearly over the <1 km and 4 km distance bands to golden eagle range centres but then declined (Figure 17.4). Raven nest density was relatively constant at distances between 0 and 6 km from eagle range centres, but then increased rapidly. In 1998, when raven numbers were higher, the density remained the same (up to 2 km from eagle range centres), but was then greater at all distances except in the 5 km band (Figure 17.4). The mean distance between the three peregrine nests active in 1998, and the nearest occupied golden eagle range centre, was 3.0 km (3.4 km, 1.4 km and 4.2 km).

17.3.2 Predictive modelling

Discriminant analyses of buzzard nests were successful (Table 17.5). There was little difference in the overall correct classification rates between habitat-only model (84.1% of cross-validated cases correctly predicted) and the enhanced (habitat plus golden eagle activity) model (87.1% correct). All nest sites misclassified (by cross-validation) by the enhanced model were also incorrectly predicted by the habitat model. However, there were important qualitative differences in the misclassified non-nest cases. The habitat-only model misclassified 11 cases while the enhanced model misclassified eight cases, four of which were common to both. The proportions of misclassified non-nest cases, with areas preferentially used by eagles, differed significantly ($z = 2.06$, $P < 0.04$) between the models. In general, the enhanced model predicted sites which had apparently suitable habitat but were unused by eagles.

Table 17.5. Cross-validated classification results from buzzard and raven nest discriminant analyses. Figures in parentheses are from re-substituted analyses. The enhanced model includes GEPref as a predictor.

Buzzard

Habitat only		Predicted group Non-nest	Nest	Total
Actual group	Non-nest	90 (93)	11 (8)	101
	Nest	10 (8)	21 (23)	31
Enhanced model				
Actual group	Non-nest	92 (94)	9 (7)	101
	Nest	8 (7)	23 (24)	31

Raven

Habitat only		Predicted group Non-nest	Nest	Total
Actual group	Non-nest	23 (23)	4 (4)	27
	Nest	3 (3)	17 (17)	20
Enhanced model				
Actual group	Non-nest	24 (24)	3 (3)	27
	Nest	3 (3)	17 (17)	20

Both Quest analyses for buzzards were more accurate than the equivalent discriminant analyses. The habitat-only model misclassified one nest and ten non-nest buffers; while the enhanced model misclassified only two non-nest buffers, both of which were misclassified by the habitat-only model. The remaining eight non-nest buffers, misclassified by the habitat-only model, all had large areas of golden eagle preferred habitat.

Discriminant (Table 17.5) and Quest analyses of raven nests were also successful. The habitat-only models made few incorrect predictions, leaving little scope for improvement when the model was augmented. Quest predictions were identical for the two models (one nest and six incorrect non-nest buffers) and golden eagle activity was not selected as a predictor in the enhanced model. All four models incorrectly predicted the inland raven nest and three coastal non-nest buffers (all of which were subsequently used when the raven population expanded further after 1998).

17.3.3 Inter-specific interactions, habitat utilisation and range overlap

The areas of the Ross of Mull identified as preferred habitat are given for six raptors (Table 17.6). Except for ravens, most of the preferred habitat was close to nests. Consequently preference maps are not shown to protect nest locations. Almost a quarter of kestrel-preferred habitat was shared with golden eagle. There was almost no overlap between golden eagle-preferred areas and those for buzzard, hen harrier and short-eared owl.

Table 17.6. Size and overlap (ha, upper triangle) in the regions used more than expected by six raptors on the Ross of Mull. Inter-specific preferred habitat overlap, as a percentage of each species preferred area, is given in the lower triangle.

	Golden eagle	Buzzard	Hen harrier	Kestrel	Raven	Short-eared owl	Total preferred habitat (ha)
Golden eagle		21.0	231.0	827.0	450.0	92	3,401
Buzzard	0.6		79.0	150.0	267.0	51	3,352
Hen harrier	6.8	2.3		459.0	50.0	715	1,508
Kestrel	24.3	4.5	30.4		375.0	312	2,549
Raven	13.2	8.0	3.3	14.7		11	2,346
Short-eared owl	2.7	1.5	47.4	12.3	0.50		1,019

A total of 648 interactions between raptors was recorded, of which 567 were inter-specific (see also Morgan *et al.*, Chapter 19). Almost 30% of the inter-specific interactions involved golden eagles, even though they only accounted for 10.3% of all observations (Table 17.3). Two species, golden eagle and kestrel, had a significantly larger than expected number of interactions. Buzzards were observed in fewer than expected interactions. Golden eagles were only classified as instigators in two inter-specific interactions (Table 17.7) and recipients in 333 inter-specific interactions. Three species, kestrel, buzzard and raven, interacted significantly more than expected with golden eagles.

Only short-eared owl appeared to use habitat that differed significantly from that used by golden eagle (Table 17.8), although there was also little similarity between habitats used

Table 17.7. Observed interactions between raptors on the Ross of Mull 1994–1999. Intra-specific interactions are in bold. Percentage of all inter-specific incidents, by the instigator, are given in parentheses.

Recipient	Golden eagle	Buzzard	Hen harrier	Kestrel	Raven	Short-eared owl	All	% inter-specific
Instigator								
Golden eagle	**8**	0 (0.0)	0 (0.0)	1 (9.1)	1 (3.2)	0 (0.0)	10	20.0
Buzzard	91 (27.3)	**35**	2 (12.5)	2 (18.2)	5 (16.1)	2 (33.3)	137	74.5
Hen harrier	19 (5.7)	15 (8.8)	**4**	1 (9.1)	2 (6.5)	2 (33.3)	43	90.7
Kestrel	116 (34.8)	63 (37.1)	12 (75.0)	**7**	22 (71.0)	2 (33.3)	222	96.8
Raven	101 (30.3)	66 (38.8)	0 (0.0)	7 (63.6)	**20**	0	194	89.7
Short-eared owl	6 (1.8)	26 (15.3)	2 (12.5)	0 (0)	1 (3.2)	**7**	42	83.3
All	341	205	20	18	51	13		
% inter-specific	97.7	82.9	80.0	61.1	60.8	46.2		

Table 17.8. Resource partitioning identified from habitat comparisons. Numbers in the table are the frequencies (from 1,000 simulations) for which the mean habitat distances from inter-specific comparisons exceeded the pooled mean from the two intra-specific comparisons (Appendix 17.3). Comparisons in which a null hypothesis 'that the inter-specific distance does not differ from the pooled intra-specific distance' can be rejected (P <0.05) are marked *.

	Golden eagle	Buzzard	Hen harrier	Kestrel	Raven	Intra-specific mean
Golden eagle						200,914
Buzzard	840					211,206
Hen harrier	916	951*				211,382
Kestrel	588	651	844			209,176
Raven	664	625	955*	559		198,640
Short-eared owl	988*	998*	578	953*	1,000*	190,160

by golden eagle and hen harrier. Three species pairs (golden eagle-kestrel, raven-kestrel and short-eared owl-hen harrier) all had considerable similarity in habitat use.

There were no examples in which co-occurrences (spatio-temporal overlap) between two species were much less than expected from their relative abundances (Tables 17.9a and 17.9b). Conversely, there were many examples of species occurring together more than expected. Two of the largest residuals (differences between observed and expected frequencies) involved

Table 17.9. Co-occurrence frequencies. (a) Data in the upper right triangle are the frequencies at which species were observed to overlap in space and time (observations less than 200 m apart and within 15 minutes of each other). The lower left triangle gives the expected frequency of inter-specific overlaps with the standardised residual in parentheses. The sign is positive if the observed frequency is larger than the expected. Expected frequencies for intra-specific overlaps are given in italics next to the observed frequencies. (b) As (a) above, except that overlap frequencies exclude behavioural interactions detailed in Table 17.7.

a)	Golden eagle	Buzzard	Hen harrier	Kestrel	Raven	Short-eared owl
Golden eagle	280.0 *38.3*	151.0	26.0	225.0	169.0	8.0
Buzzard	181.7 -(5.2)	949.0 *862.9*	60.0	309.0	375.0	50.0
Hen harrier	17.6 +(4.1)	83.4 -(6.6)	81.0 *8.1*	64.0	28.0	34.0
Kestrel	54.9 +(526.4)	260.9 -(8.9)	25.2 +(59.7)	210.0 *78.9*	190.0	25.0
Raven	69.3 +(143.2)	329.3 +(6.3)	31.8 -(0.5)	99.6 +(82.2)	304.0 *125.7*	1.0
Short-eared owl	7.9 -(0.1)	37.3 -(4.0)	3.6 +(252.7)	11.4 +(16.2)	14.4 -(12.5)	34.0 *1.6*

b)	Golden eagle	Buzzard	Hen harrier	Kestrel	Raven	Short-eared owl
Golden eagle		60.0	7.0	109.0	68.0	2.0
Buzzard	58.2 +(0.06)		43.0	244.0	304.0	22.0
Hen harrier	5.6 +(0.37)	26.5 +(10.1)		51.0	26.0	30.0
Kestrel	17.6 +(472.8)	84.1 +(303.8)	8.1 +(229.0)		161.0	23.0
Raven	22.2 +(94.9)	105.6 +(372.8)	10.1 +(25.0)	32.0 +(519.0)		0.0
Short-eared owl	2.5 -(0.1)	11.9 +(8.7)	1.1 +(734.1)	3.6 +(104.6)	4.5 -(4.52)	

golden eagles with kestrel and raven. Since inter-specific interactions contribute to the frequencies in Table 17.9a they were recalculated after removing interactions (Table 17.9b). The largest effect of the recalculation concerned buzzards, which then co-occurred much more than expected with both kestrel and raven. The recalculation had little effect on the golden eagle residuals. In other species changes to the residuals did not affect their interpretation.

17.4 Discussion

17.4.1 Golden eagle influences on raptor distribution

Lack (1946) concluded that birds of prey were an interesting assemblage in which competition for food could be studied because 'they have no serious predators' and would be limited by food supply. He appears to have overlooked the possibility that they predate each other. Since this early paper various authors (e.g. Poole & Bromley, 1988; Ratcliffe, 1993, 1997; Gainzarain *et al.*, 2000) have suggested that the threat of intraguild predation, particularly from golden eagles, may restrict the distribution and/or productivity of a number of smaller raptors. The results described in this study are strongly supportive of such an effect.

In Durant's (1998) study of Serengeti carnivores, cheetahs were said to persist by using their mobility to seek out 'competition refuges' from lions and hyenas. The situation with birds of prey is different because eagle ranges, at least on Mull, are relatively static and the only competition refuges would be away from the eagle ranges. All three species, for which sufficient island-wide data were available, appeared to avoid nesting close to occupied golden eagle nests. In common with much of the west of Scotland, peregrine density was surprisingly low (0.32 ranges 100 km²), particularly compared with other mountainous regions (Horne & Fielding, 2002) and, as with raven and buzzard, peregrines did not nest close to eagle nests. Gainzarain *et al.* (2000) studied a peregrine population in northern Spain, where only two out of 35 pairs nested closer than 2 km to an occupied golden eagle nest, an observation explained by intraguild predation. In this study the mean distance to golden eagle nests was 6.3 km, a distance that would effectively mean that no peregrines could nest on Mull. Although the trends were different, buzzard and raven nest densities increased away from golden eagle nests. However, when the raven population expanded during the study, new nests were no closer to eagle nests than the older ones. Interestingly, when there was turnover it was nests closest to golden eagle nests which were abandoned, resulting in a change in the spatial pattern of raven nests which was suggestive of territoriality. This was also highlighted by the nest density patterns, with raven nest density only increasing beyond 2 km from golden eagle range centres. The mean distances between raven and golden eagle nests in this study are comparable with those given by Ratcliffe (1997) for four other Scottish regions. Therefore, the spatial arrangement of all three species, with respect to golden eagle ranges, is consistent with a strategy which seems to exploit refuges as a means of reducing the predation threat.

Although observed nest distributions for all three species could be explained by the predation threat hypothesis there are other explanations, such as different habitat requirements. However, both ravens and peregrines are known to have similar nesting requirements to the golden eagle, and both have been observed using vacated eagle nests (Ratcliffe, 1993, 1997). In the Republic of Ireland, where golden eagles became extinct in about 1912 (O'Toole *et al.*, 2002), some former eagle sites are now occupied by peregrine falcons (L. O'Toole, pers comm.) and the first successful golden eagle nest in England for almost 150 years was usurped from a raven (Walker, 1991). Consequently, it seems unlikely that a habitat differentiation hypothesis is applicable for ravens and peregrines in relation to golden eagles. Since, in Britain, buzzards nest in a wide range of habitats, many of which would never support golden eagles, it seems less probable that they would conflict with golden eagles in their use of nesting sites. However, on Hebridean islands eagles often use low-lying habitat. The Ross of Mull's most productive golden eagle range (mean altitude 61 m) was first used in the mid-1980s. Prior to that a buzzard and/or peregrine falcon occupied the nest cliff. Therefore it seems unlikely that buzzard nest patterns were due solely to habitat differentiation. Fortunately the avoidance hypothesis can be tested for buzzard and raven using hierarchical predictive models.

Solonen's (1993) study of inter- and intra-specific nest spacing did not include golden eagles but he did observe many large inter-specific distances to larger species such as eagle owls (*Bubo bubo*) and long-eared owls (*Asio otus*). He concluded that some birds of prey failed to occupy the full range of suitable locations because of inter-specific interactions. There was, however, apparently little evidence for competitive effects, although some large species were said to 'oust' smaller species from the immediate vicinity of their nests. Solonen (1993) thought that the main process was related to predation risk, and that this was density dependent, i.e. as the density of larger species increased so did the predation threat. On Mull, golden eagles occur at a very high density and so we might expect the predation threat to be large. The two sets of predictive models support the predation-risk hypothesis since in three of four cases the introduction of a golden eagle activity predictor changed and/or reduced the misclassification of false positives (predicting non-nest locations as nest sites). Because two different modelling techniques were employed, which exploit different aspects of the data structure, we are more confident that this conclusion is not a methodological artefact. However, a simple predictor, such as distance to the nearest golden eagle nest, is inadequate. When this was tried it never improved the models. Perhaps this is unsurprising since Euclidean distances do not take account of natural barriers (e.g. lochs or large closed canopy forests) which are likely to constrain an eagle's movements. Therefore, in the absence of detailed foraging information, a better predictor might be possible if distance was replaced by a 'weighted' distance or 'cost-surface' which incorporated habitat and terrain data.

17.4.2 Prey remains

Studies of the raptors' prey could undoubtedly provide good evidence for a predation risk hypothesis. There are several examples in the literature where other raptors are included as part of a golden eagle's prey. Indeed, Watson (1997) describes finding the remains of raven, peregrine, merlin (*Falco columbarius*) and kestrel in a single golden eagle nest. Unfortunately, it was impossible to undertake a systematic prey survey on the Ross of Mull because health and safety considerations restricted the collection of pellets and prey remains from two of the five golden eagle ranges. However, some prey data were available from plucking points and from pellet analyses undertaken by ourselves and M. Madders (unpublished). Pellet and prey remains have included buzzard, raven, hen harrier, kestrel, merlin and short-eared owl. There is also circumstantial evidence that golden eagles were responsible for the regular loss of near-fledged hen harrier chicks from nests which border two eagle ranges. Thus, although the contribution that raptors make to the golden eagle diet is unknown, we are certain that all of Mull's common raptors have been taken by golden eagles at some time. It is unlikely that raptors could make a major contribution to an eagle's diet since there would be insufficient accumulated biomass. Predation of adults is probably rare because behavioural and ecological responses in an undisturbed community should minimise its incidence (Durant, 1998, 2000). However, most raptors have large dietary plasticity (Jaksić & Braker, 1983) and often show opportunistic behaviours to exploit local resources such as young birds that are easier to catch (e.g. Newton & Marquiss, 1982). Our limited prey analyses support the theory that golden eagles can exhibit considerable prey plasticity. Thus, in addition to depressing the breeding density of other raptors, it is likely that they also reduce their productivity by taking some of their young.

17.4.3 Inter-specific interactions

In common with other studies (e.g. Poole & Bromley, 1988), golden eagles were the primary target of inter-specific interactions, often involving more than one bird or species. As with the Jiménez & Jaksić (1993) study, none of our observed interactions involved prey, i.e. there was no evidence of kleptoparasitic intent in any of 567 inter-specific interactions. Poole & Bromley (1988) thought that the frequently vigorous interactions with golden eagle, irrespective of apparent niche overlap, were related to threats of predation. They observed gyrfalcons (*Falco rusticolus*), peregrines and ravens pursuing golden eagles up to 2 km from their nests, although gyrfalcons appeared to be kleptoparasitic with species other than eagles close to their own nest. It seems unlikely that the resources and risks associated with such behaviours are consistent with a competitive response. In our study there were only two inter-specific interactions apparently instigated by a golden eagle. This may be because all of the raptors on the Ross of Mull are smaller than the golden eagle. Mull's only larger raptor (white-tailed eagle, *Haliaeetus albicilla*) was observed in 12 interactions, but only one of these involved a golden eagle and it was unclear which was the instigator. Halley & Gjershaug (1998) showed that golden eagles could engage in, and usually win, vigorous interactions with white-tailed eagles at carcasses. Clouet *et al.* (1999) reported on the only known location where golden and Verreaux's eagle (*Aquila verreauxii*) coexist. In this assemblage, golden eagles were the attackers in 21 of 22 inter-specific interactions. Thus, although there is evidence that golden eagles are capable of instigating interactions in a competitive situation, our study suggests that they do not do so with smaller species, perhaps because these are not perceived as competitors, even though they apparently use the same habitat.

There was little evidence for the temporal partitioning postulated as a likely response to interference competition (Carothers & Jaksić, 1984). Only short-eared owl had a negative residual in their co-occurrence with golden eagle. Despite this, short-eared owls were a common raptor component of golden eagle prey. The most frequent inter-specific interactions with golden eagle involved kestrels. This is not too surprising since they also had the largest values for all three measures of resource overlap (preference maps, resource partitioning and co-occurrence). Ravens also had considerable overlap with golden eagles and engaged in frequent interactions. However, unlike the kestrel, these interactions often took place at considerable distances from nests. Hen harriers showed little evidence of resource overlap or interactions with golden eagles. Although buzzards had very little spatial or habitat overlap with golden eagles, there was a high interaction frequency. This suggests that the nature of buzzard-golden eagle interactions is somewhat different to those with other species.

One of the main elements of the predation risk hypothesis is that it is mediated by size. Mull is one of the few places in Britain where golden eagles coexist with a larger eagle. It has been suggested that the continued spread of the white-tailed eagle in Scotland will lead to the displacement of golden eagles through competitive effects as coastal ranges are reclaimed (Watson *et al.*, 1992; Watson, 1997; Halley & Gjershaug, 1998; Halley, 1998). However, on Mull, where both occur at relatively high densities, there is little evidence of competitive effects (Whitfield *et al.*, 2002). Unfortunately the absence of breeding white-tailed eagles from the Ross of Mull precluded any detailed resource overlap and interaction studies. However, over much of the island, both species may nest in close proximity and there have been numerous observations of close proximity between the two species with no apparent interactions (Whitfield *et al.*, 2002). Recent evidence from prey studies on Mull (Marquiss *et al.*, 2001, Chapter 36; M. Madders, pers. comm.) suggests less dietary overlap than indicated by the earlier study (Watson *et al.*, 1992). Although there have been incidents in which each species kills the other (Willgohs, 1961; Bergo, 1987; Watson, 1997), we are unaware of evidence pointing to either species depredating the other. Thus, the relationship between these two large raptors on Mull appears to be one of 'armed neutrality' and is consistent with a size-dependent predation-threat hypothesis.

17.4.4 Some implications for management

Durant's (2000) analysis of the Serengeti carnivore community suggested that intraguild predation would be rare because predator avoidance mechanisms are effective. However, she also thought that if predation risk were lifted the entire carnivore community would be altered, presumably as a consequence of mesopredator release (Crooks & Soulé, 1999). In many regions of eastern Scotland golden eagles appear to be held at low densities because of persecution (Watson, 1997; Whitfield *et al.*, in press). It would be interesting to examine the responses of the existing raptor communities if this persecution were removed. Unfortunately, several other raptor species are also persecuted in the same regions (e.g. Gibbons *et al.*, 1994; Etheridge *et al.*, 1997; Thompson *et al.*, 1997). Hence, a better opportunity to test the predation risk hypothesis may be provided by the re-introduction of the golden eagle into the Republic of Ireland (O'Toole *et al.*, 2002). The level of raptor persecution, especially poisoning, has decreased significantly and there have been recent dramatic increases in raven and buzzard numbers in regions with putative golden eagle ranges. Consequently, it should be possible to monitor the distribution of other raptors as the golden eagle population expands.

The local extinctions of several species of raptor in Britain have been attributed to persecution by game keeping and livestock interests, especially by managers of red grouse (Thompson *et al.*, 1997; Anon., 2000; Moorland Working Group, 2002). Although now illegal, such persecution still occurs on grouse moors, albeit at much lower levels than in the 19th and early 20th centuries, but is still sufficient to be a strong influence on the distribution of several species (e.g. Gibbons *et al.*, 1994; Watson, 1997; Etheridge *et al.*, 1997; Thompson *et al.*, 1997; Whitfield *et al.*, in press)). Golden eagles, buzzards, peregrines and hen harriers are killed or interfered with because they predate red grouse, but the influence of predation probably differs between species. Peregrine and, especially, hen harrier predation on red grouse has been the subject of detailed studies (e.g. Redpath & Thirgood 1997, 1999, Chapter 39), and hen harriers can affect the numbers of grouse that are shot and can keep grouse at low densities.

Habitat management has been suggested as a possible solution to the problem of hen harrier predation (Redpath & Thirgood, 1997; Smith *et al.*, 2000; Moorland Working Group, 2002; Redpath & Thirgood, Chapter 39). For example, reducing the density of meadow pipit (*Anthus pratensis*) through changes in grazing and burning regimes should reduce the density of hen harriers because harrier density is correlated with density of pipits. This would have an indirect benefit on grouse stocks through a reduction in predation by harriers and bring direct benefits through superior management of habitat for grouse. However, there is now evidence that prey species may actually benefit from the presence of top carnivores (e.g. Palomares *et al.*, 1995; Rogers & Caro, 1998). Our results suggest that positive management of golden eagles could help to maintain lower numbers of hen harrier and other avian predators of red grouse. Although red grouse are an important dietary component for many pairs of golden eagles (Watson, 1997), eagles appear to be perceived by grouse managers as less of a 'problem' than some other species. Despite this, eagles are absent from large areas of suitable habitat in Britain and are at a low density in others, largely through persecution (Watson, 1997; Watson & Whitfield, 2002; Whitfield *et al.*, in press). We suggest that if persecution were to be reduced so that golden eagles became more abundant, it could bring about an overall benefit to red grouse by lowering predation rates by medium-sized raptors.

Acknowledgements

Scottish Natural Heritage funded the raven surveys and provided a digital version of the NVC map of Mull. Roger Broad and Mike Madders did a great deal of work on eagles and ravens on Mull in the 1980s. Earthwatch helped fund the collection of bird observations. We thank three anonymous referees for comments on a draft manuscript. Alan Fielding was in receipt of a Leverhulme Fellowship during the writing of this paper.

References

Anonymous (2000). *Report of the UK Raptor Working Group*. Department of the Environment Transport and Regions/Joint Nature Conservation Council. The Stationery Office, London.

Averis, A.B.G. & Averis, A. M. (1995). The vegetation of South and East Mull - Volume 1. Unpublished report. Scottish Natural Heritage, Edinburgh.

Bechard, M.J., Knight, R.L., Smith, D.G. & Fitzner, R.E. (1990). Nest sites and habitats of sympatric hawks (*Buteo* spp.) in Washington. *Journal of Field Ornithology*, **61**, 159-170.

Bell, J.F. (1999). Tree-based methods. In *Ecological Applications of Machine Learning Methods*, ed. by A.H. Fielding. Kluwer Academic, Boston. pp. 89-106.

Bergo, G. (1987). Territorial behaviour of golden eagles in western Norway. *British Birds*, **80**, 361-376.

Besag, J.E. (1977). Comments on Ripley's paper. *Journal of the Royal Statistical Society Series B*, **B39**, 193-195.

Carothers, J.H. & Jaksić, F.M. (1984). Time as a niche difference: the role of interference competition. *Oikos*, **42**, 403-406.

Clouet, M., Barrau, C. & Goar, J.L. (1999). The golden eagle (*Aquila chrysaetos*) in the Bale Mountains, Ethiopia. *Journal of Raptor Research*, **33**, 102-109.

Crooks, K.R. & Soulé, M.E. (1999). Mesopredator release and avifaunal extinctions in a fragmented system. *Nature*, **400**, 563-566.

DeLaune, M. (1999). XTOOLS extension. Available from www.odf.state.or.us/DIVISIONS/management/state_forests/XTools.asp

Durant, S.M. (1998). Competition refuges and coexistence: an example from Serengeti carnivores. *Journal of Animal Ecology*, **67**, 370-386.

Durant, S.M. (2000). Living with the enemy: avoidance of hyenas and lions by cheetahs in the Serengeti. *Behavioural Ecology*, **11**, 624-632.

Etheridge, B., Summers, R.W. & Green, R.E. (1997). The effects of illegal killing and destruction of nests by humans on the population dynamics of the hen harrier *Circus cyaneus* in Scotland. *Journal of Applied Ecology*, **34**, 1081-1105.

Fedriani, J.M., Palomares, F. & Delibes, M. (1999). Niche relations among three sympatric Mediterranean carnivores. *Oecologia*, **121**, 138-148.

Fielding, A.H. (1999a). A review of machine learning methods. In *Ecological Applications of Machine Learning Methods*, ed. by A.H. Fielding. Kluwer Academic, Boston. pp. 1-37.

Fielding, A.H. (1999b). How should accuracy be measured? In *Ecological Applications of Machine Learning Methods*, ed. by A.H. Fielding. Kluwer Academic, Boston. pp. 209-233.

Fielding, A.H. (2002). What are the appropriate characteristics of an accuracy measure? In *Predicting Plant and Animal Occurrences: Issues of Scale and Accuracy*, ed. by J.M. Scott, P.J. Heglund, M. Morrison, J.B. Haufler, M.G. Raphael, W.B. Wall & F. Samson. Island Press, Washington DC. pp. 271-280.

Fielding, A.H. & Haworth, P.F. (1995). Testing the generality of bird-habitat models. *Conservation Biology*, **9**, 1466-1481.

Fuller, R.J. & Gough, S.J. (1999). Changes in sheep numbers in Britain: implications for bird populations. *Biological Conservation*, **91**, 73-89.

Gainzarain, J.A, Arambarri, R. & Rodriguez, A.F. (2000). Breeding density, habitat selection and reproductive rates of the peregrine falcon *Falco peregrinus* in Alava (northern Spain). *Bird Study*, **47**, 225-231.

Gibbons, D.W., Gates, S., Green, R.E., Fuller, R.J. & Fuller, R.M. (1994). Buzzards *Buteo buteo* and ravens *Corvus corax* in the uplands of Britain: limits to distribution and abundance. *Ibis*, **137**, S75-S84.

Hakkarainen, H. & Korpimäki, E. (1996). Competitive and predatory interactions among raptors: an observational and experimental study. *Ecology*, 77, 1134-1142.

Halley, D.J. (1998). Golden and white-tailed eagles in Scotland and Norway: co-existence, competition and environmental degradation. *British Birds*, **91**, 171-179.

Halley, D.J. & Gjershaug, J.O. (1998). Inter- and intra-specific dominance relationships and feeding behaviour of golden eagles *Aquila chrysaetos* and sea eagles *Haliaeetus albicilla* at carcasses. *Ibis*, **140**, 295-301.

Haworth, P.F. (1999). *Population Ecology of the raven on Mull.* Unpublished report. Scottish Natural Heritage, Perth.

Horne, G. & Fielding, A.H. (2002). The recovery of the peregrine falcon *Falco peregrinus* in Cumbria 1966-1999. *Bird Study*, **49,** 229-236.

Huberty, C.J. (1994). *Applied Discriminant Analysis.* Wiley Interscience, New York.

Jaksić, F.M. & Braker, H.E. (1983). Food-niche relationships and guild structure of diurnal birds of prey: competition versus opportunism. *Canadian Journal of Zoology*, **61**, 2230-2241.

Jiménez, J.E. & Jaksić, F.M. (1993). Observations on the comparative behavioural ecology of Harris's Hawk in Central Chile. *Journal of Raptor Research*, **27**, 143-148.

Lack, D. (1946). Competition for food by birds of prey. *Journal of Animal Ecology*, **15**, 123-129.

Lim, T.S., Loh, W.Y. & Shih, Y.S. (2000). A comparison of prediction accuracy, complexity and training time of thirty three old and new classification algorithms. *Machine Learning*, **40**, 203-229.

Loh, W.Y. & Shih, Y.S. (1997). Split selection methods for classification trees. *Statistica Sinica*, **7**, 815-840.

McGrady, M. (1997). *Aquila chrysaetos* golden eagle. *BWP Update*, **1**, 99-114.

Manel, S., Dias, J.M., Buckton, S.T. & Ormerod, S.J. (1999a). Alternative methods for predicting species distribution: an illustration with Himalayan river birds. *Journal of Applied Ecology*, **36**, 734-747.

Manel, S., Dias, J.M. & Ormerod, S.J. (1999b). Comparing discriminant analysis, neural networks and logistic regression for predicting species distributions: a case study with a Himalayan river bird. *Ecological Modelling*, **120**, 337-347.

Manly, B.J.F. (1991). *Randomization and Monte Carlo Methods in Biology*. Chapman and Hall, London.

Marquiss, M., Madders, M. & Carss, D.N. (2001). The diet of Sea Eagles in Scotland. *Sea Eagle Project Newsletter 2000*. Royal Society for the Protection of Birds, Inverness.

Moorland Working Group (2002). *Scotland's Moorland: the Nature of Change*. Scottish Natural Heritage, Perth.

Newton, I. (1998). *Population Limitation in Birds*. Academic Press, London.

Newton, I. & Marquiss, M. (1982). Food, predation and breeding season in sparrowhawks. *Journal of Zoology*, **197**, 221-240.

O'Connor, R.J. (2002). The conceptual basis of species distribution modeling: time for a paradigm shift. In *Predicting Plant and Animal Occurrences: Issues of Scale and Accuracy*, ed. by J.M. Scott, P.J. Heglund, M. Morrison, J.B. Haufler, M.G. Raphael, W.B. Wall, & F. Samson. Island Press, Washington DC. pp. 25-34.

O'Toole, L., Fielding, A.H. & Haworth, P.F. (2002). Re-introduction of the Golden Eagle *Aquila chrysaetos* into the Republic of Ireland. *Biological Conservation*, **103**, 303-312.

Palomares, F., Gaona, P., Ferreras, P. & Delibes, M. (1995). Positive effects of game species on top predators by controlling smaller predator populations: an example with lynx, mongooses and rabbits. *Conservation Biology*, **9**, 294-304.

Poole, K.G. & Bromley, R.G. (1988). Interrelationships within a raptor guild in the central Canadian Arctic. *Canadian Journal of Zoology*, **66**, 2275-2282.

Ratcliffe, D.A. (1993). *The Peregrine Falcon. Second Edition*. T. & A.D. Poyser, Calton.

Ratcliffe, D.A. (1997). *The Raven*. T. & A.D. Poyser, London.

Redpath, S.M. & Thirgood, S.J. (1997). *Birds of Prey and Red Grouse*. The Stationery Office, London.

Redpath, S.M. & Thirgood, S.J. (1999). Numerical and functional responses in generalist predators: hen harriers and peregrines on Scottish grouse moors. *Journal of Animal Ecology*, **68**, 879-892.

Rodwell, J. (ed.) (1991). *British Plat Communities. Volume 2. Moors and Heaths*. Cambridge University Press, Cambridge.

Rodwell, J. (ed.) (1992). *British Plat Communities. Volume 3. Grasslands and Montane Communities*. Cambridge University Press, Cambridge.

Rogers, C.M. & Caro, M.J. (1998). Song sparrows, top carnivores and nest predation: a test of the mesopredator release hypothesis. *Oecologia*, **116**, 227-233.

Smith, A., Redpath, S.J. & Campbell, S. (2000). *The Influence of Moorland Management on Grouse and Their Predators*. The Stationery Office, London.

Smith, D.G. & Murphy, J.R. (1982). Nest site selection in raptor communities of the eastern Great Basin Desert (USA). *Great Basin Naturalist*, **42**, 395-404.

Solonen, T. (1993). Spacing of birds of prey in Southern Finland. *Ornis Fennica*, **70**, 129-143.

Thioulouse, J., Chessel, D., Dolédech, S. & Olivier, J.M. (1997). ADE-4: a multivariate analysis and graphical display software. *Statistics and Computing*, **7**, 75-83.

Thompson, D.B.A., Gillings, S., Galbraith, C.A., Redpath, SM. & Drewitt, J. (1997). The contribution of game management to biodiversity: a review of the importance of grouse moors for uplands birds. In *Biodiversity in Scotland: Status, Trends & Initiatives*, ed. by L.V. Fleming, A.C. Newton, J.A. Vickery & M.B. Usher. The Stationery Office, Edinburgh. pp. 198-212.

Walker, D.G. (1991). *The Lakeland Eagles*. Privately published.

Watson, J. (1997). *The Golden Eagle*. Poyser, London.

Watson, J., Leitch, A.F. & Broad, R.A. (1992). The diet of the sea eagle *Haliaeetus albicilla* and golden eagle *Aquila chrysaetos* in western Scotland. *Ibis*, **134**, 27-31.

Watson, J. & Whitfield, D.P. (2002). A conservation framework for the Golden Eagle (*Aquila chrysaetos*) in Scotland. *Journal of Raptor Research,* **36**, 41-49.

Whitfield, D.P., Evans, R.J., Broad, R.A., Fielding, A.H., Haworth, P.F. & McLeod, D.R.A. (2002). Are re-introduced white-tailed eagles in competition with golden eagles? *Scottish Birds,* **23**, 36-45.

Whitfield, D.P., McLeod, D.R.A., Fielding, A.H., Haworth, P.F. (in press). Grouse moor management in Scotland is associated with the illegal use of poisoned baits to control predators. *Biological Conservation.*

Willgohs, J.F. (1961). *The White-tailed Eagle* Haliaeetus albicilla albicilla *(L.) in Norway.* Norwegian University Press, Bergen.

Appendix 17.1 Developing predictive models

All classifiers (e.g. discriminant analysis) share a common problem of selecting appropriate predictors. In this study two groups of potential predictors were available. The first (vegetation data) was obtained from a digitised 1995 NVC (National Vegetation Classification; Rodwell, 1991, 1992) survey map (Averis & Averis, 1995). The second group were indicators of golden eagle activity: distance to the nearest active golden eagle mean range centre and land identified as golden eagle preferred habitat (see Appendix 17.2). Pixel resolution for data extraction from the digital NVC maps was 50 m x 50 m. After merging some NVC class mosaics (e.g. M15-M17 was merged with M17-M15) there were 170 NVC classes, most of which were rare. Because the number of potential predictors was excessive, given the sample sizes, they were pruned using logical and statistical methods (Huberty, 1994). NVC classes were retained if they satisfied three conditions: mean areas were significantly different (P <0.05 unadjusted for multiple testing) between nest and non-nest samples; the class was present in more than 50% of cases; the class had a simple ecological interpretation. Applying these criteria produced a more parsimonious list of potential predictors. However, because of remaining correlations the retained NVC variables were subjected to a principal components analysis, resulting in a final reduced set of orthogonal predictors, each of which was primarily associated with a single NVC type (based on component loadings).

Buzzard nest predictors were the areas of ten principal components derived from the retained NVC classes (Table 17.4). Because 19 out of 20 raven ranges (two ranges on the offshore island of Iona were not used) were coastal, a slightly different approach was adopted. Since there was little unused space on the coast most non-nest buffers were inland. Inevitably class areas were smaller in the nest buffers because almost 50% of the coastal buffers were sea. In order to overcome this confounding factor, class areas were replaced by proportions of land area. The unit sum constraint did not apply because only four NVC classes satisfied the selection criteria. The four habitat proportions, plus the buffer land area, were subjected to a principal components analysis for use in the raven models.

Similarly, the proportion of the buffer classified as preferred golden eagle habitat was used instead of its area.

Discriminant analyses used direct entry of predictors with prior probabilities set to equal. Prediction accuracy was assessed using cross-validation (Leave-One-Out). Quest analyses used univariate splits identified by an exhaustive search (likelihood ratio G^2). False negatives were assigned twice the cost of false positives (Fielding, 1999b, 2002) and the best tree was selected automatically using k-fold cross validation (k = 132 for buzzards and 47 for ravens).

Appendix 17.2 Identifying preferred foraging areas

The lack of random sampling means that observations are potentially biased and unrepresentative of actual range use. For example, particularly numerous observations in one area may be due to more time spent watching that area rather than frequent use. We addressed this problem by expressing records relative to the records of all species. Data from all raptor and scavenging bird sightings (n = 19,291 observations on 14 species, five rarely recorded species were not observed interacting) were employed to identify regions used less or more than expected by each species. The proportions of sightings for each species (p_S) in the complete data set were calculated. A moving circular window (250 m radius) was applied to the Ross of Mull. In each buffer the proportion of sightings was calculated, for each species, as a proportion of all raptor sightings within the buffer (b_S). 95% confidence intervals for b_S were calculated for each buffer and compared to p_S. If a buffer's lower confidence limit was greater than p_S this was taken to indicate excess usage ('preference'), while an upper confidence limit less than p_S was indicative of under-use ('avoidance'). For example, the 1955 golden eagle observations (p_{EAGLE}) were 0.103 of all sightings. Thus, if the lower confidence interval for the proportion of golden eagle sightings within a buffer was greater than 0.103 it was assumed that this buffer was used excessively by golden eagles. This approach deals with inequalities in sampling effort because rarely visited locations have wider confidence intervals. We can be confident about under-used locations because buffers unused by one species typically had many observations from other species. The output from these analyses was a series of species-specific 'preference' maps, in which each 50 m x 50 m pixel was assigned one of four values: over-used, under-used, proportional (observed = expected) use and a rare, no data class. If preferred regions for two species do not coincide there is less potential for interference or exploitative competition. However, since overlap in preferred areas does not take account of the temporal dimension it cannot be considered as a simple measure of potential interference competition.

Appendix 17.3 Resource partitioning

If there is resource partitioning habitat associated with pairs of observations from the same species should be more similar to each other than from pairs of different species. A randomisation test was devised to test this hypothesis. Randomization tests help to avoid the pseudo-replication inherent in most pairwise comparisons (Manly, 1991). One thousand random samples of 50 observation pairs were obtained for intra- and inter-specific comparisons. In each randomisation three sample sets (n = 50) were obtained for species A and three for species B. This enabled intra-specific (A_1 v A_2 & B_1 v B_2) and inter-specific (A_3 v B_3) comparisons to be made. The area of each habitat type (see below) was measured in a 250 m buffer centred on each observation's location. For each pair of observations, within a sample of 50, the *k*-dimensional Euclidean distance between habitat class areas was calculated and summarised for the whole sample by the mean distance (d_{SS}). Intra- (d_{AA} and d_{BB}) and inter-specific (d_{AB}) distances were stored from each randomisation. If species use a narrow range of habitats the mean intra-specific distances should be small. Conversely, two species using different resources should produce a relatively large inter-specific distance. Consequently, if there is resource partitioning we should find that the mean intra-specific distance, d_{SS}, ($[d_{AA} + d_{BB}]/2$) is less than the inter-specific distance. The test statistic is significant if $d_{SS} < d_{AB}$ in more than 950 of 1,000 randomisations. In order to make the data analysis more tractable (>19,000 observations and 170 vegetation classes) the habitat data dimensionality was reduced. Because many NVC classes were rare (many zeros) a dimension reduction technique, such as principal components analysis, was inappropriate. Therefore, the areas of all NVC classes in moving 200 m circular buffers, spaced every 100 m across the Ross of Mull, were subjected to a *k*-means classification. After experimentation 30 clusters were used as a compromise between retaining habitat detail without creating many classes with small membership.

18. WINTER RANGING BEHAVIOUR AND SOCIAL INTERACTIONS IN GOLDEN EAGLES (*AQUILA CHRYSAETOS*)

Ken Crane & Kate Nellist

Summary

1. Winter ranging behaviour and social interactions by three neighbouring pairs of golden eagles *Aquila chrysaetos* in western Scotland were studied using repeated observations from fixed points over the 1995/96 winter.
2. Displays peaked prior to breeding and appeared to be primarily territorial in nature.
3. Most observed aggression was directed at non-study birds. Aggression between study pairs was observed mainly between the most recently established pair and the long established pair with which they share their only land border.
4. Males predominated both as the displaying bird and as the aggressor in aggressive interactions.
5. Intruding, unpaired eagles were recorded across the ranges.

18.1 Introduction

Golden eagles are known to be range-holding birds and strongly territorial around nest sites, but little is known of ranging behaviour outwith the breeding season. Previous studies have been hampered by the lack of individually marked birds (Watson, 1997). The aim of this study was to see what could be learnt by making more structured observations in the winter period of a small group of eagles which we have watched all year round since 1981, and which we are able to recognise confidently as individuals.

18.2 Study area and methods

18.2.1 Study area

The study location comprises 210 km squares of hill, moorland and coast in the Isle of Skye, Highland Region. The three adjacent ranges (A, B and C) centre approximately on a sea loch which forms a border between two coastal ranges (B and C); the borders between these and the third range are over low hills offering good hunting (with rabbits *Oryctolagus cuniculus* and sheep *Ovis aries* carrion) (A and B), and over a high rocky ridge with poor hunting (A and C).

18.2.2 Study pairs

Pairs A and C are old and well established; Pair B are younger birds which replaced an old pair in 1991 and bred successfully for the first time in 1995.

18.2.3 Methods

We based our methods on recognition of the six adult birds according to plumage variations and missing feathers (Crane & Nellist, 1999). Our long-term studies enabled us to site six observation points: three close to the nest sites and three close to the borders between territories.

We carried out repeated dawn to dusk watches every month from October 1995 to February 1996, and added a final series of watches spread over late March and April, timed after nesting should have started. Good visibility was essential; cloud base had to be no lower than 900 m. Rain, snow and very strong winds were avoided.

Observations were made by constantly scanning over the area in view. All flights, displays and attacks (*sensu* Watson, 1997; Crane & Nellist, 1999) were plotted on the OS 1 km square grid. Hand written notes were also kept.

Each unbroken sequence of undulating flight was recorded as a display and the number of undulations was counted. Attacks were defined as direct strikes or close chases which caused the attacked bird to take defensive or avoiding action. Non-study birds were recorded as juvenile, immature or unidentified golden eagles, adult golden eagles from neighbouring ranges not included in the study, or white-tailed sea eagles *Haliaeetus albicilla*.

We encountered problems of unequal visibility across the ranges and varying daylight hours across the months. One border observation point was not used in the first and last months (the least active) due to time constraints. In some cases we were unable to recognise individual study birds, although the majority of observations could be attributed to a particular pair.

18.3 Results

Over 34 days a total of 318 hours 50 minutes were spent watching, during which time eagles were observed for 86 hours 6 minutes. Fewest birds were seen in October and most were seen in February. Most observations of the study birds were made around nest sites and over two land borders, one of which was shared with a pair of golden eagles not included in the study. Juveniles and immatures were observed across the three ranges and were not confined to border areas. Highest juvenile activity was seen around nest sites.

18.3.1 Displays

Displays peaked as pre-breeding activity intensified and declined dramatically after incubation had started. This pattern occurred in all three pairs, despite the fact that Pair C did not prepare a nest or lay eggs in 1996. For all pairs, most displays were observed in February, but when the number of displays was examined over time spent watching, Pair A's January score was slightly higher than in February (Figure 18.1).

We observed far more displays by Pair B (101 displays comprising 673 undulations) compared with the two older pairs (Pair A, 38 displays/189 undulations; Pair C, 25 displays/230 undulations).

Males (74 displays/526 undulations) displayed slightly more than females (61 displays/416 undulations), but both sexes averaged approximately seven undulations per display.

Virtually all displays were made up of less than 20 undulations (98%). Only four had more than 20, only two more than 30, one of which, totalling 43 undulations, came in a sequence of nine displays executed by the Pair C male in response to an intruding immature golden eagle.

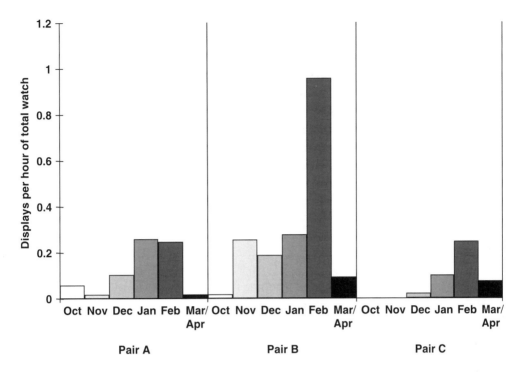

Figure 18.1. Displays per hour of total watch each month during October, November, December, January, February and March/April.

Of the 164 displays observed, at least one bird other than the displaying pair was recorded in view in 89 cases (and in 31 of these the other bird was also displaying). Some of the remaining 75 displays were probably stimulated by courtship and pair bonding.

18.3.2 Attacks

We observed 27 attacks made by study birds: 11 by Pair A, and eight each by Pairs B and C; 15 by males and 12 by females. No attack was observed on any of the females, whereas all three males were attacked at least once.

Only five attacks were made on other study birds, and all involved Pairs A and B (Pair A being the attacking birds in all cases except one). All five of these attacks occurred above the border between Pairs A and B.

The remaining 22 attacks by study birds were on non-study birds. Twelve of these attacks were made within 1 km of the nest area and only one was close to a border. There were two attacks on study birds by intruders.

18.4 Discussion

Our study observations confirmed our previous assessment of the three ranges: the apparent dominance of Pair A at its shared border with Pair B and of the other two borders as undisputed. Pair B occupied the smallest range and the only potential expansion would be over the A–B border. Possibly the younger pair of birds used their high number of displays and interactions with Pair A to test the prescribed limits of the range; Bergo (1987) suggested that establishing eagles display more intensively.

The primary function of display would appear to be territorial (Harmata, 1982). Most attacks appear to be a final response to persistent intrusion from eagles (outwith the range-holding pair). Serious aggressive interactions which involve physical contact, such as cartwheeling, are seldom observed (Ellis, 1979). In two watches we observed the Pair C male cartwheeling with an intruder in defence of his range. These major disruptions to pre-breeding activity possibly contributed to non-breeding in 1996. This could support the suggestion (Haller, 1996) that unsettled, single eagles cause territorial stress in established pairs, thereby reducing their reproduction.

The presence of immatures and juveniles was not confined to border areas or underused parts of the ranges, perhaps explaining the high incidence of attacks on these eagles. Perhaps young birds have to learn from experience the significance of displays made by range-holding birds: it is safer to heed the warning contained in displays rather than risk the more dangerous attack that may follow.

Acknowledgements

We wish to thank Jeff Watson for help in planning the study, and Mick Marquiss and Steve Redpath for comments.

References

Bergo, G. (1987). Territorial behaviour of golden eagles in Western Norway. *British Birds*, **80**, 361-376.

Crane, K. & Nellist, K. (1999). *Island Eagles*. Cartwheeling Press, Skye.

Ellis, D.H. (1979). Development of behavior in the golden eagle. Wildlife Monographs No. 70. The Wildlife Society, Bethesda, Maryland.

Haller, H. (1996). Der Steinadler in Graubunden. Langfristigte Untersuchungen zur Populationsokologie von Aquila Chrysaetos im Zentrum der Alpen. *Der Ornithologische Beobachter*, **9**, Abstract and Summary.

Harmata, A.R. (1982). What is the function of undulating flight display in golden eagles? *Raptor Research*, **16**, 103-109.

Watson, J. (1997). *The Golden Eagle*. Poyser, London.

19. Interactions Within a Raptor Assemblage: The Incidence of Interspecific Mobbing Behaviour

D.H. Morgan, P.F. Haworth & A.H. Fielding

Summary

1. The Isle of Mull supports a diverse assemblage of raptors.
2. During an observational study on the island between 1994 and 1998, 448 instances of mobbing behaviour were recorded between raptor species.
3. Larger species were mobbed far more than smaller species, and smaller species were observed to mob at a greater rate than larger species.
4. We examined the nature of the interspecific mobbing interactions and their possible function.

19.1 Introduction

Interactions between different species of birds of prey have been little studied, and then are usually investigating interactions during winter (e.g. Lein & Boxall, 1979; Bildstein & Collopy, 1985; Bildstein, 1987). In these studies, kleptoparasitism (food stealing) was the suggested primary causal factor, though predation and resource defence were also significant.

In our study we recorded 707 instances of mobbing interactions (out of 19,289 observations) between raptors and other avian species, including passerines and waders (Charadrii), of which 448 were between raptor species. We define mobbing as a suite of behaviours aimed at driving off a target bird, rather than any intent to capture (Bildstein, 1982; Pettifor, 1990).

19.2 Methods

19.2.1 Study Area

The study area comprises the Ross of Mull, a 174 km² peninsula at the south-west end of the Isle of Mull. The primary habitat is a heath and mire mosaic with patches of improved pasture and remnant woodland along with extensive areas of plantation forestry. The western part is low, rolling granite hills (to 100 m) while the eastern section is dominated by basalt plateaux and sea cliffs, rising to 400 m. Land use is largely deer *Cervus elaphus* stalking, sheep *Ovis aries* grazing and plantation forestry, though significant areas were clear of sheep during the study. There has been a steady increase in the number of small-scale deciduous woodland schemes.

19.2.2 The raptor assemblage

Breeding raptors observed during the study period included: golden eagle *Aquila chrysaetos*, common buzzard *Buteo buteo*, kestrel *Falco tinnunculus*, hen harrier *Circus cyaneus*, short-eared owl *Asio flammeus*, merlin *Falco columbarius*, sparrowhawk *Accipiter nisus*, tawny owl *Strix aluco* and barn owl *Tyto alba*. Ravens *Corvus corax* were included in the study because of their ecological position as a functional raptor (Smith & Murphy, 1982).

19.2.3 Interaction Data

During the period August 1994 to December 1998, 19,289 observations of the bird of prey assemblage were collected as part of larger study of raptor ecology, primarily in the months March to October (Fielding *et al.*, Chapter 17). Most observations were collected by two field researchers, with some additional data collected by volunteers. For each observation, a note was made of species, numbers, location, behaviour, and, if possible or appropriate, flight direction, age and sex. Data were also collected for all known breeding attempts. For the purposes of this chapter, all intraspecific interactions are excluded. Of the raptor species observed during the study, there was sufficient data to analyse mobbing for six species (golden eagle, buzzard, raven, kestrel, hen harrier and short-eared owl). For these species only, 448 mobbing interactions were recorded out of a total of 18,694 observations (Table 19.1.).

Table 19.1. Interspecific mobbing behaviour observed between five raptor species (golden eagle, buzzard, kestrel, hen harrier and short-eared owl) and the raven. N_1 = total number of observations recorded of species being mobbed; P_1 = percentage of all species observations when being mobbed; N_2 = total number of observations recorded of species mobbing; and P_2 = percentage of all species observations when mobbing.

		Mobbing										N_1	P_1
		Buzzard		Raven		Kestrel		Hen harrier		Short-eared owl			
		n	%	n	%	n	%	n	%	n	%		
	Golden eagle	79	0.85	75	2.14	103	3.71	16	1.82	4	0.99	277	14.62
Being mobbed	Buzzard			46	1.32	55	1.98	14	1.59	11	2.72	126	1.36
	Raven	2	0.02			20	0.72	2	0.23	1	0.25	25	0.71
	Kestrel	1	0.01	2	0.06			1	0.11	1	0.25	5	0.18
	Hen harrier	0	0.01	0	-	10	0.36			2	0.50	13	1.48
	Short-eared owl	0	-	0	-	2	0.07	0	-			2	0.50
N_2		83		123		190		33		19		448	
P_2		0.90		3.52		6.84		3.76		4.70			

19.3 Results

Golden eagles were never observed to mob any other raptor species (Table 19.1). However, golden eagles were the most mobbed species, (by a factor of ten; Figure 19.1) and were often simultaneously mobbed by more than one species' individual.

Buzzards concentrated most of their mobbing behaviour on golden eagles (Table 19.1) but were observed to mob less often than kestrels, hen harriers, short-eared owls and ravens (Figure 19.2).

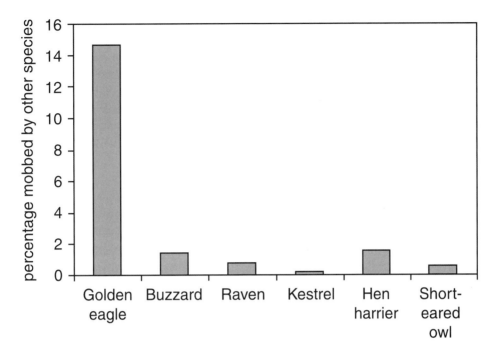

Figure 19.1. Relative proportion of target species of interspecific raptor mobbing, as a percentage of all observations of mobbing.

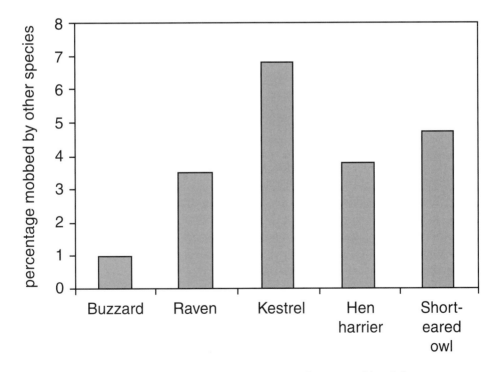

Figure 19.2. Relative proportion of species subjected to interspecific raptor mobbing behaviour, as a percentage of all observations of mobbing.

Ravens mobbed golden eagles and buzzards almost exclusively: hen harriers mobbed golden eagles and buzzards in equal proportions: and short-eared owls were observed to mob buzzards to a greater extent than they did other species (Table 19.1). Kestrels exhibited more mobbing behaviour than all other species (Figure 19.2), and mobbed all target species on occasion (though golden eagles and buzzards were the main targets, Table 19.1).

Ravens, hen harriers and short-eared owls engaged in mobbing behaviour at similar intensities, while buzzards mobbed target species at a far lower intensity (Figure 19.2).

19.4 Discussion

No observations of kleptoparasitism were made and very few observations were suggestive of kleptoparasitism. It is unlikely that kleptoparasitism was a causal factor in aggressive interactions. If prey piracy is excluded there are two other main reasons for mobbing: protection from predation (on adults themselves and their young during the breeding season) and protection of resources (food and possibly nest sites). It is likely that the first factor will be most important in interspecific interactions and the second factor most important in intraspecific interactions, with a role in territoriality.

If protection of resources was the primary factor in the mobbing behaviour observed during this study, then one would expect high levels of mobbing behaviour between species such as the kestrel and short-eared owl, which take similar prey. However, there was no evidence of this and most mobbing interactions observed were more likely to be explained by protection against predation.

Golden eagles were mobbed with far greater intensity by all other species, presumably because they are a clear threat to both adults and young of all conspecifics. Prey remains at eagle plucking points included all of the other species (buzzards, kestrels, hen harriers, short-eared owls and ravens). Although the likelihood of other raptor species falling prey to golden eagles is apparently very low, it may be sufficient to reinforce the mobbing behaviour, especially when vulnerable young have fledged.

Buzzards concentrate almost all of their mobbing effort on golden eagles, which are the only species likely to depredate them. Kestrels show the reverse, exhibiting high mobbing effort against all species, suggesting that they, or their young, are potential prey for all other species.

The raven not only mobs golden eagles and buzzards, which may be potential predators, but is also mobbed considerably by kestrels and, to a much lesser extent, by hen harriers and short-eared owls. The raven's potential for taking eggs, rather than adults or young, may account for its liability to be mobbed.

Mobbing behaviour is a hazardous undertaking and can occasionally result in the death of the mobbing bird (e.g. Walker, 1983), but its prevalence in this study suggests that its benefits far outweigh its occasionally fatal cost.

Acknowledgements

We thank two anonymous referees for comments on a draft of this manuscript.

References

Bildstein, K.L. (1982). Responses of northern harriers (*Circus cyaneus*) to mobbing passerines. *Journal of Field Ornithology*, **53**, 7-14.

Bildstein, K.L. (1987). Behavioral ecology of red-tailed hawks (*Buteo jamaicensis*), rough-legged hawks (*Buteo lagopus*), northern harriers (*Circus cyaneus*), American kestrels (*Falco sparverius*) and other raptorial birds wintering in South-Central Ohio. Biological Notes No. 18. Ohio Biological Survey, Ohio.

Bildstein, K.L. & Collopy, M.W. (1985). Escorting flight and agonistic interactions in wintering northern harriers (*Circus cyaneus*). *Condor*, **87**, 398-401.

Lein, M.R. & Boxall, P.C. (1979). Interactions between snowy and short-eared owls in Winter. *Canadian Field-Naturalist*, **93**, 411-414.

Pettifor, R.A. (1990). The effects of avian mobbing on a potential predator, the European kestrel, *Falco tinnunculus*. *Animal Behaviour*, **39**, 821-827.

Smith, D.G. & Murphy, J.R. (1982). Nest site selection in raptor communities of the eastern Great Basin Desert (USA). *Great Basin Naturalist*, **42**, 395-404.

Walker, D.G. (1983). Golden eagle killing mobbing carrion crows. *British Birds*, **76**, 312.

20. PEREGRINE (*FALCO PEREGRINUS*) PREDATION ON RACING PIGEONS (*COLUMBA LIVIA*) IN WALES

Andrew Dixon, Colin Richards, Andrew Lawrence

& Mike Thomas

Summary

1.   Peregrines *Falco peregrinus* in this study in Wales exhibited both numerical and functional responses to spatial and temporal variations in the availability of racing pigeons *Columba livia*.

2.   Peregrine breeding density, nearest neighbour distance between nest sites, and the level of territory occupation varied in line with racing pigeon availability, providing evidence of a numerical response to spatial variation in racing pigeon availability.

3.   There were seasonal and regional variations in the frequency of racing pigeons in the diet, with the greatest proportion killed during the racing season in the South Wales Valleys (84% of diet by weight).

4.   We discuss the implications for peregrine conservation of a reduction in racing pigeon availability through a decline in the number of pigeon fanciers and a possible restructuring of the race season.

20.1 Introduction

Domestic pigeons *Columba livia* are the most frequent prey species killed by peregrines during the breeding season in many parts of the United Kingdom (Ratcliffe, 1993, Chapter 4). Away from coastal and urban areas in western and northern Britain, feral pigeons *Columba livia* are relatively scarce and domestic pigeons are available mainly in the form of racing pigeons. In inland areas of South-central Wales racing pigeons comprise an estimated 92% of domestic pigeons killed by peregrines in the pigeon race season, the remainder being feral pigeons (7%) and other varieties of domestic pigeon (1%) (Dixon *et al.*, in prep.). Some authors have suggested that latitudinal variation in peregrine breeding density within Scotland is related to the availability of racing pigeons, with lower breeding densities and fewer pigeons present at higher latitudes (Ratcliffe, 1993; Redpath & Thirgood, 1999). The UK holds approximately 20% of the European peregrine breeding population (Hagemeijer & Blair, 1997), with a large proportion of the population occurring in inland Wales, Cumbria and Southern Scotland (Crick & Ratcliffe, 1994), where domestic pigeons comprise a significant proportion of the diet (Ratcliffe, 1993).

The potential importance of racing pigeons in maintaining the internationally important peregrine population of the UK is often overlooked in the debate about peregrine predation on racing pigeons (but see Anon., 2000). In this chapter we highlight the conservation issues arising from the peregrine-racing pigeon conflict and discuss the potential implications of future changes in racing pigeon availability.

20.2 Methods

We collected data on the breeding biology of peregrines within three areas of central and south Wales in 1999-2001: Central Wales; the Brecon Beacons; and the South Wales Valleys. The South Wales Valleys included peregrine sites within the vice-counties of Glamorgan (N = 49 sites) and Monmouthshire (N = 15), the Brecon Beacons included sites within the Brecon Beacons National Park (BBNP) boundary (N = 23), whilst the Central Wales study area included sites in Breconshire that were outside the BBNP boundary (N = 10) and Carmarthenshire (N = 1). In each study area breeding density and nearest neighbour distances between nest sites were calculated for core blocks within which we were confident that all territories had been located (South Wales Valleys core block = 418 km², N = 26 territories; the Brecon Beacons = 1,171 km², N = 22 and Central Wales = 948 km², N = 8).

Racing pigeon abundance is extremely difficult to quantify because of the large degree of temporal and spatial variation related to the race season, and the location of pigeon lofts and racing routes. However, it was possible to rank our study areas in terms of racing pigeon availability (Table 20.1). Pigeon lofts only occurred in the South Wales Valleys, thus pigeons on daily exercise in the loft area were only available to peregrines breeding in the South Wales Valleys. Racing pigeons were liberated on training flights from locations within the Brecon Beacons and South Wales Valleys study areas but not in the Central Wales study area. Racing pigeons could pass through all three study areas on race flights, though few race routes pass through Central Wales nowadays. Stray pigeons which have failed to return to their home lofts can occur in each of the three study areas.

Table 20.1. Availability of racing pigeons as prey within three study areas of Wales.

Study region	Pigeon availability	Circumstance of availability
South Wales Valleys	Highest	Exercising; Training; Racing, Stray
Brecon Beacons	Intermediate	Training; Racing; Stray
Central Wales	Lowest	Racing, Stray

Prey species of peregrines were identified from prey remains found in the vicinity of nesting sites. We estimated the weight contribution of each species to peregrine diet using the weights given by Snow & Perrins (1998). For domestic pigeons, we used a mean weight of 425 g. We compared the frequency and estimated weight of domestic pigeons in the diet, both during and outside the pigeon race season (April-September) between each of our study areas. In South-central Wales, peregrines usually occupy breeding sites all year round, thus we were able to obtain prey samples in each month of the year in order to compare monthly variation in the frequency and weight of domestic pigeons in the diet.

20.3 Results

Peregrine breeding density and the mean nearest neighbour distance (NND) between nest sites varied in line with the estimated availability of racing pigeons. The highest breeding density and lowest NND were found in the South Wales Valleys, where racing pigeon availability was highest. The level of territory occupation in each of the study areas provided further evidence of a numerical response to racing pigeon availability, though we found no evidence of a difference in fledged brood sizes between study areas (Table 20.2).

Table 20.2. Peregrine breeding density, mean nearest neighbour distance (NND) between nests sites, territory occupation and fledged brood sizes in 1999-2001. Breeding density and mean nearest neighbour distance were calculated for core blocks within each study area, within which we were confident that all nesting territories had been located.

Study region	No. territories checked	Territories/ 100 km²	Mean NND (km)	% Occupation	Mean fledged brood size
South Wales Valleys	144	2.8	3.4	88.2	2.3 (N = 46)
Brecon Beacons	43	1.9	4.9	79.1	2.1 (N = 17)
Mid Wales	25	1.8	5.8	56.0	2.3 (N = 10)

During the pigeon race season (April–September) domestic pigeons were the most important component of peregrine diet in all three study regions (Table 20.3). The frequency of domestic pigeons in the diet of peregrines inhabiting South-central Wales varied significantly throughout the year. Domestic pigeons were killed much more frequently during the pigeon race season than outside it (Chi square = 163.8, 1 df, P <0.0001), highlighting the importance of racing pigeons in the diet (Figure 20.1). Within the race season, the frequency of domestic pigeons in the diet varied significantly across months (Chi square = 11.8, 5 df, P = 0.05) and was lowest in April and September, probably because racing does not usually begin until mid-April and there are fewer races at the end of the race season in September. In the six months outside of the race season there was no significant difference between months in the frequency of domestic pigeons killed (Chi square = 5.8, 5 df. P = >0.3).

Table 20.3. Total number of prey items (N), the percentage frequency of domestic pigeons (% Freq) and the percentage weight of domestic pigeons (% Wt) in the diet of peregrines occupying territories in the South Wales Valleys, Brecon Beacons and Central Wales. Data are shown separately for the pigeon race season and the non-race season.

Study Area	Race season (April-September)			Non-race season (October–March)		
	N	% Freq	% Wt	N	% Freq	% Wt
South Wales Valleys	579	64.9	84.4	227	24.2	44.9
Brecon Beacons	215	37.2	63.1	111	6.4	14.4
Central Wales	137	31.6	49.6	40	7.5	19.0

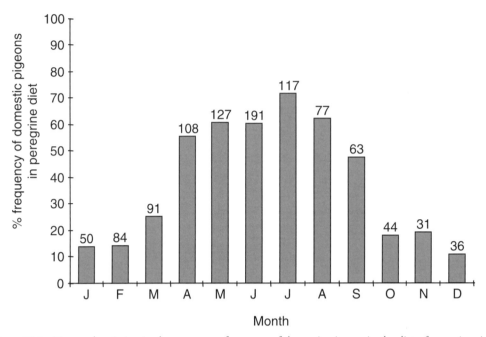

Figure 20.1. Temporal variation in the percentage frequency of domestic pigeons in the diet of peregrines in South-central Wales (all study areas combined). The number of recently killed prey items found in each month is shown above each column.

During the pigeon race season, there was a significant difference in the frequency of domestic pigeons killed in South Wales (65% of kills), the Brecon Beacons (37%) and Central Wales (32%; Chi square = 88.6, 2 df, P <0.0001; Table 20.3). In terms of prey weight, the corresponding percentages were 84%, 63% and 50%, respectively. Outside of the pigeon race season, the frequency of domestic pigeons killed was lower overall, but still significantly different between South Wales (24% of kills), the Brecon Beacons (6%) and Central Wales (8%; Chi square = 19.8, 2 df, P <0.001; Table 20.3). In terms of prey weight, the corresponding percentages were 45%, 14% and 19%, respectively.

The ten most frequent prey species killed by peregrines in South-central Wales are shown in Table 20.4.

20.4 Discussion

Our data for inland Wales suggests that peregrines show both a numerical and functional response to the availability of racing pigeons. The number of breeding pairs in each of our study areas was unlikely to be related to the availability of nest sites as there were unoccupied, but apparently suitable, cliffs in all three areas. Furthermore, persecution did not appear to influence breeding density and was most prevalent in the South Wales Valleys (unpublished data). Nevertheless, the South Wales Valleys has one of the highest recorded breeding densities of peregrines in the UK (Ratcliffe, 1993) with up to eight pairs/100 km² in the Rhondda area. The number of breeding peregrines in each of the study areas reached a ceiling in the mid-1990s (unpublished data). Given that alternative prey species are relatively scarce there (Richards & Shrubb, 1999), a reduction in racing pigeon availability could give rise to a reduction in the number of breeding peregrines. Indeed, there is some

Table 20.4. The ten most frequent prey species killed by peregrines in South-central Wales (all study areas combined). Data in columns refer to the number of individual prey items found (N), their percentage frequency in the diet (% Freq) and their estimated percentage contribution to the total weight of prey killed (% Wt) during and outside the pigeon race season.

Prey species		Summer (April-September)			Winter (October-March		
		N	*% Freq*	*% Wt*	*N*	*% Freq*	*% Wt*
Woodcock	*Scolopax rusticola*	4	0.4	0.4	30	7.9	11.2
Domestic pigeon	*Columba livia*	493	52.9	75.2	65	17.2	34.3
Magpie	*Pica pica*	7	0.8	0.6	19	5.0	5.2
Jackdaw	*Corvus monedula*	59	6.3	4.7	49	13.0	13.6
Mistle thrush	*Turdus viscivorus*	24	2.6	1.1	1	0.3	0.2
Song thrush	*Turdus philomelus*	17	1.8	0.4	8	2.1	0.7
Fieldfare	*Turdus pilaris*	5	0.5	0.2	13	3.4	1.6
Redwing	*Turdus iliacus*	5	0.5	0.1	44	11.6	3.4
Blackbird	*Turdus merula*	31	3.3	1.2	26	6.9	3.3
Starling	*Sturnus vulgaris*	106	11.4	3.0	24	6.3	2.3
Total		751	80.5	86.9	279	73.7	75.8

evidence that the switch by Welsh pigeon fanciers from northern to southern race points in the late 1990s has resulted in a reduction in the availability of racing pigeons (Dixon *et al.*, in prep.) and a higher incidence of non-breeding in Central Wales (Dixon & Lawrence, 2000).

Peregrines show a functional response to temporal variation in racing pigeon availability associated with the timing of the race season, and spatial variation in availability between study areas. Overall, only two other species accounted for more than 5% of the peregrine diet by frequency (starling, 9.8% and jackdaw, 8.0%). We had no data on the relative availability of either species between study areas but it is likely that both were most abundant in the South Wales Valleys (Gibbons *et al.*, 1993). Outside of the pigeon race season, peregrines had a more varied diet and the reduction in racing pigeon availability was possibly compensated by the influx of winter migrants. The extent to which winter migrants compensate for the reduced availability of racing pigeons is not known, but their smaller size would certainly result in less energy efficient hunting. In winter, peregrines may respond to a reduction in hunting efficiency and a possible reduction in overall prey biomass by leaving the nesting territory and hunting for food elsewhere (Mearns, 1982). Territory occupation in winter is likely to be related to food supply (Mearns, 1982), but we were unable to determine if one or both adults remained on the nesting territory, nor the amount of time they spent within the territory.

The fact that peregrines can accommodate a reduction in domestic pigeon availability in the winter does not necessarily mean that they could equally adapt to a similar reduction in the summer and still breed successfully. Food demand will be high at successful nesting territories, and hunting efficiency is particularly important because the male alone hunts for much of the breeding season (Ratcliffe, 1993). The number of pigeon fanciers in Britain is reportedly declining at a rate of approximately 5% per annum for a variety of reasons (P. Bryant, pers. comm.) and the concomitant reduction in racing pigeon availability may have a significant impact on the UK peregrine population in the near future. Raptor predation is cited as a contributory factor in the decline of pigeon racing (e.g., Scottish Homing Union, 1999) and changing the racing season is potentially one way in which peregrine predation can be reduced (Shawyer *et al.*, 2000; Anon., 2000; Galbraith *et al.*, Chapter 41). The adoption by pigeon fanciers of a strategy in which there is a hiatus in the race programme and pigeons are confined to their lofts for a period during May/June could have profound, inimical effects on peregrine breeding success. In regions such as South Wales the impact of a such a strategy on peregrine breeding success would depend on the length of confinement, the availability of alternative prey or stray pigeons, and also the ability of peregrine nestlings to survive a reduced food intake (see Boulet *et al.*, 2001).

Acknowledgements

This work is part of a long-term study of peregrines by the South Wales Peregrine Monitoring Group. We would like to thank Paul Haffield and Paul Lewis for their assistance, and two anonymous referees for comments.

References

Anonymous (2000). *Report of the UK Raptor Working Group.* Department of the Environment, Transport and the Regions and Joint Nature Conservation Committee, Peterborough.

Boulet, M., Olsen, P., Cockburn, A. & Newgrain, K. (2001). Parental investment in male and female offspring by the peregrine falcon, *Falco peregrinus. Emu*, **101**, 95-103.

Crick, H.Q.P. & Ratcliffe, D.A. (1994). The peregrine *Falco peregrinus* population of the United Kingdom in 1991. *Bird Study*, **42**, 88-94.

Dixon, A. & Lawrence, A.M. (2000). The past and present status of the peregrine *Falco peregrinus* in Breconshire (vc. 42). *Welsh Birds*, **2**, 280-291.

Dixon, A., Richards, C., Lawrence, A.M., Thomas, M. & Hartley, I.R. (in prep.). Peregrine *Falco peregrinus* predation on racing pigeons *Columba livia* in South-central Wales. *Bird Study*.

Gibbons, D.W., Reid, J.B. & Chapman, R.A. (1993). *The New Atlas of Breeding Birds in Britain and Ireland 1988-1991.* T. & A.D. Poyser, London.

Hagemeijer, E.J.M. & Blair, M.J. (eds) (1997). *The EBCC Atlas of European Breeding Birds: their Distribution and Abundance.* T. & A.D. Poyser, London.

Mearns, R. (1982). Winter occupation of breeding territories and winter diet of peregrines in South Scotland. *Ornis Scandinavica*, **13**, 79-83.

Ratcliffe, D. (1993). *The Peregrine Falcon. Second Edition.* Poyser, London.

Redpath, S.M. & Thirgood, S.J. (1999). Numerical and functional responses in generalist predators: hen harriers and peregrines on Scottish grouse moors. *Journal of Animal Ecology*, **68**, 879-892.

Richards, C. & Shrubb, M. (1999). The prey of peregrines *Falco peregrinus* in South Wales. *Welsh Birds*, **2**, 131-136.

Scottish Homing Union (1999). *Attacks by Peregrines and Sparrowhawks on Racing Pigeons in Scotland.* Scottish Homing Union, Hamilton.

Shawyer, C., Clarke, R. & Dixon, N. (2000). *A Study into the Raptor Predation of Domestic Pigeons.* Department of the Environment, Transport and the Regions, Bristol.

Snow, D.W. & Perrins, C.M. (eds) (1998). *The Birds of the Western Palearctic. Concise Edition.* Oxford University Press, Oxford.

21. CAUSES OF RACING PIGEON (*COLUMBA LIVIA*) LOSSES, INCLUDING PREDATION BY RAPTORS, IN THE UNITED KINGDOM

Colin R. Shawyer, Roger Clarke & Nicholas Dixon

Summary

1.   We investigated the principal factors responsible for losses of racing pigeons *Columba livia* in the UK, their relative significance and the extent to which raptors contributed to losses.

2.   We also designed our study to try to assist pigeon fanciers in targeting the development of measures to reduce losses.

3.   We calculated that, on average, each loft in the UK fielded 73 racing pigeons, of which 38 (52%) were lost in a year.

4.   Two raptors, the peregrine *Falco peregrinus* and sparrowhawk *Accipter nisus*, accounted for 3.5% and 3.7%, respectively, of the racing pigeon population lost in the UK.

5.   Losses due to peregrines were estimated to be greatest in Northern Ireland (21% of the racing pigeon population) and Scotland (17%).   However, 70% of pigeons found in peregrine eyries had strayed before being killed.

6.   Losses to sparrowhawks occurred mainly at or near the loft, and showed less regional variation than to peregrines, and were greatest in Northern Ireland (4.6%).

7.   Losses due to other causes (non-raptor induced), mainly straying and collision, were much higher (45%) than those due to raptors.

21.1 Introduction

Our investigation (Shawyer *et al.*, 2000) was commissioned in 1996 by the then Department of the Environment, Transport and the Regions (DETR) at the request of the UK Raptor Working Group, which sought to address recent concerns of parties (including pigeon fanciers) interested in the implications of the growth of raptor populations in the UK (Anon., 2000).

Pigeon racing unions first expressed their concern about peregrine predation in 1925. Their subsequent demand for raptor control in 1959 prompted the Home Office to commission a national peregrine survey (Ratcliffe, 1963, 1980, Chapter 4).   The results showed that the peregrine was in steep decline and led to the identification of organochlorine pesticides such as DDT as the cause of population crashes in certain raptors (Ratcliffe, 1965, 1980).   Following the withdrawal of these pesticides, peregrine and sparrowhawk numbers recovered in most regions of the UK (Gibbons *et al.,* 1993; Crick & Ratcliffe, 1995; Greenwood *et al.*, Chapter 2).

Fanciers, who generally in the UK have an ageing age profile and mostly began pigeon racing during a low in raptor populations in the 1950s-1970s, have concerns about the potential impact of the recent recovery in populations of birds of prey on their sport (also Dixon *et al.*, Chapter 20). Our investigation was initiated to provide the UK Government with data on raptor predation and to assist fanciers in accurately targeting development of measures to reduce any losses. Such measures can involve the use of raptor deterrents (see Plate 11) or varying the timing and/or locations of race routes.

21.2 Methods

21.2.1 Estimation of pigeon losses due to raptors

The impact of peregrines on racing pigeons, which usually occurs away from the loft during racing and training as a consequence of both flock disruption and direct predation, was estimated in seven regions of the UK. Pigeon losses experienced by lofts in regions where peregrines were present in varying abundance were compared with losses in Eastern England, where peregrines were largely absent and pigeons were unlikely to encounter this raptor during racing and training (Gibbons *et al.*, 1993; Crick & Ratcliffe, 1995). Assuming that the geographical distribution of other loss factors was even, the use of eastern England as a 'control' enabled us to assess the proportions of losses to peregrines (the raptor responsible for the great majority of raptor attacks away from the loft) either through direct predation or failure to return due to scattering.

By means of a questionnaire, we sought regional information on numbers of pigeons held in lofts in January, prior to training and racing, numbers remaining in lofts at the end of the year after racing had finished, age structure in each loft, race techniques used and losses attributable to attack by sparrowhawks (commonly observed by fanciers because such attacks usually occur at or near the loft). A total of 350 completed questionnaires was received, averaging 50 per region (range 23-53).

In order to determine life histories and recent flight histories of pigeons killed by peregrines, pigeon remains (mainly leg rings and less commonly flight feathers stamped with the owner's name), were collected from a random sample of occupied eyries (n = 105) in the UK in 1997 and 1998. Eyries were first cleared of prey remains early in the year, before peregrines began breeding and prior to the pigeon racing season. At the end of the breeding season, rings from 916 pigeons were collected at these eyries, and the data from these were used in our analyses.

A random sample of 700 owners, who were not made aware of how their pigeon had died, were contacted with a second questionnaire, which sought factual details about the life history of each pigeon (age, colour, experience, quality), and recent flight history (place and date pigeon last liberated, distance and route immediately prior to loss, and race technique used). Pigeon owners were identified from ring numbers with the co-operation of pigeon racing unions. A total of 366 completed questionnaires was received. Information derived from these questionnaires was used to investigate the potential vulnerability of different classes of pigeon. For each pigeon, liberation point, home loft and optimal flight trajectory were plotted on individual maps and compared with the bird's place of death. Date of liberation and the proximity of each pigeon to its intended race route prior to death enabled us to calculate the extent to which peregrine predation was the proximate cause of loss (the pigeon having first strayed or become feral) or ultimate one (pigeon killed at or near its intended race/training route).

21.2.2 Estimation of pigeon losses from other causes
In order to determine the other reasons why racing pigeons fail to return to their lofts, we analysed the detailed intake ledgers of the six RSPCA/SSPCA Wildlife Hospitals in the UK where veterinary staff record the number of pigeons and the cause of their disablement or death. Sufficient detail was provided in 417 of these records. Attacks by raptors, particularly peregrines, are likely to occur in more remote locations and be less commonly reported in these ledgers. In order to reduce this bias, any reports attributable to raptors were removed before calculating the relative proportions of pigeons lost due to other factors.

21.3 Results

In the UK, pigeon racing involves 69,000 fanciers operating from an estimated 52,000 lofts, and involving 3.8 million pigeons which are trained and raced.

At the start of the year, the average loft in the UK housed 73 pigeons destined to race; 38 (52%) of these were lost in a year during racing, training and exercising.

21.3.1 Pigeon losses to peregrines and sparrowhawks
Losses to sparrowhawks (mainly females) amounted, on average, to 2.7 pigeons per loft, or 3.7% of the racing pigeon population (ranging from 1.9% in central and southern England to 6.2% in Northern Ireland), with 63% of lofts experiencing attacks annually (see Table 21.1). Most attacks (70%) occurred between March and June mainly before or early in the sparrowhawk breeding season.

Table 21.1. Loft losses of racing pigeons to sparrowhawks.

Region	Pigeons held	Pigeons lost	% loss
England			
Eastern	74.1	1.8	2.4
Central and Southern	63.3	1.2	1.9
South-western England,			
Western England			
including Wales*	68.5	2.3	3.4
Scotland	81.8	3.5	4.3
Northern Ireland	73.8	4.6	6.2

* Regions combined to achieve sufficient sample size.

Losses to peregrines, on average, amounted to 2.6 pigeons per loft or 3.5% of the racing pigeon population. Attacks usually occurred away from lofts, when pigeons were actively involved in racing or training. Lofts in western regions of England, in Wales, Scotland and Northern Ireland experienced significantly greater annual losses to peregrines, of 7%, 10%, 17% and 21% respectively (see Table 21.2). There were significant differences between regions in losses to all causes (first-year pigeons $\chi^2_6 = 166.7$, P <0.001, older birds $\chi^2_6 = 256.9$, P <0.001) with greater losses in north and west regions, which were likely to be due to peregrines.

Of racing pigeons found in peregrine eyries, 30% were on their racing line. The other 70% had either strayed (defined as when the distance measured at right angles to their

Table 21.2. Loft losses of racing pigeons to peregrines.

Region	*Pigeons held*	*Pigeons lost*	*% loss*
England			
Eastern	74.1	(control region)	0.0
Central and Southern	63.3	1.4	2.2
Western	67.0	7.7	11.5
South-western	67.9	9.9	14.5
Wales	70.7	7.2	10.2
Scotland	81.8	13.9	17.0
Northern Ireland	73.8	15.6	21.1

expected flight line was greater than 33% of their intended race distance), or had been living a feral existence for one or more years following their liberation date. A typical example of a pigeon which had strayed was one which had been entered in a race from Eastbourne in south-east England to Newcastle in north-east England, the remains of which were found 150-250 miles away from its intended racing line at an eyrie in mid-Wales.

In the course of the 22 weeks (early/mid-April to mid/late September) of the 'old bird' and, later, the 'young bird' (first-year bird) racing seasons, most pigeons take part in and complete three to four races during their respective racing seasons. Thus, with a loft population of 3.8 million, approximately 13 million racing pigeon prey opportunities are presented annually to an estimated 3,849 to 5,132 peregrines in the UK (see peregrine population calculations in Shawyer *et al.* (2000), based on 1991 survey by Crick & Ratcliffe (1995)). The old bird racing and young bird training seasons coincide with the peak prey demands of breeding peregrines.

Comparisons were made between pigeons found in peregrine eyries and the population in UK lofts at the start of the racing season. No obvious differences were found between the live racing pigeon population and those selected by peregrines in terms of colour, sex, age or the race distance over which pigeons competed.

Evidence from race histories showed that proportionately more of those pigeons raced by the 'natural system' (pigeons of either sex flown back to the nest and their mate at the loft, or general affinity to the loft including an eagerness to be fed) were found in eyries than those raced by the 'widowhood system' (mainly males encouraged to fly back to the loft initially by being shown a potential mate with which he was not allowed to copulate, but with the expectation of copulation upon return). The latter system is the one favoured by most fanciers and appears to result in less straying and consequentially less predation.

21.3.2 Pigeon losses unrelated to raptors

On average, 33 pigeons per loft (45% of the racing pigeon population) failed to return to lofts due to factors evidently unrelated to attack by birds of prey. Such losses are due to straying and exhaustion (19%), collision with solid objects such as buildings, windows and vehicles (10%), collision with overhead wires (8%), shooting, poisoning, entanglement in netting and oiling (4%), and predation by mammals, including domestic cats (4%).

21.4 Discussion

On the basis of our data, birds of prey could be viewed as a relatively inconsequential cause of racing pigeon losses in the UK overall; pigeons are exposed to many hazards both at the loft and when training and racing. However, losses to raptors were of more significance in western and northern regions of the UK.

Steps which could be taken to reduce losses to raptors include delaying the racing season by three or four weeks to avoid the greatest prey demands of breeding peregrines, and paying greater attention to the location of lofts, liberation sites, race routes and research into the effectiveness of deterrents. This would involve a certain amount of abandonment of tradition by fanciers. In some regions there could be much more gain in addressing the ultimate causes of pigeon losses. For example, the mapping of race routes currently being used in the UK reveals a very tangled situation in the Midlands and south-west, with much criss-crossing of routes, which may give rise to widespread clashing of pigeon flocks all flying at similar height in calm winds, with consequential straying and the failure to return home. Observational studies along race routes and satellite tracking of racing pigeons could provide fruitful lines of research. As this chapter goes to press, we await with interest the results of the study funded by Scottish Natural Heritage and the Scottish Homing Union, investigating the extent and causes of racing pigeon losses in Scotland alone. This study, undertaken by the Central Science Laboratory, is also examining some mitigation measures.

Acknowledgements

We are grateful to the DETR and The Northern Ireland Environment and Heritage Service for funding this contract, and to two anonymous referees for comments. We are also grateful to all of the pigeon fanciers and their unions for their co-operation and support in the study.

References

Anonymous (2000). *Report of the UK Raptor Working Group.* Department of the Environment, Transport and the Regions and Joint Nature Conservation Committee, Peterborough.

Crick, H.Q.P. & Ratcliffe, D.A. (1995). The peregrine falcon *Falco peregrinus* breeding population of the United Kingdom in 1991. *Bird Study*, **42**, 1-19.

Gibbons, D.W., Reid, J.B. & Chapman, R.A. (eds.). (1993). *The New Atlas of Breeding Birds in Britain and Ireland: 1988-1991.* Poyser, London.

Ratcliffe, D.A. (1963). The status of the peregrine in Great Britain. *Bird Study*, **10**, 56-90.

Ratcliffe, D.A. (1965). The peregrine situation in Great Britain 1963-64. *Bird Study*, **12**, 66-82.

Ratcliffe, D.A. (1980). *The Peregrine Falcon.* Poyser, London.

Shawyer, C.R., Clarke, R. & Dixon, N. (2000). *A Study into the Raptor Predation of Domestic Pigeons* Columba livia. Department of the Environment, Transport and the Regions, London.

Plate 1. Raptors in the uplands

Adult golden eagle *Aquila chrysaetos* (Photo: Laurie Campbell).

Hen harrier *Circus cyaneus* female brooding nestlings (Photo: Laurie Campbell).

Adult merlin *Falco columbarius* female with nestlings. Just a few people have contributed substantially to our knowledge of this small falcon. In Britain, merlins commonly nest on the ground, but this is unusual in many other parts of their range (Photo: Graham Rebecca) (Chapters 14-16).

Plate 2. Raptors in the lowlands

Osprey *Pandion haliaetus* pair at nest; around 150 pairs nest in Britain. (Photo: Laurie Campbell) (Chapter 11).

Red kite *Milvus milvus* at the nest in Wales (Photo: Chris Gomersall) (Chapter 31).

Male barn owl *Tyto alba*. The world's most northern population occurs in N. Scotland (Photo: Lorne Gill) (Chapters 8, 32).

Plate 3. Forest and woodland dwelling raptors

Sparrowhawk *Accipiter nisus* female brooding nestlings (Photo: Jim Young).

Tawny owl *Strix aluco* (Photo: Laurie Campbell) (Chapter 6).

Second year goshawk *Accipiter gentilis*; the increase in numbers of this species in Britain has been hampered by persecution (Photo: Laurie Campbell) (Chapter 9).

Plate 4. Widespread raptors

Buzzard *Buteo buteo* at the nest; there has been a major expansion in the breeding range of this species in the UK (Photo: Graham Rebecca) (Chapters 12, 13, 28).

Kestrel *Falco tinnunculus* female. This is the commonest of all raptor species in Britain, though a 28% decline in population size was recorded between 1974 and 1999 (Photo: Laurie Campbell) (Chapters 2, 7).

Adult peregrine falcon *Falco peregrinus*; the 2002 national survey pointed to a 10% increase in the overall UK population, but a decline in Scotland (Photo: Laurie Campbell) (Chapters 4, 5).

Plate 5. Studying raptors in the field

Scottish Raptor Study Group workers, Keith Brockie and Bradley Yule, on a golden eagle *Aquila chrysaetos* eyrie with two eaglets (Photo: Lorne Gill).

Examining the prey remains of ringed and wing-tagged hen harrier *Circus cyaneus* youngsters in the nest (Photo: Lorne Gill).

Ian Newton (left) and Mick Marquiss (right) examining a sparrowhawk *Accipiter nisus* (Photo: Robert Rae).

Derek Ratcliffe overlooking a raven's *Corvus corax* nest in south Scotland (Photo: Des Thompson).

Plate 6. The changing nature of the uplands

The quiltwork pattern of muirburn, Abington (Photo: Patricia & Angus MacDonald).

Two fenceline boundaries (arrowed) showing the effects of grazing/burning on upland heath vegetation and erosion, N. Wales (Photo: Des Thompson) (Chapter 25).

Conifer afforestation near Merkland, Sutherland; heavily grazed woodland in the distance (Photo: Des Thompson).

Natural woodland expansion on Struie Hill, Ross-shire (Photo: Des Thompson) (Chapter 27).

Loss of heather *Calluna vulgaris* can be considerable around supplementary feeding stations used by sheep *Ovis aries* (Photo: Des Thompson) (Chapter 25).

Wind turbines - a relatively new land use in the uplands (Photo: SNH) (Chapter 25).

Plate 7. Contributors to the grouse moor debate

Signatories to the Scottish Raptor Monitoring Scheme agreement, signed on 24 June 2002 (Photo: Dougie Barnett) (Preface, Chapter 41).

Steve Redpath (left) and Simon Thirgood (right), authors of *Birds of Prey and Red Grouse*, published in 1997 (Photo: Des Thompson) (Chapter 39).

Two advisory publications produced by the Moorland Working Group (Chapter 41).

Shooting red grouse *Lagopus lagopus scoticus* in Scotland (Photo: Neil McIntyre).

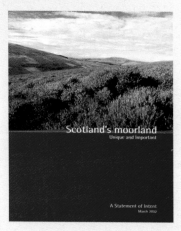

This moorland agreement was signed by 24 organisations on 25 March 2002; it led to the formation of Scotland's Moorland Forum (Chapter 41).

Plate 8. Persecution of raptors

Two poisoned first year red kites *Milvus milvus*; a hare *Lepus europaeus* carcass baited with the highly toxic poison mevinphos resulted in these deaths in the English Midlands (Photo: Ian Carter) (Chapter 37).

A dead buzzard *Buteo buteo*, which had been trapped and killed by a pole trap; both the use of the trap and killing a buzzard are illegal (Photo: Alan Ross) (Chapter 37).

Plate 11. Racing pigeons and raptors

Several deterrents have been applied to racing pigeons *Columba livia* in an attempt to reduce the impacts of raptors; these include sequins and large eye spots (above) (Photo: Colin Shawyer) (Chapters 21, 41).

The release of racing pigeons; there is considerable debate about the nature of pigeon losses during races, and around pigeon lofts (Photo: Nick Dixon) (Chapters 21, 41).

Plate 12. Two species successfully re-introduced to Britain

More than 600 pairs of red kites *Milvus milvus* nest in Britain, representing one of the conservation success stories. This plate shows an adult bird (Photo: Laurie Campbell) (Chapter 31).

An adult white-tailed eagle *Haliaeetus albicilla* hunting for fish; in 2003 there were 31 territorial pairs, with 25 confirmed breeding in Scotland (Photo: Laurie Campbell) (Chapter 30).

Plate 13. White-tailed eagles released in Scotland

Between 1975 and 1985, 80 young white-tailed eagles *Haliaeetus albicilla* (from Norway) were released on the island of Rum. The first clutch of eggs was laid in 1983, and the first successful breeding occurred in 1985. The release site had the magnificent backdrop of the Rum Cuillin (above) (Photo: John Love) (Chapter 30).

The re-introduction of Scotland's white-tailed eagle population received tremendous help from Harald Misund (pictured beside a nest in Norway). The eagle in flight provides a great spectacle, which growing numbers of people are enjoying in Scotland (Photos: John Love) (Chapter 30).

Plate 14. Golden eagles at the nest

A four-five week old eaglet *Aquila chrysaetos,* with its older sibling basking in the sun, in a tree eyrie in N.E. Scotland (Photo: Robert Rae).

Two-three week old eaglet (Photo: Jeff Watson).

Two views of the same golden eagle nest showing adults at the nest. The eaglet is three-four weeks old (upper right) and four-five weeks old (above) (Photos: Laurie Campbell).

Plate 15. Raptors seen occasionally in Britain

A portrait of an adult gyrfalcon *Falco rusticolus*, the largest falcon (50-60cm long; 130-160cm wing span). Males and females sometimes co-operate to exhaust prey, and rarely stoop from a great height like the peregrine falcon *Falco peregrinus* (Photo: Jóhann Óli Hilmarsson) (Chapter 24).

An adult male Montagu's harrier *Circus pygargus* (left) and its nest with three eggs (right). Approximately 10-12 pairs nest in Britain. These pictures were taken in western France, where the birds nest in cereal fields, pastureland and managed grasslands (Photos: Francois Mougeot (left) and Luis Palomares (right)) (Chapter 33).

Plate 16. The golden eagle hunting

An adult golden eagle *Aquila chrysaetos* hunts over Glen Spean, Scottish Highlands (Photo: Laurie Campbell).

22. THE EFFECTS OF PREDATION BY SPARROWHAWKS (*ACCIPITER NISUS*) ON THE BEHAVIOUR AND POPULATION DYNAMICS OF WINTERING REDSHANKS (*TRINGA TOTANUS*)

D. Philip Whitfield

Summary

1.   This chapter summarises a long-term study of predation on the coast in winter. The study has focused on individual differences within the prey population and how this influences its population dynamics.

2.   Sparrowhawks *Accipiter nisus* are predators on redshanks *Tringa totanus,* notably when the redshanks feed close to the high tide line .

3.   There were strong locational and density-dependent predation effects on adult and juvenile redshanks mediated by competition between individuals for feeding areas away from locations that incurred a high risk of predation by hawks.

4.   The study reveals the significant consequences of predation risk for prey population dynamics in the non-breeding season.

22.1 Introduction

A major challenge in ecology is that of determining how population density acting through effects on individuals influences the demographics of the population. Density-dependent effects are critical in affecting population dynamics and population size, but in birds clear demonstrations of these effects are difficult to document (Newton, 1998). At a rocky shore at Scoughall in south-east Scotland there is high mortality of wintering redshanks *Tringa totanus* through predation by female sparrowhawks (Whitfield, 1985, 2003a; Whitfield *et al.*, 1988). The predator-prey system involving sparrowhawks *Accipiter nisus* and redshanks on this site is particularly amenable to an examination of density-dependent mortality because, within a winter, the redshank wintering population is stable in membership, deaths can be recorded directly through recovery of kills, density-independent mortality through severe weather effects is rare, and numbers of redshanks can vary substantially from year to year.

This chapter summarises the results of a study conducted over 11 winters at Scoughall which examined how individual differences in redshank behaviour influenced the dynamics of the redshank population through its effects on risk of predation by sparrowhawks. These results are mostly unpublished but methods have been described by earlier studies at the site and at the neighbouring estuarine site of Tyninghame (Whitfield, 1985, 1988, 2003a, 2003b; Cresswell, 1994; Cresswell & Whitfield, 1994; Whitfield *et al.*, 1999).

22.2 Location of sparrowhawk attacks

The effect of feeding location on an individual redshank's risk of sparrowhawk predation was fundamental to this predator-prey system and the influence of hawk predation on the dynamics of the redshank population. Sparrowhawk attacks on redshanks feeding on beaches around the high tide mark (the strandline zone) were far more frequent than attacks on redshanks feeding seaward of the strandline zone (the intertidal zone) (Whitfield, 1985, 2003b). Attacks were also three times more successful on strandline-feeding redshanks. Flocking by redshanks in the intertidal zone was uncommon and flocking only appeared to influence the outcome of hawk attacks at shorter distances from cover on the strandline, with attacks on singletons and small flocks being more successful than attacks on larger flocks. Distance from cover appeared to have a stronger association with the likelihood of attack success than flock size. An individual redshank's likelihood of predation by a sparrowhawk declined with increasing flock size. Food intake rates of redshanks on the strandline declined with increasing flock size, indicating that redshanks probably flocked to avoid predation by hawks rather than to increase their food intake rates.

22.3 Density-dependent winter mortality

Redshank numbers at the beginning of a winter showed no trend over the study period and winter mortality rates also showed no temporal trend. Mean winter mortality through predation by sparrowhawks was 30.6% for juveniles and 5.6% for adults. The study demonstrated density-dependent winter mortality in both juvenile (first winter birds) and adult (birds in at least their second winter) redshanks due to predation by sparrowhawks (Figure 22.1) (Whitfield, 2003a).

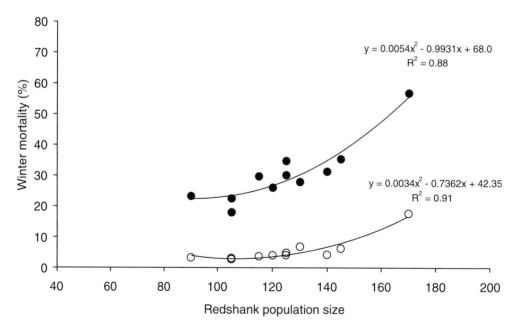

Figure 22.1. The relationship between population size (equivalent to density) and winter mortality rate due to sparrowhawk predation for adult (open circles) and juvenile (filled circles) redshank at Scoughall. Fitted lines illustrate quadratic functions.

The influence of several weather variables was also examined and wind speed was positively associated with juvenile winter mortality but had a weaker influence on adult mortality. Other results, however, suggested that weather might not have been especially influential. Hilton *et al.* (1999) found that redshanks fed further from cover (and decreased their risk of predation) when wind speed was high, in contrast to the results of the present study.

Density-dependent functions differed between adult and juvenile redshanks, consistent with differences in the competitiveness of the two age classes (Figure 22.1). It is suggested that individual differences in vulnerability to predation arose through differences in individual susceptibility to density-dependent competition during foraging.

22.4 Age-related and social class differences in redshank mortality

Adult redshanks were more likely to defend a territory on the intertidal zone than were juveniles. Juveniles were more likely to be killed by hawks than were adults (see also Whitfield, 1985; Whitfield *et al.*, 1988; Cresswell & Whitfield, 1994). Older/earlier arriving juveniles (as estimated by the stage of first winter moult) obtained those territories that were vacated by the disappearance of adults in the previous summer and had higher survival than non-territorial juveniles. When territorial adults disappeared during a winter their territories were occupied by replacement birds: most replacements which could be identified were previously non-territorial juveniles. This suggested that territory acquisition, and associated survival benefits, were restricted by the actions of territory holders. Use of the strandline, where redshanks were more likely to be killed by a hawk,

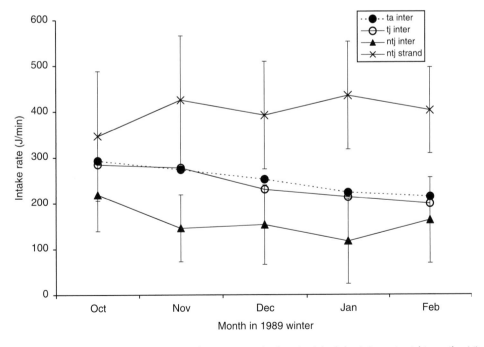

Figure 22.2. Mean intake rates (J/min: joules per minute) of territorial adults (ta), territorial juveniles (tj) and non-territorial juveniles (ntj) in the intertidal zone (inter) and strandline zone (strand) in the 1988-1989 winter. Bars illustrate standard deviations, not presented for all social classes to retain clarity in the presentation.

tended to occur mainly at high tide in mid-winter. Intake rates of redshanks feeding on the strandline were highest at high tide but even at low tide were substantially higher than intake rates of birds feeding on the intertidal zone (Figure 22.2). The preference for the intertidal zone and avoidance of the strandline was therefore probably due to the relative risk of predation rather than the relative feeding profitability.

Use of the strandline in a winter was strongly positively related to winter population density and to winter mortality rates of both adults and juveniles. This suggested that density-dependent mortality was caused by density-dependent use of the strandline. Use of the strandline was also greater in non-territorial juveniles than in territorial juveniles and adults. Intertidal food intake rates of non-territorial juveniles were lower than intake rates of territorial juveniles and adults, but did not differ between social/age classes when feeding on the strandline, when territoriality had no influence. Intertidal intake rates were negatively related to use of the strandline, so that as intertidal intake rates declined use of the strandline increased. This suggested that the low intake rates (and therefore higher use of the strandline and greater mortality due to hawk predation) of non-territorial juveniles was due to their social status rather than their age. In winters with a high population density intake rates of all social/age classes were lower. Hence, density-dependent mortality appeared to be caused by a depressive effect of population density on intertidal intake rates, forcing birds to make more use of the strandline for feeding, where risk of hawk predation was greater. Density-dependent mortality functions differed between age classes due to age-related differences in the susceptibility to competition (territoriality). Within a social/age class direct competitive interference was also thought to be responsible for density-dependent effects as rates of agonistic interactions increased with density and there was no evidence of depression of prey abundance.

22.5 Conclusion

The results of the study support theoretical models of shorebird populations which suggest density-dependent mortality and individual differences in vulnerability to predation arise through differences in individual susceptibility to density-dependent competition during foraging (e.g. Dolman & Sutherland, 1994). The results of this study also have important implications for other studies of body mass-dependent predation and cross-seasonal selection pressures on the timing of breeding in shorebirds. Indeed, the results have important consequences for cross-seasonal studies because the risk of predation to individuals in winter may have far-reaching effects in breeding seasons and population turnover for some populations thousands of miles from where they over-winter.

References

Cresswell, W. (1994). Age-dependent choice of Redshank (*Tringa totanus*) feeding location: profitability or risk? *Journal of Animal Ecology*, **63**, 589-600.

Cresswell, W. & Whitfield, D.P. (1994). The effects of raptor predation on wintering wader populations at the Tyninghame estuary, south-east Scotland. *Ibis*, **136**, 223-232.

Dolman, P. & Sutherland, W.J. (1994). The response of bird populations to habitat loss. *Ibis*, **137**, S38-S46.

Hilton, G.M, Ruxton, G.D. & Cresswell, W. (1999). Choice of feeding area with respect to predation risk in redshanks: the effects of weather and predator activity. *Oikos*, **87**, 295-302.

Newton, I. (1998). *Population Limitation in Birds*. Academic Press, London.

Whitfield, D.P. (1985). Raptor predation on wintering waders in south-east Scotland. *Ibis*, **127**, 544-558.

Whitfield, D.P. (1988). Sparrowhawks *Accipiter nisus* affect the spacing behaviour of wintering Turnstone *Arenaria interpres* and Redshank *Tringa totanus*. *Ibis*, **130**, 284-287.

Whitfield, D.P. (2003a). Predation by Eurasian sparrowhawks produces density-dependent mortality of wintering redshanks. *Journal of Animal Ecology*, **72**, 27-35.

Whitfield, D.P. (2003b). Redshank *Tringa totanus* flocking behaviour, distance from cover and vulnerability to sparrowhawk *Accipter nisus* predation. *Journal of Avian Biology*, **34**, 163-169.

Whitfield, D.P., Evans A.D, & Whitfield, P.A. (1988). The impact of raptor predation on wintering waders. *Acta XIX Congressus Internationalis Ornithologici*, 674-687.

Whitfield, D.P., Cresswell, W., Ashmole, N.P., Clark, N.A. & Evans, A.D. (1999). No evidence for sparrowhawks selecting redshanks according to size or condition. *Journal of Avian Biology*, **30**, 31-39.

23. A MODEL OF HEN HARRIER (*CIRCUS CYANEUS*) RANGING BEHAVIOUR

M. Madders

Summary

1.   A model is described that aims to predict the relative use made of different parts of local ranges occupied by hen harriers *Circus cyaneus* during the breeding season.

2.   The model uses existing data sources and takes account of nest proximity, vegetation cover and structure, and the distribution of linear habitat features.

3.   The model is a potentially important decision making tool for evaluating the impacts of land use changes and different management practices on harriers. Further work is needed so as to validate and refine the model assumptions.

4.   The need for related work to investigate the responses of hen harriers to native woodlands is discussed.

23.1 Introduction

Intensive sheep *Ovis aries* farming and maturing plantation forestry have reduced the availability of habitat suitable for foraging hen harrier *Circus cyaneus* in upland Britain. As a result, a large and increasing proportion of the UK hen harrier population occupies moorland managed for red grouse *Lagopus lagopus scoticus*, where harriers are often persecuted because of their perceived impact on grouse stocks (Redpath *et al.*, 1998; Summers *et al.*, Chapter 38; Redpath & Thirgood, Chapter 39). In Scotland, persecution is the main factor currently limiting population growth (Etheridge *et al.*, 1997). However, the impact of persecution would be far less if harriers were able to occupy more habitats where grouse management is not a priority. This can be achieved through changes to the management of land used for hill sheep farming and forestry.

At high densities, sheep limit the availability of vegetation suitable for harrier nesting and foraging. In many areas this is exacerbated by extensive burning aimed at promoting grassland development at the expense of heather (as opposed to rotational burning of small patches in order to promote heather regeneration). Imminent changes to the agricultural support system may result in a decline in sheep numbers in some areas (see Thompson *et al.*, Chapter 25). At lower densities, sheep might be used to manage habitat for the benefit of harriers by maximising the structural diversity of the vegetation. Forestry can, initially, be beneficial to harriers because of the increased prey populations that result from the lack of burning and grazing by sheep (Petty & Avery, 1990). In the longer term, however, forests are of little use to foraging harriers because the open and semi-open habitat within them is generally too small and isolated for harriers to use efficiently. However, some forests provide harriers with secure nest sites throughout the forest rotation (personal observation). There has been a marked reduction in commercial planting since 1990 (Avery & Leslie, 1990), but the establishment of native woodlands continues to have the potential for large impact.

The effects of sheep farming and forestry on harriers are compounded in some areas by existing and potential secondary land uses, such as wind farms and open cast mining. The Scottish Executive has given a commitment to secure 40% of Scotland's electricity from renewable energy sources by 2020 (Thompson *et al.*, Chapter 25). Realistically, this target can only be achieved by a massive increase in wind energy, some of which is likely to occur in upland areas which are occupied by hen harriers. Similarly, continued demand for coal will inevitably lead to further open cast activity in parts of southern Scotland. Wind farms and open cast mines both have the potential to displace harriers into less suitable habitats, although these developments sometimes offer opportunities to manage or restore land in a way that mitigates the cumulative impacts of sheep and forestry.

The recent designation of Special Protection Areas for harriers (notably Muirkirk and North Lowther, and Arran) have highlighted the need to define accurately the areas most used by foraging birds, ideally without imposing unnecessary restrictions on other land uses. In view of the existing and potential impacts on harriers, further information on harrier foraging behaviour is clearly required in order to manage populations effectively. In particular, we need to know how much land harriers require, and the importance of different habitats. These issues need to be addressed through studies of individual range size, habitat preferences and hunting success. From a conservation perspective, the aim should be to construct a predictive model of ranging behaviour which can be used to evaluate the impacts of different management practices. The model should be based on variables that a) are meaningful to harriers, and b) use data that are easily gathered (i.e. from existing data sets and remote sensing sources). This chapter describes a model used to evaluate the relative impacts of a set of woodland grant scheme applications in Perthshire (Madders, 2000a). Since the primary concern was the maintenance of breeding habitat, the model aims to predict ranging behaviour during the period April to August.

23.2 Model rationale

23.2.1 Effects of nest proximity

Hen harriers commence hunting as soon as they leave the nest area (Watson, 1977), and ground close to the nest is therefore used disproportionately more than expected by chance (Madders, 2003). Given uniform habitat, we would expect this to have a dilution by distance effect on hunting activity, with birds radiating out to the furthest parts of their ranges only when they had failed to capture prey closer to their nests. Foraging range is frequently shared with neighbouring harriers, and the use of any particular area is therefore often a function of the distance of several nests. Any model of ranging behaviour therefore needs to take account of nesting distribution.

At its simplest, a model could define the area used by foraging harriers based on fixed radii around nest locations. The aim would be to encompass either the entire area used or 'core' areas where harriers are predicted to spend most time. The main limitation of this approach is that the chosen radius is necessarily arbitrary. Picozzi (1978) estimated that the foraging range of male harriers in north-east Scotland was 14 km². However, there are no reliable estimates from other parts of Britain, while studies of the closely related northern harrier *C. c. hudsonius* in the US have indicated that male range size varies enormously between regions, e.g. 16 km² (Martin, 1987) and 72-366 km² (Thompson-Hanson, 1984). These variations are presumably a result of differences in habitat and food. It is therefore difficult to predict individual range size in a particular area with any accuracy. One way to avoid this problem would be to use a radius that is conservative in its estimate of foraging range size. However, this means that the model fails to take proper account of the overlap between the ranges of neighbouring birds, and this may distort the relative values given to different spatial components. For example, an area 1.1 km from five harrier nests is likely to be used more than a similar area that is 0.9 km from one nest. This will not be apparent from a model based on a radius of 1 km.

A better approach would be to estimate the relative use of each part of the area based on the cumulative effects of the distances of all surrounding harrier nests. This is consistent with the results of Madders (2003) and forms the basis for the model described in this chapter.

23.2.2 *Effects of habitat*

Hen harriers forage preferentially in habitats where their prey are most abundant (Redpath, 1992) and where they capture most prey (Madders, 2000b). Capture rates depend upon the interaction between the abundance of prey and its vulnerability to capture (Preston, 1990), and are largely determined by vegetation cover and structure. Capture rates are likely to be greatest where there is varied vegetation structure (Schipper *et al.*, 1975). In these situations, harriers are better able to gain insight into the vegetation than where the cover is uniformly dense, and better able to ambush prey than where the cover is more open.

In Britain, meadow pipit *Anthus pratensis* and field (short-tailed) vole *Microtus agrestis* generally predominate numerically in hen harrier diet unless there are unusually high densities of alternative prey, for example red grouse or rabbit *Oryctolagus cuniculus* (Watson, 1977; Picozzi, 1978; Redpath, 1991). Recent work has indicated that moorland with a mixture of heather and grass holds a relatively high combined density of meadow pipit and field vole (Vanhinsbergh, 2000; Smith *et al.*, 2001; Tharme *et al.*, 2001) and is therefore likely to represent the near-ideal foraging habitat for hen harriers across much of upland Britain. Heather–grass mosaics are typical of many young first rotation plantation forests and in the early stages of tree growth these are preferred foraging habitats (Madders, 2000b). In situations where there is fine-grained interspersion of heather and grass, harriers may also find it relatively easy to approach prey closely without being detected, thereby increasing the element of surprise and likelihood of successful prey capture. This may be a particular advantage when attempting to capture red grouse chicks, since the adult hens often defend their broods vigorously.

Some habitats yield little suitable prey and are seldom used by harriers even when they are distributed close to nest sites. Thus areas of closed canopy woodland and bracken are avoided, presumably because prey is scarce or difficult to detect and capture (Madders, 1997, 2000b). Disproportionate use is made of linear habitat and terrain features, such as streams, ditches and tracks (Redpath, 1992; Madders, 1997). Again, these features may have greater numbers of prey or present harriers with situations in which prey can be easily surprised.

In view of the above, the model assumes that: (i) hen harriers prefer heather–grass mosaics and pre-thicket plantation forests to other habitats; (ii) heather or grass dominated habitats have a neutral effect on foraging activity; (iii) hen harriers avoid closed canopy woodland and areas with much bracken; and (iv) hen harriers in Britain avoid agricultural habitats.

23.3 Input data

The model uses two sources of information, namely

1. nest data from long-term studies in which large areas of ground are searched annually for harrier nesting attempts, and
2. habitat data interpreted from aerial photographs.

The nest data can span any number of years where coverage has been complete. It is recommended that data from the last five years be used, at least. Such data are normally gathered by Raptor Study Groups. Ideally, a six figure grid reference is required for each nest where eggs are laid. In areas where harrier nests are routinely destroyed, it may be desirable to predict ranging behaviour in the absence of persecution. It may, therefore, be necessary to infer breeding from sightings of displaying birds and aerial food passes. In such cases, the nest grid reference should be the central point of the observed harrier activity. In areas where harriers are not thought to be persecuted, it is recommended that only proven breeding attempts be used. The minimum evidence necessary to qualify as proven breeding would be confirmation that eggs were laid.

Habitat should be mapped from contemporary stereoscopic pairs of aerial photographs of at least 1:24,000 scale. Colour photographs taken in late summer, when both heather and bracken are highly visible, are ideal. Habitat is recorded within an array of grid tiles that represent the study area. The size of tile will determine the resolution of the model. Mapping at more than one scale may be appropriate, enabling the model to be run using low resolution habitat data over a large area, and indeed using high resolution data over a smaller area. For example, where a Woodland Grant Scheme or other land use change is proposed, ranging behaviour by the population of harriers potentially affected could be predicted using habitat mapped within 1 km x 1 km tiles, whilst use of the area where development is envisaged could be predicted using habitat mapped within tiles of 200 m x 200 m or less.

23.4 Running the model

The procedure for running the model can be split into three stages (see Boxes 23.1-23.3). Calculations are easiest to make by entering the data onto a spreadsheet, and using

Box 23.1. Calculating the nest proximity index (NPI).

- The area under consideration is divided into tiles aligned to the National Grid. The size of tile chosen is the same as that used to map habitat (see Box 23.2) and will depend on the scale of detail required.

- The distance from the centre of each tile to each harrier nest recorded during the past five years (or longer if desired) is calculated. Each nest site is counted once for every time it was used. Nests greater than 5 km from the tile under consideration can be excluded on the basis that they will have negligible leverage on the *NPI*.

- The reciprocal of each tile–nest distance is calculated. Nests that fall at the centre of a tile are allocated a nominal distance (e.g. 10 m).

- For each tile, the reciprocals of nest distances are summed to create a nest proximity index (*NPI*). Tiles that represent areas very close to a hen harrier nest, or relatively close to a number of nests, therefore have large *NPI* values.

Box 23.2. Factoring in habitat effects.

- Aerial photographs of the study area are covered with a transparent overlay, grided at the scale chosen for the model. Tiles measuring 200 m x 200 m will provide sufficient detail in most cases.
- Within each tile the percentage cover of various vegetation types is estimated by eye to the nearest 10%. The vegetation types recognised are (1) heather and grass moorland; (2) open canopy woodland (>50% of ground visible); (3) closed canopy woodland (<10% of ground visible); and (4) bracken.
- Moorland is further classified according to the degree of heather-grass interspersion. Thus areas with >75% cover of either heather or grass within patches exceeding 20 m diameter are classified as heather or grass dominated, respectively. The remaining areas are classified as heather–grass mosaic. The percentage cover within each of the three classes is recorded.
- Habitats that are clearly unsuitable for harriers, such as open water and built-up areas, are classified as unused.
- In order to allow linear habitat features to have an effect in the model, the length of tracks, burns and (optionally) habitat boundaries are determined for each tile from 1:10,000 scale maps.

Box 23.3. Constructing the model.

A habitat preference index (*HPI*) is calculated for each tile as follows:

$$HPI = 1 + ([h_p - h_a])/100$$

where h_p is the percentage cover of preferred habitat (i.e. heather–grass mosaic and open canopy woodland) and h_a is the percentage cover of avoided habitat (i.e. closed canopy woodland and bracken *Pteridium aquilinum*.

A linear feature score (*LFS*) is calculated for each tile as follows:

$$LFS = 1 + (d/1000)$$

where *d* is the total length of linear features in metres.

A model combining the variables representing nest proximity, habitat and linear features is then built as follows:

$$Y = NPI \times HPI \times LFS$$

where *Y* is the predicted use by hen harriers during the breeding period. The value for *Y* will reflect the proportion of time harriers are likely to spend in a particular tile relative to other tiles in the study area. *Y* therefore provides information on relative use of habitats.

Finally, scores for *Y* are smoothed by recalculating the values for each tile using the mean value for the tile and eight surrounding tiles. This is justified because harrier activity in each tile is likely to be dependent on the use of neighbouring tiles, regardless of habitat.

Pythagorean theory to determine nest–tile distances. The model output can be displayed in a spreadsheet in which the cells represent grid co-ordinates (Figure 23.1). Setting the cell width to equal the cell height displays the data as a scaled map. It is recommended that the displayed values are inspected and the spreadsheet cells shaded or colour coded so as to help interpretation of the model output.

	2.2	2.5	2.7	2.9	3.2	3.3	3.5	3.7	3.8	4.0	4.3	4.6	4.8	5.1	5.4	5.5	5.6	5.9	6.3	6.8	7.0	7.1	7.0	7.0
2.2	2.3	2.5	2.8	3.0	3.2	3.4	3.5	3.7	3.9	4.1	4.3	4.6	4.8	5.1	5.3	5.5	5.7	6.0	6.5	6.9	7.1	7.2	7.2	7.2
2.4	2.4	2.7	2.9	3.1	3.3	3.5	3.7	3.9	4.1	4.4	4.6	4.9	5.0	5.2	5.4	5.7	6.0	6.4	6.9	7.3	7.4	7.5	7.5	7.5
2.5	2.6	2.9	3.1	3.3	3.5	3.6	3.9	4.2	4.5	4.8	5.1	5.3	5.5	5.7	5.8	6.2	6.5	7.0	7.4	7.6	7.7	7.8	7.9	8.0
2.6	2.8	3.0	3.2	3.5	3.7	3.9	4.2	4.6	5.0	5.4	5.9	6.2	6.4	6.5	6.7	6.9	7.2	7.6	7.9	8.1	8.2	8.3	8.5	8.5
2.8	2.9	3.2	3.4	3.6	3.9	4.2	4.6	5.0	5.5	6.2	7.6	8.2	8.3	7.6	7.5	7.6	7.8	8.1	8.3	8.5	8.6	8.8	9.0	9.1
2.9	3.0	3.3	3.5	3.9	4.2	4.5	4.9	5.3	5.9	6.9	9.3	10.1	10.1	8.6	8.2	8.2	8.4	8.6	8.8	9.0	9.1	9.3	9.5	9.6
3.1	3.2	3.4	3.7	4.1	4.5	4.8	5.2	5.6	6.2	7.3	9.7	**10.6**	**10.6**	9.1	8.7	8.7	8.9	9.1	9.3	9.4	9.6	9.8	10.0	10.1
3.2	3.3	3.6	3.9	4.3	4.7	5.0	5.4	5.8	6.4	7.3	9.0	9.7	9.8	9.1	9.0	9.1	9.3	9.6	9.9	10.0	10.2	10.4	**10.7**	**10.9**
3.3	3.4	3.8	4.2	4.6	4.9	5.3	5.7	6.1	6.6	7.3	8.1	8.6	8.9	9.1	9.3	9.5	9.8	10.2	10.5	**10.8**	**11.1**	**11.4**	**11.5**	**11.7**
3.4	3.6	4.0	4.4	4.9	5.2	5.6	6.0	6.5	7.0	7.5	8.1	8.5	8.9	9.3	9.7	10.0	10.4	**10.9**	**11.5**	**12.0**	**12.3**	**12.6**	**12.6**	**12.6**
3.5	3.7	4.2	4.7	5.1	5.5	5.9	6.4	6.9	7.4	7.9	8.4	8.7	9.3	9.8	10.3	**10.6**	**11.2**	**11.9**	**12.8**	**13.6**	**14.3**	**14.4**	**13.9**	**13.5**
3.7	3.9	4.4	4.9	5.3	5.8	6.3	6.9	7.5	8.1	8.6	9.0	9.2	9.8	10.3	**11.0**	**11.5**	**12.3**	**13.2**	**14.3**	**16.2**	**17.8**	**17.7**	**16.0**	**14.6**
3.9	4.1	4.6	5.1	5.6	6.2	6.8	7.5	8.2	8.9	9.4	9.8	10.0	10.5	**11.0**	**11.9**	**12.8**	**13.9**	**14.8**	**15.8**	**18.3**	**20.8**	**20.7**	**17.9**	**15.5**
4.1	4.3	4.7	5.3	5.9	6.6	7.4	8.3	9.3	**10.1**	**10.8**	**11.1**	**11.1**	**11.4**	**12.0**	**12.9**	**14.6**	**16.5**	**17.3**	**17.3**	**19.0**	**21.3**	**21.1**	**18.3**	**15.9**
4.2	4.4	4.9	5.4	6.2	7.1	8.1	9.5	**10.9**	**12.2**	**13.1**	**13.3**	**13.0**	**12.8**	**13.0**	**13.7**	**15.4**	**17.3**	**18.0**	**17.6**	**18.1**	**19.3**	**19.0**	**17.2**	**15.7**
4.3	4.5	5.0	5.6	6.5	7.5	8.8	**11.2**	**13.8**	**16.0**	**18.7**	**18.5**	**17.5**	**14.7**	**13.9**	**14.1**	**15.4**	**17.0**	**17.6**	**17.2**	**16.7**	**16.9**	**16.7**	**16.1**	**15.6**
4.4	4.6	5.1	5.8	6.7	7.8	9.3	**12.0**	**15.1**	**18.1**	**23.0**	**23.3**	**21.7**	**16.2**	**14.4**	**14.1**	**14.4**	**15.1**	**15.8**	**16.2**	**16.4**	**16.5**	**16.3**	**15.9**	**15.7**
4.4	4.6	5.2	5.9	6.9	8.0	9.5	**12.1**	**15.0**	**17.9**	**23.0**	**23.5**	**21.9**	**16.3**	**14.4**	**13.9**	**14.0**	**14.5**	**15.3**	**16.6**	**17.6**	**17.8**	**17.2**	**16.4**	**16.2**
4.5	4.7	5.3	6.1	7.0	8.3	9.7	**11.4**	**13.1**	**15.0**	**18.3**	**19.2**	**18.3**	**15.0**	**13.8**	**13.6**	**13.8**	**14.3**	**15.3**	**17.3**	**18.9**	**19.3**	**18.3**	**17.1**	**16.9**
4.5	4.8	5.4	6.2	7.2	8.5	**10.6**	**12.1**	**13.0**	**13.1**	**13.9**	**14.2**	**13.9**	**13.3**	**13.0**	**13.2**	**13.6**	**14.2**	**15.2**	**17.2**	**19.1**	**19.6**	**19.0**	**18.2**	**18.2**
4.6	4.9	5.5	6.3	7.2	8.7	**11.4**	**12.8**	**13.1**	**12.1**	**12.1**	**12.2**	**12.1**	**12.0**	**12.2**	**12.8**	**13.3**	**13.9**	**14.7**	**16.2**	**17.7**	**18.7**	**19.5**	**20.5**	**21.3**
4.6	4.9	5.5	6.2	7.0	8.4	**10.9**	**12.1**	**12.4**	**11.3**	**11.0**	**11.1**	**11.1**	**11.2**	**11.6**	**12.2**	**12.8**	**13.4**	**14.1**	**15.1**	**16.2**	**17.4**	**19.5**	**22.3**	**24.1**
4.6	4.8	5.3	6.0	6.7	7.7	9.2	10.1	**10.6**	10.2	10.2	10.3	10.4	**10.7**	**11.2**	**11.7**	**12.3**	**12.8**	**13.5**	**14.3**	**15.3**	**16.6**	**19.0**	**22.1**	**24.1**
4.5	4.8	5.3	5.8	6.5	7.2	7.9	8.6	9.2	9.6	9.8	9.9	10.1	10.5	**10.9**	**11.3**	**12.0**	**12.5**	**13.2**	**14.0**	**15.0**	**16.3**	**18.5**	**21.3**	**23.0**

E A S T I N G S

(Left row labels, reading top to bottom over rows 10–18: N O R T H I N G S)

Figure 23.1. An example of the model output in a Microsoft Excel™ spreadsheet. The cells represent grid squares measuring 200 m x 200 m. Cells containing the smoothed values for *Y* are shaded to indicate predicted relative use by harriers, from high (dark shading) to low (no shading). Refer to Boxes 23.1 to 23.3 to determine the steps involved in the model.

23.5 Discussion

The model described in this chapter can be used to classify any area for which hen harrier nest data are available. It predicts the harrier ranging behaviour using a standard index based on nest distance, without the need to make assumptions about an individual's foraging range size or 'core area'. It can be used to generate a map showing the relative importance of land to harriers at a variety of scales. The model is simple to operate and uses the available data efficiently. The areas most important to harriers can be easily identified. Unlike models based on *a priori* assumptions about foraging range size, habitat is not classified as important simply because it lies within a particular distance of a nest. This is sensible in view of the tendency for harriers in some areas to nest in mature forest plantations that provide little, if any, food.

Because it is a relative index, it is still necessary to make subjective decisions about the amount of land that harriers require. This is an important consideration when using the model to evaluate the likely impacts of land use change. In this respect, the model works best when two or more land use proposals are being compared, perhaps including one scenario where no change is envisaged.

The assumptions used in the model are based on studies carried out in a number of different situations. It is possible that habitat preferences vary regionally, and this may affect the accuracy of any predictions. For example, harriers' preference for hunting pre-thicket forest plantations was determined in a study of foraging behaviour in the west of Scotland, where birds had access to commercial Sitka spruce *Picea sitchensis* plantations (Madders, 2000b). The moorland vegetation surrounding these plantations was generally impoverished due to heavy grazing by sheep, and the young forests therefore had much higher densities of pipits and voles compared to moorland habitats. This difference is likely to be much less pronounced where moors are less affected by grazing. Further information on harriers' use of native pinewoods and broad leafed woodlands is required in order to make informed decisions on future what are now called Scottish Forestry Grant Schemes. Investigation of harriers' use of moorland habitat is also required, in particular the associations between harrier use and the interspersion of heather and grass. In Orkney, for example, Amar (2001) identified rough grassland as an optimal foraging habitat. Finally, reliable estimates of the size and shape of individual foraging ranges are needed in a variety of different landscape types. This is important because it would enable the willingness of harriers to cross areas of unsuitable habitat to be evaluated. A number of refinements are required in order to improve the efficacy of the model. For example, at present the model makes no allowance for differences in the ranging behaviours of male and female harriers, yet in most situations both range size and habitat preferences are likely to differ between sexes. Current work is focussed on practical refinements such as ways to classify habitat using Phase 1 mapping data (*sensu* Mackey *et al.*, 1998) modified to incorporate information on vegetation structure.

The model is a potentially important decision making tool for land managers, conservationists and developers alike. However, it is theoretical and untested. Field trials are now required in order to validate and refine the model. Thus, variables might be added or deleted, and the influence of the existing variables modified. It is recommended that such trials be carried out as part of a study to investigate harrier foraging preferences in relation to native pinewoods.

Acknowledgements

I am grateful to Steve Redpath and an anonymous referee for comments on earlier drafts. The model was developed whilst undertaking work funded by Scottish Natural Heritage.

References

Amar, A. (2001). Determining the cause of the hen harrier decline on Orkney. PhD thesis, University of Aberdeen.

Avery, M.I. & Leslie, R. (1990). *Birds and Forestry*. T. & A.D. Poyser, London.

Etheridge, B., Summers, R.W. & Green, R.E. (1997). The effects of illegal killing and destruction of nests by humans on the population dynamics of the hen harrier *Circus cyaneus* in Scotland. *Journal of Applied Ecology*, **34**, 1081-1105.

Mackey, E.C., Shewry, M.C. & Tudor, G.J. (1998). *Land Cover Change: Scotland from the 1940s to the 1980s.* The Stationery Office, Edinburgh.

Madders, M. (1997). The effects of forestry on hen harriers *Circus cyaneus.* PhD thesis, University of Glasgow.

Madders, M. (2000a). *Capel Hill proposed WGS: assessment of potential impacts on hen harriers.* Unpublished report. Scottish Natural Heritage, Perth.

Madders, M. (2000b). Habitat selection and foraging success of hen harriers *Circus cyaneus* in west Scotland. *Bird Study,* **47**, 32-40.

Madders, M. (2003). Hen harrier *Circus cyaneus* foraging activity in relation to habitat and prey. *Bird Study,* **50**, 55-60.

Martin, J.W. (1987). Behaviour and habitat use of breeding northern harriers in southwestern Idaho. *Journal of Raptor Research,* **21**, 57-66.

Petty, S.J. & Avery, M.I. (1990). *Forest Bird Communities – a Review of the Ecology and Management of Forest Bird Communities in Relation to Silvicultural Practices in the British Uplands.* Forestry Commission, Edinburgh.

Picozzi, N. (1978). Dispersion, breeding and prey of the hen harrier *Circus cyaneus* in Glen Dye, Kincardineshire. *Ibis,* **120**, 498-509.

Preston, C.R. (1990). Distribution of raptor foraging in relation to prey biomass and habitat structure. *Condor,* **92**, 107-112.

Redpath, S.M. (1991). The impact of hen harriers on red grouse breeding success. *Journal of Applied Ecology,* **28**, 659-671.

Redpath, S.M. (1992). Behavioural interactions between hen harriers and their moorland prey. *Ornis Scandinavica,* **23**, 73-80.

Redpath, S.M., Madders, M., Donnelly, E., Anderson, B., Thirgood, S.J., Martin, A. & McCleod, D. (1998). Nest site selection by hen harriers in Scotland. *Bird Study,* **45**, 51-61.

Schipper, W.J.A., Buurma, L.S. & Bossenbroek, P.H. (1975). Comparative study of hunting behaviour of wintering hen harriers *Circus cyaneus* and marsh harriers *Circus aeruginosus. Ardea,* **63**, 1-29.

Smith, A., Redpath, S.M., Thirgood, S.J. & Campbell, S. (2001). Habitat characteristics of managed grouse moors and the abundance of meadow pipits and red grouse. *Journal of Applied Ecology,* **38**, 390-401.

Tharme, A.P., Green, R.E., Baines. D., Bainbridge, I.P. & O'Brien, M. (2001). The effect of management for red grouse shooting on the population density of breeding birds on heather-dominated moorland. *Journal of Applied Ecology,* **38**, 439-458.

Thompson-Hanson, P.A. (1984). Nesting ecology of northern harriers on the Hanford site, south-central Washington. M.Sc. thesis, Washington State University, Pullman.

Vanhinsbergh, D. (2000). The ubiquitous meadow pipit: a useful indicator of habitat change? *BTO News,* **229**, 12-13.

Watson, D. (1977). *The Hen Harrier.* T. & A.D. Poyser, Berkhamsted.

24. The Impact of Food Availability on Gyrfalcon (*Falco rusticolus*) Diet and Timing of Breeding

Ólafur K. Nielsen

Summary

1. A gyrfalcon *Falco rusticolus* population was studied on a 5,300 km^2 area in North-east Iceland during 1981–2000. Eighty-two traditional falcon territories were known on the study area.

2. Birds formed more than 99% of the breeding season diet of this falcon population (n = 31,813 prey items). Adult rock ptarmigan *Lagopus mutus* was the most important prey for all pairs, in all years. Overall, rock ptarmigan comprised 70% by number and 72% by biomass, with synchronous changes in the proportion of ptarmigan in falcon diet and changes in ptarmigan density. The most important alternative prey for the falcons was waterfowl (Anseriformes), auks (Alcidae) and waders (Charadriiformes).

3. There was a clear seasonal pattern in prey utilization; rock ptarmigan was almost the sole food brought to nest sites during April and May (courtship through to early nestling period), and alternative prey increased in numbers in June and July. The sex ratio of rock ptarmigan prey was male-dominated in April and May (63% males) and June (59%), but in July the situation was reversed (30%).

4. The falcons bred during the annual low in number of the rock ptarmigan population. This was made possible by a) increased vulnerability of the ptarmigan associated with movements from winter to breeding habitats, b) territorial behaviour and delayed moult of males later in spring, and c) brood defence of hens in mid-summer. Rock ptarmigan chicks appeared in falcon diet when about one month old.

5. Dispersal of young falcons in late July and early August coincided with the annual peak in numbers of the harvestable part of the rock ptarmigan population.

24.1 Introduction

The gyrfalcon *Falco rusticolus* is a big and a powerful falcon of arctic and boreal alpine areas. It has long, broad, tapered wings and long tail, and is capable of making very fast and prolonged aerobic flights catching prey (Pennycuick *et al.*, 1994). The feet are strong, with thick toes and long sharp claws, and are used to knock down or grab prey, both in the air and on the ground. The gyrfalcon is a solitary hunter and searches for prey over open country, either in fast low flight or by high flying and soaring. It frequently uses perches for observations during hunting forays. It is thinly distributed within its breeding range and feeds mainly on birds, but also to some extent on mammals (Clum & Cade, 1994; Cade *et al.*, 1998). This paper describes the falcon's diet during the breeding season. Special attention is paid to how annual events within the population of its main prey, rock ptarmigan *Lagopus mutus*, affect prey selection and relate to the breeding phenology. The data come from a 20 year study in North-east Iceland (Nielsen, 1999a).

Previous studies have shown that the gyrfalcon has specialized feeding habits, relying mainly on rock ptarmigan and willow ptarmigan *Lagopus lagopus* (Bengtson, 1971; White & Cade, 1971; Mikkola & Sulkava, 1972; Pulliainen, 1975; Langvatn & Moksnes, 1979; Woodin, 1980; Bente, 1981; Lindberg, 1983; Poole & Boag, 1988; Huhtala *et al.*, 1996). Other important prey groups include waterfowl (Anseriformes), auks (Alcidae), waders (Charadriiformes), hares (Lagomorpha), and microtine rodents (Microtinae). The importance of alternative prey depends on the abundance of grouse (Nielsen, 1999a). Among bird-eating raptors in temperate regions the general rule is for juvenile birds to dominate the diet during the brood rearing period (Newton, 1979; for *Accipiters* see Opdam *et al.*, 1977; Opdam, 1978; Newton & Marquiss, 1982; Toyne, 1998). Studies have shown that the gyrfalcon is unusual in this respect by going through the breeding cycle by preying mainly on the adult segment of the ptarmigan (grouse) population during its annual low point in number (Hagen, 1952; Cade, 1960; this study). In this chapter I show that this pattern holds true during all phases of the ptarmigan cycle, and in all habitats, with predation directed mainly at ptarmigan males during the early part of the season and females later on.

24.2 Study area
The gyrfalcon study area, total 5,327 km², was in North-east Iceland, and centred on Lake Mývatn (65° 38'N, 17° 00'W). The countryside is wide and open, and dominated by heath and meadow vegetation, and sparsely or unvegetated land. Eighty-two traditional gyrfalcon territories were known, and 39–63 were occupied each year during 1981–2000. The falcons hunted in all available types of habitat. A total of 61 bird species bred in the area, and all, except for some of the larger species, were potential prey for the falcons. Rock ptarmigan was common and widespread. For more details see Nielsen (1999a).

24.3 Methods
24.3.1 Gyrfalcon food habits
Gyrfalcons carry prey back to the nesting cliff during the breeding season. This starts 2–3 weeks prior to egg laying, and continues well into the post-fledging period. The hunting bird plucks, beheads, and disembowls medium and large prey at the kill site, but small prey were carried to the nesting area more or less intact. During courtship, egg laying and incubation, prey remnants were gathered at plucking posts in the immediate area of the nesting cliff. During the nestling period most of prey remains were collected from the nest itself or on the ground beneath. After fledging, prey remains were again found on plucking posts, but as the young got older and strayed farther afield, these sites became increasingly difficult to find. Remains of medium-size to large prey consisted mostly of skeletal parts (the pectoral and pelvic girdles and the sternum). Frequently bones were disarticulated, and the keel and the distal part of the sternum and the lateral parts of the pelvis were bitten off. Remains of small prey consisted mostly of disarticulated legs and wings, but also some heads and loose feathers.

All of my data come from collections made at nest sites that successfully fledged young and where I was able to gain access to collect remains. Two or three collecting trips were made to each nest during the season. The last visit was always made after the young had fledged. During each visit I removed all remains, including all bones and pellets, and also some feathers. Prey were identified in the field, and the remains discarded. For the analysis, remains were arranged according to species, age groups, and type. Young of the year were separated from adults on down, feather pattern or bone structure. The number of individuals in each group was estimated by counting the most frequent item representing one individual. For medium-size to large birds this was most often the sternum or wing, and for small birds and young of the year one of the legs. Pellets were only collected to look for legs and skeletal remains of small birds. Problematic specimens were brought back to the laboratory and identified with the help of a reference collection. Problems and possible pitfalls in using prey remains to study gyrfalcon diet have been discussed by Hagen (1952), Langvatn (1977), Poole & Boag (1988), Huhtala *et al.* (1996), and Nielsen (1999a).

The gyrfalcon territories were divided into three groups according to the distance of nest sites from the coast or a primary waterfowl area, e.g. Lake Mývatn, Laxá River, Lake Vestmannsvatn, Lake Víkingavatn, and some other sites. These groups were termed 'heath falcons', 'lakeland falcons', and 'coastal falcons'. Heath falcons were located on average 19.2 km from primary waterfowl areas (range 7.5–33.3 km), and 29.5 km from the coast (9.3–62.0 km). Lakeland falcons only had to travel on average 3.4 km to reach primary waterfowl areas (range 0.1-9.0 km), but 33.9 km (5.5–63.0 km) to the coast. Coastal falcons were on average 3.6 km from the coast (range 0.8–7.5 km), and were situated far from inland waterfowl areas, but had ready access to both adult ducks and eider colonies and brood rearing areas (see Appendix 24.1 for scientific names of prey species).

In 1982–1985, 1987, 1988, 1990, and 1991, samples of adult rock ptarmigan in the gyrfalcon's catch were sexed. Sampling was done for three periods during the breeding season: April–May, June, and July. Sexing was done by measuring humeri, either left or right, from each sample. Measurements were done with callipers, to the nearest 0.05 mm.

In 1982–1985 only humeri length was measured (from caput humeri to condylus ventralis; terms according to Baumel, 1979). The mean length of male humeri was 59.68 mm (range 57.60–62.30 mm, n = 154, s = 0.9902) and the mean length of female humeri was 57.61 mm (range 54.60–59.90 mm, n = 193, s = 0.9846). There was considerable overlap between the sexes. To sex rock ptarmigan prey, I started by using 57.40 mm and 59.90 mm as dividing values for females and males respectively and calculating the normal cumulative distribution using the mean sex standard deviation. The mean values for humeri ≤57.40 mm was 41.4% females and 1.0% males, and for humeri ≥59.90 mm it was 41.2% males and 1.0% females. These values were used to sex birds from an independent sample of 149 humeri of known sex. Eighty (54%) could be identified to sex, of those two birds were in the wrong category (3%). The sex ratio (males/females) in the original data was 0.3925 and in sample 0.3559, the difference was not significant (χ^2 = 0.151, df = 1, P = 0.65). Using these values on the total number of humeri measured (n = 2,556) allowed me to sex 46% compared with 42% of the expected proportion. In 1987 and later two measurements were taken from each humerus, total length as before, and breadth at the distal end. A discriminate function was derived to separate the sexes. The function is:

$$(L \times -0.7529) + (B \times -1.9121) + 64.6407 > 0 = \text{male}; < 0 = \text{female}$$

where *L* is length of humerus in mm, and *B* is breadth at the distal end in mm (from epicondylus ventralis to epicondylus dorsalis). This function was tested on an independent sample of 147 sexed humeri, of which 86% were correctly categorised. Because of the large number of wrongly categorised humeri, inclusion in the sample was set at 70% for the computed probability level classification. When applied to the sexed sample, 72% were included of which 5% were wrongly categorised. The sex ratio for this derived sample was 0.3718, compared with 0.3925 in the original sample (χ^2 = 0.063, *df* = 1, P = 0.80). Nor was the difference significant in sex ratio derived using the same independent sample and humerus length versus the discriminate function (χ^2 = 0.017, *df* = 1, P = 0.89).

24.3.2 *Gyrfalcon breeding phenology*

The date on which the first egg was laid in 1981–1998 was back-calculated using the estimated age of young and assuming the following: (1) 60 hours between eggs being laid; (2) incubation period of 35 days, starting with the penultimate egg; (3) synchronous hatching; (4) clutch size of three if three or fewer young were in the nest when first observed; and (5) nestling period of 47 days (Clum & Cade, 1994; Cade *et al.*, 1998). Some broods were visited during hatching. The age of other broods, was estimated by comparing young with photographs of chicks of a known age or by measuring the length of the central tail feather (Ó.K. Nielsen, unpublished data), or the length of the seventh primary (cf. Poole, 1989). The formula for the age of young was:

$$D = 0.1894 \times T + 13.624$$

where *D* is the age of the young in days, *T* is the length of central tail feather in mm, measured with a ruler from where the feather emerges from the papilla to the tip of the feather. The formula was calculated using measurements from young of known age (*n* = 38), *r*² for the regression was 0.952.

24.3.3 *Rock ptarmigan ecology*

The breeding phenology for rock ptarmigan was estimated using data from Hrísey (66° 00'N, 18°22'W) 32 km west of the falcon study area. These data were collected by the late Finnur Gudmundsson in the 1960s and 1970s. Date on when the first egg was laid was back-calculated using information from observed date of hatch or from nests found during the laying period. The following variables were assumed: (1) 24 hours between eggs being laid; (2) incubation period of 21 day starting with the penultimate egg; and (3) synchronous hatching (Holder & Montgomerie, 1993).

Observations on the start of territorial behaviour among rock ptarmigan males in the falcon study area were made in spring 1984, 1985, 1987, 1988, 1990 and 1991 (cf. Nielsen, 1993). Territorial males were spaced, aggressive, had prominent combs and performed visual and vocal displays. Observations on the cessation of territorial behaviour were made using radio tagged males in 1995 (cf. below). The males were located once each week from late May until mid August.

A total of 22 rock ptarmigan males were trapped in late May and early June 1995 to study mortality. The birds were tagged with TW3 necklace type transmitters from

BIOTRACK, and located once each week until mid-August. A survival curve was calculated using the staggered entry design (Pollock *et al.*, 1989).

Territorial rock ptarmigan males were censused on six plots within the falcon study area in late May each year 1981–2000 (Nielsen, 1996; 1999b). The data used in this paper, as an annual index of rock ptarmigan numbers, are the total number of males on all plots.

24.4 Results

Prey remains were collected at 359 nest sites during 1981–2000. A minimum of 31,813 individuals of at least 56 species were identified as prey from these collections, which included 53 bird species, two species of mammal, and one species of fish.

24.4.1 Composition of gyrfalcon diet

Birds formed more than 99% of the breeding season diet (see Appendix 24.1 which also gives Latin names of prey species). Seventy-nine per cent of the known breeding bird species within the study area were registered in the prey collections. All except five of the quarry species belonged to the local breeding community. These five included four vagrants, coot, woodcock, wood pigeon and fieldfare, and 'carrier' pigeon. Most birds taken were adults; 88% by number and 93% by biomass. Juveniles were preyed on mainly during July (Figure 24.1). Only one case of nest robbing was established when a 'pipping' rock ptarmigan egg was found in a gyrfalcon nest.

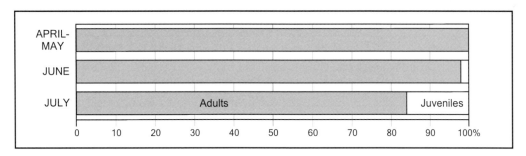

Figure 24.1. Importance (per cent frequency of all prey) of adults and juveniles in gyrfalcon breeding season diet, North-east Iceland 1987. Identified prey for April-May was 305 individuals, 600 individuals for June, and 1,405 individuals for July.

Adult rock ptarmigan was the single most important prey in all nests and in all years. Rock ptarmigan comprised 70% by frequency and 72% by biomass of the total prey sample. Three other species comprised more than 2% by frequency: wigeon (5.4%), puffin (4.1%), and whimbrel (3.7%). The mean geometric weight of prey was 471 g, and reflected the dominance of rock ptarmigan. The smallest prey were juvenile passerines that weighed less than 10 g and the largest was greylag goose at c. 3,400 g. The largest prey taken regularly was adult pink-footed goose (c. 2,500 g). The falcons were able to carry prey of this size, either whole or in pieces, as shown by complete disarticulated skeletons in nests. A few gyrfalcons were also recorded as prey, all were nestlings which had died.

Rock ptarmigan chicks were not an important prey for falcons in summer. Chicks only appeared in the diet in any numbers when they were about one month old. Smaller chicks were rarely taken.

Cross-correlation of rock ptarmigan numbers lagged by percent frequency of adult ptarmigan in falcon diet (arc-sine transformed and detrended) gave significant positive coefficients (P <0.05) for time-lags of 0 and 1 year, and a significant negative coefficient for a time lag of –6 years. The extent to which rock ptarmigan was the dominant prey item varied directly in relation to its population size. Other quarry species were alternative prey

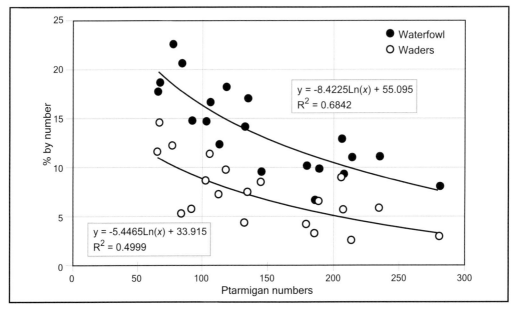

Figure 24.2. Importance of waterfowl and waders in gyrfalcon diet in relation to rock ptarmigan numbers (males on census plots), North-east Iceland 1981–2000.

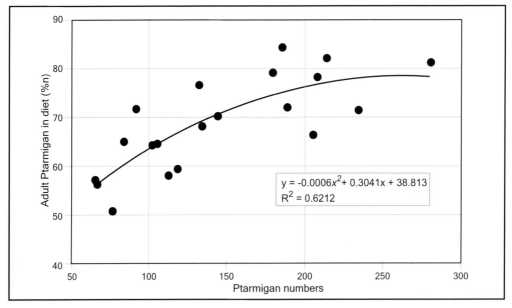

Figure 24.3. Functional response of gyrfalcons in relation to rock ptarmigan abundance (males on census plots), North-east Iceland 1981–2000.

for rock ptarmigan, as these species increased in gyrfalcon diet as ptarmigan numbers fell (cf. Nielsen, 1999a). The most important alternative prey groups were waterfowl (14% by number, 20% by biomass), and waders (7%, 3%; Figure 24.2). During years when rock ptarmigan numbers were high the importance of the grouse in the falcon's diet reached a plateau at about 80% by frequency (Figure 24.3).

24.4.2 Local changes in gyrfalcon diet

There were local differences in diet composition (Appendix 24.1). Falcons living inland and away from the main waterfowl areas ('heath falcons') relied more on rock ptarmigan than either 'lakeland falcons' ($G = 988$, $df = 1$, P <0.001) or 'coastal falcons' ($G = 75$, $df = 1$, P <0.001). The difference was most pronounced between heath and lakeland falcons (Figure 24.4). Coastal falcons relied more on rock ptarmigan than did lakeland falcons ($G = 302$, $df = 1$, P <0.001). The main alternative prey groups were waterfowl for lakeland falcons, and auks for coastal falcons. Heath falcons used mainly waterfowl as alternative prey.

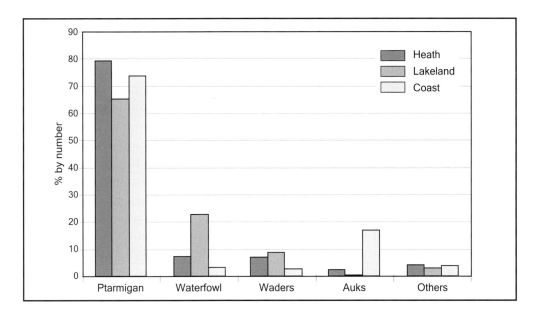

Figure 24.4. Local differences in prey selection by gyrfalcon in North-east Iceland 1981–2000.

24.4.3 Seasonal changes in gyrfalcon diet

There was a seasonal pattern of prey utilisation, which was repeated on all territories and in all years. In April and May, during courtship through to hatching, rock ptarmigan was almost the only prey brought to nests (Figure 24.5). In June during the early nestling period, alternative prey started to appear, and this became most pronounced in July, during the late nestling and the post-fledging periods. The almost total dependence on rock ptarmigan during the first phase of the breeding cycle was not due to lack of other alternative prey, at least not at lakeland and coastal sites, as all these sites had an ample selection of alternative prey from mid-April.

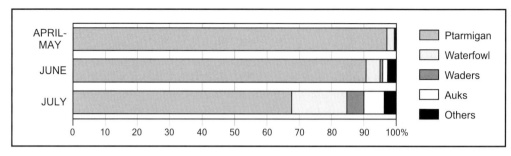

Figure 24.5. Seasonal changes in composition of the main prey groups in gyrfalcon diet in North-east Iceland 1987. The difference in composition between April-May and June was significant (G = 14.21, df = 1, P = <0.005) and also between June and July (G = 153, df = 5, P <0.001). Identified prey was 305 individuals for April-May, 600 individuals for June, and 1,405 individuals for July.

24.4.4 Sex ratio of rock ptarmigan depredated by gyrfalcons

The sex composition of adult rock ptarmigan caught by gyrfalcons showed seasonal changes that were repeated each year. Sex ratios were mainly male-dominated in April-May, but the importance of males declined in June, and again in July (Table 24.1). Combining data from all years, the mean proportion of males in rock ptarmigan diet in April-May was 63% (±4.5%; 95% confidence limits), in June 59% (±3.5%), and in July 30% (±3.0%). Observations on the survival of radio tagged rock ptarmigan males during spring and summer 1995 supported this general picture (Figure 24.6). Mortality was heavy until mid-June and then non-existent.

Table 24.1. Percent rock ptarmigan males in gyrfalcon catch, North-east Iceland. The breeding season is divided into three periods, April-May, June, and July.

Year	April-May			June			July		
	% males	95% confidence limits	n	% males	95% confidence limits	n	% males	95% confidence limits	n
1982	72	±11	61	66	±8	148	42	±12	71
1983	80	±17	25	59	±12	71	45	±13	56
1984	47	±14	53	49	±8	136	23	±9	81
1985	73	±9	99	70	±7	181	37	±7	179
1987	57	±10	103	54	±10	89	25	±5	310
1988	65	±11	75	53	±11	80	25	±6	193
1990	35	±21	23	46	±16	41	...	...	...
1991	86	±32	7	...	...	...	...	...	...
Total	63	±4	446	59	±4	746	30	±3	890

Note: comparing sex ratio (G-test) between months gave no significant differences (P >0.05) for April-May compared with June (all years and combined data); comparing June with July gave significant differences (P <0.001) for combined data and all years except for 1983 (P >0.05); comparing April-May with July gave significant differences for all years (1983 and 1984 P <0.01, other years and combined data P <0.001).

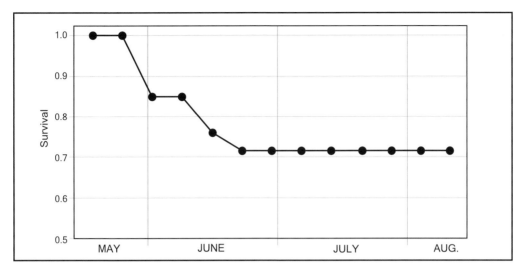

Figure 24.6. The Kaplan-Meier survival function for 22 rock ptarmigan males radio-tagged in North-east Iceland, spring and summer 1995.

All mortality of radio tagged birds ($n = 6$) was due to gyrfalcon predation. Two of those males were eaten at the kill site; the others were carried away. The leg rings of two males were subsequently found in a gyrfalcon nest 5 and 6 km from the kill sites.

24.4.5 Breeding in gyrfalcon in relation to events in the rock ptarmigan population

Gyrfalcons start their preparations for breeding early in the season, the first pairs before mid-March followed by the majority during the second half of March and the first half of April (Figure 24.7). Winter still reigns at this time of year, and rock ptarmigan are in the process of moving from winter habitat to breeding areas. Important mid-and late winter habitats for rock ptarmigan include birch *Betula pubescens* woods and scrub, and lava fields.

Most falcon pairs (c. 66%) had laid eggs before rock ptarmigan males became territorial. The onset of territorial behaviour was highly synchronous amongst males; the mean date was 23 April (range 20–28 April, $n = 6$, $s = 2.81$). Some movement of birds onto the heaths was noted in the first half of April in 1985, but not in 1984. The males advertised and defended territories vigorously throughout May and into June. Territorial activities waned in the first part of June. We used male rock ptarmigan decoys to trap territorial males (c. 450 since 1994) on the study area for banding. The latest date on which we have caught males this way was on 9 June. Radio telemetry in 1995 showed that although males had stopped advertising by mid-June, they remained on their territories throughout June and well into July, even though they were rarely seen. At the end of the territorial period, c. 10 June, more than 90% of falcons had young in the nest (Figure 24.7). Males predominated in falcon diet from start of courtship through to the end of June (Table 24.1).

Rock ptarmigan females started egg laying on 18 May (mean 29 May; Figure 24.7). The first females were incubating full clutches on 28 May and 90% by 13 June. The first chicks hatched on 17 June; 75% of hens hatched their eggs by 1 July, and 90% by 4 July. Females dominate in falcon diet in July (Table 24.1). The chicks were about one month old when they started appearing in the falcon's diet. Most chicks had reached this age by the last week

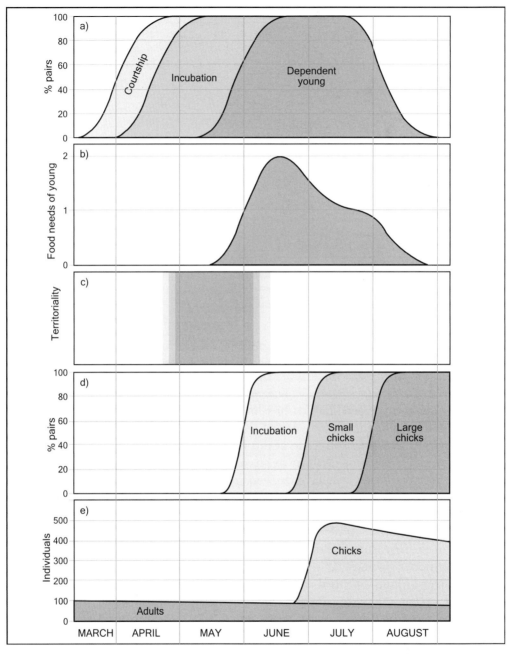

Figure 24.7. Breeding of gyrfalcon in relation to some population events in the annual cycle of the rock ptarmigan. (a) Proportion of breeding falcons courting, laying and incubating and caring for young through spring and summer. (b) Food needs of dependent young in a gyrfalcon population in North-east Iceland shown as per cent per day of total prey biomass consumed during breeding season. Data on timing of hatch and brood size are from this study; young mortality per day 0.00338, food needs of chicks of different age are according to Poole & Boag (1988). (c) The territorial phase of the rock ptarmigan population, intensity of territorial activities is shown with different shades of grey. (d) Proportion of breeding rock ptarmigan laying and incubating, caring for small young, and caring for large young (>30 days old). (e) Population size of rock ptarmigan assuming 100 adults alive 11 March (sex ratio 50/50), adult mortality per day 0.00177, brood size at hatch 10.1, chick mortality per day 0.0047.

of July and the first week of August. An important event in the annual cycle of gyrfalcons is the dispersal of young. The first falcons dispersed by mid-July and 70% were independent by 8 August, coinciding with the period when rock ptarmigan chicks become huntable (Figure 24.8).

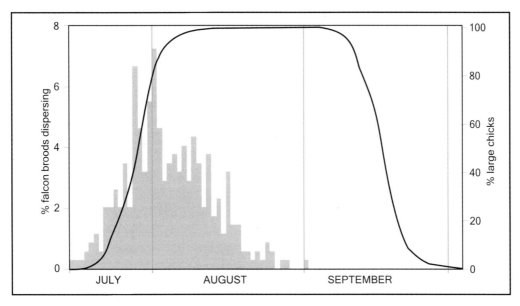

Figure 24.8. Dispersal of gyrfalcon broods (grey columns) compared with the period when rock ptarmigan chicks are large (30–80 days of age).

24.5 Discussion

The gyrfalcon population in North-east Iceland had specialized feeding habits. Rock ptarmigan were the main food during spring and summer in all years. Changes in prey selection occurred over the course of each breeding season. Rock ptarmigan were most important in the first half of the season, and somewhat less so at the end when more alternative prey were taken. The falcons killed mainly adult rock ptarmigan, predominantly males in April through to June, and females in July. Rock ptarmigan chicks became acceptable as prey when about four weeks old. The gyrfalcon's affinity to *Lagopus* grouse seems to be deeply rooted in its habits, and alternative prey species are taken in accordance with grouse numbers (this study; Nielsen, 1999a). This also applies to falcons that have an ample supply of alternative prey throughout the breeding cycle (Nielsen, 1986, 1999a).

24.5.1 Comparison with food habits of gyrfalcons in other areas
It can be difficult to compare results of other studies on gyrfalcon diet because of differences in methodology. The data must relate to the same phase of the nesting cycle, preferably the whole cycle, to be comparable. Collections of prey remnants must be made at all sites where remains gather, including the nest itself, because of seasonal changes in prey selection and in the locations where remains accumulate (perches versus nest site).

Dement'ev & Gladkov (1966) divided gyrfalcons into two distinct groups on trophic habits; namely coastal nesting falcons and inland nesting falcons. Coastal nesting falcons fed largely on aquatic birds and the interior falcons predominantly on grouse. This distinction was not supported by my data, which showed that all coastal nesting falcons were predominantly rock ptarmigan hunters and used aquatic birds only as alternative prey during the latter part of the breeding season. These findings concur with other studies. Most gyrfalcon populations base their reproduction on grouse (Figure 24.9). Depending

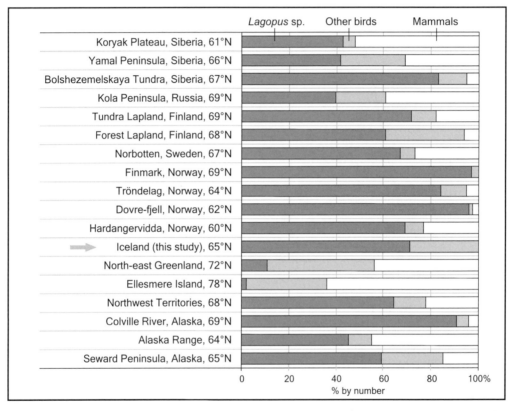

Figure 24.9. Food habits of gyrfalcons during the breeding season in different geographic areas. Data for Koryak Plateau are from Kishchinskiy (1980); Yamal Peninsula from Kalyakin & Vinogradov (1981); Bolshezemelskaya Tundra from Voronin (1987); Kola Peninsula from Kishchinskiy (1957); tundra Lapland from Mikkola & Sulkava (1972); forest Lapland from Huhtala *et al.* (1996); Norbotten from Lindberg (1983); Finmark from Haftorn (1971); Tröndelag from Langvatn & Moksnes (1979); Dovre-fjell from Hagen (1953); Hardangervidda from Hansen (1999); North-east Greenland from Fletcher and Webby (1973), Summers and Green (1974), and Cabot *et al.* (1988); Ellesmere Island from Muir and Bird (1984); Northwest Territories from Poole and Boag (1988); Colville River from White and Cade (1971); Alaska Range from Bente (1981); and Seward Peninsula from Roseneau (1972).

on location important alternative prey groups were, arctic ground squirrel *Spermophilus parryii*, waterfowl, waders, auks, microtine rodents, and hares. Seasonal changes in prey selection have followed the same general pattern as described in this chapter, namely near complete dominance of grouse in spring, alternative prey species taken during the latter part of the breeding cycle and with most avian prey being adults (Kishchinskiy, 1957; Poole &

Boag, 1988; Huhtala *et al.*, 1996; Hansen, 1999). To my knowledge, the only gyrfalcon population that does not have a grouse-based diet was from the High Arctic on Ellesmere Island (latitude 78°N). Those falcons fed mainly on arctic hare *Lepus arcticus*, collared lemming *Dicrostonyx groenlandicus* and waders (Muir & Bird, 1984). Data for gyrfalcons in North-east Greenland indicate that this might also be the case there, with arctic hare, collared lemming and snow bunting as the main prey species (Fletcher & Webby, 1973; Summers & Green, 1974; Cabot *et al.*, 1988).

24.5.2 *Food and breeding*

The gyrfalcon is able to breed by feeding on the adult sector of grouse populations during its annual trough in numbers (Hagen, 1952; Cade, 1960; Figure 24.7). Further, in Iceland the gyrfalcon is able to breed successfully during all phases of the 10 year population cycle of the rock ptarmigan, using this species as its main prey (Nielsen, 1999a). How the gyrfalcon is able to do this is not so much a question of grouse numbers as prey vulnerability.

Studies of gyrfalcon diet during the non-breeding season in North-east Iceland have shown that 'heath falcons' did not change their take of rock ptarmigan compared with the breeding season. 'Lakeland falcons' and 'coastal falcons' on the other hand ate less rock ptarmigan during the non-breeding season, the two groups increased respectively their take of waterfowl, wood mouse and snow bunting, and waterfowl and auks. The importance of rock ptarmigan increased again in March and April (Nielsen & Cade, 1990). This change in diet also marked the beginning of the falcons' courtship period. Increased predation on rock ptarmigan at this time could be due either to changes in their vulnerability associated with local movements from winter (shrublands) to breeding habitats (heaths) or by an influx of grouse wintering in other parts of Iceland. Grouse movements have been associated with the start of courtship in gyrfalcon populations in the Canadian Arctic (Poole & Boag, 1988) and Siberia (Voronin, 1987). The vulnerability of the grouse in spring culminates when males establish their territories, but it is of interest to note that by this time most gyrfalcons in Iceland have already laid (Figure 24.7). Behaviour and plumage determine differences in the vulnerability of the sexes, making the males more susceptible to predation than females at this season. Sex ratios of rock ptarmigan in Iceland are equal in spring (Gardarsson, 1988).

Faced with a diminishing number of rock ptarmigan as the season progresses, and a sharp decrease in male vulnerability as they stop defending territories and females commence incubation, the falcons turn to alternative prey. The importance of alternative prey is determined by the spring density of rock ptarmigan (Nielsen, 1999a). In mid-summer the falcons switch from hunting males to females. Again, it is behaviour of rock ptarmigan that determines their vulnerability. Most females have broods, while males have moulted to a brown summer plumage and are secretive.

These changes in movements, habitat selection and behaviour of rock ptarmigan from late winter to mid-summer are predictable and affect their vulnerability in such a way that gyrfalcons are able to use them as the predominat prey for breeding in all years.

The breeding cycle of the gyrfalcon is long and, from the start of courtship to the dispersal of young, takes around 140 days to complete. This is almost five months, and is a longer period than the growing season of plants at these latitudes. How do they fit such a long breeding cycle into the calendar; what phase of the breeding cycle is critical and *sensu* Lack (1954) are they able to match this critical phase with the peak of prey abundance?

I propose that the post-dispersal period of the young falcons is critical for the success of the breeding season, hence the weeks succeeding dispersal are when the fate of the cohort is probably determined. The falcons should strive to time their breeding in such a way as to match the post-dispersal period of juveniles with peak numbers of vulnerable young grouse. In Iceland, the peak dispersal of young falcons occurs during last week of July. Therefore, the falcons must prepare for breeding as soon as possible in late winter to be able to achieve this.

The length of the window when dispersing falcons have access to abundant young rock ptarmigan is about 50 days. It begins when rock ptarmigan chicks are large enough to be hunted in any numbers (c. 30 days old) and ends when chicks have completed their wing moult and gained full flight capabilities (c. 80 days old) by mid-September (Figure 24.8). The early part of this period should be the optimum time for the young gyrfalcons to become independent. At this time the grouse population is at its annual peak, naive young form more than 80% of the population and their flight capabilities are impaired. Thus, young falcons dispersing in early August have some weeks to master their hunting skills before rock ptarmigan become harder to catch.

Acknowledgements

These studies were funded in 1981-1993 by the National Geographic Society, the Peregrine Fund Inc., the Icelandic Science Fund, the Andrew Mellon Foundation, the Alexander Bergstrom Memorial Research Fund, and the Arctic Institute of North America. For 1986 and 1994-2000 this research was funded by the Icelandic Institute of Natural History. Many people have provided field assistance through the years including J.Ó. Hilmarsson, G. Thráinsson, I. Petersen, Ó. Einarsson, H. Bárdarson, E. Thorleifsson, Ó.H. Nielsen and A. Snæthórsson. G. Pétursson assisted with data analysis and L. Ásbjörnsdóttir produced the figures. T.J. Cade, S. Petty and an anonymous referee greatly improved the chapter with their comments.

References

Baumel, J.J. (Ed.). (1979). *Nomina anatomica avium.* Academic Press, London.

Bengtson, S.-A. (1971). Hunting methods and choice of prey of Gyrfalcons *Falco rusticolus* at Myvatn in Northeast Iceland. *Ibis,* **113**, 468–476.

Bente, P.J. (1981). *Nesting behavior and hunting activity of the Gyrfalcon,* Falco rusticolus*, in southcentral Alaska.* M.Sc. thesis. University of Alaska, Fairbanks, Alaska.

Cabot, D., Goodwillie, R. & Viney, M. (1988). *Irish Expedition to North-East Greenland 1987: Expedition Report.* Barnacle Books, Dublin.

Cade, T.J. (1960). Ecology of the peregrine and gyrfalcon populations in Alaska. *University of California Publications in Zoölogy,* **63**, 151–290.

Cade, T.J., Koskimies, P. & Nielsen, Ó.K. (1998). *Falco rusticolus* Gyrfalcon. *BWP Update,* **2**, 1–25.

Clum, N.J. & Cade, T.J. (1994). Gyrfalcon (*Falco rusticolus*). In *The Birds of North America, No. 114,* ed. by A. Poole & F. Gill. The Academy of Natural Sciences, Philadelphia, The American Ornithologists' Union, Washington, D.C.

Dement'ev, G.P. & Gladkov, N.A. (1966). *Birds of the Soviet Union, Volume 1.* Israel Program for Scientific Translations, Jerusalem.

Fletcher, D.J. & Webby, K. (1973). Observation on gyrfalcons *Falco rusticolus* in northeast Greenland. *Dansk Ornithologisk Forenings Tidsskrift,* **71**, 29–35.

Gardarsson, A. (1988). Cyclic population changes and some related events in rock ptarmigan in Iceland. In *Adaptive Strategies and Population Ecology of Northern Grouse*, ed. by A.T. Bergerud & M.W. Gratson. University of Minnesota Press, Minneapolis. pp. 300–329.

Haftorn, S. (1971). *Norges fugler.* Universitetsforlaget, Oslo.

Hagen, Y. (1952). The Gyr-Falcon (*Falco r. rusticolus* L.) in Dovre, Norway. Some breeding records and food studies. *Skrifter utgitt av Det Norske Videnskabs-Akademi i Oslo, I. Matematisk-naturvidenskapelig klasse 1952 No.* **4**, 1–37.

Hansen, R.E. (1999). Analysis of prey remains from a gyrfalcon *Falco rusticolus* nest site at Hardangervidda. *Vandrefalken*, **4**, 58–63 (in Norwegian).

Holder, K. & Montgomerie, R. (1993). Rock Ptarmigan *(Lagopus mutus).* In *The Birds of North America, No. 51*, ed. by A. Poole & F. Gill. The Academy of Natural Sciences, Philadelphia, The American Ornithologists' Union, Washington, D.C.

Huhtala, K., Pulliainen, E., Jussila, P. & Tunkkari, P.S. (1996). Food niche of the gyrfalcon *Falco rusticolus* nesting in the far north of Finland as compared with other choices of the species. *Ornis Fennica*, **73**, 78–87.

Kalyakin, V.N. & Vinogradov, V.G. (1981). On the Gyrfalcon breeding in the south of the Yamal Peninsula. *Bulletin of the Moscow Naturalist's Society, Department of Biology*, **86**, 42–50 (in Russian with English summary).

Kishchinskiy, A.A. (1957). On the biology of the gyrfalcon (*Falco gyrfalco gyrfalco* L.) on the Kola Peninsula. *Ornithology*, **1**, 61–75 (in Russian).

Kishchinskiy, A.A. (1980). *Birds of the Koryak Plateau.* Nauka, Moscow (in Russian).

Lack, D. (1954). *The Natural Regulation of Animal Numbers.* Clarendon Press, Oxford.

Langvatn, R. (1977). Characteristics and relative occurrence of remnants of prey found at nesting places of gyrfalcon *Falco rusticolus. Ornis Scandinavica*, **8**, 113–125.

Langvatn, R. & Moksnes, A. (1979). On the breeding ecology of the gyrfalcon *Falco rusticolus* in central Norway 1968–1974. *Fauna norvegica Ser. C, Cinclus*, **2**, 27–39.

Lindberg, P. (1983). *Relations between the diet of Fennoscandian Peregrines* Falco peregrinus *and organochlorines and mercury in their eggs and feathers, with comparison to the Gyrfalcon* Falco rusticolus. Ph.D. thesis, University of Göteborg, Sweden.

Mikkola, H. & Sulkava, S. (1972). The diet of the gyrfalcon. *Suomen Luonto*, **5**, 183–185 (in Finnish).

Muir, D. & Bird, D. (1984). Food of gyrfalcons at a nest on Ellesmere Island. *Wilson Bulletin*, **96**, 464–467.

Newton, I. (1979). *Population Ecology of Raptors.* T. & A.D. Poyser, Berkhamsted.

Newton, I. & Marquiss, M. (1982). Food, predation and breeding season in sparrowhawks (*Accipiter nisus*). *Journal of Zoology, London*, **197**, 221–240.

Nielsen, Ó.K. (1986). *Population ecology of the gyrfalcon in Iceland with comparative notes on the merlin and the raven.* Ph.D. thesis, Cornell University, New York.

Nielsen, Ó.K. (1993). Initiation of territoriality among Icelandic rock ptarmigan in spring. *Náttúrufrædingurinn*, **63**, 29–37 (in Icelandic with English summary).

Nielsen, Ó.K. (1996). Rock ptarmigan censuses in northeast Iceland. *Náttúrufrædingurinn*, **65**, 137–151 (in Icelandic with English summary).

Nielsen, Ó.K. (1999a). Gyrfalcon predation on ptarmigan: numerical and functional responses. *Journal of Animal Ecology*, **68**, 1034–1050.

Nielsen, Ó.K. (1999b). Monitoring of the ptarmigan population in Iceland. *Fjölrit Náttúrufrædstofnunar*, **39** (in Icelandic with English summary).

Nielsen, Ó.K. & Cade, T.J. (1990). Seasonal changes in food habits of gyrfalcons in NE-Iceland. *Ornis Scandinavica*, **21**, 202–211.

Opdam, P. (1978). Feeding ecology of a sparrowhawk population (*Accipiter nisus*). *Ardea*, **66**, 137–155.

Opdam, P., Thissen, J., Verschuren, P. & Müskens, G. (1977). Feeding ecology of a population of goshawk *Accipiter gentilis*. *Journal für Ornithologie*, **118**, 35–51.

Pennycuick, C.J., Fuller, M.R., Oar, J.J. & Kirkpatrick, S.J. (1994). Falcon versus grouse: flight adaptations of a predator and its prey. *Journal of Avian Biology*, **25**, 39–49.

Pollock, K.H., Winterstrein S.R., Bunck, C.M. & Curtis, P.D. (1989). Survival analysis in telemetry studies: the staggered entry design. *Journal of Wildlife Management*, **53**, 7–15.

Poole, K.G. (1989). Determining age and sex of nestling Gyrfalcons. *Journal of Raptor Research*, **23**, 45–47.

Poole, K.G. & Boag, D.A. (1988). Ecology of gyrfalcons, *Falco rusticolus*, in the central Canadian Arctic: diet and feeding behaviour. *Canadian Journal of Zoology*, **66**, 334–344.

Pulliainen, E. (1975). Choice of prey by a pair of gyrfalcons *Falco rusticolus* during the nesting period in Forest-Lappland. *Ornis Fennica*, **52**, 19–22.

Roseneau, D.G. (1972). *Summer distribution, numbers, and food habits of the Gyrfalcon* (Falco rusticolus L.) *on the Seward Peninsula, Alaska.* M.Sc. thesis, University of Alaska, Fairbanks, Alaska.

Summers, R.W. & Green, G.H. (1974). Notes on the food of the gyr falcon *Falco rusticolus* in north-east Greenland in 1972. *Dansk Ornithologisk Forenings Tidsskrift*, **68**, 87–90.

Toyne, E.P. (1998). Breeding season diet of the goshawk *Accipiter gentilis* in Wales. *Ibis*, **140**, 569–579.

Voronin, R.N. (1987). On the biology of the gyrfalcon (*Falco gyrfalco* L.) in the south-east of the Bolshezemelskaya tundra. *Bulletin of the Moscow Naturalist's Society, Department of Biology*, **92**, 10–15 (in Russian).

White, C.M. & Cade, T.J. (1971). Cliff-nesting raptors and ravens along the Colville River in arctic Alaska. *Living Bird*, **10**, 107–150.

Woodin, N. (1980). Observations on gyrfalcons (*Falco rusticolus*) breeding near Lake Myvatn, Iceland, 1967. *Journal of Raptor Research*, **14**, 97–124.

Appendix 24.1. The summer diet of gyrfalcon in North-east Iceland 1981–2000. The nesting territories were grouped according to location with respect to coast and primary waterfowl areas. Data for all years is combined, % n is percent by frequency and % bm is percent by biomass. Age groups are shown as adult (ad) and juvenile (juv), and … is not recorded.

Species	Scientific name	Age group	Weight (g)	Heath % n	Heath % bm	Lakeland % n	Lakeland % bm	Coast % n	Coast % bm	Total % n	Total % bm
Red-throated diver	*Gavia stellata*	juv	500	0.01	0.01	…	…	0.02	0.02	0.01	0.01
Northern fulmar	*Fulmarus glacialis*	ad	747	0.14	0.20	0.08	0.11	0.11	0.16	0.11	0.15
Pink-footed goose	*Anser brachyrhynchus*	ad	2,470	0.05	0.22	0.06	0.28	…	…	0.04	0.21
Pink-footed goose	*Anser brachyrhynchus*	juv	800	1.88	2.95	1.89	2.80	…	…	1.52	2.31
Greylag goose	*Anser anser*	ad	3,460	…	…	0.01	0.04	…	…	0.00	0.02
Greylag goose	*Anser anser*	juv	1,100	0.65	1.40	1.76	3.58	0.35	0.76	1.01	2.31
Anser sp.		juv	950	0.02	0.03	0.59	1.03	0.45	0.83	0.36	0.66
Eurasian wigeon	*Anas penelope*	ad	710	1.80	2.50	9.15	12.02	0.43	0.60	4.92	6.66
Eurasian wigeon	*Anas penelope*	juv	240	0.10	0.05	1.02	0.45	0.03	0.02	0.51	0.23
Gadwall	*Anas strepera*	ad	754	…	…	0.15	0.21	…	…	0.07	0.10
Common teal	*Anas crecca*	ad	332	0.32	0.21	0.52	0.32	0.05	0.03	0.36	0.23
Common teal	*Anas crecca*	juv	110	0.02	0.00	0.08	0.02	…	…	0.04	0.01
Mallard	*Anas platyrhynchos*	ad	1,102	0.62	1.35	1.10	2.24	0.29	0.62	0.78	1.63
Mallard	*Anas platyrhynchos*	juv	360	0.09	0.06	0.29	0.20	0.05	0.03	0.18	0.12
Pintail	*Anas acuta*	ad	793	0.02	0.03	0.03	0.05	0.03	0.05	0.03	0.04
Pintail	*Anas acuta*	juv	260	…	…	0.01	0.00	…	…	0.00	0.00
Anas sp.		juv	250	0.02	0.01	0.16	0.08	0.02	0.01	0.08	0.04
Tufted duck	*Aythya fuligula*	ad	749	0.21	0.31	2.00	2.78	0.03	0.05	1.00	1.43
Greater scaup	*Aythya marila*	ad	1,026	0.05	0.09	0.54	1.02	0.05	0.10	0.27	0.53
Aythya sp.		ad	890	0.01	0.02	0.13	0.21	…	…	0.06	0.11
Aythya sp.		juv	290	…	…	0.02	0.01	…	…	0.01	0.01
Common eider	*Somateria mollissima*	ad	1,905	0.01	0.03	…	…	0.05	0.18	0.01	0.05
Common eider	*Somateria mollissima*	juv	600	0.09	0.11	0.14	0.16	0.95	1.11	0.28	0.32
Harlequin	*Histrionicus histrionicus*	ad	618	0.76	0.92	1.20	1.37	0.11	0.14	0.84	0.98
Harlequin	*Histrionicus histrionicus*	juv	205	0.01	0.00	0.02	0.01	…	…	0.01	0.00
Long-tailed duck	*Clangula hyemalis*	ad	753	0.20	0.30	0.31	0.43	0.02	0.02	0.21	0.31
Common scoter	*Melanitta nigra*	ad	1,071	0.03	0.06	0.12	0.24	…	…	0.07	0.13

Species	Scientific name	Age group	Weight (g)	Heath %n	Heath %bm	Lakeland %n	Lakeland %bm	Coast %n	Coast %bm	Total %n	Total %bm
Barrow's goldeneye	*Bucephala islandica*	ad	1,057	0.02	0.04	0.69	1.35	0.02	0.03	0.33	0.66
Barrow's goldeneye	*Bucephala islandica*	juv	350	...	...	0.06	0.04	...	...	0.03	0.02
Red-breasted merganser	*Mergus serrator*	ad	1,079	0.11	0.23	0.26	0.52	0.16	0.34	0.19	0.39
Red-breasted merganser	*Mergus serrator*	juv	360	...	...	0.01	0.01	...	...	0.01	0.00
Goosander	*Mergus merganser*	ad	1,205	...	...	0.01	0.02	...	...	0.00	0.01
Anatinae sp.		ad	800	0.03	0.04	0.10	0.14	0.02	0.03	0.06	0.09
Anatinae sp.		juv	260	0.06	0.03	0.35	0.17	0.03	0.02	0.19	0.09
Merlin	*Falco columbarius*	ad	250	...	...	0.01	0.00	...	...	0.00	0.00
Gyr falcon	*Falco rusticolus*	juv	1,000	0.06	0.13	0.05	0.09	0.02	0.03	0.05	0.09
Rock ptarmigan	*Lagopus mutus*	ad	537	77.54	81.52	63.41	63.03	71.72	75.15	69.88	71.51
Rock ptarmigan	*Lagopus mutus*	juv	160	1.80	0.56	1.78	0.53	1.83	0.57	1.80	0.55
Common coot	*Fulica atra*	ad	775	0.01	0.01	0.01	0.01	...	...	0.00	0.00
Oystercatcher	*Haematopus ostralegus*	juv	250	0.01	0.00	...	...	...	...	0.00	0.00
Ringed plover	*Charadrius hiaticula*	ad	60	...	...	0.01	0.00	...	...	0.01	0.00
Golden plover	*Pluvialis apricaria*	ad	197	0.68	0.26	0.33	0.12	0.03	0.01	0.39	0.15
Golden plover	*Pluvialis apricaria*	juv	65	0.80	0.10	0.77	0.09	0.29	0.04	0.69	0.08
Golden plover	*Pluvialis apricaria*	?	130	0.04	0.01	0.03	0.01	...	...	0.03	0.01
Purple sandpiper	*Calidris maritima*	ad	70	0.01	0.00	...	...	0.02	0.00	0.01	0.00
Purple sandpiper	*Calidris maritima*	juv	25	0.02	0.00	...	...	...	...	0.01	0.00
Dunlin	*Calidris alpina*	ad	50	0.03	0.00	0.02	0.00	0.06	0.01	0.03	0.00
Dunlin	*Calidris alpina*	juv	20	0.01	0.00	0.02	0.00	0.03	0.00	0.02	0.00
Dunlin	*Calidris alpina*	?	35	...	...	0.01	0.00	...	...	0.01	0.00
Common snipe	*Gallinago gallinago*	ad	125	0.49	0.12	0.63	0.15	0.29	0.07	0.52	0.12
Common snipe	*Gallinago gallinago*	juv	40	0.84	0.07	1.31	0.10	0.45	0.04	0.98	0.07
Common snipe	*Gallinago gallinago*	?	80	0.16	0.02	0.07	0.01	0.02	0.00	0.09	0.01
Eurasian woodcock	*Scolopax rusticola*	ad	310	0.01	0.01	...	...	...	...	0.00	0.00
Black-tailed godwit	*Limosa limosa*	ad	320	0.06	0.03	0.09	0.05	0.03	0.02	0.07	0.04
Black-tailed godwit	*Limosa limosa*	juv	110	0.13	0.03	0.22	0.04	0.03	0.01	0.15	0.03
Whimbrel	*Numenius phaeopus*	ad	457	2.19	1.96	2.62	2.22	0.74	0.66	2.11	1.83
Whimbrel	*Numenius phaeopus*	juv	150	1.50	0.44	2.19	0.61	0.38	0.11	1.60	0.46
Redshank	*Tringa totanus*	ad	148	...	...	0.07	0.02	0.03	0.01	0.04	0.01

Species	Scientific name	Age group	Weight (g)	Heath		Lakeland		Coast		Total	
				% n	% bm	% n	% bm	% n	% bm	% n	% bm
Redshank	*Tringa totanus*	juv	50	0.06	0.01	0.22	0.02	0.11	0.01	0.14	0.01
Red-necked phalarope	*Phalaropus lobatus*	ad	35	0.01	0.00	0.01	0.00	...	...	0.01	0.00
Shorebird sp.		?	50	0.04	0.00	0.01	0.00	...	...	0.02	0.00
Arctic skua	*Stercorarius parasiticus*	ad	410	0.11	0.09	0.02	0.02	0.06	0.05	0.06	0.05
Arctic skua	*Stercorarius parasiticus*	juv	140	0.26	0.07	0.01	0.00	0.19	0.05	0.13	0.04
Great skua	*Stercorarius skua*	juv	430	0.01	0.01	...	...	...	...	0.00	0.00
Black-headed gull	*Larus ridibundus*	ad	281	0.07	0.04	0.27	0.14	0.08	0.04	0.16	0.09
Black-headed gull	*Larus ridibundus*	juv	95	0.50	0.09	1.27	0.22	0.13	0.02	0.78	0.14
Black-headed gull	*Larus ridibundus*	?	190	0.02	0.01	0.02	0.01	0.02	0.01	0.02	0.01
Common gull	*Larus canus*	ad	387	0.03	0.02	...	...	...	...	0.01	0.01
Common gull	*Larus canus*	juv	130	0.01	0.00	...	...	...	...	0.00	0.00
Lesser black-backed gull	*Larus fuscus*	ad	793	0.03	0.04	0.01	0.01	...	...	0.01	0.02
Lesser black-backed gull	*Larus fuscus*	juv	265	0.14	0.07	0.01	0.01	...	...	0.05	0.03
Great black-backed gull	*Larus marinus*	juv	480	0.01	0.01	...	...	...	...	0.00	0.00
Black-legged kittiwake	*Rissa tridactyla*	ad	402	0.40	0.32	0.10	0.07	0.35	0.28	0.25	0.19
Black-legged kittiwake	*Rissa tridactyla*	juv	120	0.45	0.11	0.13	0.03	0.35	0.08	0.28	0.06
Arctic tern	*Sterna paradisaea*	ad	104	0.06	0.01	0.34	0.07	0.79	0.16	0.33	0.07
Arctic tern	*Sterna paradisaea*	juv	30	0.20	0.01	0.10	0.01	1.17	0.07	0.35	0.02
Arctic tern	*Sterna paradisaea*	?	65	...	...	...	...	0.26	0.03	0.05	0.01
Common guillemot	*Uria aalge*	ad	1,000	...	...	0.01	0.01	0.14	0.28	0.03	0.06
Uria sp.		ad	1,000	...	...	0.01	0.01	0.02	0.03	0.01	0.01
Razorbill	*Alca torda*	ad	720	0.06	0.09	...	...	0.75	1.06	0.17	0.23
Black guillemot	*Cepphus grylle*	ad	410	0.01	0.01	0.05	0.04	0.06	0.05	0.04	0.03
Atlantic puffin	*Fratercula arctica*	ad	506	2.36	2.34	0.29	0.27	16.10	15.90	4.10	3.96
Carrier pigeon	*Columba livia*	ad	425	0.06	0.05	0.04	0.03	0.02	0.01	0.04	0.03
Common woodpigeon	*Columba palumbus*	ad	467	...	...	0.01	0.01	...	...	0.00	0.00
Short-eared owl	*Asio flammeus*	ad	300	0.01	0.01	0.01	0.00	...	...	0.01	0.00
Meadow pipit	*Anthus pratensis*	ad	20	...	...	0.01	0.00	0.02	0.00	0.01	0.00
Meadow pipit	*Anthus pratensis*	juv	10	0.01	0.00	0.03	0.00	...	...	0.02	0.00
Meadow pipit	*Anthus pratensis*	?	15	...	...	0.01	0.00	0.02	0.00	0.01	0.00
White wagtail	*Motacilla alba*	?	15	...	...	0.01	0.00	...	...	0.00	0.00

Species	Scientific name	Age group	Weight (g)	Heath % n	Heath % bm	Lakeland % n	Lakeland % bm	Coast % n	Coast % bm	Total % n	Total % bm
Northern wheatear	*Oenanthe oenanthe*	ad	30	0.01	0.00	...	...	...	...	0.00	0.00
Northern wheatear	*Oenanthe oenanthe*	juv	10	0.02	0.00	...	...	...	...	0.01	0.00
Fieldfare	*Turdus pilaris*	ad	105	...	...	...	...	0.02	0.00	0.00	0.00
Redwing	*Turdus iliacus*	ad	70	0.14	0.02	0.10	0.01	...	...	0.09	0.01
Redwing	*Turdus iliacus*	juv	25	0.73	0.04	0.21	0.01	0.10	0.00	0.36	0.02
Redwing	*Turdus iliacus*	?	50	0.42	0.04	0.05	0.00	0.02	0.00	0.17	0.02
Snow bunting	*Plectrophenax nivalis*	ad	35	...	...	...	...	0.02	0.00	0.00	0.00
Snow bunting	*Plectrophenax nivalis*	juv	15	0.01	0.00	0.01	0.00	...	...	0.01	0.00
Snow bunting	*Plectrophenax nivalis*	?	25	0.06	0.00	0.06	0.00	0.02	0.00	0.05	0.00
Passeriformes sp.		?	25	0.02	0.00	...	...	...	...	0.01	0.00
Aves sp.		?	100	0.01	0.00	0.01	0.00	...	...	0.01	0.00
Wood mouse	*Apodemus sylvatica*	ad	30	0.01	0.00	0.01	0.00	...	...	0.01	0.00
American mink	*Mustela vision*	juv	500	...	...	0.03	0.00	...	...	0.01	0.00
Brown trout	*Salmo trutta*	?	200	...	...	0.01	0.01	...	...	0.00	0.00
Total				100.00	100.00	100.00	100.00	100.00	100.00	100.00	100.00
Number of prey items				10,894		14,678		6,241		31,813	
Biomass of prey (kg)				5,564		7,930		3,198		16,692	
Collections				131		162		66		359	

THEME FOUR

IMPLICATIONS OF LAND USE CHANGE

THEME FOUR

IMPLICATIONS OF LAND USE CHANGE

Across Europe, human influences have had a defining impact on birds of prey (e.g. Newton, 1979). Various forms of land use change have affected habitat and food supplies, both directly and indirectly, and persecution and conservation-related activities have impacted on the changing fortunes of different species. Perhaps more than any other group of birds, numbers, distribution and productivity of raptors have been most influenced by these human activities (Tucker & Heath, 1994). Thompson *et al.* (Chapter 25) provide an overview of the main impacts of land use change on raptors. It is striking, but perhaps not surprising, how few studies have actually managed to disentangle the direct and indirect impacts of land uses such as farming, forestry, agriculture, recreation and game management on the behaviour and ecology of many raptor species. Instead, most studies have focussed on one species, and on one aspect of land use management.

Two studies deal with land use change and golden eagles *Aquila chrysaetos*. In Chapter 26, Fielding *et al.* use two Geographical Information System (GIS)-based models to examine the effects of land use changes on golden eagle productivity. They stress that regional variation between eagle ranges can be considerable and can have an important bearing on observed and modelled responses to land use. In Chapter 27, McGrady *et al.* examine specifically the potential impacts of native woodland expansion on golden eagles in Scotland. They argue that the main impact of such woodland expansion is to reduce the amount of food available to eagles. However, we find that there are subtle changes in food availability as woodland matures, and the authors make the point that we still know very little about the impacts of woodland expansion on the non-breeding part of the eagle population. The study is timely because the Forestry Commission Scotland (http://www.forestry.gov.uk/forestry/HCOU-4U4J33) has recently introduced a Scottish Forestry Grants Scheme, which offers payments for managing native woodland planting as well as the management of existing woodland areas and some open areas. Chapters 26 and 27 should assist in guiding the nature of such grants.

The final study concerns common buzzards *Buteo buteo* in the Welsh Marches. Sim (Chapter 28) has examined several datasets for buzzards between 1983 and 1996 to understand the significant increase in density and distribution of buzzards across Britain. He found that an increase in rabbit *Oryctolagus cuniculus* abundance and a reduction in persecution levels (notably poisoning) coincided with higher productivity in buzzards, with high breeding densities associated with high proportions of unimproved pasture and mature woodland within territories. His study found the highest breeding density of buzzards so far recorded in Europe (81 territorial pairs per 100 km^2). Sim suggests that buzzards should continue to expand their range in the UK, especially if rabbit numbers continue to increase and persecution levels continue to decline.

These four chapters look in different ways at how land use change affects birds of prey. Whilst such studies can be classified as falling within upland, lowland/agricultural or woodland/forested environments, it is striking how complex the interactions between the birds and human activities can be (e.g. Newton, 1979; Anon., 2000). An important challenge for the future will be to identify those land management practices which benefit raptors and the rest of wildlife, and the policies and land uses which support these.

References

Anonymous (2000). *Report of the UK Raptor Working Group.* Department of the Environment, Transport and Regions, and Joint Nature Conservation Committee, Peterborough.

Newton, I. (1979). *Population Ecology of Raptors.* Poyser, Berkhamsted.

Tucker, G.M. & Heath, M.F. (1994). *Birds in Europe: their conservation status.* Birdlife International, Cambridge.

25. AN OVERVIEW OF LAND USE CHANGE AND IMPLICATIONS FOR RAPTORS

D.B.A. Thompson, P. Shaw, H.T. Riley, M.C. Shewry, E.C. Mackey, P. Robertson & K. Morton

Summary

1. Major land use changes have occurred over most of Europe, resulting in land cover, habitat and species changes. Land cover/land use changes in Britain since the 1940s have involved intensification of agriculture, declines in the extent of natural and semi-natural habitats (notably in the uplands) and, more recently, increases in woodland cover.

2. In Scotland, we examined trends in raptor populations and considered associations with land use changes. There are currently approximately 30,000-36,000 pairs of 18 raptor species breeding in Scotland each year. Seven species are increasing, four are decreasing, three appear to be stable, and trends for the remaining four species are uncertain.

3. There are no clear trends in raptor species' populations in relation to their principal habitats during the breeding or non-breeding seasons. We have identified and ranked four major land use 'drivers' of population change in raptors. We suggest that these are, in order of decreasing scale of impact across species: agricultural intensification, persecution (largely associated with game management), afforestation/deforestation, and grazing pressure. Persecution is not implicated as a causal factor for three of the four raptor species which are currently declining in Scotland (sparrowhawk *Accipiter nisus*, barn owl *Tyto alba* and kestrel *Falco tinnunculus*).

4. Changes in the breeding ranges of raptors between 1968-72 and 1988-91 are broadly similar to those of 76 other widespread, terrestrial bird species in Scotland. Buzzard *Buteo buteo*, hen harrier *Circus cyaneus*, merlin *Falco columbarius*, peregrine *Falco peregrinus* and, in particular, the goshawk *Accipiter gentilis* showed at least a 10% increase in the number of 10 km squares occupied over the 20 year study period.

5. A broadscale analysis of changes in the distribution of 22 bird species which breed widely in the Scottish uplands (including 6 raptor species) between 1968-72 and 1988-91, showed no clear patterns in terms of range changes in 'centre' and 'edge' areas. Five of six raptor species showed range increases or stability in both centre and edge areas.

6. Suggestions are made for further research, (i) to explore relationships between land cover/habitat/prey base and bird population changes at different scales; (ii) for scenario modelling; and (iii) for experimental investigations of land use/management impacts. We note in particular the current dearth of information on renewable energy developments (notably wind farms) in relation to raptors.

25.1 Introduction

"The conservation problems of recent years have repeatedly shown that it is not enough to let nature alone, nor merely to protect against direct human interference. Research may often be needed to define the problem and some form of active management to rectify it. Effective conservation usually entails some assessment of breeding stocks, of numbers, distribution and nest success. Only in this way can the most endangered stocks be identified and funds used to best effect." From *Population Ecology of Raptors* (Newton, 1979).

Across Europe during the last two centuries there have been substantial changes in the use of the land, and in wildlife associated with this (e.g. Meyer & Turner, 1994; Birdlife International/European Census Council, 2000; Mackey 2002; Birnie *et al.*, 2002). Raptors, at the upper reaches of the food chain, reflect many of the impacts of human land use on food supplies, habitat and quality of the environment.

In this chapter, we use data and information on raptors, land cover and land use change in Scotland to investigate some of the associations which appear to underlie variation in the distribution, numbers and status of raptors. The data are derived from a number of different sources and time frames, including: the latest available estimates of the breeding populations of raptors in Scotland (some as yet unpublished, referenced as Scottish Raptor Monitoring Group (2003)); data from the two breeding bird surveys of Britain and Ireland (Sharrock, 1976; Gibbons *et al.*, 1993); and land cover data (see Mackey *et al.*, 2001).

Complex inter-relationships exist between human influences, environmental characteristics and raptors. We have presented these relationships in Figure 25.1 using a basic 'Pressure-State-Response' model (*sensu* Stanners & Bordeau, 1995). In particular, with respect to the potential 'limiting' factors, persecution is an issue which does not impact to the same extent on many other groups of birds (e.g. Newton, 1979; Newton, Chapter 1; Fielding *et al.*, Chapter 26; Viñuela & Villafuerte, Chapter 40).

This chapter aims to identify those issues which should be investigated further: the variable scale and importance of land use and land management changes; the lack of information on interactions between land use and raptor populations; and time lags between land use change and responses in raptors.

25.2 Land use change and raptors

Many of the chapters in this book focus on the specifics of associations between land use change and raptors. Of all the changes on land, agricultural intensification has arguably influenced more populations of more raptor species than any other. However, some of the more subtle changes are difficult to measure: a spread of housing, growing access to 'wild' and indeed peri-urban areas, various forms of forestry and woodland cover changes, and most recently, wind farm developments, have all had varying effects on predatory birds and their prey. Other environmental changes have also been difficult to quantify. For instance, increases in the acidification of soils, losses of organic matter through soil erosion, climate change, and indeed sea level rise may all have had (or be having) significant impacts on the prey base of some raptors in some areas. Some of these factors have still to be investigated, let alone determined (e.g. Meyer & Turner, 1994; Stanners & Bordeau, 1995).

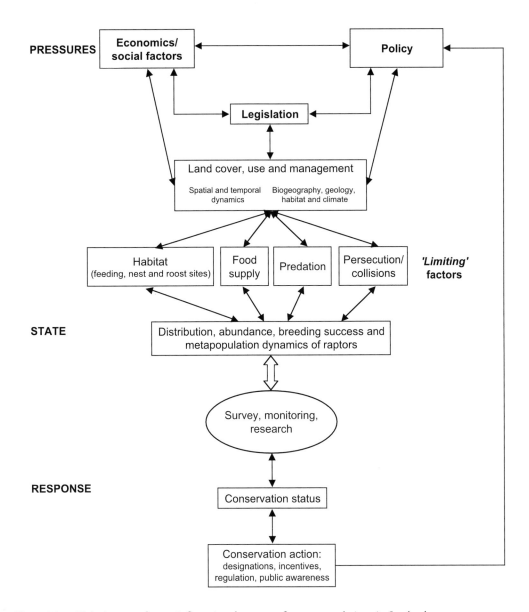

Figure 25.1. Links between factors influencing the status of raptor populations in Scotland.

25.2.1 Land cover changes

Mackey *et al.* (2001) provide a substantial overview of natural heritage trends in Scotland. The broad land cover of Scotland in 1988 consisted of grassland (26%), heather moorland (21%), peatland (17%), woodland (15%), arable (11%), built environment (2%), freshwater (2%) and other features (5%). Changes in these habitats have been quantified over a range of temporal and spatial scales. For instance, between the 1940s and 1980s, the area of heather moorland in Scotland declined by about 23%, and it would appear that this decline has continued through to the late 1990s (Moorland Working Group, 2002). McGowan *et al.* (2001) provide statistics on net changes in the major broad habitats of

Scotland, estimating that the greatest increases between 1990 and 1998 have been in fen, marsh and swamp (18.7%), broad-leaved, mixed and yew *Taxus baccata* woodland (9%), and arable and horticulture land (6.7%), while the greatest decreases over the same time period have been in neutral grassland (-14.8%), dwarf shrub heath (-5.4%) and acid grassland (-4.9%). Much of this type of reporting contributes to updates on progress in meeting targets under the UK Biodiversity Action Plan (Anon., 1994), which stems from the Earth Summit held in Rio de Janeiro in 1992.

25.2.2 *Changes in raptor numbers*

We estimate that there are currently 30,000-36,000 pairs of 18 raptor species breeding in Scotland each year. An overview of the status and recent trends in Scottish raptor populations is given in Table 25.1. This builds on the detailed analyses presented in the UK Raptor Working Group report (Anon., 2000) and Greenwood *et al.* (Chapter 2). We have included some population estimates for 2003 (Scottish Raptor Monitoring Group, 2003), in order to provide as up-to-date a picture as possible. Information on trends over the past decade or so indicate that populations of seven species are increasing, four are decreasing, and populations of three raptor species appear to be stable. For a further four species the trend in Scotland is uncertain.

25.2.3 *Associations between changes in land use and raptor numbers*

It is difficult to equate changes in raptor numbers and distribution with changes in land cover. Often, the management practices applied to the land can have more of a significant impact than changes in land cover *per se*. For instance, looking at the uplands, while heather *Calluna vulgaris* cover has declined, sheep *Ovis aries* numbers have increased by approximately 18% during the period 1982-1998; numbers of red deer *Cervus elaphus* have almost doubled between 1959 and 1989; and the mean number of red grouse *Lagopus lagopus scoticus* shot per km² of moorland between 1947 and 1999 has varied eightfold, with a marked decline evident from the 1970s onwards (Moorland Working Group, 2002). The studies by Tharme *et al.* (2001) and Whitfield *et al.* (2003) show the highly variable effects of management for red grouse shooting on populations of several upland breeding birds.

We have sought to discern any patterns in the trends of Scottish raptor populations, by comparing the principal habitats occupied by each raptor species during the breeding and non-breeding seasons with four factors considered to be the main 'drivers' of land-use change on birds: afforestation/deforestation, grazing pressure (mainly from sheep, deer and rabbits *Oryctolagus cuniculus*), agricultural intensification (principally increases in the scale and turnover of cropping and harvesting regimes, losses of field boundaries and margins, and the use of pesticides and herbicides), and persecution (largely arising from game management). Judgements on principal habitats used and the effects of land use 'drivers' were made on the basis of key references on raptors and other birds (e.g. Brown, 1976; Gibbons *et al.*, 1993; information in the other chapters of this book and the references cited for this chapter). The scale of effects of each 'driver' were assigned to three categories (Table 25.2, columns 5-8): negligible (blank), moderate and high.

There are no clear trends in terms of changes in status and principal breeding habitat (Table 25.2). During the breeding season, six raptor species are predominantly lowland, five are upland, four are woodland, two are wetland, and one is coastal. In the non-breeding

Table 25.1. Status and recent trends (over approximately the last 10 years) in Scottish raptor populations. European population estimates, which include Russia, are from BirdLife International/EBCC (2000).

Species	Scottish population	UK or GB$ population	Measure	Scottish as % of UK or GB population	European population (pairs)	Scottish as % of European population	Recent trend in Scotland	Source
Honey buzzard *Pernis apivorus*	14	69	Probable/possible pairs	20%	100,000-150,000	<1%	Uncertain	2
Red kite *Milvus milvus*	57	600	Breeding pairs	10%	19,000-24,000	<1%	Increase ↗	2
White-tailed eagle *Haliaeetus albicilla*	25	25$	Breeding pairs/ trios	100%	4,000-4,700	<1%	Increase ↗	2
Marsh harrier *Circus aeruginosus*	6-8	183-206$	Breeding pairs	3-4%	52,000-88,000	<1%	Increase ↗	1
Hen harrier *Circus cyaneus*	365-506**	499-640	Territorial pairs	73-78%	22,000-31,000	1-2%	Stable ⇔	3
Goshawk *Accipiter gentilis*	80	405-410	Occ. home ranges/pairs with nests	20%	130,000-180,000	<1%	Increase ↗	3
Sparrowhawk *Accipiter nisus*	7,000	34,400	Pairs with nests	20%	280,000-380,000	2%	Stable ⇔	3
Buzzard *Buteo buteo*	4,600-6,500*	12,000-17,000	Apparently territorial pairs	38%	690,000-1,000,000	<1%	Increase ⇔	3
Golden eagle *Aquila chrysaetos*	421	422	Home ranges occ. by pairs	100%	6,600-12,000	3-6%	Stable ⇔	3
Osprey *Pandion haliaetus*	147	151	Pairs with nests	97%	8,000-10,000	1-2%	Increase ↗	1
Kestrel *Falco tinnunculus*	11,000	51,600	Pairs producing eggs	22%	300,000-440,000	2-4%	Decline ↘	3
Merlin *Falco columbarius*	800	1,305-1,320	Pairs with nests	61%	37,000-55,000	1-2%	Increase ↗	3
Hobby *Falco subbuteo*	0-6	2,200$	Territories/breeding pairs	<1%	65,000-120,000	<1%	N/A	2
Peregrine *Falco peregrinus*	544	1,402	Territorial pairs	39%	7,600-11,000	5-7%	Decline ↘	2
Barn owl *Tyto alba*	300*	4,140-4,210	Pairs producing eggs/ territorial pairs	7%	100,000-200,000	<1%	Decline ↘	3
Tawny owl *Strix aluco*	3,900	20,000$	Territorial pairs	20%	380,000-810,000	1%	Decline ↘?	3
Long-eared owl *Asio otus*	530-1,750	1,620-5,320	'Pairs'	33%	190,000-780,000	<1%	Uncertain	3
Short-eared owl *Asio flammeus*	780-2,700	1,000-3,500$	'Pairs'	77-78%	17,000-130,000	2-5%	Uncertain	3

Sources:[1] Ogilvie & RBBP (2002);[2] Scottish Raptor Monitoring Group (2003);[3] Greenwood *et al.* (Chapter 2).

* We consider these to be underestimates, but there appear to be no more up-to-date estimates for these species in Scotland.

** Site-specific surveys indicate a decline over parts of eastern and southern Scotland; there will be a comprehensive UK survey of the hen harrier in 2004.

Table 25.2. Recent trends in Scottish raptor populations, in relation to main habitat and land use 'drivers'. Information on trends in population comes from Table 25.1. Many of the entries for this table come from other studies detailed throughout the book (notably Chapters 5-7, 9, 10-12, 14, 18, 20, 23, 26-29, 31-34, 38 and 39).

Species	Principal habitat in		Trend	Main drivers			
	Breeding season	Non-breeding season		Afforestation/ deforestation	Grazing	Agricultural intensification	Persecution
Buzzard	Lowland	Lowland	Increase		Moderate	High	Moderate
Goshawk	Woodland	Woodland	Increase	High			High
Marsh harrier	Wetland	Wetland	Increase			High	
Merlin	Upland	Lowland	Increase	Moderate	Moderate	Moderate	
Osprey	Wetland	Absent	Increase				Moderate
Red kite	Lowland	Lowland	Increase			Moderate	High
White-tailed eagle	Coastal	Coastal	Increase			High	Moderate
Golden eagle	Upland	Upland	Stable	Moderate	Moderate	Moderate	High
Hen harrier	Upland	Upland	Stable	High	High	Moderate	High
Sparrowhawk	Woodland	Woodland	Stable	Moderate		High	
Peregrine	Upland	Coastal	Decline			Moderate	Moderate
Barn owl	Lowland	Lowland	Decline			High	
Kestrel	Lowland	Lowland	Decline			High	
Tawny owl	Woodland	Woodland	Decline	Moderate			
Honey buzzard	Lowland	Absent	Uncertain				Moderate
Long-eared owl	Woodland	Woodland	Uncertain	Moderate			
Short-eared owl	Upland	Coastal	Uncertain	Moderate		Moderate	Moderate
Hobby	Lowland	Absent	-			Moderate	

High, medium and low indicate the known impact of these land use drivers on raptor populations.
In other parts of its UK range the honey buzzard can be regarded as woodland.

season, the osprey, honey buzzard and hobby are absent, the merlin moves into the lowlands, and short-eared owl and peregrine move towards the coast (scientific names are given in Table 25.1). Of the predominantly lowland raptors, two species have increased and two have declined, and in the uplands one has increased, one has declined and two are stable (though the hen harrier may actually be declining, and is to be surveyed comprehensively in 2004). The two wetland raptors (marsh harrier and osprey) have increased.

The main land use 'drivers' can be ranked in terms of the assessment of the number of species affected. We suggest that agricultural intensification has influenced 13 species, followed by persecution (10 species), afforestation/deforestation (eight species) and grazing pressure (four species). Agricultural intensification is considered a moderate/high driver for all the upland breeding raptors and five out of the six lowland breeding raptors; persecution is judged to influence 60% of the upland raptor species and 50% of the lowland raptor species. Grazing is considered to influence only one of the lowland raptors (buzzard, through changes in rabbit abundance) but three of the five upland raptors (merlin, golden eagle and hen harrier, through influencing their food supplies). Afforestation/deforestation may have influenced the upland (four species) and woodland (three species) raptors, but evidently not any of the lowland or wetland raptors.

No clear associations are evident in relation to trends in raptor populations and the land use drivers. A given driver may have contrasting effects on different species; for example afforestation is thought to have benefited goshawks through increasing potential breeding habitat (Sharrock, 1976) but adversely affected golden eagles by reducing the availability of foraging habitat (see Marquiss *et al.*, Chapter 9; Fielding *et al.*, Chapter 26; McGrady *et al.*, Chapter 27). The same factor can also have different effects on a given species at different times. Sticking with afforestation, the post-1940s' expansion of forestry in the Scottish uplands is thought to have been a key factor allowing hen harriers to re-colonize the Scottish mainland (Sharrock, 1976; Bibby & Etheridge, 1993). More recently, as plantations have matured and the habitat has become unsuitable, the number of hen harriers breeding in plantations has declined (Sim *et al.*, 2001). Instead, there has been an increase in the numbers of harriers breeding on grouse moors suggesting that the hen harrier population is currently under greater threat from persecution than it was 10 years ago (Summers *et al.*, Chapter 38). Persecution is, however, not implicated as a causal factor for three of the four raptors which are declining in Scotland (sparrowhawk, barn owl and kestrel). Declines in the latter two species are thought to be attributable to agricultural intensification affecting prey supplies and nesting habitat availability (Greenwood *et al.*, Chapter 2; Taylor & Walton, Chapter 34).

25.3 Population trends of raptors in relation to other birds

Having considered broad population trends in raptors and associations with land use drivers, we have compared their population trends with other birds breeding in Scotland. We analysed data collected by volunteers for the British Trust for Ornithology for the Breeding Bird Atlas studies of 1968-72 and 1988-91 (Gibbons *et al.*, 1993) in order to contrast changes in numbers and distributions of breeding birds in Scotland.

Figure 25.2 shows the numbers of surveyed 10 km squares in Scotland occupied by individual bird species during 1968-72 and 1988-91. A regression line is drawn for 86 widespread, terrestrial breeding bird species for the two survey periods; points above the line indicate an increased range for a given species in 1988-91 compared with 1968-72.

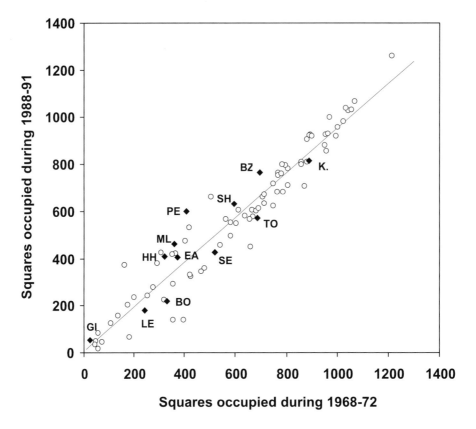

Figure 25.2. The number of 10 km squares occupied in Scotland during 1988-91, compared with 1968-72. O = Non-raptor, terrestrial species. ◆ = Raptor species, as follows: BO, barn owl; BZ, buzzard; EA, golden eagle; GI, goshawk; HH, hen harrier; K., kestrel; LE, long-eared owl; ML, merlin; PE, peregrine; SE, short-eared owl; SH, sparrowhawk. Regression relationship: y = 5.236 + 0.949x, N = 86 species.

Over the 20 year period between the two surveys, five widespread raptor species (buzzard, hen harrier, merlin, peregrine and goshawk) showed at least a 10% increase in the number of 10 km squares occupied, while four species (barn owl, short-eared owl, long-eared owl and tawny owl) showed a decline of at least 10%. The greatest proportional increase was that of goshawk, which doubled its range, re-colonising parts of lowland Scotland during the 1970s and 1980s (see Marquiss *et al.*, Chapter 9). The pattern of change in range size shown by raptor species was broadly similar to that of 76 other widespread, terrestrial bird species, with notable increases being observed in the peregrine and buzzard (Figure 25.2).

25.4 Changes in the uplands: comparisons between bird populations in central and edge regions

25.4.1 Centre and edge areas in the uplands

The Scottish uplands support substantial populations of raptors (Greenwood, Chapter 2; Table 25.1). We have investigated changes in raptor populations and the populations of 16 other species which breed widely in the uplands: red grouse, black grouse *Tetrao tetrix*, golden plover *Pluvialis apricaria*, dunlin *Calidris alpina*, common snipe *Gallinago gallinago*, whimbrel *Numenius phaeopus*, curlew *Numenius arquata*, redshank *Tringa totanus*, greenshank

Tringa nebularia, skylark *Alauda arvensis*, meadow pipit *Anthus pratensis*, whinchat *Saxicola rubetra*, wheatear *Oenanthe oenanthe*, ring ouzel *Turdus torquatus*, raven *Corvus corax* and twite *Carduelis flavirostris*. We have already used these data to investigate changes in bird distributions in relation to different land uses (e.g. grouse moor cf. non-grouse moor areas; Thompson *et al.*, 1997a) and with regard to specific regions (e.g. Cairngorms; Thompson *et al.*, 1997b).

We examined the hypothesis that species dependent on upland habitats during the breeding season are likely to have more stable distributions in areas where upland habitats predominate. We investigated changes in the area of occupancy of upland species between 1968-72 and 1988-91. Two sets of 10 km squares were compared: 'centre' squares, containing at least 80 km^2 of upland or marginal upland habitats, and 'edge' squares, containing 20-79 km^2 of upland or marginal upland habitat, as defined in Haines-Young *et al.* (2000). For each species, changes in the number of centre and edge squares occupied during each time period were compared. In the following analysis, a species area of occupancy is said to have changed only if the number of squares it occupied increased or decreased by at least 10%.

25.4.2 Observed changes in distribution 1968-72 to 1988-91: raptors and other upland birds

Over the time period between the two breeding atlases, raptors appear to have generally fared better than other upland birds, with four out of six species increasing their ranges in centre or edge squares (Table 25.3, Figure 25.3). The exceptions to this are buzzard, which showed gains of less than 10% in centre and edge squares, and short-eared owl, a species for which population size and trends in the UK are poorly known (Gibbons *et al.*, 1993).

Looking at raptors and other species in the round, of the 22 upland species examined, four increased their range in centre and edge squares, two increased in the centre, but

Table 25.3. Comparison of changes in the range (number of 10 km squares occupied) of bird species breeding widely in the uplands between 1968-72 and 1988-91 within 'centre' and 'edge' upland areas (see text for explanation of terms, and Figure 25.3 for details of the scale of change for each species). Text in brackets after each species name indicates the main breeding habitat (see Gibbons *et al.*, 1993; Thompson *et al.*, 1995).

	Edge increase	*Edge no change*	*Edge decline*
Centre increase	Merlin (heather) Peregrine (mixed) Whimbrel (mixed) Hen harrier (grassland)	Golden eagle (heather) Dunlin (mixed)	
Centre no change	Greenshank (mixed)	Golden plover (mixed) Curlew (grassland) Twite (grassland) Snipe (grassland) Skylark (grassland) Meadow pipit (grassland) Wheatear (grassland) Buzzard (grassland) Whinchat (mixed)	Black grouse (heather) Red grouse (heather)
Centre decline		Redshank (grassland) Raven (grassland)	Ring ouzel (heather) Short-eared owl (grassland)

showed no change in the edge, one showed no change in the centre, but increased in the edge, two showed no change in the centre, but declined in the edge, two declined in the centre but showed no change in the edge, and two declined in both centre and edge (Table 25.3). The remaining nine species showed no change in centre or edge squares. Overall, ten species showed a change in their occupancy of centre squares, while nine species showed a change in their occupancy of edge squares. The initial hypothesis is not supported at this level of analysis.

These mixed results may reflect changes in each species' population status between the two surveys; as well as changes in the habitat composition of centre and edge squares. One of the key factors implicated in land use change in the uplands is increased grazing pressure resulting in losses of heather to grassland (Thompson *et al.*, 1995). However, while half of

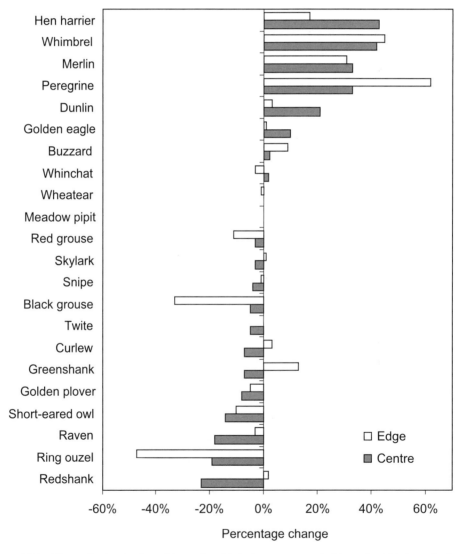

Figure 25.3. Change in the number of 'centre' and 'edge' squares occupied by upland bird species between 1968-72 and 1988-91.

the species examined were grassland birds, they accounted for seven of the nine species showing no change in the centre or edge, three of the four species declining in the centre, and only one of the six species increasing in the centre (Table 25.3).

One of the most difficult aspects of this type of investigation is an appreciation of the complexity of the influences of land management and land use on bird populations. Range changes of birds in upland areas need to be considered in the context of overall changes in population size and distribution between the two survey periods – which for species that move away from the uplands during the non-breeding season may be influenced by factors acting outside the uplands. The possibility that habitat or land cover change may not be an

overriding influence for some species must also be considered. For example, the distribution of poisoning incidents where raptors were thought to be the intended victim during 1987-2000 is shown in Figure 25.4. In Scotland, there would appear to be a strong association between incidents of illegal poisoning and grouse moors (Whitfield *et al.*, 2003); and a population model of golden eagles in Scotland has indicated that persecution is a key limiting influence on the population (Whitfield *et al.*, in press). Conversely, in some parts of Britain grouse moor management can be beneficial to some upland birds, notably through effective management of habitat and the control of pest species (e.g. Thompson *et al.*, 1997b; Tharme *et al.*, 2001). The important point with regard to the above analyses, however, is that factors such as the persecution of raptors may compound associations between habitat change, the prey base and population size and distribution of raptors (e.g. Rebecca & Cosnette, Chapter 14; Fielding *et al.*, Chapter 26; Summers *et al.*, Chapter 38; Redpath & Thirgood, Chapter 39).

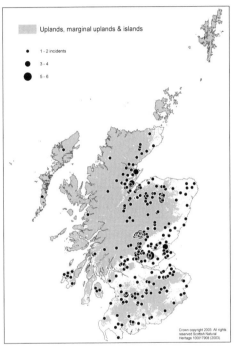

Figure 25.4. Poisoning incidents in which raptors were killed or considered to have been at risk, 1987-2000. The RSPB provided the map, based on information from the public, Scottish Raptor Study Groups, the Scottish Agricultural Science Agency and the Scottish Police Forces; see also Whitfield *et al.* (2003).

25.5 Discussion

Using several data and information sources we examined broadscale changes in numbers and distribution of raptors in Scotland. The most telling result is that, at a landscape scale, there appear to be no clear relationships between land use change and changes in the numbers and distribution of raptors. Instead, an array of social, environmental and chance events have given rise to the present day distribution of raptors, and appear to have accounted for the variable status of the different raptor species (e.g. Figure 25.1).

At least three issues emerge. First, over the past 50 or so years in Scotland there have been major changes in land cover, notably in terms of losses of natural and semi-natural habitats, increases in grazing pressure – particularly in the uplands, intensification of agriculture (losses of field boundaries and margins, more rapid transitions between crop regimes, and the use of pesticides and herbicides) and a steady increase in woodland cover (e.g. Thompson *et al.*, 1995, 1997a; McGowan *et al.*, 2001; Mackey *et al.*, 2001; Birnie *et al.*, 2002). Quantitative data for changes in bird populations across the UK, and indeed across Scotland, date mostly from the late 1960s, whereas some habitat data derived from aerial photographs go back to the early–mid twentieth century. Based on key published information about raptors and their habitats (including information presented in other chapters of this book), we have identified agricultural intensification, afforestation/deforestation, grazing pressure and persecution as the four main land use drivers of population change in raptors.

The second issue is that, with the exception of a small number of localised studies, largely by volunteer/part-time field workers, we have little information on the interactions between land use, land management practices and raptors (Amar, 2001; and see Petty & Thomas, Chapter 6; Marquiss *et al.*, Chapters 9 and 36; Jardine, Chapter 13; Rebecca & Cosnette, Chapter 14; Sim, Chapter 28; Amar. *et al.*, Chapter 29; Summers *et al.*, Chapter 38). This makes it particularly difficult to determine those land uses/management practices which are likely to benefit raptors as a whole, and to support these through legislative and policy changes (Figure 25.1; Stroud, Chapter 3).

A third issue is that time lags between changes in land use, land management impacts on the ground and responses in raptors must vary considerably, ranging from a few years (e.g. Petty & Thomas, Chapter 6; Sim, Chapter 8) to several decades (e.g. Ratcliffe, Chapter 4; Amar *et al.*, Chapter 29; Viñuela & Villafuerte, Chapter 40). It is, therefore, difficult to reach firm conclusions about the importance of habitat, food and land use *per se* in determining raptor numbers and changes in these (e.g. Newton, Chapter 1; Redpath & Thirgood, Chapter 39).

Looking ahead we suggest that at least three lines of work should be pursued:-

- *Linking land cover changes to wildlife.* For specific areas it would be valuable to analyse habitat and bird population changes in order to determine underlying causes (e.g. Tharme *et al.*, 2001; Moorland Working Group, 2002). The type of detailed analyses done in relation to interactions between peregrines and racing pigeons *Columba livia* (Dixon *et al.*, Chapter 20; Shawyer *et al.*, Chapter 21; Central Science Laboratory, in press), and between hen harriers and their habitat and prey (Amar *et al.*, Chapter 29; Redpath & Thirgood, Chapter 39) are needed for other areas and raptor species.
- *Scenario modelling.* With impending changes in the EC Common Agricultural Policy, increases in the number of wind farms (the Scottish Executive has indicated that by 2020 40% of Scotland's electricity supply should come from renewable sources; currently, Scottish Natural Heritage is commenting on approximately 220 wind farm proposals (SNH, unpublished)) and recent projections regarding climate change (e.g. Mackey *et al.*, 2001; Moorland Working Group, 2002), it is timely to undertake modelling studies to indicate the potential scale and magnitude of impacts on raptors. However, these studies have to make gross assumptions given the sorts of data limitations referred to earlier in this chapter, and elsewhere (e.g. Watson *et al.*, Chapter 10; Fielding & Haworth, Chapter 15; Fielding *et al.*, Chapter 26).

- *Experiments to determine land use/management impacts.* With a few exceptions there is little experimental evidence linking land use/land management changes to raptor population dynamics (Anon., 2000; Newton, Chapter 1; Amar *et al.*, Chapter 29; Redpath & Thirgood, Chapter 39). Given the growing recognition amongst land management organisations of the need to share and promote good land management practices (e.g. Scotland's Moorland Forum, 2003), it is timely to investigate rigorously those practices which benefit raptors, especially the rarer and more vulnerable species. As Figure 25.4 and Whitfield *et al.* (2003, in press) indicate, illegal persecution is a potentially damaging and limiting factor for some raptors.

Beyond these suggested studies and approaches, we need more detailed studies to determine the nature of metapopulation dynamics, and in particular the behaviour of 'source' and 'sink' populations (e.g. Lennon *et al.*, 2001; Holt *et al.*, 2002; He *et al.*, 2002; Whitfield *et al.*, in press). Looking ahead, we hope that in ten years' time there will be more published studies of raptors which have investigated the relationships between habitat, prey and metapopulation changes. It is important to begin this work now, by identifying which raptor populations are increasing, stable or declining; and drawing together relevant information and data on potentially limiting factors. If conservation actions are taken to halt population declines, and even to address concerns about some stable populations, it would be valuable to have baseline, control and 'subsequent-change' data on the birds and their environment. There are particularly exciting opportunities to collect such data for the re-introduced and expanding species, notably red kite, white-tailed eagle and osprey.

Acknowledgements

We are grateful to the following for earlier discussions about this work: Dick Birnie, Brian Etheridge, Nigel Buxton, Alan Fielding, Paul Haworth, Susan Haysom, John Orr, Adam Smith, Derek Ratcliffe, Steve Redpath and Phil Whitfield. We thank the volunteers who collected the data for the British Trust for Ornithology atlases; the many raptor workers who are now contributing to the Scottish Raptor Monitoring Scheme; and two referees for their comments.

References

Amar, A. (2001). *Determining the cause of the hen harrier decline on Orkney*. PhD thesis. University of Aberdeen, Aberdeen.

Anonymous (1994). *Biodiversity: The UK Action Plan.* Cm 2428. HMSO, London.

Anonymous (2000). *Report of the UK Raptor Working Group.* Department of the Environment, Transport and Regions and the Joint Nature Conservation Committee, Peterborough.

Bibby, C.J. & Etheridge, B. (1993). Status of the Hen Harrier *Circus cyaneus* in Scotland in 1988-89. *Bird Study*, **40**, 1-11.

BirdLife International/European Bird Census Council (2000). *European Bird Populations. Estimates and Trends.* BirdLife International, Cambridge.

Birnie, R.V., Curran, J., MacDonald, J.A., Mackey, E.C., Campbell, C.D., McGowan, G., Palmer, S.C.F., Paterson, E., Shaw, P. & Shewry, M.C. (2002). The land resources of Scotland: trends and prospects for the environment and natural heritage. In *The State of Scotland's Environment and Natural Heritage*, ed. by M.B. Usher, E.C. Mackey & J.C. Curran. The Stationery Office, Edinburgh. pp. 41-82.

Brown, L. (1976). *Birds of Prey*. Collins, London.

Central Science Laboratory (in press). Interactions between raptors and racing pigeons *Columba livia*. Report to Scottish Natural Heritage and the Scottish Homing Union. Scottish Natural Heritage, Perth.

Gibbons, D.W., Reid, J.B. & Chapman, R.A. (1993). *The New Atlas of Breeding Birds in Britain and Ireland: 1988-1991*. Poyser, London.

Haines-Young, R.H., Barr, C.J., Black, H.I.J., Briggs, D.J., Bunce, R.G.H., Clarke, R.T., Cooper, A., Dawson, F.H., Firbank, L.G., Fuller, R.M., Furse, M.T., Gillespie, M.K., Hill, R., Hornung, M., Howard, D.C., McCann, T., Morecroft, M.D., Petit, S., Sier, A.R.J., Smart, S.M., Smith, G.M., Stotti, A.P., Stuart, R.C. & Watkins, J.W. (2000). *Accounting for Nature: Assessing Habitats in the UK Countryside*. Department of the Environment, Transport and the Regions, London.

He, F., Gaston, K.J. & Wu, J. (2002). On species occupancy-abundance models. *Ecoscience*, **9**, 119-126.

Holt, A.R., Warren, P.H. & Gaston, K.J. (2002). The importance of biotic interactions in abundance: occupancy relationships. *Journal of Animal Ecology*, **71**, 846-854.

Lennon, J.J., Kileff, P., Greenwood, J.J.D. & Gaston, K. (2001). The geographical structure of British bird distributions: Diversity, spatial turnover and scale. *Journal of Animal Ecology*, **70**, 966-979.

Mackey, E.C. (2002). Scotland in a European context: environmental and natural heritage trends. In *The State of Scotland's Environment and Natural Heritage*, ed. by M.B. Usher, E.C. Mackey & J.C. Curran. The Stationery Office, Edinburgh. pp. 5-18.

Mackey, E.C., Shaw, P., Holbrook, J., Shewry, M.C., Saunders, G., Hall, J., Ellis, N.E. (2001). *Natural Heritage Trends Scotland (2001)*. Scottish Natural Heritage, Perth.

McGowan, G.M., Palmer, S.C.F., French, D.D., Barr, C.J., Howard, D.C. & Smart, S.M. (2001). *Trends in broad habitats: Scotland 1990-1998*. Report to Scottish Natural Heritage. Scottish Natural Heritage, Perth.

Meyer, W.B. & Turner, B.L. (Eds.) (1994). *Changes in Land Use and Land Cover: a Global Perspective*. Cambridge University Press, Cambridge.

Moorland Working Group (2002). *Scotland's Moorland: The Nature of Change*. Scottish Natural Heritage, Perth.

Newton, I. (1979). *Population Ecology of Raptors*. Poyser, Berkhamsted.

Ogilvie, M.A. & Rare Breeding Birds Panel (2002). Rare breeding birds in the United Kingdom in 2000. *British Birds*, **95**, 542-582.

Scotland's Moorland Forum (2003). *Scotland's Moorland Forum: Principles of Moorland Management*. Scottish Natural Heritage, Perth.

Scottish Raptor Monitoring Group (2003). Population estimates for honey buzzard *Pernis apivorus*, red kite *Milvus milvus*, white-tailed eagle *Haliaeetus albicilla*, hobby *Falco subbuteo* and peregrine *Falco peregrinus*. Scottish Natural Heritage, Perth.

Sharrock, J.T.R. (1976). *The Atlas of Breeding Birds in Britain and Ireland*. Poyser, Berkhamsted.

Sim, I.M.W., Gibbons, D.W., Bainbridge, I.P. & Mattingley, W.A. (2001). Status of the Hen Harrier *Circus cyaneus* in the UK and the isle of Man in 1998. *Bird Study*, **48**, 341-353.

Stanners, D. & Bordeau, P. (Eds.) (1995). *Europe's Environment: The Dobris Assessment*. European Environment Agency, Copenhagen.

Tharme, A.D., Green, R.E., Baines, D., Bainbridge, I.P. & O'Brien, M. (2001). The effect of management for red grouse shooting on the population density of breeding birds on heather-dominated moorland. *Journal of Applied Ecology*, **38**, 439-457.

Thompson, D.B.A., Gillings, S.D., Galbraith, C.A., Redpath, S.M. & Drewitt, J. (1997a). The contribution of game management to biodiversity: a review of the importance of grouse moors for upland birds. In *Biodiversity in Scotland: Status, Trends and Initiatives*, ed. by L.V. Fleming, A.C. Newton, J.A. Vickery & M.B. Usher. The Stationery Office, Edinburgh. pp. 198-212.

Thompson, D.B.A., MacDonald, A.J., Marsden, J.H. & Galbraith, C.A. (1995). Upland heather moorland in Great Britain: a review of international importance, vegetation change, and some objectives for nature conservation. *Biological Conservation*, **71**, 163-178.

Thompson, D.B.A., Watson, A., Rue, S. & Boobyer, G.A. (1997b). Recent changes in breeding bird populations in the Cairngorms. *Botanical Journal of Scotland*, **48**, 99-110.

Whitfield, D.P., Macleod, D.R.A., Watson, J., Fielding, A.H. & Haworth, P.F. (2003). The association of grouse moor in Scotland with the illegal use of poisons to control predators. *Biological Conservation*, **114**, 157-163.

Whitfield, D.P., Fielding, A.H., McLeod, D.R.A. & Haworth, P.F. (in press). Modelling the effects of persecution on the population dynamics of golden eagles *Aquila chrysaetos* in Scotland. *Biological Conservation*.

26. Modelling the Impact of Land Use Change on Golden Eagles (*Aquila chrysaetos*)

Alan Fielding, D. Phil Whitfield, David R.A. McLeod,
Mike J. McGrady & Paul F. Haworth

Summary

1.   The distribution and productivity of golden eagles *Aquila chrysaetos* in Scotland is thought to be closely related to current and historical land uses.

2.   Ecological models are one of the tools which land managers can use to assess the potential impacts of land use changes on golden eagles over a range of spatial and temporal scales.

3.   Two existing Geographical Information Systems (GIS)-based models, the RIN and the PAT, are described. The PAT model was derived from the RIN model by incorporating the eagles' apparent preference for certain topographic features and their avoidance of other features such as closed canopy forests and human habitation. Possible extensions to the PAT model are suggested, including the incorporation of prey maps, movement costs and predicting the consequences of climate change.

4.   Particular attention is paid to the importance of dealing with the regional variation between golden eagle ranges. One such example is the use of classification and regression trees (C&RT) to highlight the different factors which may influence range productivity.

26.1 Introduction

Golden eagles *Aquila chrysaetos* were once much more widespread and common throughout Britain and Ireland. Their population declined to a historical minimum prior to the 1940s (Watson, 1997), but since the 1950s there has been a recovery to an apparently stable population of approximately 420 pairs (Green, 1996). This recovery has coincided with considerable environmental change including detrimental factors such as the spread of commercial conifer forests and reductions in live prey, including red grouse *Lagopus lagopus scoticus* and mountain hare *Lepus timidus*. Future variation in the numbers of large grazers, such as sheep *Ovis aries* and red deer *Cervus elaphus*, expansion of windfarms and native woodland schemes, together with climate change, are all likely to impact on golden eagles. Although the two most recent national golden eagle surveys (Dennis *et al.*, 1984; Green, 1996) suggest a relatively stable population, albeit with some regional losses and gains in range occupancy, the actual occupancy of a range may not be a reliable indicator of future population trends. Relatively few pairs appear to contribute a disproportionately large share of the national production of fledged young. For example, between 1981 and 2000, on the island of Mull, four out of 35 ranges fledged 24% of the young.

If current land uses and persecution levels remain unchanged there seems little opportunity for range expansion (Watson, 1997). If any of the extant ranges, particularly the more productive ones, are detrimentally affected the resultant decreases in eagle productivity could have important consequences for future population trends. British golden eagles are, effectively, isolated from other European populations and there is little scope for natural immigration in the event of a decline. The only exception to this is the potential for migration from Ireland if the current re-introduction programme meets its aims (O'Toole *et al.,* 2002). Unfortunately, surplus Irish birds are unlikely to become available until the middle of the 21st century. Therefore, the future of the Scottish golden eagle population is dependent on the continuing success of existing productive ranges or the management of unproductive ranges in order to increase their output.

Ecological models can support the monitoring and management of environmental change, and possibly even contribute to policy and land use decisions at local, regional and national scales. Ideally, such models would assist with the practical conservation of golden eagles, since land managers frequently have to make decisions under severe budget constraints and meet deadlines with incomplete and uncertain information (Scott *et al.,* 2002). For example, models could be used to assess the impact of a development, such as a windfarm, on a single range, or to predict the impact on landscape-level land use changes on a number of eagle ranges. Models could also be used to guide proactive interventions so as to increase local golden eagle productivity.

Any model that we develop and implement for practical conservation should be accurate, robust and cost-effective; users need to have confidence in its applicability. This confidence can only be achieved if robust accuracy measures of the model's predictions are developed (Fielding & Bell, 1997). We also need to be clear about the model's rationale. If it is to be used to achieve management objectives it must be a forecasting model rather than the more common exploratory type (O'Connor, 2002). The main problem with modelling golden eagle ranges is that, although their broad ecological requirements are quite well known (e.g. Watson, 1997; McGrady, 1997; Watson *et al.,* Chapter 10), the details needed to set parameters for a model are rather sketchy. For instance, there is evidence of considerable between-range variability, operating at many scales (e.g. Fielding & Haworth, 1995; Fielding *et al.,* Chapter 17; Crane & Neillist, Chapter 18). Indeed, Marzluff *et al.* (1997) have stated that if between-range variation is ignored, by focusing on population averages, then conservation strategies and biological descriptions will be inaccurate and ineffective.

A number of potentially causal links between golden eagle productivity and land use can be seen if the broad Scottish biogeographical regions are examined (Watson & Whitfield, 2002). In the absence of persecution, the greatest breeding success occurs where red grouse and mountain hare are numerous (low intensity grazing and relatively high dwarf shrub heath development). Locally, particularly within the Hebrides, high eagle productivity may be seen where seabirds or rabbits *Oryctolagus cuniculus* replace grouse and hare as the main food item. In other regions, where live prey is scarce, productivity is low. Reductions in live prey have been linked to current and historical heavy grazing by sheep and red deer, combined with repeated burning in a wet oceanic climate, which severely restricts the 'semi-natural' heaths which replaced the cleared forests (McVean & Lockie, 1969; Thompson *et al.,* Chapter 25).

In this chapter we examine existing models in order to investigate and then manage the impact of land use change on golden eagles in Scotland. We also suggest ways in which these models could be extended.

26.2 Existing eagle range models

Two models have been developed using ranging data from Argyll and, more recently, from the Island of Mull. These are somewhat technical models so the details are summarised. More detailed information can be found in McGrady *et al.* (1997) and McLeod *et al.* (2002). In both models, golden eagle home ranges are approximated as Thiessen polygons from range or territory 'centres' (mean location of recently used nest sites, weighted by use) by constructing boundaries at mid-points between range centres. If there are no eagle neighbours, a 6 km cut-off from the range centre is used as the notional range boundary (Figure 26.1). Because Thiessen boundaries may lie beyond the actual maximum ranging distances they should not be used to indicate that ranging occurs up to the polygon boundary, only that ranging is assumed not to extend beyond the boundary. A 'core area', within which 50% of eagle activity occurs, can be further delimited by a circle of 2-3 km radius (McGrady *et al.*, 1997).

This first modelling approach, termed the RIN (Research Information Note) model (McLeod *et al.*, 2002) has advantages because it can be applied in cases where the possible effect of a proposed development needs to be assessed with the minimum of information (McGrady *et al.*, 1997; McLeod *et al.*, 2002). However, the RIN model has a tendency to over-predict range limits compared with observational data (McLeod *et al.*, 2002) because estimated range and core area boundaries include unused areas. The more recently developed PAT (Predicting Aquila Territories) model takes account of local features, such as altitude and unsuitable terrain, in order to assess range use more realistically.

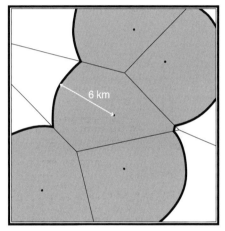

Figure 26.1. Five home ranges with limits imposed by Thiessen polygon boundaries or 6 km radial limits from nest locations.

The PAT model begins with the RIN's Thiessen polygons but also incorporates a combination of excluded (Boolean) areas and categorised variables. Because eagle eyrie use within a range can vary between years, the mean position of nest sites used in the previous ten years (see also McGrady *et al.*, 1997; Kochert *et al.*, 1999; McLeod *et al.*, 2002) is used as the range centre. If these data are unavailable an unweighted mean of the alternative nest sites can be used. A preliminary examination of ranging observations suggested that eagle activity tends to be centred around nest sites.

26.3 Modelling eagle ranges

26.3.1 Data sources and exclusion areas

Neighbouring occupied golden eagle ranges, human-made features (roads, settlements), water bodies (including the sea) and closed canopy commercial forests are used as Boolean (sharp-boundary exclusion) factors. Distances to the range centres and terrain features (ridges, cliff edges) are treated as categorised variables. The principal source of terrain data is the Ordnance Survey's (OS) 1:50,000 raster digital elevation model. During model development the forestry data came from the Forestry Commission and field surveys

(Whitfield *et al.* (2001) provide details). Land cover data were generated from the Land Cover of Scotland 1988 (LCS88) (Macaulay Land Use Research Institute, 1993). Road data came from the OS, and human settlement information was created by enhancing OS data, and spatially correcting them to a 1:50,000 reference data set.

Golden eagles are sensitive to human disturbance and, depending on the level of human activity, tend to avoid areas such as settlements and roads (Anderson *et al.,* 1990; Watson & Dennis, 1992; McGrady, 1997; McGrady *et al.,* 1997, Chapter 27; Watson, 1997; Petty, 1998). In the absence of specific information on disturbance distances, buffer zones around human settlements, within which eagles are assumed not to range, are created as follows: single building, 250 m; cluster of buildings, 400 m; village, 600 m; and town, 800 m. These distances are based on limited observations of ranging behaviour within the study areas and experience of golden eagles elsewhere in Scotland. Roads are more complex to buffer since, in the Scottish Highlands, there is unlikely to be a strong link between traffic volume and road category. In addition, it is the road visibility, rather than the presence or proximity of the road *per se*, that may impact on eagle ranging. However, as a simplistic representation, 300 m buffer distances were introduced for category A and B roads.

Water bodies and the sea are treated as exclusion areas because they provide few air currents that golden eagles can exploit, and they provide few prey sources (Watson, 1997). Water bodies (not including rivers and streams) were derived from LCS88. The sea is excluded by clipping at the coastline using an OS data source. Although it may be possible to use vegetation classes as surrogates for prey availability (see Appendix 26.1) they were not incorporated in the PAT model. However, forestry and woodland are modelled as exclusion factors because there is evidence from several areas that golden eagles avoid or overfly large areas of woodland (McGrady *et al.,* 1997, Chapter 27) and do not feed appreciably on prey typical of tree plantations (e.g. Marquiss *et al.,* 1985). The PAT model assumes that golden eagles avoid commercial forestry (or other closed canopy woodland) once trees reach an age at which eagles are unable to access the open ground between trees (Watson *et al.,* 1987, 1992; McGrady *et al.,* 1997, 2000; Whitfield *et al.,* 2001). The model assumes that closure occurs when forests are 12 years and older (see Whitfield *et al.,* 2001). Non-commercial woodlands are treated as permanent and either modelled as closed or open, subject to field survey.

26.3.2 *Further adjustments to models*
All available observations of range use, collected year-round, were used in order to derive the PAT rule-base for the categorical variables. It was apparent from these observations, and earlier modelling (McGrady *et al.,* 1997; Marzluff *et al.,* 1997; McLeod *et al.,* 2002), that eagles tended to use central parts of their home range most frequently, and that this feature should be incorporated into the PAT model. The amount of land available within consecutive 500 m wide annuli from the range centres was estimated for each range (up to the Thiessen range boundary) and summed for each distance class across all ranges. Ranging data were aggregated for all ranges, plotted for Euclidean distance to the range centre, and assigned to the appropriate 500 m annulus. The numbers of ranging points observed within annuli (or distance classes) were converted to density values per annulus. The density of ranging observations underwent a sigmoidal decay with increasing distance away from the centre.

The relationship between ranging observation density and distance to centre is too complex to model within the current PAT model, so a simpler representation has been developed that involves plotting ranging observations per annulus as percentages of all observations (rather than as density values). The percentage count method revealed considerable variation between ranges, but combining all data regionally produced a relationship that was linear and easier to model (Figure 26.2). A higher concentration of ranging activity close to the range centre was apparent on Mull, and ranging activity varied less within regions than between regions. From the relationship between percentage ranging observations and distance ranged, it follows that if the maximum ranging distance (the x intercept in Figure 26.2) can be estimated for a range then the slope can be predicted since the area below the slope should total 100%. Hence, numerous factors were explored as potential estimators of maximum ranging distance.

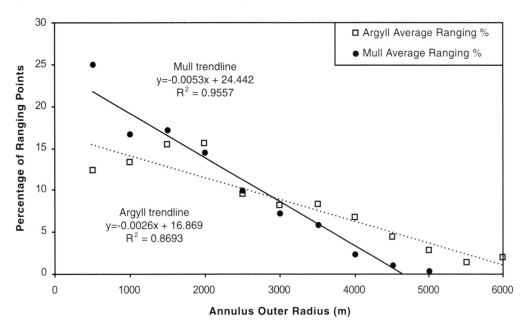

Figure 26.2. The density of ranging observations per km², per 500 m annulus, averaged for each of Argyll and Mull study areas. Ranging observation counts were converted to percentages of totals.

The peripheral area of a home range, where maximum ranging distances are recorded, had the least empirical data (a general finding: see Seaman *et al.*, 1999) and this may lead to errors in the measurement of home range area and maximum ranging distance. Most studies attempt to overcome this by reporting home range area as ≤95% estimates. Consequently, in the search for an estimator of maximum ranging distance, maximum values for each study home range were calculated by linear extrapolations from the more reliable 90% values. The best estimator for maximum ranging distance in a range was the range's Thiessen polygon area, clipped at 6 km in the absence of neighbours or other exclusions (Figure 26.1). Logically this reflects the notion that maximum ranging distance and range area are both proximately influenced by neighbouring ranges and any constraints caused by coastlines or other exclusion factors. In the relationship between ranging distance and percentage of ranging points, therefore, the maximum ranging distance is estimated from the Thiessen polygon's area. This in turn allows an estimation of the slope of the relationship, and hence the derivation of the percentage of range use points per distance annulus from the range centre.

In a species such as the golden eagle, adapted for soaring flight (McGrady, 1997; Watson, 1997), it is likely that terrain features affect range use. For example, in the cool Scottish climate thermal air currents are rare but wind deflected upwards off terrain features is probably an important aid for flight. In keeping with this argument, Chalmers (1997) found a strong relationship between eagle activity and ridge features, which is consistent with the use of deflected wind currents on slopes. Jiménez & Jaksić (1993) observed a similar relationship between topographic features, likely to favour updrafts, and the movement of Harris' hawk *Parabuteo unicinctus* in Central Chile. This may be a widespread feature of many raptors' ranging behaviour (Strickland *et al.*, 2000).

In order to incorporate terrain features into the PAT model an automated recognition method was developed and applied to every pixel within a radius set by the maximum ranging distance. In a raster digital terrain model each pixel has an elevation value that can be compared with its neighbours to determine which type of terrain feature it represents. For example, if a pixel's neighbours all have lower elevations it is a candidate 'peak' pixel. Ridges and plateau/cliff edges, are recognized by comparing a source pixel's elevation with those of five neighbouring pixels along two opposing (180°) directions or radial arms. This comparison is repeated at three further 45° orientations to give a total of four orientations and four pairs of opposing radial arms (NE-SW, N-S, SE-NW, E-W). A rule base or formulae approach is used to compare a measure of elevation between each opposing radial arm and the source pixel, giving a measure of convexity in elevation about the source pixel. Cliff and plateau edges have a convex relative angle (<168°) about the source pixel. 'Cliff' pixels are identified by first deriving the mean elevation along each opposing radial arm, and using this to generate a relative angle (about the source pixel) between radial arms. If the relative angle is less than the threshold (168°) the source is a cliff or plateau edge i.e. a 'convex feature'. Ridges are a special form of convex feature where, in addition to a convex relative angle (<168°) about the source, the pixels of any one pair of opposing radial arms must all be lower than the source pixel. Experimentation showed that 'ridge pixels' were best identified using a method where the relative angle was derived from mean slope along each radial arm (rather than a raw difference in elevation). Relative angle is determined by measuring and comparing slope for each opposing radial, which in turn are derived from the source elevation and mean elevation of the radial arms. Each source pixel is a ridge if, in any one of its opposing radials, the elevation angle relative to the source pixel is less than 168°. More complex scenarios, where source pixels have multiple relationships with neighbours, were not modelled.

Observed ranging locations were more frequently within 200 m of a terrain feature (i.e. ridge or convex feature) than would be expected if they were evenly distributed within a 1,200 m buffer from terrain features (this buffer was chosen as almost every point in a home range was within 1,200 m of a terrain feature). Golden eagles were three times more likely to be seen close to ridge or convex feature pixels than expected if observations were randomly distributed. The distribution of observed ranging points relative to terrain features was used within the model for assigning predicted use relative to terrain features.

Areas outside the Thiessen polygon and internal exclusion areas (coastline, forestry, water, and road and settlement buffers) were assigned a usage value of zero. It is more difficult to assign usage values when categorised variables (distance to range centre, and distance to terrain feature) are considered. In order to implement the rule-base for categorised variables, each range is divided into 500 m zones from the range centre, and independent 100 m buffer intervals from terrain features. The rule-base assumes that range use decreases linearly away from the range centre (to a maximum distance defined by Thiessen polygon size). Within each 500 m annulus, range use is distributed between the 100 m terrain buffer zones according to the observed distributions relative to terrain features (i.e. use is geographically biased towards certain terrain features). This method generates an idealised representation of predicted range use, but does not account for perturbation of ranging in response to exclusion areas (water, closed forestry, road buffers, settlement buffers). Hence, a subjective rule base is used to generate plasticity in predicted ranging, by partitioning the range use predictions between the 500 m annuli, depending on the geographic area of each annulus and the location of the excluded area. The foundation of this plasticity is that any reduction in the area within an annulus, caused by an exclusion area, results in a proportional over-prediction of range use, and so this excess of predicted range use is redistributed within and between annuli.

The output of the PAT model is a raster representation of predicted range use: each 50 m x 50 m pixel having a predicted 'use value' constrained so that they sum to 100 for each range. Pixels with higher use values are located near the range centre and around terrain features, and pixels with the lowest values are further away from the centre and terrain features (Figure 26.3). A 'use surface' can be generated if pixels, predicted as being used, are ordered in decreasing use value and then sequentially summed. Isolines can then be fitted to this surface, encompassing notional percentages of predicted ranging. For example, the 80% isoline encompasses the 80% highest use value pixels, and represents the geographic area required to encompass 80% of a pair's predicted ranging.

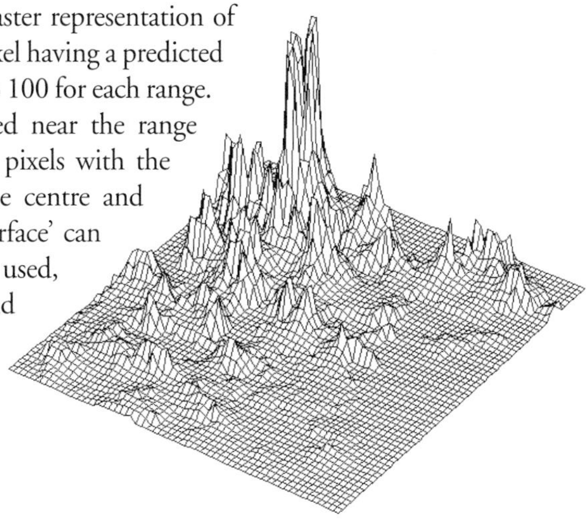

Figure 26.3. Sample 3-D PAT output. The height of the surface indicates its relative use. The range centre is close to the tallest peak.

The PAT model was evaluated by comparing predicted 'use surfaces' with observed range usage for six Argyll and five Mull ranges. There was a good fit between observed and predicted usage and the PAT model consistently captured the same percentage of actual range usage observations in a smaller area than the RIN model, confirming that it was a more 'efficient' model.

26.4 Future developments of eagle ranging models

Although the RIN and PAT models represent considerable advances over previous subjective range-use models there is still much potential for refinement. For example, with the exception of the PAT model's exclusion of closed canopy forest, existing models have limited abilities to predict the effects of environmental change. Some changes may be relatively simple to incorporate into future models, e.g. habitat changes resulting from conifer and Woodland Grant Scheme (WGS) schemes, and construction schemes such as road building and reservoir construction. Other changes may be more difficult, e.g. the responses of prey to changes in grazing pressure or climate change. More details are given in the Appendix 26.1.

The models have the difficult task of mapping an eagle's perception of its environment (Boone & Krohn, 2002). In order to be successful the model must incorporate information about prey distributions and factors that increase the energetic costs of an eagle's movements across its range. Although detailed prey maps will be rarely available, we could consider using habitat maps as surrogate prey maps. For example, Marzluff *et al.* (1997) used habitat variables as surrogates for jack rabbit *Lepus californicus* density, and Gorman & Reynolds (1993) showed how vole *Microtus arvalis orcadensis* density varied with habitat on Orkney. However, it may be necessary to weight such maps to take account of the influence that patch size has on the creation of 'dead ground' that could facilitate hunting. There is also evidence from this study, and the work of Jiménez & Jaksić (1993), that some birds of prey avoid flatter areas and exploit the extra lift provided by the interaction between prevailing winds or thermal updrafts and certain topographic features. Therefore, the model may need to incorporate energetic, rather than Euclidean, distances between the nest and prey sources (Figure 26.4). Thus, although path c in Figure 26.4 is the longest, it is the least costly for the bird. It is unclear how energetic costs could be objectively determined, although it may be possible to use the PAT model's pixel usage values to construct least-cost routes across a range.

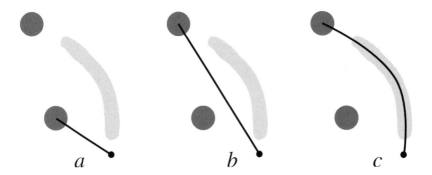

Figure 26.4. Hypothetical flight paths and terrain features from a nest site to prey 'hotspots'. Large shaded circles represent prey 'hot-spots' and the curved light grey region is a ridge. Distances from the nest (small shaded circle) for flight paths a, b and c are 10, 20 and 25 respectively. However, the notional energetic costs for the same paths are 20, 40 and 15.

Significant land use change within a range will probably affect prey abundance and availability, for example reductions in grazing by sheep, cattle or deer may reduce rabbit density (Cowan, 1991). Unfortunately we have little information on the plasticity of an eagle's responses to dietary change. For example, what are the time scales and consequences of such changes (see, for example, Fernandez, 1993; Kochert *et al.*, 1999; Steenhof & Kochert, 1988)? Although the general habitat preferences of most potential prey are relatively well known we rarely have sufficiently precise quantitative assessments of prey abundance over a range of habitat types.

Finally, if a model is to be used to guide range enhancement then information about the relationships between range characteristics and range productivity is needed. Good historical range productivity data are important here because land use change tends to occur gradually and it is rarely possible to establish clear pre- and post-change boundaries, particularly when other factors such as weather (Watson *et al.*, Chapter 10) may influence productivity.

Acknowledgements

We are grateful to Mike Madders, Richard Evans, Fiona Harmer and Sean Morris for collecting much of the data on eagle productivity, and two referees for comments on the manuscript. The development of the RIN model was funded by the Royal Society for the Protection of Birds and the Forestry Commission. Scottish Natural Heritage funded development of the PAT model. The collection of the Mull ranging data was part-funded by EarthWatch International. Dom Morgan assisted in the collection of the Mull ranging data. Alan Fielding was in receipt of a Leverhulme Fellowship whilst writing the manuscript.

References

Anderson, D.E., Rongstad, O.J. & Mytton, W.R. (1990). Home-range changes in raptors exposed to increasing human activity levels in southeastern Colorado. *Wildlife Society Bulletin*, **18**, 134-142.

Averis, A.B.G. & Averis, A.M. (1995). The vegetation of South and East Mull - Volume 1. Unpublished report. Scottish Natural Heritage, Perth.

Bell, J.F. (2000). Tree-based methods. In *Ecological Applications of Machine Learning Methods*, ed. by A. Fielding. Kluwer Academic, Boston, MA. pp. 89-106.

Boone, R.B. & Krohn, W.B. (2002). Modeling tools and accuracy assessment B: introductory comments. In *Predicting Plant and Animal Occurrences: Issues of Scale and Accuracy*, ed. by J.M. Scott, P.J. Heglund, M. Morrison, J.B. Haufler, M.G. Raphael, W.B. Wall & F. Samson. Island Press, Covello CA. pp. 265-270.

Chalmers, S. (1997). Detection and characterisation of terrain features for incorporation in golden eagle (*Aquila chrysaetos*) territory models. M.Sc. thesis. University of Edinburgh, Edinburgh.

Cowan, D.P. (1991). Rabbit, *Oryctolagus cuniculus*. In *The Handbook of British Mammals, Third Edition*, ed. by G.B. Corbet & S. Harris. Blackwell Scientific Publications, Oxford. pp. 146-154.

Dennis, R.H., Ellis, P.M., Broad, R.A. & Langslow, D.R. (1984). The status of the golden eagle in Britain. *British Birds*, **77**, 592-607.

Fernandez, C. (1993). Effect of the viral haemorrhagic pneumonia of the wild rabbit on the diet and breeding success of the golden eagle *Aquila chrysaetos*. *Rev. Ecologie (Terre Vie)*, **48**, 323-329.

Fielding, A.H. (2002). What are the appropriate characteristics of an accuracy measure? In *Predicting Plant and Animal Occurrences: Issues of Scale and Accuracy*, ed. by J.M. Scott, P.J. Heglund, M. Morrison, J.B. Haufler, M.G. Raphael, W.B. Wall & F. Samson. Island Press, Covello CA. pp. 271-280.

Fielding, A.H. & Bell, J.F. (1997). A review of methods for the assessment of prediction errors in conservation presence/absence models. *Environmental Conservation*, **24**, 38-49.

Fielding, A.H. & Haworth, P.F. (1995). Testing the generality of bird-habitat models. *Conservation Biology*, **9**, 1466-1481.

Gargett, V. (1990). *The Black Eagle.* Acorn Books, Johannesburg.

Gorman, M.L. & Reynolds, P. (1993). The impact of land use change on voles and raptors. *Mammal Review*, **23**, 121-126.

Green, R.E. (1996). The status of the golden eagle in Britain in 1992. *Bird Study*, **43**, 20-27.

Huston, M.A. (2002). Introductory essay: critical issues for improving predictions. In *Predicting Plant and Animal Occurrences: Issues of Scale and Accuracy*, ed. by J.M. Scott, P.J. Heglund, M. Morrison, J.B. Haufler, M.G. Raphael, W.B. Wall & F. Samson. Island Press, Covello CA. pp. 7-21.

Jiménez, J.E. & Jaksić, F.M. (1993). Observations on the comparative behavioural ecology of Harris hawk in Central Chile. *Journal of Raptor Research*, **27**, 143-148.

Kochert,. M.N., Steenhof, K., Carpenter, L.B. & Marzluff, J.M. (1999). Effects of fire on golden eagle territory occupancy and reproductive success. *Journal of Wildlife Management*, **63**, 773-780.

McGrady, M.J. (1997). *Aquila chrysaetos* Golden Eagle. *Birds of the Western Palearctic Update*, **1**, 99-114.

McGrady, M.J., McLeod, D.R., Petty, S.J., Grant, J.R. & Bainbridge, I.P. (1997). *Golden Eagles and Forestry.* Forestry Commission Research Information Note. Forestry Commission, Roslin.

McLeod, D.R.A., Fielding, A.H., Haworth, P.F., Whitfield, D.P., McGrady, M.J. (2002). Predicting home range use by golden eagles *Aquila chrysaetos* in western Scotland. *Journal of Avian Science*, **2**,183-198.

McLeod, D., Whitfield, D.P. & McGrady, M.J. (2002). Improving prediction of golden eagle (*Aquila chrysaetos*) ranging in western Scotland, using GIS and terrain modelling. *Journal of Raptor Research*, **36 (1 Supplement)**, 70-77.

McVean, D.N. & Lockie, J.D. (1969). *Ecology and Land Use in Upland Scotland.* Edinburgh University Press, Edinburgh.

Marquiss, M., Ratcliffe, D.A. & Roxburgh, R. (1985). The numbers, breeding success and diet of Golden Eagles in southern Scotland in relation to changes in land use. *Biological Conservation*, **33**, 1-17.

Marzluff, J.M., Knick, S.T., Vekasy, M.S., Scheuck, L.S. & Zarriello, T.J. (1997). Spatial use and habitat selection of golden eagles in southwestern Idaho. *Auk*, **114**, 673-687.

Macaulay Land Use Research Institute (1993). *Land Cover of Scotland 1988. Final Report.* Macaulay Land Use Research Institute, Aberdeen.

O'Connor, R. J. (2002). The conceptual basis of species distribution modeling: time for a paradigm shift. In *Predicting Plant and Animal Occurrences: Issues of Scale and Accuracy*, ed. by J.M. Scott, P.J. Heglund, M. Morrison, J.B. Haufler, M.G. Raphael, W.B. Wall & F. Samson. Island Press, Covello CA. pp. 25-34.

O'Toole, L., Fielding, A.H. & Haworth, P.F. (2002). Re-introduction of the Golden Eagle *Aquila chrysaetos* into the Republic of Ireland. *Biological Conservation*, **103**, 303-312.

Petty, S.J. (1998). *Ecology and Conservation of Raptors in Forests. Forestry Commission Bulletin 118.* The Stationery Office, London.

Scott, M.J., Heglund, P.J., Morrison, M.J., Haufler, J.B., Raphael, M.G., Wall, W.B. & Simpson, F. (2002). Introduction. In *Predicting Plant and Animal Occurrences: Issues of Scale and Accuracy*, ed. by J.M. Scott, P.J. Heglund, M. Morrison, J.B. Haufler, M.G. Raphael, W.B. Wall & F. Samson. Island Press, Covello CA. pp. 1-5.

Seaman, D.E., Millspaugh, J.L., Kernohan, B.J., Brundige, G.C., Raedeke, K.J. & Gitzen, R.A. (1999). Effects of sample size on kernal home range estimates. *Journal of Wildlife Management*, **63**, 739-747.

Steenhof, K. & Kochert, M.N. (1988). Dietary responses of three raptor species to changing prey densities in a natural environment. *Journal of Animal Ecology*, **57**, 37-48.

Strickland, M.D., Young, D.P., Johnson, G.D., Derby, C.E., Erickson, W.P. & Kern, J.W. (2000). Wildlife monitoring studies for the Sea West Power Development, Carbon County, Wyoming. In *Proceedings* of the National Avian-Wind Power Planning Meeting III, San Diego, CA, May 1998. NWCC c/o RESOLVE Inc., Washington, DC and LGL Ltd., King City, Ontario. pp. 55-63.

Watson, J. (1997). *The Golden Eagle*. T. & A.D. Poyser, London.

Watson, J. & Dennis, R.H. (1992). Nest site selection by golden eagles *Aquila chrysaetos* in Scotland. *British Birds*, **85**, 469-481.

Watson, J., Langslow, D.R. & Rae, S.R. (1987). *The impact of land-use changes on golden eagles in the Scottish Highlands. CSD Report No. 720*. Nature Conservancy Council, Peterborough.

Watson, J., Rae, S.R. & Stillman, R. (1992). Nesting density and breeding success of golden eagles in relation to food supply in Scotland. *Journal of Animal Ecology*, **61**, 543-550.

Watson, J. & Whitfield, P. (2002). A conservation framework for the golden eagle *Aquila chrysaetos* in Scotland. *Journal of Raptor Research*, **36**, (1 Supplement), 41-49.

Whitfield, D.P., Evans, R.J., Broad, R.A., Fielding, A.H., Haworth, P.F. & McLeod, D.R.A. (2002). Is there competition between the re-introduced white-tailed eagle and the golden eagle in western Scotland? *Scottish Birds*, **23**, 36-45.

Whitfield, D.P., McLeod, D.R.A., Fielding, A.H., Broad, R.A., Evans, R.J. & Haworth, P.F. (2001). The effects of forestry on golden eagles on the island of Mull, western Scotland. *Journal of Applied Ecology*, **38**, 1208-1220.

Appendix 26.1

The model building process can be broken down into a number of simplified stages:-

Step 1 Define the maximum ranging distance (*r*) from observations. The RIN and PAT models use 6 km. This could be further refined by imposing RIN or PAT range limits (Figure 26.1).

Step 2 Exclude uncontentious habitats (shaded) that are unlikely to be used by golden eagles, e.g. lakes, open sea, urban development. If the different habitat types, within the notional range, are quantified relationships between range characteristics and range productivity could be investigated.

Step 3 Assuming an unchanging habitat, 'preferred' (dark grey), and 'avoided' (light grey) regions could be identified if sufficient and appropriate ranging and habitat data are available.

Step 4 Finally, land use change could be simulated and used to predict the impact on prey abundance and availability. However, this requires reliable information on the relationships between habitat, grazing and prey. Note, that except for quarrying and major construction schemes, topography is immune to change over the appropriate time scale for such models.

Potential approaches to steps 2 and 3 are illustrated using examples based on the golden eagles and habitat of the island of Mull.

Productivity data (1981-2000) and PAT range predictions were available for 32 ranges on Mull. Using the PAT range limits, habitat data (area in hectares) were extracted from the LCS88 dataset (Macaulay Land Use Research Institute, 1993) for each range and pooled into 17 habitat classes. Although a correlation or regression approach might appear to be the best way of looking for productivity-habitat relationships, it has many problems. In the absence of external interference it seems likely that productivity will be proportional to the food supply. However, total prey is unlikely to be correlated with a single habitat type that acts as a reliable surrogate variable across all ranges. For example, the habitat needed to support ptarmigan *Lagopus mutus* or mountain hare is quite different from that needed by seabirds or rabbits. This is less likely to be a problem if the predator is more specialised, as illustrated by the work on black eagles *Aquila verreauxii* (Gargett, 1990) where a good relationship has been found between range size and a surrogate for prey availability (rock outcrops for hyrax (Procaviidae)). In addition, we need to be very cautious about making predictions on the effects of management options if the model is based on some analysis of a correlation matrix. This is because the management process itself is likely to disrupt the correlation structure that is the model's basis (O'Connor, 2002). Huston (2002) argued that we should concentrate on an analysis of constraints rather than correlates. This allows the constraints to be ranked and management can then concentrate on the most severe local constraint operating for a particular range, thus providing the flexibility needed to overcome the between-range heterogeneity highlighted by Marzluff *et al.* (1997). One way of undertaking this type of analysis is via a classification and regression tree analysis (Bell, 2000). The fledging rates of the 32 Mull ranges were subjected to a classification and regression tree analysis (SPSS Answer Tree, version 2.0.1) using pooled LCS88 habitat classes as predictors. The results (Figure A26.1) are presented to illustrate the methodology and should be treated with caution since the sample size is rather small.

The dichotomies identified by the regression tree (Figure A26.1) highlight the potential failure of management options based on a single management prescription since there are several 'routes' to good productivity. The first split separates a small unproductive group with a range size greater than 27 km² from the more productive group with smaller ranges. Larger ranges tend to occur where there are few neighbours and are suggestive of either a shortage of nesting sites or prey. The most productive ranges are between 11 and 28 km² in size and are not dominated by heath. If the amount of scrub exceeds approximately 2 km² this is also associated with a reduction in productivity.

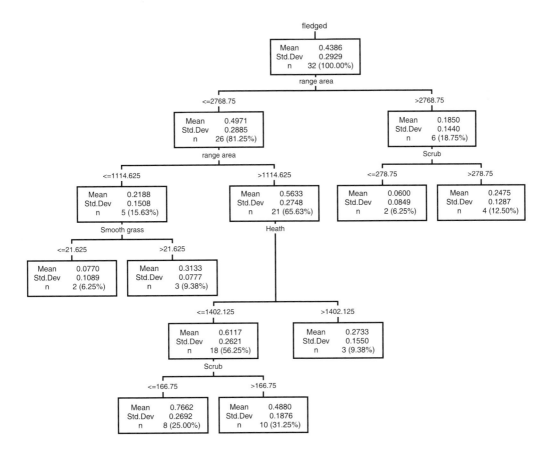

Figure A26.1. Decision tree for fledging rate (given as the mean in the boxes) of 32 golden eagle ranges on Mull. Predictor variables are habitat areas (ha). The C&RT analysis used five-fold cross-validation and post-pruning to produce a more parsimonious tree.

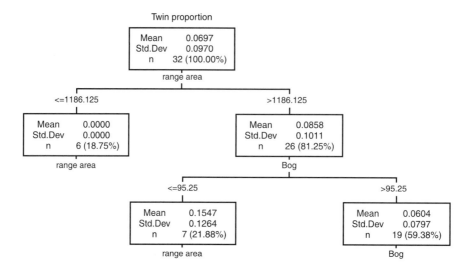

Figure A26.2. Decision tree for the proportion of successful breeding attempts that fledged twins of 32 golden eagle ranges on Mull. Predictor variables are habitat areas (ha).

A similar analysis (Figure A26.2) was undertaken using the proportion of successful nests with twins, a potentially important contributor to overall productivity. This again highlighted the small ranges (<11.9 km²) as the least successful, none of these had twins between 1981 and 2000. The remaining 26 ranges had twins at least once during the survey period. They were more likely to have twins if the area of bog was less than 1 km².

The next step in the modelling process is concerned with identifying habitats or regions that are used more or less frequently than expected from their areas. Presumably, over-used regions are important for the eagle. On Mull, observations of golden eagle location and behaviour were obtained as part of a larger long-term study of the Ross of Mull raptor and scavenging bird assemblage (Fielding & Haworth, 1995). In an area encompassing five ranges, 1,895 records of eagles were gathered opportunistically by two experienced field workers supported by 200 volunteers between August 1994 and December 1998 inclusive. Random sampling was not possible because of access and safety constraints. Sampling effort was greatest, and approximately constant, between July and October. Observations were collected using binoculars and spotting telescopes and recorded on 1:25,000 maps. Records of range holding adults (both sexes) were used in the subsequent analysis (*n* = 1,382), pooled across ranges and months. Data from all raptor and scavenging bird sightings (*n* = 19,291 observations on 14 species) were employed to identify regions that were used by eagles less or more than expected. The 1,382 observations of adult golden eagles represented an overall proportion of 7.2% of all sightings of raptors and scavengers. A moving circular window (250 m radius, 50 m centre) was applied to the whole of the Ross of Mull. In each buffer the number of golden eagle sightings, as a proportion of all raptor sightings within the buffer, was calculated. Ninety-five per cent confidence intervals for the proportion of golden eagle sightings were calculated for each buffer and compared to the overall proportion of golden eagle sightings. If the lower confidence limit was greater than 0.072 this was taken to indicate excess usage, while an upper confidence limit of less than 0.072 was indicative of under-use. A small number of buffers had no sightings, either because no raptors had been seen or the location was rarely visited. In all other locations usage did not differ from the expected proportion. This method does not depend on correct allocation of golden eagle sightings to ranges. It also deals with inequalities in sampling effort because rarely visited locations will have wide confidence intervals. We could be confident about under-used locations because buffers typically had many observations from other species (e.g. 9,284 buzzard *Buteo buteo*, 2,807 kestrel *Falco tinnunculus* and 3,543 raven *Corvus corax* sightings). The output from these analyses was a 'preference' map in which each 50 m pixel was assigned to one of four possible values: over-used, under-used, proportional (observed = expected) use, no data. There is a good fit between the over-used locations on the Ross of Mull and the pooled ranges predicted by the PAT model for the five occupied ranges, the only exception is a region apparently used by surplus, non-breeding adults that was not included in the PAT predictions. Two habitat data sets were available for the Ross of Mull: the LCS88 data (Macaulay Land Use Research Institute, 1993) and a digitized version of a recent National Vegetation Classification (NVC) survey (Averis & Averis, 1995). The areas (ha) of 17 LCS88 and 18 NVC classes were extracted for under- and over-used locations on the Ross of Mull. Only 14 NVC classes were used because the other four classes had very small areas.

The LCS88 (Table A26.1) and NVC (Table A26.2) habitat classes that are disproportionately present in both over- and under-used regions are generally consistent with existing ecological knowledge about golden eagles. For example, there is more bog and

Table A26.1. Proportional composition of over- and under-used pooled LCS88 classes by golden eagles on the Ross of Mull (1994-1998). The overall proportions include regions used in proportion to their availability or for which there was no bird data (42.5 km²). In the calculation of the log ratio (over/under), zero values for over-use were replaced by 0.0001. Values close to 0 indicate equal proportions. Preference indices were calculated as $\log(U_i+1)/A_i$, where U_i is over- or under-used proportion and A_i is the overall proportion. Preference index values >0.3 are said to indicate over-representation of a habitat class, while values <0.3 are indicative of under-representation.

Pooled LCS88 class	Proportions			Log ratio (over/under)	Preference indices	
	Under-used	Over-used	All		Under-used	Over-used
Cliffs (montane)	0.000	0.031	0.008	2.314	0.008	1.639
Dry heath	0.000	0.024	0.007	2.809	0.002	1.538
Montane	0.002	0.055	0.015	1.500	0.050	1.528
Smooth grass	0.083	0.171	0.098	0.314	0.354	0.701
Bog	0.185	0.178	0.169	-0.015	0.436	0.422
Heathland	0.322	0.410	0.354	0.105	0.342	0.421
Pre-thicket forest	0.071	0.068	0.110	-0.018	0.271	0.261
Broadleaf woodland	0.034	0.011	0.022	-0.489	0.666	0.218
Smooth grass/rush	0.092	0.030	0.072	-0.484	0.531	0.179
Improved pasture	0.109	0.016	0.064	-0.836	0.707	0.108
Bracken	0.041	0.004	0.028	-0.997	0.624	0.064
Dune	0.006	0.000	0.004	-1.141	0.703	0.051
Water	0.002	0.000	0.002	-1.184	0.322	0.000
Productive forest	0.036	0.000	0.040	-2.560	0.391	0.000
Wet heath	0.017	0.000	0.008	-2.227	0.903	0.000
Saltmarsh	0.001	0.000	0.000	-0.718	0.639	0.000

Table A26.2. Proportional composition of over- and under-used pooled NVC classes by golden eagles on the Ross of Mull (1994-1998). Other details are as for Table A26.1.

Pooled NVC class	Proportions			*Log ratio*	Preference indices	
	Under-used	*Over-used*	*All*	*(over/under)*	*Under-used*	*Over-used*
Coastal grassland	0.014	0.059	0.025	0.630	0.242	1.011
Heathland	0.051	0.097	0.062	0.279	0.348	0.649
Mire	0.533	0.656	0.562	0.090	0.330	0.390
Water	0.003	0.002	0.003	-0.077	0.451	0.378
Young plantation	0.053	0.034	0.048	-0.196	0.463	0.298
Conifer plantation	0.114	0.065	0.102	-0.242	0.458	0.268
Bracken	0.066	0.032	0.058	-0.314	0.480	0.236
Deciduous woodland	0.036	0.013	0.031	-0.436	0.503	0.186
Agrostis-Festuca	0.092	0.033	0.078	-0.442	0.490	0.182
Managed grassland	0.030	0.007	0.025	-0.613	0.522	0.129
Beach	0.007	0.001	0.005	-1.047	0.553	0.050
Cliff	0.000	0.000	0.000	-0.473	0.572	0.000
Saltmarsh	0.001	0.000	0.000	-0.750	0.570	0.000
Deciduous plantation	0.000	0.000	0.000	-0.090	0.570	0.000

improved pasture than expected in the under-used regions and over-used regions are characterized by more montane cliffs, dry heath and montane habitat than expected from their availabilities. Unfortunately, few of these highlighted habitats are amenable to simple management. However, the greater refinement of the NVC habitat classes, combined with the advantages arising from field surveys, produces a clearer picture of over- and under-used habitats. For example, the large value for coastal grassland in over-used regions is a consequence of its association with rabbit colonies. This exploratory analysis suggests that the incorporation of habitat preference information into a model may be worth pursuing and that, where the data are available, NVC classes should be used.

It seems inevitable that all of Scotland's golden eagle ranges will be affected by climate changes. The environmental consequences of a changing climate for a particular range will depend on its location (in particular its oceanicity), altitude (to take account of altitudinal decline in temperature), vegetation (some vegetation types will be more susceptible than others) and existing land uses. It may be possible, albeit difficult, to construct models that attempt to predict how prey would respond to climatically induced vegetation changes.

The preliminary results presented here are encouraging since they suggest that further model development may be possible. In particular, the incorporation of habitat information may be useful because of its link to potential eagle productivity. However, it is important to recognise the trade-off between the additional expenditure needed to produce the improvements derived from gathering more data and extending the PAT model, i.e. we need to consider the balance between model improvement and the amount of additional accuracy. There will be an upper limit to any model's achievable accuracy and, if this is approached asymptotically, the later improvements require a disproportionate expenditure (Figure A26.3). Although most ecologists feel uncomfortable about including economic considerations in their models (Fielding, 2002) it would be better if objective constraints were pre-determined, rather than arising indirectly from budget allocations. Therefore, determining the acceptable model accuracy is a decision that managers must take after balancing budgetary constraints with the requirements of this and other competing demands for expenditure.

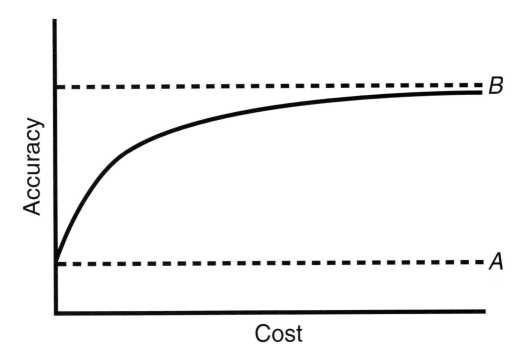

Figure A26.3. Hypothetical relationship between model accuracy and the cost of model development. Line A is the limit achieved by 'guessing' while line B is the limit imposed by unpredictable 'noise'.

The RIN and PAT models are the first important stages in the development of land use change models for golden eagles. The end point of this potentially lengthy process should be better models that are built on a greater understanding of golden eagle ecology. We have the possibility of testing the new and existing models by looking at range use in the re-introduced Irish eagles (O'Toole *et al.*, 2002). Unlike the white-tailed eagle *Haliaeetus albicilla* re-introduction to Scotland (Whitfield *et al.*, 2002) there is no complication of potential competition for nest sites or prey. Even if the eventual conclusion is that resources would be better targeted at individual range studies rather than further model development, there will still be a need for historical range and productivity data. This is an important role for Raptor Study Group data.

27. Potential Impacts of Native Woodland Expansion on Golden Eagles (*Aquila chrysaetos*) in Scotland

Michael J. McGrady, Steve J. Petty, David R.A. McLeod,

Greg Mudge & Ian P. Bainbridge

Summary

1.   Golden eagles *Aquila chrysaetos* prefer open country, though some live in partially forested landscapes with widely spaced, old trees. Eagle densities are generally lower in woodlands than in open habitats, but productivity can be high in woods, especially when medium-sized prey are plentiful. Woodlands can extend the breeding range of golden eagles by providing nesting places in areas that lack nesting opportunities on crags.

2.   The main impact of increasing the area of native woodlands in Scotland will be to reduce the amount of food available to golden eagles. In the short to medium term, the impact on potential food biomass will be similar to that of commercial afforestation, but there may be subtle advantages in the medium to long term. The impact on the non-breeding sector of the eagle population is unknown.

3.   The Forestry Commission's Scottish Forestry Grant Scheme (SFGS) will only fund up to 20% of the area of a new native woodland as open ground. This factor alone limits the ability of the SFGS to create eagle-friendly woodlands.

4.   A revised SFGS that funds much larger areas of open ground, especially within the context of proposed forest networks, would have a far greater potential to benefit those prey species that are important for eagles and upland habitats that are threatened by over-grazing and afforestation.

27.1 Introduction

The golden eagle *Aquila chrysaetos* is an open country species, which sometimes occupies landscapes that are partially forested (deciduous and coniferous) (Watson, 1997). Such woods are characterised by old, widely spaced trees and are associated with extensive open areas. Woods can influence eagle distribution and breeding success by providing nest sites and affecting prey availability. Woodland types that are beneficial to eagles have high densities of medium-sized prey (0.5-2.0 kg body mass) (Tjernberg, 1981; Watson, 1997; Sulkava *et al.*, 1999).

Commercial forestry is an important land use in Scotland. The 'UK Forestry Standard' (Anon., 1998a) provides the framework for judging forestry proposals and managing existing forests. The Scottish Forestry Grant Scheme (SFGS) is the principal means for funding the establishment and management of new and existing woodlands (Scottish Executive and Forestry Commission, 2003); it succeeded the Woodland Grant Scheme

(WGS) in 2003. In addition, it has been proposed that native and coniferous forests in Scotland should be integrated into a Forest Habitat Network (Peterken *et al.*, 1995).

Grants currently available in the uplands are not particularly eagle-friendly. The SFGS encourages the establishment of woodland, but only allows up to 20% of the area to be managed as open habitat (Scottish Executive and Forestry Commission, 2003). On the other hand, vast areas of open upland habitats are overgrazed by red deer *Cervus elaphus* and domestic animals, the latter being encouraged by agricultural grants. Although high stocking levels of sheep *Ovis aries* and deer (mostly red deer) result in ample carrion, which in turn is linked to relatively high breeding densities of eagles, heavy grazing and burning regimes only lead to further impoverishment of a relatively fragile ecosystem (Thompson *et al.*, 1995, Chapter 25; Scotland's Moorland Forum, 2003), and appear to have an adverse effect on eagle productivity.

In this chapter we summarise the findings from a recent review on the potential impacts on golden eagles of expanding the area of native woodland in Scotland (see McGrady *et al.*, in press). The review was based on studies in Scotland and other countries to try to evaluate these impacts and provide guidance on how to create 'eagle-friendly' forests.

27.2 Food availability

Food supply has a great influence on the demography of golden eagles. Although their diet is varied, golden eagles prey mainly on the most abundant species of a profitable size (Watson, 1997). When these prey are abundant they form a high proportion of eagle diet, as with red grouse *Lagopus lagopus scoticus* in the Eastern Highlands. However, when prey are scarcer, eagle diet becomes far more varied as they switch to a range of less abundant prey species, as in the Western Highlands (Watson *et al.*, 1993). In such areas, the abundance of alternative prey species determines how well eagles breed when preferred prey are scarce.

Live prey can be divided into preferred, alternative and occasional prey. In any particular area, preferred prey are the most abundant and vulnerable medium-sized species. Eagles feed upon alternative prey when preferred prey are scarce, and occasional prey comprise a small proportion of eagle diet and are hunted opportunistically. Likely changes in the abundance of these three prey categories as a result of converting relatively large areas of open hill ground to new native woodland are summarised in Table 27.1.

The two most important mammalian species for eagles in Scotland are rabbit *Oryctolagus cuniculus* and mountain hare *Lepus timidus* (Watson, 1997). Rabbits prefer short dry grassland, particularly when it is heavily grazed by domestic stock. Some of the highest mountain hare densities in Scotland occur on heather moorland that is managed for red grouse (Watson *et al.*, 1973). Heather *Calluna vulgaris* is the main winter food of mountain hares, with grasses being more important in other seasons. Young deer (mostly roe deer *Capreolus capreolus*, but occasionally red and sika deer *Cervus nippon*) are taken as live prey. Although only available to eagles for a short period, young deer are important during the time that eagle nestlings are large, and as such are an important source of food for some pairs. Red grouse is the most important avian prey of eagles, although in some localities ptarmigan *Lagopus mutus*, crows *Corvus* spp. and seabirds are important. Carcasses of sheep and deer provide a source of food for eagles throughout the year, particularly in winter, and at other times when live prey are scarce.

Table 27.1. Subjective assessment of possible changes in abundance of the most important prey of golden eagles as a result of converting open hill ground into new native woodlands.

Species	East Highlands		West Highlands		Hebrides	
	Category[1]	change[2]	Category[1]	change[2]	Category[1]	change[2]
Rabbit	O	-	A	-	P/A[3]	-
Mountain hare	P	-	A	=	A/P	=
Red fox	O	+	O	+	O[3]	+
Roe deer kids[5]	A	+	A	+	O[3]	+
Sheep carrion	O	-	P	-	P	-
Deer carrion[6]	A	-	P	-	O	-
Seabirds	N		O	=	P/O[4]	=
Wildfowl	O	=	O	=	O	=
Red grouse	P	-	P	=	O	=
Ptarmigan	P	=	O/A	=	O[3]	=
Black grouse	O	+	O	+	N[3]	=
Pheasant	O	+	O	+	O[3]	+
Waders	N	-	O	-	O	-
Woodpigeon	N	+	O	+	N	+
Corvids	O	+	A	+	O	+

Notes

1   P = primary prey, A = alternative prey, O = occasion prey, N = not recorded or rarely recorded as prey.
    Scientific names given in text, except for pheasant *Phasianus colchicus* and woodpigeon *Columba palumbus*.
2   - decrease in abundance, + increase in abundance, = no change in abundance.
3   Absent from some Hebridean islands where golden eagles are present.
4   Primary prey only for coastal pairs.
5   Roe deer kids are more frequently killed (particularly during May/June) by golden eagles than much larger red deer calves. Roe deer numbers will increase with woodland cover.
6   Mostly red deer.

Food supply and diet are closely linked to the breeding density and success of eagles in that the highest breeding densities occur where carrion is most abundant, but the most productive pairs are in areas with the highest live prey densities (Watson *et al.*, 1987). Thus, the Western Highlands are characterised by high breeding densities, but poor breeding success, whilst in the Eastern Highlands eagle densities are lower, but breeding success is higher.

27.3 The effect of new native forestry

Today, only 4% of eagles in Scotland nest in trees, mostly in the Eastern Highlands, and these pairs are some of the most productive in the country (Green, 1996; Watson, 1997). New native woodland can extend the breeding range of eagles by providing nesting places in areas where these are lacking. However, only large, old trees (80-400 years old) with substantial branches are used, and these are usually located at the upper edge of widely spaced stands associated with more extensive open upland areas. In the Alps, golden eagles have recently established new breeding territories at lower elevations in relatively close proximity to human habitation, where forest cover is greater (Haller, 1996). An abundance of non-territorial birds and high occupancy of preferred open-habitat territories may result in the population expanding into forest areas, provided that a suitable prey base exists.

The main effect on eagles of increases in the area of native woodlands is on prey availability. Carrion biomass will decline to virtually zero due to the exclusion of sheep and the reduction in deer density that is necessary for forest establishment (i.e. approximately <5 deer km^2) (Holloway, 1967; Staines, 1995). The loss of carrion is not entirely negative because fox *Vulpes vulpes* and crow numbers are likely to decline and their contribution to the breeding failure in grouse and other eagle prey should be reduced. However, crows and foxes can be important prey for some eagle pairs (Watson, 1997). During the establishment phase, red grouse will initially outnumber black grouse *Tetrao tetrix*, but the position may be reversed once suitable vegetation recovers from overgrazing. During thicket stage, open areas within forests will be the only habitat left for grouse and hares, but by then the carrying capacity of the area will have been substantially reduced.

These effects will vary both within and between regions and will be influenced by previous land management. The greatest loss of potential food biomass will occur in the Western Highlands and Hebrides, where the loss of carrion will be almost complete, and where rabbit numbers will most probably decline. Eagles in these regions are more dependent on carrion than in the Eastern Highlands. At the landscape scale, no new eagle prey species will be attracted to new native woodland, instead it will be the relative abundance of existing foods that changes. The impact of woodland establishment on red grouse, one of the most important prey species, is likely to vary geographically. In the East Highlands, grouse numbers are likely to decrease after woodland establishment on grouse moors. In the Western Highlands and Hebrides, red grouse numbers could increase when heather regenerates following a reduction in grazing pressure. Increases could also occur in the Eastern Highlands on moors that have been overgrazed.

Black grouse often increase following woodland establishment, thus providing food for eagles, but much depends on woodland design at the landscape scale. Some avian prey of eagles occur in habitats that are unlikely to be greatly affected by the establishment of new native woodlands; these include ptarmigan, wildfowl and seabirds.

In very simplistic terms, the carrying capacity for live prey (e.g. grouse and mountain hare) is likely to decline by about 80% at 15-30 years after planting/regeneration, assuming 20% of land is left unplanted. This suggests that the impact of new native woodland on potential food biomass may be similar to that of commercial conifer forests. Incorporating suitable design features into the SFGS based on what is known about grouse and hare requirements may slightly moderate the scale of this decline. Therefore, the establishment of large areas of new native woodland in areas with eagles may result in the loss of some eagle pairs, but much depends on the extent and quality of open habitats that remain within home ranges.

Some aspects of the SFGS are 'beneficial' to eagles, but the level of benefit varies depending upon the situation. The SFGS encourages woodland establishment on lowland sites that are unlikely to be at elevations preferred by eagles (McGrady *et al.*, 1997). Such woodlands might encourage potential eagle prey that may become available to eagles once they venture out of the forest onto adjacent open habitats (e.g. black grouse (Swenson & Angelstam, 1993; Schmitz, 1997) and young deer (Bergo, 1987)). The SFGS encourages the use of native trees, so providing more scope for increasing the abundance of some prey species, such as black grouse, through appropriate design and management (Picozzi *et al.*, 1992; Cayford, 1993). Specific initiatives within the framework of the WGS in the Cairngorms, Speyside and Deeside have funded some operations that are likely to be, on balance, eagle-friendly, including the creation of open spaces, removal of deer fences, increased deer culling, the creation of a local forest network and removal of non-native tree species where they threaten habitat quality (Anon., 1999).

27.4 Designing new native woodlands to benefit eagles

Policy statements about how to achieve a balance between forested and open landscapes exist in draft (Anon., 1998b, 2000), but an integrated Forest Network is not yet extant. Furthermore, details of how these proposals might be integrated for the benefit of eagles, while trying to achieve other objectives, are only at the discussion stage (e.g. Watson & Whitfield, 2002; Fielding *et al.*, Chapter 26). Woodlands that support eagles are, for the most part, old but there is no provision under the SFGS to ensure that some woodlands progress to old age (>200 years) to provide foraging and breeding habitat for eagles. Draft policy documents by the Scottish government environment agency, Scottish Natural Heritage, encourage such beneficial aspects at the landscape level by encouraging woodland biodiversity and promoting integrated grazing, continuous cover management of forests and sustainable management in cooperation with the Forestry Commission and others involved in forestry (Anon., 2000). Boxes 27.1 and 27.2 provide guidance on designing and managing new native forests to benefit eagles and their prey.

Box 27.1. Managing disturbance and creating new nest sites (see also, McGrady *et al.* (1997) and Petty (1998)).

- **Avoid disturbance** – All potentially disturbing activities within 900-1,100 m of the nest should be avoided during February to July inclusive. The most sensitive times are during nest building, hatching and the early nestling stage. New forest roads should not be routed within 1,000 m of an eagle nest.
- **Conserve nest sites** - Conserve existing nesting trees and the surrounding forest. Establish and manage new stands as future nest sites. Existing old trees should be protected in suitable sites. Potential nest trees should be located at or near the edge of the forest-moorland boundary, in stands >10 ha in size. Trees are suitable for nesting from >80-100 years of age and are often larger than other trees in the stand. Eagles prefer trees with large open crowns with substantial branches. Scots pine *Pinus sylvestris* is a particularly valuable species. Good flight access into the stand is required. Avoid planting trees that will obstruct flight lines into crag nests.
- **Opportunities during harvesting operations** - During tree felling consider leaving trees that could be used as future nest sites, particularly small stands in ravines or on craggy slopes. In such locations it is often economical to leave trees because they are of low value and/or difficult to harvest and extract.

Box 27.2. Designing forests and managing open ground to benefit eagles and their preferred prey (see also McGrady *et al.* (1997) and Petty (1998)).

- **Open ground** - Design forests that link suitable open areas within the SFGS to adjacent open moorland. Avoid creating open areas that are small or linear. Think big! Open areas should be >20 ha, over 300 m wide and on higher elevation sites
- **Encourage habitats for prey** – Black grouse, red grouse and mountain hares are the prey species on which to concentrate.
  - Locate open areas where regeneration will be slow due to a lack of seedlings or seed trees. If necessary use seasonal grazing, controlled burning and tractor-mounted swiping to control vegetation.
  - Encourage food plants and vegetation structure to benefit eagle prey. Areas of dwarf shrub vegetation and cotton grass *Eriophorum vaginatum* should be encouraged for grouse and hares. Ericaceous vegetation should be tall (40-50 cm). Grouse eat tree buds/flowers in spring, particularly from birch *Betula* spp., and Scots pine. Fruits of dwarf shrubs and rowan are important in autumn.
  - Conserve and expand invertebrate-rich areas, which are crucial for grouse chick survival. These include damp sites with grasses, bog myrtle *Myrica gale* and herbs, which should be linked to larger patches of ericaceous vegetation.
  - Maintain deer densities at 2-4 km^2.
  - Wide ecotones with low density tree planting should be encouraged between native woodland and open areas. Low growing *Salix* spp., juniper *Juniperus* spp. and other shrubs should be promoted on the open side. Aim for <40% canopy cover, varying from inner to outer edge of the ecotone.
- **Reduce mortality in grouse** - Collisions with deer fences are an important cause of mortality in grouse. Aim to manage deer by culling rather than fencing. Remove existing fences whenever possible.

27.4.1 Scale

Individual SFGSs are likely to be much smaller than individual eagle home ranges. Previous publications offer guidance on amounts and location of forests within eagle home ranges; these were based on research that considered the effect of coniferous forests on eagles (Watson *et al.*, 1987; McGrady *et al.*, 1997) which, as we have indicated, may not be all that different from new native woodlands, at least in the short to medium term.

The present limit of 20% open ground within a SFGS is a major constraint on designing forests to benefit eagles. One way in which the current SFGS system could be made more eagle-friendly would be to allow much larger areas of open ground, for which a grant would be paid. This would counter some of the negative effects of fragmentation caused by having relatively small areas of open ground embedded within a forest. Moreover, such a change could make a substantial contribution to meeting government targets on threatened species and habitats, such as black grouse, blanket bogs and upland heathland.

Managing individual schemes within the context of a forest network is likely to provide some flexibility, although achieving an eagle-friendly balance may be difficult with constraints imposed by land ownership and economics. Without landscape level planning that includes the management of woodlands and deer, both within forests and on adjacent moorland, benefits of native woodlands for eagles will not be realised. A long-term management strategy is urgently needed to ensure that woodlands fit for eagles will be available in the future. Such forests would be of great benefit to other species that are dependent on old woodlands and susceptible to woodland fragmentation, such as the capercaillie *Tetrao urogallus*.

27.4.2 Extending the breeding range of golden eagles

The SFGS will only contribute to the extension of the breeding range of golden eagles in Scotland if forest management promotes: (i) the creation of large areas of old forests (for foraging and breeding) in suitable locations for eagles, and (ii) the linking of these old forests to open areas rich in live prey. In other countries, eagles nest on man-made structures (M. Kochert, pers. comm.), and nesting platforms (Ivanovsky, 2000) may sometimes encourage early nesting in young woodlands. However, these should not be seen as a replacement for long-term management to encourage trees large enough for eagles to nest in. Unfortunately, persecution is still a factor in limiting range expansion by eagles, particularly in southern and eastern Scotland (e.g. Watson, 1997; Watson & Whitfield, 2002).

27.4.3 Increasing prey abundance in new native woodlands

The value of new native woodlands as foraging habitats for eagles depends initially on the success of incorporating open areas into woodland design. Consideration also needs to be given to adjacent open areas that are used by eagles, including how to balance different land uses at landscape and regional scales.

New, native woodlands are dynamic habitats where successional changes influence prey abundance and the ability of eagles to utilise them. Open habitats are dynamic too, but the rate of change is less rapid than within woodland. Open areas will naturally progress to woodland in the absence of significant grazing and it may be necessary to consider using seasonal grazing, controlled burning or tractor-mounted swiping to control vegetation. The SFGS provides support for maintaining open space (Scottish Executive and Forestry Commission, 2003). Within open areas food plants and a vegetation structure that benefit eagle prey need to be encouraged. Some of the best habitats for grouse and hares comprise dwarf shrubs (Hewson, 1962; Moss, 1969). Wet areas should be protected and enlarged whenever possible as they are often rich in invertebrates, which provide an important food source for grouse chicks during their first few weeks of life (Baines *et al.*, 1996; Scotland's Moorland Forum, 2003).

Following woodland establishment and providing dwarf shrubs regenerate, habitats become increasingly suitable for grouse (Moss, 1969) and mountain hare (Watson *et al.*, 1973). Initially, red grouse and hare numbers will increase for up to 10-15 years (Hewson, 1962; Swenson & Angelstam, 1993). Once dwarf shrubs become taller than 20-30 cm, red grouse densities will often decline while black grouse densities will continue to increase. Black grouse prefer young forest up to about 20 years of age, after which numbers decline (Swenson & Angelstam, 1993). Open areas with dwarf shrub vegetation will continue to provide suitable habitat for black grouse after canopy closure within the woodland part of the SFGS. Low densities of red grouse and mountain hare will often persist in these open areas too. Ideally, deer numbers should be controlled by culling, rather than fencing, to reduce damage to trees and ground vegetation because fences increase grouse mortality (Baines & Summers, 1997).

Acknowledgements

This manuscript is a product of cooperation between Scottish Natural Heritage, the Royal Society for the Protection of Birds and the Forestry Commission. The authors would like to thank Gordon Patterson for his support. Mike Madders and an anonymous referee provided comments which improved this chapter.

References

Anonymous (1998a). *The UK Forestry Standard: the Government's Approach to Sustainable Forestry*. Forestry Commission, Edinburgh.

Anonymous (1998b). Reasonable balance between afforestation and open moorland habitats in the uplands: preliminary guidance. Unpublished report. Scottish Natural Heritage, Perth.

Anonymous (1999). *A Guide to the Woodland Grant Scheme*. Forestry Commission, Edinburgh.

Anonymous (2000). Scottish Natural Heritage Position Statement on Forestry (Draft).

Baines, D. & Summers, R.W. (1997). Assessment of bird collisions with fences in Scottish forests. *Journal of Applied Ecology*, **34**, 941-948.

Baines, D., Wilson, I.A. & Beeley, G. (1996). Timing of breeding in black grouse *Tetrao tetrix* and capercaillie *Tetrao urogallus* and the distribution of insect food for the chicks. *Ibis*, **138**, 181-187.

Bergo, G. (1987). Eagles as predators on livestock and deer. *Fauna Norvegica Ser. C, Cinclus*, **10**, 95-102.

Cayford, J. (1993). *Black grouse and forestry: habitat requirements and management. Technical Paper 1*. Forestry Commission, Edinburgh.

Green, R.E. (1996). The status of the golden eagle in Britain in 1992. *Bird Study*, **43**, 20-27.

Haller, H. (1996). Der Steinadler in Graubünden: Langfristige Untersuchungen zur Populationsökolgie von *Aquila chrysaetos* im der Zentrum der Alpen. *Der Ornitholgishe Beobachter*, **9**.

Hewson, R. (1962). Food and feeding habits of the mountain hare *Lepus timidus scoticus* Hilzheimer. *Proceedings of the Zoological Society of London*, **139**, 515-526.

Holloway, C.W. (1967). *The Effects of Red Deer and Other Animals on Naturally Regenerating Scots Pine*. University of Aberdeen, Aberdeen.

Ivanovsky, V.V. (2000). Construction of artificial nest as conservation measure for rare birds of prey. *Buteo*, **11**, 131-138.

McGrady, M.J., McLeod, D.R., Petty, S.J., Grant, J.R. & Bainbridge, I.P. (1997). *Golden eagles and Forestry. Research Information Note 292*. Forestry Commission, Farnham.

McGrady, M.J., Petty, S.J. & McLeod, D.R. (in press). Potential impacts of new native woodland expansion on golden eagles in Scotland – a desk study. Final Report. Scottish Natural Heritage Contract No. R/LD7/HT/99/02.

Moss, R. (1969). Comparison of red grouse (*Lagopus l. scoticus*) stocks with the production and nutritive value of heather (*Calluna vulgaris*). *Journal of Applied Ecology*, **38**, 103-122.

Peterken, G.F., Baldock, D. & Hampson, A. (1995). A forest habitat network for Scotland. Scottish Natural Heritage Research, Survey and Monitoring Report. No. 44.

Petty, S.J. (1998). *Ecology and Conservation of Raptors in Forests. Forestry Commission Bulletin 118*. The Stationery Office. London.

Picozzi, N., Moss, R. & Catt, D.C. (1992). *Blaeberry and Heather in Conifer Forests* (Report to Eagle Star). Institute of Terrestrial Ecology, Banchory.

Schmitz, L. (1997). Black grouse *Tetrao tetrix*. In *The EBCC Atlas of European Breeding Birds*, ed. by W. Hagemeijer & M.J. Blair. T. & A.D. Poyser, London. pp. 200-201.

Scotland's Moorland Forum (2003). *Scotland's Moorland Forum: Principles of Moorland Management*. Scottish Natural Heritage, Perth.

Scottish Executive and Forestry Commission (2003). *Scottish Forestry Grants Scheme Applicants Booklet*. Scottish Executive and Forestry Commission, Edinburgh.

Staines, B.W. (1995). The impact of red deer on the regeneration of native pinewoods. In *Our Pinewood Heritage*, ed. by J.R. Aldhous. Forestry Commission, The Royal Society for the Protection of Birds and Scottish Natural Heritage, Farnham. pp. 107-114.

Sulkava, S., Huhtala, K., Rajala, P. & Tornberg, R. (1999). Changes in the diet of the golden eagle *Aquila chrysaetos* and small game populations in Finland in 1957-1996. *Ornis Fennica*, **76**, 1-16.

Swenson, J.E. & Angelstam, P. (1993). Habitat separation by sympatric forest grouse in Fennoscandia in relation to boreal forest succession. *Canadian Journal of Zoology*, **71**, 1303-1310.

Thompson, D.B.A., Hester, A.J. & Usher, M.B. (Eds) (1995). *Heaths and Moorland: Cultural Landscapes*. HMSO, Edinburgh.

Tjernberg, M. (1981). Diet of the golden eagle *Aquila chrysaetos* during the breeding season in Sweden. *Holarctic Ecology*, **4**, 12-19.

Watson, A., Hewson, R., Jenkins, D. & Parr, R. (1973). Population densities of mountain hares compared with red grouse on Scottish moors. *Oikos*, **24**, 225-230.

Watson, J. (1997). *The Golden Eagle*. T. & A.D. Poyser, London.

Watson, J., Langslow, D.R. & Rae, S.R. (1987). *The Impact of Land-Use Changes on Golden Eagles in the Scottish Highlands. CSD Report No. 720*. Nature Conservancy Council, Peterborough.

Watson, J., Leitch, A.F. & Rae, S.R. (1993). The diet of golden eagles *Aquila chrysaetos* in Scotland. *Ibis*, **135**, 387-393.

Watson, J. & Whitfield, P. (2002). A conservation framework for the golden eagle Aquila chrysaetos in Scotland. *Journal of Raptor Research*, **36 (1 Supplement)**, 41-49.

28. LAND USE, COMMON BUZZARDS (*BUTEO BUTEO*) AND RABBITS (*ORYCTOLAGUS CUNICULUS*) IN THE WELSH MARCHES

I.M.W. Sim

Summary

1.   Buzzard *Buteo buteo* density and distribution increased significantly in the Welsh Marches between 1983 and 1996.

2.   The number of soaring buzzards counted in spring increased by 118% in the main range, 348% in the edge range and 231% overall.

3.   Although there was no significant linear trend in breeding success between 1950 and 1995, numbers of young fledged per breeding attempt were highest in the period 1980-95. This high productivity coincided with an increase in rabbit *Oryctolagus cuniculus* abundance.

4.   Persecution levels, especially poisoning, appear to have been lower more recently (comparing the 1990s with this period).

5.   Breeding densities of 81 and 22 territorial pairs per 100 km^2 in two areas 40 km apart were found: the former is the highest density recorded in Europe. High buzzard breeding densities were associated with high proportions of unimproved pasture and mature woodland within estimated territories.

6.   Buzzards laid earlier clutches at lower altitudes and with high proportions of unimproved pasture close to nests. Large clutches and high numbers of fledged young were associated with high rabbit abundance close to nests.

7.   Most nest failures occurred during incubation and were probably due mainly to corvid predation. Brood reduction was associated with low proportions of deciduous woodland close to nests and small clutch sizes, although the causes of chick mortality were uncertain.

8.   Rabbits were the main prey item found at nests with passerines, especially young corvids, also appearing frequently.

28.1 Introduction

Until the beginning of the 19th century the common buzzard *Buteo buteo* was found throughout Britain and Ireland, but by 1900 it had become restricted to Wales, Scotland and western England. This range contraction was probably due to persecution. A slight population recovery occurred from 1915, but from 1953 a catastrophic decline in populations of the main prey, rabbit *Oryctolagus cuniculus*, due to myxomatosis, and the introduction of organochlorine pesticides which contaminated other prey species in the 1950s and 1960s, may have prevented buzzards expanding further (Moore, 1957; Newton, 1979). There was little change in distribution in Britain between 1968-72 and 1988-91, but there was a considerable expansion in Ireland (Gibbons *et al.*, 1993).

Persecution is often proposed as one of the main reasons why buzzards were unable to re-occupy much of their former range. Elliott & Avery (1991) showed that buzzards were especially vulnerable to persecution at the edge of their range, and claimed that this limited the number of birds available to colonise new areas. However, it is possible that the removal of hedgerows, pasture improvement and the increased use of pesticides in recent decades may have reduced suitable breeding habitat and prey abundance in these areas.

The first aim of this study was to discover whether buzzard numbers and distribution had changed since 1983, when the British Trust for Ornithology (BTO) carried out a survey of soaring buzzards in spring (Taylor *et al.*, 1988). Data on breeding success, survival, persecution, and abundance of rabbits were analysed to discover any strong correlates of change in buzzard population size in this area. The second aim was to discover the main habitat correlates of buzzard density and breeding success in an area of the Welsh Marches close to the edge of the present-day range. This chapter is partly a synthesis of two published papers (Sim *et al.*, 2000, 2001).

28.2 Methods

The 10 km squares used in the 1996 Soaring Survey are shown in Figure 28.1. The same tetrads within each 10 km square were visited for the same amount of time as in 1983, and within five days of the 1983 survey date. The 1983 survey was stratified to sample buzzard numbers in both the main range and the edge range, defined using criteria obtained from Sharrock (1976). We have retained this classification here, even though these definitions may no longer correctly define present day buzzard distribution. We examined buzzard breeding density and productivity in detail in 10 km squares SO37 and SO77. Land use in these squares was predominantly agricultural, with a mixture of pasture and arable land, but also shooting estates, forestry plantations and grazing commons.

Breeding success over the period 1950 to 1995 was analysed using 938 BTO Nest Record Cards from Wales, Shropshire, Hereford & Worcester and Gloucestershire. This constituted the area from which most recruits to the population of our study area were likely to have originated. This analysis included our own data on breeding success from 1994 and 1995. Breeding success was assessed using the Mayfield Maximum Likelihood Estimate (Bart & Robson, 1982). County bird reports for the period 1983-95 were examined for evidence of trends in breeding buzzard numbers. Records of buzzard persecution incidents from Gloucestershire, Hereford & Worcester and Shropshire for the periods 1975-89 and 1990-95 were obtained from the Royal Society for the Protection of Birds (RSPB) Investigations Department. Instances of deliberate pesticide abuse during 1980-95 for the same counties, and reported to the Wildlife Incident Investigation Scheme (WIIS), were obtained from the Ministry of Agriculture, Fisheries and Food (MAFF).

Historical data on rabbit abundance in Wales and the West Midlands were obtained from The Game Conservancy Trust. The annual index of abundance in this data set was the mean number of rabbits shot per 100 ha. An index of rabbit abundance in buzzard 'territories' was obtained by walking a 4 km transect (a 1 km x 1 km square) centred on the nest, and counting all rabbits seen within 200 m each side of the observer. Counts were carried out between 05.30 and 08.30 BST from 15 August to 30 September in 1995 and 1996, avoiding wet and windy weather which reduces lagomorph activity (Langbein *et al.*, 1995). We measured rabbit abundance for all territories where pairs laid either one or four

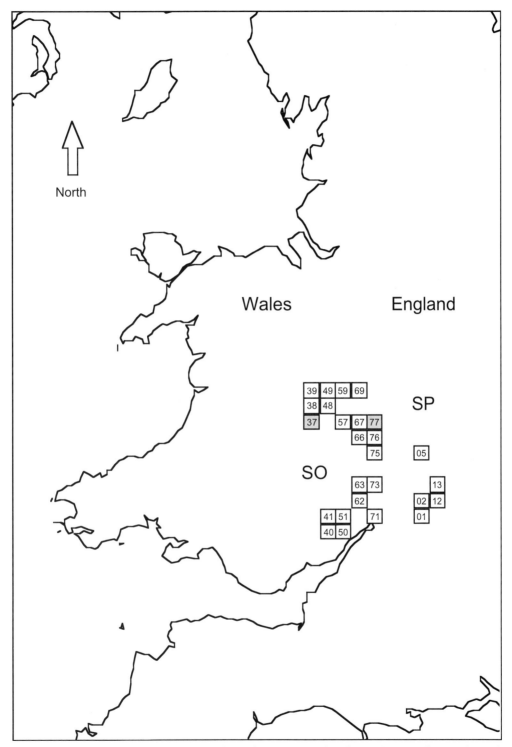

Figure 28.1. Location of study area, showing the 10 km squares used in the 1996 survey of soaring buzzards. Intensive breeding studies were carried out in SO37 and SO77 (SO77 was not included in the Soaring Survey). Letters refer to Ordnance Survey reference system.

eggs, but due to time and access limitations only 45 out of 66 (68%) territories where pairs laid two or three eggs were surveyed.

Likely nesting areas were identified from February to April by watching for displaying birds, and this was followed by intensive nest searches in all potentially suitable areas from April to July. Territorial pairs were defined as pairs which built nests, but did not necessarily lay eggs, and breeding pairs were defined as pairs that definitely laid eggs. Nearest neighbour distances were obtained by measuring distances between nests, or centres of groups of nests belonging to the same pair, to the nearest 25 m from 1:25,000 Ordnance Survey (OS) maps. We did not have sufficient time to measure territory size directly, but estimated this in SO37 by using Dirichlet tessellation. It was not considered appropriate to use this method to estimate territory size in SO77 since the buzzard population here was relatively low and still expanding, and territory boundaries were more likely to change between years.

Laying dates were estimated using formulae relating chick age to wing length and laying date to chick age, derived by Austin (1992). Clutch size was determined either by using a mirror mounted on telescopic aluminium poles, or by climbing to the nest if possible. Nests were checked soon after hatching was expected; this allowed us to measure hatching success and to determine clutch size more accurately, since unhatched eggs remained in the nest for at least two weeks after hatching. Nests were climbed to when chicks were three to five weeks old in order to ring them, and to measure their wing length (maximum chord) to the nearest 1 mm using a steel rule. A final visit was made to successful territories soon after fledging so as to determine how many chicks actually fledged. In order for comparisons to be made with studies in other regions we also measured apparent nest success, where the number of surviving nests is simply derived by subtracting the number of failed nests from the total number of nests monitored.

Prey remains were identified at all nests that were climbed. Prey identification was to the species level where possible, but in some cases it was necessary to combine remains into groups (e.g. corvids). Approximate numbers of each prey item were estimated from, for example, the number of legs or wings. No pellets were collected, as too few were found.

Habitats were mapped by field visits during July-September 1995, and divided into 11 types. The area of each habitat type was measured within a 1,000 m radius of nests using a Quora digitiser. All environmental parameters measured, and their definitions, are listed in Table 28.1. Fifty territory sizes in SO37 could be estimated by tessellation; the remaining 31 could not as they were close to the edge of the study area, outside which we did not know the locations of all buzzard nests. Since we did not have data on various aspects of breeding biology for several of these 50 territories, the sample sizes for modelling laying date, clutch size, fledged brood size, complete failure of nests with eggs, and partial brood mortality would have been unacceptably low. Hence, instead of tessellation, we measured environmental parameters at four different radii (400, 600, 800 and 1,000 m) from all nests, and compared the variance explained by the models at each radius. One might expect that the variance explained by each model would increase up to a certain radius, approximating to the radius of a buzzard territory, and then fall off sharply at greater radii as habitat composition of the 'territory' becomes increasingly determined by areas never used by that breeding pair.

Proportional data were transformed by calculating the arcsine of each proportion prior to analysis. Log transformations were performed on variables that were not normally distributed, and are indicated by the prefix 'log'. In all models we assumed that the response

Table 28.1. Independent variables and factors used in the analyses.

Area of arable farmland
Area of improved pasture (rolled flat, fertiliser added, bright green)
Area of unimproved pasture (all other pasture, including most orchards)
Area of shrubs, brambles etc. less than 3 m high
Area of mature coniferous woodland
Area of mature deciduous woodland
Area of mature mixed woodland
Area of mature deciduous and mixed woodland
Area of mature coniferous, deciduous and mixed woodland
Area of plantation more than five years old but before first thinning
Area of plantation less than five years old
Area of mature coniferous woodland and plantation more than 5 years old but before first thinning
Area of shrubs, brambles etc. less than 3 m high and plantation less than five years old
Number of other pairs of territorial buzzards within different radii
Altitude of nest site above sea level (m)
Shannon-Weiner habitat diversity index
Index of rabbit abundance
Height of nest above ground (m)
10 km square e.g. SO37
Size of nest wood (single tree, small (<5 ha), medium (>5 ha <10ha), large (>10 ha))
1994, 1995 or 1996
Nest easily seen, partly hidden or well-hidden from ground level
Full-time, part-time or no gamekeeper present
Deciduous or coniferous nest tree
Nearest-neighbour distance
Clutch size
Laying date of clutches

---

variable followed a normal error distribution. Note that sample sizes in the models differ occasionally due to missing data. We examined the relationship between environmental parameters and six aspects of buzzard breeding biology: territory size, laying date, clutch size, fledged brood size, complete failure of nests with eggs, and partial brood mortality. Multiple regression models were produced in order to examine variation in territory size, laying date, clutch size and fledged brood size, using the statistical package MINITAB (version 11). Logistic regression models were used to examine variation in complete failure of nests with eggs and partial brood mortality, using the statistical package GLIM4 (Francis *et al.*, 1993). Two-tailed probabilities are quoted throughout.

28.3 Results

28.3.1 Survey of soaring buzzards

The results are summarised in Table 28.2. Numbers of soaring buzzards increased by 118% in the main range, 348% in the edge range, and 231% overall. The estimated mean annual population increase was 9.6%, assuming a constant growth rate. The median number of soaring buzzards per tetrad was significantly higher in 1996 than in 1983 in both the main and edge range (Wilcoxon matched pairs tests: $Z = 5.09$, $P < 0.001$ [main]; $Z = 7.58$,

Table 28.2. Numbers of soaring buzzards per 10 km square in 1983 and 1996. Total percentage increases are mean values. +++ denotes squares where no buzzards were seen in 1983 but where one or more were seen in 1996. See section 28.2 Methods for details of the 10 km squares.

10 km square	1983	1996	% increase ± C.I.	No. of tetrads surveyed
SO37	3	17	467	3
SO38	12	25	108	14
SO39	9	16	77	7
SO40	5	7	40	6
SO41	11	14	27	7
SO48	3	13	333	5
SO49	7	17	143	9
Total (main range)	50	109	118 ±18	51
SO50	2	8	300	4
SO51	6	13	117	5
SO57	0	18	+++	21
SO59	9	25	177	13
SO62	3	17	467	18
SO63	0	8	+++	3
SO66	0	4	+++	1
SO67	2	18	800	7
SO69	5	28	460	19
SO71	0	3	+++	4
SO73	2	6	200	1
SO75	10	20	100	7
SO76	3	10	233	4
SP01	0	8	+++	10
SP02	0	7	+++	13
SP05	4	7	75	3
SP12	0	12	+++	10
SP13	2	3	50	2
Total (edge range)	48	215	348 ± 25	145
Overall total	98	324	231 ± 11	196

$P < 0.001$ [edge]). Soaring buzzards were seen in 29% of tetrads in 1983 and 74% of tetrads in 1996. In the main range, soaring buzzards were seen in 63% (1983) and 84% (1996) of tetrads. Comparable figures for the edge range were 17% (1983) and 70% (1996).

28.3.2 *Temporal variations in breeding success*
Buzzard breeding success during the period 1950-1995 is summarised in Table 28.3. Mean clutch size did not vary significantly with time ($F_{1,40}$ = 1.41, $P > 0.10$), but the mean number of young fledged per successful nest showed a significant quadratic regression with time:

Mean number of young fledged per successful nest = 6.518 - 0.134 [Year] + 0.001 [Year²]

Table 28.3. Buzzard breeding success during 1950-1995. Calculation of the percentage of nests failing to fledge at least one chick assumes 35 days incubation and 49 days nestling period (Cramp 1985).

Period	Mean clutch size ± se (n)	Mean no. of young fledged per successful nest ± se (n)	Daily nest failure rates during incubation ± se (n)	Daily nest failure rates during chick rearing ± se (n)	% of nests failing to fledge at least one chick ± se (n)	Mean no. of young fledged per breeding attempt ± se (n)
1950-54	2.37 ± 0.38 (8)	2.06 ± 0.29 (16)	0.0137 ± 0.0079 (14)	0.0034 ± 0.0034 (10)	47.78 ± 17.22 (10)	1.08 ± 0.39 (10)
1955-59	2.00 ± 0.32 (8)	1.43 ± 0.22 (23)	0.0128 ± 0.0057 (19)	0.0068 ± 0.0048 (11)	54.40 ± 14.36 (11)	0.65 ± 0.23 (11)
1960-64	2.79 ± 0.44 (14)	2.00 ± 0.29 (24)	0.0124 ± 0.0049 (24)	0.0042 ± 0.0029 (18)	47.43 ± 11.89 (18)	1.05 ± 0.28 (18)
1965-69	2.42 ± 0.15 (12)	1.72 ± 0.18 (43)	0.0112 ± 0.0046 (24)	0.0053 ± 0.0037 (18)	48.04 ± 12.79 (18)	0.89 ± 0.24 (18)
1970-74	2.42 ± 0.26 (12)	1.48 ± 0.12 (63)	0.0537 ± 0.0109 (27)	0.0038 ± 0.0026 (23)	87.98 ± 5.12 (23)	0.18 ± 0.08 (23)
1975-79	2.12 ± 0.21 (34)	1.51 ± 0.10 (79)	0.0108 ± 0.0039 (41)	0.0059 ± 0.0026 (38)	48.83 ± 9.68 (38)	0.77 ± 0.15 (38)
1980-84	2.10 ± 0.11 (40)	1.55 ± 0.07 (121)	0.0036 ± 0.0016 (69)	0.0006 ± 0.0006 (68)	14.41 ± 5.43 (68)	1.33 ± 0.11 (68)
1985-89	2.08 ± 0.23 (39)	1.76 ± 0.07 (117)	0.0068 ± 0.0022 (67)	0.0030 ± 0.0013 (71)	32.03 ± 6.84 (67)	1.20 ± 0.13 (67)
1990-95	2.31 ± 0.12 (94)	1.86 ± 0.06 (190)	0.0113 ± 0.0021 (143)	0.0020 ± 0.0007 (167)	39.10 ± 4.99 (143)	1.13 ± 0.10 (143)

$F_{2,43} = 7.43$, $R^2_{adj} = 0.26$, $P < 0.005$]. The mean number of young fledged per successful nest was high in 1952-53, the early 1960s and in the late 1980s-early 1990s, but was low in the 1970s (Figure 28.2).

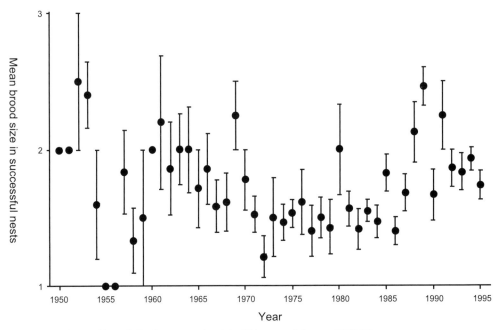

Figure 28.2. Buzzard brood size (mean ± se bars) in 681 successful nests 1950-95.

Mean daily nest failure rates during incubation showed no significant linear trend with time ($F_{1,7} = 0.05$, $P > 0.10$), nor was the quadratic regression significant ($F_{2,6} = 0.28$, $P > 0.05$). However, there was a significant variation among five year periods ($\chi^2 = 30.4$, df = 8, $P < 0.001$). Daily nest failure rates during incubation were very high in the period 1970-74, and very low in the period 1980-84. Mean daily nest failure rates during chick-rearing showed no significant linear trend with time ($F_{1,7} = 4.00$, $P > 0.05$), nor was the quadratic regression significant ($F_{2,6} = 1.77$, $P > 0.05$). There was no significant variation among five year periods ($\chi^2 = 12.6$, df = 8, $P > 0.05$). The mean number of young fledged per breeding attempt was significantly higher in the periods 1980-84, 1985-89 and 1990-95 than in the period 1970-74, but there were no significant differences between any of the other time periods (Games and Howell approximate test of equality of means).

28.3.3 Persecution

Recorded buzzard deaths due to persecution are summarised in Table 28.4. Mean annual recorded deaths fell from 1.87 during 1975-89 to 0.47 during 1990-95, correcting the figures to deaths per year per buzzard. Recorded annual deaths by poisoning fell from 1.80 in 1975-89 to 0.20 in 1990-95, but recorded annual shooting and trapping incidents increased from 0.07 to 0.27 between 1975-89 and 1990-95. Annual incidents of deliberate pesticide abuse reported to WIIS averaged 8.50 (range 3-13) during 1980-1991, but then fell to 4.25 (range 3-6) during 1992-95.

Table 28.4. Confirmed buzzard persecution incidents in Gloucestershire, Hereford & Worcester and Shropshire 1975-95. The population in 1993 was estimated to have been 2.51 times greater than in 1983, assuming a constant rate of population increase.

| | *Total deaths* | | *Deaths per year* | | *Deaths per year 1990-95 divided by 2.51* |
	1975-89	*1990-95*	*1975-89*	*1990-95*	
Poisoned	27	3	1.80	0.50	0.20
Shot/trapped	1	4	0.07	0.67	0.27
Total	28	7	1.87	1.17	0.47

28.3.4 Rabbit abundance

The index of rabbit abundance (from shooting bags) increased dramatically from 1985 in the West Midlands and from 1989 in Wales (Figure 28.3). Rabbit abundance (as measured by transects) did not vary significantly, within habitats, between SO37 and SO77 (Mann-Whitney tests). However, there was a significant difference in abundance between different habitats (Kruskall-Wallis ANOVA = 143.1, df = 3, P <0.001); rabbits were numerous in unimproved pasture but scarce in arable farmland and woodland (Table 28.5).

Table 28.5. Index of rabbit abundance per km of transect in different habitats in SO37 and SO77 (see also Figure 28.1).

| *Habitat* | *SO37* | | | *SO77* | | | *Overall* | | |
	Median	*Range*	*n*	*Median*	*Range*	*n*	*Median*	*Range*	*n*
Unimproved pasture	21	4-56	20	15.0	7-25	10	17	4-56	30
Improved pasture	5	0-44	68	6.5	1-23	30	5	0-44	98
Arable farmland	0	0-9	39	0.0	0-4	17	0	0-9	56
Mature woodland	0	0-4	29	0.0	0-1	19	0	0-4	48

28.3.5 Breeding density and territory occupancy

Buzzard densities and nearest-neighbour distances are summarised in Table 28.6. The number of territorial pairs in SO37 and SO77 were 81 and 22 respectively; the number of pairs that bred in either 1994 or 1995 were 71 (SO77) and 20 (SO77). Estimated territory size in SO37 ranged from 39 to 221 ha (mean 119.65 ± 36.30 sd) (Figure 28.4). There was a significant effect on territory size of habitat composition ($F_{5,45}$ = 3.31, P <0.05). Small territories, and thus high buzzard densities, were associated with high proportions of unimproved pasture and mature woodland (territory size = 2.381 scrub and young plantation + 1.956 arable + 1.315 improved pasture + 0.828 mature woodland + 0.774 unimproved pasture, n = 50).

a)

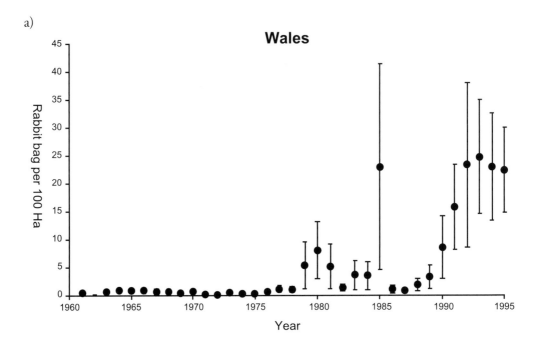

b)

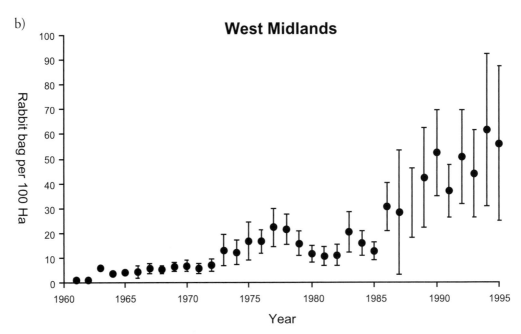

Figure 28.3. Index of rabbit abundance (mean ± se bars) in the West Midlands (a) and Wales (b) during 1961-1995.

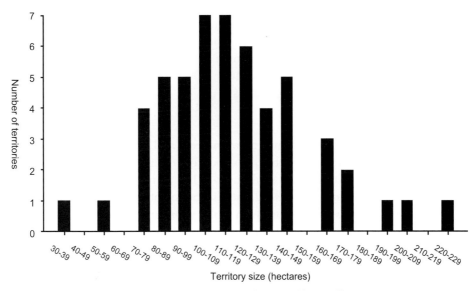

Figure 28.4. Frequency of buzzard territory size estimated by Dirichlet tessellation.

Table 28.6. Numbers of territorial and breeding pairs, and nearest neighbour (NN) distances (km) in SO37 and SO77 (see also Figure 28.1).

Square	Territorial pairs	Breeding pairs	NN (mean ± se)	n
SO37	81	71	0.83 ± 0.27	70
SO77	22	20	1.33 ± 0.27	12

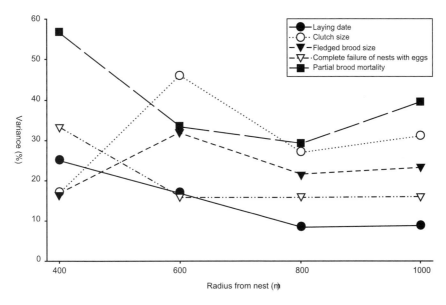

Figure 28.5. Proportion of variance explained by the models at different radii from nests, indicating that environmental parameters within 600 m of nests had the biggest influence on measures of breeding success.

28.3.6 *Variance explained by different models*
The variance explained in the laying date, complete failure of nests with eggs and partial brood mortality models peak at 400 m radius, whereas the variance in the clutch size and fledged brood size models peak at 600 m, before falling off sharply (Figure 28.5). Thus it appears that it is environmental parameters within 400-600 m of nests that most strongly correlate with our measures of breeding success.

28.3.7 *Laying date and clutch size*
Mean laying date did not differ significantly between years ($t = 1.78$, df = 58, $P > 0.05$). Earlier clutches were laid at low altitude and with high proportions of unimproved pasture within 400 m of the nest (laying date = 0.910 + 0.047 altitude - 6.180 unimproved pasture, $R^2_{adj} = 0.25$, $n = 31$, $P = 0.007$). Mean clutch size was 2.2; the distribution of clutch sizes is shown in Table 28.7. Large clutches were associated with high rabbit abundance within 600 m of the nest (clutch size = 0.165 + 1.56 log (rabbit abundance), $R^2_{adj} = 0.46$, $n = 57$, $P = 0.0001$).

Table 28.7. Distribution of clutch size, and brood size at hatching and fledging.

	Number of eggs or chicks					
	1	*2*	*3*	*4*	*Mean*	*se*
Clutch size	5	53	23	1	2.2	0.06
Brood size (hatched)	11	45	14	1	2.1	0.08
Brood size (fledged)	25	32	6	1	1.7	0.08

28.3.8 *Nest survival rates*
There were no significant differences between years in daily nest survival rates during either incubation ($z = 0.25$, $P > 0.10$) or chick-rearing ($z = 0.14$, $P > 0.10$). However, daily nest survival rates were significantly lower during incubation than during chick-rearing ($z = 2.22$, $P < 0.02$) (Table 28.8). The proportions of nests predicted to have survived using Mayfield estimates were 67% during incubation, 85% during chick-rearing, and 57% overall. This contrasts with apparent nest survival rates of 86%, 92%, and 79%, respectively. We found no evidence of deliberate human disturbance to nests, but three nests with eggs probably failed due to nearby tree-felling. Predation of eggs was probably mainly due to corvids, but at least two large chicks were predated by either goshawks *Accipiter gentilis* or other buzzards. Total nest failures during incubation were more likely with decreasing amounts of unimproved pasture within 400 m of the nest and lower nearest neighbour distances (complete failure of nests with eggs = -1.404 - 17.260 unimproved pasture - 3.243 nearest-neighbour, $\chi^2 = 12.54$, df = 2, $P < 0.005$).

28.3.9 *Fledging success and chick mortality*
Mean brood size at hatching was 2.1 (Table 28.7). Mean numbers of young fledged were 1.2, 1.4 and 1.7 per territorial, breeding and successful pair respectively. High numbers of young fledging were associated with high rabbit abundance within 600 m of nests (fledged brood size = 0.463 + 1.550 log (rabbit abundance)), $R^2_{adj} = 0.32$, $n = 49$, $P = 0.0001$).

Table 28.8. Summary of nest survival rates in 1994 and 1995. Total period of survival over incubation (35 days), chick rearing (49 days) and overall (84 days).

	Incubation	*Chick rearing*	*Overall*
Daily survival rate	0.988649	0.996730	0.985416
Standard error of daily rate	0.003576	0.001161	0.003288
Total period	0.671137	0.851827	0.571693
Number of nests	68	80	90

Causes of chick deaths were largely unknown as corpses were rarely found; most mortality occurred soon after hatching and corpses were probably eaten by the adults or other chicks. Brood reduction was associated with small amounts of deciduous woodland within 400 m of the nest and small clutch sizes (partial brood mortality = -1.574 - 279.4 deciduous woodland - 1.393 clutch size, χ^2 = 18.47, df = 2, P <0.001).

28.3.10 Prey remains at nests

Rabbits were by far the most common prey item found at nests, comprising 56.1% of all prey remains (Table 28.9). Corvids comprised 18.2%, small passerines 9.9% and pheasants *Phasianus colchicus* 5.1% of prey remains respectively. The majority of rabbits taken were young and most bird remains were of fledglings. Although moles *Talpa europaea* comprised 3.5% of prey remains, they were mostly untouched. Voles *Microtus* spp. comprised only 1.2% of prey remains at nests.

Table 28.9. Prey remains found at 77 buzzard nests 1994-1995. Scientific names given for species not mentioned in text.

Prey Item	*Number*	*Percentage*
Rabbit	142	56.1
Corvids	46	18.2
Small passerines	25	9.9
Pheasant	13	5.1
Mole	9	3.5
Tawny owl *Strix aluco*	6	2.4
Wood pigeon *Columba palumbus*	6	2.4
Voles	3	1.2
Lamb Ovis aries	1	0.4
Rat *Rattus norvegicus*	1	0.4
Slow worm *Anguis fragilis*	1	0.4
Totals	253	100.0

28.4 Discussion

28.4.1 Soaring Survey and temporal variations in breeding success

Numbers of soaring buzzards in our study area increased dramatically between 1983 and 1996; the increase was much higher (348%) on the edge of the range than in the main range

(118%). There was no clear time trend in clutch size, but brood sizes declined from the early 1950s to reach a low in the early 1970s, before recovering in the 1980s and 1990s. No clear trend in nest failure rates was apparent, but failure rates during incubation were unusually high in 1970-74 (due mainly to egg collecting – see Sim *et al.* (2001) for details), and unusually low in 1980-84. Daily nest failure rates during both incubation and chick rearing were lowest in the period 1980-95, resulting in the highest numbers of young fledging per breeding attempt during this period. It would thus appear that increased buzzard breeding success since 1980 was associated with lower nest failure rates, especially during incubation, rather than increased brood sizes.

Raptor breeding success is strongly influenced by prey availability, and rabbits are a major prey of buzzards during the breeding season in Britain (Newton, 1979). Swann & Etheridge (1995) found that buzzards bred more successfully in an area where rabbits were common, and Graham *et al.* (1995) showed that buzzard breeding densities were positively correlated with lagomorph abundance in south-west Scotland. We used rabbit bags to provide an index of abundance, and the indications are that there have been substantial increases in rabbit numbers in Wales and the West Midlands since at least the early 1980s.

28.4.2 Persecution
Persecution of buzzards, especially poisoning, on the edge of their range may have prevented colonisation of new areas in the past (Elliott & Avery, 1991). Our results show that the percentage of the population reported as killed by man in Gloucestershire, Hereford & Worcester and Shropshire was 75% lower in 1990-95 than in 1975-89. This was mainly due to a 72% decrease in reported poisonings and an estimated 151% increase in population size. The number of cases of deliberate pesticide abuse reported to the WIIS dropped sharply after 1991, probably due to a combination of stiffer penalties for offenders and the MAFF-led campaign against illegal poisoning implemented in 1990 (Batten *et al.*, 1991). An additional factor may have been the introduction of Larsen traps in 1990, which provided an alternative to illegal poisoning as a means of controlling corvids. The Game Conservancy Trust, who developed this trap, had sold 5,930 sets of springs for traps by the end of 1991 (S. Tapper, pers. comm.).

28.4.3 Population trends in other regions
Elsewhere in England, buzzards have returned to breed in several counties after many years' absence (e.g. Bedfordshire, Hertfordshire, Leicestershire, Lincolnshire, Norfolk, Durham and Sussex), and have increased markedly in many others (e.g. Berkshire, Sussex, Derbyshire, Northamptonshire, Northumberland and West Yorkshire) (Clements, 2000). Buzzards have also become more numerous in much of Scotland and in the Republic of Ireland in recent years. No detailed explanations are given, but factors thought to be important include reduced persecution and increased rabbit numbers. Hence it appears that the increase in the buzzard population in our study area since 1983 has been mirrored in other parts of Britain and Ireland (see also Holling, Chapter 12; Jardine, Chapter 13).

28.4.4 Breeding density and territory occupancy
At 81 territorial pairs per 100 km², buzzard density in SO37 was the highest yet recorded in Europe. Densities of up to 78 pairs per 100 km² have been recorded in rich wooded areas

in central Europe (Melde, 1956; Thiollay, 1967), but the previous highest density found over a large area in Britain was 41 pairs per 100 km² in mid-Wales (Newton *et al.*, 1982). Mean territory size in SO37 estimated by tessellation was about 120 ha; similar to values of 130 and 140 ha found at high breeding densities in Germany (Mebs, 1964) and Devon (Dare, 1961). Even where buzzards bred at lower densities, mean territory size was typically in the range 180-190 ha (Picozzi & Weir, 1974; Tubbs, 1974; Halley, 1993), although it could be as high as 319 ha in upland North Wales (Dare, 1995). Evidence from our study (Figure 28.5) suggests that environmental parameters measured within 400-600 m of nests were most important in predicting aspects of buzzard breeding success. Since the area contained within a circle of radius 600 m is 113 ha, this implies that buzzards in our study area were foraging mainly within hunting territories of around that size.

At 22 territorial pairs per 100 km², breeding density in SO77 was in the upper range of the 10-22 pairs per 100 km² found elsewhere in Britain (Holdsworth, 1971; Tubbs, 1974; Weir & Picozzi, 1983; Dare & Barry, 1990; Halley, 1993). This was surprising considering that this area was close to the edge of the range and breeding was unproven in 1988-91 (Gibbons *et al.*, 1993). Densities would probably have been higher but for the Wyre Forest, which occupied approximately 16 km², and where only one pair held territory. Buzzards were continuing to colonise this area during the study period; several territories had only been re-occupied within the last five years after many years absence, according to local landowners.

Within SO37 small territories (as defined by the tessellation method), and thus high buzzard densities, were associated with high proportions of unimproved pasture and mature woodland within polygons. Rabbit abundance was highest in unimproved pasture, and mature woodland holds a high diversity of other favoured prey such as corvids and small passerines. In their broader scale analysis of factors influencing buzzard abundance in upland Britain, Gibbons *et al.* (1994) found that there was a positive association with mature woodland and grazed pasture, a very similar result to our own.

28.4.5 *Laying date and clutch size*

The laying date model was rather poor, explaining only 25% of the variation in laying date. Egg laying was earlier at low altitude, and with high proportions of unimproved pasture within 400 m of the nest. Climatic conditions are less harsh at lower altitudes, especially in early spring, which may have enabled earlier laying, and unimproved pasture provides an abundance of rabbits. Austin (1992) found that buzzards in Argyll laid earlier at low altitudes and with small amounts of forest plantation within 1,500 m of the nest; they tended to avoid agricultural land and preferred to forage in perennial grassland. Similarly, Newton *et al.* (1996) found that red kites *Milvus milvus* in mid-Wales laid clutches earlier at lower altitudes.

The mean clutch size of 2.2 in our study area was similar to the 2.1-2.4 found in Argyll, Dartmoor and Wales (Dare, 1961; Newton *et al.*, 1982; Austin, 1992; Dare, 1995), though less than the 2.9-3.0 recorded in Moray, Speyside and Yorkshire (Holdsworth, 1971; Picozzi & Weir, 1974; Swann & Etheridge, 1995). Within our study area, large clutches were associated with high rabbit abundance within 600 m of the nest. This model was more robust than the one predicting laying date, explaining 46% of the variation in clutch size.

Our findings agree with those of Swann & Etheridge (1995), who showed that buzzards laid larger clutches and produced twice as many young in an area where rabbits were common than in a nearby area where few rabbits were found. Austin (1992) found that large clutches were laid at medium altitude (100-200 m), with large amounts of perennial grassland and small amounts of forest plantation.

28.4.6 Nest survival rates

Nest survival rates estimated by Mayfield analyses were much lower than those obtained by the apparent nest success method. Previous studies of buzzard breeding success have used the apparent nest success method, and we used this method in order to compare results with other studies. The percentages of nests in our study area apparently surviving incubation, chick rearing and the total breeding period were 86%, 92% and 79% respectively. In north Wales, Dare (1995) found comparable values of 68%, 93% and 63%, but Austin (1992) noted much higher values of 92%, 100% and 92% respectively in Argyll. In an analysis of nest record cards from the whole of Britain, Tubbs (1972) found that 84% of nests survived incubation, very similar to our figure of 86%.

Nest failure at the egg stage was more likely with small amounts of unimproved pasture within 400 m of the nest and at high breeding densities. The main cause of egg loss was probably corvid predation, since several damaged eggs examined had puncture marks typical of crows. This predation would have been made easier if incubating buzzards were forced to leave their nests to hunt more frequently, and this would be more likely when prey availability close to nests was low. Rabbit densities were highest in unimproved pasture, and a lack of this habitat close to nests may thus have contributed to a higher rate of failure at the egg stage. In addition, territorial disputes between neighbouring buzzard pairs were probably more common at higher breeding densities, and frequent disputes may have allowed corvids more opportunities to raid nests.

28.4.7 Fledging success and chick mortality

Our figure of 1.2 young fledged per territorial pair was about twice that found in Dartmoor, Wales and the New Forest (Dare, 1961; Tubbs, 1974; Newton *et al.*, 1982), but lower than values of 1.5 and 1.8 noted in Moray and Speyside (Picozzi & Weir, 1974; Swann & Etheridge, 1995). Although clutch size in Wales, Dartmoor and the New Forest was similar to that in our study area, higher failure rates resulted in fewer young fledging per pair in these areas. Conversely, buzzards in Moray and Speyside produced more fledged young per pair than in the Welsh Marches because of higher initial clutch sizes rather than higher nest survival rates. In our study area, higher numbers of fledged young were associated with high rabbit abundance within 600 m of nests. This result was expected, since rabbits were by far the most common prey item recorded in nests.

Most chick deaths occurred within the first two weeks after hatching but it was difficult to be certain about the causes of death. We think it unlikely that they were predated, and starvation or sibling aggression are more plausible explanations. Brood reduction was associated with low proportions of deciduous woodland within 400 m of nests and small clutches. Mature deciduous woodland holds large numbers of suitable prey, such as corvids and small passerines, and also provides a habitat in which prey may be more easily surprised and captured. A lack of this habitat close to nests may thus have resulted in a higher probability of chick starvation. Smaller clutches were associated with low rabbit abundance close to nests, and the fact that nests with small clutches were more likely to suffer brood reduction may indicate that chicks in such nests were starving to death, or suffering siblicides.

28.4.8 Prey

Rabbits were by far the most important prey item for breeding buzzards in our study area. Fledgling corvids also appear to have been an important prey item, especially during chick rearing. Some nests were almost completely covered in corvid remains, eight legs being found in one nest. Pheasant rearing was carried out on a large scale in SO37, where three shooting estates released a total of about 30,000 poults, but pheasants were less common in SO77 where there were no shooting estates. Despite the abundance of pheasants they comprised only 5.1% of prey remains in nests, and these were perhaps more likely to have been scavenged from road kills rather than predated by buzzards. We found only three voles in nests in our study area, perhaps because most of those taken to nests may be swallowed whole by chicks. Our method of recording prey items at nests will undoubtedly be biased towards large prey items, but even allowing for this it seems that voles were not important for breeding buzzards in our study area.

Several studies in continental Europe have shown that small mammals were the most frequent prey item of buzzards (e.g. Mebs, 1964; Newton, 1979; Spidso & Selas, 1988). Medium-sized birds, such as corvids and pigeons, were also important, especially in poor vole years (Spidso & Selas, 1988; Jedrzejewski *et al.*, 1994). However, in Britain rabbits are generally thought to be the most important prey, especially for breeding buzzards (e.g. Dare, 1961; Tubbs, 1974; Newton, 1979; Swann & Etheridge, 1995; Jardine, Chapter 13). Tubbs (1974) found that birds predominated in the diet of New Forest buzzards, but in this area few rabbits were found and productivity was low. As in our study area, corvids were found to be a common prey item in north Scotland and Wales (Newton *et al.*, 1982; Dare, 1989; Swann & Etheridge, 1995).

28.5 Conclusions

Buzzard density and distribution in the Welsh Marches increased significantly between 1983 and 1996, a situation that has been mirrored in several other areas within Britain and Ireland in recent years. Increased productivity, probably associated with increased rabbit abundance and a reduction in persecution, especially poisonings, are thought to be the main factors involved. Rabbit abundance, as measured by bag data, in Britain has increased markedly since the mid-1960s (Tapper, 1992), and there can be little doubt that this has contributed to the increase in the buzzard population since the 1970s (Gregory *et al.*, 2000). A reduction in persecution levels since the MAFF-led campaign against illegal poisoning and the introduction of Larsen Traps, both implemented in 1990, has undoubtedly also enabled buzzards to re-occupy much of their former range in central and eastern Britain. We found buzzards breeding at high densities in an area which was close to the edge of the species' range in 1988-91 (Gibbons *et al.*, 1993). High rabbit abundance, and the widespread availability of suitable habitats such as unimproved pasture and mature woodland were probably major factors contributing to these high breeding densities.

The rate of spread of the population may have been relatively slow, at least until relatively recently, due to the apparent tendency for buzzards to breed at high densities in favoured areas. We found record densities in one 10 km square, and moderate densities in another square that apparently held no breeding pairs 10 years previously. Evidence from wing tagging and radio tagging suggests that, although buzzards may disperse considerable distances in their first winter, the majority tend to return close to their natal area in the following spring (Davis & Davis, 1992; Walls & Kenward, 1995). These birds are then likely to establish breeding territories nearby in subsequent years. Hence the colonisation of new areas may only occur once all the suitable territories in established areas have been occupied. It is likely that buzzards will continue to expand their range in the UK in the future, especially if rabbit numbers continue to increase and persecution levels continue to decrease.

Acknowledgements

We would like to thank all the landowners who gave us access to their land. Tony Cross, Dave Lamacraft, Mike Thornley, Cliff Smout, Len Campbell, Richard Knight, Kirsty Allen, Peter Dutta and Alan Leitch provided valuable advice and assistance with fieldwork. Drs Rhys Green, Debbie Pain, Jerry Wilson, Ken Norris and Norman Ratcliffe provided advice on project design and statistical analyses. The following people helped with the 1996 Soaring Survey: J. Armstrong, M. Avery, P. Dymott, G. Hall, E. Marrs, P. Morris, S. Nelson, A. Remfry, C. Train, M. Williams. Dr Humphrey Crick (BTO) provided the Nest Record Card data, Dr Stephen Tapper (The Game Conservancy Trust) provided the data on rabbit abundance, and Mark Fletcher (WIIS) provided the data on pesticide abuse.

References

Austin, G.E. (1992). *The distribution and breeding performance of the buzzard* Buteo buteo *in relation to habitat: an application using remote sensing and Geographical Information Systems.* Unpublished PhD thesis, University of Glasgow, Glasgow.

Bart, J. & Robson, S.R. (1982). Estimating survivorship when the subjects are visited periodically. *Ecology,* **63**, 1078-1090.

Batten, L.A., Douse, A.F.G. & Nugent, M.J. (1991). The abuse of pesticides: illegal poisoning continues in 1989. In *Britain's Birds in 1989/90: the Conservation and Monitoring Review,* ed. by D.A. Stroud. & D. Glue. British Trust for Ornithology/Nature Conservancy Council, Thetford. pp. 35-37.

Clements, R. (2000). Range expansion of the common buzzard in Britain. *British Birds,* **93**, 242-248.

Cramp, S. (1985). *The Birds of the Western Palearctic. Volume 2.* Oxford University Press, London.

Dare, P.J. (1961). *Ecological observations on a breeding population of the common buzzard* Buteo buteo. Unpublished PhD thesis, University of Exeter, Exeter.

Dare, P.J. (1989). Aspects of the breeding biology of the buzzard *Buteo buteo* in north Wales. *Naturalist,* **114**, 23-31.

Dare, P.J. (1995). Breeding success and territory features of buzzards *Buteo buteo* in Snowdonia and adjacent uplands of North Wales. *Welsh Bird Report,* **1**, 69-78.

Dare, P.J. & Barry, J.T. (1990). Population size, density and regularity in nest spacing of buzzards *Buteo buteo* in two upland regions of Wales, *Bird Study,* **37**, 23-29.

Davis, P.E. & Davis, J.E. (1992). Dispersal and age of first breeding of buzzards in Central Wales. *British Birds,* **85**, 578-587.

Elliott, G.D. & Avery, M.I. (1991). A review of reports of buzzard persecution 1975-1989. *Bird Study,* **38**, 52-56.

Francis, B., Green, M. & Payne, C. (1993). *GLIM4.* Oxford University Press, Oxford.

Gibbons, D.W., Reid, J.B. & Chapman, R.A. (1993). *The New Atlas of Breeding Birds in Britain and Ireland.* Poyser, Berkhamsted.

Gibbons, D.W., Gates, S., Green, R.E., Fuller, R.J. & Fuller, R.M. (1994). Buzzards *Buteo buteo* and ravens *Corvus corax* in the uplands of Britain: limits to distribution and abundance. *Ibis,* **137**, S75-S84.

Graham, I.M., Redpath, S.M. & Thirgood, S.J. (1995). The diet and breeding density of common buzzards *Buteo buteo* in relation to indices of prey abundance. *Bird Study,* **42**, 165-173.

Gregory, R.D., Noble, D.G., Campbell, L.H. & Gibbons, D.W. (2000). *The State of the UK's Birds 1999.* Royal Society for the Protection of Birds and British Trust for Ornithology, Sandy.

Halley, D.J. (1993). Population changes and territorial distribution of common buzzards *Buteo buteo* in the Central Highlands, Scotland. *Bird Study,* **40**, 24-30.

Holdsworth, M. (1971). Breeding biology of buzzards at Sedburgh during 1937-67. *British Birds,* **64**, 412-420.

Jedrzejewski, W., Szymura, A. & Jedrzejewska, B. (1994). Reproduction and food of the buzzard *Buteo buteo* in relation to the abundance of rodents and birds in Bialowieza National Park, Poland. *Ethology, Ecology and Evolution,* **6**, 179-190.

Langbein, J., Hutchings, M.R., Harris, S., Stoate, C., Tapper, S.C. & Wray, S. (1995). Techniques for assessing the abundance of brown hares *Lepus europaeus. Mammal Review,* **29**, 93-116.

Mebs, T. (1964). Zur Biologie und Populations-dynamik des Mausebussards *Buteo buteo. Journal fur Ornithologie,* **105**, 247-306.

Melde, M. (1956). *Die Mausebussard.* Neue Brehm Bucherei, Leipzig.

Moore, N.W. (1957). The past and present status of the buzzard in the British Isles. *British Birds,* **50**, 173-197.

Newton, I. (1979). *Population Ecology of Raptors.* Poyser, Berkhamsted.

Newton, I., Davis, P.E. & Davis, G.E. (1982). Ravens and buzzards in relation to sheep farming and forestry in Wales. *Journal of Applied Ecology,* **19**, 681-706.

Newton, I., Davis, P.E. & Moss, D. (1996). Distribution and breeding of red kites *Milvus milvus* in relation to afforestation and other land-use in Wales. *Journal of Applied Ecology,* **33**, 210-224.

Picozzi, N. & Weir, D. (1974). Breeding biology of the buzzard in Speyside. *British Birds,* **67**, 199-210.

Sharrock, J.T.R. (1976). *The Atlas of Breeding Birds in Britain and Ireland.* T. & A.D. Poyser, Berkhamsted.

Sim, I.M.W., Campbell, L., Pain, D.J. & Wilson, J.D. (2000). Correlates of the population increase of common buzzards *Buteo buteo* in the West Midlands between 1983 and 1996. *Bird Study,* **47**, 154-164.

Sim, I.M.W., Cross, A.V., Lamacraft, D.L. & Pain, D.J. (2001). Correlates of common buzzard *Buteo buteo* density and breeding success in the West Midlands. *Bird Study,* **48**, 317-329.

Spidso, T.K. & Selas, V. (1988). Prey selection and breeding success in the common buzzard *Buteo buteo* in relation to small rodent cycles in southern Norway. *Fauna Norvegica, Series C,* **11**, 61-66.

Swann, R.L. & Etheridge, B. (1995). A comparison of breeding success and prey of the common buzzard *Buteo buteo* in two areas of northern Scotland. *Bird Study,* **42**, 37-43.

Tapper, S. (1992). *Game Heritage.* Game Conservancy Ltd., Hampshire.

Taylor, K., Hudson, R. & Horne, G. (1988). Buzzard breeding distribution and abundance in Britain and Northern Ireland in 1983. *Bird Study,* **35**, 109-118.

Thiollay, J.M. (1967). Ecologie d'une population de rapaces diurnes en Lorraine. *Terre et la vie,* **114**, 116-183.

Tubbs, C.R. (1972). Analysis of nest record cards for the buzzard. *Bird Study,* **19**, 96-104.

Tubbs, C.R. (1974). *The Buzzard.* David & Charles, Newton Abbot.

Walls, S.S. & Kenward, R.E. (1995). Movements of radio-tagged common buzzards *Buteo buteo* in their first year. *Ibis,* **137**, 177-182.

Weir, D.N. & Picozzi, N. (1983). Dispersion of buzzards in Speyside. *British Birds,* **76**, 66-78.

THEME FIVE

CONSERVATION AND MANAGEMENT

THEME FIVE

CONSERVATION AND MANAGEMENT

Some of the highest profile conservation and management schemes for animals have been devised for birds of prey. Taken as a whole, conservation management activities have tended to focus on the birds, their habitat and food, or on their wider environment, and have been given added impetus because of national/local extinctions or population declines of individual raptor species. As a rule, we can categorise conservation and management activities on the ground as addressing: (a) habitat reduction/deterioration (affecting food supplies and/or nesting areas); (b) human persecution; and (c) toxic chemical contamination (in the food chain, and having a cumulative effect on raptors) (e.g. Newton, 1979).

Amar *et al.* (Chapter 29) provide an elegant examination of the causes of the decline of the hen harrier *Circus cyaneus* population in Orkney. In the early 20th century, when the hen harrier became extinct as a nesting species on mainland Britain, the Orkney population was significant in underpinning the ensuing recolonisation throughout Britain (Watson, 1977). Since 1960 on Orkney, the increase in the proportion of land re-seeded as pasture, and a decline in the amount of rough grassland, has reduced the amount of food available to hen harriers, giving rise to a steady decline in the population. Amar *et al.* carried out an experiment involving the provision of supplementary food to some males (which provide food for females and chicks), resulting in an increase in the number of breeding females, and also the amount of polygynous breeding. Indeed, whereas all supplementary-fed males were mated with at least one breeding female, around 20% of unfed (control) males had no breeding females. Since completion of this research, Scottish Natural Heritage has introduced a 'Natural Care' positive management scheme to increase the amount of food available to harriers through habitat improvements (notably the re-creation of rough grassland).

Two chapters deal with major raptor re-introduction programmes, of white-tailed eagles *Haliaeetus albicilla* in Scotland (Bainbridge *et al.*, Chapter 30), and of red kites *Milvus milvus* (Carter *et al.*, Chapter 31) in Britain. Both chapters explain in considerable detail the history and complexity of high profile species re-introduction programmes. It would appear that whilst the prospects for the white-tailed eagle programme are reasonable, those for red kites will depend upon the cessation of poisoning of raptors in parts of Scotland and north England. Such is the concern about the impacts of poisoning of red kites, notably using agricultural pesticides such as Carbufuran, that the UK Raptor Working Group recommended that the Control of Pesticides Regulations (1996) should be amended to require those who possess pesticides to be licenced (Recommendation 26 in Anon., 2000).

Four chapters consider a range of conservation challenges for birds of prey. Taylor & Walton (Chapter 32) have studied the importance of nest site provision for the conservation of barn owls *Tyto alba* in south Scotland. This builds on Taylor's long-term study of barn owls since 1978 (Taylor, 1993). Artificial nest sites have been put out to counteract the loss of traditional nest sites, and by the year 2000 artificial sites comprised around 70% of all sites available to breeding birds. The study suggests that in the absence of artificial sites, the study population would have been limited by nest site availability by 1997, and might have begun to decline thereafter. The study stresses the importance of artificial nest sites as a management tool, and urges that they should be used in areas of high habitat quality, where birds should breed particularly successfully. Barn owls, like many farmland birds in western Europe, have declined due to intensification of farming methods (e.g. Tucker & Heath, 1994; Siriwardena *et al.*, 1998; Donald *et al.*, 2001). The study of barn owls is particularly important because the species is dependent upon both specialised nesting structures as well as suitable feeding habitat. It is heartening, therefore, that research has shown provisioning of artificial nest sites in suitable areas can benefit this rather enigmatic, nocturnal and crepuscular owl.

Game bird management is a significant land use in the lowlands of Britain, and much of the woodland and, to a lesser extent, farmland areas there are now managed for the shooting of pheasant *Phasianus colchicus* and red-legged partridges *Alectoris rufa*. Indeed, each year in Britain approximately 20 million pheasants and 1 million red-legged partridges are released for game shooting (Robertson, 1997; Thompson *et al.*, 1997; Anon., 2000). Allen & Feare (Chapter 33) review the impacts of raptors on lowland game birds, and management measures which can reduce these. Research continues to investigate these interactions (also Anon., 2000). Recently, several management techniques have been deployed effectively to reduce raptor impacts on game birds (e.g. British Association for Shooting and Conservation, 2002). However, as Newbery *et al.* (Chapter 34) show, other aspects of land management in the lowlands are an increasing problem for red kites. Specifically, they have found that rodenticides are increasingly associated with high mortality in red kites.

The theme of conservation and management is concluded with a fascinating study of practices put into place to reduce the conflict between agricultural land use and the conservation of Montagu's harrier *Circus pygargus* (Arroyo *et al.*, Chapter 35). In western Europe around 60% of harrier nestlings in agricultural areas may perish in the absence of conservation measures. Such measures include maintaining food supplies through improving habitat management measures, developing novel agricultural practices, and protecting nest sites and nestlings during the harvesting period. The holistic and imaginative approach deployed in managing this vulnerable raptor sets an important standard for lowland conservation and management programmes involving raptors throughout Europe.

References

Anonymous (2000). *Report of the UK Raptor Working Group*. Department of the Environment, Transport and Regions, and Joint Nature Conservation Committee, Peterborough.

British Association for Shooting and Conservation (2002). *Birds of prey at pheasant release pens*. British Association for Shooting and Conservation, Rossett.

Donald, P.F., Green, R.E. & Heath, M.F. (2001). Agricultural intensification and the collapse of Europe's farmland bird populations. *Proceedings of the Royal Society of London* (B), **268**, 25-29.

Newton, I. (1979). *Population Ecology of Raptors*. T. & A.D. Poyser, Berkhamsted.

Robertson, P. (1997). Naturalised introduced game birds in Britain. In *The Introduction and Naturalisation of Birds*, ed. by J.S. Holmes & J.R. Simons. HMSO, London. pp. 63-69.

Siriwardena G.M., Baillie, S.R. & Wilson, J.D. (1998). Variation in the survival rates of some British passerines with respect to their population trends on farmland. *Bird Study*, **45**, 276-292.

Taylor, I.R. (1993). *Barn Owls: Predator-Prey Relationships and Conservation*. Cambridge University Press, Cambridge.

Thompson, D.B.A., Gillings, S.D., Galbraith, C.A., Redpath, S.M. & Drewitt, J. (1997). The contribution of game management to biodiversity: a review of the importance of grouse moors for upland birds. In *Biodiversity in Scotland: Status, Trends and Initiatives,* ed. by L.V. Fleming, A.C. Newton, J.A. Vickery & M.B. Usher. The Stationery Office, Edinburgh. pp. 198-212.

Tucker, G.M. & Heath, M.F. (1994). *Birds in Europe: their conservation status*. Birdlife International, Cambridge.

Watson, D. (1977). *The Hen Harrier*. T. & A.D. Poyser, Berkhamsted.

29. COULD THE HEN HARRIER (*CIRCUS CYANEUS*) DECLINE ON ORKNEY BE DUE TO A SHORTAGE OF FOOD?

Arjun Amar, Steve Redpath, Xavier Lambin & Eric Meek

Summary

1.   The population of hen harriers *Circus cyaneus* in Orkney has declined dramatically over the last 20 years. One hypothesis for this decline is that there has been a reduction in the amount of food available.

2.   Harriers in Orkney were found to hunt areas with more rough grass during both the spring and summer.

3.   Agricultural records revealed that, since 1960, there has been an increase in the proportion of land under pasture and a decrease in the amount of rough grazing. Additionally, since the start of the 1980s, stocking densities of sheep *Ovis aries* have more than doubled on mainland Orkney. These changes are likely to have been detrimental to harriers and could have reduced the amount of food available.

4.   Male harriers in Orkney provisioned food to their females during the pre-lay period at a lower rate than did males in another Scottish population, where the population was breeding far more successfully.

5.   A supplementary feeding experiment showed that males provided with extra food had more breeding females than control males.

6.   Observational and experimental data therefore suggested that the population is indeed limited by food and that a reduction in prey is a likely explanation for this population's decline.

29.1 Introduction

The Orkney hen harrier *Circus cyaneus* population was once the stronghold for this species in Britain, but the population is currently in decline (Meek *et al.*, 1998). The hen harrier became extinct as a breeding species on mainland Britain at the start of the 1900s, due to human persecution, and it is believed that birds from the Orkney population aided in the re-colonisation of the British mainland (Watson, 1977).

Hen harriers on parts of mainland Britain are persecuted because they kill red grouse *Lagopus lagopus scoticus* and can limit the numbers available for shooting in autumn (Thirgood *et al.*, 2000; Redpath & Thirgood, Chapter 39). Persecution of this species continues despite the fact they are legally protected under international and UK legislation (e.g. Etheridge *et al.*, 1997; Stroud, Chapter 3). However, in Orkney persecution does not occur due to the absence of commercial grouse shooting. The decline of the hen harrier in Orkney is therefore alarming, and if levels of persecution on mainland Britain were to increase, this population may no longer be able to act as a sustainable refuge in the future.

Hen harriers in Orkney have been monitored with varying degrees of intensity for the last 50 years (Balfour, 1957; Balfour & Cadbury, 1979; Picozzi, 1984a; Downing, 1990; Meek *et al.*, 1998), and this continuous effort has allowed this population's decline to be revealed. Meek *et al.* (1998) found that numbers of males and females had declined by around 70% and that productivity had decreased by 60%, from the peak figures of the 1970s.

During previous research, male hen harriers in Orkney were found to be highly polygynous (Balfour & Cadbury, 1979; Picozzi, 1984a,b). Both authors considered that the female biased sex ratio of the population was an important factor in causing this high level of polygyny. One of the major features associated with the decline of this population has been the reduction in polygynous breeding, defined as a male mated with more than one female, which lays at least one egg. Picozzi (1984a) found that from 1976-1981, an average of 77% of adult males were polygynous breeders. Current levels of polygyny in Orkney are far lower (only 17% in 1998-2000) and some males fail to breed at all (Amar *et al.*, in press). Despite the fact that polygynous breeding is low there is still a female biased sex ratio in the population. The female:male sex ratio in 1998 was estimated to be 1.8:1 in Orkney's West Mainland, which is similar to the average bias found during 1976-1981, which was 2.2:1 (Picozzi, 1984a). These figures suggest that a shortage of males is not the only factor involved in influencing levels of polygyny on Orkney.

A shortage of food during the early breeding period may be responsible for the reduced levels of polygyny and also for the poor productivity of the population, factors that may ultimately be responsible for this population's decline. Polygynous breeding is often associated with productive habitats (Verner & Willson, 1966). If levels of food have decreased in Orkney, males may not be able to supply adequate food to allow more than one female to breed. Changes in land use, such as the destruction of habitats and the intensification of farming, may be factors responsible for the shortage of prey.

In this chapter we explore the hypothesis that a shortage of food during the early breeding period could be responsible for the population's decline. We examine the changes in land use on Orkney and investigate the implications of these changes for harriers by examining which habitats and habitat characteristics are important to hunting harriers. We compare the provisioning rates of male harriers in Orkney with the rates from males at Langholm, in south-west Scotland, where the population breeds more successfully (Amar *et al.*, 2003), in order to examine whether differences in breeding performance are reflected in provisioning rates. Finally, we examine the effect of a supplementary feeding experiment on the breeding performance of the hen harriers in Orkney.

29.2 Methods

29.2.1 *Changes in land use*

In Orkney, the following parishes in the West Mainland have breeding hen harriers: Birsay, Harry, Evie, Rendall, Firth, Ophir and Stenness. Data from the June Agricultural Census from 1960 until 1998 in these parishes were used to assess changes in land use. Data were collected on the total area under pasture and under rough grazing, the total area of land from which records were taken in each parish and the total number of sheep *Ovis aries* in each parish. These latter two measures were then used to calculate the number of sheep per hectare for each parish in each year.

29.2.2 Habitat use by hunting harriers

The relative use of three habitat types by hunting harriers was investigated. These habitats were as follows: i) upland moorland – dominated by *Calluna vulgaris;* ii) semi-natural lowland – principally a mixture of *Calluna vulgaris* and rough grass, similar to the transitional land between moorland and farmland; and iii) intensive lowland farmland – dominated by sheep and cattle *Bos taurus* pasture, but also with small areas of semi-natural lowland, primarily rough grazing. Squares of 1 km dominated by each habitat types were chosen subjectively based on appearance. Although ideally squares would have been chosen randomly, the limited areas of certain habitat types (principally the semi-natural lowland) combined with suitable topography to achieve sufficiently good observations meant that these factors constrained selection of squares. However, as we had no previous knowledge of harrier hunting intensity, potential bias in site selection was unlikely. No squares had active harrier nests within them during a watch period and all squares were located within 5 km of an active harrier nest. In summer, a nest proximity index for each square was then calculated as the sum of the reciprocals of the squared distance to each nest site. In spring, a similar territory proximity index was calculated, using the same methods, but replacing distance to nests with the distance to the centre of male territories in the subsequent breeding season.

Data on habitat use by harriers were collected in summer 1998, spring and summer 1999 and spring 2000. Data were collected in spring between 28 February and 29 March and during summer from 12 July until 16 August. Nine squares, three of each habitat type, were used in all periods, except for the three moorland squares in summer 1999 (due to the presence of active harrier nests). Data in summer 1999 and spring 2000 were also recorded from a further nine squares, again, three in each habitat type. Data were therefore collected from a total of 18 squares.

Watches of squares were conducted from suitable locations that were close to the edge of the square and also offered good views over the whole square. The relatively flat landscape of mainland Orkney allowed continuous observations of harriers within a square. Watches were conducted at squares until a total of ten hours watching per square had been accumulated (usually in two to three hour watch blocks). During a watch, squares were continuously scanned using 10 x 42 binoculars for hunting harriers. Harriers were classified as hunting if they were flying approximately <10 m from the ground (estimated visually). Harriers tend to hunt by flying low and quartering across the ground (Schipper *et al.*, 1975) and <10 m was the criterion chosen to exclude harriers which may not have been actively searching for prey. Previous work by Madders (1997) showed that there was a high degree of agreement between two observers, independently recording the height of an individual harrier and that this close level of agreement also existed between habitat types. A tape recorder, set to run continuously for the duration of each foraging bout, was used to record the duration of hunting within a square.

Vegetation composition and height were recorded between the same dates as the hunting watches were conducted and were performed in both spring and summer. For squares observed during the same season in two years, vegetation measures were only recorded in the first year as vegetation was assumed not to have altered greatly between years. Quadrats, measuring 25 cm² were placed every 40 m along two parallel transect lines within a square, each located 250 m and 750 m away from one side of a watch square, thus giving information from 50 quadrats per square. The dominant type of vegetation in each quadrat was recorded and the highest live point of this vegetation type measured. Vegetation was recorded at species level, except for grass species, which were classified categorically as either smooth or rough grass. A build up of dead vegetation adequate to conceal a moving vole (Hewson, 1982) defined rough grass.

Habitat use by hunting harriers was examined in relation to the three main habitat types in the two seasons. At a finer scale we examined the amount of hunting in an area in relation to the abundance of the main vegetation types (i.e. those that were dominant in over 10% of the quadrats in a squares), the mean vegetation height and the proximity of nests or territories in spring and summer, respectively.

29.2.3 *Comparative breeding success and provisioning rates*

Possible harrier territories in Orkney and Langholm were checked at the start of the breeding season for signs of occupancy, which was identified from either perched or displaying males or females. During this study some birds in Langholm and Orkney were provided with supplementary food (see later, but see also Redpath *et al.*, 2001; Amar & Redpath, 2002). All data relating to birds provided with supplementary food were excluded from these analyses, as was information relating to the second breeding attempt of birds which re-laid following the failure of their initial clutches.

The rate at which males provisioned their females with food in Orkney and Langholm was recorded during both the pre-lay and incubation period. The pre-lay period was defined as four weeks prior to laying, or if no clutch was produced, until the mean laying date for that year. Watches were conducted at times with good visibility and little precipitation.

In Orkney, an effort was made after a food pass to search for prey remains in the area where the female fed and the prey types were identified to provide information on the diet of the birds in this area. Similar data were not collected in Langholm, but observations indicated that all items delivered were small, probably almost exclusively small mammals and meadow pipits *Anthus pratensis* or other small passerines (Redpath & Thirgood, 1997).

So as to investigate whether there were large differences in the average sizes of prey between the areas, we estimated the average biomass of prey items delivered in the two localities. In order to calculate these we used the percentage of prey types identified from remains in Orkney, and for Langholm we assumed an equal representation in the diet of field voles *Microtus agrestis* and passerines. However varying this assumption for Langholm would have little effect as passerines and field voles weights only differed by 13 g. Rabbit *Oryctolagus cuniculus* biomass was calculated from the regression equation from Carss (1995), using the mean hind foot length of rabbits found in the nest during a previous study on Orkney (Picozzi, 1980). A quarter of this biomass was used to account for the fact that only part of a rabbit was usually delivered by the males. Biomass of Orkney vole *Microtus arvalis orcadensis* or field vole was taken from Corbett & Harris (1991) and the meadow pipit's weight from Picozzi (1978) was used for passerines.

29.2.4 *Supplementary feeding experiment*

A short-term trial in 1998 to provide supplementary food to hen harriers in Orkney found that scavenging birds, particularly hooded crows *Corvus corone corone*, quickly removed all the food intended for the harriers. So as to achieve supplementary feeding of the harriers it was therefore necessary to remove crows from the immediate areas. This, however, potentially confounded the effect of feeding and therefore an additional group from which crows were removed was also included in the experiment. This additional removal group therefore allowed assessment of the effect of crow removal independently of food provision. If the removal of crows had no effect on breeding parameters, we could then realistically conclude that any effect in the fed group was most likely attributable to the provision of food rather than from the removal of crows. We also had a third control group where neither crow removal nor supplementary feeding occurred. Our experiment therefore had three treatments, namely:-

1. Fed group, where supplementary food was provided and crows were removed;
2. Removal group, where crows were removed from harrier territories; and
3. Control group, where neither crow removal nor supplementary feeding occurred.

The experiment was conducted during 1999 and 2000, but we also used data from un-manipulated nests in 1998 in order to increase sample size of the control group and to test for territory effects. Territories used by harriers in 1998 were randomly assigned to one of the three treatments in 1999 before the start of the breeding season. Subsequently in 2000, territories were randomly assigned to one of the other two treatments. Supplementary food was placed on feeding posts and at likely perching places from 6 April and continued throughout the incubation period in both years. Supplementary food mainly consisted of dead day old cockerel chicks but also some pieces of rabbit and hare *Lepus europaeus.* For full methods of the supplementary feeding experiment see Amar & Redpath (2002).

All harrier territories were watched throughout the pre-lay and laying period both to count numbers of females associated with males and to find nests. Males were not individually marked, so synchronous watches by multiple observers were performed in adjacent valleys, sometimes with the aid of short-wave radios. Using overlapping and sequential sightings of males, we were confident that we were able to ascertain which males were mated to which females. The maximum number of females associated with each male during the pre-lay period was based on courtship flights, birds perched together, food passes and nest building. The pre-lay period was defined separately for each year as the period from the start of April until the median lay date for that year. This period was used to account for the many females that did not lay and so allowed this period to be standardised between all males. In this chapter, breeding females were defined as those that were confirmed to have laid at least one egg. The breeding status of a female was classified as either monogamous, primary or secondary (the last category including both beta (secondary) and gamma (tertiary) females). Polygynous females were classified according to lay date, with the earliest laying female being considered the primary female. Nests were usually located during egg laying or early incubation, and both lay date (first egg) and clutch size recorded. For full methods on how lay date was calculated see Amar & Redpath (2002). Nests that had either uncertain lay date or clutch size were excluded from any analysis relating to these measures.

29.2.5 *Statistical analysis*
All statistical analyses were performed using SAS, version 6.12 (SAS Institute, 1990). Generalised linear mixed models were implemented using the GLIMMIX macro (Littell *et*

al., 1996) and generalised linear models, using the GENMOD procedure. Data on habitat use were analysed using a gamma error structure and a log link function. The properties of the gamma distribution mean that zero figures cannot be accommodated; to accommodate this we added half of the smallest value of the response variable being examined to each observation. We chose this value because the analyses were conducted using a log link function; values at the lower end of the range would therefore have had a disproportionate effect in the analyses. Because some squares had repeat observations in the different years, we analysed the data using GLIMMIX with the non-independent effect of individual squares set as a random term in the model. There were, however, insufficient replicates in the data set to examine the summer data using GLIMMIX; so instead GENMOD was used. To accommodate the potential pseudo-replication from repeated observations on the same sites, squares with repeat observations carried half of the weight in the analysis. Provisioning rates of male harriers were analysed using GENMOD, with a Poisson error structure and a log link function. The effect of experimental treatment on breeding parameters was analysed using GLIMMIX, with the non-independent effects of the different male territories incorporated into the analysis as a random term in the model. In this analysis data from un-manipulated nests in 1998 were also used to increase sample size and to further control for territory effects. Count data such as the maximum number of females associated per male and the number of breeding females per male were analysed with a Poisson error structure and a log link function. Lay date and clutch size were analysed with a normal error structure, and an identity link function and hatching success, a binary measure, was analysed with a binomial error structure and a logit link function. All models had year and treatment as permanent fixed effects because 1998 lacked any data for fed and removal territories. For models analysing breeding parameters determined at a female level, such as lay date, clutch size or hatching success, we also tested for the effect of female breeding status.

All models were constructed using a backward elimination procedure, dropping the least significant term in the subsequent model until only terms significant at the 10% level, using type III analyses, remained. All pair-wise comparisons were conducted in the GLIMMIX models, through t-tests of the differences in least square means (DLSM) and in generalised linear models using specific contrast statements. For the models implemented using the GLIMMIX procedure, denominator degrees of freedom were estimated, using Satterthwaite's formula (Littell *et al.*, 1996).

29.3 Results

29.3.1 *Change in land use*

Figure 29.1 shows the mean changes in land use and sheep stocking density from the seven parishes in West Mainland that were investigated. Since 1960 there has been an increase in the amount of land under pasture from 36% to 54% in 1990. Over this same period there has been a corresponding decline in the amount of land under rough grazing by 11%, equivalent to a loss of 22 km². Over the same period, numbers of sheep have changed dramatically. Numbers remained relatively constant between 1960 and 1980 but they then increased sharply from 1981 onwards. During the period 1960-1980 the mean stocking density was 0.95 sheep per hectare, by 1998 stocking densities were over twice this level at 2.14 sheep per hectare.

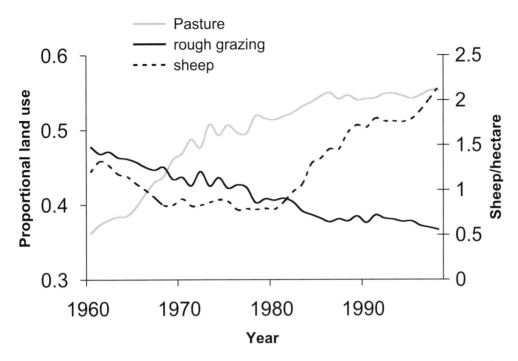

Figure 29.1. Proportion of land under pasture (pale line) and rough grazing (solid line) and the density of sheep (dashed line) in Orkney from 1960–1998. Data are mean values from seven parishes on West Mainland Orkney which have breeding hen harriers.

29.3.2 *Habitat use by hunting harriers*

The total time for which harriers were observed hunting in the squares did not vary significantly between spring and summer ($F_{1,33}$ = 1.20, P = 0.10). During the spring there was a positive association between harrier hunting and territory proximity ($F_{1,21}$ = 6.47, P <0.02). In other words, squares were generally hunted more the closer they were to the eventual breeding territories. Therefore, in subsequent analyses examining hunting in spring, territory proximity was controlled for by having it as a permanent fixed effect in the models. After controlling for this variable, the habitat type in which squares were located did not significantly explain the variation in the amount of time that squares were hunted ($F_{2,17}$ = 0.77, P >0.40). Examining the amount of time that squares were hunted in relation to the vegetation within the squares revealed that, in spring, there was a near-significant positive association with the amount of quadrats dominated by rough grass ($F_{1,16}$ = 3.68, P <0.08), once the proximity of territories were controlled for.

In summer, there was no effect of nest site proximity on the amount of time that a square was hunted. However, the habitat in which squares were located did explain a significant amount of the variation in hunting time between the squares ($F_{2,21}$ = 4.54, P <0.05), with semi-natural lowland habitats being hunted significantly more than either farmland ($F_{1,21}$ = 7.00, P <0.05) or moorland ($F_{1,21}$ = 4.62, P <0.05) (Figure 29.2.). In summer, the amount of time that an area was hunted by harriers was significantly positively associated with the amount of rough grass ($F_{1,21}$ = 12.5, P <0.01) after controlling for the near-significant effect of heather cover ($F_{1,21}$ = 3.34, P <0.10).

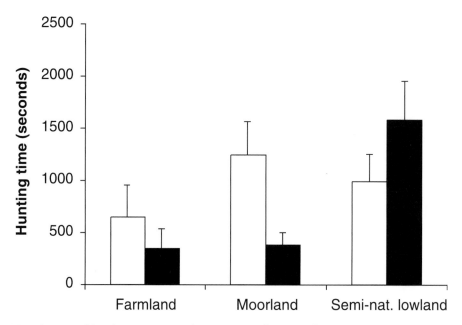

Figure 29.2. Amount of time harriers were seen hunting per ten hours in 1 km squares in the three habitat types in spring (clear bars) and summer (filled bars). Sample size for each bar is nine, except moorland in summer where sample size is six. Data are given as means with one standard error.

29.3.3 Breeding success and male provisioning rates in Orkney and Langholm

In the Langholm study area, between 1992 and 2000, 100% of the females that settled on a territory subsequently laid a clutch. The situation in Orkney was remarkably different. Between 1998 and 2000, over 50% of females that were on territories failed to lay a clutch. Hatching success also differed between Orkney and Langholm, although the difference was less striking. In Langholm, between 1993 and 2000, 13% of females failed to hatch their clutch, whereas in Orkney, between 1998-2000, 35% of breeding females were unsuccessful at hatching their clutch.

The frequency with which prey items were delivered to females by male harriers in Langholm was significantly higher than in Orkney, during both the pre-lay ($F_{1,44}$ = 69.7, P <0.001) and incubation periods ($F_{1,46}$ = 19.3, P <0.001) (Figure 29.3). Between the pre-lay and incubation periods, there was an approximate four-fold increase in the rate at which food was delivered by males in Orkney and this increase was statistically significant ($F_{1,56}$ = 14.69, P <0.001). In Langholm, however, provisioning rates did not vary between these two periods ($F_{1,34}$ = 0.19, P >0.50).

Remains from 13 prey items were found after food passes during the pre-lay and incubation periods in Orkney (Table 29.1a). From the remains of young rabbits found, it was evident that males usually only delivered a part of the rabbit, often only a leg or a head. After calculating the average biomass of prey items it did appear that males in Orkney tended to provide more biomass per prey delivery. We calculated an average biomass per prey item of 47.6 g and 23.7 g for Orkney and Langholm, respectively.

If the respective provisioning rates in the two localities are multiplied by the average biomass of prey items, we can derive the approximate average biomass (g) delivered per hour

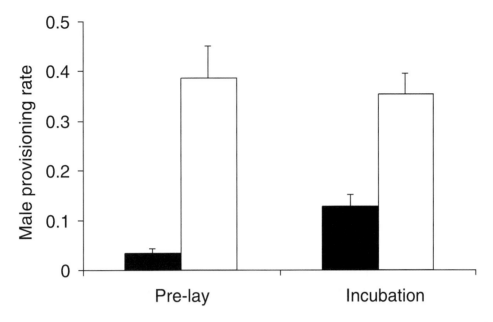

Figure 29.3. Provisioning rate (items delivered per hour) of male harriers in Orkney (filled bars) and Langholm (clear bars) during the pre-lay and incubation periods. Data given as means with one standard error.

(Table 29.1b). After accounting for these biomass differences, provisioning rates during the pre-lay period appeared to be around six times higher in Langholm than in Orkney. However the differences between the two locations during the incubation period appears to be less marked. Therefore, during the incubation period, there is a possibility that although items are delivered less frequently in Orkney, the amount of food delivered does not differ greatly.

Table 29.1. (a) Prey items identified from sites where females fed after food passes, during the pre-lay and incubation periods in Orkney, 1998, 1999 and 2000. Sample size of prey types in parentheses. (b) Estimation of the average biomass (g) delivered per hour in Orkney and Langholm during the pre-lay and incubation periods. Data are derived from the mean provisioning rates in the respective areas and the average biomass of prey delivered (see text for more details).

(a)	Prey type	Percentage	Biomass (g)
	Young rabbit	38 (5)	277
	Orkney vole	38 (5)	39
	Passerine	23 (3)	17

(b)	Study site	Provisioning rate (g per hour)	
		Orkney	Langholm
	Pre-lay	1.61	9.17
	Incubation	6.09	8.36

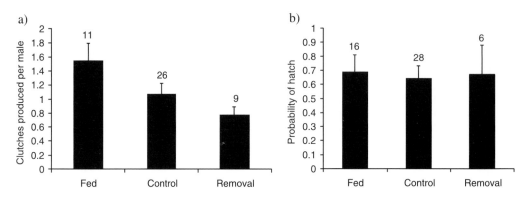

Figure 29.4. a) Mean number of breeding females shown as clutches produced per male in each of the treatment groups for all years combined. N = number of males. b) Probability of a female hatching a clutch in relation to which treatment their male was receiving for all years combined. Data are presented as means with one standard error and sample size. N = number of females.

29.3.4 Supplementary feeding experiment

The number of females associated with males during the pre-lay period, varied significantly between years ($F_{2,29}$ = 10.12, P <0.001). Although, experimental treatment had no significant effect on the number of females associated with males ($F_{2,32}$ = 2.43, P >0.10), it did have a significant effect on the number of females breeding per male ($F_{2,31}$ = 7.71, P <0.005) (Figure 29.4a), with fed males having significantly more breeding females than controls (DLSM: P = 0.003). There were no differences in the number of females breeding per male between the removal and control groups (DLSM: P = 0.87). There was also a significant effect of year ($F_{2,28}$ = 3.69, P <0.05), with fewer breeding females per male in 1999 compared with either 1998 (DLSM: P <0.01) or 2000 (DLSM: P <0.05).

There was no significant effect of treatment on lay date ($F_{2,33}$ = 0.46, P >0.50), nor was there any effect of year ($F_{2,27}$ = 1.68, P >0.10). There was, however, a near-significant effect of female breeding status ($F_{2,32}$ = 3.22, P <0.10), with primary females laying significantly earlier than monogamous females (DLSM: P = 0.02) and there was also a tendency to lay somewhat earlier than secondary females (DLSM: P <0.10). So neither the provision of supplementary food nor the removal of crows significantly affected lay date. There was no significant effect of treatment ($F_{2,30}$ = 0.21, P >0.80), year ($F_{2,24}$ = 0.50, P >0.60) or breeding status ($F_{2,29}$ = 1.42, P >0.20) on clutch size.

Hatching success was also unaffected by treatment ($F_{2,38}$ = 0.87, P >0.40) (Figure 29.4b). However, there was a significant effect of year on hatching success ($F_{2,39}$ = 3.43, P <0.05), with clutches more likely to hatch in 2000 than in 1999 (DLSM: P = 0.01). Breeding status of the female also significantly affected hatching success, with secondary females being significantly less likely to hatch their clutch than either primary (DLSM: P <0.01) or monogamous females (DLSM: P <0.005). There were insufficient data to consider the interaction between female status and treatment on hatching success in the GLIMMIX model. However, if the hatching success of secondary females, mated with fed and control males, was pooled between all years, we found that no secondary females mated with controls were successful (n = 5), whereas 66% of secondary females mated to males supplied with food were successful (n = 6), a difference that was found to be statistically significant (Fisher exact test P = 0.045).

29.4 Discussion

Large-scale changes in land use in Orkney have occurred since 1960. Based on the pattern of habitat use by hunting harriers, these changes are likely to have been detrimental to harriers in Orkney. The decrease in the amount of rough grazing and the increase in sheep numbers will have reduced the amount of rough grass in the environment, which is the favoured habitat for hunting harriers in the spring and the summer. The loss of rough grazing habitat and the increase in the amount of intensive pasture may have resulted in a shortage of food for the harriers, as voles and meadow pipits are more abundant in moorland and semi-natural lowland habitat than they are in intensive farmland. Indeed vole and meadow pipit abundance are known to correlate with the amount of rough grassland in some of these habitat types (Amar, 2001).

Observational data supported the idea that there was a shortage of food for the harriers in Orkney. Males in Orkney delivered food less frequently during both the pre-lay and incubation periods than males in Langholm, where the population breeds more successfully. After accounting for the differences in prey biomass between these populations, there was a suggestion that it was only during the pre-lay period that these large differences remained. However, young rabbits are relatively large prey items and formed 38% of the prey remains found in Orkney and were therefore largely responsible for harriers in Orkney receiving more biomass per prey delivery. Their importance might, however, be overestimated, since remains of rabbits may be easier to find than smaller items, such as passerines or small mammals, which may be completely eaten (Picozzi, 1980). However, the average biomass of prey delivered by males during the nestling period, extrapolated from Reynolds (1992) and Picozzi (1980), is 57.1 g and is therefore not particularly different from the estimate of 47.6 g used in this study. It is not known to what degree the size of prey items varies between individuals within Orkney, which therefore makes any statistical testing of biomass provisioned problematic.

It appears, therefore, that the discrepancy in provision rates between the two populations may be most acute during the pre-lay period. This is especially interesting, since the most striking difference in breeding success between these two populations was in the proportion of settled females which subsequently bred. In Langholm, all females that were on territory in spring went on to lay a clutch, suggesting that males were able to provide them with adequate food during the pre-lay period. This contrasts sharply with Orkney, where 50% of the females failed to lay. The large differences in pre-lay provisioning rates between these two populations may well explain these differences in breeding success and indicates that the breeding success in Orkney could have been reduced as a result of a shortage in food. Another interesting feature in the comparison between these two populations was that, in Orkney, provisioning rates during the incubation period were significantly higher than during the pre-lay period, whereas in Langholm no such difference was found. This further suggests that the shortage of food for the harriers in Orkney may be particularly acute during the earlier stages of breeding.

It therefore appears that the rate at which food is supplied to the females during the pre-lay period may have declined over the last 20 years and that this may be responsible for the reduced breeding success currently seen in the population. Unfortunately there is no quantitative data available from earlier times which would allow this assumption to be tested. Interestingly, Nick Picozzi, who studied this population during the late 1970s, considered that food provisioning was never prolific in this population (N. Picozzi, pers. comm.). If provisioning rates have not changed dramatically then an alternative explanation, evoking the same ultimate factor of food shortage, might be that the females are currently in a poorer condition prior to the period of pre-lay courtship feeding due to the overall shortage of food in the environment. In that case the rate at which prey is delivered, although not different from previously when the population bred more successfully, is now no longer sufficient to allow as many females to breed. Regardless of which scenario is actually occurring, the ultimate cause of the reduced breeding success is still a shortage of food available in the environment.

The provision of supplementary food to male hen harriers increased their number of breeding females, and therefore provided the necessary experimental evidence to show that breeding performance in this population is currently limited by food. The increase in breeding females resulted from a reduction in the number of males failing to breed and also an increase in the amount of polygynous breeding. All fed males were mated with at least one breeding female, whereas around 20% of both controls and removal males had no breeding females. Over the two experimental years, 36% of fed males bred polygynously, including two cases of trigamy. In the other two groups there was only one case of polygyny, representing only 5% of un-fed males.

Territorial polygyny in birds is rare (Lack, 1968; Møller, 1986). Where it does occur, it is often associated with areas or years of high food abundance (Verner & Willson, 1966; Hamerstrom *et al.*, 1985; Korpimäki, 1989). For species in which breeding females are dependent on males for food, the association between territorial polygyny and food is often thought to result from conditions that allow males to support more than one breeding female (Orians, 1969). In our study, similar numbers of females were associated with fed males as were associated with males in the other two experimental groups, yet fed males bred with significantly more females. This suggests that they were able to provision food at a sufficient level to allow more of their associated females to breed. These results are consistent with findings from correlative studies of northern harrier populations (Hamerstrom *et al.*, 1985; Simmons *et al.*, 1986), whose main prey, *Microtus* voles, undergo large cyclic fluctuations in abundance. The highest levels of harrier polygyny were associated with years of high *Microtus* abundance. Simmons *et al.* (1986) suggested that polygynous breeding by northern harriers was only possible when males were able to supply food to secondary females above a certain threshold rate during the pre-lay period. Previous studies of the Orkney population found that, on average, around 75% of adult males were polygynous (Balfour & Cadbury, 1979; Picozzi 1984a) whereas current levels are far lower. That supplementary feeding increased polygynous breeding therefore suggests that in Orkney there is currently insufficient food available to harriers during the pre-lay period to allow many of the polygynous associations to be expressed as polygynous breeding.

Food had no significant effect on lay date or clutch size. We believe this was related to the time that males first started to take the supplementary food. Only 50% of all females breeding with fed males, for which we had accurate lay dates, were paired with males that were seen taking food before laying commenced. So food levels for many of the fed males may not have been effectively increased until after laying had started. However, in all cases of secondary females with accurate lay dates, males were seen to take food before laying had commenced. This seems to be a likely explanation for the observation that supplementary feeding caused fed males to have more breeding females yet had no significant effect on lay date or clutch size. In a supplementary feeding experiment conducted on the hen harriers in Langholm, Scotland (Redpath *et al.*, 2001), most males were seen to take supplementary food before laying commenced (S. Redpath, pers. obs.). This experiment again found no significant effect on lay date, but supplementary feeding did significantly increase clutch size (Redpath *et al.*, 2001). The difference in the effect of feeding on clutch size between the two experiments may be explained by the fact that males started taking food relatively earlier in the experiment at Langholm. Another interesting difference between these two experiments was that, unlike in Orkney, feeding males in Langholm did not increase the number of breeding females. This reinforces the suggestion that breeding success in the two areas is influenced by the rate at which males provisioned food. Males in Langholm are able to provision food at an adequate rate, and so may not be as limited by food.

The lack of effect of supplementary food on hatching success was surprising, but could perhaps be due to the same reasons. If food levels were not effectively increased for many of the females before laying commenced, then their condition may also not have been increased before laying. Newton (1986) found that female sparrowhawks *Accipiter nisus* in better condition before incubation were more likely to successfully hatch their clutch. This may be the case with Orkney hen harriers. This possibility is supported by the fact that hatching success of secondary females was significantly higher if they were mated with fed males rather than with control males. As all fed males with secondary females were seen to take food before their secondary females laid, the condition of these females may have been higher before laying than the controls or the primary females of the fed males.

The main experimental finding was that the number of females breeding per male was food limited. It should be noted, however, that because crows were also removed on fed territories, the additive effect of supplementary food and decreased predation could not be completely eliminated as a potential cause of this result (see also Amar & Burthe, 2001). However, the fact that crow removal had no effect on any of the breeding parameters in the removal group suggests that crow removal was of little overall consequence and was therefore unlikely to have had a strong confounding effect in the fed group.

In conclusion, both comparative and experimental data supported the idea that the hen harrier population in Orkney is currently limited by food availability during the early part of the breeding season. A reduction in the prey available to harriers is therefore the most likely explanation for this population's decline. This reduction in food may be attributable to a decrease in the amount of rough grazing which harriers selectively hunted in the spring and summer, and the increase in sheep stocking density which is also likely to have decreased the amount of rough grass and therefore also potentially the amount of food. Management for this population should be directed toward increasing the amount of rough grass and rough grazing (Scottish Natural Heritage, 2003). This management might be best achieved through the exclusion or reduction of grazing within the farmland areas close to the moorland sites where the harriers breed, and a decrease in the grazing pressures in areas of rough grazing which are currently overgrazed. In January 2003, Scottish Natural Heritage launched a land management incentive scheme (Orkney Moorlands Natural Care Scheme) to create more such rough grassland habitat for harriers.

Acknowledgements

We are grateful to Brian Ribbands, Kerry Lock, Rory Gordon, Sarah Burthe, Gaetan Bottin, Maxime Esnault, Jacqui Todd, Keith Fairclough and Andy Knight for their tremendous help with fieldwork. Special thanks are also due to Donnie Littlejohn for making the crow traps. We would also like to thank the landowners in Orkney for permission to work on their land. Advice on many aspects was gratefully received from Ron Summers, Mick Marquiss, Ian Bainbridge, Audun Stien, Steve Albon, Beatriz Arroyo, Isla Graham, Nick Picozzi and two anonymous referees. Special thanks are also due to Dave Elston for advice relating to experimental design and statistics. This research was funded through an Aberdeen Research Consortium studentship to Arjun Amar and an RSPB grant to Steve Redpath.

References

Amar, A. (2001). *Determining the cause of the hen harrier decline on Orkney.* PhD thesis. University of Aberdeen, Aberdeen.

Amar, A. & Burthe, S. (2001). Observations of predation of hen harrier nestlings by hooded crows in Orkney. *Scottish Birds*, **22**, 65-66.

Amar, A. & Redpath, S. (2002). Determining the cause of the hen harrier decline on the Orkney Islands: an experimental test of two hypotheses. *Animal Conservation*, **5**, 21-28.

Amar, A., Redpath, S. & Thirgood, S. (2003). Evidence for food limitation in the declining hen harrier population on the Orkney Islands, Scotland. *Biological Conservation*, **111**, 377-384.

Amar, A., Picozzi, M., Meek, E.R., Redpath, S.M. & Lambin, X. (in press). Decline of the Orkney Hen Harrier *Circus cyaneus* population: do changes to demographic parameters and mating system fit a declining food hypothesis? *Bird Study.*

Balfour, E. (1957). Observations on the breeding biology of the hen harrier in Orkney. II. *Bird Notes*, **27**, 216-224.

Balfour, E. & Cadbury, C.J. (1979). Polygyny, spacing and sex ratio among hen harrier *Circus cyaneus* in Orkney, Scotland. *Ornis Scandinavica*, **10**, 133-141.

Carss, D.N. (1995). Prey brought home by two domestic cats (*Felis catus*) in northern Scotland. *Journal of Zoology (London)*, **237**, 678-686.

Corbett, G.B. & Harris, S. (1991). *The Handbook of British Mammals. Third Edition.* Blackwell Scientific Publications. Oxford.

Downing, R. (1990). Orkney hen harriers – 1989. In *Orkney Bird Report 1989*, ed. by C. Booth, M. Cuthbert & E.R. Meek. Orcadian, Kirkwall. pp. 57-58.

Etheridge, B., Summers, R.W. & Green, R.E. (1997). The effects of illegal killing and destruction of nests by humans on the population dynamics of the hen harrier *Circus cyaneus* in Scotland. *Journal of Applied Ecology*, **34**, 1081-1105.

Hamerstrom, F., Hamerstrom, F.N. & Burke, C.J. (1985). Effect of voles on mating systems in a Central Wisconsin population of harriers. *Wilson Bulletin*, **97**, 332-346.

Hewson. R. (1982). The effect upon field vole (*Microtus agrestis*) habitat on removing sheep from moorland in west Scotland. *Journal of Zoology (London)*, **197**, 304-307.

Korpimäki, E. (1989). Mating system and mate choice of Tengmalm's Owls *Aegolius funereus*. *Ibis*, **131**, 41-50.

Lack, D. (1968). *Ecological Adaptations for Breeding in Birds.* Methuen, London.

Littell, R.C., Milliken, G.A., Stroup, W.W. & Wolfinger, R.D. (1996). *SAS System for Mixed Models.* SAS Institute Inc., Cary, NC.

Madders, M. (1997). *The effect of forestry on hen harriers* Circus cyaneus. PhD thesis. University of Glasgow, Glasgow.

Meek, E.R., Rebecca, G.W., Ribbands, B. & Fairclough, K. (1998). Orkney hen harriers: a major population decline in the absence of persecution. *Scottish Birds*, **19**, 290-298.

Møller, A.P. (1986). Mating systems among European passerines: a review. *Ibis*, **124**, 234-250.

Newton, I. (1986). *The Sparrowhawk*. T. & A.D. Poyser, Calton.

Orians, G.H. (1969). On the evolution of mating systems in birds and mammals. *American Naturalist*, **103**, 589-603.

Picozzi, N. (1978). Dispersion, breeding and prey of hen harrier *Circus cyaneus* in Glen Dye, Kincardineshire. *Ibis*, **120**, 498-509.

Picozzi, N. (1980). Food, growth, survival and sex ratio of nestling hen harriers *Circus c. cyaneus* in Orkney. *Ornis Scandinavica*, **11**, 1-11.

Picozzi, N. (1984a). Sex ratio, survival and territorial behaviour of polygynous hen harriers *Circus c. cyaneus* in Orkney. *Ibis*, **126**, 356-365.

Picozzi, N. (1984b). Breeding biology of polygynous hen harriers *Circus c. cyaneus* in Orkney. *Ornis Scandinavica*, **15**, 1-10.

Reynolds, P. (1992). *The impact of changes in land-use in Orkney, on the vole* Microtus arvalis orcadensis *and its avian predators*. PhD. thesis, University of Aberdeen, Aberdeen.

Redpath, S.M. & Thirgood, S.J. (1997). *Birds of Prey and Red Grouse*. The Stationery Office, London.

Redpath, S.M., Thirgood, S.J. & Leckie, F. (2001). Does supplementary feeding reduce predation of red grouse by hen harriers? *Journal of Applied Ecology*, **37**, 1157-1168.

SAS Institute (1990). *SAS/STAT Users' Guide, Version 6*. SAS Institute Inc., Cary, NC.

Schipper, W.J.A., Buurma. L.S. & Bossenbrock, P. (1975). Comparative study of hunting behaviour of wintering hen harriers *Circus cyaneus* and marsh harriers *Circus aeruginosus*. *Ardea*, **63**, 1-29.

Scottish Natural Heritage (2003). The Orkney Vole A Management Guide. Unpublished report. Scottish Natural Heritage, Perth.

Simmons, R., Barnard, P., MacWhirter, B. & Hansen G.L. (1986). The influence of microtines on polygyny, productivity, age, and provisioning of breeding northern harriers: a 5-year study. *Canadian Journal of Zoology*, **64**, 2447-2456.

Thirgood, S.J., Redpath, S.M., Rothery, P. & Aebischer, N.J. (2000). Raptor predation and population limitation in red grouse. *Journal of Animal Ecology*, **69**, 504-516.

Verner, J. & Willson, M.F. (1966). The influence of habitat on mating systems in North American passerine birds. *Ecology*, **47**, 143-147.

Watson, D. (1977). *The Hen Harrier*. T. & A.D. Poyser. Berkhamsted.

30. RE-INTRODUCTION OF WHITE-TAILED EAGLES (*HALIAEETUS ALBICILLA*) TO SCOTLAND

I.P. Bainbridge, R.J. Evans, R.A. Broad, C.H. Crooke, K. Duffy, R.E. Green, J.A. Love & G.P. Mudge

Summary

1.   The white-tailed eagle *Haliaeetus albicilla* became extinct in Britain in 1918 following a prolonged period of human persecution. Due to a decrease in raptor persecution and changes in legislation, conditions were deemed suitable for the species to be reintroduced by the 1950s. After two brief attempts, a large-scale release programme was initiated in 1975.

2.   Between 1975 and 1985, 82 young white-tailed eagles from Norway were released on the island of Rum, off the west coast of Scotland. The first clutch of eggs was laid in the wild in 1983 and the first successful breeding occurred in 1985.

3.   By 1992, eight territories were occupied, but overall breeding performance was not high and the likelihood of chance effects leading to eventual extinction was considered high enough to justify a second series of releases.

4.   Between 1993 and 1998 a further 58 young eagles from Norway were released on the Scottish mainland. The first of these birds bred in 1998.

5.   Wild-bred progeny from the first release raised young for the first time in 1996 and by 2000, 22 territories were occupied, 21 by territorial pairs.

6.   A re-analysis of breeding performance and survival data suggests that the population is now securely established.

7.   The Scottish population at 2000 was likely to number at least 80–90 individuals.

8.   By 2002, 26 territories were occupied, 25 by territorial pairs, and half of the territory-holding birds were wild-bred offspring of first-phase released birds. In 2001, 11 young fledged, and in 2002, 12 young fledged.

30.1 Introduction

After 70 years of absence as a breeding bird in the British Isles, a population of the white-tailed eagle *Haliaeetus albicilla* has been re-established in western Scotland through a partnership between conservationists in Scotland and Norway. Accounts of some of the earlier stages of the re-introduction have already been published (Love & Ball, 1979; Love, 1983, 1988; Evans *et al.*, 1994). This chapter sets out the context for the re-introduction, summarises and updates earlier work and outlines progress made since 1975, when the project began.

The white-tailed eagle is regarded as a near-threatened species at a global level (Collar *et al.*, 1994; Tucker & Heath, 1994). The species is distributed from Greenland to eastern

Siberia. However, its world population of 8,500–11,000 pairs (Mizera, 1999) has been highly fragmented by persecution, habitat loss and pollution. Europe now holds around 4,400 pairs (Mizera, 1999; Greenwood *et al.*, Chapter 2).

The former distribution, population decline and eventual extinction of the species were documented by Love (1983). After the last individual was shot in Shetland in 1918, the bird occurred in Scotland only as an occasional vagrant (Thom, 1986). There were two attempts to re-introduce white-tailed eagles to Scotland prior to the current project. A total of seven white-tailed eagles were released in 1959 in Argyll and in 1968 on Fair Isle, but no breeding pairs were established (Sandeman, 1965; Dennis, 1968, 1969). However, these attempts were useful tests of release techniques used in the subsequent project.

30.2 Decision to begin reintroduction

IUCN guidelines current at the initiation of the project in 1975 stated merely that "re-introductions of species into their original habitats [were] considered generally unobjectionable" (IUCN, 1968). UK policy guidelines on re-introductions (Green, 1979 – based on the WWF Manifesto on Re-introductions, 1976) were largely fulfilled by the white-tailed eagle re-introduction, in spite of the fact that the project pre-dated the new guidelines. Seven key points applied to the programme:–

1. There was a clear understanding of the reasons for the loss of the species (persecution) and these conditions were considered to have been reduced to an insignificant level.
2. The habitats in the release area were considered still capable of supporting a re-introduced population of white-tailed eagles.
3. The released birds were as genetically and morphologically close as possible to the extinct population and could be obtained at no risk to the donor population.
4. A risk assessment was carried out.
5. The re-introduced population could be controlled if necessary.
6. The release sites were within the species' former range and in sympathetic management.
7. The translocations complied with the Convention on International Trade in Endangered Species of fauna and flora.

Additionally, the white-tailed eagle was classified as globally threatened (King, 1978). Populations around the Baltic and in central Europe were suffering greatly reduced productivity (e.g. Helander *et al.*, 1982) and, in some regions, population decline due to the effects of chemical pollutants in the environment (Stjernberg & Saurola, 1983). As well as a wish to restore to Scotland a species that had become extinct solely through human action, there would be international benefits from the re-establishment of a population of white-tailed eagles in the relatively unpolluted highlands and islands of Scotland.

The historical evidence of the species' occurrence in Scotland was indisputable, as was the cause of extinction (Love, 1983). The nearest population of white-tailed eagles is largely sedentary, so it was doubtful that the species would re-colonise naturally (Love, 1983), having shown no signs of doing so in the 57 years since the last individual was shot. The main factors causing extinction had been greatly reduced, as changes in legislation since the

Protection of Birds Act (1954) and in public attitudes had led to a reduction in the persecution of raptors in Britain during the 20th century. There was enough suitable habitat in Scotland to accommodate a viable population of white-tailed eagles. A suitable, healthy donor population existed in Norway, the nearest neighbour population.

The main reservations raised at the planning stage were possible detrimental effects of marine pollutants on future breeding success, possible competition with golden eagle *Aquila chrysaetos*, possible predation of livestock, in particular young sheep *Ovis aries*, and the possibility of the re-introduction failing.

The likelihood of serious problems due to environmental pollutants was considered to be low in the west of Scotland. Golden eagles and white-tailed eagles co-exist in Norway and elsewhere (Willgohs, 1961; Halley, 1998) and had co-existed in Scotland in the 19th

Table 30.1 Numbers of young white-tailed eagles (male, female, sex unknown and total) imported from Norway and released in Scotland, 1975–1998. Note that some birds were not released in their year of importation.

Imported	1975-1985	1993-1998	Total
Male	40	25	65
Female	45	28	73
Unknown		5	5
Total	85	58	143
Released			
Male	39	25	64
Female	43	28	71
Unknown	0	5	5
Total	82	58	140

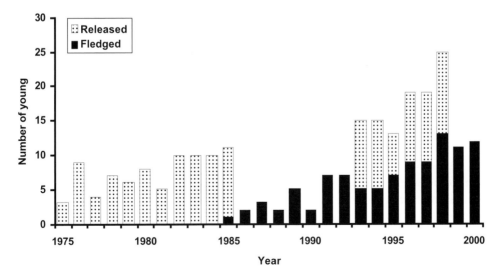

Figure 30.1. Numbers of white-tailed eagles released and fledged in the wild, Scotland 1975-2000.

century (Gray, 1871; Harvie-Brown & Buckley, 1892; Baxter & Rintoul, 1953). Studies of white-tailed eagle diet elsewhere (e.g. Willgohs, 1961, 1984; Wille & Kampp, 1983) suggested that mammalian prey was relatively unimportant and that white-tailed eagles tended to feed on mammals mainly as carrion rather than as live prey. The possibility of eventual failure remained, but mechanisms were put in place in order to monitor both the progress of re-establishment and any problems that might be caused by the re-introduction.

Importation of young birds from Norway, to be released by the falconry technique of 'hacking back', was considered to be the best method of re-introduction. Captive breeding was considered, but rejected, though not before a small number of birds had been retained for this purpose and eventually released. (Love, 1983, 1988). The releases took place in two phases, 1975-85 and 1993-98 (Table 30.1 and Figure 30.1).

30.3 The donor population

The population of white-tailed eagles in Norway in 1968 was estimated to be between 700 and 800 pairs (Helander & Mizera, 1997). All 140 eagles released in Scotland came from the area around Bodø, in the Salten district of Nordland County, Norway. White-tailed eagles are common in this area, which holds the highest breeding density in the country (Folkestad, 1994). Hundreds of small offshore islands and many streams and fjords provide good nesting and feeding habitat in Salten. Prey consists mainly of fish and waterbirds.

Birds in the Bodø area are tolerant of human presence and one pair nests only 5 km from Bodø itself, a town of 40,000 inhabitants. Bodø is home to the Havørn (sea eagle) Club, and there is local pride in the fact that the area has provided young eagles for the Scottish project.

30.4 Methods used for first re-introduction

The island of Rum was selected as the first release site. Rum is in the heart of the species' former range and held breeding white-tailed eagles until 1907. The island is large (10,820 ha) and human disturbance was low (Love, 1983).

Eaglets, aged six to eight weeks, were collected under special licence from nests in Norway. Single eaglets were taken from broods of two or three. Use of the same nests in successive years was avoided as far as possible so as to ensure genetic diversity in the founder population. Time spent by the young eagles in captivity before translocation to Scotland was kept to a minimum. The only human contact was for feeding (three or four times a day) and for a veterinary inspection on the day of departure. The eaglets were hand-fed on fish and extra food was left for the birds to feed themselves.

The birds were flown from the Royal Norwegian Air Force base at Bodø to RAF Kinloss in Scotland and then transported by road and boat to their release site (Love, 1988). Under UK law, the birds had to undergo a five-week quarantine period after their arrival.

On Rum, eaglets were housed in cages 4 m square and 2 m high, constructed of 3 cm chain link mesh attached to a framework of wood. Each cage was provided with a perch and a 1 m square wooden box for shelter. Apart from short daily feeding visits, there was no human contact, although the keepers were visible to the caged birds. Some birds were transferred from the cages to an open area, where they were kept tethered for a short while before being liberated. Long-term captives were also kept in this manner (Love & Ball, 1979; Love, 1983, 1988).

Birds were released on Rum when four to six months old. Three birds retained for captive breeding purposes were liberated at three and a half years old. Eagles were weighed, measured and marked before release. Between 1975 and 1981, each bird was fitted with colour rings, in addition to a standard metal ring. From 1982, all eagles were fitted with patagial wing-tags instead of colour rings so as to allow easier identification after release. Food provided for captive eagles consisted largely of fish, particularly scraps obtained at no cost from fish dealers. Meat from culled red deer *Cervus elaphus* and feral goat *Capra hircus* was provided, as well as birds (Love, 1983). White-tailed eagles are gregarious (Cramp & Simmons, 1980). Because these congregations are thought to facilitate selection of future mates, supplementary food was provided at the release site during the autumn and winter, in order to encourage this behaviour.

30.5 Development of the wild population from the first phase of re-introduction

Of the 82 eagles released between 1975 and 1985 (Table 30.1), eight were reported dead from a variety of causes. One bird died in Caithness, in north-east Scotland, after feeding on bait poisoned with phosdrin, and at least one other bird found dead was thought to have been poisoned. One bird died probably as a result of colliding with power cables. The other five birds died from unknown causes. Other deaths have certainly occurred undetected.

The first nest-building behaviour by released birds was recorded in 1981. The first breeding attempts were proved in 1983, when two pairs laid eggs. One of the attempts in 1983 was by a short-lived trio of birds, comprising one male and two females. These attempts and those in 1984 failed. Successful breeding occurred for the first time in 1985, when a single chick was reared (Love, 1988) and has occurred in every year from 1985 onwards (Table 30.2).

Table 30.2 Numbers of territorial, breeding and non-breeding, successful and unsuccessful pairs of white-tailed eagles, numbers of young fledged and mean breeding success, mean fledged brood size and productivity in Scotland, 1981-2000.

	1981-1985	*1986-1990*	*1991-1995*	*1996-2000*	*Total:* *1981-2000*
Territories occupied by pair or trio	16	43	46	87	192
Breeding attempts	8	31	38	74	151
Successful attempts (%)	1 (12.5)	9 (29.0)	21 (55.3)	35 (47.3)	66 (43.7)
Failed attempts	7	22	17	39	85
Territorial pairs with breeding not proved	8	12	8	12	40
Fledged young	1	14	31	54	100
Mean fledged brood size	1.00	1.56	1.48	1.54	1.52
Young fledged per breeding pair	0.13	0.45	0.82	0.73	0.66
Young fledged per territorial pair	0.06	0.33	0.67	0.62	0.52

Between 1981 and 1987, the breeding population increased rapidly from one to nine territorial pairs (Figure 30.2), but breeding success remained relatively low with no more than four successful pairs in any one year before 1992. During this period, 34% of nesting attempts were successful (Figure 30.3). Twenty-nine young fledged during this period, with a mean fledged brood size of 1.61; mean annual productivity for the period 1981–1992 was 0.38 young fledged/territorial pair/year (Figure 30.4 and Table 30.2). Although the proportion of males and females released was not significantly different (G = 0.097, *P* = 0.76, Williams' correction), at least one other trio of birds, comprising a male and two females, was well established by 1992; the birds were different from those involved in the 1983 breeding attempt. By the same time, five out of 15 areas previously occupied by

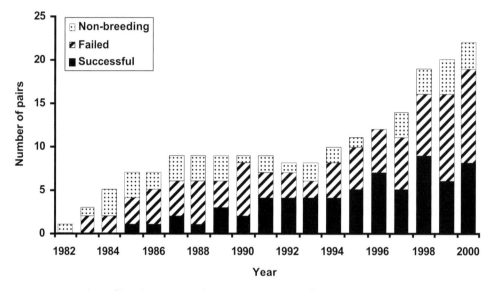

Figure 30.2. Numbers of breeding and non-breeding pairs or trios of white-tailed eagles, Scotland, 1982–2000 (total number of pairs: r_s = 0.93, *P* <0.001, n = 19).

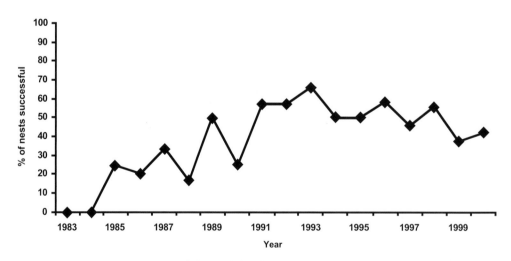

Figure 30.3. Mean annual nest success of white-tailed eagles, Scotland, 1983–2000 (r_s = 0.61, n = 18, *P* <0.02).

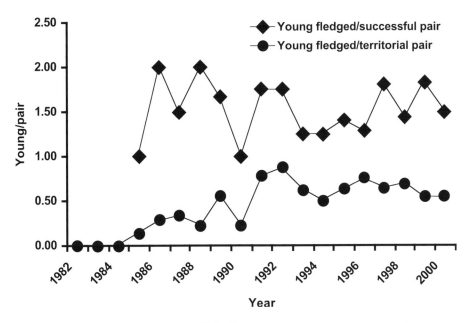

Figure 30.4. Mean fledged brood size (young fledged/successful nest: r_s = 0.007, n = 16, ns) and mean annual productivity (young fledged/territorial pair or trio: r_s = 0.72, P <0.001, n = 19) of white-tailed eagles breeding in Scotland 1982-2000.

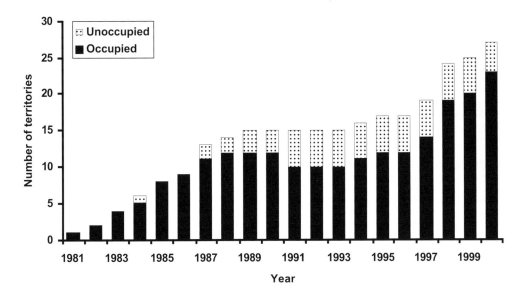

Figure 30.5. Numbers of occupied and unoccupied white-tailed eagle territories, Scotland 1981-2000.

white-tailed eagles were no longer tenanted by pairs (Figure 30.5), and another area was occupied by a single adult only. Up to 1992, only five territories had produced fledged young and all but three of the 29 fledged young had come from three female birds.

30.6 Decision to make supplementary releases

During 1991-1992, a detailed analysis was carried out of the progress of the re-introduction: Green *et al.* (1996) examined annual productivity and estimated survival of Scottish white-tailed eagles at 73% for young birds and 94% for birds settled on territory. These were similar to estimates for bald eagles *Haliaeetus leucocephalus* in north America (e.g. Buehler *et al.*, 1991). A mean annual productivity rate of 0.47 fledged young/pair/year for adults at least six years old (cf. 0.38 for birds of all ages, above) was similar to depressed rates for parts of north-west Europe in the early 1980s (Stjernberg & Saurola, 1983). However, the small size of the population left it vulnerable to stochastic effects, including chance deaths, particularly of productive adults, and the failure of some adults to form pairs due to chance differences in numbers of males and females surviving. Green *et al.* (1996) concluded that, with realistic assumptions about the variation in breeding success and survival among individual birds and territories, there was a probability of about 60% that the population derived from the first releases would become extinct within 100 years. It was on this basis that a second release programme was started; simulations indicated that the release of a further 60 juveniles would reduce the risk of extinction considerably, and increase the size of the breeding population in the long term (see Green *et al.*, 1996 for detailed analysis).

30.7 Methods used for supplementary releases

The site selected for the supplementary releases was in Wester Ross, on the mainland of Scotland. Compared with Rum, the new site offered logistical advantages, as well as the likelihood of creating a new nucleus of white-tailed eagle activity adjacent to the range established by the first series of releases. The area surrounding the new release site provided a wider range of habitat types than Rum, including broad-leaved woodland and freshwater lochs.

There were some differences from the first phase of releases, based in part on experience gained during the re-introduction programme for red kites *Milvus milvus* to Britain from 1989 onwards (Evans *et al.*, 1994). The cages were 4 m square and 2.5 m high, and solid wood, apart from mesh roofs and fronts so that eaglets could see, and imprint on, their local environment through the mesh cage front, but were prevented from seeing their keeper approaching from the rear or sides by the solid walls. Eaglets were grouped in 'broods' of two or three to a cage and each 'brood' was fed through a small hatch. Food was given in excess to ensure that the smaller members of broods had enough to eat: 1,000–1,600 g were provided daily for each individual. Food items not used in the first series of releases included rabbits *Oryctolagus cuniculus,* and Atlantic salmon *Salmo salar* heads obtained from fish-processing factories.

Fifty-eight birds were released at the second site between 1993 and 1998 (Table 30.1 and Figure 30.1). The birds were released directly from their cages, during the first half of August, at approximately 10-12 weeks old. Marking and measuring was carried out seven to 14 days before release. The cages were opened at night and the birds were free to leave the cages after dawn. Food was placed on the cages to allow the birds to feed after release. As on Rum, a regular supply of supplementary food was provided at the release site through the winter.

30.8 Development of the population since 1992

Between 1993 and 2000, the breeding population increased from eight to 22 territorial pairs, of which 19 bred in 2000 (Figure 30.2). By 2000, the majority of pairs were either phase one released birds or their offspring (Figure 30.6). A third trio comprising a single male and two females had formed by 1995, but all trios broke up by 2000, due to the arrival of additional males. Wild-bred birds reared young for the first time in 1996. Between 1993 and 2000, there were 48 successful breeding attempts (compared with 18 for the period 1985–1992), mean annual nest success was 48% (Table 30.2 and Figure 30.3), 71 young fledged, mean fledged brood size was 1.48 and mean annual productivity was 0.61 young fledged/territorial pair/year (Table 30.2 and Figure 30.4). By 2000, a total of 27 territories had been occupied by white-tailed eagles and 23 of these were occupied in 2000, an occupancy rate of 85%, compared with 67% in 1992 (Figure 30.5).

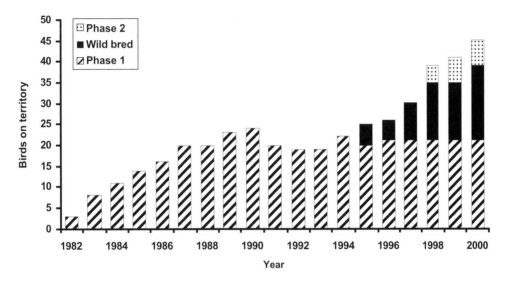

Figure 30.6. Origin (phase 1 release, wild bred, phase 2 release) of white-tailed eagles confirmed on territory, Scotland 1982-2000.

The first breeding attempts by birds released during the second phase took place in 1998, when two pairs of birds bred successfully. Of the four birds involved, only one (a female) was fully adult (five years old); both of the males and the second female were four years old. At the end of the 2000 breeding season, 75 individual white-tailed eagles (either territorial adults or identified, wing-tagged immatures and juveniles) were known to be alive. Given that a number of young fledge annually without wing tags, as their nests are not accessible for ringing, and that only a small proportion of re-sightings of wing-tagged birds are of identified individuals, a conservative estimate might put the whole population in the order of 80-90 individuals.

Unsurprisingly for a re-introduced population, both population size (r_s = 0.93, P <0.001, n = 19) and annual productivity per territorial pair (r_s = 0.72, P <0.001, n = 19) showed strong upward trends for the period 1982–2000. Mean fledged brood size between 1985 and 2000 showed no trend (r_s = 0.007, n = 16, ns); therefore, increased productivity resulted from an increased proportion of pairs breeding successfully each year (r_s = 0.615, n = 18, P <0.02). Mean annual productivity for the period 1993-2000 was broadly similar to rates reported for Norway (Folkestad, 1994), Finland (Stjernberg & Koivusaari, 1995),

Estonia (Randla & Tammur, 1996) and Mecklenburg-Vorpommern, Germany (Hauff, 1996), but lower than those most recently reported for Poland (Mizera, 1999) and Schleswig-Holstein, Germany (B. Struwe-Juhl, pers. comm.).

A further review of data up to and including 1997 suggested higher estimated annual survival rates (75% for unsettled immatures and 97% for adults) than for the period up to 1992. These survival rates are broadly similar to those recently reported for bald eagles in Alaska and California (Bowman *et al.*, 1995; Jenkins *et al.*, 1999). Between 1995 and 2000, mean age of first breeding of Scottish white-tailed eagles was 6.00 ± 2.34 years old for seven females and 4.33 ± 0.86 years old for nine males: the difference between the sexes was not significant and there were no significant differences between ages of first breeding of phase 1 and 2 released and wild-bred birds (Table 30.3). These ages are lower than those recently reported for Norway and Sweden (D. Halley, pers. comm.): recruitment of individuals at an early age (relative to larger, established populations) appears to be a feature of depleted, re-introduced or naturally re-establishing raptor populations (Newton, 1979; Sarrazin *et al.*, 1996; Wylie & Newton, 1991; Evans *et al.*, 1999).

Table 30.3 Mean ages of first breeding (± 95% C.I.) of female and male white-tailed eagles released in Scotland in 1975-85 (phase 1), 1993-98 (phase 2) and bred in Scotland 1985 onwards (wild bred).

	Female	*Male*
Phase 1 release	6.00 (± 2.13, n = 8)	5.40 (± 1.82, n = 5)
Phase 2 release	4.25 (± 0.50, n = 4)	4.00 (± 0.00, n = 2)
Wild bred	5.50 (± 0.58, n = 4)	4.60 (± 1.35, n = 10)
All birds	5.44 (± 1.10, n = 16)	4.76 (± 1.44, n = 17)

30.9 Conclusions and prospects

The first phase of releases resulted in the occupation by released birds of 15 territories, five of which had been abandoned by 1992. Recruitment into the breeding population of offspring of first phase released birds resulted in the occupation of a further ten territories by 2000 (Figure 30.5): two of these territories can be considered re-occupations of previously abandoned territories and another two 'new' territories were created by the pairing of young male birds with the 'spare' first phase released females, which had previously made up trios. By the end of 2000, a further three territories were occupied by pairs derived from the second phase of releases.

Although overall breeding success is satisfactory, some long-established territorial pairs have not yet produced young and breeding success of the whole population has relied on a small number of regularly productive pairs. Thirteen territories have contributed young to the population, but 76% of wild-bred young have come from only five territories. Only in 1996 did more than 50% of territorial pairs breed successfully. Although the number of territorial pairs more than doubled between 1994 and 2000, some of the new, young pairs have yet to breed successfully. Nevertheless, the fact that a small number of the new, young pairs (including all three pairs from the second phase of releases) bred successfully at an earlier age than birds from the first phase of the release bodes well for the future. Just under half of all of the breeding attempts recorded occurred during the five year period 1996-2000 and produced 54 out of the 100 young fledged since the start of the project, reflecting increased numbers of breeding and successful pairs.

Territory occupancy by single birds accounted for 20 bird-years in seven territories, and that by additional birds forming trios for 15 bird-years in three territories, out of a total of 423 bird-years of territory occupation. The initial formation of at least three trios, each comprising one male and two females suggest that there may have been chance differences in mortality between males and females. The fact that, in two cases, new additional pairs were formed upon the arrival of additional males suggests that occupation of territories by trios and single birds might have been lower if a greater number of birds had been released during the first phase of the project (cf. Griffith *et al.*, 1989; Green, 1997).

A further two birds are known to have been illegally killed since 1992 (one shot in Lochaber, one poisoned with carbofuran in Caithness). Three breeding attempts are known to have failed and a further two have lost part clutches due to interference from egg collectors. Some predation of lambs has been recorded (Marquiss & Madders, 2000), but this would appear to be both localised and limited in scale compared with other causes of lamb mortality in north-west Scotland. Unhatched eggs continue to be screened and have been found invariably to contain pesticide and other chemical residues, though levels of DDE and PCBs recorded in Scottish eggs were lower than levels suggested as critical in Sweden by Helander *et al.* (1982).

To date, few effects have been observed of competition between golden eagles and white-tailed eagles, either for nest sites or for prey. Although white-tailed eagles probably outnumbered golden eagles in Scotland during the first half of the 19th century (Gray, 1871), it is unlikely that direct competition between the species will result in a serious decline in golden eagle numbers. To date, there have been three possible instances of displacement of breeding golden eagle pairs by white-tailed eagles, but at least two of these occurred in golden eagle home ranges occupied by individual golden eagles thought to have been in poor condition (Nellist & Crane, 1999; Whitfield *et al.*, 2002). The two pairs of re-established white-tailed eagles with the longest history of successful breeding regularly use nests between 1.5 and 3.5 km from long-established golden eagle nest sites, which have had a record of good breeding success since the establishment of white-tailed eagle territories. On the island of Mull, no effect of increased white-tailed eagle activity was detected in golden eagle breeding success during 1981-99, when white-tailed eagles were in the process of re-establishment (Whitfield *et al.*, 2002).

30.10 Update to 2002

By 2002, a cumulative total of 31 different territories had been occupied by white-tailed eagles, and the breeding population had increased to 26 territorial pairs, of which 24 bred that year. In 2002, half of the territory-holding birds were wild-bred offspring of first-phase released birds. In 2001, there were seven successful breeding attempts, fledging 11 young, and in 2002 there were eight successful breeding attempts, fledging 12 young. Productivity for the 5 years up to and including 2002 was 0.54 young fledged/territorial pair/year (0.64 young fledged per confirmed breeding attempt) and mean fledged brood size was 1.55 young per nest for the same period.

Acknowledgements

The re-introduction programme would have been impossible without the international collaboration of the governmental and conservation bodies involved.

In Norway, we thank Harald Misund, without whose help in providing eaglets over 25 years the project would not have been possible. We thank the Norwegian Directorate for Nature Management, the local landowners and the County Governor, Department of the Environment in Salten district for permitting eaglets to be collected for the project. We also thank the fieldworkers and the Havørn Club, Bodø, who assisted the project in Norway. We thank the Royal Air Force (especially 120 Squadron) and the Royal Norwegian Air Force for transporting the eaglets from Norway to Scotland.

In Scotland, we thank Paul van Vlissingen, the owner of the second release site, and the estate staff. SNH is grateful to Anheuser-Busch European Trade Ltd. for their support to the project. We also thank a huge number of individual fieldworkers, landowners, farmers, crofters, foresters and many others for their help in re-establishing the white-tailed eagle as a breeding species in the United Kingdom.

Comments from Paul Haworth and from two anonymous referees improved earlier versions of this paper.

The reintroduction programme has been managed by the UK Sea Eagle Project Team, which has comprised staff of SNH, RSPB, ITE (now CEH) and JNCC. The authors have produced this paper on behalf of the UK Sea Eagle Project Team.

References

Baxter, E.V. & Rintoul, L.J. (1953). *Birds in Scotland.* Oliver and Boyd, Edinburgh.

Buehler, D.A., Fraser, J.D., Seegar, J.K.D, Therres, G.D. & Byrd, M.A. (1991). Survival rates and population dynamics of bald eagles in Chesapeake Bay. *Journal of Wildlife Management,* **55**, 608-613.

Bowman, T.D., Schempf, P.F. & Bernatowicz, J.A. (1995). Bald eagle survival and population dynamics in Alaska after the *Exxon Valdez* oil spill. *Journal of Wildlife Management,* **59**, 317-324.

Collar, N.J., Crosby, M.J. & Stattersfield, A.J. (1994). *Birds to Watch 2: The World List of Threatened Birds.* Birdlife International, Cambridge.

Cramp, S. & Simmons, K.E.L. (1980). *Handbook of the Birds of Europe, the Middle East and North Africa Vol. II.* Oxford University Press, Oxford.

Dennis, R.H. (1968). Sea eagles. *Fair Isle Bird Observatory Report,* **21**, 17-21.

Dennis, R.H. (1969). Sea eagles. *Fair Isle Bird Observatory Report,* **22**, 23-29.

Evans, I.M., Love, J.A., Galbraith, C.A. & Pienkowski, M.W. (1994). Population and range restoration of threatened raptors in the United Kingdom. In *Raptor Conservation Today,* ed. by B.-U. Meyburg & R.D. Chancellor. World Working Group on Birds of Prey, Berlin. pp. 447-457.

Evans, I.M, Summers, R.W., O'Toole, L., Orr-Ewing, D.C., Evans, R., Snell, N. & Smith, J. (1999). Evaluating the success of translocating red kites *Milvus milvus* to the UK. *Bird Study,* **46**, 129-144.

Folkestad, A.O. (1994). *Prosjekt Havørn: Organisering, bestandforhold, populasjonsdynamikk, forvaltningsproblematikk.* Unpublished report. Direktoratet for Naturforvaltning, Trondheim.

Gray, R. (1871). *The Birds of West Scotland including the Outer Hebrides.* Thomas Murray and Son, Glasgow.

Green, B.H. (1979). *Wildlife Introductions to Great Britain.* Report by the Working Group on Introductions of the UK Committee for International Nature Conservation, Nature Conservancy Council, London.

Green, R.E. (1997). The influence of numbers released on the outcome of attempts to introduce exotic bird species to New Zealand. *Journal of Animal Ecology,* **66**, 25-35.

Green, R.E., Pienkowski, M.W. & Love, J.A. (1996). Long-term viability of the re-introduced population of the white-tailed eagle *Haliaeetus albicilla* in Scotland. *Journal of Applied Ecology*, **33**, 357-368.

Griffith, B., Scott, J.M., Carpenter, J.W. & Reed, C. (1989). Translocation as a species conservation tool: status and strategy. *Science*, **245**, 477-480.

Halley, D.J. (1998). Golden and white-tailed eagles in Scotland and Norway: coexistence, competition and environmental degradation. *British Birds*, **91**, 171-179.

Harvie-Brown, J.A. & Buckley, T.E. (1892). *A Vertebrate Fauna of Argyll and the Inner Hebrides.* David Douglas, Edinburgh.

Hauff, P. (1996). Der Seeadler *Haliaeetus albicilla* in Mecklenburg-Vorpommern: Vorkommen und Entwicklung 1981-1990. In *Eagle Studies*, ed. by B.-U. Meyburg & R.D. Chancellor. World Working Group on Birds of Prey, Berlin. pp. 117-124.

Helander, B. & Mizera, T. (1997). White-tailed eagle (*Haliaeetus albicilla*). In *The EBCC Atlas of European Breeding Birds: their Distribution and Abundance*, ed. by W.J.M. Hagemeijer & M.J. Blair. Poyser, London. pp. 136-137.

Helander, B., Olsson, M. & Reutergårdh, L. (1982). Residue levels of organochlorine and mercury compounds in unhatched eggs and the relationships to breeding success in white-tailed sea eagles *Haliaeetus albicilla* in Sweden. *Holarctic Ecology*, **5**, 349-366.

IUCN (1968). Problems in species introductions. *IUCN Bulletin New Series,* **2**, 70-71.

Jenkins, J.M, Jackman, R.E. & Hunt, W.G. (1999). Survival and movements of immature bald eagles fledged in northern California. *Journal of Raptor Research*, **33**, 81-86.

King, W.B. (1978-79). *Red Data Book Volume 2, Aves.* IUCN, Morges, Switzerland.

Love, J.A. (1983). *The Return of the Sea Eagle.* Cambridge University Press, Cambridge.

Love, J.A. (1988). *The reintroduction of the white-tailed sea eagle to Scotland: 1975-1987.* NCC Research and Survey in Nature Conservation Report No. 12. Nature Conservancy Council, Peterborough.

Love, J.A. & Ball, M.E. (1979). White-tailed sea eagle (*Haliaeetus albicilla*). Reintroduction to the Isle of Rhum, Scotland 1975-1977. *Biological Conservation*, **16**, 23-30.

Marquiss, M. & Madders, M. (2000). *White-tailed eagle diet, Mull 1999.* Unpublished report. Scottish Natural Heritage, Perth.

Mizera, T. (1999). *Bielik.* Wydawnictwo Lubuskiego Klubu Przyrodnikow, Swiebodzin, Poland.

Nellist, K. & Crane, K. (1999). *Island Eagles.* Cartwheeling Press, Glenbrittle.

Newton, I. (1979). *Population Ecology of Raptors.* Poyser, Berkhamsted.

Randla, T. & Tammur, E. (1996). The white-tailed sea eagle *Haliaeetus albicilla* population and breeding productivity in Estonia and some regions of NW Europe. In *Eagle Studies*, ed. by B.-U. Meyburg & R.D. Chancellor. World Working Group on Birds of Prey, Berlin. pp. 51-56.

Sandeman, P. (1965). An attempted reintroduction of the white-tailed eagle to Scotland. *Scottish Birds*, **3**, 411.

Sarrazin, F., Bagnolini, C., Pinna, J.L. & Danchin, E. (1996). Breeding biology during establishment of a reintroduced griffon vulture *Gyps fulvus* population. *Ibis*, **138**, 315-325.

Stjernberg, T. & Koivusaari, J. (1995). Merikotkat palaavat? Merikotkakannan kehitys ja pesimätulos Suomessa 1970-1994. *Linnut*, **3**, 5-14.

Stjernberg, T. & Saurola, P. (1983). Population trends and management of the White-tailed eagle in Northwestern Europe. In *Biology and Management of Bald Eagles and Ospreys*, ed. by D.M. Bird. McGill University and Raptor Research Foundation, Montreal. pp. 307-317.

Thom, V.M. (1986). *Birds of Scotland.* Poyser, Calton.

Tucker, G.M. & Heath, M.F. (1994). *Birds in Europe: their Conservation Status.* BirdLife International, Cambridge.

Whitfield, D.P., Evans, R.J., Broad, R.A, Fielding, A.H, Haworth, P.F., Madders, M. & McLeod, D.R.A. (2002). Are reintroduced white-tailed eagles in competition with golden eagles? *Scottish Birds*, **23**, 36-45.

Wille, F. & Kampp, K. (1983). Food of the white-tailed eagle *Haliaeetus albicilla* in Greenland. *Holarctic Ecology*, **6**, 81-88.

Willgohs, J.F. (1961). *The White-tailed Eagle* Haliaeetus albicilla albicilla *(Linné) in Norway*. Norwegian Universities Press, Bergen.

Willgohs, J.F. (1984). *Havørn I Norge: næring, forplantningsøkologi, konkurrenter og fiender*. WWF Norway, Trondheim.

Wylie, I. & Newton, I. (1991). Demography of an increasing population of sparrowhawks. *Journal of Animal Ecology*, **60**, 749-766.

31. RE-INTRODUCTION AND CONSERVATION OF THE RED KITE (*MILVUS MILVUS*) IN BRITAIN: CURRENT THREATS AND PROSPECTS FOR FUTURE RANGE EXPANSION

I. Carter, A.V. Cross, A. Douse, K. Duffy, B. Etheridge, P.V. Grice, P. Newbery, D.C. Orr-Ewing, L. O'Toole, D. Simpson & N. Snell

Summary

1.   Efforts to conserve the red kite *Milvus milvus* in Britain have achieved considerable success, and self-sustaining populations are now well-established in several different areas.

2.   Although annual survival rates are relatively high, the most important mortality factors are connected to human activities, particularly illegal persecution. The loss of birds due to such factors is slowing the rate at which populations can increase, and hence reducing the potential for natural recolonisation of currently unoccupied areas.

3.   Certain aspects of the red kite's ecology, including its social behaviour and high degree of natal philopatry, also reduce the rate of natural recolonisation.

4.   In order to ensure that all suitable areas within Britain are recolonised within a reasonable period of time, further release projects may be required.

31.1 Introduction

The red kite *Milvus milvus* was formerly one of the most common and widespread birds of prey in Britain. As an extremely adaptable species with no specialist food or habitat requirements, the red kite was able to exploit a wide range of different landscapes across Britain and was even common in some urban areas during medieval times.

Several aspects of the red kite's lifestyle make it highly vulnerable to human persecution. As a result of its preference for animal carrion it is easy to trap and poison using meat baits, and its habit of flying slowly, low over the ground, with little evident fear of man make it easy to shoot. Intensive human persecution by game- and livestock-keepers resulted in the extinction of the red kite in England and Scotland by the end of the 1800s. Only a few pairs managed to survive in remote parts of central Wales where levels of persecution were lower, but the landscape and climate were far from ideal.

As a result of a long-term conservation programme in Wales and, more recently, a re-introduction programme in England and Scotland, self-sustaining populations are now well-established and increasing in several parts of Britain. The prospects for the species in Britain are now brighter than at any time since the early 1800s. Despite such an encouraging recovery, the red kite is still relatively rare in Britain and currently breeds in only a tiny part of the suitable countryside available. Monitoring of the re-introduced and

Welsh populations has identified several factors which are slowing population growth and hence the potential for spread to new areas. This chapter reviews the progress that has been made with work to improve the status of the red kite in Britain and assesses the prospects for future range expansion.

31.2 Overview of conservation efforts

Intensive efforts to conserve the surviving population of red kites in Wales began in the late 1800s (Lovegrove, 1990) and have continued to the present day. A major focus has been on identifying nest sites and protecting them from disturbance and interference. This has been successful in preventing extinction and encouraging a slow but steady increase in the population from a low point of only a handful of birds to an estimated 259 breeding pairs in 2000 (Welsh Kite Trust, 2000). Monitoring and research suggest that one of the main factors preventing a more rapid recovery is low breeding productivity resulting from a poor food supply, exacerbated by frequent periods of cool and damp weather during the breeding season (Lovegrove *et al.*, 1990).

In 1989 a programme began with the aim of re-introducing the red kite to England and Scotland (Evans *et al.*, 1997). Over a six year period, 93 young birds were released at each of two sites, one in the Chiltern Hills (Oxfordshire) in southern England and another on the Black Isle in northern Scotland. Birds were taken as nestlings of four to six weeks old from northern Spain for release in southern England, and from southern Sweden for release in northern Scotland. Survival rates of released birds were high and self-sustaining breeding populations quickly became established in both areas. Breeding productivity in the newly-established populations has averaged about two young per breeding pair, equivalent to the breeding populations from which the young birds were taken, and roughly twice as high as the average productivity in Wales. The high survival rates and breeding productivity demonstrate that the countryside in the release areas is well suited to the red kite (Evans *et al.*, 1999; Carter & Grice, 2000).

In order to increase the rate at which the red kite is able to recolonise all suitable areas in Britain, further release projects have been carried out since 1995 in the English Midlands (1995-98), central Scotland (1996-2000), Yorkshire (1999-ongoing) and south-west Scotland (2001-ongoing). Nestlings collected for these projects have been taken from central Spain (for release in the English Midlands), eastern Germany (released in central Scotland and south-west Scotland), southern England (English Midlands, Yorkshire and south-west Scotland) and northern Scotland (south-west Scotland). A breeding survey was carried out in 2000 (Wotton *et al.*, 2002) and the estimated number of breeding pairs in each of the kite areas in Britain is given in Table 31.1.

31.3 Survival rates

Released and wild-fledged red kites in Britain have been fitted with coloured, plastic wing tags and, in the case of the re-introduction projects, radio-transmitters, as an aid to monitoring. This has allowed useful data on survival rates to be collected and has also improved the chances of dead birds being located while still fresh so that a full post-mortem can be carried out. There is some variation in survival rates between the different kite populations, as shown by the figures in Table 31.2. These figures should be regarded as minimum values as some surviving individuals may be unrecorded due to tag loss or dispersal.

Table 31.1. Breeding red kites in Britain in 2000.

Area	*Breeding (egg-laying) pairs*
Northern Scotland	32
Central Scotland	7
Yorkshire	3
English Midlands	16
Southern England	112
Wales	259
Total	429

Table 31.2. Annual survival rates for red kites in Britain (released and wild-fledged birds in England and Scotland, wild-fledged birds in Wales).

Area		*Survival rates (%)*	*Source*
English Midlands:	First-year	52 (n=46)	Carter & Grice (2000)
	Adult	74 (n=19)	
Central Scotland:	First-year	57 (n=37)	O'Toole *et al.* (2000)
Southern England:	First-year	80 (n=153)	Evans *et al.* (1999)
	Adult	95 (n=134)	
Northern Scotland:	First-year	52 (n=93)	Evans *et al.* (1999)
	Adult	76 (n=88)	
Wales:	First-year	60 (n=70)	Newton *et al.* (1989)
	Adult	95[1]	

[1] Derived from the number of territorial birds located in each year (maximum 112) and estimates of recruitment by young fledged in previous years.

Note that for English and Scottish populations 'adult' is used to mean birds in their second year and older.

Taking levels of breeding productivity into account, annual survival rates have been sufficiently high to allow each of the kite populations to increase. The mortality factors discussed below have not, therefore, prevented red kite populations from recovering. However, they have undoubtedly slowed the rate at which populations have increased and so reduced the potential for recolonisation of suitable but currently unoccupied countryside.

31.4 Current threats

The main threats faced by the red kite in Britain result either directly or indirectly from various forms of human activity. This includes direct persecution in the form of egg collecting, shooting and illegal poisoning, together with accidental secondary poisoning, electrocution on overhead powerlines and collision with vehicles when scavenging on road casualties. The following sections provide a summary of three of the most serious threats using information derived from intensive monitoring of the Welsh and re-introduced populations.

31.4.1 *Illegal poisoning*

In all three countries within Britain, illegal poisoning results in considerably more deaths of full-grown red kites than any other factor. Because the red kite is primarily a scavenger, it is highly vulnerable to poison baits placed out in the open, either with the intention of killing birds of prey or, more often, to kill pest species such as corvids and foxes *Vulpes vulpes* (Anon., 2000). Kites often forage in loose groups and so a single carcass laced with poison may result in the death of a number of birds.

In England, 20 kites have been found illegally poisoned between the start of the re-introduction project in 1989 and 2000 (Plate 8). It is estimated from population studies that only about one in five of the birds that die are recovered so that a full post-mortem can be carried out (see Holmes *et al.*, 2000). The true number of deaths from this cause is therefore estimated at approximately 100 individuals.

In Wales, over 60% of birds found freshly dead between 1950 and 1996 were either definitely or probably poisoned. This involved a total of 49 birds and, as in England, this is undoubtedly only a small proportion of the total number of deaths from this cause (Cross & Davis, 1998).

In Scotland, the problem is even greater and poisoning is one of the main factors that has led to the far slower rate of population increase in northern Scotland than in southern England (see Table 31.1), despite the same number of birds being released in both areas. In the three years from 1997 to 2000, 13 individuals were found illegally poisoned and if, as in England, only one in five of the birds that died were recovered, this may represent as many as 65 actual deaths in just three years.

31.4.2 *Shooting*

It is very difficult to estimate the true number of deaths from this cause, as when birds are killed or severely wounded, the evidence is likely to be concealed by the perpetrator, knowing such actions to be illegal. Only when a bird is injured but manages to evade immediate capture and is found later do such incidents come to light, and these probably represent only a small proportion of the actual number of birds shot. In England there were four such incidents in the period 1995-2000, all involving birds that were wounded by pellets from a shotgun cartridge. Three of these birds were successfully rehabilitated and released back into the wild, whilst the fourth died in captivity after rehabilitation attempts failed.

Two further birds have been found dead with single lead pellets lodged in their bodies but it was impossible to determine from the post-mortem whether they had been shot or had ingested the pellet when feeding on shot prey.

31.4.3 *Accidental secondary poisoning*

As is the case with illegal poison baits, the scavenging habits of the red kite make it vulnerable to accidental secondary poisoning when feeding on animals that have themselves been poisoned. In Britain, the major problem in recent years has been with highly toxic second generation anticoagulant rodenticides that are now widely used to control rats. These are used in place of less toxic first generation products, such as Warfarin, as they are effective against rats that have developed resistance to Warfarin and, even in areas where resistance has not developed, they are seen as more effective due to their higher potency. Red kites are known to scavenge on rat carcasses throughout the year, and often forage close to farm buildings where poisoning campaigns are frequent (Carter & Burn, 2000).

From tissue analysis of red kites that have died from a variety of different causes, it is apparent that a high proportion of individuals have residues of rodenticides in their bodies. In England, 70% of a sample of 20 birds analysed had residues in the liver (Shore *et al.*, 2000), and in Scotland five out of a sample of nine birds (56%) contained residues (Sharp & Hunter, 1999). It is not known how many of these individuals had died from the effects of the rodenticides as there is little information available to relate red kite liver residue levels to likely adverse effects on the bird. However, post-mortems of freshly dead birds, found to have high residue levels in the liver, have shown that the ingestion of rodenticides does, at times, lead to death as a result of internal bleeding. At least seven individuals in England and eight in Scotland are believed to have died in this way in 1998-2000. As in the case of illegal poisoning, this is likely to be only a small proportion of the true number of deaths from this cause. Rodenticides are not currently thought to pose a significant threat to red kites in Wales as the majority of the breeding range is within a mainly pastoral landscape where rodenticide use is relatively low.

31.5 Natural recolonisation

In addition to suffering unnecessary deaths as a result of factors relating to human activities, there are certain aspects of the red kite's behavioural ecology that act to slow down the rate at which unoccupied, but suitable, habitat is recolonised. These are dealt with below.

31.5.1 Natal philopatry

Despite the dispersive behaviour of a proportion of birds in their first year, red kites are reluctant to breed far from their natal site and birds that have moved away from their nest (or release) site often return before making their first breeding attempt. For example, although 35% of the 70 birds released in the English Midlands dispersed in their first autumn, many subsequently returned and there have been only four records of such individuals attempting to breed more than 20 km away from the release site (see Carter & Grice, 2000). A similar pattern has been found in Scotland where, up to 2000, only a single bird was found breeding away from its population of origin. In Wales, the average distance from birthplace to subsequent breeding site for a sample of 139 individually-marked birds was only 12.5 km (Cross & Davis, 1998).

Faithfulness to natal areas means that populations may be expected to increase by a gradual spreading out from a core breeding range with first-time breeders not moving far away from the site where they themselves were fledged. In southern England, despite a rapid population increase to at least 112 pairs in 2000, only six breeding pairs were found more than 15 km away from the site where all 93 birds were released in 1989-94. The majority of the population increase during the last five years has been within a radius of about 8 km of the release point. The 10 km x 10 km square at the centre of the breeding area (and containing the release site) supported 14 breeding pairs in 1995 but this had increased dramatically to 58 pairs by 2000 (Wotton *et al.*, 2002). Although this may be considered a relatively high density for a large bird of prey it is by no means exceptional and is easily exceeded, for example, by red kites in parts of central Europe (Nicolai, 1997) and the common buzzard *Buteo buteo* in several areas of its European range (Bijlsma, 1997). In the red kite areas of northern Scotland and Wales there has been a similar pattern of gradual range expansion, along with increasing density within the core breeding area, although overall breeding densities in these areas are far lower than is the case in southern England.

31.5.2 Social behaviour

The red kite is a highly social species. This is particularly evident in winter when groups of birds concentrate in favoured foraging areas or at specific food sources, and large numbers of birds gather at the end of each day at communal roost sites. The social nature of the species is less apparent in the breeding season but the red kite is not highly territorial and only a small area close to the nest is defended against other kites. In Britain, active nests have been found within 100 m of each other (Evans *et al.*, 1999) and large woodlands may support several active nests.

The kite's strong social tendencies reduce the likelihood that areas of vacant but suitable habitat will be recolonised quickly as birds are reluctant to move into these areas, well away from others of their own kind. The few birds that have been found breeding away from their population of origin have, in most cases, recruited into established populations rather than recolonising vacant areas that are well separated from other breeding red kites. Since the start of the re-introduction programme in 1989 at least eight individually identifiable wing-tagged birds have been recorded breeding away from their population of origin (Table 31.3). Only one of these was found breeding in isolation, in this case about 55 km from the edge of the established Chilterns' population.

Table 31.3. Red kites breeding more than 20 km away from their natal or release area in Britain.

Original population	Population where found breeding	Number of individuals
Northern Scotland	Central Scotland	1
English Midlands	Southern England	3
Southern England	English Midlands	2
English Midlands	Wales	1
Southern England	Isolated breeding	1

Even when isolated pairs do breed in an area that is well away from the main population centres, the social nature of the red kite means that these are unlikely to result in the establishment of a new breeding population. A good example is provided by a pair of untagged birds, of probable continental origin, that bred successfully in Suffolk in 1996 and 1997, rearing a total of five young (Carter, 1998). This pair was more than 140 km from the nearest red kite population, and it was hoped that a small population might become established in the area as a result of the fledged young remaining faithful to their natal site and breeding in the same area. However, all of the young birds (identifiable from their wing tags) dispersed away from the area, four of the five being recorded in other kite areas in England and Wales. None returned to breed in Suffolk. For these young birds, the instinct to breed in an area already supporting a well-established population apparently proved to be stronger than the instinct to breed close to the natal site.

Further evidence for the social nature of the red kite comes from radio-tracking studies of young kites released as part of the re-introduction programme. In southern England, the English Midlands and northern Scotland, more of the released birds dispersed in the early years of projects when there were few kites in the area than in later years when small breeding populations had become established (Evans *et al.*, 1999; Carter & Grice, 2000). Table 31.4 shows this reduction in the tendency to disperse as the various re-introduction projects developed.

Table 31.4. Dispersal of released red kites in southern England (SE), English Midlands (EM)[1] and northern Scotland (NS) in their first year.

Year of release programme	Territorial pairs in local population			Proportion of released birds dispersing >50 km (sample size)		
	SE	*EM*	*NS*	*SE*	*EM*	*NS*
1	0	0	0	100 (5)	60 (10)	100 (6)
2	0	1	0	38 (13)	37 (16)	79 (19)
3	2	5	0	40 (15)	40 (20)	60 (20)
4	7	8	2	35 (20)	15 (20)	38 (24)
5	12		8	35 (20)		25 (24)

[1] Figures for English Midlands include birds dispersing in first autumn only.

The red kite's habit of communal winter roosting further reduces the likelihood of individuals settling in vacant habitat. Figure 31.1 shows the distribution of first-year kites in the English Midlands in the winter of 1996/97. All birds roosted at the same site each night and were only rarely recorded more than 4 km from the roost during the day. By the winter of 2000/01, although the Midlands' population had increased to approximately 70 birds, the general pattern of distribution remained much as in Figure 31.1. By associating in loose groups, scavenging birds such as the kite may improve their foraging efficiency, and because carcasses are often sufficient to feed many individuals, there is no overall disadvantage in having to share located food. One of the most obvious advantages of communal roosting is that it ensures that groups of birds are together in the same area at the beginning of each day so that social foraging is possible (Hiraldo *et al.*, 1993). Individual kites are unlikely to move into vacant habitat, well away from the nearest communal roost, as the advantages of social foraging are then no longer available.

In larger populations, such as in southern England, Wales and northern Scotland, there are now several communal roosts, and because birds move between roosts during the course of the winter, they utilise a larger overall area than is the case in the Midlands. Nevertheless, the basic pattern of major concentrations of birds within relatively small areas remains the same.

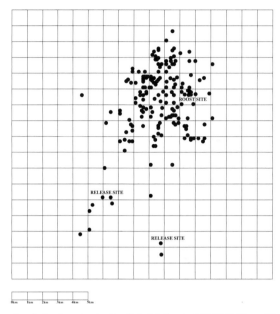

Figure 31.1. Winter ranging behaviour in the English Midlands 1996/97 (from Carter & Grice, 2000). Each dot is a radio-tracking location for one of 16 first-year kites released in summer 1996 (the background is a 1 km x 1 km grid).

31.6 Discussion

The red kite is an extremely popular species and attracts considerable publicity in the areas into which it has been re-introduced and in central Wales. Conservation work has undoubtedly helped to increase awareness of the most serious threats resulting from human activities, and action taken to tackle these issues will benefit a wide range of species in addition to the red kite. For example, the ongoing Government Campaign Against Illegal Poisoning (Anon., 2000) has been boosted by publicity associated with the red kite, including a high profile court case in 1997 concerned with kites killed by poison baits in southern England. The large fine that resulted from the successful prosecution will hopefully act as a deterrent to others considering using the same methods. Guidance on the safe use of anticoagulant rodenticides has been provided to landowners in the red kite areas and, on a wider scale, through articles in the national media. This too is likely to benefit a range of scavengers and predators in addition to the kite.

Detailed monitoring is a vital part of any well planned species conservation programme. Monitoring has been invaluable during work on the red kite in order to identify the main threats facing the species in our modern landscapes and in providing some indication of the potential for future population increase and range expansion. Such work has shown that although survival rates of released birds are high, the most important mortality factors result from human activities, particularly deliberate persecution. Unnecessary deaths from such causes will undoubtedly result in a slower rate of population increase and thus a reduced potential for range expansion.

Natal philopatry and a reluctance to breed far from others of their own kind are common factors for many raptors (Newton, 1979; Poole, 1989). Once such species have been lost from an area it requires not only a cessation of the factors that caused extinction but also a sufficiently long period of time to allow natural recolonisation to take place. This poor ability to recolonise vacant but suitable habitat is one of the main reasons why large raptors are frequent subjects for re-introduction programmes.

The red kite has particularly poor powers of natural recolonisation. Young birds show a high degree of natal philopatry and the social nature of the species further reduces the likelihood of breeding away from established population centres. Until the start of the re-introduction programme in 1989 there had been no records of successful breeding outside of Wales, despite the steadily increasing population and the regular dispersal of first-year kites into England. Since the re-introduction programme began, red kites have occasionally been found breeding in Britain away from the main population centres but these have not, so far, led to the founding of new populations away from the release areas. Where the young from such isolated pairs have been monitored, they are known to have dispersed, in some cases joining up with established kite populations in England and Wales, rather than remaining in the natal area to breed.

In the future, as populations continue to increase, there may be more breeding attempts away from current centres of populations. Elsewhere in Europe this has led to the natural recolonisation of countries from which kites had been wiped out by human persecution, including Austria, the Czech Republic and Belgium (Tucker & Heath, 1994). The extent to which new populations become established in this way in Britain will have a major impact in determining the rate at which the red kite is able to recolonise the large areas of currently unoccupied countryside. If continued monitoring shows that there is only a gradual spread from the main population centres then natural recolonisation of all suitable habitats will take a very long period of time. If this situation prevails then further release projects in other parts of the country should be considered in order to facilitate a more rapid recovery.

Acknowledgements

Work to conserve the red kite in Britain has been a joint effort with many different organisations and individuals making important contributions. The following organisations have helped to fund and carry out the work during recent years: the Welsh Kite Trust coordinates monitoring of the expanding breeding population in Wales; the RSPB, Scottish Natural Heritage and English Nature have jointly co-ordinated the re-introduction programme in England and Scotland; British Airways, Conoco, Forest Enterprise, The Harewood Estate, The Royal Air Force, The Southern England Kite Group, and Yorkshire Water have provided support; and Gobierno de Navarra, Gobierno de Aragón, Junta de Castilla y León, WWF-Sweden, Skånes Ornitologiska Förening, The Swedish National Environment Protection Board, Sachsen-Anhalt Lande, Martin Luther University, and Halle and Vogelschutzwarte Steckby have helped to translocate young kites from Germany, Spain and Sweden. Two anonymous referees commented on a draft of the manuscript.

References

Anonymous (2000). *Report of the UK Raptor Working Group.* Department of the Environment, Transport and the Regions and the Joint Nature Conservation Committee. Joint Nature Conservation Committee, Peterborough.

Bijlsma, R.G. (1997). Common buzzard (species account). In *The EBCC Atlas of European Breeding Birds: their Distribution and Abundance*, ed. by W.J.M. Hagemeijer & M.J. Blair. Poyser, London. pp. 160-161.

Carter, I. (1998). The changing fortunes of the red kite in Suffolk. *Suffolk Birds*, **46**, 6-10.

Carter, I. & Burn, A. (2000). Problems with rodenticides: the threat to red kites and other wildlife. *British Wildlife*, **11**, 192-197.

Carter, I. & Grice, P. (2000). Studies of re-established red kites in England. *British Birds*, **93**, 304-322.

Cross, A.V. & Davis, P.E. (1998). *The Red Kite of Wales*. The Welsh Kite Trust, Llandrindod Wells.

Evans, I.M., Dennis, R.H., Orr-Ewing, D.C., Kjellén, N., Andersson, P-O., Sylvén, M., Senosiain, A. & Carbo, F.C. (1997). The re-establishment of red kite breeding populations in Scotland and England. *British Birds*, **90**, 123-138.

Evans, I.M., Summers, R.W., O'Toole, L., Orr-Ewing, D.C., Evans, R., Snell, N. & Smith, J. (1999). Evaluating the success of translocating red kites to the UK. *Bird Study*, **46**,129-144.

Hiraldo, F., Heredia, B. & Alonso, J.C. (1993). Communal roosting of wintering red kites: social feeding strategies for the exploitation of food resources. *Ethology*, **93**, 117-124.

Holmes, J., Walker, D., Davies, P. & Carter, I. (2000). The illegal persecution of raptors in England. *English Nature Research Report* No. 343. English Nature, Peterborough.

Lovegrove, R. (1990). *The Kite's Tale: the Story of the Red Kite in Wales*. RSPB, Sandy.

Lovegrove. R., Elliot, G. & Smith, K. (1990). The red kite in Britain. *RSPB Conservation Review* No. 4. RSPB, Sandy.

Newton, I. (1979). *Population Ecology of Raptors*. Poyser, London.

Newton, I., Davis, P.E. & Davis, J.E. (1989). Age of first breeding, dispersal and survival of red kites in Wales. *Ibis*, **131**, 16-21.

Nicolai, B. (1997). Red kite (species account). In *The EBCC Atlas of European Breeding Birds: their Distribution and Abundance*, ed. by W.J.M. Hagemeijer & M.J. Blair. Poyser, London. pp. 134-135.

O'Toole, L., Orr-Ewing, D.C., Stubbe, M., Schönbrobt, R. & Bainbridge, I.P. (2000). Interim report on the translocation of red kites from Germany to central Scotland. *Populationsökologie Greifvogel-und Eulenarten*, **4**, 233-242

Poole, A.F. (1989). *Ospreys: A Natural and Unnatural History*. Cambridge University Press, Cambridge.

Sharp, E.A. & Hunter, K. (1999). *The occurrence of second generation anticoagulant rodenticide residues in red kites in Scotland*. Unpublished report. Scottish Agricultural Science Agency, Edinburgh.

Shore, R.F., Afsar, A., Horne, J.A. & Wright, J. (2000). *Rodenticide and Lead Concentrations in Red Kites*. Centre for Ecology and Hydrology, Huntingdon.

Tucker, G.M. & Heath, M.F. (Eds). (1994). *Birds in Europe: Their Conservation Status*. Birdlife International, Cambridge.

Welsh Kite Trust (2000). *The Newsletter of the Welsh Kite Trust, Winter 2000*. The Welsh Kite Trust, Llandrindod Wells.

Wotton, S.R., Carter, I., Cross, A.V., Etheridge, B., Snell, N., Duffy, K., Thorpe, R. & Gregory, R.D. (2002) Breeding status of the Red Kite *Milvus milvus* in Britain in 2000. *Bird Study*, **49**, 278-286.

32. CONSERVATION OF BARN OWLS (*TYTO ALBA*) AND THE ROLE OF NEST SITE PROVISIONING IN SOUTH SCOTLAND

Iain R. Taylor & Andrew Walton

Summary

1.   During the 1980s and 1990s, traditional nest sites of the barn owl *Tyto alba* were lost at the rates of 2.3%, 3.8% and 3.1% per annum in three study areas in South Scotland. In one area, the Esk catchment, 47 artificial nest sites were provided between 1980 and 1996, matching the loss of traditional sites.

2.   By 2000, artificial sites comprised 60% of all sites available, and between 1990 and 2000 the percentage of the owl population breeding in these sites fluctuated between 50% and 70%. In the absence of artificial sites, the population would have been limited by nest site availability by 1997, and presumably would have decreased thereafter.

3.   In a sample section of the Esk area, the percentage of years that nest sites were occupied by breeding owls was not correlated with site quality, defined by breeding performance and foraging habitat around the site. There were 'sink' and 'source' areas at the level of individual nest sites, which were used indiscriminately by the owls.

4.   The use of artificial nest sites as a management tool will be essential for the future conservation of barn owls, but this use will have to take into account differences in habitat quality.

5.   The random location of artificial nest sites has the potential to exacerbate population decline if too many are placed in low quality 'sink' areas.

6.   Artificial nests should be placed in habitat of good enough quality to ensure that gains through breeding at least match losses through mortality.

32.1 Introduction

The history of barn owls *Tyto alba* in Europe is largely unknown, but presumably they spread and became more abundant as humans cleared the original forest cover. In the early phases, when human habitations were modest in size, barn owls probably nested mostly in hollow trees at the edges of cleared land, but as rural buildings became more numerous and complex, and the numbers of large trees declined, they must have switched their preferences progressively towards buildings. By the latter part of the 20th century the use of tree nest sites had declined to low levels throughout most of Europe, with perhaps the exception of England, where 30-40% of reported sites were in tree hollows (Sharrock, 1976; Shawyer, 1987). The main nesting places for barn owls throughout Europe are now buildings of various kinds, including church bell towers, hay and grain storage lofts in farms, dovecotes, and abandoned dwellings (Honer, 1963; Braaksma & De Bruijin, 1976; Kaus, 1977; Braaksma, 1980; Bunn *et al.*, 1982; Juillard & Beuret, 1983; Pikula *et al.*, 1984; Baudvin, 1986; Taylor, 1994).

The loss of breeding sites has frequently been suggested as a significant cause of declines in barn owl populations during the second half of the 20th century, although usually with little direct quantitative evidence (Kragenow, 1970; Braaksma & De Bruijin, 1976; Kaus, 1977; Bunn *et al.*, 1982; Juillard & Beuret, 1983; Shawyer, 1987). Modernisation of farm buildings, a desire for greater hygiene within them, and a decrease in the abundance of old, large trees with suitable hollows, are often cited as some of the main causes of nest site loss. In some areas, the provision of 'artificial' nest sites has been used successfully to reverse these losses and prevent further population declines, and in some cases, dramatic increases in numbers have been achieved (Petty *et al.*, 1994; De Bruijin, 1994).

In this chapter we describe the types of nest site used by barn owls in three study areas in South Scotland, their rate of loss, and the results of providing artificial nest sites. We also describe ways in which the conservation value of such provisioning can be maximised.

32.2 Study area and methods

The main study area, investigated from 1978 to 2000, encompassed the catchments of the Rivers Esk and Liddle in South Scotland, a total area of 1,600 km², ranging from fertile coastal plains to uplands of around 500 m above sea level (Figure 32.1). Below about 150 m the area was predominantly pastoral farmland for dairy, beef and sheep production. Most

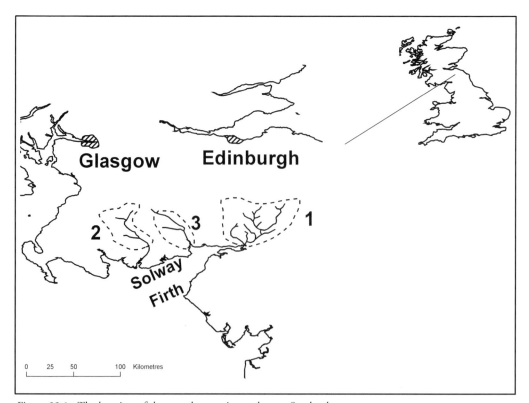

Figure 32.1. The location of three study areas in south-west Scotland.

fields were short rotation pastures, silage and hay with little arable land. Interspersed among the fields were numerous small coniferous, deciduous and mixed species woodlands covering about 20% of the total area. Rough grassland areas that could support populations of small mammal prey for barn owls were restricted to edge habitats, especially woodland edges, along tracks, and occasional ditches. Because of livestock grazing, most fence lines and hedge headlands were closely cropped and hence lacked suitable long grassland for small mammals.

Above about 150 m the land rapidly graded into hill margin land and uplands devoted to sheep production and plantation forestry. Human habitation was concentrated along the numerous small valleys, which supported narrow strips of enclosed fields of pasture and hay. These were flanked by moist, semi-natural rough grassland, grazed by low densities of sheep. From the 1950s onwards, but especially during the 1960s and 1970s, large areas of these uplands were drained and planted with even-aged woodlands of exotic conifers, especially Sitka spruce *Picea sitchensis*. These forests occurred at altitudes from 120 to 300 m above sea level.

Most of the farm buildings throughout the area dated from the 19th century and so had structures within them such as hay and grain storage lofts required of the farming practices of those times. However, during the 1950s and 1960s, because of the increasing mechanisation and efficiency of farming, many such structures progressively became redundant and disused. Reductions in farm labour forces and major changes in land use, such as afforestation, resulted in the abandonment of many farms and workers' cottages, and these were the main nesting places for barn owls. There were few trees large enough to form suitably sized hollows for the owls.

Two additional study areas were established in the upper part of the River Dee catchment from New Galloway northwards (200 km²) and the River Nith catchment (190 km²). These had similar land uses, habitat types and histories to the Esk area and were investigated from 1980 to 1988. These three study areas together are referred to subsequently as the intensive study areas. In addition, records were also kept of any barn owl nests found casually in areas between and adjacent to these study areas, referred to as the extensive study area.

The intensive study areas were searched systematically by IRT with volunteers in order to locate all suitable barn owl nesting places. For the Esk area these searches were undertaken between May 1978 and March 1979 and in the other areas between September 1979 and March 1980. During these searches all buildings within the study areas, except those in towns and villages, were visited. Those that could potentially have contained a suitable nesting site for barn owls were inspected in detail, and discussions were held with the owners for any information on the occurrence of owls. Thus all farm buildings, disused and derelict buildings, haysheds, dovecotes and other such structures were examined. In the great majority of cases the sites actually used by the owls were in attic or loft spaces of disused or rarely visited buildings, but in a few cases they nested in very small cavities (0.3 m x 0.5 m x 0.5 m), such as between layers in walls, where a missing stone allowed entry and fallen masonry formed a hollow. Thus, searches for potentially suitable sites had to be meticulous. None of the study areas had a great abundance of deciduous trees that might have contained large enough hollows for nesting barn owls, and most trees were sycamore *Acer pseudoplatanus* and beech *Fagus sylvatica* that rarely formed suitable hollows. Ash *Fraxinus excelsior* was the main hollow-forming species and most of these occurred as individual trees around farmhouses or on the lower slopes of hillsides. All isolated or woodland edge trees were inspected for hollows, from the ground, by teams of volunteers. After initial identification of potential sites, all were examined at least twice each year to establish their continued suitability for nesting and whether or not they were occupied by breeding owls. Additionally, while driving around the study areas a constant check was made for any changes in the use of buildings that might have changed their suitability as nest sites. As further checks to ensure discovery of breeding owls, farmers, gamekeepers, foresters and interested members of the public throughout the study areas were asked to look out for breeding or roosting owls and report any sightings to local contacts. These observers reported independently the majority of the pairs discovered by our routine checks, but only twice reported pairs that had been missed. In both cases they were late nesters that bred for only one season between bales in haysheds. We were therefore confident that our methodology for finding pairs was reliable.

Artificial nest sites were provided only in the Esk area. Between 1979 and 1993, when an intensive population study was undertaken in the area, the objective was to maintain a more or less equal number of nest sites from year to year (Taylor, 1994). Wherever possible, losses of individual sites were anticipated and artificial sites erected as close as possible to the original, before or immediately after loss. Where no suitable location existed nearby, an equivalent artificial site was erected elsewhere in the study area. The most frequently chosen locations were haysheds or other similar buildings that were subject to low levels of human activity, especially in the spring when established pairs were laying and new pairs settling in.

Between 1980 and 1996, 47 nest boxes were provided. Initially, low cost boxes such as tea chests with a minimum floor area of 60 cm x 45 cm were used, but these were gradually replaced by more robust plywood boxes. These had a long entrance tunnel into which an automatic trapping device could be inserted so as to catch the adult birds when they were feeding young (see Taylor, 1994). Entrances to boxes were at the top of one side, thereby allowing for an accumulation of pellets over a number of years without becoming blocked. A layer of wood shavings was provided initially. Boxes were placed within the buildings as high as possible on tie-beams. An A-framed box was specifically designed for use on the outside walls of buildings, or in trees (Taylor, 1993), but their use was abandoned in the study area as they invariably became occupied by jackdaws *Corvus monedula*. Two instances were recorded where boxes within buildings, that had been occupied for several years by barn owls, were taken over by jackdaws, even though both members of the barn owl pair were still alive at the time. It seems likely that jackdaws were able to supplant nest sites used by barn owls. The A-shaped boxes were used successfully by barn owls in an area of conifer plantations to the west of the study area where jackdaws were scarce (Petty *et al.*, 1994).

Nest site selection of the birds in relation to the quality of the foraging habitat around potential nest sites was examined in the low farmland section of the Esk study area between 1980 and 1993. The quality of sites was assessed by identifying the components of the habitat used by foraging birds and quantifying the amount of such habitat within the foraging range of each pair, and also by examining the relationship between the density of preferred foraging habitat at each site and the birds' breeding performance. Breeding performance has been used widely to assess breeding site quality (Newton, 1986; Korpimäki, 1988). The percentage of years that each site was occupied by breeding owls over the 20 year study period was compared with these measures of site quality.

32.3 Results

32.3.1 Types of nest site used by barn owls

Sites used by the owls that were not deliberately provided by the researchers are referred to as 'traditional' sites, even though most were of human origin. In the intensive study areas of the Esk, Nith and Dee river catchments, a total of 101 separate traditional nest sites (i.e. not including artificial sites) were used by breeding barn owls, of which 10 (9.9%) were in tree hollows, 42 (41.6%) in abandoned cottages, 44 (43.6%) in farm buildings, and 5 (4.9%) in other situations such as castles, a dovecote and a church. In the extensive study areas, 45 sites were found, of which 3 (6.7%) were in trees, 16 (35.6%) in abandoned cottages, 18 (40.0%) in farm buildings, and 8 (17.8%) in other locations. A high dependence on buildings was apparent throughout the entire area, as was the relative scarcity of tree nest sites. When nesting in abandoned cottages the owls mostly used either the attic space or blocked chimneys, invariably selecting the most secluded parts of attic spaces such as between floorboards and the ceiling, behind panelling or in dry water tanks. Generally, they only laid in the open space of the attic where the building was either so remote that it was rarely visited by humans, or where the attic space was exceptionally dark. When nesting in farms the owls most often selected hay or grain lofts that were no longer in use. A common characteristic of most sites selected was a low frequency of direct human visitation within the loft or attic space used by the owls, but they were clearly able to tolerate considerable activity within the general area around the nest building. For example, on many sheep farms, there was often a great deal of noise from lambing activities, and tractors shifting animal feed, less than 10 m from the lofts where the owls were nesting. They were also able to tolerate infrequent direct disturbance at all stages of the breeding season, with no deleterious effects (Taylor, 1991).

32.3.2 Rates of loss of traditional nest sites

Traditional nest sites were lost through a variety of causes. Buildings unused by humans were not maintained, so their roofs gradually deteriorated and eventually collapsed. Some were renovated, and others demolished (with the stone used elsewhere). On farms, old barns were often modified in such a way that the former loft spaces were removed. Trees with hollows large enough to attract barn owls were exceptionally vulnerable to collapse during strong winds.

Rates of loss of traditional sites were quantified for the Esk study area over 22 years, from 1978 to 2000, and for the Nith and Dee study areas, over eight years from 1980 to 1988. In all areas losses were progressive, as would be expected from the causes of loss (Figure 32.2). In the Esk area, 33 sites of an initial 64, or 51.6%, were lost over the 22 year study (2.3% per annum) and a minimum of a further ten of the 31 sites remaining in 2000 were considered highly vulnerable to loss within five to ten years (Figure 32.3a). The Nith and Dee study areas both showed slightly higher rates of loss, although they were studied over shorter time spans. Ten of 33 sites (30.3%, 3.8% per annum.) were lost in the Nith area, and six of 24 (25%, 3.1% per annum) in the Dee area were lost, over eight years.

32.3.3 Use of artificial sites

At the start of the study, in 1978, 64 traditional nest sites were located within the study area, all of which were occupied by breeding barn owls at some time during the following 22

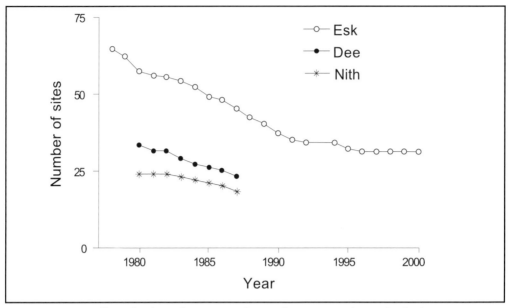

Figure 32.2. Rates of loss of traditional nest sites in three study areas in south-west Scotland.

years, although never all in any single year. By 2000, only 31 of these sites remained. Artificial sites provided an increasing percentage of the available sites, rising from zero in 1979 to 50% by 1992 and 60% in 2000 (Figure 32.3b). Excluding 1980 and 1981, when only three artificial sites were available, the percentage of the total population breeding in artificial sites increased steadily to 1990 and thereafter fluctuated between about 50% and 70% depending on the stage of the vole cycle and total population size. The percentage of these artificial sites that were occupied by breeding owls also increased steadily to 50% in 1990, thereafter fluctuating between 30 and 70% (Figure 32.3b).

The long-term effect of artificial nest site provision on total breeding population size can be assessed by comparing the numbers of traditional sites remaining each year with the numbers of breeding pairs. The number of breeding barn owls in the study area was affected mainly by annual variations in the densities of field voles *Microtus agrestis*, their main prey, and also by exceptionally severe winter weather (Taylor, 1994). Thus, they exhibited three-yearly cycles of abundance, of varying amplitude, superimposed upon any longer term changes (Figure 32.3b.c). The maximum number recorded during the study, 55 breeding pairs, was in 1981, the highest peak vole year, which had also been preceded in 1980 by a year of reasonably high vole density. In 1981 only six nest sites in suitable habitat remained unoccupied throughout the study area, so nest sites came very close to limiting population size. During the mid- to late 1980s, four out of five consecutive years were recorded with exceptionally low vole populations. These were reflected in low productivity and survival in the owl population (Taylor, 1994). Consequently, breeding numbers during this time were below the numbers of traditional nest sites available to the birds. During the early 1990s vole populations, although still cyclic, remained at higher densities during the low phases and the owl population increased. By 1993 there were 32 breeding pairs, a single non-breeding pair and two unmated males occupying nest sites. Only 34 traditional sites remained. Data on population size were not obtained for 1994 but, as this was a peak vole year, numbers should

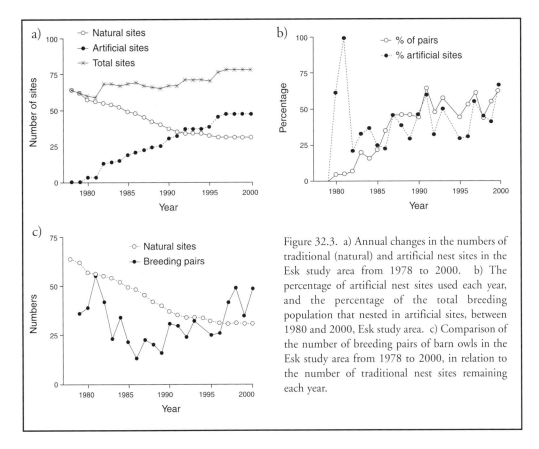

Figure 32.3. a) Annual changes in the numbers of traditional (natural) and artificial nest sites in the Esk study area from 1978 to 2000. b) The percentage of artificial nest sites used each year, and the percentage of the total breeding population that nested in artificial sites, between 1980 and 2000, Esk study area. c) Comparison of the number of breeding pairs of barn owls in the Esk study area from 1978 to 2000, in relation to the number of traditional nest sites remaining each year.

have risen above 1993 levels. Thus by 1993/94, in the absence of artificial nest site provisioning, the number of breeding pairs would have been close to, or limited by, the numbers of remaining traditional sites. From 1997 to 2000 the number of breeding pairs had returned to around the levels of the early 1980s and considerably exceeded the number of traditional sites still available to them (Figure 32,3c). Thus, these population levels could not have been reached had artificial nest sites not been provided in earlier years.

32.3.4 Occupancy of sites in relation to site quality.

The provision of artificial nests sites can be used to reverse the declining availability of natural sites, but it also has the potential to alter population demography by encouraging pairs to breed in the best remaining areas of habitat. There could be two approaches to this; artificial nest sites could be provided wherever possible, allowing the birds to chose those in the best areas, or they could be provided only in the best areas. The former depends on the birds being able to differentiate site quality and the latter depends on the observers being able to do likewise. It has been shown that the most important aspect of habitat responsible for determining site quality in the study area was the amount of rough grassland, woodland edge habitat within the birds' normal breeding range of about 1 km radius around the nest site. Woodland edges of this type supported populations of small mammal prey and were the birds' main foraging areas. The mean number of young reared at each site was significantly correlated with the length of woodland edge at each site, while annual survival was independent of woodland edge (Taylor, 1994, 2002).

Occupancy by breeding owls at the different sites ranged from 8% to 100% of the years the sites were available, but was not correlated with the quality of the site assessed by the amount of woodland edge around the nest (r = 0.1, $P > 0.50$). There was also no correlation between the percentage of years each site was occupied and the quality of the site, assessed by the mean number of young fledged from the site (r = -0.19, $P > 0.45$). Sites with the lowest amounts of preferred foraging habitat and lowest long-term breeding success were occupied just as frequently as those with the most foraging habitat and highest breeding success.

32.4 Discussion

Barn owls, like many farmland birds in Western Europe, must have increased in numbers with the initial spread of agriculture and, like most, their abundance is now decreasing with modern intensification of farming (Marchant *et al.*, 1990; Fuller *et al.*, 1995; Siriwardena *et al.*, 1998; Thompson *et al.*, Chapter 25). However, unlike most species, barn owls have come to depend closely on man-made structures for their nesting places, so they are now threatened by the loss of both nest sites and suitable foraging habitats. This study has shown that there has been a high rate of loss of traditional nesting places throughout south-west Scotland during the 1980s and 1990s, and given that most remaining traditional nest sites are in disused buildings which are no longer maintained, the trend is expected to continue.

The effect of nest site loss on barn owl population size cannot be assessed over short time periods, as changes in numbers are complex, with short-term cycles related to fluctuations in field vole abundance, and medium-term changes associated with variations in the magnitude of these fluctuations, as well as winter weather conditions (Taylor, 1994). In this study the implications of nest site loss were apparent only over the full 22 year span of the research programme, in which it was demonstrated that, in the absence of artificial nest sites, there would have been a significant long-term decline in the size of the breeding population. The provision of nest sites prevented such a decline. There seems to be little doubt that the maintenance of viable populations of barn owls in South Scotland will rely on the continued provision and management of artificial nest sites, and the important question is how can this conservation technique be used to maximum effect.

Nest boxes were accepted by barn owls in the study area but this relied on the availability of undisturbed situations for their installation, such as haysheds that were at a distance from the main centres of activity on farms. Modern multi-purpose sheds, that are increasingly replacing traditional haysheds, are unsuitable because of the high levels of activity in them. Also, the high densities of nest competitors, such as jackdaws, throughout most of the farmed area precluded the use of boxes attached to trees. Thus, the choice of sites for artificial nests was somewhat constrained by the availability of suitable locations and this may become an increasing problem as farm modernisation progresses.

One obvious strategy to maximise the chances of achieving sustainable populations would be to encourage as many pairs as possible to breed in the best quality habitat available, quality being most appropriately defined as the net outcome of breeding output and survival. There are two possible ways of achieving this objective: either by providing artificial nest sites only in the best quality areas, or by providing sites throughout, and allowing the birds to select the best areas. In the lowland farm section of the study area, it was shown that the percentage of years during which each site was occupied by breeding owls was independent of site quality. The poorest quality sites, defined by productivity, were occupied just as frequently as the best quality sites. The birds apparently did not distinguish between them. It was estimated that, in this habitat, a long-term mean production of around 3.2 young per breeding pair would be needed to maintain long-term population stability (Taylor & Masseder, 1992). About 40% of the nest sites used regularly for breeding had a long-term productivity below the required maintenance levels and 20% had substantially higher values. Thus, throughout the study area, there were 'source' and 'sink' areas (Pulliam, 1988) at the level of individual breeding sites. Source and sink habitats have also been identified in barn owl populations in Holland (De Bruijin, 1994).

Given that the birds did not distinguish poor quality from good quality sites in the low farm area (Taylor, 2002), the only way to ensure that overall productivity at least balanced mortality losses would be to ensure that nest sites are available only in habitat at, or above, the minimum necessary quality. The long-term objective should be to achieve a gradual shift of population distribution to occupy as much as possible of the existing best quality foraging habitat but, at the same time, it might also be necessary to undertake some enhancement of habitat at these sites so as to achieve the required quality and abundance of them. Presumably, concentrating habitat management activity in this way would be more cost effective than attempting a less targeted improvement of habitat more widely across the study area. The siting of artificial nests in the best quality habitat requires that the observers are able to identify the characteristics of such habitat and that suitable locations for the installation of artificial nest sites are available in these areas. It might also be advisable to remove existing nest sites in poor quality sink areas, as leaving significant numbers of such sites could cause population declines. The main determinant of habitat quality in the low farmland was the amount of woodland edge consisting of rough grassland, suitable for the owls' foraging, within a 1 km radius of potential nest sites, a characteristic that can be assessed rapidly in the field (Taylor, 1994, 2002).

The dynamic nature of farmland has an important bearing on the long-term conservation strategies for species, such as the barn owl, which occur mostly in this habitat. The provision of artificial nest sites could be undertaken flexibly in response to such temporal changes in habitat. Within the present study area, the most obvious changes occurred through woodland management. New woodlands were planted and existing ones felled. Felling and replanting created suitable foraging habitat until canopy closure, and also offered opportunities to modify the edge areas of new woodlands to be more suitable as hunting areas for barn owls over a longer time period. Thus, an area that may have been poor quality habitat could improve in quality in both the short- and long-term, and could be exploited by ensuring that artificial nest sites are made available to match the change in habitat. Dynamic conservation of this nature requires a detailed and ongoing knowledge of the areas involved and is probably best achieved by local amateur ornithologists, funded by, and working in conjunction with conservation agencies.

Acknowledgements
We thank the many interested landowners, farmers, gamekeepers, foresters and members of the public who helped us with this study, Simon McDonald for help with Figure 32.1, and two anonymous referees for comments on the manuscript.

References

Baudvin, H. (1986). La reproduction de la Chouette Effraie (*Tyto alba*). *Le Jean le-Blanc*, **22**, 1-125.

Braaksma, S. (1980). Gegevens over de achteruitgang van de kerkuil (*Tyto alba guttata* Brehm) in West-Europa. *Wielwaal*, **46**, 421-428.

Braaksma, S. & De Bruijin, O. (1976). De kerkuilstand in Nederland. *Limosa*, **49**, 135-187.

De Bruijin, O. (1994). Population ecology and conservation of the barn owl *Tyto alba* in farmland habitats in Liemers and Achterhoek (The Netherlands). *Ardea*, **82**, 1-109.

Bunn, D.S., Warburton, A.B. & Wilson, R.D.S. (1982). *The Barn Owl.* Poyser, Calton.

Fuller, R.J., Gregory, R.D., Gibbons, D.W., Marchant, J.H., Wilson, J.D., Baillie, S.R. & Carter, N. (1995). Population declines and range contraction among lowland farmland birds in Britain. *Conservation Biology*, **9**, 1425-1441.

Honer, M.R. (1963). Observations on the barn owl *Tyto alba guttata* in the Netherlands in relation to its ecology and population fluctuations. *Ardea*, **51**, 158-195.

Juillard, M. & Beuret, J. (1983). L'aménagement des sites de nidification et son influence sur une population de Chouettes Effraie, *Tyto alba,* dans le nord-ouest de la Suisse. *Nos Oiseaux*, **37**, 1-70.

Kaus, D. (1977). Zur populationsdyamik ökologie, und Brutbiologie der Schleiereule in Franken. *Anzeiger der Ornithologischen Gellsellschaft in Bayern*, **16**, 18-44.

Korpimäki, E. (1988). Effects of territory quality on occupancy, breeding performance and breeding dispersal in Tengmalm's Owl. *Journal of Animal Ecology*, **57**, 97-108.

Kragenow, P. (1970). Die Schleiereule in den Nordbezeirken der DDR. *Falke*, **17**, 256-259.

Marchant, J.H., Hudson, R., Carter, S.P. & Whittington, P. (1990). *Population Trends in British Breeding Birds.* British Trust for Ornithology, Tring.

Newton, I. (1986). *The Saprrowhawk.* Poyser, Calton.

Petty, S.J., Shaw, G. & Anderson, D.I.K. (1994). Value of nest boxes for population studies and conservation of owls in coniferous forests in Britain. *Journal of Raptor Research*, **28**, 134-142.

Pikula, J., Beklova, M. & Kubik, V. (1984). The breeding bionomy of *Tyto alba.* *Acta Scientisiarum Naturalium, Academiae Scientiarum Bohemoslovacae Brno*, **18**, 1-53.

Pulliam, H.R. (1988). Sources and sinks, and population regulation. *American Naturalist*, **132**, 652-661.

Ramsden, D. (1998). Effect of barn conversions on local populations of barn owl *Tyto alba. Bird Study*, **45**, 68-76.

Sharrock, J.T.R. (1976). *The Atlas of Breeding Birds in Britain and Ireland.* Poyser, Berkhamsted.

Shawyer, C. (1987). *The Barn Owl in the British Isles - its Past, Present and Future.* The Hawk Trust. London.

Siriwardena, G.M., Baillie, S.R. & Wilson, J.D. (1998). Variation in the survival rates of some British passerines with respect to their population trends on farmland. *Bird Study*, **45**, 276-292.

Taylor, I.R. (1991). Effects of nest inspections and radio-tagging on barn owl breeding success. *Journal of Wildlife Management*, **55**, 312-315.

Taylor, I.R. (1993). *Barn Owls: An Action Plan and Practical Guide for their Conservation in Scotland.* University of Edinburgh, Edinburgh.

Taylor, I.R. (1994). *Barn Owls: Predator Prey Relationships and Conservation.* Cambridge University Press, Cambridge.

Taylor, I.R. (2002). Occupancy in relation to site quality in Barn Owls (*Tyto alba)* in south Scotland. In *The Ecology and Conservation of Owls*, ed. by I. Newton, R.P. Kavanagh, J. Olsen & I.R. Taylor. CSIRO, Melbourne. pp. 30-41.

Taylor, I.R. & Masseder, J. (1992). The dynamics of depleted and introduced farmland barn owl *Tyto alba* populations: a modelling approach. In *The Ecology and Conservation of European Owls*, ed. by C.A. Galbraith, I.R. Taylor & S. Percival. Joint Nature Conservation Committee, Peterborough. pp. 104-109.

33. BIRDS OF PREY AND LOWLAND GAMEBIRD MANAGEMENT

David S. Allen & Chris J. Feare

Summary

1. Three gamebird species, grey partridge *Perdix perdix*, red-legged partridge *Alectoris rufa* and pheasant *Phasianus colchicus*, are widespread in lowland Britain, with wild populations heavily augmented by birds bred in captivity and subsequently released to be shot.

2. Game management, aimed at maximising the number of birds available to be shot, benefits some species of raptor through the provision of food. Game managers are concerned that raptors reduce the availability of reared game, both directly and indirectly, giving rise to the illegal killing of some raptor species.

3. The impact of raptors on lowland gamebirds depends upon the geographical and habitat overlap of the species, and on the diet and foraging behaviour of raptors.

4. Evidence for raptor predation of lowland gamebirds comes mainly from studies of diet, but this is difficult to interpret in terms of impact on gamebirds. Game manager responses to questionnaires and studies of carcasses are also difficult to interpret.

5. Attempts to reduce raptor predation of gamebirds include scaring (largely unsuccessful), management of vegetation in and near release pens, and physical barriers to prevent raptor ingress. Further research is needed on all of these management aspects to maximise their efficiency.

33.1 Introduction

Gamebirds have been managed for shooting since at least the 19th century and game managers have long considered raptors to be damaging to their birds. During this period game shooting and its associated management practices have changed, as have legislation and other external factors, such as the intensification of agriculture and its effects on both bird of prey and gamebird populations. All of these have influenced the relationship between birds of prey and gamebirds (Anon., 2000; Thompson *et al.*, Chapter 25).

In the late 1800s and 1900s, the perceived impact on gamebirds and livestock of birds of prey led to the extermination of many such species from large parts of Britain (Newton, 1979). Control of predators was a major role of the large numbers of gamekeepers. Since the introduction of legislation prohibiting the killing of birds of prey and the withdrawal of organochlorine pesticides, which had been associated with the declines of several species, the populations of some raptors have recovered and have reoccupied areas from which they had been extirpated. Whilst this recovery has been seen as a conservation success, game managers are concerned about the potential for increased conflict with game (Harradine *et al.*, 1997; Anon., 2000). Illegal killing of birds of prey has not stopped since protective legislation was enacted and is considered a factor contributing to the continued absence of species such as buzzard *Buteo buteo* and hen harrier *Circus cyaneus* from parts of their former ranges (Gibbons *et al.*, 1993; Thompson *et al.*, Chapter 25).

Whilst the killing of a gamebird by a bird of prey or the killing of a bird of prey by a game manager are two of the most obvious interactions that can occur between game interests and birds of prey, there are also less direct interactions. This chapter considers the range of interactions that might occur, and attempts to assess the extent to which they represent threats or benefits to raptors. Data on many relevant aspects are sparse, however, in marked contrast to the wealth of anecdotal and subjective opinion on the subject as evidenced, for example, by numerous articles and letters in the popular shooting press.

33.2 Lowland gamebirds in Britain

The native grey partridge *Perdix perdix* was the species shot most commonly in the early 1900s (Tapper, 1999). Following its decline since the 1950s, resulting from various aspects of agricultural intensification (Potts, 1986), the pheasant *Phasianus colchicus* and red-legged partridge *Alectoris rufa*, both introduced to Britain as sporting birds, have become the most frequently shot game species.

All three species are widespread in Britain (Gibbons *et al.*, 1993), especially the pheasant, which is absent over large areas only in north-west Scotland. Grey partridges are still widely distributed, although between the early 1970s and 1990s their distribution contracted away from western areas. Red-legged partridges have always been most abundant in southern and eastern England, but their range extended northwards during the period that the range of grey partridge contracted. The current distributions and local abundance of pheasants and red-legged partridges (grey partridge to a lesser extent) are strongly influenced by the release of captive-reared birds (Thompson *et al.*, 1997).

33.3 Lowland gamebird management

Game are managed over much of lowland Britain (Figure 33.1). This management has considerable potential to impact on lowland landscapes, through the provision of habitats for game, including cover, over-winter food, and pesticide-free field margins to provide insect food for young gamebirds. The primary aim of game management is to increase the number of birds available to be shot in a given area during the shooting season. Three main approaches are used (Robertson & Rosenberg, 1988), namely:-

1. Increasing the size and/or productivity of populations: achieved through habitat management, provision of food and shelter, predator control, and management of diseases and parasites;
2. Minimising non-hunting losses of adult gamebirds: achieved primarily through predator control and habitat management to control immigration and emigration; and
3. Supplementing wild populations with released birds through captive rearing and release of poults, generally six to seven weeks old, into open-topped (pheasants) or enclosed (partridges) release pens in which food, water and any necessary medication are supplied. Released pheasants remain here for up to six weeks, during which they increasingly switch from roosting on the ground to roosting in trees and bushes, so becoming less vulnerable to ground predators.

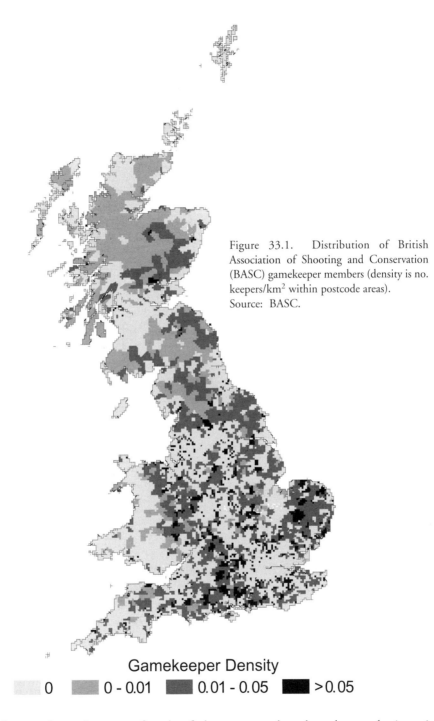

Figure 33.1. Distribution of British Association of Shooting and Conservation (BASC) gamekeeper members (density is no. keepers/km² within postcode areas). Source: BASC.

Gamekeeper Density
0   0 - 0.01   0.01 - 0.05   >0.05

Many shoots adopt elements of each of these approaches, but the emphasis varies depending on whether priority is given to the management of wild birds or to released birds, or to a combination of the two. Approximately 20 million pheasants are released each year, with wild pheasants thought to make up only c. 10% of the 12 million birds shot annually (Tapper, 1999).

Below, we emphasise the two ends of the management spectrum - shoots relying wholly on wild-bred birds and shoots relying wholly on released birds. We focus on interactions between birds of prey and released pheasants, given their predominance in modern shoots.

33.4 Interactions between raptors and lowland gamebirds

Figure 33.2 illustrates potentially beneficial and detrimental aspects of game management for birds of prey, and potentially damaging influences of birds of prey on game.

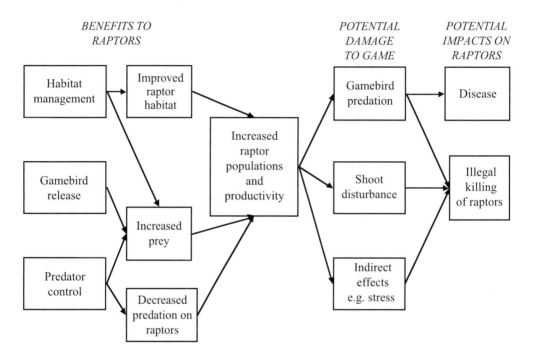

Figure 33.2. Hypothetical interactions between birds of prey and lowland gamebirds.

33.4.1 *Benefits to raptors*

Many studies have demonstrated a relationship between food availability and both breeding density and success of birds (Newton, 1998), and successful game management can increase food availability for raptors, at least locally and temporarily, through the provision of large numbers of gamebirds. The large number of released birds, however, is not available until late summer/autumn, which may not be a critical time of year for the raptors. The control of predators, other than raptors, by gamekeepers could leave larger numbers of bird and mammal prey available to raptors; if undertaken when food supplies are limiting, this might influence the productivity, survival and distribution of raptors. Enhancement of post-breeding numbers of small birds through predator control has been considered to increase prey availability for sparrowhawks *Accipiter nisus* (Côté & Sutherland, 1997).

Habitat management for the benefit of game commonly involves: i) the provision of cover, both in woodland and as field crops (Vesey-Fitzgerald, 1946); ii) the provision of feeding stations in which cereal and other seeds are available; and (iii) more recently, the creation of 'conservation headlands', which are field margins left unsprayed so as to encourage insect populations and the growth and seeding of arable weeds (Sotherton *et al.*, 1985; Sotherton & Self, 2000). Cover may encourage the proliferation of small mammal populations (Jacob & Halle, 2001) and seed available from feeders benefits small mammals and birds (Brickle & Harper, 2000; Moorcroft & Wilson, 2000). The insects intended as food for gamebird chicks in spring are available to other farmland birds during their breeding season, and seeds may enhance the over-winter survival of granivorous birds. Many of the practical measures currently being promoted as means of reversing the decline of many farmland bird populations derive from game management practices (Boatman *et al.*, 2000).

Other potential benefits to raptors include enhanced breeding success following reduction in numbers of nest predators, especially corvids. The creation of new woodlands may increase the availability of nest sites, initially for open nesters but later for hole-nesting species, e.g. owls (Strigiformes). Although Village (1990) recorded kestrels *Falco tinnunculus* occupying crow *Corvus corone* nests which had become vacant following control by gamekeepers, any benefit of nest-site provision would depend upon nest sites being a limiting resource; Newton (1979) cited examples where this appeared to be the case.

33.4.2 Impact on gamebirds

The right-hand side of Figure 33.2 shows areas of conflict between raptors and game interests. Such conflicts arise when gamebird numbers are reduced either directly as a result of predation or indirectly as a consequence of stress, disease, or dispersal resulting from raptor activity. Disruption of shoot days by raptors may also be a cause of conflict (although equivalent claims for upland grouse moors appear not to be borne out by recent study (Robson & Carter, 1999)). Gamekeepers variously attempt to manage such losses through habitat management and the use of deterrents.

33.4.3 Threats to raptors

The main threat to raptors from game management lies in illegal killing, by trapping, shooting or the deliberate misuse of organophosphorus and carbamate pesticides (Barnett *et al.*, 2000; Anon., 2000), to which raptors are particularly susceptible (Minot *et al.*, 1999). The impact of illegal persecution on raptor populations is difficult to quantify, although it is considered to be a constraint on the re-colonisation of parts of Britain from which some species were extirpated by game interests in the 19th and 20th centuries (Gibbons *et al.*, 1993; Anon., 2000; Carter *et al.*, Chapter 31). Holmes *et al.* (2000) considered that during the 1990s illegal killing was mainly an upland activity, where hen harriers were subjected to high levels of persecution. In lowland areas, impacts on sparrowhawk and buzzard populations were assessed as 'negligible' and 'low' respectively, while effects on goshawks and red kites were 'moderate' (see also Thompson *et al.*, Chapter 25).

Both wild and captive gamebirds are susceptible to viral, bacterial and protozoan diseases (Beer, 1988; Pennycott, 1996), some of which have also been recorded in raptors (Morishita *et al.*, 1997). Some studies have suggested that raptors can contract diseases through feeding on infected birds, e.g. Newcastle Disease (Forbes & Simpson, 1997) and trichomoniasis (Pepler & Oettlé, 1992; Boal *et al.*, 1998). Boal *et al.* (1998) attributed a high incidence of trichomoniasis in Cooper's hawks *Accipiter cooperii* in Arizona (leading to increased nestling mortality), to their feeding on infected doves. Trichomoniasis in pigeons and doves, however, is caused by *Trichomonas gallinae* (which has been linked to disease in raptors) and not by *T.*

phasiani which is the parasite responsible for the gamebird disease. We have found no evidence of *T. phasiani* being identified in raptors. Generally, disease is considered an insignificant cause of mortality in raptors (Newton, 1979), and Newton *et al.* (1999) confirmed that disease was responsible for the deaths of only 2% of sparrowhawks and 5% of kestrels examined by between 1963 and 1997, though mortality caused by disease might be underestimated.

33.5 Predicting levels of interaction

The extent to which different species of raptor are likely to interact with lowland game-birds, and the magnitude of any impact, depends on the distributional overlap between raptor populations and gamebird interests, biological factors that influence the likelihood of raptor species impacting upon gamebirds, and game management practices that influence the opportunities for interaction.

33.5.1 Distribution of raptors and lowland gamebird interests

The degree of overlap between the distribution of raptor populations and lowland game interests will determine the geographical extent of any interaction. Of the raptor species that breed regularly in Britain, six species - honey buzzard *Pernis apivorus*, red kite *Milvus milvus*, goshawk *Accipiter gentilis*, marsh harrier *Circus aeruginosus*, Montagu's harrier *C. pygargus* and peregrine *Falco peregrinus* - currently have restricted distributions and/or small populations in the lowlands (although they may be locally abundant, and peregrines and red kites are increasing in numbers and range; Greenwood *et al.*, Chapter 2). A further nine species – sparrowhawk, buzzard, kestrel, tawny owl *Strix aluco*, hobby *Falco subbuteo*, little owl *Athene noctua*, barn owl *Tyto alba,* short-eared owl *Asio flammeus* and long-eared owl *Asio otus* - have widespread distributions that overlap considerably with lowland game interests. The remaining species have distributions that overlap with lowland game interests in only a very limited way.

33.5.2 Biological factors

Habitat preferences influence the extent to which lowland birds of prey encounter gamebirds, and these can vary seasonally. Sparrowhawk, goshawk, buzzard and tawny owl, predators which commonly hunt in woodlands, will have different opportunities to take gamebirds compared with other predators which tend to hunt mostly over open terrain, e.g. harriers, kestrel and barn owl. The former group of species comprises those most likely to encounter gamebirds in or close to release pens.

Pheasants and/or partridges (especially young birds) have been recorded in the diets of most British raptors (e.g. Cramp & Simmons, 1980; Mikkola, 1983; Cramp, 1985; Cotgreave, 1995). They usually constitute only a small component, suggesting that predation on gamebirds is opportunistic. Larger predators, such as buzzard and goshawk, can take adult pheasants whilst smaller species, such as kestrel and little owl, probably take only young birds, especially chicks. Sexual size dimorphism may also influence the size of prey taken; female sparrowhawks regularly take prey up to 500 g (and female pheasants of 600-800 g have been recorded in their diet) whilst males rarely take prey over 120 g (Newton, 1986).

The appearance of large numbers of young, naïve pheasants and partridges in and around release pens in late summer presents a source of highly concentrated prey that several raptor species seem well suited to exploit (Thompson *et al.*, 1997; Anon., 2000). However, the territorial behaviour of most of the predator species, some throughout the year, will limit the number of individuals able to exploit these localised concentrations. Nevertheless, individuals of some raptor species appear to specialise on certain prey types (Cramp & Simmons, 1980) and localised abundances of gamebird prey could encourage this trait. Raptor foraging strategies influence the impact that birds of prey have on gamebird production. However, the fact that some gamebird remains occur at nests and roosts of buzzards and red kites could indicate scavenging of dead birds, rather than predation on live game.

33.5.3 Influence of management practices

Wild gamebirds and released birds differ in their vulnerability to raptor predation. On wild bird shoots, the habitat preferences of breeding and foraging gamebirds largely determine opportunities for predation. By contrast, on shoots where captive bred birds are released, the release programme dictates opportunities for predation. The location of release pens, the timing of release, the age of released birds and the period for which they are encouraged to stay within the pen will influence the exposure of released birds to predation.

On wild-bird shoots, gamebirds are present and vulnerable to raptor predation from immediately after hatching from April to June (pheasant) or May to June (both partridges) (and some species have been recorded taking gamebird eggs (Cramp & Simmons, 1980)) through to adulthood. By contrast, released birds are largely protected during the early stages of their life and only become available to predators when placed in release pens (pheasants) or following release from pens (partridges). Reports of little owls being particularly adept at getting into buildings where gamebird chicks are raised (Tapper, 1999) suggest inadequate proofing of buildings rather than any particular expertise of little owls. Pheasant release pens in woodland are open to exploitation mostly by those species that commonly hunt in woodland. Following release, they become available to a wider range of raptors as they disperse onto open farmland. Thus species such as sparrowhawk, that feed primarily in woodland, are likely to encounter released pheasant poults when at their most vulnerable, whilst species that favour open terrain for hunting encounter released pheasants when more fully grown.

33.5.4 The potential for conflict between raptors and game management

Table 33.1 illustrates the potential impacts of British birds of prey on lowland game, especially pheasants, based on our knowledge of the raptors' biology. It is clear that of the widespread species, two – sparrowhawk and buzzard – have the potential to impact upon pheasants, mainly young birds, over most of lowland Britain. The tawny owl, by virtue of its size and ability to take relatively large prey, might also be expected to take chicks and poults but this is not borne out by dietary studies (Cramp, 1985; Anon., 2000). Of the more locally distributed species, goshawks take adults as well as young and could exploit poults within release pens and larger birds soon after release (see Marquiss *et al.*, Chapter 9).

33.6 Evidence for predation of released gamebirds

33.6.1 Evidence from raptor diets

Although avian dietary studies are prone to bias, most studies of raptor diets, based on analysis of regurgitated pellets, show that gamebirds do not figure prominently (Cramp, 1985). However, gamebirds, especially young pheasants, formed 25-37% (by weight) of the diet of marsh harriers during the breeding season in East Anglia (Underhill-Day, 1985) and

Table 33.1. UK breeding raptors and aspects of their ecology that influence the likelihood of significant interaction with pheasants. Species ranked according to their estimated population size (number of pairs, from UK Raptor Working Group (Anon., 2000), Gibbons *et al.* (1993) and Greenwood *et al.* (Chapter 2).

Species	Habitat	Lowland distribution	Occurrence of pheasants and partridges in diet[1]	Potential for impact on pheasants
Kestrel	Open	Widespread	Young	Limited, mainly chicks of wild birds
Sparrowhawk	Wooded & open	Widespread	Mainly young, but adult female pheasant recorded	Extensive, wild-bred and released young/poults
Tawny owl	Wooded	Widespread	Not recorded	Potential predator of young birds, especially released poults but not recorded in diet
Buzzard	Open & wooded	Widespread	Young	Extensive and increasing, wild-bred and released young/poults, some adults, possibly scavenged
Little owl	Open	Widespread	Young	Limited, wild chicks
Barn owl	Open	Widespread	Not recorded	Negligible, chicks
Merlin	Open	None	Young	Negligible
Peregrine	Open	Local	Young and adults	Negligible, adults in winter
Long-eared owl	Wooded	Local	Young (rarely)	Limited, young birds, especially released poults
Short-eared owl	Open	Local	Recorded attacking adult pheasant; partridge also	Negligible
Hobby	Open	Widespread	Partridge only	None
Hen harrier	Open	None	Young and adults	Negligible
Golden eagle	Open	None	Not recorded	Negligible
Goshawk	Wooded	Local	Young and adults	Locally significant, young and adults
Osprey	Open aquatic	Local	Not recorded	None
Marsh harrier	Open	Local	Eggs and young	Locally significant, young, wild-bred
Red kite	Open & wooded	Local	Partridge only	Negligible, scavenger
Montagu's harrier	Open	Very local	Eggs and young	Locally significant, young, wild-bred
Honey buzzard	Wooded & open	Very local	Eggs and young	None
White-tailed eagle	Open	None	Not recorded	None

[1] Based on all listed references.

9-13% for Montagu's harriers (Underhill-Day, 1993). Raptor diets vary according to prey availability; Swann & Etheridge (1995) found a higher incidence of gamebirds in prey remains on an estate where large numbers of pheasants were released than on an estate without this sporting interest. In a study at Langholm, Scotland, pheasants were found amongst prey remains in 9% of buzzard nests (Graham *et al.*, 1995) but the extent to which these pheasants were predated and scavenged is unknown. Goshawks too appear to prey on gamebirds partly in relation to their abundance (Kenward, 1981).

33.6.2 Evidence from game losses

From a game manager's perspective, the proportion of a sparrowhawk's diet that is made up of pheasants is of less concern than the percentage of his game stock that has been taken (British Association for Shooting and Conservation, 2002). Currently, the greatest area of concern to gamekeepers is predation at and around release pens, yet there have been few attempts to quantify levels of predation by raptors. This may be a reflection of the difficulty of data collection; direct observation of predation is difficult, especially in wooded habitat in which most pheasant release pens are sited. Two recent studies have attempted to address game losses.

Harradine *et al.* (1997) analysed data from 996 completed questionnaires from gamekeeper members of the British Association for Shooting and Conservation. Despite the occurrence of birds of prey on most estates, 39% of respondents reported no serious problems from raptors. Whether this reflects a degree of acceptance of the level of predation experienced (i.e. it occurs but is not considered 'serious'), or whether keepers have employed management strategies that have been successful in minimising predation, is not known.

Over 70% of reported incidents were attributed by gamekeepers to sparrowhawk, buzzard and tawny owl (Figure 33.3). Most of the incidents involving these three species were associated with pheasant release pens and/or poults (Figure 33.4). For a shoot that relies heavily on released birds this is the critical period for raptor predation. It is the period when birds are most vulnerable and the effects of predation are also most visible to keepers at this time. Figure 33.4 also shows that, of the three species, only the sparrowhawk is considered to be a serious predator of partridges (39% of sparrowhawk incidents related to partridges).

In the second recent study, Allen *et al.* (2000) used standardised descriptions of pheasant carcasses provided by keepers from 14 estates in order to estimate levels of predation during the release period. Whilst carcasses can usually be ascribed to predation by birds or mammals with a high degree of confidence, there are difficulties in identifying the species involved in a kill (Thirgood *et al.*, 1998).

The proportion of released pheasants killed by raptors was estimated at c. 1% (median from 28 pens), but ranged up to a maximum of c. 5% at individual pens. This contrasts with total losses of c. 2% (median) and up to c. 18%. In pens with the highest total loss, the greatest cause of mortality was predation by mammals, probably foxes *Vulpes vulpes*,

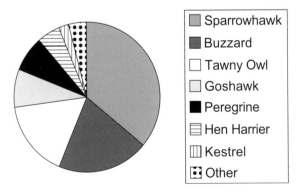

Figure 33.3. Percentage of game-killing incidents attributed by BASC respondents to different raptor species. The 'other' category includes merlin *Falco columbarius*, marsh harrier, long-eared owl, little owl, short-eared owl and red kite (each <1% of all incidents). From: Harradine *et al.* (1997).

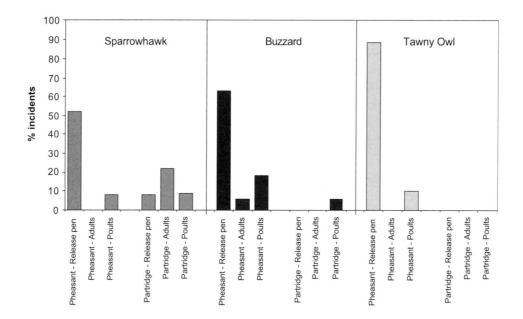

Figure 33.4. Percentage of game-killing incidents attributed by BASC respondents to three raptor species associated with different aspects of game management. From: Harradine *et al.* (1997).

rather than birds. These data are broadly similar to estimates available from other studies. On the basis of observations made by gamekeepers on 154 estates between 1973 and 1975, Lloyd (1976) estimated that 0.9% of released pheasants were taken by raptors (albeit whilst many of the participating estates acknowledged actively controlling raptors). More recent alternative estimates by keepers put levels of raptor predation at 'mostly under 5%, often under 1% but sometimes over 10% of released birds' (Harradine *et al.*, 1997).

Non-shooting losses are not confined to the release period. An average of c. 40% of released birds are shot each year (Robertson & Hill, 1986). The majority of the remaining c. 60% are lost to a variety of causes including traffic, predators and emigration; only a small proportion of released birds survive until the following spring. On one estate in Ireland, most mortality of released pheasants occurred within ten days of leaving the release pen, and was due largely to foxes (Robertson, 1988). Thus the loss of 1-5 % of released pheasants to raptors during the release period appears small compared to other losses. Further losses to raptors outside of the release period are likely to be low as pheasants become too big for most raptors to handle easily.

Game managers are also concerned about raptor predation of adult partridges. Few data are available, however, to quantify the scale of predation by raptors either on released or wild birds. Whilst Potts (1986) did not consider this to be an important factor in the decline of the grey partridge, recent contrary evidence has led to calls for further research (Aebischer. 1999).

33.7 Managing interactions between raptors and gamebirds
Gamekeepers use a wide range of deterrent techniques, including lights, mirrors, noises and plastic bags hung at pens, in an attempt to reduce levels of predation at release pens (see

British Association for Shooting and Conservation, 2002). Allen *et al.* (2000) found that hanging bags, hanging mirrors, and especially the use of mylar reflective tape, might offer some protection against raptor predation, but accepted that more detailed studies are needed to confirm this. However, most keepers have little confidence in the effectiveness of scarers (Harradine *et al.*, 1997).

Management in order to increase the density of vegetation inside pens may reduce levels of predation. Allen *et al.* (2000) found an inverse relationship between predation by birds and foliage density (measurement technique followed Redpath & Thirgood, 1997) 1.5 m above ground level inside pens (Figure 33.5). Enhancement of cover is generally seen as an important means of reducing raptor predation (Kenward, 1999). Unfortunately, less emphasis tends to be placed on habitat management the more release of captive birds is the dominant management method (Robertson & Rosenberg, 1988).

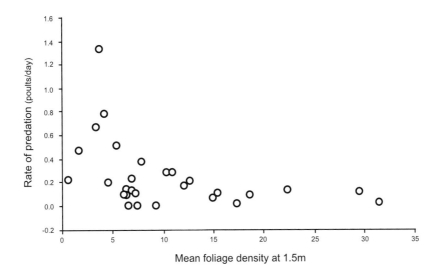

Figure 33.5. Rate of avian predation (poults per day) in relation to vegetation density 1.5 m above ground level in 28 release pens (after Allen *et al.*, 2000).

There are some variations in release techniques in different countries. In Denmark, the composition of vegetation is regarded as a vital component of release sites, where dense cover includes tall grasses, cover crops, and conifers in which birds can roost. Food is available along mown grass tracks or patches. Release in Denmark takes two basic forms. In one, poults are taken in their heated rearing houses to the release site. Outside the houses, food and water are available, together with small cages containing broody hens. The poults are released on a warm sunny day, and their first encounter with the outside world includes 'parents' in addition to sustenance. In the second release system, poults may be taken in their rearing houses, as above, to large (0.5–1.0 ha) release pens, or may be placed in these release pens within smaller holding cages, sometimes with netted roofs. The poults are allowed to settle in the new conditions before slow release into the large pens (T.H. Christensen, pers. comm.).

33.8 Conclusions

On theoretical grounds, one can predict likely interactions between birds of prey and gamebird management. However, there is a paucity of good information on both the rates of predation by raptors on gamebirds, and also on the effect of any predation on the productivity of game rearing concerns, and especially on the number of birds ultimately available for shooting. Information on diets of birds of prey have generally been collected as components of ornithological studies, rather than addressing game issues, and more directed research is needed in relation to lowland gamebirds. The contention of game managers that tawny owls are important predators at release pens (Harradine *et al.*, 1997) is not supported by the data as gamebirds have not been found in dietary studies of these owls (Cramp, 1985). Investigations of impact have relied on questionnaires to game managers, and on the finding of carcasses from which interpretations of cause of death are difficult. New techniques are needed to quantify both of these impacts so that the conflict, if real, can be addressed using measures that are effective in resolving the problems, economically realistic, and benign in terms of conservation concerns (British Association for Shooting and Conservation, 2002).

Although game managers employ scaring devices at or near release pens, they place little faith in the effectiveness of these (Harradine *et al.*, 1997). There are good theoretical grounds for believing that resident, territorial raptors will habituate to deterrents that rely on scaring (see review in Allen *et al.*, 2000) and thus that these deterrents will not be effective. Experiments with deterrents that combine behavioural deterrence with physical protection of release pens are needed. The use of overhead netting at pens is reportedly effective (Harradine *et al.*, 1997) but there appears to be resistance to its use as it interferes with the ability of pheasants to leave the pen. Alternative forms of release, involving improved designs of pen, need urgent investigation, and practices used elsewhere in the world might help in the search for alternatives. For some keepers, culling, licensed removal or translocation are viewed as preferred options for managing raptor predation (Harradine *et al.*, 1997). However, there is no evidence that these techniques enhance shooting bags, and the development of effective and economically viable means of reducing perceived threats from raptors would help to alleviate this emotive area of conflict.

In conservation terms, perhaps the greatest threat is not to the widespread and common raptor species that are most frequently considered by gamekeepers to take gamebirds. Instead, it is the hen harriers and goshawks, whose ability to kill gamebirds is well documented (Kenward 1981; Underhill-Day, 1985, 1993) but which have localised distributions and small population sizes, which may be least able to withstand persecution. This has been clearly demonstrated for upland hen harriers *Circus cyaneus* (Etheridge *et al.*, 1997; Green & Etheridge, 1999), whose distribution and/or productivity has been suppressed by human persecution.

The management of predation can also be a problem for those concerned with biodiversity conservation. The >80% decline in grey partridge numbers from 1970 to 1998 has led to its placement on the red list of birds of conservation concern (Gibbons *et al.*, 1996; Gregory *et al.*, 2002) and being targeted for specific conservation action in the UK Biodiversity Action Plan, although the targets for its recovery are unlikely to be met (Gregory *et al.*, 2001). Predation of this species by raptors is arguably now more a concern from a conservation than from a shooting perspective.

Acknowledgements

The results on predation of released pheasants are taken from a study undertaken by the authors on behalf of the British Association for Shooting and Conservation (BASC), with funding from BASC, the Department for the Environment, Transport and the Regions, Scottish Natural Heritage, the National Trust and the Royal Society for the Protection of Birds. We thank BASC for providing information on their gamekeeper membership. Brian Etheridge and Mark Fletcher provided some valuable references, Thoman Holst Christensen provided information on release systems in Denmark, and two anonymous reviewers made helpful suggestions for the improvement of the manuscript.

References

Aebischer, N. (1999). Grey partridges, lowland raptors and the Sussex study. *The Game Conservancy Trust Review of 1999.* Game Conservancy Trust, Fordingbridge. pp. 61-65.

Allen, D.S., Packer, J.J., Feare, C.J. & Blanchard, C. (2000). Raptors and the rearing of pheasants: problems and management needs. Unpublished report. British Association for Shooting and Conservation, Rossett.

Anonymous (2000). *Report of the UK Raptor Working Group.* Department for the Environment, Transport and the Regions and Joint Nature Conservation Committee, Peterborough.

Barnett, E.A., Hunter, K., Fletcher, M.R. & Sharp, E.A. (2000). *Pesticide Poisoning of Animals 1999: Investigations of Suspected Incidents in the United Kingdom.* CSL, Sand Hutton, York and SASA, Edinburgh.

Beer, J.V. (1988). *Diseases of Gamebirds and Wildfowl.* The Game Conservancy, Fordingbridge.

Boal, C.W., Mannan, R.W. & Hudelson, K.S. (1998). Trichomoniasis in Cooper's hawks from Arizona. *Journal of Wildlife Diseases,* **34**, 590-593.

Boatman, N.D., Stoate, C. & Watts, P.N. (2000). Practical management solutions for birds on lowland arable farmland. In *Ecology and Conservation of Lowland Farmland Birds,* ed. by N.J. Aebischer, A.D. Evans, P.V. Grice & J.A. Vickery. British Ornithologists' Union, Tring. pp. 105-114.

Brickle, N.W. & Harper, D.G.C. (2000). Habitat use by corn buntings *Miliaria calandra* in winter and summer. In *Ecology and Conservation of Lowland Farmland Birds,* ed. by N.J. Aebischer, A.D. Evans, P.V. Grice & J.A. Vickery. British Ornithologists' Union, Tring. pp. 156-164.

British Association for Shooting and Conservation (2002). *Birds of Prey at Pheasant Release Pens: a Practical Guide for Game Managers and Gamekeepers.* British Association for Shooting and Conservation, Wrexham.

Côté, I.M. & Sutherland, W.J. (1997). The effectiveness of removing predators to protect bird populations. *Conservation Biology,* **11**, 395-405.

Cotgreave, P. (1995). Relative importance of avian groups in the diets of British and Irish predators. *Bird Study,* **42**, 246-252.

Cramp, S. (ed.) (1985). *Birds of the Western Palearctic. Volume 4.* Oxford University Press, Oxford.

Cramp, S. & Simmons, K.E.L. (Eds) (1980). *Birds of the Western Palearctic. Volume 2.* Oxford University Press, Oxford.

Etheridge, B., Summers, R.W. & Green, R.E. (1997). The effects of illegal killing and destruction of nests by humans on the population dynamics of the hen harrier *Circus cyaneus* in Scotland. *Journal of Applied Ecology,* **34**, 1081-1105.

Forbes, N.A. & Simpson, G.N. (1997). A review of viruses affecting raptors. *Veterinary Record,* **141**, 123-126.

Gibbons, D.W., Reid, J.B. & Chapman, R.A. (1993). *The New Breeding Atlas of Breeding Birds in Britain and Ireland: 1988-1991.* T. & A.D. Poyser, London.

Gibbons, D., Avery, M., Baillie, S., Gregory, R., Kirby, J., Porter, R., Tucker, G. & Williams, G. (1996). Bird species of conservation concern in the United Kingdom, Channel Islands and the Isle of Man: revising the Red Data List. In *RSPB Conservation Review* 10, ed. by C.J. Cadbury. Royal Society for the Protection of Birds, Sandy. pp. 7-18.

Graham, I.M., Redpath, S.M. & Thirgood, S.J. (1995). The diet and breeding density of common buzzards *Buteo buteo* in relation to indices of prey abundance. *Bird Study*, **42**, 165-173.

Green, R.E. & Etheridge, B. (1999). Breeding success of the hen harrier *Circus cyaneus* in relation to the distribution of grouse moors and the red fox *Vulpes vulpes*. *Journal of Applied Ecology*, **36**, 472-483.

Gregory, R.D., Noble, D.G., Cranswick, P.A., Campbell, L.H., Rehfisch, M.M. & Baillie, S.R. (2001). *The State of the UK's Birds 2000*. Royal Society for the Protection of Birds, British Trust for Ornithology and Wildfowl & Wetlands Trust, Sandy.

Gregory, R.D., Wilkinson, N.I., Noble, D.G., Robinson, J.A., Brown, A.F., Hughes, J., Procter, D.A., Gibbons, D.W. & Galbraith, C.A. (2002). The population status of birds in the United Kingdom, Channel Islands and Isle of Man: an analysis of conservation concern 2002-2007. *British Birds*, **95**, 410-450.

Harradine, J., Reynolds, N. & Laws, T. (1997). *Raptors and Gamebirds. A Survey of Game Managers Affected by Raptors*. BASC, Rossett.

Holmes, J., Walker, D., Davies, P. & Carter, I. (2000). *The Illegal Persecution of Raptors in England*. English Nature Research Report No. 343. English Nature, Peterborough.

Jacob, J. & Halle, S. (2001). The importance of land management for population parameters and spatial behaviour in common voles (*Microtus arvalis*). In *Advances in Vertebrate Pest Management 2*, ed. by J. Pelz, D.P. Cowan & C.J. Feare. Filander, Fürth. pp. 319-330.

Kenward, R.E. (1981). Goshawk predation on game and poultry: some problems and solutions. In *Understanding the Goshawk*, ed. by R.E. Kenward & I.M. Lindsay. The International Association for Falconry and Conservation of Birds of Prey, Oxford. pp. 152-162.

Kenward, R.E. (1999). Raptor predation problems and solutions. *Journal of Raptor Research*, **33**, 73-75.

Lloyd, D.E.B. (1976). *Avian Predation of Reared Pheasants*. Report to The British Field Sports Society, The Game Conservancy, The Royal Society for the Protection of Birds and The Wildfowlers' Association of Great Britain and Ireland.

Mikkola, H. (1983). *Owls of Europe*. T. & A.D. Poyser, Calton.

Minot, P., Fletcher, M.R., Glaser, L.C, Thomas, N.J., Brassard, C., Wilson, L.K., Elliott, J.E., Lyon, L., Henny, C.J., Bollinger, T. & Porter, S.J. (1999). Poisoning of raptors with organophosphorus and carbamate pesticides with emphasis on Canada, US and UK. *Journal of Raptor Research*, **33**, 1-37.

Moorcroft, D.M. & Wilson, J.D. (2000). The ecology of linnets *Carduelis cannabina* on lowland farmland. In *Ecology and Conservation of Lowland Farmland Birds*, ed. by N.J. Aebischer, A.D. Evans, P.V. Grice & J.A. Vickery. British Ornithologists' Union, Tring. pp. 173-181.

Morishita, T.Y., Aye, P.P. & Brooks, D.L. (1997). A survey of diseases in raptorial birds. *Journal of Avian Medicine and Surgery*, **11**, 77-92.

Newton, I. (1979). *Population Ecology of Raptors*. T. & A.D. Poyser, Berkhamsted.

Newton, I. (1986). *The Sparrowhawk*. T. & A.D. Poyser, Calton.

Newton, I. (1998). *Population Limitation in Birds*. Academic Press, London.

Newton, I., Wyllie, I. & Dale, L. (1999). Trends in the numbers and mortality patterns of sparrowhawks (*Accipiter nisus*) and kestrels (*Falco tinnunculus*) in Britain, as revealed by carcass analyses. *Journal of the Zoological Society, London*, **248**, 139-147.

Pennycott, T. (1996). Gamebird diseases: the need for more research. In *Game Conservancy Review 28*. The Game Conservancy Trust, Fordingbridge. pp. 63-65.

Pepler, D. & Oettlé, E.E. (1992). *Trichomonas gallinae* in wild raptors on the Cape Peninsula. *South African Journal of Wildlife Research*, **22**, 87-88.

Potts, G.R. (1986). *The Partridge: Pesticides, Predation and Conservation.* Collins, London.

Redpath, S.M. & Thirgood, S.J. (1997). *Birds of Prey and Red Grouse.* The Stationery Office, London.

Robertson, P.A. (1988). Survival of released pheasants, *Phasianus colchicus*, in Ireland. *Journal of the Zoological Society, London*, **214**, 683-695.

Robertson, P.A. & Hill, D.A. (1986). The role of predation in pheasant release. *Proceedings of the International Wild Pheasant Association Symposium* No 3, Thailand, January 1986. World Pheasant Association, Reading.

Robertson, P.A. & Rosenberg, A.R. (1988). Harvesting gamebirds. In *Ecology and Management of Gamebirds*, ed. by P.J. Hudson & M.R.W. Rands. BSP Professional Books, Oxford. pp. 177-201.

Robson, G. & Carter, I. (1999). Do raptors disturb driven grouse shoots? A pilot study in northern England. *English Nature Research Report* No. 342. English Nature, Peterborough.

Sotherton, N.W. & Self, M.J. (2000). Changes in plant and arthropod biodiversity on lowland farmland: an overview. In *Ecology and Conservation of Lowland Farmland Birds*, ed. by N.J. Aebischer, A.D. Evans, P.V. Grice & J.A. Vickery. British Ornithologists' Union, Tring. pp. 26-35.

Sotherton, N.W., Moreby, S.J. & Rands, M.W. (1985). Comparison of herbicide treated and untreated headlands on the survival of game and wildlife. In *Proceedings of the 1985 British Crop Protection Conference*. British Crop Protection Council, Farnham. pp. 991-998.

Swann, R.L. & Etheridge, B. (1995). A comparison of the breeding success and prey of the common buzzard *Buteo buteo* in two area of northern Scotland. *Bird Study*, **42**, 37-43.

Tapper, S. (ed.) (1999). *A Question of Balance. Game Animals and their Role in the British Countryside.* The Game Conservancy Trust, Fordingbridge.

Thirgood, S.J., Redpath, S.M., Hudson, P.J. & Donnelly, E. (1998). Estimating the cause and rate of mortality in red grouse *Lagopus lagopus scoticus*. *Wildlife Biology*, **B**, 65-71.

Thompson, D.B.A., Gillings, S.D., Galbraith, C.A., Redpath, S.M. & Drewitt, J. (1997). The contribution of grouse management to biodiversity: a review of the importance of grouse moors for uplands birds. In *Biodiversity in Scotland: Status, Trends and Initiatives*, ed. by L.V. Fleming, A.C. Newton, J.A. Vickery & M.B. Usher. The Stationery Office, Edinburgh. pp. 198-212.

Underhill-Day, J.C. (1985). The food of breeding marsh harriers *Circus aeruginosus* in East Anglia. *Bird Study*, **32**, 199-206.

Underhill-Day, J.C. (1993). The foods and feeding rates of Montagu's harriers *Circus pygargus* breeding in arable farmland. *Bird Study*, **40**, 74-80.

Village, A. (1990). *The Kestrel.* T. & A.D. Poyser, Calton.

Vesey-Fitzgerald, D. (1946). *British Game.* Collins, London.

34. ARE RODENTICIDES AN INCREASING PROBLEM FOR RED KITES (*MILVUS MILVUS*)?

Peter Newbery, Ian Carter, Keith Morton & Andy Tharme

Summary

1.   Red kites *Milvus milvus* are being re-introduced into England and Scotland in an ambitious programme co-ordinated by the RSPB, English Nature and Scottish Natural Heritage, and expanding populations have been established in both countries. The native population in Wales is also increasing.

2.   Two-thirds of a sample of 29 dead red kites from England and Scotland were found to have rodenticide residues in their livers, a far higher figure than has been found in any other species tested.

3.   Although poisoning by rodenticides does not appear to be preventing an increase in the red kite population, there may be sub-lethal effects in individuals. We propose that best practice guidelines should be followed in all rat eradication campaigns.

34.1 Introduction

The red kite *Milvus milvus* was once widespread in the UK, but by the late 19th century persecution had confined the entire UK population to remote parts of central Wales. In 1989, an experimental re-introduction project set out to improve the situation, and the 1990s saw populations becoming well established in four areas of England and Scotland (with a fifth, in Yorkshire, at an early stage) (Carter *et al.*, Chapter 31).

Red kites depend mainly on carrion, and dead rats are a key element of their diet all year round in some areas (Carter & Grice, 2000). Kites will forage readily around farm buildings - often the site of rodent poisoning activity. As scavengers, they take mainly dead and possibly moribund rats which are more likely to contain rodenticide residues than healthy, living rats (Anon., 2003). This makes them particularly vulnerable to secondary poisoning.

34.2 Is rodenticide poisoning an increasing problem?

Infestations of rats are a widespread problem, which may increase if climate change results in fewer cold winters. The first generation rodenticide poison Warfarin had been the principal rodent poison until the 1980s, and its toxicity was relatively low, so secondary poisoning occurred only infrequently. Tolerance to Warfarin has developed in some populations of rats, and manufacturers have therefore developed second-generation rodenticides. These chemicals are up to 600 times more toxic than Warfarin (Newton & Wyllie, 1992), and subsequently incidents of secondary poisoning have increased.

Alarmingly, recent analysis of tissue samples from a random sample of 29 dead kites found that 66% contained rodenticide residues, a far higher figure than has been found in any other tested species. All of these were in England or Scotland (see Table 34.1). In Wales, the problem of secondary poisoning by rodenticides does not appear to be a serious one - rats are not prominent in the diet there and only a small number of incidents, mainly involving Warfarin, have been reported. Birds not killed outright by rodenticide poisoning may still suffer sub-lethal effects which could, for example, reduce foraging efficiency or increase the likelihood of collision with road traffic or powerlines.

34.3 The way forward

34.3.1 Best practice
We believe that Warfarin should be used in preference to second-generation rodenticides, except in areas where Warfarin resistance is known to be established. Rodenticides must be used in accordance with their label instructions - this is a legal requirement (Anon., 1999). The most toxic products, containing Brodifacoum and Flocoumafen, are licensed for indoor use only. When using any rodenticide, the bait must be placed within a secure container, and every effort must be made to find dead rats so that they do not become available to scavengers (Anon., 2001). Methods of control other than rodenticides (such as trapping) should be used wherever possible (Anon., 2003).

34.3.2 Monitoring
It is essential that all dead red kites are analysed for rodenticides. There is a particular need to determine residue levels in birds found during post-mortems to show internal bleeding. This may help to establish what constitutes a lethal level of second generation rodenticides. Rodenticide poisoning may not be preventing populations of red kites from becoming established and increasing at the release site, but it may compromise the rate of increase and the overall re-colonisation process.

34.3.3 Legislation
If further monitoring reveals secondary poisoning by rodenticides to be a serious problem, legislative changes may be needed to govern the use of these chemicals more effectively, perhaps even requiring their replacement with less damaging alternatives.

Acknowledgements
We thank the agencies involved with these analyses: Central Science Laboratory Wildlife Incident Unit, the Institute of Zoology, the Centre for Ecology and Hydrology, and the Scottish Agricultural Science Agency. An anonymous referee commented on the manuscript.

Tables 34.1. Results of analysis of the livers of a sample of dead red kites found in the wild in the UK 1994-2000, showing the levels of rodenticide residues, in England and Scotland.

a) England

Age/ Origin	Date found/ Location	Bromadiolone (mg/kg live)	Difenacoum (mg/kg liver)	Brodifacoum (mg/kg liver)	Cause of death/comments
2nd year Chilterns	Jan 1994 Chilterns	0.04	0.03	0.01	Aspergillosis (a fungal respiratory disease)
3rd year Chilterns	Jan 1996 Chilterns	0.01	-	0.05	*Trichomonas* (a protozoan digestive tract disease)
1st year Chilterns	Nov 1996 Chilterns	0.16	0.02	-	Probably killed by vehicle
2nd year Chilterns	Jan 1997 Chilterns	-	0.02	0.21	Under powerlines but true cause not known
2nd year Chilterns	Jan 1997 Chilterns	0.01	0.03	0.19	Avian tuberculosis
3rd year Chilterns	Mar 1998 mid-Wales	-	0.21	-	Also 0.01 mg/kg Flocoumafen; under powerlines, electrocution likely
3rd year Chilterns	May 1998 Chilterns	-	-	0.98	Probably rodenticide
Nestling Midlands	Jun 1998 Midlands	0.14	-	-	Also residue of Bendiocarb, true cause of death not known; 7 of 10 chicks died at time of fledging
1st year Chilterns	Nov 1998 Chilterns	0.06	-	-	Not known
3rd year Chilterns	Jan 1999 Chilterns	Small residue	Small residue	-	Aldicarb poisoning
6th year Chilterns	Feb 1999 Chilterns	0.02	0.12	-	Aspergillosis and traumatic wing injury
2nd year central Scotland	Mar 1999 Gloucestershire	0.1	-	-	Haemorrhaging after collision with vehicle and/or rodenticide
6th year Chilterns	Mar 1999 Chilterns	0.05	0.16	0.3 (CSL)* 0.46 (ITE)*	Point of egg laying - killed by rodenticide
2nd year Chilterns	Mar 1999 Chilterns	0.1	0.05	-	Death attributed to rodenticide
2nd year Chilterns	Apr 1999 Chilterns	-	0.2	0.04	Death attributed to rodenticide
Recently fledged Midlands	Jul 1999 Midlands	0.19	-	-	Calcium deficiency
2nd year Chilterns	May 1999 Chilterns	-	0.06	-	Shot and wounded- later destroyed
Unringed adult	Sept 1999 Chilterns	0.03	0.04	-	Under powerlines – true cause not known
Nestling	July 2000 Midlands	0.27	-	-	Bromadiolone exposure?
2nd year Yorkshire	April 2001 Yorkshire	0.18	-	-	Alphachloralose poisoning, bait was rat

*   CSL = Central Science Laboratory
     ITE = Institute of Terrestrial Ecology, now Centre for Ecology and Hydrology

b) Scotland

Age/ Origin	Date found/ Location	Bromadiolone (mg/kg live)	Difenacoum (mg/kg liver)	Brodifacoum (mg/kg liver)	Cause of death/comments
10/6/97	Trochry	0.22	-	-	Carbofuran poisoning. 1996 wild bred bird.
3/1/98	Muir of Ord	-	0.13	-	Alphachloralose poisoning
22/2/98	Muir of Ord	0.40	0.05	-	Alphachloralose poisoning
23/3/98	Muthill	-	-	-	Alphachloralose poisoning
17/4/98	Black Isle	-	0.08	-	Unknown. Tideline corpse
27/2/99	Dunblane	0.25	-	-	Alphachloralose poisoning
12/7/99	Black Isle	0.24	-	-	Bromadiolone poisoning. Chick
12/7/99	Black Isle	0.21	-	-	Bromadiolone poisoning. Chick
12/7/99	Black Isle	0.20	-	-	Bromadiolone poisoning. Chick
30/4/00	Doune	0.24	-	-	Bromadiolone poisoning. Dead on nest.
31/5/00	Black Isle	0.36	-	-	Bromadiolone poisoning. Chick
26/6/00	Muir of Ord	-	0.35	-	Difenacoum poisoning. Chick
26/6/00	Muir of Ord	-	0.38	-	Difenacoum poisoning. Chick
4/8/00	Garve	0.14	-	-	Carbofuran poisoning. 1998 wild-bred bird.
22/9/00	Muir of Ord	0.2	-	-	Collision with car? 2000 Wild-bred chick
29/9/00	A836 near Alness	0.1	-	-	Carbofuran poisoning. Breeding female
14/02/01	Highland	-	-	-	Carbofuran poisoning. 15.8 mg/kg liver
01/04/01	C Scotland	-	0.07	-	Carbofuran poisoning. 9.8 mg/kg liver
12/04/01	Tayside	-	-	-	Alphachloralose poisoning
20/04/01	Highland	-	-	-	Carbofuran poisoning. Rabbit/pigeon baits
16/04/01	Highland	-	-	-	Carbofuran poisoning. 961 mg/kg gullet
21/07/01	Highland	-	-	-	Carbofuran poisoning

References

Anonymous (1999). Safe use of rodenticides on farms and holdings. *HSE Information Sheet* No. 31. Health and Safety Executive, London.

Anonymous (2001). *Guidelines for the Safe Use of Anticoagulant Rodenticides by Professional Users.* British Pest Control Association, Derby.

Anonymous (2003). *Rat Poison and the Threat to Birds of Prey.* Royal Society for the Protection of Birds and English Nature, Peterborough.

Carter, I. & Grice, P.V. (2000). Studies of re-established Red Kites in England. *British Birds,* **93**, 304-322

Newton, I. & Wyllie, I. (1992). Effects of new rodenticides on owls. In *The Ecology and Conservation of European Owls,* ed. by C.A. Galbraith, I.R. Taylor & S. Percival. Joint Nature Conservation Committee, Peterborough. pp 49-54.

35. LAND USE, AGRICULTURAL PRACTICES AND CONSERVATION OF THE MONTAGU'S HARRIER (*CIRCUS PYGARGUS*)

Beatriz Arroyo, Vincent Bretagnolle & Jesús T. García

Summary

1.   The Montagu's harrier *Circus pygargus* breeds mainly in cereal crops in western Europe. This represents a habitat shift from the original grasslands occupied, evidently due to impacts on the land.

2.   Montagu's harrier reproduction is primarily dependent on food supply in natural conditions, so biodiversity decline in agricultural areas might affect harrier sustainability in the long term.

3.   In addition, combine harvesters can kill harrier nestlings if they are unfledged by harvest time. In western Europe (which holds the stronghold of the breeding population, excluding Russia), around 60% of nestlings in agricultural areas could die like this in the absence of conservation measures.

4.   There is therefore a need to develop sustainable and effective conservation measures, which should include a) maintaining food supplies, as well as b) minimising the impact of harvesting activities on harrier productivity. Large scale agro-environmental measures should be implemented to maintain food supplies. Protection of harrier nestlings from harvesting activity, in contrast, could be implemented through a network of relatively small protected areas.

5.   In the short term, priority actions include a) promoting the protection of natural vegetation areas, b) identifying and protecting the most productive and stable harrier colonies in agricultural areas, and c) testing experimentally factors which are likely to attract and maintain harriers in protected areas.

35.1 Introduction

The Montagu's harrier *Circus pygargus* is arguably the most characteristic raptor of agricultural habitats in continental Europe. This ground nesting raptor originally nested in wet (marshes or meadows) and dry (steppe) grasslands (Cramp & Simmons, 1980). However, the harrier may also use crops, building nests mainly within winter cereal fields (wheat and barley), but also rye-grass, alfalfa and, occasionally, rapeseed fields (Cramp & Simmons, 1980). Use of crops by harriers as a nesting habitat in south-western Europe was described early in the 20th century (Larrinúa, 1908; Frionnet, 1925). First recorded observations of harrier nests in crops in other parts of Europe were made during the 1970s in England, Germany and the Netherlands (Davies, 1977; Clemens, 1993; Koks *et al.*, 2001), and during the 1980s in Poland and Russia (Krogulec, 1993; Ivanovski, 1993). In all of these parts of Europe, the proportion of Montagu's harriers breeding in crops increased rapidly after the first recorded cases. By the end of the 20th century the proportion of Montagu's harriers breeding in crops exceeded 15-20% in north-eastern Europe (Flint *et al.*, 1984; Krogulec, 1993; Ivanovski, 1993), 50% in Italy (Martelli & Parodi, 1992), 70% in Germany, the Netherlands and France (Salamolard *et al.*, 1999; Holker, 1999; Koks *et al.*, in press), and exceeded 90% in Spain and Portugal (Ferrero, 1995). Given that France, Spain and Portugal hold about 80% of the European population, excluding Russia (Tucker & Heath, 1994), cereal crops now appear to be the most typical nesting habitat of Montagu's harriers in Europe.

The harrier's dependence on such a man-made environment makes this species particularly vulnerable to land use change in this habitat. Agricultural habitats have changed drastically over the last decades (e.g. review in Pain & Pienkowski, 1997), and this trend may continue in the near future. Successful management of the harrier populations therefore requires an understanding of how these changes affect the harriers.

At the European level, the Montagu's harrier is included in conservation category SPEC 4 (species with a favourable conservation status, but concentrated in Europe, Tucker & Heath, 1994). However, the conservation status for the species in France and the Iberian Peninsula, the stronghold of western Europe, is 'vulnerable' (SNPRCN, 1990; Blanco & González, 1992; Salamolard *et al.*, 1999). Knowledge of the relationship between agricultural practices and Montagu's harrier ecology is therefore vital in order to develop conservation plans. Additionally, given that resources for conservation are limited, assessment of the potential conservation measures should help in the best deployment of resources.

This chapter reviews all published (and some unpublished) data related to factors that influence reproduction in the Montagu's harrier. It considers how the use of agricultural habitats may affect population sustainability, the conservation measures currently applied in France and Spain, and conservation methods which could be implemented to best effect in the future.

35.2 Methods

Most of the results presented here come from six to 12 years studies carried out in three areas in western France (Marais de Rochefort, 45°57'N, 0°55'W; south of Deux Sèvres, 46°11'N, 0°28'W; and Baie de l'Aiguillon, 46°24'N, 1°24'W), and in one area located north-east of Madrid, central Spain (40°38'N, 3°30'W). Most Montagu's harriers in Rochefort nested in natural vegetation (pastures and grassland), whereas in the other three areas they bred mainly in cereal fields.

Quantitative data on the abundance of the main prey in western France, the common vole *Microtus arvalis*, were based on line trapping (Butet & Leroux, 1993) each study year in the three areas in western France, and are expressed as captures/100 night-traps.

Land use in Deux Sèvres was monitored in the field each year and incorporated in a Geographical Information System (GIS, ArcView 3.0), which allowed calculation of the area of each crop type in the whole study area. Additionally, long-term data on land use in the Rochefort and Deux Sèvres study areas were available through the Recensement Général Agricole (1970-1989).

Nests were located each year in each study area, and were visited regularly to collect data on breeding parameters (timing of nesting, hatch success, number of fledglings, etc.).

Additionally, a wing-tagging programme of nestlings and adults has been carried out in these areas for several years, allowing estimates of juvenile and adult dispersal and survival rates. Demographic parameters (breeding rates, age of first breeding, adult and juvenile survival) estimated from the study areas were used to model population dynamics using Vortex 7.0, a stochastic simulation programme (Lacy *et al.*, 1995). Age of first breeding was set at two years for females, and three years for males, which are the averages observed for the species, and adult survival was estimated as 80 ±7% (A. Leroux & V. Bretagnolle, unpublished data). No accurate measures of juvenile survival were available, but we used 50 ±20% for the simulations. Simulations were run for 100 years, and we performed 100 iterations per simulation. Except when otherwise stated, simulations were performed starting from an initial population size of 50 pairs, as this is the average population size for a 200 km^2 area in the study sites. More information on how simulation analyses were carried out, and the premises used for the simulations, can be found in the original papers (Arroyo & Bretagnolle, 2000; Arroyo *et al.*, 2002).

We have also used published data collected in other areas of western Europe when necessary: in these cases, data sources are duly acknowledged.

35.3 Food and breeding performance in the Montagu's harrier

35.3.1 *Relationships between food and breeding performance*

The main prey of Montagu's harrier in western France is the common vole (Butet & Leroux, 1993), which constitutes 60-90% of the diet in biomass, with insects being the main alternative prey (5-40% in biomass, Salamolard *et al.* (2000)). In that area, vole abundance influenced all breeding parameters: breeding density increased with increasing vole abundance, as did clutch size and fledging success (Salamolard *et al.*, 2000). The number of fledglings per brood varied, from 0.57 fledglings per pair in poor vole years to 2.64 fledglings per pair in peak vole years. The median date of onset of laying also varied among years (by 20 days), and was earlier when spring vole abundance was high.

In eastern France and the Netherlands, Montagu's harriers are less dependent on voles, which constitute only 40-50% of the diet (in biomass), the rest of the prey being formed mainly by passerines (Koks *et al.*, 2001; Millon *et al.*, 2002). Nevertheless, relationships were found in that area also between vole abundance (as determined through occurrence in pellets) and breeding parameters, especially number of fledglings per brood (Koks *et al.*, 2001; Millon *et al.*, 2002). In contrast, at least in eastern France, breeding density and clutch size did not vary with year or vole abundance over the eight years of the study (Millon *et al.*, 2002).

In areas where voles are not the main prey, there is evidence that reproductive parameters are also dependent on food supply. For example, the Montagu's harrier's diet in central Spain is varied, with the most important prey (in terms of biomass) being young hares *Lepus granatensis* (Arroyo, 1997). In that area, breeding numbers did not change significantly between years (similar to eastern France), but all reproductive parameters considered did vary between years (laying date, clutch size, hatching success, number of fledglings per pair) (García & Arroyo, 2001). Annual values for reproductive parameters were significantly correlated with the proportion of hares in pellets each year, and such a relationship was also found within years: individual pairs eating a higher proportion of hares had better reproductive success (Arroyo, 1998).

In south-eastern Spain, the main prey are insects (Corbacho *et al.*, 1995). In that area, clutch size and chick survival were highest in rainier years (Corbacho & Sanchez, 2000), associated with a higher primary productivity, particularly of insects then (Lucio, 1990; Suarez *et al.*, 1992; Borralho *et al.*, 1998).

In summary, despite a high level of behavioural plasticity in relation to diet (from lagomorphs to insects through small mammals and birds), Montagu's harrier reproduction is strongly influenced by food abundance. The effect of food abundance is mainly observed in parameters related to breeding performance (laying date, clutch size or, particularly, breeding success), but it may also influence breeding density if fluctuations in food abundance are strong enough.

35.3.2 *Food supplies in agricultural environments: long term trends*

Despite the annual fluctuations observed, a long term decline in vole abundance is apparent in Marais de Rochefort, over the period 1987-2000 (Figure 35.1), with the amplitudes of the vole cycles getting progressively smaller. Similar patterns were observed in Deux-Sèvres (Figure 35.1a). These declines are associated with a strong reduction in the area covered with grassland and/or pasture land (Figure 35.1b and see Delattre *et al.*, 1992). Land use changes in agricultural habitats may therefore have an impact of food supply.

Such patterns of long-term declines are not restricted to voles. Insect abundance has also been found to decline in agricultural habitats in recent decades (Potts, 1991), and the abundance of many farmland passerines has declined in farmland (e.g. Tucker & Heath, 1994; Pain & Pienkowski, 1997; Gregory *et al.*, 2002). Such changes are associated with modifications in agricultural practices such as increasing use of pesticides or herbicides, and reduction of field margins (Pain & Pienkowski, 1997; Newton, 1998). Overall, agricultural intensification (increasing production per unit area), particularly of cereal crops, may be responsible for all these changes, and it can explain 30% of the variation in bird population trends in farmland (Donald *et al.*, 2000).

Therefore, agricultural habitats are associated with impoverished food supplies and this trend might continue, particularly in countries such as Spain or Portugal (or those of eastern Europe) which have recently entered the more productive agricultural markets.

35.3.3 *Implications for harrier sustainability*

As food supply is the main factor regulating breeding performance in the Montagu's harrier, and food supply may be impoverished in agricultural habitats, what are the implications for harrier populations? Simulations showed that when productivity decreased below 1.8 fledglings per pair, the probability of harrier populations becoming extinct increases. Additionally, for any value of harrier productivity, extinction probability was higher when the carrying capacity of the environment (i.e. the maximum number of pairs being able to breed) decreased by as little as 1 or 2% annually (Arroyo *et al.*, 2002).

Average harrier productivity observed in our study areas ranged between 1.8 and 2.2 fledglings per pair (all years combined). This figure is similar to that observed in other areas of Europe when deaths due to harvesting activities (see below) are unimportant (e.g. Underhill-Day, 1990; Biljsma *et al.*, 1993, Krogulec & Leroux, 1993; Jiménez & Surroca, 1995; Corbacho *et al.*, 1997). Therefore, under prevailing conditions, harrier populations should be sustainable if values of fledgling production are maintained.

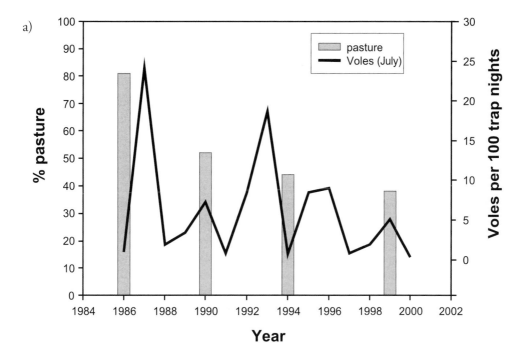

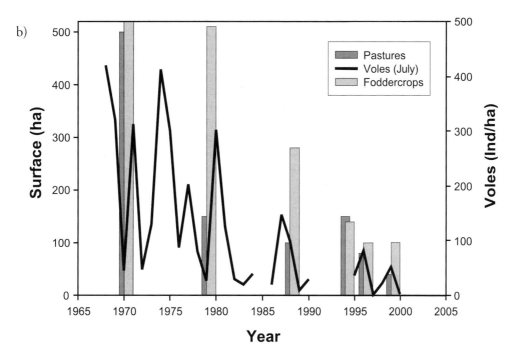

Figure 35.1. Trends in land use and vole abundance in a) Marais de Rochefort and b) Deux Sèvres. Data for Marais de Rochefort from Salamolard *et al.* (2000) and CNRS. Land use data for Deux Sèvres from CNRS and RGA (corresponding to Saint-Blandine parish); vole data for Deux Sèvres from Quéré *et al.* (1991) and CNRS (corresponding to Beauvoir parish).

However, if food abundance decreases further in agricultural environments, both average productivity and breeding numbers (i.e. carrying capacity) might decline. In the long-term, therefore, impoverishment of food supplies caused by changes in land use and intensification of agriculture may render harrier populations in agricultural areas unsustainable.

In many agricultural areas the Montagu's harrier breeds sympatrically with increasing populations of hen harrier *Circus cyaneus* (García & Arroyo, 2001; Millon *et al.*, 2002), and food resources used by both species are very similar (Arroyo & García, 1999; Millon *et al.*, 2002). Therefore, interspecific competition for limited food resources may accentuate the problem for one or both of these species.

35.4 Other factors reducing harrier productivity: harvesting activity

As outlined above, harrier productivity in 'natural' conditions is mainly regulated by food abundance. However, in agricultural areas another factor strongly influences harrier productivity: harvesting activity. Because harrier nests are on the ground, any 'combine' harvesting (or mowing) occurring before the nestlings are able to fly can be detrimental. This problem has been highlighted by harrier conservationists for almost 20 years (e.g. Berthemy *et al.*, 1983; Palma, 1985), and nestling mortality due to this factor has been quoted to be very high (>80-90%) in some areas (e.g. Pérez *et al.*, 1971; Martelli, 1987; Pandolfi & Pino d'Astore, 1990). This problem has been accentuated in recent years due to the increased mechanisation of agriculture. Additionally, intensification of agriculture (use of nitrates and other varieties of cereal) has also favoured earlier and faster growing crops, allowing earlier harvesting.

Risk of death by harvesting activities depends on timing of harrier breeding and timing of harvesting. Timing of harrier breeding depends on latitude, which influences the time of arrival from winter quarters (Arroyo, 1995) and, additionally, on food conditions at arrival (Salamolard *et al.*, 2000). Timing of harvesting, on the other hand, depends on weather (and thus also latitude and altitude), but also on socio-economic variables such as the most common cereal variety in a given area, or whether the harvesting is carried out by the farmers themselves or contractors. Factors affecting timing of breeding and timing of harvesting are not necessarily correlated, thus the risk of nestling death at harvest time should vary annually, as has been observed in many areas (e.g. Arroyo *et al.*, 1995; Castaño, 1995; Arroyo & Bretagnolle, 2000; Millon *et al.*, 2002).

Overall, between 30 and 98% of nestlings in agricultural areas in France and the Iberian Peninsula were potentially at risk from harvesting activities (i.e. were unfledged at harvest time), with the highest values being observed in the south-western Iberian Peninsula, and also in areas where barley is the predominant crop (e.g. Arroyo *et al.*, 2002). On average, c. 60% of harrier nestlings were unfledged at harvest time, so the average productivity of the harriers could be reduced by up to 60%, if we assume that all unfledged nestlings will be killed by combine harvesters if unprotected. However, some nestlings (5-25%) may survive by chance, even in the absence of conservation measures, at least in some areas (Castaño, 1995; Arroyo, 1996). Nevertheless, even a 40% reduction in productivity renders harrier populations unsustainable in the absence of conservation measures (Arroyo & Bretagnolle, 2000; Arroyo *et al.*, in press). Therefore, harvesting activities represent a major threat for harrier sustainability even in the short term.

35.5 Conservation campaigns directed to nest saving

The urgency of harvesting problems have long mobilised conservationists in many areas to protect nests at harvest time. For example, in France, a national conservation campaign co-ordinated by the Fond d'Intervention pour les Rapaces (FIR-LPO) has been carried out since the 1980s (Pacteau, 1999). These campaigns use voluntary people to locate harrier nests each year, and then different measures are implemented if the nests are at risk. Protective measures include removing the nestlings from the field during harvesting, and building an artificial nest with straw or bales after harvesting has finished; leaving a 4 m² (or more) unharvested area around the nest, which is sometimes subsequently protected by a fence; or moving the nestlings to a close-by field (see Berthemy *et al.*, 1983; Millon *et al.*, 2002). In the extreme, if none of those measures are applicable, nestlings are taken to captive rearing centres, and subsequently released by hacking (Pacteau, 1999; Amar *et al.*, 2000). In total, over 1,000 Montagu's harrier nests are managed in this way each year in France, and such an effort represents more than 5,000 person days (Pacteau, 1999). Some 5,000-10,000 are spent each year to cover the expenses (e.g. petrol) of the volunteers, but this campaign would represent approximately 225,000 per year (at an hourly cost of 7.00) if volunteers were paid.

In Spain, similar measures have been implemented in different regions (or Autonomous Communities) since the late 1980s, although there is not a national campaign. In many areas, conservation budget includes salaries for the people locating the nests and contacting the farmers, and/or money for the farmers for leaving an unharvested area of up to 1 ha around each nest. Captive rearing centres also exist in some regions, to rear and release Montagu's harrier nestlings unable to be saved otherwise (Pomarol, 1994). More than 70,000 a year are spent in harrier conservation campaigns in Spain, involving over 90 people.

Overall, important resources are used every year to protect harrier nests from harvesting activities. Because resources for conservation are limited, and may dwindle in the future (as other priorities develop), the question arises as to how these resources could be used in the most effective and sustainable way. Such a question is obviously not new to conservation managers, and is difficult to answer. Several aspects of harrier biology provide some insight into how to explore and eventually develop such effective conservation schemes.

35.5.1 *Optimising conservation effort: where to use the resources?*

Montagu's harrier populations are not isolated. Data from wing-tagged juveniles showed that at least 15% of juveniles disperse >50 km away from their natal site (Arroyo & Bretagnolle, 2000). This figure is without doubt an underestimate because the probability of detecting wing-tagged harriers away from natal areas (where no strong monitoring exists) is small.

Simulation analyses showed that connectivity through juvenile dispersal between two populations, one of them having normal productivity (two fledglings per pair), and the other one suffering 50% mortality due to harvesting activities, would allow persistence of the second population, even in the absence of conservation measures (Arroyo & Bretagnolle, 2000; Arroyo *et al.*, 2002). These results imply that conservation measures applied to a given area also impact on all other areas connected to it through juvenile dispersal. Therefore, if resources are limited and do not allow for full protection of all breeding areas, the choice exists as to how to distribute resources in the most efficient way. This raises the following question: "Is it better to concentrate resources for conservation in a particular area, or to share them among as many areas as possible?". We assessed this question by running some simulation analyses. Figure 35.2 represents the probability of extinction of four hypothetical populations and the whole metapopulation under four scenarios (representing the same amount of conservation resources used, but distributed differently among the populations). If resources are insufficient to protect all nests in four populations, the most effective situation (in terms of maximising harrier persistence) would be the one in which one of the populations is fully protected (Arroyo *et al.*, 2002).

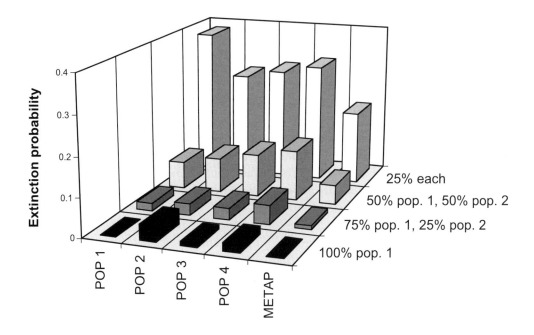

Figure 35.2. Probability of extinction of four hypothetical populations (and the whole metapopulation) of Montagu's harriers connected bilaterally through juvenile dispersal (1% of fledglings produced in each area would settle in each of the other three areas each year). Each population initially held 80 breeding pairs, had a potential productivity of two fledglings per pair, and suffered 50% nestling mortality through harvesting activities in the absence of conservation measures. The simulation presents four potential scenarios, assuming that there are only resources to save 40 nests per year. The first scenario (25% each) contemplates that those resources would be used equally among all areas, thus saving 25% of affected nests in each area. In the second and third scenarios (75% pop 1, 25% pop 2 and 50% pop 1, 50% pop 2), the resources would be distributed among only two of the populations (saving either 50% of affected nests in each population, or 75% of affected nests in one, and 25% in the other). In the last scenario (100% pop 1), all resources would be concentrated in only one of the four populations, saving 100% of the affected nests there, but leaving the other three areas unprotected (From: Arroyo *et al.*, 2002).

These results highlight the importance of maintaining fully productive populations. The first way to attain this in a sustainable and economic way would be to protect the populations which are naturally productive and unaffected by harvesting problems, such as those breeding in natural vegetation. Second, the results suggest that if resources are limited, and do not to allow for full protection of all breeding areas, it is more efficient to concentrate conservation efforts in a given area, making sure that most of the nests are saved there, rather than working less intensively in larger areas.

The most efficient and sustainable way of protecting Montagu's harrier nestlings from harvesting activity, however, should probably involve habitat management, for example through agro-environmental measures (e.g. delaying harvesting until most nestlings have fledged), which would protect the nestlings without the need for locating the nests (which involves considerable human resources). This would be possible in areas where the difference between timing of harvesting and timing of fledging is small, as is the case in many areas of Spain (Arroyo *et al.*, 2002).

However, it is not always easy to apply habitat measures (e.g. agro-environmental measures) over large land surfaces. By considering another aspect of the harrier's biology – semi-colonial nesting – we can provide pointers to the spatial scale of conservation measures needed.

35.5.2 *Harriers as semi-colonial species*
Montagu's harriers, as opposed to many raptors that are territorial, breed semi-colonially. This means that even if some nests appear isolated, the majority of pairs (85% in our study areas, n = 1,007 nests) breed in small colonies of two to 27 pairs each (mean 7 ±4 pairs). Nests are distributed in a highly clumped fashion, sometimes as close as a few metres apart. The average between-nest distance in colonies is 183 ±140 m (n = 794). Given, among other things, the variability of the agricultural habitat between years, the location of the colonies is not fixed. However, areas where colonies settle may be used persistently over several years if conditions for breeding are favourable.

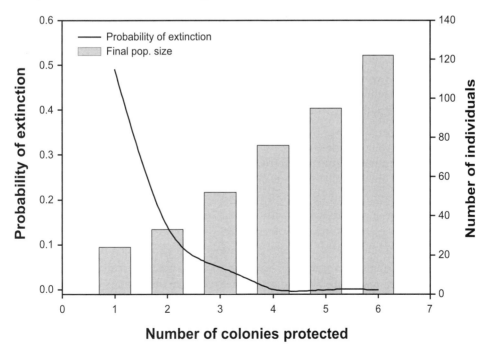

Figure 35.3. Probability of extinction and final population size of a hypothetical population of Montagu's harrier, organized in 12 colonies each with seven to 15 pairs, according to the number of those colonies protected. (From: Arroyo *et al.*, 2002).

We can consider harrier populations as a compound of subpopulations (the colonies) connected through dispersal in a metapopulation. Simulation analyses were undertaken for a population of Montagu's harriers composed of 12 colonies. These colonies were connected through juvenile dispersal, with each one holding seven to 15 pairs, having an average productivity of two fledglings per pair, but suffering 50% nestling loss due to harvesting activities if unprotected. Under these assumptions, the whole metapopulation would persist (to a level of at least 70% of initial population size) with as few as five (40%) colonies protected (Arroyo *et al.*, 2002 and Figure 35.3).

These results are indicative, and should not be taken literally given that the premises used for simulation analyses are simplistic. Nevertheless, they show that, at least theoretically, a relatively small network of small protected areas could be effective in maintaining harrier populations.

However, another problem arises. As stated above, colony location is not fixed, and Montagu's harriers may move considerable distances between one nesting event and the next one. Even if a network of protected areas were in place, it would be difficult to ensure that the harriers use these instead of settling nearby. In other words, how could we attract and then maintain harriers within protected areas? Knowledge about factors influencing nest area choice in this species may help to answer this question.

35.5.3 Parameters affecting choice of nest site

Ground-nesting species are particularly vulnerable to predators. Coloniality in the Montagu's harrier provides advantages against predators (Arroyo *et al.*, 2001). Nevertheless, for a species that nests on the ground, vegetation structure and/or height may also be very important in determining choice of nest site, as a well concealed nest may be more difficult to detect by predators. In the Deux Sèvres study area, cereal crops with nests were taller (89 ±11 cm, n = 169) than cereal crops without nests measured at the same time (79 ±13 cm, n = 78). Rye-grass fields are usually mowed in late April, and are thus unsuitable for breeding at the moment when Montagu's harriers build their nests (early May in that area). However, if mowing is delayed (because of rainy weather, for example), Montagu's harriers often settle in rye-grass fields. Before mowing, vegetation in rye-grass fields in late April is taller on average (58 ±17 cm, n = 23) than in cereal crops (48 ±11 cm, n = 36). In another study, in Portugal, nests of Montagu's harriers were found more frequently than expected in oats, which were on average taller than wheat and set-aside, the other crops used for nesting. Additionally, nests were found in parts of the fields which had vegetation around 88 ±10 cm height, and were not in areas with higher or shorter vegetation (Claro, 2000). Therefore, height is apparently important in determining choice of nest areas.

In many raptors, when nest sites are not limiting, food abundance is also important in determining nest location. Large-scale vole trapping in Deux Sèvres, together with the mapping of land use each year, allowed an estimate of vole abundance in 1 km² quadrats throughout the study area. Harriers preferentially bred in areas with high vole abundance (Arroyo *et al.*, 2002).

In many colonial species, conspecific attraction is also important in determining nest area choice, as is conspecific breeding success (Boulinier & Danchin, 1997). We looked at whether the total number of fledglings produced in a given 1 km² in the previous breeding seasons influenced where harriers settled (once controlling for vole abundance) and found this variable to be highly significant in all years of the study (Arroyo *et al.*, 2002). Considering that young harriers do not tend to return to their natal area, this result suggests that harriers are attracted to areas where young harriers are produced each year, and which contain good food supplies.

All of these above variables (vegetation height, food abundance, fledging success) could potentially be used to attract and maintain harriers to protected areas. Experimental evaluations could be developed in order to determine the most attractive vegetation heights or land uses which maximise food abundance in each area. Additionally, traditionally productive colonies could be protected as a priority, given that they are more likely to be used in subsequent years. Finally, in some circumstances, breeding success could even be manipulated artificially (e.g. boosted) in protected areas.

An example of the potential use of manipulating breeding success comes from a conservation programme in Catalunya (NE Spain). In that area, harvesting occurs very early in the season (late May or early June on average), and therefore more than 95% of nestlings are unfledged at harvest time, and many nests (around 40%) are still at the incubation stage (Pomarol *et al.*, 1995). In 1988, a programme was started in that region in which eggs or young nestlings from nests which could not be protected on the field were taken to a captive rearing centre; nestlings were reared there by foster mothers (captive Montagu's harrier females), and subsequently released at fledging by the method of 'hacking' (Pomarol, 1994; Pomarol *et al.*, 1995). The hacking site was an area with natural vegetation potentially suitable for harrier breeding, located 190 km away from the original breeding area where eggs/young were collected. The purpose of that programme was to 'fix' some of the released fledglings to that area (as happens with many other raptor species, such as falcons, Falconidae, or kites *Milvus* spp.), thus helping to create a long-term breeding population in natural vegetation, unaffected by harvesting problems. Released birds were wing-tagged so as to enable monitoring. The programme was successful, but for reasons different from those expected. Given the (at the time unknown) relatively low philopatry of the species, very few of the released birds came back to the hacking area to breed. However, a few years after the start of the hacking programme, some unmarked (thus unreleased) birds were attracted to the hacking area and subsequently settled to breed (Pomarol & Heredia, 1994). In 2000, a small colony (c. eight pairs) existed in that area, mainly (but not only) formed of unmarked birds (M. Pomarol, pers. comm.). The unmarked birds were probably attracted to the release area because the released birds were perceived by the prospectors to signify that the area was productive.

Obviously, captive rearing and release by hacking is a very intrusive form of management, and is unnecessary in many cases. In most cases, manipulation of habitat characteristics or the protection or enhancement of natural productivity should be sufficient to attract or maintain harriers in protected areas. However, in cases when egg or nestling recovery is necessary (such as the Catalunya case, and in some areas in France and south-western Spain), there exists the option of where to release, and such an option should be used in management programmes.

35.6 Conclusions

In the present day agricultural regime, the Montagu's harrier is clearly dependent on conservation measures for its sustainability in the long term. There is, therefore, a need to develop sustainable and efficient conservation plans. Such measures should include ones directed towards maintaining food supplies, as well as those directed towards minimising impacts of harvesting activities on harrier productivity. Maintenance of biodiversity (thus food supply for the harriers) in agricultural areas is a highly important issue, but not just for the Montagu's harriers. Large scale agri-environmental measures should be implemented to benefit biodiversity. Protection of harrier nestlings from harvesting activity, in contrast, could be effectively implemented through a network of relatively small protected areas. The following should be priorities in the short term: promoting protection of natural vegetation areas; identifying and protecting the most productive and stable colonies in agricultural areas; and testing experimentally factors which are likely to attract and maintain harriers in protected areas.

Finally, we should stress the importance of research for developing conservation strategies. Knowledge about the ecology of the species of concern, but also about its behaviour and social relationships, is needed to implement efficient conservation measures (also Madders, Chapter 23; Redpath & Thirgood, Chapter 39). Modelling techniques, even simple ones such as the one presented here, are very useful for evaluating the efficacy of different conservation scenarios, and field experimentation may subsequently be used to test the validity of the best options.

Acknowledgements

Many people helped with fieldwork in our study areas throughout the years, and particular thanks are due to Marc Salamolard, Marie-Helene Froger and Luis Palomares. Alain Leroux started the wing tagging programme, and helped both in the field and with advice throughout the project. Carole Attié helped in many stages of the work (and thanks are also due for last minute assistance). We thank all participants of the Iberian Working Group on Harriers, for discussion and for allowing the use of unpublished data. Two anonymous referees improved the manuscript.

References

Amar, A., Arroyo, B.E. & Bretagnolle, V. (2000). Post-fledging dependency and dispersal in hacked and wild Montagu's harriers *Circus pygargus*. *Ibis*, **142**, 21-28.

Arroyo, B.E. (1995). *Breeding ecology and nest dispersion of Montagu's Harrier* Circus pygargus *in central Spain*. PhD thesis. University of Oxford, Oxford.

Arroyo, B. (1996). Reproductive success of Montagu's harrier (*Circus pygargus*) and hen harrier (*Circus cyaneus*) in agricultural habitats. In *Biology and Conservation of Mediterranean Raptors, 1994*, ed. by J. Muntaner & J. Mayol. Monografias SEO/Birdlife, 4. pp. 459-463.

Arroyo, B.E. (1997). Diet of Montagu's harrier *Circus pygargus* in central Spain: analysis of temporal and geographical variation. *Ibis*, **139**, 664-672.

Arroyo, B.E. (1998). Effect of diet on the reproductive success of Montagu's harriers *Circus pygargus*. *Ibis*, **140**, 690-693.

Arroyo, B.E. & Bretagnolle, V. (2000). Evaluating the long-term effectiveness of conservation practices in Montagu's harrier *Circus pygargus*. In *Raptors at Risk*, ed. by R.D. Chancellor & B.-U. Meyburg. Pica Press, Cornwall. pp. 403-408.

Arroyo, B. & García, J.T. (1999). Los aguiluchos cenizo (*C. pygargus*) y pálido (*C. cyaneus*) en las áreas cerealistas del Jarama: resúmen de 8 años de estudio. *Anuario Ornitológico de Madrid*, **1998**, 14-25.

Arroyo, B.E., García, J.T & Bretagnolle, V. (2002). Conservation of the Montagu's harrier *Circus pygargus* in agricultural areas. *Animal Conservation*, **5**, 283-290.

Arroyo, B.E., Mougeot, F. & Bretagnolle, V. (2001). Coloniality and costs of nest defence in the Montagu's harrier *Circus pygargus*. *Behavioural Ecology and Sociobiology*, **50**, 109-115.

Arroyo, B., Palomares, L. & Pinilla, J. (1995). Situación y problemática de los Aguiluchos cenizo (*Circus pygargus*) y pálido (*C. cyaneus*) en la Comunidad de Madrid. *Alytes*, **7**, 365-372.

Berthemy, B., Dabin, P. & Terrasse, M. (1983). Recensement et protection d'une espèce protégée: le busard cendré. *Le Courier de la Nature*, **Jan/Fev**, 10-16.

Biljsma, R.G., Blomert, A.M., Van Manen, W. & Quist, M. (1993). *Ecologische Atlas van de Nederlandse Roofvogels*. Schuyt, Harlem.

Blanco, J.C. & González, J.L. (Eds) (1992). *Libro Rojo de los Vertebrados de España*. ICONA-M.A.P.A., Madrid.

Borralho, R., Rito, A., Rego, F., Simoes, H. & Vaz Pinto, P. (1998). Summer distribution of red-legged partridges *Alectoris rufa* on Mediterranean farmland. *Ibis*, **140**, 620-625.

Boulinier, T. & Danchin, E. (1997). The use of conspecific reproductive success for breeding patch selection in terrestrial migratory species. *Evolutionary Ecology*, **11**, 505-517.

Butet, A. & Leroux, A. (1993). Effect of prey on a predator's breeding success. A 7-year study on common vole (*Microtus arvalis*) and Montagu's harrier (*Circus pygargus*) in a west of France Marsh. *Acta Oecologica*, **14**, 857-865.

Castaño, J.P. (1995). Efecto de la actividad de siega y causas de fracaso reproductivo en un población de Aguilucho cenizo *Circus pygargus* en el SE de Ciudad Real. *Ardeola*, **42**, 167-172.

Claro, J.C. (2000). *Ecologia reproductiva do Tartaranhão-caçador* Circus pygargus *(L.) na região de Evora*. MSc thesis. University of Evora, Portugal.

Clemens, C. (1993). International Conference on Montagu's Harrier. *WWGBP Bulletin*, **18**, 12.

Corbacho, C. & Sánchez, J.M. (2000). Clutch size and egg size in the breeding strategy of Montagu's harrier *Circus pygargus* in a Mediterranean area. *Bird Study*, **47**, 245-248.

Corbacho, C., Muñoz, A. & Bartolome, P. (1995). Espectro trófico del Aguilucho cenizo *Circus pygargus* en Extremadura. *Alytes*, **7**, 433-440.

Corbacho, C., Sánchez, J.M. & Sánchez, A. (1997). Breeding biology of Montagu's harrier (*Circus pygargus*) L. in agricultural environments of southwest Spain; comparison with other populations in the western Paleartic. *Bird Study*, **44**, 166-175.

Cramp, S. & Simmons, K.E.L. (Eds) (1980). *The Birds of the Western Paleartic, Vol. 2*. Oxford University Press, Oxford.

Davies, S. (1977). Summer with the harriers. *Birds*, **6**, 68-69.

Delattre, P., Giraudoux, P., Baudry, J., Mussard, P., Toussaint, M., Truchetet, D., Stahl, P., Poule, M.L., Artois, M., Damange, J.P. & Quéré, J.P. (1992). Land use patterns and types of common vole (*Microtus arvalis*) population kinetics. *Agriculture, Ecosystems and Environment*, **39**, 153-169.

Donald, P.F., Green, R.E. & Heath, M.F. (2000). Agricultural intensification and the collapse of Europe's farmland bird populations. *Proceedings of the Royal Society*, **268**, 25-29.

Ferrero, J.J. (1995). La población ibérica de Aguilucho Cenizo *Circus pygargus*. *Alytes*, **7**, 539-560.

Flint, V.E., Boehme, R.L., Kostin, Y.V. & Kuznetsov, A.A. (1984). *A Field Guide to Birds of the USSR*. Princeton University Press, New Jersey.

Frionnet, C. (1925). *Les Oiseaux de la Haute-Marne*. Bulletin de la Société des Sciences Naturelles de Haute-Marne, Chaumont.

García, J.T. & Arroyo, B.E. (2001). Abiotic factors influencing reproduction in the centre and periphery of breeding ranges: a comparative analysis in sympatric harriers. *Ecography*, **24**, 393-402.

Gregory, R.D., Noble, D.G., Robinson, J.A., Stroud, D.A., Campbell, L.H., Rehfisch, M.M., Cranswick, P.A., Wilkinson, N.I., Crick, H.Q.P. & Green, R.E. (2002). *The State of the UK's Birds 2001*. The Royal Society for the Protection of Birds, British Trust for Ornithology, Wildfowl & Wetland Trust and Joint Nature Conservation Committee, Sandy.

Holker, M. (1999). Zur Umsetzung der EU-Vogelschutzrichtlinie in Ackerbaugebieten. *Berichge zum Vogelschutz*, **37**, 85-92.

Ivanovski, V. (1993). International Conference on Montagu's Harrier. *WWGBP Bulletin*, **19**, 13.

Jiménez, J. & Surroca, M. (1995). Evolución poblacional y reproducción del Aguilucho Cenizo *Circus pygargus* en la provincia de Castellón. *Alytes*, **7**, 287-296.

Koks, B.J., Van Scharenburg, K.W.M. & Visser, E.G. (2001). Grauwe kiekendieven *Circus pygargus* in Nederland: balanceren tussen hoop en vrees. *Limosa*, **74**, 121-136.

Krogulec, J. (1993). International Conference on Montagu's Harrier. *WWGBP Bulletin*, **18**, 13.

Krogulec, J. & Leroux, A. (1993). Breeding ecology of Montagu's harrier *Circus pygargus* on natural and reclaimed marshes in Poland and France. In *Raptor Conservation Today*, ed. by B.-U. Meyburg & R.D. Chancellor. Pica Press, Cornwall. pp. 151-152.

Lacy, R.C., Kimberly A.H. & Miller, P.S. (1995). *Vortex: A Stochastic Simulation of the Extinction Process. Version 7 User's Manual*. IUCN/SSC Conservation Breeding Specialist Group, Apple Valley, MN, USA.

Larrinúa, A. (1908). *Catálogo descriptivo de la colección de aves e insectos legada a la Excma. Diputación de Guipúzcoa*. Imprenta de la Provincia, San Sebastian.

Lucio, A.J. (1990). Influencia de las condiciones climáticas en la productividad de la perdiz roja (*Alectoris rufa*). *Ardeola*, **37**, 207-218.

Martelli, D. (1987). Datti sull'ecologia riprodutiva dell'albanella minore (*Circus pygargus*) in Emila-Romana. Nota preliminare. *Supplement Ricerca Biologia Selvaggina*, **12**, 125-137.

Martelli, D. & Parodi, R. (1992). Albanella minore Circus pygargus. In *Fauna d'Italia. Ucelli I*, ed. by P. Bichetti, P. De Franceschi & N. Baccetti. Calderini, Milan. pp. 541-550.

Millon, A., Bourrioux, J.L., Riols, C. & Bretagnolle, V. (2002). Comparative breeding biology of Hen and Montagu's harriers: an eight-year study in north-eastern France. *Ibis*, **144**, 94-105.

Newton, I. (1998). *Population Limitation in Birds*. Academic Press, London.

Pacteau, C. (1999). Busards en France, 20 ans de protection. *FIR Bulletin*, **33**, 38-39.

Pain, D.J. & Pienkowski, M.W. (Eds) (1997). *Farming and Birds in Europe. The Common Agricultural Policy and its Implications for Bird Conservation*. Academic Press, London.

Palma, L. (1985). The present situation of birds of prey in Portugal. In *Conservation Studies of Raptors*, ed. by I. Newton & R.D. Chancellor. International Council for Bird Preservation, Cambridge. pp. 3-14.

Pandolfi, M. & Pino d'Astore, P.R. (1990). Analysis of breeding behaviour in Montagu's harrier *Circus pygargus* in a site of Central Italy. *Avocetta*, **14**, 97-102.

Perez Chiscano, J.L. & Fernandez Cruz, M. (1971). Sobre *Grus grus* y *Circus pygargus* en Extremadura. *Ardeola*, **Vol esp**, 509-574.

Pomarol, M. (1994). Releasing Montagu's harrier (*Circus pygargus*) by the method of hacking. *Journal of Raptor Research*, **28**, 19-22.

Pomarol, M. & Heredia, G. (1994). Wiesenweihen (*Circus pygargus*) in Catalonien (Spanien) – Schutzmaßnahmen und Auswilderungen. *Greifvögel und Falknerei*, **1993**, 126-130.

Pomarol, M., Parellada, X. & Fortia, R. (1995). El aguilucho cenizo Circus pygargus en Cataluña: historia de 10 años de manejo. *Alytes*, **7**, 253-268.

Potts, G.R. (1991). The environmental and ecological importance of cereal fields. In *The Ecology of Temperate Cereal Fields*, ed. by L.G. Firbank, N. Carter, J.F. Darbyshire & G.R. Potts. Blackwell, Oxford. pp. 3-21.

Quéré, J.P., Delattre, P., Toussaint, M. & Musard, P. (1991). Le campagnol des champs. *Bulletin Technique d'Information*, N°3. Ministère de l'Agriculture et de la Forêt, Paris. pp. 17-26.

Salamolard, M., Leroux, A.B.A. & Bretagnolle, V. (1999). Le Busard cendré. In *Les oiseaux à statut de conservation défavorable ou fragile en France. Listes rouges et priorités nationales*, ed. by G. Rocamora, G. Jarry & D. Yeatman-Berthelot. SEOF, Paris. pp. 388-389.

Salamolard, M., Butet, A., Leroux, A. & Bretagnolle, V. (2000). Responses of an avian predator to variations in prey density at a temperate latitude. *Ecology*, **81**, 2428-2441.

Suárez, F., Sainz, H., Santos, T. & González Bernaldez, F. (1992). *Las Estepas Ibéricas*. Ministerio de Obras Públicas y Transportes, Madrid.

SNPRCN (1990). *Livro Vermelho dos Vertebrados de Portugal. Vol 1 - Mamiferos, Aves Repteis e Anfibios.* Secretaria de Estado do Ambiente e Defesa do Consumidor, Lisbon.

Tucker, G.M. & Heath, M.F. (1994). *Birds in Europe: their Conservation Status.* BirdLife International. Cambridge.

Underhill-Day, J. (1990). *The status and breeding biology of Marsh Harrier and Montagu's Harrier in Britain since 1900.* PhD Thesis. CNAA, London.

THEME SIX

CONFLICTS AND THE SEARCH FOR SOLUTIONS

THEME SIX

CONFLICTS AND THE SEARCH FOR SOLUTIONS

In his important study of Britain's 24 diurnal raptors, Brown (1976) noted that complaints made against birds of prey shared three main characteristics: (a) they were rarely based on factual evidence; (b) when they were painstakingly investigated they were found to be without substance, or even exaggerated; and (c) when factual information was made available and published, and this disagreed with the complaints about raptors, the conclusions were seldom accepted and "often very rudely rejected". Almost 30 years after publication of Brown's book we still find conflicts and a familiar polarity of views over raptors (e.g. Anon., 2000). In the concluding part of *Birds of Prey in a Changing Environment* there are six studies, each searching for a solution to the alleged conflict between raptors and other interests.

Marquiss *et al.* (Chapter 36) investigated white-tailed eagle *Haliaeetus albicilla* predation on lambs of sheep *Ovis aries*. Their study was stimulated by concerns amongst some farmers in the west of Scotland, primarily on Mull, that many of their lambs were being taken by eagles. Marquiss *et al.* studied the diet of 11 pairs of eagles on Mull, and concluded that the number of lambs killed by eagles was small compared with the overall mortality of lambs. This research demonstrates the type of meticulous science required to address allegations about the impacts of predatory birds on land use interests.

In England, several raptor species are being persecuted, and the hen harrier *Circus cyaneus* is on the verge of extinction as a breeding bird because of this. Holmes *et al.* (Chapter 37) have drawn together information on persecution incidents involving diurnal raptors in England during the 1990s. They have devised a simple persecution index in order to compare the susceptibility of different raptor species and populations, and conclude that the hen harrier, followed by Montagu's harrier *Circus pygargus*, red kite *Milvus milvus*, peregrine *Falco peregrinus*, goshawk *Accipiter gentilis* and marsh harrier *Circus aeruginosus* are the six species most heavily persecuted. Holmes *et al.* conclude that the number of reported persecution incidents is likely to be an under-estimate; for instance, 31 persecution incidents were reported for the peregrine falcon (with 21 birds shot, nine poisoned and one trapped) but raptor study groups identified more than 300 incidents where persecution was 'suspected but not confirmed' by subsequent investigations. Developing the theme of persecution impacts, Summers *et al.* (Chapter 38) quantify in detail the apparent significant impact of persecution of hen harriers nesting on grouse moors (see also Etheridge *et al.*, 1997). In Chapter 39, Redpath & Thirgood link models with field data to develop an understanding of the impacts of hen harrier predation on red grouse *Lagopus lagopus scoticus* populations. Building on their highly publicised report *Birds of Prey and Red Grouse* (Redpath & Thirgood, 1997), the authors suggest that some of the so-called conflict between driven grouse moor management and hen harriers can be resolved. Their model suggests that supplementary (or diversionary) feeding of hen harriers could reduce the impact of harrier predation on red grouse chicks (see Redpath *et al.*, 2001), to the extent that driven grouse shooting could occur on moors with a broader range of harrier densities than previously realised. Redpath & Thirgood stress that their model needs to be subject to sensitivity analysis and careful examination of its assumptions. However, there do appear to be at least some potential ways of reducing this particular conflict, which appears to have given rise in some cases to the sorts of persecution induced effects on harriers reported in the previous two chapters (see Moorland Working Group, 2002).

Virtually every country in Europe experiences conflicts between birds of prey and some other interest. Viñuela & Villafuerte (Chapter 40) summarise the complexity of issues affecting some of the 25 raptor species breeding in Spain. Here, we find a wide-ranging account linking the changing fortunes of the rabbit *Oryctolagus cuniculus*, red-legged partridges *Alectoris rufa* and persecution of raptors. The study shows the complexity of human-predator-prey relationships, and the interdependency of each element. Two of the world's most endangered predators – the Spanish imperial eagle *Aquila adalbertii* and the Iberian lynx *Lynx pardinus* – are implicated in this plight, both of which could benefit through the legal control of generalist and abundant predators, notably the fox *Vulpes vulpes*.

In the final chapter, Galbraith *et al.* reflect on the ingredients of the raptor-human conflict. In many ways, such conflict is a distraction from the undoubted enjoyment most people derive from seeing birds of prey in the wild. Galbraith *et al.* suggest that resolution of the conflicts lies in developing open and inclusive routes of communication between the protagonists, gaining agreement on the numbers of birds of prey, factors affecting their productivity, and the extent to which they have any impact on particular prey groups, and in devising novel management techniques. It is important to develop an acceptance of the need for change in land management and conservation actions, and to trial novel management techniques which may reduce the impact of some predators on human interests (also Anon., 2000; Moorland Working Group, 2002).

The 'Evil Quartet' refers to the four major causes of biodiversity loss: habitat loss and degradation; killing of plants and animals by people; introduction of alien species; and the secondary effects of extinctions (Diamond, 1984). We could add to this the failure of humans to communicate to one another their concerns and aspirations for the environment, and then to unite in action. The future security of raptors in Europe will depend as much on co-operation between land mangers and the rest of the public as on conservation schemes.

References

Anonymous (2000). *Report of the UK Raptor Working Group.* Department of the Environment, Transport and Regions, and Joint Nature Conservation Committee, Peterborough.

Brown, L. (1976). *Birds of Prey.* Collins, London.

Diamond, J. (1984). Normal extinctions of isolated populations. In *Extinctions*, ed. by M.H. Nitecki. University of Chicago Press, Chicago. pp. 191-246.

Etheridge, B., Summers, R.W. & Green, R.E. (1997). The effects of illegal killing and destruction of nests by humans on the population dynamics of the hen harrier *Circus cyaneus* in Scotland. *Journal of Applied Ecology*, **34**, 1081-1105.

Moorland Working Group (2002). *Scotland's Moorland: the nature of change.* Scottish Natural Heritage, Battleby.

Redpath, S.N. & Thirgood, S.J. (1997). *Birds of Prey and Red Grouse.* The Stationery Office, London.

Redpath, S.M., Thirgood, S.J. & Leckie, F.M. (2001). Does supplementary feeding reduce predation of red grouse by hen harriers? *Journal of Applied Ecology,* **38**, 1157-1168.

36. WHITE-TAILED EAGLES (*HALIAEETUS ALBICILLA*) AND LAMBS (*OVIS ARIES*)

Mick Marquiss, Mike Madders & David N. Carss

Summary

1.   There is a perception amongst some farmers in Western Scotland that re-introduced white-tailed eagles *Haliaeetus albicilla* kill lambs *Ovis aries*. An attempt was made to estimate the numbers of lambs consumed by eagles and the proportion killed, as opposed to scavenged, by examining carcasses recovered from eagle nests.

2.   The diet of eleven pairs of eagles during the breeding season was species-diverse but included lambs. Most pairs took few lambs but one pair took twice as many lambs as any other pair under study.

3.   Heavy, localised subcutaneous bruising associated with talon punctures suggested that some lambs were killed by eagles. Other carcasses had no such subcutaneous bruising and sometimes signs of other scavengers (mainly corvids *Corvus* spp. and gulls *Larus* spp.).

4.   For three pairs of white-tailed eagles investigated intensively, one pair took few lambs, another pair took many but mainly scavenged them, and a third pair took most and could have killed 28 lambs in 1999, and six or seven in 2000. A lack of alternative prey (rabbits *Oryctolagus cuniculus*) and the proximity of the nest to a lambing area in 1999 may have been responsible for higher lamb predation then.

5.   The numbers of lambs killed is small compared with overall lamb mortality, but sufficient to be an important loss to an individual farmer if eagle predation of lambs is additive and concentrated on one farm.

36.1 Introduction

White-tailed eagles *Haliaeetus albicilla* were re-introduced to Scotland in the 1970s and by 2002, at least 26 pairs were established with at least 22 pairs breeding (Bainbridge *et al.*, Chapter 30). On the island of Mull, Scotland, white-tailed eagles have recently increased to nine pairs, though to date no more than four have reared young in any one year. Eagles consume lambs *Ovis aries* during the breeding season and local farmers claim that at least some of these are killed. The anecdotal evidence includes lamb carcasses seen in eagle nests, eagles disturbed from freshly dead (sometimes bloody) lambs, eagles seen attacking live lambs, and well-grown live lambs with injuries from eagle talons. It is thought that some of the lambs killed by eagles would have otherwise survived, so eagle predation could represent a direct economic loss to the farmers concerned. Some farmers claim that eagles kill lambs from birth (~3 kg weight) through to August (~25 kg).

The present work aimed to: (i) quantify eagle diet during the period when lambs are available (late April to August); and (ii) search for evidence of lamb predation, as opposed to scavenging, by examining relatively fresh remains collected frequently from eagle nesting areas. The intensive study was confined to Mull, the site of the perceived problem, but we also looked at the foods of white-tailed eagles elsewhere in Scotland to give context.

Hill sheep farming in Western Scotland differs from elsewhere in Europe (Houston, 1977; Hewson & Wilson, 1979; Hewson & Verkaik, 1981; Hewson, 1984). The sheep are mainly 'Scottish Blackface' and live on upland hill pastures year-round. For free-ranging sheep, stocking densities can be high – up to 60 breeding females (ewes) per km^2. Lambs are born in late April and May as grass starts to grow, and productivity varies between 65 and 90 lambs per 100 breeding ewes (Gunn & Robinson, 1963; Mather, 1978; Hewson, 1984). Such productivity levels are relatively low compared with those in lowland, enclosed and improved pastureland in the UK, where 140-190 lambs per 100 breeding ewes are not uncommon (Eadie, 1970). Most male lambs from hill flocks are removed in the autumn for sale, whereas most female lambs are retained for breeding when two years of age.

36.2 Methods

A broad description of the Island of Mull, its land use and vegetation is given in Whitfield *et al.* (2001). On Mull, the diet of white-tailed eagles in the breeding season was assessed using the remains of food recovered from nests and nearby (<250 m) perches. We visited nests every week during the period when eaglets were three to nine weeks old (early May to early July) and again after they had fledged (August). On each occasion the nest and its lining material was thoroughly searched and food remains removed. The flesh on some of the prey remains had not been fully consumed and to compensate for this potential loss of food, the eaglets were given two to four mackerel *Scomber scombrus*. Food remains were identified to species, categorised as juvenile or full-grown, and stored frozen. In the laboratory, items from all weekly collections were compared to ensure that the same individual was not counted more than once. These methods probably recorded most if not all food items delivered to eaglets, under-estimating only occasional soft-tissued items (e.g. sheep 'afterbirths' or small, soft-bodied fish). We cannot be sure, but these records probably also included most items eaten by the adults, which were seen to consume items at the nest or in the vicinity.

Elsewhere in Scotland, white-tailed eagle diet was assessed from food remains recovered from the nest in August or September after the eaglets had fledged. These 'end of season' collections are biased towards robust bones, feathers and fur, and against fish, small birds and small mammals (Wille & Kampp, 1983; Mersmann *et al.*, 1992). However, the method enabled us to estimate the number of lambs in nests because their bones are large, robust and survive well in the nest.

Most of the flesh had been stripped from even the freshest of lamb remains. The viscera were absent and stomachs rarely present. Thus lamb remains mostly comprised four intact limbs and the dorsal portion of the skull, often still attached by the animal's whole skin. By July, the remains of many of the carcasses retrieved were dismembered and some lambs were represented only by shoulder blades (scapulae) or a single leg. Remains were measured; their size was indexed using the length of the hind foot, which is highly correlated with live weight (Marquiss *et al.*, 2003). Where remains were rotten or incomplete, the size of lamb was estimated from curvilinear regression equations of hind foot length against the length of bones (metatarsal, tibia, metacarpal, radius, ulna and scapula). The final tally of lambs was the minimum number that could account for all remains, taking size into consideration.

The state of decay of lamb remains varied and was classified on a four point scale from fresh to decomposed (only bones and wool). Where the hooves were present, we examined the foot membrane for evidence of wear to determine whether the lamb had walked. We categorised membranes as intact, or broken and eroded. Where the animal's skin was present and reasonably fresh, the inside was examined for eagle talon punctures. It was assumed that the presence of bleeding was reasonable evidence that an injury had been sustained when the lamb was alive or close to the point of death. Lamb remains were therefore classified as showing evidence of predation by eagles if talon punctures were associated with localised bruising and haemorrhaging (Rowley, 1970). They were classified as showing evidence of having been scavenged by eagles if there were talon punctures but no localised bruises or haemorrhage. Also, where there was enough material, remains were examined for evidence of other scavengers or predators (e.g. eyes removed by raven *Corvus corax* or hooded crow *Corvus corone*, 'V'-shaped marks on the neck skin from gull *Larus* spp. pecks, and canine tooth wounds on the legs from dog bites). Where such evidence was associated with bruising it showed that the lamb had been attacked or killed prior to it being scavenged by eagles.

Statistical analyses used ANOVA (GLM) packages, in Minitab (Minitab Release 13.2 for Windows™, 2000). The probability of frequencies in contingency tables was estimated using observation randomisation tests (Brown & Rothery, 1993) with 1,200 iterations.

36.3 Results

We examined material from 22 successful nests, representing all but one of those known to have reared young in Scotland during 1998, 1999 and 2000. White-tailed eagles took a large variety of foods. The 1,338 items identified included nine species of mammal, 37 of bird, 18 of fish, a toad, an octopus and a crustacean. Thus, diet in Scotland (as elsewhere) was highly species-diverse, suggesting that these eagles are 'generalist' predators and scavengers. Nevertheless, only four species constituted almost three-quarters of items collected, due mainly to the apparent 'specialism' of the eleven eagle pairs sampled. Northern fulmar *Fulmarus glacialis* was the predominant food species for seven pairs and rabbit *Oryctolagus cuniculus* or mountain hare *Lepus timidus* were predominant for two pairs. One of the remaining pairs fed mainly on lamb, the other on fish.

36.3.1 The numbers of lambs in nests of individual pairs

Away from Mull, the lamb bones recovered from successful nests at the end of the breeding season gave minimum estimates of the numbers taken by each pair in that year, and are directly comparable between pairs and years. They are also roughly comparable with the numbers collected from multiple visits to Mull nests. For example, in 2000, we calculated that single end of season collections on Mull would have underestimated the tally of lambs by three individuals (6% of the 51 recorded). The three lambs that would have been unaccounted for (had we relied solely on an end of season collection) were represented by a single leg or scapular and were of a size that matched another lamb that we knew from the collection date had been taken earlier.

Figure 36.1 gives the average number of lambs at the nests of the eleven white-tailed eagle pairs. For direct comparison, lamb numbers at Mull nests were adjusted to those that would have been estimated had food remains been removed from nests after the young had fledged. In an Analysis of Variance, the numbers of lambs varied considerably between pairs

($F_{10, 21}$ = 23.0, P <0.0001). Some nests contained only one or two lambs, but pair A on Mull was exceptional, taking almost twice as many as any other pair. There was also a small but significant difference between years ($F_{2, 21}$ = 5.7, P <0.05). In 1999 more lambs were present on nests than in 1998 and in 2000. However, the difference between years was substantially less than the difference between eagle pairs. Only 19% of the variation in lamb numbers at nests was explicable by differences between years compared with 77% by differences between pairs.

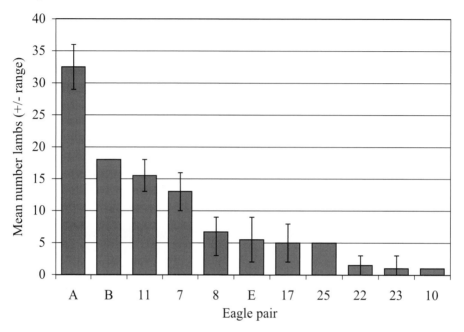

Figure 36.1. Number of lambs estimated from bone remains in successful nests of eleven pairs of white-tailed eagles. Data from 22 nests over three years, 1998-2000. Pairs A, B and E were on Mull, the rest were elsewhere in Scotland.

36.3.2 *The numbers of lambs brought to nests on Mull, and seasonal trends*

On Mull, the numbers of lambs recovered from or nearby white-tailed eagle nests was much higher for pair A (45 in 1999, 31 in 2000) than for pair B (20 in 1999), and least for pair E (1 in 1998, 10 in 2000).

We calculated the rate at which lambs accrued at nests by dividing the number of lambs recovered in any one visit by the number of days since the previous nest clearance. It is rare for items to be left on the nest before hatch (pers. obs. and R.J. Evans, pers. comm.) so we assumed that the lambs recovered at the first visit to a nest were delivered since hatching. We also assumed that those recovered at the last visit had been delivered prior to the young fledging, though this provided maximal rates because fledged eaglets sometimes return to the nest to be fed. The maximum delivery rate was one lamb every two days. In three of the four successful nests examined, there were marked seasonal trends: most lambs were delivered in May, far fewer in June and almost none in July and August (Figure 36.2). Lamb deliveries by pair E were less than half of those by pairs A and B. At one nest (pair A in 1999), despite a similar seasonal decline, more lambs accrued overall because the delivery rate declined less steeply after May.

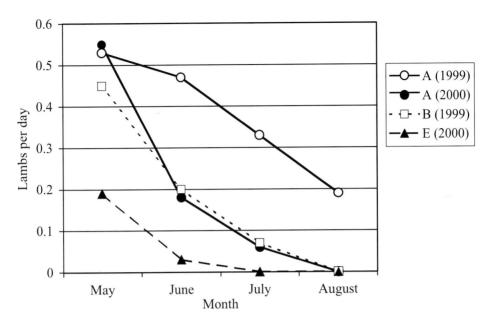

Figure 36.2. Seasonal trends in the daily delivery rates of lambs to nests of three pairs of white-tailed eagles on Mull. Two nests in 1999 (A and B) and in 2000 (A and E).

Table 36.1. The numbers of lamb carcasses with evidence of predation or scavenging at nests of white-tailed eagles on Mull. WTE = white-tailed eagle.

	1999 Pair B	1999 Pair A	2000 Pair A
Number of lamb carcasses retrieved	20	45	31
Number of carcasses diagnosed	11	21	19
Number with evidence of WTE predation Talon punctures with associated bruising	1	13	4
Number with evidence of WTE scavenging*	10	8	15
Talon punctures but no bruising	(2)	(4)	(15)
With evidence of other predators/scavengers	(3)	(4)	(13)
Rotten when delivered to the nest	(3)	(1)	(3)
With intact foot membranes	(3)	(2)	(9)
% lambs predated**	9%	62%	21%

* Some carcasses had more than one sort of evidence of scavenging, so totals are less than the sum of the figures in parentheses.

** Significant difference between nests A & B (observation randomisation test; P = 0.004) and between years 1999 and 2000 for nest A (P = 0.009).

36.3.3 Lamb predation and scavenging by two eagle pairs on Mull

Of the three eagle pairs examined on Mull, sufficient fresh lamb carcasses were retrieved from the nests of pairs A and B to estimate the proportion predated as opposed to scavenged (Table 36.1). The two pairs clearly differed in 1999: pair A apparently killed lambs whereas pair B mainly scavenged them. The situation changed in 2000 when far fewer lambs from the nest of pair A showed evidence of predation. Unfortunately, we had no data for pair B in 2000 because they did not breed successfully.

36.3.4 The size of lambs brought to nests

In 1999 and 2000, we retrieved 127 lambs from the nesting areas of five pairs of white-tailed eagles (from nesting attempts including four where eaglets had hatched but died). The hind foot length was estimated for 124 of these lambs and it varied between nests and years (Table 36.2). However, this was largely due to the time of year at which lambs were taken. The week during which a lamb was delivered to the nest was either known (those retrieved on weekly visits) or could be estimated (on the basis of 'freshness') for those retrieved on the first nest visit. When delivery date was taken into account, the differences between sites and between years were small and statistically insignificant (difference between pairs, $F_{5,124}$ = 1.29, P <0.30, and years, $F_{1,124}$ = 0.22, P <0.70). Fewer large lambs were taken to nests in 2000 because fewer lambs were taken in June, July and August (Figure 36.3). The three largest lambs were taken in late June or early July and were an estimated seven to eight weeks of age and 15-18 kg in weight. Eagles would have had difficulty in carrying intact lambs of this weight (Watson, 1997) so they may have been dismembered prior to delivery to the nest.

Taking season into account, there were marginal differences in hind foot length between lambs showing evidence of having been scavenged (mean $\pm$se = 162.5 $\pm$4.6 mm), those with evidence of predation (166.3 $\pm$5.9 mm) and those remaining undiagnosed (172.0 $\pm$ 4.4 mm)

Table 36.2. Average sizes of lambs from white-tailed eagle nests on Mull.

Year	Nest	Number of lambs	Mean hindfoot length (mm)	Standard deviation	Range
1999	A	45	185.0	26.1	137-242
	B	20	172.3	21.0	138-214
	C	4	160.2	6.9	151-166
	D	3	166.6	5.8	162-173
	E	3	168.0	31.1	136-199
2000	A	31	173.6	26.7	107-238
	C	1	134.7	-	-
	D	8	154.5	11.9	141-170
	E	9	156.3	16.4	126-179
	F	1	123.5	-	-

Comparing variation within and between nests, $F_{5,124}$ = 3.98, P <0.005, and years, $F_{1,124}$ = 5.60, P <0.05.

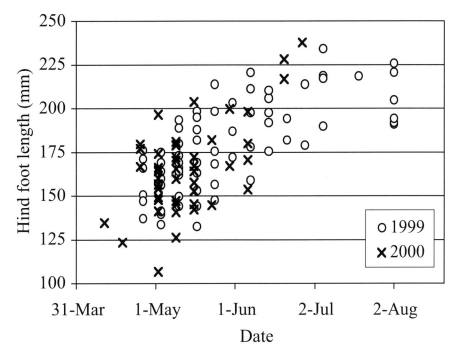

Figure 36.3. The seasonal trend in size of 124 lambs recovered from white-tailed eagle nests.

($F_{2, 114}$ = 2.92, P <0.06). The quoted mean values are those adjusted to May 25th (using a General Linear Model Analysis of Variance; see section 36.2), the midpoint of lamb deliveries.

36.4 Discussion

White-tailed eagles in Scotland are generalist predators, taking a large variety of foods, and only a few consume lambs in numbers. Nevertheless, there is now evidence that the perceptions of some Mull farmers are well founded. Some pairs of white-tailed eagles do consume many lambs, some of which are killed by the eagles. However, the majority of white-tailed eagles do not kill many lambs. We have examined the successful nests of eleven pairs (what was, during the study, just over half of the Scottish population) and only four pairs took more than ten lambs. Intensive nest visits on Mull endorsed these results; one pair (E) took few lambs, another two (A and B) consumed many. Of these two pairs, B predominantly scavenged lambs in 1999, whereas A mainly killed them. In 2000, pair A killed far fewer than in the previous year and the seasonal pattern of lamb deliveries was similar to that of pair B in 1999. Most lambs are taken in May, when they are small, and most are scavenged, associated with the high lamb mortality then (Houston, 1977; Hewson, 1984). It seemed that pair A maintained a high delivery rate of lambs to the nest in 1999 by killing more.

The main difference between the two years was that pair A nested in the centre of a hill lambing area in 1999, but on the nearby coast in 2000. The food remains at the nest differed in 2000 when coastal items and large numbers of rabbit replaced lamb as the main food in July and August. In 1999, rabbits were reputed to be locally scarce due to disease, and this reduction could have resulted in the higher predation of lambs that year. Rabbits are smaller than lambs and may be easier to kill and transport. However, the proximity of the nest to lambs does not necessarily result in eagles killing them. For example, pair E consumed few lambs in both 1998 and 2000 despite being close to areas of intensive lamb birth and rearing. Although this pair nested well inland, the adults frequently flew over lambing areas to take seabirds on the coast 15 km distant.

If we assume that our sample of diagnosed lambs (i.e. killed or scavenged) was typical of all those taken on Mull, we can calculate a figure for the numbers killed by white-tailed eagles. Pair B in 1999 took 20 lambs to the nest but only killed 9%, i.e. one or two. Similarly, we calculate that pair A killed about 28 lambs in 1999, but only six or seven in 2000. Pair E only took one lamb in 1998 and ten in 2000, so it cannot have killed many. Even if we consider the worst case, i.e. that another two pairs of eagles on Mull killed as many lambs as did pair A, and more were taken by subadults and adults away from the nest, the numbers of lambs killed annually on the island amounted to 'tens'. By comparison, the annual losses of hill lambs to all sources of mortality involve 'thousands' (Mather, 1978). During each year of the study, there were over 20,000 breeding ewes on Mull, and total lamb losses from birth to June were in excess of 13 per 100 breeding ewes (Marquiss *et al.* 2003). Thus the loss of lambs attributable to eagles is small on a landscape scale. However, this does not preclude a significant impact on the economy of specific farms if lamb killing is concentrated in localised areas and killed lambs would have otherwise survived. Future studies will therefore attempt to estimate the diet of more pairs of eagles in further years and determine the area within which specific eagle(s) kill lambs.

We cannot be sure that the lambs killed by eagles would otherwise have survived. There is evidence that other predators, such as foxes and corvids, tend to take weak individuals, many of which would have died shortly afterwards anyway (Houston, 1977; Hewson, 1984, 1990). We therefore need to quantify lamb losses close to pair A in contrast to lamb losses elsewhere. Finally, we need information on factors which might predispose lambs to eagle predation: only some lambs are killed, and many are apparently ignored, so we need to compare the circumstances of lambs taken with those 'available', alive and dead.

Acknowledgements
Studies of eagle diet were funded by Scottish Natural Heritage, and of lamb mortality were funded by the Scottish Executive Environment and Rural Affairs Department. We are grateful to the landowners and farming tenants of Mull for their co-operation and support for the study. We thank Richard Evans, Fiona Harmer, Justin Grant, Rob Forrest, Alison McLennan, Martin Carty, Steven MacDonald, Viv de Fresnes, David Miller, Colin Crooke, Andrew Stevenson, John Love, Gwen Evans and Brian Etheridge for assistance in collecting samples. Alan Poole (Forest Enterprise), Roger Broad and Colin Crooke (Royal Society for the Protection of Birds) provided invaluable assistance. Peter Rothery (CEH, Monkswood) devised the 'observation randomisation test' statistical program. Andrew Douse and Philip Whitfield (Scottish Natural Heritage), Toby Willison (Scottish Executive Environment and Rural Affairs Department), David Houston (Glasgow University) and an anonymous referee commented on earlier drafts of this chapter.

References

Brown, D. & Rothery, P. (1993). *Models in Biology: Mathematics, Statistics and Computing.* Wiley, New York.

Eadie, J. (1970). Sheep production and pastoral resources. In *Animal Populations in Relation to their Food Resources, British Ecological Symposium Number 10*, ed. by A. Watson. Blackwell Scientific. Oxford. pp. 7-24.

Gunn, R.G. & Robinson, J.F. (1963). Lamb mortality in Scottish hill flocks. *Animal Production*, **5**, 67-76.

Hewson, R. (1984). Scavenging and predation upon sheep and lambs in West Scotland. *Journal of Applied Ecology*, **21**, 843-868.

Hewson, R. (1990). *Predation Upon Lambs by Foxes in the Absence of Control.* League Against Cruel Sports. London.

Hewson, R. & Verkaik, A.J. (1981). Body condition and ranging behaviour of blackface hill sheep in relation to lamb survival. *Journal of Applied Ecology*, **18**, 401-415.

Hewson, R. & Wilson, C.J. (1979). Home range and movements of Scottish Blackface sheep in Lochaber, North-west Scotland. *Journal of Applied Ecology*, **16**, 743-751.

Houston, D. (1977). The effect of hooded crows on hill sheep farming in Argyll, Scotland. *Journal of Applied Ecology*, **14**, 17-29.

Mather, A.S. (1978). The alleged deterioration in hill grazings in the Scottish Highlands. *Biological Conservation*, **14**, 181-195.

Marquiss, M., Madders, M., Irvine, J. & Carss, D.N. (2003). *The Impact of White-tailed Eagles on Sheep Farming on Mull.* Final Report to Scottish Executive Environment and Rural Affairs Department on Contract No. ITE/004/99. http://www.scotland.gov.uk/publications.

Mersmann, T.J., Buehler, D.A., Fraser, J.D. & Seegar, J.K.D. (1992). Assessing bias in studies of bald eagle food habits. *Journal of Wildlife Management*, **56**, 73-78.

Minitab (2000). *Release 13.2 for Windows.* Minitab Inc., PA. USA.

Rowley, I. (1970). Lamb predation in Australia: incidence, predisposing conditions, and the identification of wounds. *CSIRO Wildlife Research*, **15**, 79-123.

Watson, J. (1997). *The Golden Eagle.* T. & A.D. Poyser, London.

Whitfield, D.P., McLeod, D.R.A., Fielding, A.H., Broad, R.A., Evans, R.J. & Haworth, P.F. (2001). The effects of forestry on golden eagles on the island of Mull, western Scotland. *Journal of Applied Ecology*, **38**, 1208-1220.

Wille, F. & Kampp, K. (1983). Food of the white-tailed eagle *Haliaeetus albicilla* in Greenland. *Holarctic Ecology*, **6**, 81-88.

37. RAPTOR PERSECUTION IN ENGLAND AT THE END OF THE TWENTIETH CENTURY

John Holmes, Ian Carter, Malcolm Stott, Julian Hughes,
Peter Davies & David Walker

Summary

1.   Most raptor populations in England are recovering from past persecution and other adverse factors. However, several species are either absent or occur at lower than expected densities in some, seemingly suitable, parts of the country.

2.   This chapter reports on information collected on persecution incidents during the 1990s and includes the use of a simple persecution index in order to help assess the likely impact of persecution on raptor populations in England.

3.   Illegal persecution remains a serious problem for several raptors in England. The hen harrier *Circus cyaneus* is on the verge of extinction as a breeding bird, and the red kite *Milvus milvus*, buzzard *Buteo buteo* and marsh harrier *Circus aeruginosus*, are among the species whose population recoveries are being hampered.

37.1 Introduction

In general, levels of raptor persecution are thought to have declined during recent decades in response to changing attitudes, the introduction of effective legal methods of pest control and stronger legislation. However, despite the welcome increase in most raptor populations during the last few decades, there is a perception that persecution remains a significant problem for certain species and in certain parts of the country. In order to quantify the current impact of persecution on raptor populations in England, in part to inform the work of the UK Raptor Working Group (Anon., 2000), a desk study was undertaken in 1999 and 2000.

Information on the persecution of all raptor species was sought from questionnaires to Raptor Study Groups and through an analysis of the RSPB's Investigations Database. Because persecution incidents are often difficult to interpret (for example, where nest contents are destroyed and the evidence removed) incidents reports were included in the analysis only if there was clear evidence of illegal persecution (Holmes *et al.,* 2000). The study focussed on direct persecution through killing adult birds or the destruction of nest contents: it did not consider egg or chick thefts for collections, or falconry, which are reported elsewhere (e.g. RSPB, 2000).

37.2 The impact of persecution

In order to compare the relative impact of persecution on species with differing population sizes, a simple 'persecution index' was calculated for each species as the total number of persecution incidents in 1990-99 as a percentage of the population estimate for England

(Table 37.1). Hence, ten incidents reported for a species estimated to have a population of 100 pairs gives an index of 10. The inclusion of a small number of incidents involving non-breeding/passage birds from populations outside of England is not thought to have altered the results unduly. Hen harrier *Circus cyaneus*, Montagu's harrier *Circus pygargus*, red kite *Milvus milvus*, peregrine *Falco peregrinus*, goshawk *Accipiter gentilis* and marsh harrier *Circus aeruginosus* are the six species with the highest persecution indices.

Table 37.1. The illegal persecution of diurnal raptors in England, based on confirmed persecution incidents 1990-1999 (based on Holmes *et al.*, 2000).

Species	*England*		*No. poisoned*	*No. Shot*	*No. trapped*	*Persecution index*[2]
	Year	*Population*[1]				
Hen harrier	1998	19 f	4	9	0	68.4
Montagu's harrier	1999	4-11 p	0	2	0	18.0–50.0
Red kite[3]	2000	131 p	20	4	0	18.3
Peregrine	1991	283 p	9	21	1	11.0
Goshawk	1996	120 p	0	7	5	10.0
Marsh harrier	1995	153 f	2	5	0	4.6
Buzzard	1988-91	4-6,000 p	34	50	10	1.6-2.4
Merlin	1993-94	401 p	0	3	0	0.7
Sparrowhawk	1988-91	22,000 p	3	34	5	0.2
Hobby	1988-91	500-900 p	0	1	0	0.1-0.2
Kestrel	1988-91	35,500 p	4	22	6	0.1
Honey buzzard	1997	12-32 p	0	0	0	0.0

[1] p = breeding pairs: f = breeding females; see Holmes *et al.* (2000) for main sources. Scientific names of species not mentioned in text: merlin *Falco columbarius*, sparrowhawk *Accipiter nisus*, hobby *F. subbuteo*, kestrel *F. tinnunculus*, honey buzzard *Pernis apirorus*.

[2] Persecution index calculated as total number of persecution incidents in 1990-99 as a percentage of the population estimate for England.

[3] Figures for red kite are for 1989-2000.

37.2.1 Hen harrier

The hen harrier's high persecution index reflects the fact that it is being suppressed at an artificially low population size in England, as a direct result of persecution. Although Potts (1998) estimated that there is sufficient habitat for over 230 territorial females in England, only 19 territorial females were found during a national survey in 1998 (Sim *et al.*, 2001). Table 37.2 compares the breeding productivity of hen harriers on a) moors managed with nature conservation as a major objective, with b) moors managed primarily for commercial grouse shooting during the period 1994-2000. Summing the results for all years, 72% of nesting attempts on nature conservation moors were successful whereas only 40% of nesting attempts on commercial grouse moors were successful. These results are similar to those of Etheridge *et al.* (1997) and Summers *et al.* (Chapter 38) for Scotland and suggest that, in England too, game rearing interests are associated with much illegal persecution.

Table 37.2.   Success of female hen harriers breeding on moorland in England, 1994-2000 (updated from Holmes *et al.*, 2000).

Year	Moorland managed for nature conservation (128 km²)			Commercial grouse moors (1767 km²)		
	Territorial females	Nesting attempts[1]	Successful nests[2] (%)	Territorial females	Nesting attempts[1]	Successful nests[2] (%)
1994	10	5	5 (100)	27	12	9 (75)
1995	4	4	4 (100)	26	19	8 (42)
1996	5	5	4 (80)	30	18	8 (44)
1997	11	11	8 (73)	15	11	3 (27)
1998	9	9	7 (78)	6	3	0
1999	14	14	9 (64)	7	4	0
2000	10	10	5 (50)	6	3	0

[1] At least one egg laid

[2] At least one young fledged

37.2.2 Red kite

Species that are increasing in numbers and range may still suffer adverse effects from illegal persecution. Following extinction, due to widespread persecution, the red kite is now recovering in England as a result of an ongoing re-introduction project (Carter & Grice, 2000; Carter *et al.*, Chapter 31). The population has increased rapidly since the project started in 1989 to an estimated 131 breeding pairs in 2000 (Wotton *et al.*, 2002). Despite this success, the red kite currently occupies a tiny fraction of the suitable available countryside in England and is expanding its range only very slowly. Persecution is the main cause of death for red kites in England and, in the period up to 2000, a total of 20 birds was found to have been killed by illegal poisoning (Table 37.1). Estimates based on detailed population studies have shown that only about one in five dead birds is recovered for post mortem, suggesting that as many as 100 birds may actually have been killed by illegal poisoning in the same period (see Holmes *et al.*, 2000 and Carter *et al.*, Chapter 31 for more details). Losses on this scale are undoubtedly slowing the rate of population expansion as well as the potential for recolonisation of currently unoccupied habitat, thus reducing the effectiveness of the re-introduction programme.

37.2.3 Other raptors

Even species with low persecution indices, for example the buzzard, encounter problems due to illegal persecution; indeed, its persecution has been cited as a factor preventing more rapid population recoveries (Elliot & Avery, 1991; Holling, Chapter 12). Buzzards Buteo buteo are still absent, or present at low density, in large areas of suitable countryside in central and eastern areas despite population increases in western England. It has also been suggested that persecution is the most likely reason for the very low numbers of golden eagle *Aquila chrysaetos* in England (e.g. Thompson *et al.*, 1995). Poison baits are regularly used in northern England (Holmes *et al.*, 2000) and work in Scotland showed that golden eagles are vulnerable to this form of illegal persecution (Watson, 1997; Moorland Working Group, 2002). Of the species with a high persecution index not yet discussed, it is likely that persecution is greatly limiting population size and range for the goshawk (see Marquiss *et al.*, Chapter 9), is restricting peregrine numbers in at least parts of its range (see Hardey *et al.*, Chapter 5) and is slowing the rate of population increase and recolonisation in the marsh harrier (see Holmes *et al.*, 2000 for more details). Montagu's harrier has a high persecution index but this is based on only two confirmed incidents during the 1990s. This species has a very small English population and the number of breeding pairs fluctuates unpredictably from year to year, making a realistic assessment of the impact of persecution very difficult.

37.3 Conclusion

Raptors are generally considered to be doing well in the UK, with many species recovering from past heavy persecution and the effects of organochlorine pesticides in the 1950s and 1960s. However, the situation varies geographically, and although the persecution index used here is a crude measure of impacts on raptor populations, it is clear that persecution remains a serious problem for several species. The hen harrier is on the verge of extinction in England and several other species are either absent or occur at lower than expected densities across large areas of suitable countryside.

Those responsible for killing birds of prey are aware that they are acting illegally and are therefore likely to conceal the results of their activities. Proven incidents therefore represent only a small proportion of the actual total. It is clear, for example, that in order to hold the hen harrier population at such an artificially low level, persecution incidents must be far more frequent than indicated in Table 37.1. The comparison between breeding productivity on different types of moors (Table 37.2) emphasizes the hidden nature of much persecution and gives an indication of the motives of some of those responsible (see also Summers *et al.*, Chapter 38).

The same problem of under-reporting of persecution is apparent with the peregrine. There are 31 confirmed incidents of peregrine persecution in Table 37.1, yet Raptor Study Groups identified more than 300 incidents during the same period where persecution was 'suspected but not confirmed' by subsequent investigations (see also Pickford, 2002). Incidents involving the destruction of nest contents or even nest sites in species which often breed in remote areas with little public access are particularly difficult to confirm, and this should be taken into account when comparing the persecution indices of different species.

Acknowledgements

The authors wish to thank the many individuals and groups that supplied information on persecution incidents in England. Graham Elliot and Keith Morton helped to analyze information from the RSPB's Investigations database. Phil Whitfield provided detailed comments on an earlier draft and we are grateful to him and an anonymous referee.

References

Anonymous (2000). *Report of the UK Raptor Working Group.* Department of the Environment, Transport and the Regions and Joint Nature Conservation Committee, Peterborough.

Carter, I. & Grice, P. (2000). Studies of re-established red kites in England. *British Birds,* **93**, 304-322.

Elliot, G.D. & Avery, M.I. (1991). A review of reports of buzzard persecutions 1975-1989. *Bird Study,* **38**, 52-56.

Etheridge, B., Summers, R.W. & Green, R.E. (1997). The effects of illegal killing and destruction of nests by humans on the population dynamics of the hen harrier (*Circus cyaneus*) in Scotland. *Journal of Applied Ecology,* **34**, 1081-1105.

Holmes, J., Walker, D., Davies, P. & Carter, I. (2000). *The illegal persecution of raptors in England.* English Nature Research Report No. 343. English Nature, Peterborough.

Moorland Working Group (2002). *Scotland's moorland: the nature of change.* Scottish Natural Heritage, Perth.

Pickford, T. (2002). To the brink of extinction. *Bird Watching,* **March**, 6-12.

Potts, G.R. (1998). Global dispersion of nesting hen harriers (*Circus cyaneus*); implications for grouse moors in the UK. *Ibis,* **140**, 76-88.

RSPB (2000). *Birdcrime '99.* RSPB, Sandy.

Sim, I.M.W., Gibbons, D.W., Bainbridge, I.P. & Mattingley, W.A. (2001). Status of the hen harrier (*Circus cyaneus*) in the UK and the Isle of Man in 1998. *Bird Study,* **48**, 341-353.

Thompson, D.B.A., MacDonald, A.J., Marsden., J.H. & Galbraith, C.A. (1995). Upland heather moorland in Great Britain: a review of international importance, vegetation change and some objectives for nature conservation. *Biological Conservation.,* **71**, 163-178.

Watson, J. (1997). *The Golden Eagle.* Poyser, London.

Wotton, S.R., Carter, I., Cross, A.V., Etheridge, B., Snell, N., Duffy, K., Thorpe, R. & Gregory, R.D. (2002). Breeding status of the red kite *Milvus milvus* in Britain in 2000. *Bird Study,* **49**, 278-286.

38. CHANGES IN HEN HARRIER (*CIRCUS CYANEUS*) NUMBERS IN RELATION TO GROUSE MOOR MANAGEMENT

R.W. Summers, R.E. Green, B. Etheridge & I.M.W. Sim

Summary

1.   The hen harrier *Circus cyaneus* is one of Britain's rarer birds of prey, and one of the most persecuted because it comes into conflict with managers of red grouse *Lagopus lagopus scoticus* sporting estates.   As a result, there is concern amongst conservationists about the status of this species.

2.   Surveys of breeding hen harriers on the Scottish mainland provided maximum estimates of 523 breeding pairs in 1988-89 and 517 in 1998. Although there was no change in population size, numbers increased on grouse moors and decreased in young conifer plantations between 1988-89 and 1998, so that 55% of the population is now found on grouse moors compared with 26% in 1988-89. The decline in use of plantations coincides with the reduced availability of young conifers.

3.   Our understanding of the population dynamics (breeding productivity, natal dispersal and female survival) of hen harriers shows that grouse moors are a 'sink' habitat, whilst productivity on other moorlands is sufficient to offset losses in this habitat.

4.   Combining data across habitats, a 6% decline per annum (95% confidence limits, 25% decline to 12% increase) was predicted under the current level of human persecution, but a 13% increase per annum (95% CLs, 11% decline to 36% increase) is predicted if persecution stops.   However, with no change in the population size between 1988-89 and 1998, and wide confidence limits in the predictions for population change, it is not possible to say that levels of persecution have changed or remained the same.

5.   Given that relatively more hen harriers now breed on grouse moors, it is possible that the hen harrier population is currently under greater threat from persecution than it was 10 years ago.

38.1 Introduction

The hen harrier *Circus cyaneus* is a medium-sized bird of prey. It is sexually dimorphic with respect to colour (the males are grey and females brown) and size (the males are smaller than the females). The size dimorphism has implications for the diet of these birds; males feed on smaller prey like songbirds, whilst the females feed on larger prey; for example, rabbits *Oryctolagus cuniculus* (Cramp & Simmons, 1980). In Britain, hen harriers breed largely in the Scottish Highlands on moorland between 200 and 600 m above sea level. This is an artificial habitat created from Neolithic times to the present day by the felling of the woodland of Scots pine *Pinus sylvestris* and birch *Betula* spp. which once grew in this part of Scotland (Bennett, 1988; Thompson *et al.*, 1995; Smout, 1997). Now, the treeless landscape is maintained by grazing and burning. Grazing is largely by sheep *Ovis aries*, of which there are approximately eight million in Scotland (Fuller & Gough, 1999), and at least 350,000 red deer *Cervus elaphus* (Deer Commission for Scotland, 2000). The burning of moorland (muirburn) is carried out in order to encourage the growth of young heather *Calluna vulgaris* for the benefit of red grouse *Lagopus lagopus,* shot for sport on Highland estates (e.g. Scotland's Moorland Forum, 2003). On these grouse moors, the hen harrier comes into conflict with the sporting estates because it is perceived to be a threat by gamekeepers to the viability of red grouse stocks (e.g. Redpath, 1991; Redpath & Thirgood, 1997; Anon., 2000; Moorland Working Group, 2002; Galbraith *et al.*, Chapter 41).

The hen harrier was once widespread throughout Britain but persecuted during the 19th and 20th centuries, reaching its most restricted range during the 1930s when it occurred only on the Western Isles and Orkney (Watson, 1977). With the relaxation of persecution as the number of gamekeepers in Scotland declined (Hudson, 1992), the hen harrier spread back onto mainland Scotland. The British population increased, and by the mid-1970s it was estimated to be at least 500 pairs, with a further 250-300 pairs in Ireland (Watson, 1977). However, despite this increase there was still concern that the hen harrier's range was not as complete as it should be and that numbers were being limited by persecution on many grouse moors (Thom, 1986). In order to provide a more accurate estimate of population size and distribution in Scotland, a survey was undertaken in 1988-89 (Bibby & Etheridge, 1993). This was followed up ten years later with a repeat survey (Sim *et al.*, 2001) as part of the long-term monitoring of Britain's red-listed birds (Gregory *et al.*, 2002). In the intervening years, a study was carried out on the population dynamics on mainland Scotland, examining productivity, natal dispersal and survival of full-grown harriers (Etheridge *et al.*, 1997). Thus, the two surveys provide information on the patterns of distribution and numbers, whilst the study of their population dynamics helps us to understand the processes that operate to determine these patterns.

This chapter examines changes in harrier numbers and distribution, and aspects of their population ecology. We focus only on the hen harriers breeding on mainland Scotland, where comparative data exist and where 70% of the British population breeds.

38.2 Methods

38.2.1 Survey designs

In 1988-89, a population estimate of the breeding hen harriers on mainland Scotland was obtained by surveying a random sample of 10 km squares from all of the suitable 10 km squares within Scotland, as judged from the map in the 1968-72 *Atlas of Breeding Birds in Britain and Ireland* (Sharrock, 1976). A stratified sampling system was devised, with the sampling intensity being higher across those squares with probable and confirmed breeding (25% coverage), and a lower intensity for possible (10%) and no breeding (5%) (Bibby & Etheridge, 1993). In addition, many squares which were not part of the formal sample were also checked, largely by experienced amateur raptor workers.

As in the 1988-89 survey, the recording unit in the 1998 survey was the 10 km square. The range of the hen harrier was defined as all squares with records of hen harriers in the breeding season since 1968, using primarily the Atlas studies (Sharrock, 1976; Gibbons *et al.*, 1993). These squares were split into two categories; 1) 10 km squares regularly watched by experienced raptor fieldworkers and which were known to hold breeding harriers, and 2) 10 km squares chosen at random from all of the remaining squares in Scotland with records of hen harriers. The latter comprised 373 squares, from which 57 random squares were selected, thus providing a sampling intensity of 15.3%. (Sim *et al.,* 2001).

38.2.2 Fieldwork methods

The fieldwork methods were the same in the two surveys in order to ensure comparability between the two surveys. Observers were asked to make a minimum of two visits to all suitable habitat below 600 m above sea level in the 10 km squares between early April and early June Suitable habitat was defined as moorland, both heather-dominated and grass-dominated, and upland young (pre-canopy closure) conifer plantation. Observers were required to use a combination of walking over and scanning suitable habitat in order to observe harriers. Where visibility was restricted, observers were advised to pass within 250 m of any point in the sample square. Records of hen harriers were classified as either 'proved', 'probable' or 'possible' breeding, following the criteria used in the 1968-72 *Breeding Bird Atlas* (Sharrock, 1976).

Mainland Scotland was split into the following regions: North Highlands - Highland Region except Nairn District, Morvern and Ardnamurchan; East Highlands - Grampian, Tayside and Fife Regions, and Nairn District of Highland Region; West Highlands - Central Region and Strathclyde north and west of the Firth of Clyde and including the Morvern and Ardnamurchan areas of Highland Region; Southern Uplands - all mainland south of the central lowlands.

Four habitats or land management classes (LMCs) were defined: grouse moor, other heather moor, young conifer plantation and grass moor (Etheridge *et al.,* 1997). Young conifer plantation was the most dynamic habitat in terms of distribution and age structure of trees. In order to assess the amount of this habitat available to hen harriers during the two surveys, the area of new conifer plantings in Scotland between 1973 and 1997 was obtained from the Forestry Commission. This allowed an estimate to be made of the cumulative area of conifers planted over the previous ten years for each year, from 1988 to 1997 (Sim *et al.,* 2001). This time period was chosen because the suitability of conifers for hen harriers is thought to last for about ten years from planting (Watson, 1977; Madders, 1997). These data provided the maximum area of new conifer plantations available, since an unknown proportion will have been unsuitable for nesting hen harriers.

38.2.3 Calculation of population estimates

The survey count units were expressed as pairs (i.e. a breeding female and male), even though polygyny occurs (e.g. Watson, 1977; Balfour & Cadbury, 1979; Amar *et al.,* Chapter 29). Population estimates were made by adding the number of pairs counted in census squares (i.e. those special squares surveyed by raptor workers) to the extrapolated estimates from the rest of the range. These extrapolated estimates were made by multiplying the mean number of pairs found in the random squares by the total number of squares from which the random sample was taken. Estimates for regions and land management classes were made using only those squares relevant to them. Confidence intervals were estimated by boot-strapping (Efron, 1982). The method used to test for significant changes in numbers between the two surveys is given in Sim *et al.* (2001).

Two population estimates were obtained, based on the criteria for breeding. The figure given as the minimum population size was the number of proven breeding pairs plus probable breeding pairs, and the maximum population size was the sum of the proven, probable and possible pairs.

Although it is possible that some pairs that failed early in the breeding attempt, either naturally or through persecution, may have gone unrecorded, the evidence suggests that the possible effect on the population estimate was low. It was possible that many of the apparently single birds (possible breeders) did not refer to breeding pairs, especially in areas that were well covered. However, the proportion of non-breeders is difficult to measure because they are likely to be more mobile than breeding birds, moving between areas and exploiting temporarily abundant food sources (Newton, 1979; Greenwood *et al.*, Chapter 2).

38.2 4 Population dynamics

During the period 1988-1995, 1,459 nests were located. Nest visits were made to determine egg volume, clutch and brood sizes, and to determine whether the nest was successful. From the number of 'exposure' days, Mayfield estimates were made for the percentage of successful nests (Mayfield, 1975).

When chicks were three to four weeks old, they were sexed and fitted with unique permutations of coloured and lettered patagial wing tags, so that subsequent sightings could be made when they returned as breeding adults. Such sightings provided information on natal dispersal and estimates of survival (Clobert *et al.*, 1985; Etheridge *et al.*, 1997). There were insufficient data from males, so estimates of survival were based solely on females, of which 592 were tagged.

Breeding males were classified as either first year (with brown plumage) or adult (grey and white plumage) (Cramp & Simmons, 1980), providing an index of the age composition of the breeding population. First year and adult females have similar plumages (brown) so could not be distinguished.

Population multiplication rates (PMRs) refer to the factor by which a population changes annually, and were calculated only for females; there were insufficient data for males. PMRs were derived from the product of the proportion of fledglings that were female, the mean annual productivity and survival of females in their first year, added to the annual survival of breeding females (Etheridge *et al.*, 1997).

38.3 Results

38.3.1 Population estimates for 1988-89 and 1998

Summaries of the population estimates are given in Table 38.1. The estimates for minimum and maximum breeding pairs were very similar for the two surveys, and there were no significant changes. In both surveys, a high percentage of the estimated breeding population was actually seen by observers. In 1998, 310 pairs were located, being 77% of the minimum population estimate. In 1988-89, 389 pairs were located, being 95% of the minimum estimate. These high values are a result of many of the main areas being known and surveyed by the raptor workers.

Regional estimates of harrier numbers for Scotland are given in Table 38.1. In 1988-89, most hen harriers occurred in the West Highlands (148 pairs), with smaller numbers in the East Highlands (109), North Highlands (85) and Southern Uplands (80). In 1998, the West

Table 38.1. The size of the breeding population (number of pairs) of hen harriers on mainland Scotland during the two surveys. The 95% confidence limits are in brackets. The regional splits refer to minimum estimates whereas the splits for the different land management classes (LMCs) refer to maximum estimates. Data from Bibby & Etheridge (1993) and Sim *et al.* (2001).

	1988-89		1998		P*
Total pairs (maximum)	523	(369-689)	517	(440-613)	-
Total pairs (minimum)	408	(279-551)	402	(331-472)	0.67
Region					
North Highlands	85	(21-165)	30	(13-53)	0.10
East Highlands	109	(61-158)	82	(64-99)	0.15
West Highlands	148	(73-236)	159	(107-218)	0.64
Southern Uplands	80	(20-152)	117	(97-153)	0.17
North and East Scotland	194	(108-290)	113	(88-140)	0.05
South and West Scotland	228	(124-336)	276	(217-344)	0.23
LMC					
Grouse moors	140	(69-220)	286	(222-366)	0.002
Other moorland	202	(109-303)	148	(107-195)	0.16
Conifer plantations	177	(97-265)	54	(30-86)	0.006
Grass moors	10	(1-30)	29	(5-61)	0.14

* Sim *et al.* (2001) provide details of the test between the two periods.

Highlands and Southern Uplands held the highest numbers, with an estimated 159 and 117 pairs, respectively. The East Highlands held 82 pairs, and a smaller number was found in the North Highlands (30). There were no significant differences in the number of pairs between the two surveys for any of the individual Scottish regions. However, when the two northern regions were combined, there was a significant decline in the North and East Highlands, but no significant difference in the Southern Uplands and West Highlands combined (the two southern regions), between 1988-89 and 1998 (Table 38.1). In 1988-89, 54% of the population was in Southern Uplands plus West Highlands, and 46% in the North plus East Highlands. In 1998, however, the Southern Uplands plus West Highlands held 71%, but the North plus East Highlands held only 29% of the total Scottish mainland population.

38.3.2 Numbers found in different land management classes

The total number of birds found in different LMCs in 1988-89 and 1998 are shown in Table 38.1. In both surveys, the vast majority occurred on three LMCs: grouse moors, other heather moors, and young conifer plantations (98% in 1988-89 and 94% in 1998); very few harriers occurred on grass moors. There was a significant increase in the number on grouse moors, and a significant decrease in young plantations, between 1988-89 and 1998. There was no significant change in the numbers on either other heather moors or grass moors.

It is likely that the decrease in the number of hen harriers breeding in young plantations can be partly explained by the decrease in the area of young plantations (Figure 38.1).

There were no records of birds from second-rotation forestry in 1998, suggesting that they favour young plantation only at the first planting.

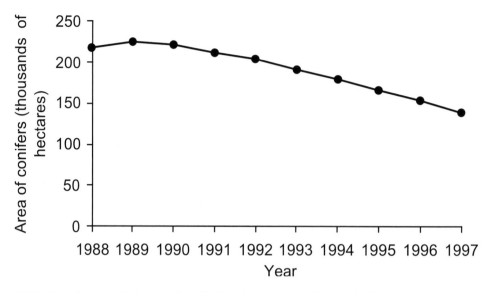

Figure 38.1. Annual changes in the area of conifers less than ten years old in Scotland.

38.3.3 Population dynamics

a) Breeding productivity

Clutch and brood sizes were found to vary according to LMC, with largest clutches and broods found on grouse moors (Table 38.2). Further, the egg volumes on the moorland habitats were higher than in plantations (Table 38.2). Clearly, the heather moorland habitats and in particular grouse moor, are well suited to hen harriers.

In contrast, nest success was lowest on grouse moors and highest on other moorland. The difference in nest success between the different LMCs was attributed to the amount of human interference experienced at nests on grouse moors; a minimum of 30% of failed nests on grouse moors had signs of human interference, compared with 7% for other moorland and 11% in conifer plantations (Etheridge *et al.*, 1997).

Hen harriers may relay after failure of the initial nest. It was assumed that the late nesting was due to relays, so the skewed distribution of laying dates allowed estimates of the percentage relaying. The combination of brood size at fledging, nest success and percentage relaying allowed estimation of the overall productivity. The figures for the different land management classes were: 0.84 fledglings per breeding female per year on grouse moors, 2.39 on other moorland and 1.41 in young plantations (Table 38.2) (Etheridge *et al.*, 1997).

b) Survival

Estimates of survival were derived only for females, and primarily for the moorland habitats. The return rates of first year birds was thought to be independent of land management class, so a common figure of 36% was derived for this age group. Thereafter, when females entered the breeding population, those nesting on grouse

Table 38.2. Productivity and survival of hen harriers breeding in different land management classes on mainland Scotland. SEs are in brackets. Data from Etheridge *et al.* (1997).

	Grouse moors		Other moorlands		Conifer plantations		P*
Clutch size (n = 600)	5.41	(0.06)	4.90	(0.06)	4.81	(0.11)	<0.001
Egg volume (length x breadth²) (n= 139)	57.80	(0.66)	58.40	(0.67)	54.80	(1.35)	<0.05
Brood size (n = 845)	3.34	(0.08)	3.18	(0.06)	3.03	(0.08)	<0.001
Proportion of clutches that hatched	0.34	(0.03)	0.71	(0.03)	0.51	(0.07)	<0.001
Proportion of broods that fledged	0.58	(0.04)	0.85	(0.04)	0.81	(0.02)	<0.001
Proportion of successful attempts	0.20	(0.02)	0.60	(0.03)	0.41	(0.05)	<0.001
Number of fledglings per attempt	0.66	(0.08)	1.91	(0.10)	1.24	(0.16)	<0.001
Attempts per female per year	1.28	(0.09)	1.25	(0.05)	1.13	(0.10)	n.s.
Fledglings per female per year	0.84	(0.12)	2.39	(0.19)	1.41	(0.18)	<0.001
First year female survival	0.36		0.36				-
Adult female survival	0.40		0.78				<0.02

* Etheridge *et al.* (1997) provide details of the statistical testing.

moors had half the survival rate of females nesting on other moorland (Table 38.2). We inspected the survival of females according to the outcome of their nests, and found that if a nest was unsuccessful on a grouse moor, the survival of the breeding female was extremely low (14.6%). If the nest was successful, on the other hand, the survival of the female was as high as on other moorland, where there was no difference in the survival of females according to nest success. We conclude that nests and breeding females were being persecuted together (also Etheridge *et al.,* 1997).

c) Natal dispersal

Natal dispersal was found to vary markedly between LMCs. Almost all birds hatched on grouse moors settled to breed there, and a disproportionately high percentage of birds hatched on other moorland and in plantations settled on grouse moors (Table 38.3).

Table 38.3. Estimated percentages of birds which fledged from a given land management class (LMC) and either settled in the same LMC or moved to another LMC to breed for the first time. The percentages have been adjusted to account for uneven sampling of the three LMCs. Data from Etheridge *et al.* (1997).

Natal LMC		LMC of first breeding		
	Sex	Grouse moors	Other moorlands	Conifer plantations
Grouse moors	Male (n = 9)	100	0	0
	Female (n = 45)	89	5	6
Other moorlands	Male (n = 10)	32	44	24
	Female (n = 49)	35	26	39
Conifer plantations	Male (n = 2)	48	52	0
	Female (n = 18)	38	17	46

Clearly, grouse moors were preferentially selected by hen harriers.

First year males do not attain their grey adult plumage until their second year when most start to breed for the first time. However, some do breed as one year old birds when in brown plumage. We found that during 1991-95 the percentage of the male population that was brown was highest on grouse moors (5.6 %), but very low on other moorland (0.6%) and plantations (1.0%) (Etheridge *et al.*, 1997). A very similar pattern was found during the 1998 survey: the percentage of brown males was significantly higher on grouse moors (8.1%) than on other heather moors (0.4%), young plantations (2.7%) and grass moors (2.3%) (Sim *et al.*, 2001). Thus, the situation on grouse moors is symptomatic of one where birds are being attracted to a preferred habitat where the population is being continually depleted.

d) Population multiplication rates (PMRs)

PMRs were calculated only for females. It was assumed that all females breed for the first time at one year old. PMRs were estimated for each LMC, assuming that the birds breeding on them were in closed populations. PMRs varied from 0.54 for grouse moors to 1.19 for other moorland, indicating that the former is a 'sink' habitat and the latter a 'source' habitat. Productivity in conifer plantations was sufficient to balance mortality. Combing all LMCs, an annual decline of 6% would be expected (Table 38.4). However, in a hypothetical harrier population in which the survival rate on grouse moors was the same as on other moorland, one would expect the population to increase by 13% per annum (Table 38.4).

Table 38.4. Female population multiplication rates (PMRs) in relation to land management class. Data from Etheridge *et al.* (1997).

Land management class	PMR	95% confidence limits
Grouse moors	0.54	0.35-0.75
Other moorlands	1.19	0.91-1.46
Conifer plantations	1.02	0.78-1.24
All classes	0.94	0.75-1.12
All classes (no persecution)	1.13	0.89-1.36

38.4 Discussion

The two population estimates for the size of the breeding population of hen harriers on mainland Scotland show that there has been no change over a ten year period. In fact, the two estimates are virtually identical. The first survey (Bibby & Etheridge, 1993) was designed to give the first ever population figure based on a scientific methodology, and there was little idea then what the variance might be. The sampling effort varied between 5 and 25% depending on the breeding category, and resulted in confidence limits, which were about 30% of the mean. In the second survey (Sim *et al.*, 2001), the sampling effort was 15.3% and the confidence limits were reduced, but still large (c. 17% of the mean). Clearly, if one wishes to detect small changes by field survey, a greater sampling effort is required.

Based on productivity and survival estimates, Etheridge *et al.* (1997) made predictions about how the hen harrier population would change on the different LMCs if they were closed populations, and how the population as a whole would change. These predictions were in the form of population multiplication rates (PMRs) (Table 38.4). The results indicated that hen harrier numbers on grouse moors would decline at between 25% and 65% per annum. The data on natal dispersal and the percentage of young males on grouse moors was consistent with this habitat being a 'sink'. The PMRs for the populations on other moorland and in plantations indicated that they could either decline or increase, though the mean values indicated stability in plantations, and an increase (19% per annum) on other moorlands.

When the data for all the land management classes were combined, it gave a PMR of 0.94 (95% CLs 0.75-1.12) under continuing human persecution. This would have meant that a population of 408 hen harriers breeding in 1988-89 would have fallen to about 230 pairs in 1998. However, given the large confidence limits of the PMR, we cannot use the result of no change in the population as evidence for a decline in the level of persecution. We are faced with the same problem in predicting population change if persecution ceases. The PMR indicated a population increase of 13% per annum, but the confidence limits varied between 0.89 and 1.36. Thus, even if the population estimates were accurate, the large confidence limits on the PMRs mean that we cannot say whether persecution is the same or has changed during our studies.

The perceived threat that hen harriers pose to red grouse stocks appears to have remained unchanged. Therefore, it is likely that human persecution continues to limit the numbers and range of hen harriers (Etheridge *et al.*, 1997; Potts, 1998; Stott, 1998). Illegal nest destruction is widespread on grouse moors, and killing of females was estimated to account annually for 11-15% of their numbers in Scotland (excluding Orkney) during 1988-1995 (Etheridge *et al.*, 1997). It has been calculated that the population of hen harriers in the UK could more than double in the absence of persecution (Potts, 1998). In one study, following the cessation of suspected human persecution on four study moors in Scotland, there was an increase from two to 20 breeding females between 1992 and 1997 at one site (Redpath & Thirgood, 1997, 1999, Chapter 39), though numbers have since declined.

Although there has been no change in the total population size on the Scottish mainland, there have been changes in the distribution of hen harriers. The trend has been towards a decrease in the North and East Scotland. In terms of LMCs, there are less hen harriers in young plantations and more on grouse moors. Can these changes be accounted for based on our knowledge of population dynamics and habitat change?

Many of the plantations where hen harriers were found breeding during the 1980s have now reached canopy closure and are unsuitable because the interlocking branches shade out the heather nesting habitat. In addition, an increasing proportion of young plantations consist of restocked plantation, which appears to be largely unsuitable for nesting harriers because of the lack of dense heather (Petty & Anderson, 1986; Redpath *et al.*, 1998; Madders, 2000). In South and West Scotland the largest areas of conifers have been planted, and in the Western Highlands most nests were found in young plantations (Etheridge *et al.*, 1997). One would therefore expect to see declines in the Western Highlands associated with the decline in young plantations (Figure 38.1). Yet, we found no significant change in breeding numbers in South and West Scotland, perhaps because the losses to plantations have been offset by gains to grouse moors within these areas.

The decline in the hen harrier population on North and East Scotland is less easy to understand, given that much of the habitat is grouse moor, which has seen an increase in numbers of harriers nationally (Table 38.1). It seems that the increase in harrier numbers on grouse moors was mainly due to the increase on grouse moors in the Southern Uplands. In contrast, there have been losses of harriers on grouse moors in the North and East Highlands, and it is likely that intense human persecution is the reason for this localised decline. There are also some conifer plantations in North and East Scotland, which would have declined in suitability for nesting harriers.

It is a cause for concern that there is a greater proportion of the Scottish population now breeding on grouse moors (Table 38.1) because of the risks posed there. Clearly, grouse moors provide attractive habitat for hen harriers, perhaps because of the high availability of prey. However, this LMC is known to be a 'sink' habitat (Etheridge *et al.*, 1997), which means that the Scottish hen harrier population is possibly at greater risk to persecution than it was ten years ago.

Acknowledgements
Full acknowledgements to field workers and others involved in the three studies on hen harriers reported here are given in the original papers. Comments on this manuscript were gratefully received from D.W. Gibbons, S. Redpath and an anonymous referee.

References
Anonymous (2000). *The Report of the UK Raptor Working Group*. Department of the Environment, Transport and the Regions and Joint Nature Conservation Committee, Peterborough.

Balfour, E. & Cadbury, C.J. (1979). Polygyny, spacing and sex ratio among hen harriers *Circus cyaneus* in Orkney, Scotland. *Ornis Scandinavica*, **10**, 133-141.

Bennett, K.D. (1988). A provisional map of forest types for the British Isles 5000 years ago. *Journal of Quaternary Science*, **4**, 141-144.

Bibby, C.J. & Etheridge, B. (1993). Status of the hen harrier *Circus cyaneus* in Scotland in 1988-89. *Bird Study*, **40**, 1-11.

Clobert, J., Lebreton, J-D., Clobert-Gillet, M. & Coquillart, H. (1985). The estimation of survival in bird populations by recaptures or sightings of marked individuals. In *Statistics in Ornithology*, ed. by P.M. North & B.J.T. Morgan. Springer-Verlag, Berlin. pp. 197-214.

Cramp, S. & Simmons, K.E.L. (Eds) (1980). *The Birds of the Western Palearctic, Volume 2*. Oxford University Press, Oxford.

Deer Commission for Scotland (2000). *Wild Deer in Scotland: a Long-term Vision*. Deer Commission for Scotland, Inverness.

Efron, B. (1982). *The Jacknife, the Bootstrap and other Resampling Plans*. Society of Industrial and Applied Mathematics, Philadelphia.

Etheridge, B., Summers, R.W. & Green, R.E. (1997). The effects of illegal killing and destruction of nests by humans on the population dynamics of the hen harrier *Circus cyaneus* in Scotland. *Journal of Applied Ecology*, **34**, 1081-1105.

Fuller, R.J. & Gough, S.J. (1999). Changes in sheep numbers in Britain: implications for bird populations. *Biological Conservation*, **91**, 73-89.

Gibbons, D.W., Reid, J.B. & Chapman, R.A. (1993). *The New Atlas of Breeding Birds in Britain and Ireland: 1988-1991*. Poyser, London.

Gregory, R.D., Wilkinson, N.I., Noble, D.G., Robinson, J.A., Brown, A.F., Hughes, J., Procter, D.A., Gibbons, D.W. & Galbraith, C.A. (2002). The population status of birds in the United Kingdom, Channel Islands and Isle of Man: an analysis of conservation concern 2002-2007. *British Birds*, **95**, 410-448.

Hudson, P.J. (1992). *Grouse in Space and Time.* The Game Conservancy Ltd., Fordingbridge.

Madders, M. (1997). The effects of forestry on hen harriers *Circus cyaneus.* PhD Thesis. University of Glasgow. Glasgow.

Madders, M. (2000). Habitat selection and foraging success of hen harriers *Circus cyaneus* in west Scotland. *Bird Study*, **47**, 32-40.

Mayfield, H.F. (1975). Suggestions for calculating nest success. *Wilson Bulletin*, **87**, 456-466.

Moorland Working Group (2002). *Scotland's moorland: the nature of change.* Scottish Natural Heritage, Perth.

Newton, I. (1979). *Population Ecology of Raptors.* Poyser, Berkhamsted.

Petty, S.J. & Anderson, D. (1986). Breeding by hen harriers *Circus cyaneus* on restocked sites in upland forests. *Bird Study*, **33**, 177-178.

Potts, G.R. (1998). Global dispersion of nesting hen harriers *Circus cyaneus*: implications for grouse moors in the U.K. *Ibis*, **140**, 76-88.

Redpath, S.M. (1991). The impact of hen harriers on red grouse breeding success. *Journal of Applied Ecology*, **28**, 659-671.

Redpath, S., Madders, M., Donnelly, E., Anderson, B., Thirgood, S., Martin, A. & McLeod, D. (1998). Nest site selection by hen harriers in Scotland. *Bird Study*, **45**, 51-61.

Redpath, S.M. & Thirgood, S.J. (1997). *Birds of Prey and Red Grouse.* The Stationery Office, London.

Redpath, S.M. & Thirgood, S.J. (1999). Functional and numerical responses in generalist predators: hen harriers and peregrines on Scottish grouse moors. *Journal of Animal Ecology*, **68**, 879-892.

Scotland's Moorland Forum (2003). *Scotland's Moorland Forum: principles of moorland management.* Scottish Natural Heritage, Perth.

Sharrock, J.T.R. (1976). *The Atlas of Breeding Birds in Britain and Ireland.* Poyser, Berkhamsted.

Sim, I.M.W., Gibbons, D.W., Bainbridge, I.P. & Mattingley, W.A. (2001). Status of the hen harrier *Circus cyaneus* in the UK and the Isle of Man in 1998. *Bird Study*, **48**, 341-353.

Smout, T.C. (1997). Highland land-use before 1800: misconceptions, evidence and realities. In *Scottish Woodland History*, ed. by T.C. Smout. Scottish Cultural Press, Edinburgh. pp. 5-23.

Stott, M. (1998). Hen harrier breeding success on English grouse moors. *British Birds*, **91**, 107-108.

Thom, V.M. (1986). *Birds in Scotland.* Poyser, Calton.

Thompson, D.B.A., Hester, A.J. & Usher, M.B. (Eds) (1995). *Heaths and Moorlands: Cultural Landscapes.* The Stationery Office, Edinburgh.

Watson, D. (1977). *The Hen Harrier.* Poyser, Berkhamsted.

39. THE IMPACT OF HEN HARRIER (*CIRCUS CYANEUS*) PREDATION ON RED GROUSE (*LAGOPUS LAGOPUS SCOTICUS*) POPULATIONS: LINKING MODELS WITH FIELD DATA

Steve Redpath & Simon Thirgood

Summary

1.   In the absence of human persecution the densities of breeding hen harrier *Circus cyaneus* on heather-dominated moorland appear to be determined by the abundance of passerines and small mammals.

2.   Small prey are important in the diet of harriers in the spring, whilst the chicks of red grouse *Lagopus lagopus scoticus* form an important component of the diet during the summer. This predation brings harriers into conflict with grouse managers, who seek to maximise the number of grouse available for shooting in the autumn.

3.   We build on published data on the functional response of harriers to grouse chicks and use a deterministic model to understand how the numbers of harriers breeding on grouse moors influence the average density of autumn grouse populations.

4.   The model suggests that driven shooting could coexist with breeding harriers over a range of grouse brood sizes and harrier densities. If the effect of supplementary feeding on grouse predation rates observed at Langholm hold more widely across grouse populations, then the model suggests that driven shooting could occur across an even broader range of harrier densities. The model now needs to be subject to sensitivity analysis and its assumptions examined.

39.1 Introduction

Hen harriers *Circus cyaneus* have long been persecuted in Scotland because of their perceived threat to red grouse *Lagopus lagopus scoticus* populations and shooting bags (Watson, 1977; Etheridge *et al.*, 1997; Anon., 2000; Moorland Working Group, 2002). This perception was partly supported by recent studies which found strong evidence that high densities of breeding harriers limited grouse populations at low density, suppressed population cycles and reduced shooting bags (Redpath & Thirgood, 1999; Thirgood *et al.*, 2000a,b). However the same studies found that grouse moors where harriers occurred at low density were able to support driven shooting. An understanding of the factors important in determining harrier density and the amount of grouse in the diet is therefore important if we are to make predictions about which grouse populations are vulnerable to high levels of harrier predation and what level of harrier predation causes grouse populations to be limited at low density.

In this chapter we build on previously published data and consider the importance of small mammals and passerines in determining harrier breeding density and diet during the spring. We then examine the diet of harriers during the nestling period and examine how the rate at which red grouse chicks are taken varies with grouse chick density. Using these field data we then build a simple deterministic model to examine the effect of varying the breeding density of harriers on the autumn density of grouse. The aim of the model is primarily to provide an estimate of the maximum density of harriers that can co-exist with driven grouse shooting. Our recent work has demonstrated that predation on grouse chicks can be reduced through the provision of supplementary food to harriers (Redpath *et al.*, 2001a). In light of this, we use the model to estimate the effect on grouse populations of providing harriers with supplementary food.

39.2 Hen harrier and red grouse ecology

Hen harriers breeding in Scotland are confined almost exclusively to moorland (e.g. Gibbons *et al.*, 1993). Within these moors, harriers selectively nest in tall heather (notably *Calluna vulgaris*) (Redpath *et al.*, 1998) and heather moorland is therefore important in determining their distribution and breeding density. The other critical factor which limits the distribution and density of nesting harriers in Scotland is human interference. Harriers are still persecuted on the majority of moors that are managed for red grouse despite their legal protection (Etheridge *et al.*, 1997; Scottish Raptor Study Groups, 1997, 2003; Holmes *et al.*, Chapter 37; Summers *et al.*, Chapter 38).

Harriers return to their breeding sites in February and March and generally lay their eggs in late April. Eggs are incubated for 34 days, and the chicks spend four to five weeks in the nest and a further three to four weeks on the moor before they disperse away from the uplands. Adult males also leave the breeding grounds during the winter, but some females stay throughout the year. During the summer, hen harriers in the Scottish uplands eat a wide variety of prey, with meadow pipits *Anthus pratensis*, field voles *Microtus agrestis*, grouse chicks and young lagomorphs being the most frequent (Watson, 1977; Picozzi, 1978; Redpath, 1991; Redpath & Thirgood, 1999; Redpath *et al.*, 2001b; Amar *et al.*, Chapter 29).

Red grouse feed almost exclusively on heather and their distribution is therefore confined to heather-dominated moorland (e.g. Jenkins *et al.*, 1963; Gibbons *et al.*, 1993). Hen grouse lay their clutches in late April, and chicks hatch after four weeks. After hatching the broods forage widely with their parents, feeding mainly on insects in the first two weeks (Hudson, 1986). Grouse are shot in autumn either over pointing dogs or by driving the birds over butts. Driven shooting tends to occur above densities of 60 birds per km^2 (Hudson, 1992).

39.3 Methods

Most of the data described here were collected from 1992 to 2000 on Langholm Moor in the Scottish Borders. Some additional data came from five other study areas across Scotland. Sites were selected on the basis that they were managed for red grouse, and raptors were not killed by humans on these. The methods and study areas have been described in detail elsewhere (Redpath & Thirgood, 1997, 1999; Redpath *et al.*, 2001a,b; Thirgood *et al.*, 2000a).

39.3.1 Prey counts

Grouse were counted on Langholm Moor with pointing dogs on 12 areas of 0.5 km^2 in April, July and October and the number of chicks in grouse broods were counted in early June. Meadow pipits were counted on two transects of 1 km in each of 12 areas of 1 km^2 in June and small mammals were trapped using 12 lines of 50 snap traps set for two nights in April and October. On other study areas grouse were counted on two areas of 1 km^2, pipits on four areas of 1 km^2, and small mammals on four trap lines (50 traps set for two nights).

39.3.2 Harrier diet

Harrier pellets were collected during late winter and early spring (February to April) from 1997 to 1999 at a communal roost at Langholm. Prey in the pellets were identified to species, and are expressed as the proportion of identified items; no grouse chicks were available as prey during the spring. From 1993-99 (excluding 1997) hides were set up within 10 m of harrier nests during the nestling period, and summer prey were identified as they were delivered to chicks. Watches from hides allowed us to obtain provisioning rates of grouse chicks during the harrier nestling period. The functional response curve was derived from the relationship between predation rate of grouse chicks over this period and the initial grouse chick density.

39.3.3 Harrier breeding numbers

The study area was searched each spring for displaying harriers and any area where birds were seen displaying or involved in courtship behaviour or nest building was checked for subsequent breeding attempts. There was an estimated 41.5 km^2 of heather-dominated moorland at Langholm and harrier densities were expressed as the number of breeding females per km^2 of heather moorland.

39.3.4 The model

The model uses relationships derived from the Langholm grouse population and does not incorporate any stochasticity or delayed density-dependence, which can lead to population cycles (Figure 39.1). We start with an initial spring grouse density of 30 pairs km^2, though the model outcomes did not vary with initial density. Each run of the model iterates the steps 50 times, by which time an asymptote of autumn grouse density is reached. Essentially, therefore, the model can be considered as presenting average densities of grouse in autumn under given harrier breeding densities.

From April to July adult grouse are lost from the population according to the density dependent equation in Thirgood *et al.* (2000a):

$$\text{July density} = (1.78)\ (\text{April density}^{0.67}) \qquad (1)$$

The density is for grouse per 0.5 km^2. We assume that sex ratios in the grouse population in April and in the grouse lost during spring are equal. We also assume that spring predation is 100% additive, and that all females that survive spring losses have broods varying from two to seven chicks per brood. At Langholm, measured brood sizes in June ranged from 4.0 to 6.6 (Thirgood *et al.*, 2000a). The average clutch size of grouse is usually

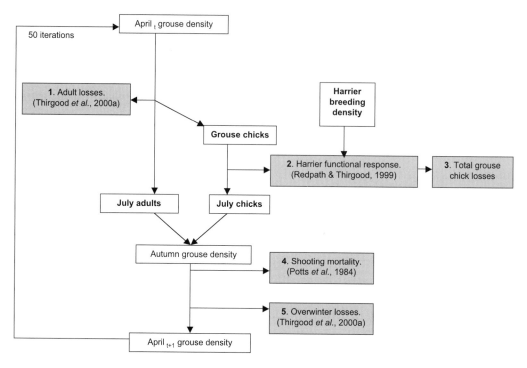

Figure 39.1. Diagrammatic representation of the model examining the impact of harrier predation on red grouse populations. Shaded boxes indicate losses to the grouse population and numbers refer to equations in text.

about nine eggs (Hudson, 1986), and the reduced brood sizes reflect some loss of young chicks to density independent factors during the first few days after hatch. Grouse chick density is determined from the product of female density and brood size. The grouse chicks are subject to predation by harriers according to the functional response (Redpath & Thirgood, 1999, and results below):

$$\text{Grouse delivered to each nest per hr} = \frac{(0.21)(\text{initial grouse chick density}^{5.1})}{51^{5.1} + \text{initial grouse chick density}^{5.1}} \quad (2)$$

Sixty days is the average length of time that harrier young are on territory and 15 hrs is the amount of time available for hunting per day (Redpath & Thirgood, 1999). Hence:

$$\text{Total grouse chick losses} = (\text{grouse per hr})\,(60\text{ days})\,(15\text{ hrs})\,(\text{harrier density}) \quad (3)$$

The surviving chicks join the adult birds in the July population. In August, the number shot was determined by the equation in Potts *et al.* (1984):

$$\text{Number shot} = \frac{(\text{autumn density})(0.55)}{(1 + e^{(5.7-(0.04\cdot\text{autumn density}))})} \quad (4)$$

The surviving birds formed the October grouse population. The number of birds surviving from October to April was determined from the density dependent equation in Thirgood *et al.* (2000a):

$$\text{Spring density} = (3.91)(\text{October density}^{0.45}) \tag{5}$$

The density is for grouse per 0.5 km². This model therefore includes the overwinter predation on adult grouse observed at Langholm from 1992 to 1997. Managing winter predation is problematic, although some potential solutions have been suggested (Anon., 2000). However, it is possible to manage levels of raptor predation on grouse chicks through a range of measures (e.g. Thirgood *et al.*, 2000b; Scotland's Moorland Forum, 2003). In this chapter we have taken the approach of incorporating the observed high levels of adult grouse mortality, but manipulating levels of predation on chicks, and examined the impact on autumn grouse densities.

39.3.5 Main assumptions of the model
Our model makes five main assumptions.

1. Spring predation. The model assumes that sex ratios are equal and that spring predation of adult grouse is additive and results in the loss of potential grouse broods.
2. Adult mortality rates. The density dependent relationships for spring and winter losses at Langholm were derived from relatively low grouse population densities. We have assumed that these relationships are maintained at higher densities. In addition, the shape of the density-dependent relationships may vary between populations, but there is too little information from other populations where raptor persecution is absent to include such information here.
3. Functional response. The functional response takes no account of depletion of grouse chick numbers by harriers and in certain instances (high densities of harriers and intermediate densities of grouse) may lead to all of the grouse chicks being killed. In reality there is likely to be some effect of depletion at high harrier density with harriers altering their diet as grouse chick numbers are reduced. However, initial analysis found little evidence for reductions in predation rate over the summer (Redpath & Thirgood, 1999) and for the purposes of this chapter we have assumed that predation rates stay constant over the 60 days from hatch to dispersal and that there was no interference competition between harriers, as supported by earlier analyses (Redpath & Thirgood, 1997, 1999).
4. Delayed density-dependence and stochasticity. The model assumes that many of the demographic parameters are constant for each run of the model. Clearly, mortality and reproductive rates will vary between years due to stochastic and density-dependent factors, but we have deliberately excluded such effects for the sake of clarity. The next step in the modelling will be to include the delayed density-dependent effects of spacing behaviour and parasitism on grouse population dynamics as these factors are considered important in determining density (Moss *et al.*, 1996; Hudson *et al.*, 1998; Mougeot *et al.*, 2003).

5. Grouse chick losses. For the sake of clarity, we have assumed that harrier mortality is the only form of grouse chick loss after the first few days of life. Harriers are one of the main mortality factors at this stage of the grouse life-cycle, but clearly other factors (parasites, weather, other predators) can also be important in certain populations/areas (e.g. Hudson, 1986, 1992).

39.4 Results

39.4.1 Harrier breeding density

On areas where heather is abundant and human persecution is absent, the available evidence suggests that harrier breeding density is determined not by the abundance of grouse but by the abundance of small prey. At Langholm, there is a clear relationship between the numbers of breeding harriers in one year and the abundance of field voles (Redpath *et al.*, 2002; Figure 39.2). Across study areas Redpath & Thirgood (1999) found a positive correlation between harrier density and meadow pipit abundance. Harrier breeding densities vary widely (from 0–0.48 per km^2) and are not affected by the abundance of red grouse, thus there was no need to build a feedback mechanism into the model (see Figure 39.1).

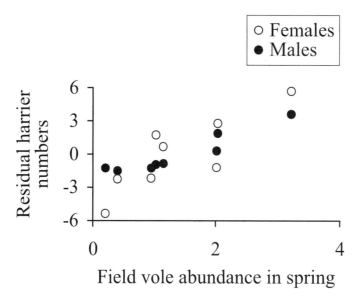

Figure 39.2. Relationship between residual harrier breeding numbers (controlling for the effects of time since persecution ended) and field vole abundance in spring (numbers caught per 100 trap nights). Males: $r_s = 0.96$, $P < 0.001$. Females: $r_s = 0.90$, $P < 0.01$.

39.4.2 Harrier diet

Harrier diet appears to differ widely from spring to summer (Figure 39.3). In the spring, analysis of pellets indicated that field voles predominated in the diet, particularly in the years of peak and declining vole abundance. However, during the summer, birds dominated the nestling harrier diet and the principal prey by biomass was red grouse chicks. This dependence on voles in spring may account for the temporal relationship between vole abundance and harrier breeding densities at Langholm.

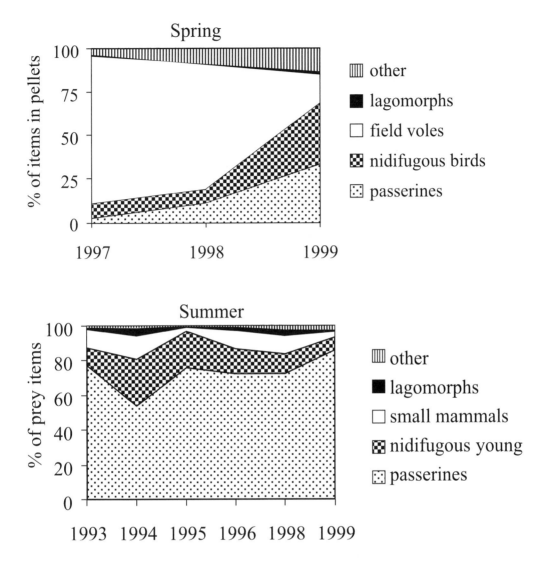

Figure 39.3. Diet of hen harriers at Langholm as estimated from pellets collected in spring 1997-99 and from direct observations at nests during summer 1993-99 (excluding 1997). Field vole abundance peaked in spring 1993/94 and 1997. Field voles were identified in pellets but could only be classed along with shrews *Sorex* spp. as small mammals during the summer.

39.4.3 Harrier functional response

Redpath & Thirgood (1999) presented a functional response curve for harriers feeding on red grouse chicks. Since that relationship was published we have collected two further data points that provide support for the shape of the original curve (Figure 39.4). This sigmoidal relationship is termed a Type III functional response and such patterns have the capacity to regulate prey populations at low density (Begon *et al.*, 1986).

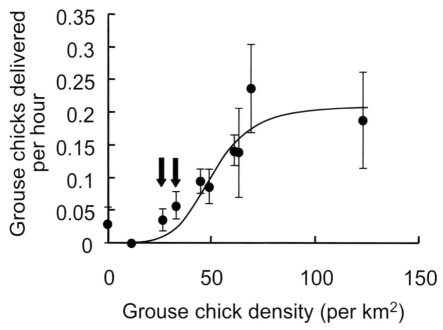

Figure 39.4. Relationship between the rate at which grouse chicks are delivered to harrier nests and the density of grouse chicks in early June. Each point represents data collected on one moor in one year. Arrows indicate data collected since figure first published. Based on Figure 6 in Redpath & Thirgood (1999).

39.4.4 Model outputs

We first ran the model for a range of harrier densities (0-0.5 per km²) and grouse brood size (two to seven chicks per pair) values (Figure 39.5a). The model suggests that autumn density of grouse generally increased as brood size increased and harrier density decreased. However, at high harrier densities autumn densities were slightly higher for lower grouse brood sizes. The model also predicts that the relationship between harrier density and autumn grouse population size will not be linear, but that autumn density declines rapidly below harrier densities of 0.4 per km².

The model suggests that there are ranges of harrier densities and grouse brood sizes at which driven grouse shooting is possible (at densities over 60 grouse per km² (Hudson, 1992)). However, once harrier densities rise over 0.3 per km² the model suggests that grouse will not reach these densities. At Langholm, grouse brood sizes in early June from 1993-96 averaged 5.5 (Thirgood *et al.*, 2000c). Over the same time period harrier densities averaged 0.23 per km². For these values, the model estimates autumn density as 56 grouse per km². In 1993 autumn densities of grouse were 66 per km², declining to 56 per km² in 1997. The figure for 1997 is therefore similar to the model's estimate. Over the last three years (1997 to 2000) autumn densities of grouse have averaged 38 per km² (Thirgood & Redpath, unpublished).

Data from a study where supplementary food was provided to harriers suggested that fed birds reduced their predation on grouse chicks by 86% (Redpath *et al.*, 2001a). If this reduction in grouse predation was consistent across grouse populations then the benefits to grouse populations could be important, with predation on grouse chicks largely being prevented (Figure 39.5b).

a) Without supplementary feeding

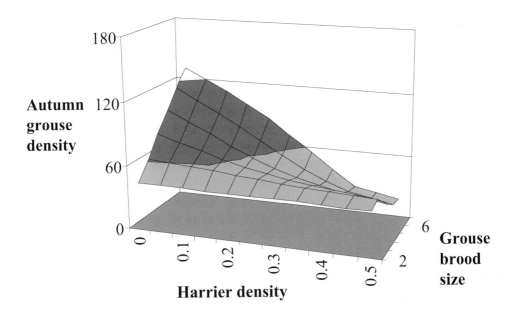

b) With supplementary feeding

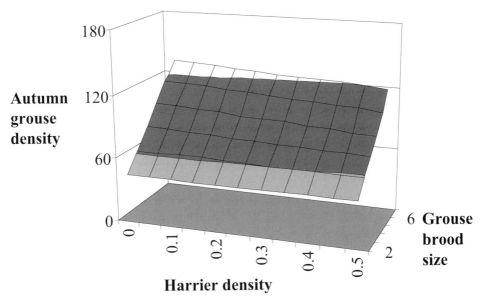

Figure 39.5. Outputs from model giving autumn densities of grouse after 50 iterations over a range of harrier densities and grouse brood sizes. Outputs presented without (a) and with (b) supplementary feeding. Driven grouse shooting generally occurs above densities of 60 grouse per km^2 (Hudson, 1992).

39.5 Discussion

What density of breeding harriers is compatible with a grouse density sufficient for driven grouse shooting? Questions such as this are increasingly being asked by conservationists and land managers who are keen to resolve the conflict between harrier conservation and grouse management (e.g. Anon., 2000; Galbraith *et al.*, Chapter 41). Potts (1998) suggested that a density of 0.04 breeding females per km² (or one nest per 25 km²) would be an appropriate target density to fulfil both harrier conservation and grouse management purposes. Here we attempt a more quantitative approach to the question using a simple deterministic model. Even though our model incorporates the density dependent losses found at Langholm, it still suggests that breeding densities of harriers below 0.3 per km² (or one nest per 3.3 km²) can co-exist with driven grouse shooting, depending on the breeding success of the grouse prior to harrier predation. In areas where adult losses are lower than at Langholm, autumn grouse densities will inevitably be higher.

Two patterns are at the root of the conflict between hen harriers and red grouse (Thirgood *et al.*, 2000c). First, breeding densities of harriers are related to small prey abundance and not to grouse numbers, therefore harriers can occur at high density on moors where grouse are relatively scarce. The relationship between harrier breeding density and vole abundance is not surprising given that harriers prey mainly on voles during the spring (Redpath *et al.*, 2001; Amar *et al.*, Chapter 29; Figure 39.3) and that males feed their females with small prey items during courtship and incubation (Redpath & Thirgood, 1997). A positive relationship between harriers and voles has also been found elsewhere in Europe (Korpimäki, 1985) and North America (Hamerstrom, 1979). The second factor important to the harrier-grouse conflict is that the rate at which individual harriers eat grouse chicks is primarily determined by grouse density. Harriers eat more grouse as the density of grouse chicks increases, but their impact is greatest at grouse chick densities of approximately 67 chicks per km² (Redpath & Thirgood, 1999). These two patterns mean that harriers can have a large impact on grouse populations, although the effects are likely to vary across Britain according to variation in the habitat and associated small prey (Redpath & Thirgood, 1999; Smith *et al.*, 2001).

At Langholm, the adult grouse losses were due largely to predation by raptors in the winter and spring (Thirgood *et al.*, 2000a). Without managers resorting to a few un-tested management practices to reduce this loss (such as the use of dovecots (Anon., 2000)), little can be done to reduce these predation levels. We have therefore maintained those winter and spring grouse losses in the model and concentrated on the effects of manipulating harrier predation on grouse chicks. Despite this, the model does suggest that there are ranges of harrier densities and grouse brood sizes within which driven grouse shooting is possible. Furthermore, reducing predation rates on grouse chicks by providing supplementary food could increase the likelihood that grouse reach densities sufficient for driven shooting to occur.

The aim of grouse management is to maximise the number available for shooting, and many grouse managers may consider that the autumn densities predicted here are not financially viable. However, Hudson (1992) suggested that the costs of grouse management would be covered when grouse density exceeded 60 birds per km². Such densities were reached over a wide range of harrier densities in our model, suggesting that there is the potential for driven grouse shooting and breeding harriers to coexist.

In our model we have used our previously published density dependent and functional response equations to estimate losses of grouse. There is, however, a considerable amount of variation around these relationships, so consequently the level of uncertainty around our predictions will be large. Nevertheless, we feel that the model provides a useful first step in estimating the densities at which harriers may occur with grouse management. The next step should be to examine the confidence limits around the estimates and examine how sensitive the model outputs are to variation in the parameters. It may also be appropriate to split the harrier functional response by sex, as males and females appear to respond slightly differently to variation in grouse chick abundance (Redpath & Thirgood, 1999). Finally, we would like to include a range of parameter values from other grouse populations and try to model the effects of delayed density dependence in the grouse population in addition to variation in harrier numbers.

Acknowledgements

We are grateful to the many field assistants and volunteers who have helped us with the collection of field data over the years and we thank Roger Clarke for his analysis of the harrier pellets. This work was based on data collected during a field study funded by Scottish Natural Heritage, Buccleuch Estates, The Game Conservancy Trust, The Game Conservancy Scottish Research Trust, The Centre for Ecology and Hydrology, The Royal Society for the Protection of Birds, English Nature, The Joint Nature Conservation Committee and The Scottish Landowners' Federation. Two anonymous referees improved the manuscript.

References

Anonymous (2000). *Report of the UK Raptor Working Group*. Department of the Environment, Transport and the Regions and Joint Nature Conservation Committee, Peterborough.

Begon, M., Harper, J.L. & Townsend, C.R. (1986). *Ecology: Individuals, Populations and Communities*. Blackwell Scientific Press, London.

Etheridge, B., Summers, R.W. & Green, R.E. (1997). The effects of illegal killing and destruction of nests by humans on the population dynamics of the hen harrier *Circus cyaneus* in Scotland. *Journal of Applied Ecology*, **34**, 1081-1105.

Gibbons, D.W., Reid, J.B. & Chapman, R.A. (1993). *The New Atlas of Breeding Birds in Britain and Ireland*. Poyser, London.

Hamerstrom, F. (1979). Effect of prey on predators: voles and harriers. *Auk*, **96**, 370-374.

Hudson, P.J. (1986). *Red Grouse: the Biology and Management of a Wild Gamebird*. The Game Conservancy Trust, Fordingbridge.

Hudson, P.J. (1992). *Grouse in Space and Time: the Population Biology of a Wild Gamebird*. The Game Conservancy Trust, Fordingbridge.

Hudson, P.J., Dobson, A.P. & Newborn, D. (1998). Prevention of population cycles by parasite removal. *Science*, **282**, 2256-2258.

Jenkins, D., Watson, A. & Miller G.R. (1963). Population studies on red grouse, *Lagopus lagopus scoticus* (Lath.) in north-east Scotland. *Journal of Animal Ecology*, **32**, 317-376.

Korpimäki, E. (1985). Rapid tracking of microtine populations by their avian predators: possible evidence for stabilising predation. *Oikos*, **45**, 281-284.

Moorland Working Group (2003). *Scotland's Moorland: the nature of change*. Scottish Natural Heritage, Perth.

Moss, R., Watson, A. & Parr, R. (1996). Experimental prevention of a population cycle in red grouse. *Ecology*, **77**, 1512-1530.

Mougeot, F., Redpath, S.M., Leckie, F. & Hudson, P.J. (2003). The effect of aggressiveness on the population dynamics of a territorial bird. *Nature*, **421**, 737–739.

Picozzi, N. (1978). Dispersion, breeding and prey of the hen harrier *Circus cyaneus* in Glen Dye, Kincardineshire. *Ibis*, **120**, 489-509.

Potts, G.R. (1998). Global dispersion of nesting Hen Harriers *Circus cyaneus*; implications for grouse moors in the U.K. *Ibis*, **140**, 76-88.

Potts, G.R., Tapper, S.C. & Hudson, P.J. (1984). Population fluctuations in red grouse: analysis of bag records and a simulation model. *Journal of Animal Ecology*, **53**, 21-36.

Redpath, S.M. (1991). The impact of hen harriers on red grouse breeding success. *Journal of Applied Ecology*, **28**, 659-671.

Redpath, S.M. & Thirgood, S.J. (1997). *Birds of Prey and Red Grouse.* The Stationery Office, London.

Redpath, S.M., Madders, M., Donnelly, E., Anderson, B., Thirgood, S.J., Martin, A. & McLeod, D. (1998). Nest site selection by hen harriers in Scotland. *Bird Study*, **45**, 51-61.

Redpath, S.M. & Thirgood, S.J. (1999). Functional and numerical responses in generalist predators: hen harriers and peregrines on Scottish grouse moors. *Journal of Animal Ecology*, **68**, 879-892.

Redpath, S.M., Thirgood, S.J. & Leckie, F.M. (2001a). Does supplementary feeding reduce predation of red grouse by hen harriers? *Journal of Applied Ecology*, **38**, 1157-1168.

Redpath, S.M., Clarke, R.G., Madders, M. & Thirgood, S.J. (2001b). Assessing raptor diet: comparing pellets, prey remains and observational data at hen harrier nests. *The Condor*, **103**, 184-188.

Redpath, S.M., Thirgood, S.J. & Clarke, R. (2002). Influence of Field Voles *Microtus agrestis* abundance on hen harrier *Circus cyaneus* diet and breeding in Scotland. *Ibis,* **144**, E33-E39.

Scotland's Moorland Forum (2003). *Scotland's Moorland Forum: principles of moorland management.* Scottish Natural Heritage, Perth.

Scottish Raptor Study Groups (1997). The illegal persecution of raptors in Scotland. *Scottish Birds*, **19**, 65-85.

Scottish Raptor Study Groups (2003). Raptor round-up for 2000 and 2001. *Scottish Birds* (in press).

Smith, A., Redpath, S.M., Thirgood, S.J. & Campbell, S. (2001). Habitat characteristics of managed grouse moors and the abundance of meadow pipits and red grouse. *Journal of Applied Ecology*, **38**, 390-401.

Thirgood, S.J., Redpath, S.M., Rothery, P. & Aebischer, N. (2000a). Raptor predation and population limitation in red grouse. *Journal of Animal Ecology*, **69**, 504-516.

Thirgood, S.J., Redpath, S.M., Haydon, D.T., Rothery, P., Newton, I. & Hudson, P.J. (2000b). Habitat loss and raptor predation: disentangling long- and short-term causes of red grouse declines. *Proceedings of the Royal Society, Series B*, **267**, 651-656.

Thirgood, S., Redpath, S., Newton, I. & Hudson, P. (2000c). Raptors and grouse: conservation conflicts and management solutions. *Conservation Biology*, **14**, 95-104.

Watson, D. (1977). *The Hen Harrier.* Poyser Press, Berkhamsted.

40. Predators and Rabbits (*Oryctolagus cuniculus*) in Spain: A Key Conflict for European Raptor Conservation

Javier Viñuela & Rafael Villafuerte

Summary

1.   This chapter considers conflicts between raptors and rabbits *Oryctolagus cuniculus* in Spain. As many as 29 predatory species eat rabbits in Spain.

2.   Rabbits influence the population ecology of some generalist as well as specialist raptor species, with some exhibiting finely tuned adaptations to variation in rabbit availability.

3.   Disease-related declines in rabbit populations, and coincidental declines in some other small games species, notably the red-legged partridge *Alectoris rufa,* have given rise to conflicts between hunters and predators.

4.   Poisoning and other forms of persecution have impacted heavily on some raptor species, notably the scavenging species, nesting in Spain. Migrants have also been heavily impacted on, and some central European (notably German) populations of red kite *Milvus milvus* may have declined as a result of this persecution of winter birds.

5.   The ANTIDOTE project was established to combat the illegal persecution of raptors in Spain. This has quantified substantial levels of poisonings (notably of Griffon vulture *Gyps fulvus*, red kite and black vulture *Aegypius monachus*; 1,365 poisoned carcasses found in two years), and pointed to a particular concern regarding the Spanish imperial eagle *Aquila adalberti* (68 birds found dead in two years out of a national population of about 140 breeding pairs). In the last ten years, there were only 15 successful criminal prosecutions for killing raptors.

6.   Studies of predator impacts on rabbits are reviewed, pointing to evidence that predation may control some rabbit populations, and that inter-specific competition or predation between predators may influence rabbit numbers.

7.   Effective habitat management measures and, in some areas, fox *Vulpes vulpes* control, and varying the hunting season, could benefit rabbit numbers and reduce the predator conflict with game managers.

40.1 Introduction

The rabbit *Oryctolagus cuniculus* is the most abundant mid-size herbivore of the food chain in the Iberian Mediterranean region (Valverde, 1967), and as such is considered by many to be the 'cornerstone' species. As many as 29 predatory species eat rabbit in Spain (Delibes & Hiraldo, 1981; Moreno *et al.*, 1996) where there is a varied community of predators, many of which are absent from more northern areas (e.g. large snakes, Serpentes, or lizards, Sauria). Furthermore, some of these predators are alien species, such as genets *Genetta*

genetta or mongooses *Herpestes icneumon*, which were introduced in historical times to the Iberian ecosystems by invaders from north Africa (Blanco, 1998). Among predators of rabbits, two species deserve special attention, the Iberian lynx *Lynx pardinus*, currently considered the most endangered cat in the world (Nowell & Jackson, 1996), and the Spanish imperial eagle *Aquila adalberti*, one of the most endangered raptors in the world (Collar *et al.*, 1994). Both of these predators tend to specialise on rabbits, to the point that the relatively small size of the lynx or the high breeding productivity of the eagle may be specific adaptations to predation on rabbits (González, 1989; Blanco, 1998). As well as being a key prey species, the rabbit is one of the main small game species in Spain, and is highly valued by hunters (Blanco & Villafuerte, 1993; Calvete *et al.*, 1997). Indeed, more than 80% of a sample of randomly selected areas in Andalucía (southern Spain) are currently managed to increase rabbit populations for hunting (Gortázar *et al.*, 2000a).

Spain holds one of the most varied and dense raptor assemblages in Europe (Table 40.1). As in other European countries, Spanish raptor populations suffered dramatic declines in the first half of the 20th century, mainly due to human persecution, which included government campaigns sponsoring the killing of predators (Bijleveld, 1974; Garzón, 1977). Following the implementation of protection laws in the mid-1970s, populations of most species recovered during the 1980s, sometimes slowly, as in the case of imperial eagles (González, 1996), and sometimes rapidly, as in the case of griffon vultures *Gyps fulvus* (Donázar & Fernández, 1989) (Table 40.1).

Given the importance of the rabbit as prey, its availability is an important factor affecting the population ecology of raptors in Spain, not only for specialist predators, such as the imperial eagle (González, 1989), but for more generalist species also. The case of black kites *Milvus migrans* in Doñana, perhaps the most generalist raptor in the Palearctic (Brown & Amadon, 1968; Cramp & Simmons, 1980), is enlightening. The breeding success of black kites in south-western Spain is affected by the availability of young and ill rabbits (Viñuela & Veiga, 1992; Viñuela, 2000), and the nesting dispersion of kites is determined by the location of rabbit warrens (Viñuela *et al.*, 1994). Furthermore, black kites breeding in territories with high rabbit availability lay larger last-laid eggs, and hatch their clutches more synchronously, thus promoting survival of last hatched chicks and increasing the number of young fledged (Viñuela, 1997, 2000). Therefore, this population of a highly generalist predator seems to have evolved finely tuned mechanisms so as to regulate productivity on the basis of rabbit availability near the nesting site.

This chapter considers several facets of the conflict between game management and raptors, much of this centred around the changing fortunes of the rabbit.

The bio-geographical origin of the European rabbit is in the western Mediterranean area, probably in the Iberian peninsula (Zeuner, 1963; Villafuerte *et al.*, 2000). The optimal ecosystems for this species are the Mediterranean ones of Spain, Portugal and southern France (e.g. Flux & Fullagar, 1983). The rabbit was extremely abundant in Spain in historical times. Even the name of the country comes from rabbit abundance, because Phoenician sailors reaching the Spanish coast confused the abundant rabbits with east-Mediterranean Hyrax *Procavia* spp., calling the country 'land of Hyrax' ('I-shepham-im', later romanized as 'Hispania'; Zeuner, 1963). Rabbits were such a pest in Spain that the inhabitants of the Balearic Islands asked Caesar to bring in the Roman Legions to eradicate rabbits or, if impossible (as they assumed), to give the people new

Table 40.1. Raptor species breeding in Spain, estimated population sizes in the late 1980s/early 1990s, and population trends during the 1980s (Tucker & Heath, 1994; Purroy, 1997). ? denotes not known.

Species	**Population (No. of pairs**	**Population trend in the 1980s**
Black-winged kite *Elanus caeruleus*	1,000	Increase
Black kite *Milvus migrans*	9,000	Stable/increase
Red kite *Milvus milvus*	3,300-4,000	Stable/increase
Lammergeier *Gypaetus barbatus*	62	Large increase
Honey buzzard *Pernis apivorus*	1,000	?
Egyptian vulture *Neophron percnopterus*	1,300-1,400	Stable/decrease
Griffon vulture *Gyps fulvus*	7,500-8,100	Large increase
Black vulture *Aegypius monachus*	770	Large increase
Short-toed eagle *Circaetus gallicus*	1,700-2,100	Stable
Hen harrier *Circus cyaneus*	837-999	Stable/Increase
Montagu's harrier *Circus pygargus*	3,500-4,500	Stable/increase
Marsh harrier *Circus aeruginosus*	481-522	Increase/stable
Goshawk *Accipiter gentilis*	2,300-3,000	?
Sparrowhawk *Accipiter nisus*	3,000-8,000	?
Common buzzard *Buteo buteo*	5,000-5,500	Increase/stable
Spanish imperial eagle *Aquila adalberti*	146	Increase
Golden eagle *Aquila chrysaetos*	1,192-1,265	Stable/increase
Booted eagle *Hiearaetus pennatus*	2,000-4,000	Stable/increase
Bonnelli's eagle *Hieraetus fasciatus*	675-751	Decrease
Osprey *Pandion haeliaetus*	29-31	Stable/decrease
Lesser kestrel *Falco naumanni*	7,000-8,000	Decrease/Stable
Common kestrel *Falco tinnunculus*	25,000-30,000	Stable/decrease
Hobby *Falco subbuteo*	900-1,600	?
Eleonora's falcon *Falco eleonorae*	640	Large increase
Peregrine *Falco peregrinus*	1,628-1,751	Stable/decrease

lands to crop in areas free of rabbits, no matter the distance from their homes (Estrabon, I. in García y Bellido, 1945).

40.2 The problem arrives: rabbit and partridge population crashes

40.2.1 Two diseases in rabbits

Two diseases have dramatically reduced rabbit populations in the 20th century. First, myxomatosis during the 1950s caused large decreases in populations (Valverde, 1967; Villafuerte *et al.*, 2000), as it did in other European countries. Rabbits in Spain had probably acquired resistance to this disease, and their populations were recovering, when the second disease, rabbit haemorrhagic disease (RHD), irrupted in the country. RHD had a major effect on rabbit populations, reducing these to between one-half and two-thirds in just five years (1988-1993), or even inducing local extinctions where rabbit populations had low densities (Blanco & Villafuerte, 1993; Villafuerte *et al.*, 1994, 1995).

40.2.2 Some direct impacts on predators

Initially, the irruption of RHD probably favoured generalist predators. For example, in the year following the arrival of this disease to the Doñana National Park, black kites brought larger rabbits to the nests than in previous years, probably because the high availability of dead or ill rabbits induced by RHD gave the kites access to a size group previously inaccessible (Villafuerte & Viñuela, 1999). However, reductions in rabbit populations, induced by RHD, have subsequently negatively affected the breeding success or population densities of some predators, including generalist species such as foxes *Vulpes vulpes*, eagle owls *Bubo bubo* and golden eagles *Aquila chrysaetos* (Fernández, 1993; Villafuerte *et al.*, 1996; Martínez & Calvo, 2001). Rabbit scarcity may represent a serious conservation problem for the Iberian lynx and the Spanish imperial eagle. Lynx density in some areas of the Doñana National Park and imperial eagle breeding success in some areas of the country may both have been reduced due to rabbit scarcity (e.g. Oria, 2000). During recent years, management measures for some pairs of imperial eagles have included artificial feeding, which has improved poor breeding success induced by low rabbit availability (Oria, 2000). Raptors in Spain, therefore, have an important problem now due to scarcity of the basic prey in the ecosystem.

40.2.3 Decline in numbers of red-legged partridges and links to rabbit availability

At least since the 1980s, and coinciding with the irruption of RHD, populations of the other important small game species in Spain, notably the red-legged partridge *Alectoris rufa*, have also declined (Nadal, 1992; Notario, 1992). This reduction in red-legged partridge numbers has been a common problem in other countries during recent decades (Potts, 1980; Office Nationale de la Chasse, 1986; Tucker & Heath, 1994). Red-legged partridges have many conservation problems in Spain, such as poor management by hunters, introduction of farmed and hybrid partridges, changes in agricultural practices (pesticide applications, hedgerow reduction, overgrazing), increases in wild boar *Sus scrofa* populations, and diseases (Nadal, 1992; Notario, 1992). Predation, especially by generalist species such as foxes or magpies *Pica pica*, is often cited as a problem for partridge populations (Herranz, 2000). Studies of the diet of predators in Spain indicate that red-legged partridges are not the main prey of any predator, but are included in the diet of many species (eggs, chicks or adult partridges are eaten by at least 39 species; Yanes *et al.*, 1998). Although predation rates on red-legged partridge nests can be high in Spain (15.2-74.3% of nest attempts; Yanes *et al.*, 1998), scientific studies of the relative importance of predation with respect to the other possible conservation problems do not exist. Hunters go even further, however, claiming that rabbit scarcity has induced a switching of predation pressure onto partridges, and that the recovery of rabbit populations could be beneficial for partridges (Costa-Batllori, 1992); to our knowledge, no scientific evidence supporting this claim has yet been published (see also Mañosa 2002).

40.3 Persecution of raptors: links to small game decline

40.3.1 Intensification of raptor persecution

As well as inducing prey shortages, the scarcity of the two main small game species in Spain has brought about a second, probably more serious, problem for Spanish raptors. When human hunting success decreases, predators are commonly blamed, and hunting lobbies call for intensification of predator control (Franzmann, 1993; Anon., 2000; Redpath & Thirgood, Chapter 39; Galbraith *et al.*, Chapter 41). Spain is no exception, but hunters have not been satisfied by the government response to calls for greater predator control, and consequently the level of illegal control, particularly through poisoning, has increased over the last ten years. Furthermore, hunters have reacted to the scarcity of red-legged partridge and rabbit by promoting massive releases of farm-bred animals (currently more than 3 million partridges per year; Gortázar *et al.*, 2000b). These releases are usually accompanied by predator control campaigns which are often urged by game managers in order to achieve a successful release (Costa-Batllori, 1992; Nadal,1998). This widespread, increasing management technique may have worsened the problem of illegal predator control.

40.3.2 *Poisoning and declines in scavenging raptors*

Increased rates of poisoning were first detected in red kites *Milvus milvus*, during the national census carried out between 1992 and 1994 (Viñuela, 1996; Viñuela *et al.*, 1999). The red kite has almost disappeared as a breeding species in those areas of Spain where small game hunting is economically more important and where the illegal persecution of predators by poisoning is a more common activity (Castilla-La Mancha and Andalucía, southern Spain) (Villafuerte *et al.*, 1998). Most populations of red kite, for which information was available, were declining during the early 1990s, apparently due mainly to persecution. These declines again coincided with areas where hunting was economically important, particularly in the core range of the rabbits (Villafuerte *et al.*, 1998). The situation has not improved during recent years. Data from the northern plateau indicates a statistically significant reduction of about 50% in breeding numbers between 1994 and 2000 (IBERIS, 2001). In the Segovia province, one of the most important breeding areas

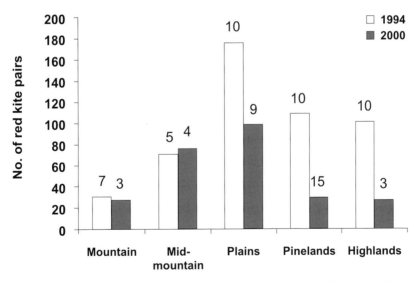

Figure 40.1. Estimated populations of red kites during the breeding season in five areas of Segovia province (central Spain, overall area of 6,900 km²). Estimates were obtained from road transects in 100 km² U.T.M. squares or by detection of territorial pairs. Comparison was given between data from 1994 (white bars; Viñuela *et al.*, 1999) and from 2000 (black bars; Contreras, 2001). Data classified according to natural regions within the province (see Viñuela *et al.*, 1999). Number of squares sampled given above bars.

in the world, breeding populations of red kite appear to have been reduced by a similar proportion (Contreras, 2001; Figure 40.1). Red kites appear to be particularly sensitive to human persecution due to their life history. They feed on small carrion items and thus are very sensitive to poisoning (see Carter *et al.*, Chapter 31; Holmes *et al.*, Chapter 37). They also spend long periods flying low and slowly, often near human settlements, and are thus an easy target for shooters (Viñuela, 1996; Viñuela *et al.*, 1999; Carter, 2001). Although the red kite is probably the species most seriously affected by this problem, populations of other carrion-eating raptors such as Egyptian vultures *Neophron percnopterus* are also affected. Most recent data on this species suggest an overall reduction of 20-30% in the Spanish population during the last decade (F. Hiraldo, pers. comm.; see http://fapas.netcom.es/ANTIDOTO.html, and http://www.wwf.es).

In recent years poisoning has also affected imperial eagles, because they also scavenge carrion outside of the breeding season (González, 1996, 1997). Poisoning is a serious problem in Spain, and this is well illustrated by the discovery of an illegal business distributing poisoned eggs. In just three months, this operation had sold more than one million poisoned eggs to several landowners, mainly in southern Spain (ADENA/WWF, unpublished report).

40.3.3 Impacts on migratory species

Spain is also the main wintering area for several species of European raptors, including red kites (Cramp & Simmons, 1980; Sunyer & Viñuela, 1996; Viñuela *et al.*, 1999). The breeding population of red kites in Germany started to decline slightly between 1992 and 1993, and then suffered a decline estimated at 25% between 1994 and 1997 (Mammen, 2000). German researchers think that this is due to a decrease in kite productivity operating through agricultural changes, occurring mainly in Eastern Germany, which have reduced food availability for red kites (Hille, 1995; Mammen, 2000). However, such a rapid population decrease in a long-lived species like the red kite is more likely to be related to increasing adult mortality than to falling productivity (Newton, 1979). During 1992-1994, 25 cases of shooting at winter roosts were recorded in Spain (based on approximately 500 visits to 268 roosts; Viñuela & Hiraldo, in press). Extrapolating this rate of shooting to the overall winter population, and assuming one bird is killed per shooting event (probably a conservative criteria for shooting in roosts), we estimate that several thousand red kites may be killed in Spain each winter. To this number we should also add birds that are killed out of roosts, and those poisoned (e.g. 17 ringed German kites found poisoned in north Burgos in one year; WWF/ADENA, unpublished data).

We suggest that the illegal killing of red kites in Spain in winter is perhaps the most important mortality source of this species in Europe. The decline of the German population occurred soon after the increase in raptor persecution in Spain was detected (early 1990s), but with a slight delay. The winter census performed in Spain during 1992-1994 suggested that there was a large floating population among wintering red kites (Viñuela *et al.*, 1999). The high mortality during winter in Spain in the early 1990s may have been partially compensated by a large floating population replacing lost breeding birds. However, after only several years of high winter mortality, a reduction in the number of breeding pairs would have been detectable in Germany, as the supply of floaters expired. Other red kite populations in central Europe that presumably also spend the winter in Spain

(France, Denmark, Austria, Czech Republic) have suffered strong declines during the same period (J.M. Thiollay & Libor Schröpfer, pers. comm.). In contrast, other populations which do not spend the winter in Spain (UK and Italy) remain stable or increasing (Allavena *et al.*, 2001; Carter & Ottway, 2001; Carter *et al.*, Chapter 31), also suggesting that the problems facing wintering birds in Spain could be a major explanation for the widespread decline in central Europe. Unfortunately, no data are available for other species which could be suffering the same problem during winter in Spain, such as common buzzard *Buteo buteo*, hen harrier *Circus cyaneus*, or merlin *Falco columbarius*.

40.4 Looking for a solution: the 'ANTIDOTE' project

In 1997 the main Spanish conservation organisations mounted a campaign against the illegal killing of predators (the 'ANTIDOTE' project). The main aim of this project is to encourage the use of a standard reporting protocol when a predator's carcass is found in the field. This should support the identification of hunting lands where illegal persecution occurs, and may increase the number of successful criminal prosecutions. The first important objective of this project was to establish a better information base on the extent of illegal persecution and, unfortunately, our worst expectations have been realised (Table 40.2). Of particular concern are the 68 imperial eagles that have been found dead during the last ten years. Poisoning rates must be higher than given in Table 40.2 because many cases remain undetected. The real number of Spanish imperial eagles poisoned during that

Table 40.2. Poisoned raptors found in Spain between 1990 and 2000. Data from ANTIDOTE project (Hernández, 2000; http://ecologistasenaccion.org; http://www.wwf.es).

Species	No. Poisoned
Griffon vulture *Gyps fulvus*	566
Red kite *Milvus milvus*	408
Black vulture *Aegypius monachus*	391
Black kite *Milvus migrans*	152
Egyptian vulture *Neophron percnopterus*	112
Golden eagle *Aquila chrysaetos*	72
Spanish imperial eagle *Aquila adalberti*	68
Common buzzard *Buteo buteo*	57
Common kestrel *Falco tinnunculus*	50
Bonnelli's eagle *Hieraetus fasciatus*	21
Lesser kestrel *Falco naumannii*	20
Eagle owl *Bubo bubo*	15
Booted eagle *Hieraetus pennatus*	12
Marsh harrier *Circus aeruginosus*	10
Lammergeier *Gypaetus barbatus*	8
Montagu's harrier *Circus pygargus*	5
Sparrowhawk *Accipiter nisus*	5
Long-eared owl *Asio otus*	5
Barn owl *Tyto alba*	2

period is estimated to be between 100 and 600 birds from a population of about 140 breeding pairs (Criado, 2000; J. Oria, pers. comm.). The ANTIDOTE project has also confirmed that the red kite is one of the species more seriously affected by this problem, with more than 400 birds found poisoned in ten years (Table 40.2).

The data gathered also seem to support the idea that the main reason poison is placed in the environment is to supposedly benefit small game species through the control of foxes and corvids, because 79% of poisoning cases were found on small game hunting lands. Furthermore, 70% of the poisoning cases have been detected during spring months when gamekeepers and hunters prepare the estates for the hunting season ahead. The breeding season is the time of year when predation has a major impact on red-legged partridge and rabbit populations (Villafuerte, 1994; Herranz, 2000), so the game managers' actions may be an effective way of striving to maximise small game productivity. The higher incidence of poisoning during the breeding season could partially explain why declines of the resident Spanish red kite populations appear to be greater than the population declines found in the other European migrating red kite populations (see Mañosa, 2002).

The main aim of the ANTIDOTE project was to reduce the illegal killing of predators by improving the prosecution of offenders. However, the results have proved to be relatively poor so far. In the last 10 years, there have been only about 15 successful prosecutions for the illegal poisoning of raptors, and fewer than 20 are currently under consideration (C. Cano, pers. comm.). Although this project is an urgent initial step in trying to solve the problem, it cannot be considered a robust and long-term solution to the conflict.

40.5 Effects of predation on small game in Spain

40.5.1 *Predator impacts on prey populations: limitation of prey numbers*

The first step to a long-term resolution of this conflict, is to improve our knowledge of the effect of predators on small game populations in Spain (c.f. Anon., 2000 for the UK). Food supply is one of the main factors regulating the population density and breeding productivity of animals, and thus the effect of prey abundance on populations of predators is often very clear (Newton, 1979, 1998, Chapter 1). In contrast, the role of predators in the dynamics of prey populations seems to be much more varied, from having no effect at all to a clear regulation of prey numbers by predators (Newton, 1998, Chapter 1; and see Redpath & Thirgood, Chapter 39). Errington (1946) suggested that predation could have little impact on prey populations because predators would be removing the surplus individuals from the population that would be lost anyway (the so-called 'doomed surplus'). However, recent experimental and correlational data suggest that predators may indeed limit prey abundance, particularly under conditions of low prey densities and when the predator communities are complex (e.g. Sih *et al.*, 1985, 1998; Marcström *et al.*, 1989; Newsome *et al.*, 1989; Newton, 1993, 1998; Korpimäki & Krebs, 1996; Klemola *et al.*, 1997; Redpath & Thirgood, 1997; Banks, 2000; Thirgood *et al.*, 2000a,b).

Extensive research on the effect of predators on rabbits has been undertaken in Australia and New Zealand, where this alien species has become a pest and where it seems that rabbit populations can escape predatory regulation of numbers (e.g. Newsome *et al.*, 1989; Pech *et al.*, 1992; Banks *et al.*, 1998; Banks, 2000). However, the results of these studies cannot necessarily be applied to Spain, where the predator community is more complex than in Australia. In fact, it has been suggested that one of the main reasons explaining the success of rabbits colonizing Australia could have been the paucity of mammalian predators, and in particular those species which kill rabbits inside their warrens (Williams *et al.*, 1995). Furthermore, experimental research has shown that predation by carnivores can control rabbit numbers when populations have a low density (human control) in Australia (Banks, 2000), or when adverse environmental conditions do not allow high rabbit densities in New Zealand (B. Reddex, pers. comm.).

40.5.2 Predator impacts on rabbit numbers in Spain

Little is known in Spain about the effect of predators on small game populations (reviews in Villafuerte (1994) and Herranz (2000)). To our knowledge, the only study on the effect of predation on rabbit populations in Iberia was that undertaken in Doñana National Park (Villafuerte, 1994; Villafuerte *et al.*, 2000). This is a protected area where there is no game hunting (except occasional poaching), and where there is a high density of rabbit predators. During the study as many as 11 individual lynx used the study area (Villafuerte, 1994). This study was performed over a three year period which included the year in which RHD arrived at the National Park. Although a high proportion of radio-tracked rabbits and monitored warrens or litter holes were predated before the arrival of RHD (Figure 40.2), Doñana maintained one of the highest densities of rabbits recorded in Spain (Blanco & Villafuerte, 1993; Villafuerte, 1994; Villafuerte *et al.*, 1998). The predators which caused a higher loss of reproductive potential in rabbit population were opportunistic species, such as black kites or foxes, while specialist predators on rabbits, such as imperial eagle or Iberian lynx, had relatively low impacts (Villafuerte, 1994).

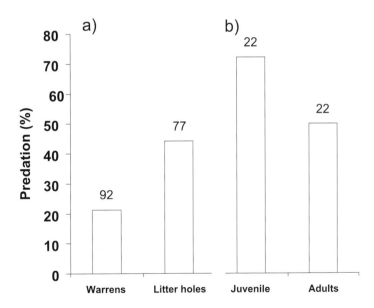

Figure 40.2. a) Percentage of rabbit warrens and litter holes predated per year, estimated by visits every two days during the year. Predation was considered to have occurred when warrens/litter holes were found excavated and the nest material was outside. b) Percentage of juvenile and adult rabbits radio-marked that were predated. Data pooled for 1989-1991 for the Doñana study area, before the arrival of rabbit haemorrhagic disease (RHD) in one of the highest recorded density populations in Spain. Sample sizes given above bars.

When RHD arrived to Doñana in 1990, rabbit populations were reduced by about 60%, and they have remained constantly low over ten years (Villafuerte, 1994; Villafuerte *et al.*, 2001). This could be an example of the predator-pit hypothesis: rabbits populations were reduced by causes other than predation, but predation pressure could be suppressing numbers after the crash (Newsome *et al.*, 1989; Trout & Tittensor, 1989; Banks, 2000). In contrast, in other areas of Spain where game hunting is commonplace and where predator control is likely to occur, rabbit populations are already recovering (Blanco & Villafuerte, 1993) because rabbits acquire natural resistance to RHD (Villafuerte *et al.*, 2000).

Experimental evidence also suggests that predation can control rabbit populations in Doñana. Experimental suppression of predation by carnivores, kept out of experimental areas by low-energy electric lines, was correlated with marked increases in numbers of rabbits to the point that food was exhausted and starvation followed (Moreno & Villafuerte, 1994). Predation pressure by raptors in this study was not reduced, as the time spent by raptors flying above the fenced areas increased three-fold as rabbit populations grew (R. Villafuerte, unpublished data). Additional research is necessary in order to assess the effect of raptors on population dynamics of rabbits.

Some workers have suggested that the presence of Iberian lynx may benefit rabbits, because lynx displace or kill smaller carnivores, such as mongooses or genets, thus reducing overall predation rates on rabbits, and increasing the density of the prey (Palomares *et al.*, 1995, 1996a). The possible effect of lynx on fox populations remains unclear (Palomares *et al.*, 1996a). These studies have been considered 'good news' by Spanish conservationists, because of the positive message that can be presented to land-owners about the presence of lynx. However, the Iberian lynx is a very scarce species, absent from most of the country, and game managers could claim that the absence of the lynx may induce a 'mesopredator release' effect, and that predator control is a necessary management tool in most of the country.

More research is needed before it is generally accepted that the presence of lynx can induce a higher density in rabbit populations (see Litvaitis & Villafuerte, 1996; Palomares *et al.*, 1996b). Lynx can control numbers of smaller carnivores (Palomares *et al.*, 1996a, 1998), but it is still unclear whether a reduction in mongoose numbers (this is the only small carnivore controlled by lynx which is an important predator of rabbits in the area; Palomares *et al.*, 1995), has a real effect on rabbit populations. The studies by Palomares *et al.* in this area of Doñana (Coto del Rey) did not take into account the effect of habitat selection by rabbits. Rabbits are most common in the Mediterranean bushlands and pasturelands with cork oaks *Quercus suber* near marshes, locally called 'La Vera' (Moreno & Villafuerte, 1995; Palomares *et al.*, 2001). In these areas the density of lynx was high, while areas further from marshes are less favourable for rabbits, particularly pine *Pinus* spp. forests, and where there were fewer lynx.

Palomares *et al.* (1995) compared the density of rabbits in two different habitat types: continuous optimal habitat, and good habitat within a matrix of unfavourable habitat. They argued that high rabbit densities in the good habitat was promoted by a reduction in mongoose numbers alone. It is possible that lynx density would depend on rabbit density, which is determined mainly by habitat quality (Palomares *et al.*, 2001; P. Ferreras *et al.*, submitted), and if this is the case then the reduction in mongoose numbers induced by the presence of lynx may have no influence on rabbit abundance. Furthermore, Palomares *et al.* (1995) did not consider that in their study area there was a dense population of raptors (several hundred pairs of black kites, and some red kites, booted eagles *Hierateus pennatus*, imperial eagles and buzzards), all taking rabbits as their main prey (Valverde, 1967). In fact, the density of black kites was highest in areas where lynx were present, probably because this raptor also selects areas with a high density of rabbits (Viñuela *et al.*, 1994). Less than 5 km away from Coto del Rey, in the Reserva Biológica de Doñana, a similar raptor community with a lower density of black kites killed about the same proportion of rabbits (53% of the total number of rabbits killed) as did a diverse population of carnivores (47%), with a lower density of lynx, and thus probably higher densities of smaller carnivores (Villafuerte, 1994; Moreno *et al.*, 1996). Without further data on mongoose predation rates on rabbits it is difficult to see how the simple reduction in mongoose numbers can benefit rabbit density when so many raptors are removing rabbits from the population.

In conclusion, while intraguild population control induced by lynx could increase rabbit abundance, we suggest that predation by raptors, and more importantly habitat selection by rabbits and risk of predation in different habitats, should be included in attempts to model rabbit abundance (Litvaitis & Villafuerte, 1996).

40.6 Prospects for a solution to the raptor-game conflict

It is possible that abundant generalist predators such as foxes, with populations probably supplemented by human activities and not experiencing intra-guild predation by wolf and lynx, can suppress the number of rabbits after the population crash induced by RHD (Gortázar *et al.*, 2000a). If this is the case, both hunters and conservationists should collaborate in fox control. A legal, regulated, and selective predator control scheme could favour the recovery of rabbit populations and reduce the use of illegal, non-selective methods, thus favouring the recovery of populations of non-targeted predators (see Sim *et al.*, 2000, Chapter 28). However, setting management targets will depend on knowing the relative importance of predation in determining rabbit numbers. A good habitat management programme can increase rabbit density four-fold (Moreno & Villafuerte, 1995), and is one of the best management techniques for increasing rabbit density. If the problem for rabbits in a given area is habitat structure, predator control would not provide benefits and would be a waste of resources. Even where predator control appeared to be necessary, it is not clear how it should be carried out. For example, intense non-selective predator control can reduce the number of less common, more specialised predators, thus favouring foxes which are the main target species of the predator control (J. Casanovas, pers. comm.).

In general, a 'truce' in the long 'war' between conservationist and hunting movements may, after all, benefit the conservation of endangered predators. Both hunters and conservationists may have a common interest: well preserved habitats holding high numbers of small game (prey for endangered predators and hunters) (see also Anon., 2000; Galbraith *et al.*, Chapter 41).

An example of how research and collaboration between these two sectors may improve the situation is found in Andalucía with respect to the season for rabbit hunting. Models of the population dynamics of rabbits in this area of Spain suggested that the traditional hunting season (October to January) is the worst time of the year for rabbit hunting if the aim is to keep high numbers of rabbits throughout the years (Angulo & Villafuerte, 2003). Before the arrival of diseases, rabbits were probably a pest, and the hunting season in Spain was set to reduce numbers of rabbits by as much as possible. However, when the objective is enhancing rabbit populations, the best hunting season predicted by modelling could be May to August. Given that hunting from May to July may cause disturbance to other species during the breeding season, researchers have recommended a new hunting season between August and November, as a compromise. Future surveys in Andalucía should provide insights on the success of this management measure, for rabbit populations, as well as for raptor conservation.

Acknowledgements

We thank two anonymous referees and the editors for comments on an earlier draft of the manuscript.

References

Allavena, S., Angelini, I. & Pellegrini, M. (2001). The red kite in Italy. In *Abstracts of the 4th Eurasian Congress on Raptors*, Sevilla, 2001. Estación Biológica de Doñana/Raptor Research Foundation, Sevilla. pp. 4-5.

Angulo, E. & Villafuerte, R. (2003). Modelling hunting strategies for the conservation of wild rabbit populations. *Biological Conservation,* **115**, 291-301.

Anonymous (2000). *Report of the UK Raptor Working Group.* Department of the Environment, Transport and the Regions and Joint Nature Conservation Committee, Peterborough.

Banks, P.B. (2000). Can foxes regulate rabbit populations? *Journal of Wildlife Management,* **64**, 401-406.

Banks, P.B., Dickman, C.R. & Newsome, A.E. (1998). Ecological costs of vertebrate pest control: foxes and rabbits. *Journal of Wildlife Management,* **60**, 766-772.

Bijleveld, M. (1974). *Birds of Prey in Europe.* MacMillan, London.

Blanco, J.C. & Villafuerte, R. (1993). *Factores ecológicos que influyen sobre las poblaciones de conejos. Incidencia de la enfermedad hemorrágica.* Unpublished report. ICONA, Madrid.

Blanco, J.C. (1998). *Mamíferos de España.* Planeta, Barcelona.

Brown, L.H. & Amadon, D. (1968). *Eagles, Hawks and Falcons of the World.* Hamlyn, Feltham.

Calvete, C., Villafuerte, R., Lucientes, J. & Osacar, J.J. (1997). Effectiveness of traditional wild rabbit restocking in Spain. *Journal of Zoology (London),* **241**, 271-277.

Carter, I. (2001). *The Red Kite.* Arlequin Press, Chelmsford.

Carter, I. & Ottway, D. (2001). Rates of spread of reintroduced red kites in the United Kingdom. In *Abstracts of the 4th Eurasian Congress on Raptors*, Sevilla, 2001. Estación Biológica de Doñana/Raptor Research Foundation, Sevilla. pp. 39.

Collar, N.J., Crosby, M.J. & Stattersfield, A.J. (1994). *Birds to Watch 2: the World List of Threatened Birds.* Birdlife Conservation Series No. 4. Birdlife International, Cambridge.

Contreras, A. (2001). *Impacto sobre la avifauna de la implantación del Plan de Gestión de los Resíduos Sólidos Urbanos en Segovia.* XII Becas de Medio Ambiente Caja Segovia. Caja Segovia, Segovia.

Costa-Batllori , P. (1992). El mantenimiento de las poblaciones de conejo silvestre como protección a la perdiz roja. In *La Perdiz Roja. Gestión del Hábitat.* Fundación La Caixa, Barcelona, Spain. pp. 61-62.

Cramp, S. & Simmons, K.E.L. (1980). *The Birds of the Western Palearctic, Vol. II.* Oxford University Press, Oxford.

Criado, J. (2000). Aguila imperial ibérica. El ave del año necesita ayuda. *La Garcilla,* **107**, 10-12.

Delibes, M. & Hiraldo, F. (1981). The rabbit as prey in the Iberian Mediterranean ecosystem. In *Proceedings of the I World Lagomorph Conference*, ed. by K. Myers & C.D. MacInnes. University of Guelph Press, Guelph. pp. 614-622.

Donázar, J.A. & Fernández, C. (1989). Population trends of the Griffon vulture (*Gyps fulvus*) in northern Spain between 1969 and 1989 in relation to conservation measures. *Biological Conservation,* **53**, 83-91.

Errington, P.L. (1946). Predation and vertebrate populations. *Quarterly Review of Biology,* **21,** 144-177, 221-245.

Fernández, C. (1993). Effect of the viral haemorrhagic pneumonia of the wild rabbit on the diet and breeding success of the golden eagle *Aquila chrysaëtos (L.)*. *Revue d'Ecologie, Terre et Vie,* **48,** 323-329.

Ferreras, P., Travaini, A., Zapata, S.C. & Delibes, M. (submitted). Short term responses of mammalian carnivores to a sudden collapse of rabbits in Mediterranean Spain.

Flux, J.E.C. & Fullagar, P.J. (1983). World distribution of the *rabbit (Oryctolagus cuniculus)*. *Acta Zoologica Fennica,* **174,** 75-77.

Franzmann, A.W. (1993). Biopolitics of wolf management in Alaska. *Alces,* **29,** 9-26.

García y Bellido, A. *(1945). España y los españoles hace dos mil años según la 'Geografía' de Estrabón.* Espasa Calpe, Madrid.

Garzón, J. (1977). Birds of prey in Spain: their present situation. In *Proceedings of the I World Conference on Birds of Prey,* ed. by R.D. Chancellor. ICBP, London. pp. 159-170.

González, L.M. (1989). *Historia natural del Aguila imperial ibérica.* Ph.D. Thesis. Universidad Autónoma, Madrid.

González, L.M. (1996). Tendencias poblacionales y estatus de conservación del Aguila imperial ibérica *Aquila adalberti* en España durante los últimos 20 años. In *Biology and Conservation of Mediterranean Raptors,* ed. by J. Muntaner & J. Mayol. Monografía No. 4. SEO/Birdlife, Madrid. pp. 61-76.

González, L.M. (1997). Aguila imperial ibérica. In *Atlas de las Aves de España (1975-1995),* ed. by F.J. Purroy. Lynx Ed., Barcelona. pp. 118-119.

Gortázar, C., Fernández de Luco, D., Pages, A., Feliu, C. & Lucientes, J. (2000a). Actuaciones para la recuperación de las poblaciones de conejo. In *Enfermedades del Conejo, Vol. II,* ed. by J.M. Rosell. Mundi-Prensa, Madrid. pp. 493-512.

Gortázar, C., Villafuerte, R. & Martín, M. (2000b). Success of traditional restocking of red-legged partridge for hunting purposes in areas of low density of northeast Spain, Aragón. *Z. Jagdwiss.* **46,** 23-30.

Herranz, J. (2000). *Efectos de la depredación y del control de predadores sobre la caza menor en Castilla-La Mancha.* Ph.D. Thesis. Universidad Autónoma, Madrid.

Hille, S. (1995). Nahrungswahl und Jagdstrategien des Rotmilans (*Milvusmilvus*) im Biosphärenreservat Rhon/Hessen. *Vogel and Umwelt,* **8,** 99-126.

IBERIS, Estudios y Actividades Medioambientales (2001). *Estudio de las poblaciones reproductoras del Milano Real (Milvus milvus) en Castilla y León 2001.* Unpublished report. Consejería de Medio Ambiente y Ordenación del Territorio de la Junta de Castilla y León, Valladolid.

Klemola, T., Koivula, M., KorpimäkI, E. & Norrdahl, K. (1997). Small mustelid predation slows population growth of *Microtus* voles: a predation reduction experiment. *Journal of Animal Ecology,* **66,** 607-614.

Korpimäki, E. & Krebs, C.J. (1996). Predation and population cycles of small mammals. *Bioscience,* **46,** 754-764.

Litvaitis, J.A. & Villafuerte, R. (1996). Intraguild predation, mesopredator release, and prey stability. *Conservation Biology,* **10,** 676-677.

Mammen, U. (2000). Bestandsabnahme beim Rotmilan *Milvus milvus* von 1994 bis 1997 in Deutschland. *Ornithologische Mitteilungen,* **52,** 4-13.

Mañosa, S. (2002). The conflict between gamebird hunting and raptors in Europe. Unpublished report. REGHAB project, European Commission, Brussels.

Marcström, V., Keith, L.B., Engren, E. & Cary, J.R. (1989). Demographic responses of Arctic hares (*Lepus timidus*) to experimental reductions of red foxes (*Vulpes vulpes*) and martens (*Martes martes*). *Canadian Journal of Zoology,* **67,** 658-668.

Martínez, J.E. & Calvo, J.F. (2001). Diet and breeding success of eagle owl in southeastern Spain: effect of rabbit haemorrhagic disease. *Journal of Raptor Research,* **35,** 259-262.

Moreno, S. & Villafuerte, S. (1994). Estudio de la influencia de la enfermedad hemorrágico vírica sobre las poblaciones de conejos en el Parque Nacional de Doñana. Report. ICONA-CSIC, Estación Biológica de Doñana, Sevilla.

Moreno, S. & Villafuerte, R. (1995). Traditional management of scrubland for the conservation of rabbits *Oryctolagus cuniculus* and their predators in Doñana National Park, Spain. *Biological Conservation,* **73**, 81-85.

Moreno, S., Villafuerte, R. & Delibes, M. (1996). Cover is safe during the day but dangerous at night: the use of vegetation by European wild rabbits. *Canadian Journal of Zoology,* **74**, 1656-1660.

Nadal, J. (1992). Problemática de las poblaciones de perdiz roja, bases ecoetológicas para tener éxito con las repoblaciones. In *La Perdiz Roja. Gestión del Hábitat.* Fundación La Caixa, Barcelona. pp. 87-100.

Nadal, J. (1998). La bioecología de la perdiz roja. In *La Perdiz Roja. Gestión del Hábitat.* Fundación La Caixa, Barcelona. pp. 33-48.

Newsome, A.E., Parer, I. & Catling, P.C. (1989). Prolonged prey suppression by carnivores. Predator-removal experiments. *Oecologia,* **78**, 458-467.

Newton, I. (1979). *Population Ecology of Raptors.* T. & A.D. Poyser, London.

Newton, I. (1993). Predation and limitation of birds numbers. *Current Ornithology,* **11**, 143-198.

Newton, I. (1998). *Population Limitation in Birds.* Academic Press, London.

Notario, A. (1992). Panorámica de la perdiz roja en España. Análisis de los factores de amenaza de sus poblaciones. In *La Perdiz Roja. Gestión del Hábitat.* Fundación La Caixa, Barcelona. pp. 5-14.

Nowell, K. & Jackson, P. (1996). *Wild Cats: Status Survey and Conservation Action Plan.* IUCN, Gland.

Office Nationale de la Chasse (1986). *La Perdix rouge.* Notes techniques. Bulletin No. 106. ONC, París.

Oria, J. (2000). Una especie sensible a las agresiones. *La Garcilla,* **107**, 20-21.

Palomares, F., Gaona, P., Ferreras, P. & Delibes, M. (1995). Positive effect on game species of top predators by controlling smaller predator populations: an example with lynx, mongooses, and rabbits. *Conservation Biology,* **9**, 295-305.

Palomares, F., Ferreras, P., Fedriani, J.M. & Delibes, M. (1996a). Spatial relationships between Iberian lynx and other carnivores in an area of south-western Spain. *Journal of Applied Ecology,* **33**, 5-13.

Palomares, F., Delibes, M., Ferreras, P. & Gaona, P. (1996b). Mesopredator release and prey abundance: reply to Litvaitis and Villafuerte. *Conservation Biology,* **10**, 678-679.

Palomares, F., Ferreras, P., Travaini, A. & Delibes, M. (1998). Co-existence between lynx and Egyptian mongooses: estimating interaction strength by structural equation modelling and testing by an observational study. *Journal of Animal Ecology,* **67**, 967-978.

Palomares, F., Delibes, M., Revilla, E., Calzada, E. & Fedriani, J.M. (2001). Spatial ecology of Iberian lynx and abundance of European rabbits in southwestern Spain. *Wildlife Monographs,* **148**, 1-36.

Pech, R.P., Sinclair, A.R.E., Newsome, A.E. & Catling, P.C. (1992). Limits to predator regulation of rabbits in Australia: evidence from predator-removal experiments. *Oecologia,* **89**, 102-112.

Potts, G.R. (1980). The effects of modern agriculture, nest predation and game management on the population ecology of partridges (*Perdix perdix* and *Alectoris rufa*). *Ecological Research,* **2**, 2-79.

Purroy, F.J. (1997). *Atlas de las Aves de España (1975-1995).* Lynx Edicions, Barcelona.

Redpath, S.M. & Thirgood, S.J. (1997). *Birds of Prey and Red Grouse.* The Stationery Office, London.

Sih, A., Crowley, P., McPeek, M., Petranka, J. & Strohmeie, R.K. (1985). Predation, competition, and prey communities: a review of field experiments. *Annual Review of Ecology and Systematics,* **16**, 269-311.

Sih, A., Englund, G. & Wooster, D. (1998). Emergent impacts of multiple predators on prey. *Trends in Ecology and Evolution,* **13**, 350-355.

Sim, I.M.W., Campbell, L., Pain, D.J. & Wilson, J.D. (2000). Correlates of the population increase of common buzzards *Buteo buteo* in the West Midlands between 1983 and 1996. *Bird Study*, **47**, 154-164.

Sunyer, C. & Viñuela, J. (1996). Invernada de rapaces (*O. Falconiformes*) en España peninsular y Baleares. In *Biology and Conservation of Mediterranean Raptors*, ed. by J. Muntaner & J. Mayol. Monografía No. 4. SEO/Birdlife, Madrid. pp. 361-370.

Thirgood, S.J., Redpath, S.M., Rothery, D.T. & Aebischer, N.J. (2000a). Raptor predation and population limitation in red grouse. *Journal of Animal Ecology*, **69**, 504-516.

Thirgood, S.J., Redpath, S.M., Haydon, S.M., Rothery, D.T., Newton, I. & Hudson, P.J. (2000b). Habitat loss and raptor predation: disentangling long- and short-term causes of red grouse declines. *Proceedings of the Royal Society B*, **267**, 651-656.

Trout, R.C. & Tittensor, A.M. (1989). Can predators regulate wild rabbit *Oryctolagus cuniculus* population density in England and Wales? *Mammal Review*, **19**, 153-173.

Tucker, G.M. & Heath, M.F. (1994). *Birds in Europe: Their Conservation Status*. Birdlife Conservation Series No. 3. Birdlife International, Cambridge.

Valverde, J.A. (1967). *Estructura de una comunidad de Vertebrados terrestres*. Monografías de la Estación Biológica de Doñana, No. 1. CSIC, Sevilla.

Villafuerte, R. (1994). *Riesgo de predación y estrategias defensivas del conejo Oryctolagus cuniculus, en el Parque Nacional de Doñana*. Ph.D. Thesis. Universidad de Córdoba, Spain.

Villafuerte, R., Calvete, C., Gortázar, C. & Moreno, S. (1994). First epizootic of rabbit haemorrhagic disease in free living populations of *Oryctolagus cuniculus* at Doñana National Park, Spain. *Journal of Wildlife Diseases*, **30**, 176-179.

Villafuerte, R., Calvete, C., Blanco, J.C. & Lucientes, J. (1995). Incidence of viral haemorrhagic disease in wild rabbit populations in Spain. *Mammalia*, **59**, 651-659.

Villafuerte, R., Luco, D.F., Gortázar, C. & Blanco, J.C. (1996). Effect on red fox litter size and diet after rabbit haemorrhagic disease in north-eastern Spain. *Journal of Zoology (London)*, **240**, 764-767.

Villafuerte, R., Viñuela, J. & Blanco, J.C. (1998). Extensive predation persecution caused by population crash in a game species: the case of red kites and rabbits in Spain. *Biological Conservation*, **84**, 181-188.

Villafuerte, R. & Viñuela, J. (1999). Size of rabbits consumed by black kites increased after a rabbit epizooty. *Mammal Review*, **29**, 261-264

Villafuerte, R., Jordán, G. & Angulo, E. (2000). Biología y factores de riesgo en el conejo silvestre. In *Enfermedades del Conejo, Vol. II*, ed. by J.M. Rosell. Mundi-Prensa, Madrid. pp. 459-472.

Villafuerte, R., Calvete, C., Angulo, E., Moreno, S., dela Puente, M. & Branco, M.S. (2001). *Análisis de la efectividad de las repoblaciones del conejo y otras medidas de gestión en el Parque Nacional de Doñana*. Unpublished report. Parque Nacional de Doñana, Spain.

Viñuela, J. (1996). Situación del Milano Real (*Milvus milvus*) en el Mediterráneo. In *Biology and Conservation of Mediterranean Raptors*, ed. by J. Muntaner & J. Mayol. Monografía No. 4. SEO/Birdlife, Madrid. pp. 91-100.

Viñuela, J. (1997). Adaptation vs. constraint: intraclutch egg-mass variation in birds. *Journal of Animal Ecology*, **66**, 781-792.

Viñuela, J. (2000). Opposing selective pressures on hatching asynchrony: egg viability, brood reduction, and nestling growth. *Behavioural Ecology and Sociobiology*, **48**, 333-343.

Viñuela, J. & Veiga, J.P. (1992). Importance of rabbits in the diet and reproductive success of black kites in southwestern Spain. *Ornis Scandinavica*, **23**, 132-138.

Viñuela, J., Villafuerte, R. & De Le Court, C. (1994). Nesting dispersion of a black kite population in relation to location of rabbit warrens. *Canadian Journal of Zoology*, **72**, 1680-1683.

Viñuela, J., Martí, R. & Ruiz, A. (Eds) (1999). El Milano Real en España. Monografía No. 6. SEO/Birdlife, Madrid.

Viñuela, J. & Hiraldo, F. (in press). Conservation problems of wintering red kites in Spain. *Vogel and Unwelt.*

Williams, K., Parer, I., Coman, B., Burley, J. & Braysher, M. (1995). *Managing Vertebrate Pests: Rabbits.* Australian Government Publishing Service, Canberra.

Yanes, M., Herranz, J., De La Puente, J. & Suárez, F. (1998). La perdiz roja. Identidad de los depredadores e intensidad de la depredación. In *La Perdiz Roja. I Curso.* Fedenca, Madrid. pp. 135-150.

Zeuner, F.E. (1963). *A History of Domesticated Animals.* Hutchinson, London.

41. TOWARDS RESOLVING RAPTOR-HUMAN CONFLICTS

Colin A. Galbraith, David A. Stroud & D.B.A. Thompson

Summary

1.   This concluding chapter examines aspects of human-raptor conflicts.

2.   Three aspects are considered: numbers and status of raptors; research on predation; and the complexity of land use change.

3.   Perceptions and the history of human-raptor interactions have an important bearing on the involvement of different parties in the debate.

4.   We argue that fora are effective in bringing protagonists together in order to address areas of conflict, and to devise practical and policy measures to provide some resolution.

41.1 Introduction

Over the past century raptors have figured significantly in the psyche of conservation, and in considerations of how the countryside should be managed. Indeed, in recent decades the history of raptor conservation in the UK has parallels with the wider history of nature conservation (e.g. Marren, 2002). The interplay between raptors and some sections of human society has been problematic over much of this time (e.g. Brown, 1976; Anon., 2000). As with many such issues, there has been much conjecture, speculation and debate concerning the policies and management practices which have been put in place to ensure effective conservation. This book provides many significant examples of studies which address key areas in the so-called 'raptor debate'. It is an important development, building on the UK Raptor Working Group Report (Anon., 2000). That report made 25 recommendations for action, dealing with: a) raptor populations and conservation status; b) illegal killing of raptors; c) gaps in research; d) moorland issues; e) racing pigeon issues; f) birds of prey in the lowlands; and g) raptors and songbirds.

Many raptor populations declined to low levels in the 1950s and 1960s because of pesticides, to recover only slowly through the 1970s until recent times (e.g. Newton, 1979; Anon., 2000; Greenwood *et al.*, Chapter 2). The decline to near extinction within the UK has clearly contributed to some raptor species becoming figureheads or conservation icons. At the same time, the overall quality of rural habitats has declined (e.g. Tucker & Heath, 1994; Stanners & Bordeau, 1995; Mackey *et al.*, 2001; Usher *et al.*, 2002; Moorland Working Group, 2002), and some people have linked the changing fortunes of raptors to this change (e.g. Brown, 1964, 1976). In relation to the economic stability of the rural environment, it is arguable that a more precarious situation exists now than perhaps at any time in recent decades; for example, the numbers of people directly engaged in land management has fallen to the lowest level since the 1940s (Moorland Working Group, 2002). It is important, therefore, that land managers and owners are able to find ways of balancing the economics of managing the countryside with maintaining biodiversity overall. In this context, an increasing public interest in raptors, and in the countryside in general, linked to a greater degree of leisure time available to individuals, is significant. More than a million people in Britain now routinely bird-watch, and many have a deep fascination and interest in birds of prey. There is, therefore, the potential for considerable debate and disagreement over the relevance and value of birds of prey to the countryside.

41.1.1 *Some key studies of raptors*

Many of the earlier chapters describe some of the significant contributions of work on raptors to conservation as a whole in the UK. For example, the re-introduction programmes of white-tailed eagles *Haliaeetus albicilla* (Bainbridge *et. al.*, Chapter 30) and red kite *Milvus milvus* (Carter *et al.*, Chapter 31) have been at the forefront of nature conservation work in the UK (Marren, 2002). Research on hen harriers *Circus cyaneus* (Amar *et al.*, Chapter 29; Summers *et al.*, Chapter 38; Redpath & Thirgood, Chapter 39), golden eagles *Aquila chrysaetos* (Watson, 1997; Watson *et al.*, Chapter 10; Fielding *et al.*, Chapter 17; Whitfield *et al.*, 2003, in press), peregrines *Falco peregrinus* (Ratcliffe, 1993, Chapter 4, Hardey *et al.*, Chapter 5) and owls (Strigiformes*)* (Petty & Thomas, Chapter 6; Shaw & Riddle, Chapter 7; Taylor & Walton, Chapter 32) continues to make significant contributions to ecological work underpinning wider conservation activities. Moreover, there are important studies from outwith the UK (Nielsen, Chapter 24; Arroyo *et al.*, Chapter 35; Viñuela & Villafuerte Chapter 40) which provide important directions for further research across Europe. All of these studies, and others, form a significant pedigree of research which builds on earlier advances in ecology and conservation generally arising from work on raptors (e.g. Newton 1979, 1998, Chapter 1; Ratcliffe, 1993; Redpath & Thirgood, 1997; Anon., 2000).

41.1.2 *Land use and management: stewardship*

There have been major changes in land use and land management across Britain over recent decades (e.g. Tucker & Heath, 1994; Thompson *et al.,* Chapter 25). In the uplands, large areas (often estates) have been managed for red grouse *Lagopus lagopus scoticus* (as well as red deer *Cervus elaphus* in Scotland) and/or sheep *Ovis aries* and forestry, and there have been significant changes in the areas under each of these land uses (e.g. Usher & Thompson, 1988; Thompson *et al.,* 1995; Moorland Working Group, 2002). The situation in the lowlands is perhaps more complex, with a variety of regimes being maintained throughout lowland Scotland to varying degrees of intensity. However, the principle of stewardship, where essentially the current owners manage the land in a way which passes on benefits to future generations, is well-established in land management practices throughout Scotland (e.g. Warren, 2001). There is, therefore, a deep involvement of landowners in the care of the land and its wildlife, and a long history of traditional land management practices, particularly in the uplands.

The link between land stewardship and birds of prey is clear, and in many cases birds of prey populations are maintained, or indeed enhanced, through particular land management practices (e.g. Tharme *et al.*, 2001; Scotland's Moorland Forum, 2003; Taylor & Walton, Chapter 32; Marquis *et al.*, Chapter 36; Redpath & Thirgood, Chapter 39). For example, the management regime for an area in the uplands may serve to maintain populations of golden eagle and hen harrier at sustainable numbers. But in some parts we have seen a culture of destruction of birds of prey which persists to this day (Thompson *et al.*, Chapter 25; Whitfield *et al.*, 2003, in press; Redpath *et al.*, in press). Tensions between different sectors of society which place different values on birds of prey have led on the one hand to a significant level of illegal persecution and killing throughout the second half of the twentieth century (Moore, 1957; Brown, 1964, 1976; RSPB & NCC, 1991a,b; RSPB, 1999a,b; Whitfield *et al.*, 2003; Redpath *et al.,* in press), whilst (and partly in response to this) national and international conservation legislation has been developed to give birds of prey some of the highest levels of legislative protection of any of Europe's wildlife (Tucker & Heath, 1994; Stroud, Chapter 3).

It is likely that persecution of wildlife will be punished more severely in the future, and the latest legislative proposals in Scotland point to tougher sentences being introduced to combat wildlife crime (e.g. Part 3 of the Nature Conservation (Scotland) Bill, as introduced in the Scottish Parliament on 29 September 2003). Encouragingly though, there is also a history in recent decades of dialogue between interested groups attempting to align land management practices with the ecological needs of birds of prey and, in particular, to eradicate persecution while maintaining other management practices (e.g. Moorland Working Group, 2002; Scotland's Moorland Forum, 2003; Redpath *et al.*, in press). The nature of legislative change, but also a realisation that conflicts are damaging all interests, is paving the way for more attempts at consensus building (see also Viñuela & Villafuerte's study in Spain, Chapter 40).

41.2 Raptor numbers and status

This book has been divided into six themes to highlight the various facets of research, conservation and management at the heart of many ecological studies. If any overall solution to achieving a balance between managing the countryside for raptors and people is to be achieved, then there are key areas where early agreement is required. For example, all parties involved should agree on the numbers and status of birds of prey throughout the country. Indeed, if we cannot agree on how many birds there are, and whether their populations are increasing, declining or stable, then the prospects of any wider agreement on how to resolve conflicts must be doubtful. Greenwood *et al.* (Chapter 2) and Table 25.1 in Thompson *et al.* (Chapter 25) provide the most up-to-date estimates of numbers and trends. As Greenwood *et al.* explain, a substantial amount of work has gone into verifying data and information sources, and peer-reviewing the work generally. In many ways Scotland is leading the way in Europe in drawing together data and information on raptors in a robust and systematic way. Seven bodies have signed a formal agreement to systematically collect, store, analyse and report on raptor information (Scottish Raptor Monitoring Scheme Agreement, 2002). This scheme will facilitate the sharing of raptor information between organisations and make data/information available for policy purposes and to inform practical action on the ground.

Gathering information on numbers is, of course, only part of the overall activity needed to underpin any decisions and to achieve a resolution of different opinions. It is important also to have longer-term studies which examine the ecology of a species in order to consider what its population trends are, and whether, in fact, numbers are being maintained through recruitment, or whether numbers are declining. Recent studies have highlighted that there may be many subtleties here, indicating, for example, that peregrine falcon numbers may be increasing in some parts of Scotland, level in others, and declining in some parts of the north-west Highlands (e.g. Ratcliffe, Chapter 4; Hardey *et al.*, Chapter 5; Scottish Raptor Monitoring Group, 2003).

41.3 Research on the predatory behaviour of raptors

Much of the research in this book focuses on predation: the prey taken (e.g. Shaw & Riddle, Chapter 7; Nielsen, Chapter 24; Marquiss *et al.*, Chapter 36), the habitats used whilst feeding (e.g. Petty & Thomas, Chapter 6; Crane & Nellist, Chapter 18; Fielding *et al.*, Chapter 26) and overall impacts on prey numbers or distribution (e.g. Newton, Chapter 1; Dixon *et al.*, Chapter 20; Redpath & Thirgood, Chapter 39). These studies are vital in developing our understanding of the nature of raptor predation, but also the particular nature of the so-called conflict. As Thompson *et al.* (Chapter 25) show, it is extremely difficult to quantify the impacts of land use change on raptor numbers, range use and behaviour. Much of the raptor debate focuses on numbers of raptors, when in fact it is the nature of any impact on game or agricultural interests which is the key. There remains a need for studies to evaluate the impacts of raptors on their prey, but also to quantify the impacts of habitat and prey base changes on the raptors (e.g. Redpath & Thirgood, 1997).

41.4 Land use change

Land use changes, such as the conversion of grouse moor to forestry, changes in lowland areas from one crop regime to another, or increases in public access, are of key importance in determining which species of raptor may be found in any area (e.g. Thompson *et al.*, Chapter 25; Viñuela & Villafuerte, Chapter 40). The need to be clear about any significant changes taking place is of fundamental importance to predict how raptor populations may change in response to policy, land use and management shifts. For example, on a grouse moor, the extent and quality of heather-dominated versus grass-dominated habitats may be key determinants of numbers of meadow pipits *Anthus pratensis* and other prey species for hen harriers (Redpath & Thirgood, 1997, Chapter 39; and see Tharme *et al.*, 2001). The balance between heather and other habitats will therefore be of significance in determining not just the nature conservation value of a given upland block, but perhaps also its potential economic viability overall (e.g. Thompson *et al.*, 1995, 1997; Redpath & Thirgood, Chapter 39; Redpath *et al.,* in press). The ensuing balance could be manipulated to achieve different economic and wildlife gains. For instance, it may be possible to redress any take of grouse by hen harriers by providing suitable habitat for other prey species on areas currently less preferred by hen harriers, or by providing some form of supplementary or diversionary food supply (e.g. Moorland Working Group, 2002; Redpath & Thirgood, Chapter 39; Redpath *et al.*, 2001, in press).

A challenge for land users and for behavioural scientists in the future must be to work together to examine whether habitat-based solutions are more widely applicable. One useful example of such habitat manipulation is suggested in a booklet dealing with pheasant *Phasianus colchicus* release pens, published by the British Association for Shooting and Conservation (2002) (see also Allen & Feare, Chapter 33). Increasingly, of course, conservation management itself is a land use in its own right with agricultural and other support mechanisms aimed at enhancing the particular quality of land for biodiversity.

In some cases, these inducements focus on birds of prey, in particular. A prime example here are the Natural Care habitat and species management schemes introduced and managed by Scottish Natural Heritage. These schemes make positive payments to land managers for activities which directly benefit nature conservation interests in protected areas. For example, on Orkney such a scheme is targeted at recovering important, traditional rough grassland habitats required by the Orkney vole *Microtus orcadensis* and hen harriers (see Amar *et al.*, Chapter 29). Does such a targeted support regime have a wider applicability? We think so.

From the above examples it is apparent that obtaining clarity on the numbers, status and ecology of birds of prey is of fundamental importance to reaching any agreement. Detailed studies of behavioural interactions, in particular, but also consideration of the implications of land use change and of conservation management overall, are important, and have contributed greatly to our understanding of raptor ecology.

41.5 Examples of research which is helping resolve conflicts

Many of the key raptor-human issues have been examined in detail through research (e.g. Anon., 2000; Chapters 20-24, 33-36, 38-40 in this book). We can consider two of these in some detail.

41.5.1 Moorlands

The debate involving grouse moor owners/managers and raptor conservationists has a high public and media profile, and has been running for at least 50 years (Brown, 1976; Thompson *et al.*, 1995, 1997; Redpath & Thirgood, 1997; Anon., 2000; Tharme *et al.*, 2001; Moorland Working Group, 2002; Redpath *et al.*, in press). In November 1997, Scottish Natural Heritage (SNH) established a Moorland Working Group (MWG) to address these areas of conflict in Scotland. This group comprised SNH (in the chair), The Royal Society for the Protection of Birds, The Game Conservancy Trust, and its Scottish Research Trustees, Scottish Landowners' Federation and Buccleuch Estates (on whose land much of the Joint Raptor Study was undertaken; see Redpath & Thirgood, 1997); The Scottish Office (now Scottish Executive) had 'observer' status in the MWG. This group worked alongside the UK Raptor Working Group (Anon., 2000) and some common membership ensured that the groups worked together well.

In July 1998 the MWG initially produced a high-level statement of intent, summarising the main issues related to the conservation of grouse moors in Scotland (*Action for Scotland's Moorlands: a Statement of Intent*). Subsequently, the MWG worked to produce a series of non-technical publications which outlined best practice management of grouse moorland for biodiversity (Moorland Working Group, 1998) as well as the underlying trends in Scottish moorlands (Moorland Working Group, 2002); these were aimed at owners and mangers of grouse moors and sought to develop understanding of habitat management options.

The Group developed an experimental protocol to trial supplementary feeding of hen harriers as a means of reducing raptor impacts on red grouse. A major field experiment was undertaken in spring and summer 1998 (Redpath *et al.*, 2001), and a popular 'how-to-do-it' guide was subsequently produced to encourage the uptake of this effective technique (Moorland Working Group, 1999).

The MWG was succeeded by Scotland's Moorland Forum (chaired by SNH) in 2002. The Forum comprises 22 member organisations working together to improve the care and management of moorland (24 organisations signed *Scotland's Moorland; Unique and Important: a Statement of Intent* in March 2002). In 2003 the Forum published a 'good practice' guide for moorland management (Scotland's Moorland Forum, 2003). An important next step for the Forum will be to trial novel conservation and management activities across several moors to determine whether or not these can help resolve the moorland game-raptor conflicts.

41.5.2 *Raptors and racing pigeons*

As Ratcliffe (1993, Chapter 4), the UK Raptor Working Group (Anon., 2000), Dixon *et al.* (Chapter 20) and Shawyer *et al.* (Chapter 21) detail, there have been long-standing disagreements between racing pigeon *Columba livia* 'fanciers' and raptor conservationists. As a result of a cross-party meeting of Members of the Scottish Parliament with the Scottish Homing Union (SHU) representing pigeon fanciers and SNH (in Edinburgh, in January 2001), a small working group was formed to address the issues. The group comprises members of the SHU and SNH, and is chaired by a Member of the Scottish Parliament, Alex Neil. The Group developed a research proposal which SNH, along with the SHU, subsequently commissioned to the Central Science Laboratory (CSL).

The research had three objectives, to: a) quantify the nature and extent of racing pigeon losses to raptors, primarily sparrowhawks *Accipiter nisus* around rearing 'lofts', b) quantify the nature and extent of losses to raptors, primarily peregrines, along race routes, and c) determine the efficiency of deterrents. CSL is due to report on this research towards the end of 2003.

41.6 Some common threads emerge

In considering the above examples, it is clear that there are a number of common threads underpinning these problems. In many cases, the historic perceptions of birds of prey being seen as a major problem have not stood the test of time or the test of rigorous, scientifically objective research (e.g. Brown, 1976; Marquiss *et al.*, Chapter 36). However, there are still occasions where birds of prey do have an effect on the overall management of the countryside, whether it be in relation to grouse moor management, pheasant shooting or some livestock interests. It does not seem obvious that any action should necessarily lead to the illegal killing or, indeed, to the legalised killing of birds of prey as part of any apparent short-term solution. There is clearly a need in each case to clarify if damage is actually being caused and then to quantify this accurately. We know that grouse moor management, for instance, was worth £14.8 million to the Scottish economy in 2000 (Moorland Working Group, 2002), and that open-air recreation was worth £730 million, supported by 29,000 full time equivalent jobs, in Scotland 1998 (Mackey *et al.*, 2001). This provides some context for finding sustainable, long term solutions to resolving any conflicts between different facets of countryside management. There is a rapidly increasing public interest in the conservation of raptors; any solution to raptor and land-use problems has to take this on board. There is likely to be more demand for visitor facilities to help enjoy raptors in the wild. This public interest is indeed likely to be an important driver in taking forward raptor conservation. Equally, it is likely to mean that the killing of raptors will remain abhorrent to the vast majority of the public in Scotland.

How then do we achieve any resolution to conflicts, or develop an agreed way forward? Communication between all parties, be they gamekeepers, conservationists or walkers in the uplands, or pheasant release managers, farmers or conservationists in the lowlands, needs to involve a dialogue which is open and inclusive. Perhaps the best examples come from the Moorland Working Group, and now Scotland's Moorland Forum, and from a similar forum established in Spain (Viñuela & Villafuerte, Chapter 40). In these fora, the key interested parties discuss the policy, public relations and research agendas. Developing ownership of such work in this way should lead to a more considered way forward and to a more participative approach.

Fundamentally, such fora need to achieve agreement on the numbers of birds of prey and their breeding success, the extent and significance of any predation, and alternative management measures (e.g. Redpath *et al.*, in press). Indeed, even to gain a shared understanding of the current legal situation affecting birds of prey has been important. This may seem self-evident, but has not been so in the past. Recent progress has been good and it is particularly important to stress the importance of openness and of sharing information and ideas.

The solution to many problems lies in the provision of funding and in creating opportunities for land managers to adapt their management, if necessary. Continued policy support for sympathetic management is important and here again, perhaps, SNH's Natural Care Programme, which is appropriately targeted on key habitats and species, and on their ecological requirements, primarily within protected areas, is a good model.

Public relations and perceptions do matter, however, and a recognition of the important role of land managers in helping to determine the overall direction and implementation of countryside change is important. Perhaps the conservation community could recognise more freely and openly the valuable role that land managers, gamekeepers and others play in the overall well-being of our countryside. In dealing with perceptions, many of the studies in this book have actually countered prejudices, and challenged the views held by some. Clearer recognition of and active support for independently-done, objective research, quantifying areas where there is a conflict in terms of the extent of damage, and in researching novel techniques to resolve this, are important for progress.

Perhaps more fundamental than anything is the need to develop an acceptance for change in land management practices. Importantly, this change needs to relate to conservation action and to the development of novel management techniques dealing with the problems outlined above. No one idea will solve all these problems; but bringing many organisations together to tackle the problem is perhaps going to lead to the greatest benefits in the long term.

References

Anonymous (2000). *Report of the UK Raptor Working Group.* Department for the Environment, Transport and the Regions/Joint Nature Conservation Committee, Peterborough.

British Association for Shooting and Conservation (2002). *Birds of Prey at Pheasant Release Pens – a Practical Guide for Game Managers and Gamekeepers.* British Association for Shooting and Conservation, Rossett.

Brown, L. (1976). *Birds of Prey.* Collins, London.

Brown, P. (1964). *Birds of Prey.* Andre Deutsch, London.

Mackey, E.C., Shaw, P., Holbrook, J., Shrewry, M.C., Saunders, G., Hall, J. & Ellis, N.E. (2001). *Natural Heritage Trends, Scotland 2001.* Scottish Natural Heritage, Perth.

Marren, P. (2002). *Nature Conservation.* The New Naturalist, Collins, London.

Moore, N.W. (1957). The past and present status of the buzzard in the British Isles. *British Birds,* **50**, 173–197.

Moorland Working Group (1998). *Good Practice for Grouse Moor Management.* Scottish Natural Heritage, Perth.

Moorland Working Group (1999). *Substitute feeding of Hen Harriers on Grouse Moors.* Scottish Natural Heritage, Perth.

Moorland Working Group (2002). *Scotland's Moorland: the Nature of Change.* Scottish Natural Heritage, Perth.

Newton, I. (1979). *Population Ecology of Raptors.* Poyser, Berkhamsted.

Newton, I. (1998). *Population Limitation in Birds.* Academic Press, London.

Ratcliffe, D.A. (1993). *The Peregrine Falcon. 2nd edition.* T. & A.D. Poyser, London.

Redpath, S.M. & Thirgood, S.J. (1997). *Birds of Prey and Red Grouse.* The Stationery Office, London.

Redpath, S.M., Thirgood, S.J. & Leckie, S.J. (2001). Does supplementary feeding reduce predation of red grouse by hen harriers? *Journal of Applied Ecology* **38**, 1157-1168.

Redpath, S.M., Arroyo, B.E., Leckie, F.M., Bacon, R., Bayfield, N., Gutiéerrez, R.J. & Thirgood, S.J. (in press). Using decision modelling with stakeholders to reduce human-wildlife conflict: a raptor-grouse case study. *Conservation Biology.*

RSPB (1999a). *Persecution: a Review of Bird of Prey Persecution in Scotland in 1998.* Royal Society for the Protection of Birds, Edinburgh.

RSPB (1999b). *Birdcrime '98. Offences Against Wild Bird Legislation 1998.* Royal Society for the Protection of Birds, Edinburgh.

RSPB & NCC (1991a). *Death by Design. The Persecution of Birds of Prey and Owls in the UK 1979–1989.* Royal Society for the Protection of Birds/Nature Conservancy Council, Sandy.

RSPB & NCC (1991b). *Persecution. Birds of Prey and Owls Killed in the UK 1979–1989.* Royal Society for the Protection of Birds/Nature Conservancy Council, Sandy and Peterborough.

Scotland's Moorland Forum (2003). *Scotland's Moorland Forum: Principles of Moorland Management.* Scottish Natural Heritage, Perth.

Scottish Raptor Monitoring Group (2003). Population estimates for peregrine *Falco peregrinus.* Scottish Natural Heritage, Perth.

Scottish Raptor Monitoring Scheme Agreement (2002). Agreement involving Scottish Natural Heritage, Joint Nature Conservation Committee, Scottish Raptor Study Groups, British Trust for Ornithology (Scotland), Rare Breeding Birds Panel, Royal Society for the Protection of Birds (Scotland) and Scottish Ornithologists' Club. Scottish Natural Heritage, Perth.

Stanners, D. & Bordeau, P. (eds.) (1995). *Europe's Environment: The Dobris Assessment.* European Environment Agency, Copenhagen.

Tharme, A.D., Green, R.E., Baines, D., Bainbridge, I.P. & O'Brien, M. (2001). The effect of management for red grouse shooting on the population density of breeding birds on heather-dominated moorland. *Journal of Applied Ecology,* **38**, 439-457.

Thompson, D.B.A., Gillings, S.D., Galbraith, C.A., Redpath, S.M. & Drewitt, J. (1997). The contribution of game management to biodiversity: a review of the importance of grouse moors for upland birds. In *Biodiversity in Scotland: Status, Trends and Initiatives,* ed. by L.V. Fleming, A.C. Newton, J.A. Vickery & M.B. Usher. The Stationery Office, Edinburgh. pp. 198-212.

Thompson, D.B.A., MacDonald, A.J., Marsden, J.H. & Galbraith, C.A. (1995). Upland heather moorland in Great Britain: a review of international importance, vegetation change, and some objectives for nature conservation. *Biological Conservation,* **71**, 163-178.

Tucker, G.M. & Heath, M.F. (1994). *Birds in Europe: their Conservation Status*. Birdlife International, Cambridge.

Usher, M.B., Mackey, E.C. & Curran, J.C. (eds) (2002). *The State of Scotland's Environment and Natural Heritage*. The Stationery Office, Edinburgh.

Usher, M.B. & Thompson, D.B.A. (eds.) (1988). *Ecological Change in the Uplands*. Blackwell, Oxford.

Warren, C. (2001). *Land Management Scotland*. Edinburgh University Press, Edinburgh.

Watson, J. (1997). *The Golden Eagle*. Poyser, London.

Whitfield, D.P., Fielding, A.H., McLeod, D.R.A. & Haworth, P.F. (in press). The effects of persecution on age of breeding and territory occupation in golden eagles in Scotland. *Biological Conservation*.

Whitfield, D.P., McLeod, D.R.A., Fielding, A.H., Watson, J. & Haworth, P.F. (2003). The association of grouse moors in Scotland with the illegal use of poisons to control predators. *Biological Conservation*, **114**, 157-163.

INDEX

Note: **Emboldened** page numbers indicate entire chapters. References
are to Scotland and England, unless otherwise indicated.